Western Engraving Co. Chicago.

A. Lincoln

ABRAHAM LINCOLN.

President of the United States.

ENGRAVED EXPRESSLY FOR PATRIOTISM OF ILLINOIS. CLARKE & CO. PUBLISHERS.

PRESIDENT LINCOLN'S HOME, SPRINGFIELD, ILLINOIS.

THE

PATRIOTISM OF ILLINOIS.

A RECORD OF THE

CIVIL AND MILITARY HISTORY

OF THE STATE IN THE

WAR FOR THE UNION,

WITH A

HISTORY OF THE CAMPAIGNS IN WHICH ILLINOIS SOLDIERS HAVE BEEN CONSPICUOUS,

SKETCHES OF DISTINGUISHED OFFICERS, THE ROLL OF THE ILLUSTRIOUS DEAD, MOVEMENTS OF THE SANITARY AND CHRISTIAN COMMISSIONS.

BY T. M. EDDY, D. D.,
Editor N. W. Christian Advocate.

ILLUSTRATED WITH STEEL ENGRAVINGS OF EMINENT MEN.

IN TWO VOLS.—VOL. I.

CHICAGO:
CLARKE & CO., PUBLISHERS.

1865.

Entered according to Act of Congress, in the year 1865,
By CLARKE & CO.,
In the Clerk's Office of the District Court of the United States for the Northern District of Illinois.

Stereotyped by
JOHN CONAHAN

TO ILLINOIS SOLDIERS,

FROM THE LIEUTENANT GENERAL

TO THE

SMALLEST DRUMMER-BOY:

TO THE

GALLANT LIVING AND HEROIC DEAD

WHO HAVE MADE THE STATE ILLUSTRIOUS

ON EVERY BATTLE-FIELD,

THESE VOLUMES

ARE GRATEFULLY INSCRIBED.

PUBLISHERS NOTICE.

IT gives us pleasure to present to the public, and especially to the citizens of Illinois, the FIRST volume of the military history of the State. The work has been prepared, we think, with marked ability and impartiality, and the Publishers have spared no pains or expense to make it attractive and permanent. As it is a record of the part our noble State has borne in the great struggle to maintain our glorious government and to hand down our institutions untarnished and unimpaired, therefore every family will be interested to possess a copy of the work. Much care has been taken to combine incidents and statistics, sketches of persons and battles, thus embodying the essential and important facts of our great history, so that the work shall be instructive to all classes of readers.

The second volume will follow in as close proximity as possible. It will be issued in the same style, so that when completed it will make an interesting standard work for both private and public libraries; containing, as far as possible, a complete record of our brave men who have fallen in their country's cause.

PREFATORY NOTES.

PATRIOTISM is the love of country. It has ever been recognized among the cardinal virtues of true men, and he who was destitute of it has been considered an ingrate. Even among the icy desolations of the far north we expect to find, and *do* find, an ardent affection for the land of nativity, the HOME of childhood, youth and age. There is much in our country to create and foster this sentiment. It is a country of imperial dimensions, reaching from sea to sea, and almost "from the rivers to the ends of the earth." None of the empires of old could compare with it in this regard. It is washed by two great oceans, while its lakes are vast inland seas. Its rivers are silver lines of beauty and commerce. Its grand mountain chains are the links of God's forging and welding, binding together north and south, east and west.

It is a land of glorious memories. It was peopled by the picked men of Europe, who came hither "not for wrath but conscience' sake." Said the younger Winthrop to his father, "I shall call that my country where I may most glorify God and enjoy the presence of my dearest friends." And so came godly men and devoted women, flying from oppressive statutes, where they might find

"Freedom to worship God."

There are spots on the sun, and the microscope reveals flaws in burnished steel, and so there were spots and flaws in the early records of the founders of this land, but with them all, our colonial history is one that stirs the blood and quickens the pulse of him who reads.

And then the glorious record of that Revolutionary struggle gives each American a solid historic platform on which he may plant his foot. It was an era of high moral heroism, and for principle, against theoretical usurpation, rather than practical (though of the latter there wanted not enough to give to our fathers' lips a full and bitter cup), the men of the Revolution drew their swords, and entered the field against the most powerful nation of the world, and fought on and on, through murky gloom, until triumph came. It was also an era of Providential agencies and deliverances, and each right feeling American, realizes that not more truly did God raise up Moses and Aaron and lead Israel with the pillar of cloud and fire, than He raised up *our* leaders and led *our* fathers. And reverent is our adoration, when we remember how he guided the deliberations of our Constitutional Convention and poured the peaceful spirit, in answer to ascending prayer, down upon that august convocation

There are later memories, when again measuring strength with Britain, our gallant tars showed on the Sea and on the Lakes that the empire of the deep was not henceforth conceded to the so-called "Mistress of the Seas." It was a new sensation experienced by the old nations, when the youngest of them all dared lift the glove of the power which "ruled the waves," and defy her on the field of her greatest prowess. Yet so it was, and the achievements of Decatur, McDonough, Paul Jones and Porter gave luster to our navy to be brightened by Foote, Farragut, Porter, Dahlgren and Worden in our own times. For it is no idle boast to say that to-day the United States floats the most powerful navy of the world. These and other memories invest our land with sacredness, and commend it to the reverent love of its sons, native or adopted.

Its institutions of civil and religious freedom, guaranteeing the rights of citizenship, education and worship, extending the blessings of beneficent law silently and extensively as the atmosphere about us, demand our love. True, one dark blot, one iron limitation, one cruel exception was in our organization, one tolerated by our fathers in the faith that it would soon die, endured as a necessary but transient evil, but which from toleration, soon claimed protection, from protection, equality, and from equality, supremacy; one deplored by the good, and destined to bring its terrible harvest upon us, reminding the world that, as truly of nations as of individuals, is it written that whatsoever is sown shall be reaped, and "with what measure ye mete, shall it be measured to you again." But with this, there was much that was great and elevating in our institutions, so that with more than ancient Roman pride could the traveler in far-off lands exclaim, "I am an American citizen."

It is a land of innumerable resources. Extending through so many parallels of latitude, and isothermal lines, its soil yields almost an infinite variety of productions. It gives the fruits and grains of all zones. Within its bosom lie hid all minerals, the iron, the copper, vast fields of coal, the gold, the silver, the platina, the quicksilver, while the very "rock pours out rivers of oil." Its forests are rich in exhaustless stores of timber, while its prairies are the granaries of the world.

It is the land of the free school, the free press, and the free pulpit. It is impossible to compute the power of this trio. The free schools, open to rich and poor, bind together the people in educational bonds and in the common memories of the recitation-room and the play-ground, and how strong *they* are, you, reader, well know, as some past recollection tugs at your heart-strings. The free press may not always be altogether as dignified or elevated as the more highly cultivated may desire, but it is ever open to the complaints of the people; is ever watchful of popular rights and jealous of class encroachments, and the highest in authority know that it is above President or Senate. The free pulpit, sustained not by legally exacted tithes wrung from an unwilling people, but by the free-will offerings of loving supporters, gathers about it the millions, inculcates the highest morality, points to brighter worlds, and when occasion demands, will not be silent before political wrongs. Its power, simply as an educating agency can scarcely be estimated. In this country its freedom gives a competition so vigorous that it must remain in direct popular sympathy. How strong it is, the country saw when its voice was lifted in the old cry, "Rebellion is as the sin of witchcraft." Its words started the slumbering, roused the careless, and called the "sacramental host," as well as the "men of the world to arms." These three grand agencies are not rival but supplementary, each doing an essential work in public culture.

Ours, above all others, is the land of homes. Local attachment is essential to patriotism. Give a man a bit of ground and let him build a house, though it be scarce larger than Queen Mab's, and he becomes a permanent part of the country. He has something to live for, vote for, fight for. Here there is no system of vast land-ownerships, with lettings and sub-lettings, but, on the contrary, the abundance and cheapness of land, and the prevalence of wise homestead exemptions, give a large proportion of the population proprietary interests. To all this, add the freedom of elective franchise, which invests the humblest citizen with the functions of sovereignty, and opens to his competition the highest places of trust and profit, and is there not reason for loving such a country? Is there not reason why its home-born sons should swear upon its holy altars that this trust received from their fathers, shall be transmitted, pure and whole, to their children? Is there not reason why each adopted son should see that the land which gives him sanctuary, refuge and citizenship shall not be rent in twain? Especially that it shall not be divided in the interest of class-distinctions, of distinction between labor and capital, based upon a difference of birth and ancestry?

Above all: When we assume the higher doctrine that civil government is divinely appointed, "that the powers that be, are ordained of God," and the maintenance of lawfully established government becomes a duty, God, the King of Nations, summons us to prevent its overthrow; and He declares that the hour when it is imperiled, the magistrate shall not bear the sword in vain, but shall be "the minister of God, a revenger to execute wrath upon him that doeth evil," and that they who rise up against lawful authority and "resist the power, resist the ordinance of God, and they that resist shall receive to themselves damnation."* Patriotism then comes to the baptism of Christian duty, and for the hour when just government and righteous authority are periled, the duty is one of sternness, and the sword of the magistrate is its symbol.

The civilization of the West is in some respects peculiar. Its growth has been so rapid as to be almost incredible. Into it have come the active young of Eastern and Middle States, young men portionless or desiring a wider field than their narrow patrimony

* Romans xiii. 1–4.

afforded. They are not the men to settle in quiet dignity. We know not who originated the use of "push" as a noun, but it expresses the characteristic of these "younger sons"—younger but not "prodigal"—who come to our Western States. "Push"—they will stop for no obstacle and brook no difficulty. Before that "push" forests disappear, prairies are decked with cultivated beauty, railways are projected of length sufficient to open the eyes of grave eastern directors, which yet, somehow, secure eastern capital for their construction. These are not men to be held in leading strings, and kept in subjection to effete systems.

The traveler from the Eastern States, will find in each Western frontier village the evidences of highest culture. In the cabin of unhewn logs or "ended" slabs he will find music and painting. With this, there is, of course, the endless variety of foreign population. German, Irish, Scandinavian are its chief elements, though in the Northwest there is a large infusion of the genuine English. This population must be fused, and that work has been going on under the combined influence of the educating trio of powers above indicated, with the additive influence of business and politics.

To these is now being added the uniting influence of the WAR FOR THE UNION. Together are we all being "baptized in the cloud and in the sea," and we shall emerge more than ever ONE PEOPLE.

Illinois has full share of all Western peculiarities. Its size and elements of material wealth have long since caused it to be conceded that it was destined to rank with the foremost of the States of the Union. When, therefore, the tocsin of war was sounded, it was proper, it was natural, that the nation should turn its eyes upon this, with other large States, and ask, "What will Illinois do?" The answer is given in the offering of more than a quarter of a million of soldiers and untold millions of money to the country.

It is proper that each State should, in some form, make its own record during the war. No general history can do the individual States justice; nay, no complete, comprehensive history can be written until, at the end of the war, the States have made up their annals. For these the Irvings, Bancrofts and Prescotts of the Union must wait. In each State should be written the deeds of its sons; the achievements of its regiments, the deeds of its officers and citizen soldiery. If delayed, much will be lost; if issued at once, there cannot be perfect symmetry and complete finish. Between these alternatives, it seems better to seize the present and accept the artistic sacrifice.

When the proposition was made to the author to undertake the preparation of the present work he promptly declined. He had enough work upon his hands to tax all his strength and consume all his time. But the proposition was renewed and so pressed upon him by numerous and influential gentlemen whose judgment he highly respects, that it became a question of duty. The entire business management has been with the publishers, the author declining any participation in its details.

As to *material*, of course all published works are procured, regardless of expense, and the uninitiated would wonder at the amount of war literature from massive octavos down to pamphlets, already produced.

His Excellency, Governor Yates, placed at the author's disposal a valuable collection of State papers and other documents, and for his uniform courtesy the author renders this public acknowledgment. Adjutant-General Fuller courteously tendered access to the documentary stores of his office. Major-General McClernand placed in his possession his full memoranda of the movements of his command. Major-General Hurlbut kindly furnished important information.

Learning that Rev. F. Senour, of Rockford, Illinois, had contemplated a similar work and had already collected considerable *material*, a correspondence was opened, followed by a personal interview, resulting in the transfer to the writer of Mr. Senour's MSS., principally biographical and regimental sketches. These have been of much service, and their use is thus acknowledged.

In a very few instances pamphlet sketches of single regiments have been published and made available. The "History of the Old Second Division," by Wm. Sumner Dodge, and the "annals of the Army of the Cumberland," by John Fitch, have afforded valuable assistance. Col. James Grant Wilson's "Sketches of Illinois Officers," have aided in personal biography. But the principal reliance for regimental and personal sketches has been upon the Adjutant-General's reports, official reports of commanders, and MSS. furnished the author.

In giving *regimental sketches* there is a difference in the space given. This may need explanation. There is a wide difference in the service rendered by regiments equally meritorious. One has been from "muster" almost constantly with the same brigade and division, while another has been on detached service, or thrown from division to division, from one department to another.

The same principle will explain the difference in personal notices. One officer has performed service so varied in kind and field that any just notice requires much detail—another has served as well, as bravely, but his career has been with one corps or division.

There has been a difference also in accessible materials which no industry could prevent. The history of very few regiments is yet completed, and among the most difficult to reach, the author has found the regiments out of service. It will be remembered that the work is yet incomplete, and that for regiments with scanty mention there is ample record in store.

Much regimental history is found in the record of campaigns, battles and sieges. Indeed it is such as is the most satisfactory. You find a regiment, as for instance the 13th at Chickasaw Bayou, or the 19th at Stone River, and what special record does it need to tell its gallantry?

Illinois troops have seldom been brigaded together, at least this was so early in the war. This adds to the labor of the historian and prevents that unity which is desirable. From the manner in which the regiments were distributed it has not been practicable to treat them in numerical order.

Furthermore, in the preparation of regimental sketches, the author has followed very closely the authorities before him, editing rather than preparing them. Hence they sometimes seem bald and rugged, but there was only space for the rugged statement of facts.

Care has been taken to secure accuracy, and corrections have been made at much expense, subsequently to stereotyping—in some instances chapters canceled and rewritten on receiving later or more satisfactory authorities; and yet, in such a work, it is too much to hope that entire accuracy, especially in names and dates, has been secured. Proper names are the terror of printers and proof-readers and the vexation of authors. "What's in a name?" Much, and no man wishes to see his deeds assigned to some respectable person of whom he has no knowledge.

The lists of killed and wounded are not given. In the case of regiments and batteries yet in the field, the present publication would, alas! be premature. In the regiments mustered out, the casualty reports of the Adjutant's office are not brought down to date of expiration of service, and to have secured them from the officers would have demanded a delay disappointing and vexatious to patrons. It has therefore been thought best—necessary indeed—to defer such publication until the second volume shall appear. Efforts were made to prevent this, but they would have been successful only by further delay.

The reader will be struck with the difference of space assigned the campaigns of the West and those of the East, but the reason is clear. These volumes do not profess to be a complete history of the war, but of the work of Illinois in the war. It has so happened that most of the Illinois troops have been in the West, and until the recent battles of Franklin and Nashville and the capture of Savannah and Charleston, we have had but few of them on the Potomac, Shenandoah, the James, or the coast of the Carolinas. How could the record of our men be written without the battles of Shiloh, Corinth, the Hatchie, the siege of Vicksburg, Stone River, Chickamauga, Mission Ridge and Lookout Mountain? They were there! It was absolutely necessary, either to sketch the campaigns at once, or to go over them again and again with the several regiments. We have, for instance, given much space to Donelson and Shiloh. How could that be avoided when so many from Illinois fought those battles; when Grant, and McClernand, and Hurlburt were the master spirits, and Wallace poured out his life?

Here is made a personal acknowledgment. In the midst of pressing cares and overwork, the health of the author threatened to give way so seriously, as to peril the completion of the first volume months beyond the promised time. In this emergency he was so fortunate as to secure the assistance of Mr. George Upton, now one of the *Chicago Tribune* staff, a gentleman who, as reporter was with the Western army in its early campaigns, and is familiar with military movements. Mr. Upton's assistance has been of great value, lightening the author's labors at a time when they were prostrating him.

By a Providential coincidence, a former Illinois lawyer is Commander-in-chief of our Army and Navy, and the former Colonel of the 21st Illinois Infantry is, as Lieutenant General, in immediate command of our armies. The former has passed through four years of an eventful administration, and having been proven by the people, has been re-commissioned. The nation has recognized in him a divinely chosen leader, and believes, that with all his liability to mistake, the President has been divinely directed. It was a sublime moment when that tall form was seen on the platform of the car as the train was about to carry him from his quiet home in Springfield to the cares and perils which awaited him, and the President elect, with choked utterance, asked his old friends to pray for him! So they did. It seemed proper to follow our Illinois citizen with some particularity, until he became actually the Nation's Chief Magistrate.

Our scarcely less distinguished fellow-citizen, the Lieutenant-General, merits ampler notice than has yet been given him. But the time for it is not yet. When time shall have fully tested his plans and his generalship will be the hour of his record.

This volume has brought down the history of the State in the war to the close of 1864, and the close of the administration of Governor Yates. It was providential that a man with his spirit and activity was in the chair executive. He was as fully committed to freedom as against slavery, nor did he ever falter in his position. He stood as an iron pillar, when locally in a minority, and waited for the day when truth should triumph. As Governor he was the soldier's friend. On the field he went with them under fire, used every possible exertion to forward them sanitary supplies, to bring the wounded into hospitals and to their homes. The soldier's wife or widow could secure audience when officers were turned away. It was no wonder that when his official term as governor expired that so strong a popular demand was made for his election to another position of eminence. His messages and proclamations, so far as they bear on the war, are fully given, for they indicate the State history.

His successor is a gallant officer of the Union, wounded on more than one field, an ardent patriot and able administrator. His official doings are not before the reader as yet, but there have been enough to foreshadow a wise and patriotic administration. In Richard J. Oglesby, Illinois has a trustworthy leader.

At the termination of four years of war, is Illinois exhausted and desponding? Can it afford to go on? It has given answer as to what it meant to do in the popular elections of the autumn of 1864! The purpose of the people is unalterable to restore the authority of the general government and to maintain the federal Union. As to "exhaustion," a few facts presented in Governor Yates's last message should be conclusive answer.

"Notwithstanding the war, we have prospered beyond all former precedents. Notwithstanding nearly two hundred thousand of the most athletic and vigorous of our population have been withdrawn from the field of production, the area of land now under cultivation is greater than at any former period, and the census of 1865 will exhibit an astounding increase in every department of material industry and advancement; in a great increase of agricultural, manufacturing and mechanical wealth, in new and improved modes for production of every kind; in the substitution of machinery for the manual labor withdrawn by the war; in the universal activity of business in all its branches; in the rapid growth of our cities and villages; in the bountiful harvests, and in unexampled material prosperity, prevailing on every hand; while at the same time the educational institutions have in no way declined. Our colleges and schools of every class and grade are in the most flourishing condition; our benevolent institutions, State and private, are maintained; and, in a word, our prosperity is as complete and ample as though no tread of armies or beat of drum had been heard in our borders."

Surely these are not the ordinary indices of exhaustion! As to resources for the future struggle the resources of the State will meet each legitimate call. Illustrative of this are some additional paragraphs from the same document:

"The physical resources of a State are the foundation of all others. They make it great or little. They shape its destiny. They even affect its moral and religious character. History teaches this truth. All the great nations of ancient and modern times demonstrate it.

Egypt, Syria, Greece, Rome; Great Britain, France, the United States, are so many proofs that favorable physical situations and resources are absolutely necessary to material and moral development. Illinois, in this respect, stands pre-eminent among the States of the Union. She is the heart of the Northwest. In agricultural resources she is unsurpassed. In manufacturing and commercial facilities she has no superior. On the east, south and west, the great river of the continent and its tributaries water her border counties, while their branches penetrate to every part of the State, irrigating her soil, draining her low lands, and affording water power for her manufactures. The Illinois River runs for over two hundred miles through the State, from northeast to southwest, forming a natural highway between the Lakes and the Mississippi, the key of which is entirely in our possession. This highway is one of the most important of the physical resources of the State; while, in a military point of view, it enables us to dominate the Lakes on the one hand, and the Father of Waters on the other. A State, holding this great waterway, must always be a power on the continent, as well as in the Union. Then, we have, on the northeast, an outlet to the ocean through the great Lakes, those inland seas of the continent; while that one of them, Michigan, which laves our northeastern border, is almost land-locked, and thus the least liable to hostile incursions from foreign powers. This secures to us the site for a naval depot, for dock-yards, for the building and repair of vessels, for foundries for cannon, for workshops for all descriptions of war material, at some point on Lake Michigan, between the Wisconsin and Indiana State lines. Our State is also on the direct route of the Pacific Railroad, which must intersect it from east to west; thus making it a portion of the great highway between Europe and the Indies. Then, again, all our lines of communication, from the interior of the State to shipping points connected with tide-water, at which bulky articles of merchandise or agricultural products can be received or delivered, are short. This saves the cost of lengthy transportation of such articles by railway, which must always be expensive. At present, in some of the States to the west and northwest of us, large quantities of grain have been stored on the navigable rivers for the last two seasons. On account of low water it cannot be sent to market by steamboat, while the cost of railway transportation would eat up its value. This can never be the case in Illinois, as long as water runs in the Mississippi, and that of the great Lakes flows unobstructed to the sea. But not alone do we possess agricultural resources of an almost unlimited character: we have also within the limits of our State, facilities for manufactures, which equal those of nearly all the other States of the Union combined. Beneath the surface of our blooming prairies and beautiful woodlands are millions of tons of coal, easy of access, close to the great centers of commerce and manufactures, on great navigable rivers, and intersected by railway facilities of the best description.

"Illinois, in 1860, was the fourth State in the Union in the number of tons of coal produced. But what has been produced bears no comparison to what may be. Our State geologist assures me that in a single county in this State there are a thousand millions tons of coal awaiting the various uses to which the civilization of the future will apply it. It will thus be seen that Illinois possesses within itself the physical resources of not only a great State but a great nation."

Guiding all these is the intelligent purpose of the people, and Illinois will continue to demand the vigorous prosecution of the war, until the authority of the Government of the United States is acknowledged over every State and Territory of the Republic.

It were ungrateful for rendered service, and untrue to facts were, not mention made of the devoted patriotism of the women of the State. They have not their record in the organization and marching of regiments, but theirs was nevertheless real and a noble work. They inspired the love of country by their own spirit. They would hear nothing of cowardice, or worldly prudence. They threw the halo of love of country over all social life. They gave their best loved to the altar of the State. They organized sewing circles, aid societies, etc., in every neighborhood; they organized and managed fairs; they opened and sustained Homes or Rests for the weary and wounded soldier. This record is a meager one, and does scanty justice to the devoted women of Illinois. Many a soldier has said "God bless them."

The people of this State have seen, in common with their fellow-citizens elsewhere, that God is in this contest. They have heard His speech and were afraid; they have seen His hand and have trusted. They have believed that He was leading the nation through the Red Sea and the desert to the Canaan of liberty. They have steadily believed that ere their ABRAHAM should return to dwell in his Springfield home; the ISAAC of Freedom should be born! So they still believe, and they are sanguine that the day cometh!

In these notes the author must mention two facts with peculiar satisfaction, which did not come within the scope of the text of the first volume, facts which are to the honor of the State.

The first is the repeal, by the Legislature, of the odious black laws. They were passed when prejudice against the colored race was at its hight. The African was a pariah, an outlaw, and only by ostracizing him could there be safety for the State. The cry of "Amalgamation" was raised, forgetting that it is slavery that mingles the races; slavery that makes each plantation as many colored in its population as Joseph's famed coat of ancient days; slavery that bleaches African slavery out by bleaching Anglo-Saxon slavery in!

And so a code unchristian and inhuman crept into the statute-books. It made Illinois virtually a slave state. Fortunately its most odious features were decided by the Supreme Court to be at variance with the constitution of the State. The remnant had come to be a dead letter, and so little attention was directed to it that it might have gone unrepealed but that certain "sons of Belial" in whom was little of the love of God or country saw fit to prosecute Union officers, who, on temporary return from the field, brought with them each his servant, "confiscated" by the sword, made free perhaps for service rendered the army. No matter—bringing him into the State was illegal, and prosecution followed. It was mean and dastardly as the selling of Joseph into Egypt, but like that event was overruled for good. A demand swept from Cairo to Waukegan from Quincy to Paris, from Old Kaskaskia to Galena that the code should be repealed. Governor Yates urged the popular demand with fiery vehemence; Governor Oglesby threw his influence in its favor, and the 1st day of February 1865, the General Assembly voted the repeal. The Governor promptly appended his signature, and the black laws of Illinois were consigned to the tomb of dead monstrosities!

The other was the prompt approval of the proposed amendment to the Constitution of the United States, rendering human slavery forever impossible in all the States and Territories of the Union. After a protracted debate on it in Congress it received the constitutional majority, and of course the signature of the President.

The telegraph flashed the news over the country, and immediately Gov. Oglesby sent a special message to the Legislature, recommending its concurrence. In spite of parliamentary strategy, a joint resolution was put upon its passage, and within twenty-four hours of the Congressional vote, Illinois had given, first of all the States, her approval! The capitol at Springfield rang with cheer after cheer when the result was announced, and throughout the State there was most intense rejoicing. Bonfires blazed, cannon roared and people shouted. Illinois had placed herself in the van of the States in demanding freedom for man *as man*. It is an honor the Prairie State may justly place upon her crest and proudly wear. These two events merit record in the volumes which chronicle the Patriotism of Illinois.

It is amazing to contemplate the imperial contributions the State has made in this war. With the completion of the call now pending, more than one quarter of a million of men will have gone from her homes. They were not her pauper population sent away that she might find for them cheap burial and cheaper graves, but the sons of the hearths and homes of the State of broad prairies. They went with the blessing of wives, mothers, sisters and betrothed upon them.

The Sanitary Commission at Chicago credits the citizens of Chicago with contributions amounting to $40,331.13, and the citizens of the State outside of Chicago with $55,541.68, and nine thousand five hundred and thirty-nine packages of various kinds, while immense amounts of stores have gone forward from other centers.

The Christian Commission has received and expended $145,844; a single farmer, Jacob Strawn, giving his check, and one that would be honored anywhere, for ten thousand dollars, the citizens of Morgan county sending with it an equal amount! And this to provide religious instruction to the men in the army! The people saw an army of *souls*, not of fighting machines! In addition the Illinois donations to the Freedmen's Aid Commission amount to $81,865.81.

In what follows it is not claimed that other states have not done nobly, for they have. In the patriotic sisterhood Illinois claims to be second to none. She is worthy to clasp them by the hand, for she has not disgraced them. She has not faltered when they called, nor deserted in the hour of extreme peril. With Peninsular Michigan, glorious Indiana, gallant Wisconsin, Iowa, whose rolling prairies resemble some vast ocean suddenly solidified, and with Missouri lately made free by her own act; with these her immediate neighbors she is well worthy to clasp hands, to exchange greetings, and when the day of victory shall come, to mingle congratulations.

Illinois is justly proud of the eminent leaders she has given to the country. There is Grant, of cool persistence and undying purpose; McClernand, whose early record was so brilliant; Prentiss, who suffered from wasting captivity; Pope, whose military genius shone brilliantly in the campaign of Island No. 10 and Corinth; Hurlbut, whose fighting 4th division stood as a wall on the bloody plain of Pittsburg Landing and whose admirable generalship won the battle of the Hatchie; Logan, whose shout has many a time steadied the waving column; Palmer, whose reputation rests upon a solid basis, with many others of lower rank, but not lower bravery.

The official action of churches deserves permanent record in these volumes, and will receive it, but in the present is omitted.

It has not been possible to speak of surgeons and chaplains as their services demand. The surgeon has no promotion ahead; nothing to cheer or stimulate, but the stern sense of duty. The chaplain has no promotion, and during the earlier part of the war had no rank, and was made the foot-ball of contrary and sometimes oppressive decisions. But with these drawbacks, statements yet to be made will show that the service owes much to these officers. The surgeons have saved life, the chaplains have pointed to the higher life.

With the exception of two who rose from the ranks to the chaplaincy, special mention has been avoided from a purpose to collect and generalize certain facts and suggestions in the second volume.

The burdens of a chaplain's life, early in the service were very onerous, and with the shifting orders in reference to his rank and pay, no wonder he was sometimes driven to resignation. The vexations culminated in giving such a construction to the law, that if a chaplain was absent from active duty, though it might be from wounds or sickness contracted in actual service, all allowances of pay and rations were stopped! In one instance a chaplain refused to leave the hospital when he was serving the wounded, and worked on until prostrated. His conduct merited honorable mention in official reports, and promotion if such a thing had been possible. What it brought him was deduction of fifty days' pay! No wonder so many were driven out of the army. The law has been amended, but is yet vague and too indefinite, and is susceptible of improvement.

Richmond, the rebel capital, has surrendered, and the Libby prison has opened its gloomy portals; the tramp of Weitzel's armed freedmen has been heard in its streets, and Mr. Lincoln lived to give audience in the departments of Davis. The iron chamber has been compressing its walls; General Lee has surrendered his grand army, and this volume goes to its patrons with the glad prophecy of early peace. The country is saved, and before it are long days of peace and quietness.

"God bless our native land."

The author sends out this volume, craving for it such modification of severe criticism as the circumstances suggest. Our regiments are a-field—forty-six are with Sherman as he marches through the sea-board States of the Confederacy, and in many instances communication with them is impossible. Matter designed for this volume is unavoidably delayed until the second.

There has been honesty of intention, close and faithful application, and free expenditure of means in gathering information. Error has been guarded against, but 'twere too much to hope that it is entirely excluded. * * * * The author craves indulgence to state that the delay of sending this volume to press, gives opportunity to say that Charleston, which fired the first gun of the rebellion has yielded to Federal authority and without any desperate resistance, and the U. S. colored troops, South Carolina freedmen, were first to parade its streets, singing as they marched, the Glory Halleluiah of the John Brown song!

CONTENTS OF VOLUME I.

CHAPTER I.

INTRODUCTORY.

CHAPTER II.

THE ILLINOIS PRESIDENT.

CHAPTER III.

THE GREAT UPRISING.

CHAPTER IV.

EARLY WAR MEASURES.

CHAPTER V.

EARLY STATE MOVEMENTS—ORGANIZATION.

CHAPTER VI.

THE STATE AUTHORITIES AND WAR DEPARTMENT.

CHAPTER VII.

THE STATE AND THE ARMY—'61 TO '64.

CHAPTER VIII.

THE PRECEDING CHAPTERS.

CHAPTER IX.

FREMONT'S ADMINISTRATION.

CHAPTER X.

U. S. GRANT.

CHAPTER XI.

THE CUMBERLAND AND TENNESSEE.

PAGE.

CHAPTER XII.

COLUMBUS: ISLAND NO. 10: PEA RIDGE.

CHAPTER XIII.

PITTSBURG LANDING—SHILOH.

CHAPTER XIV.

PERSONAL AND INCIDENT.

CHAPTER XV.

CORINTH CAMPAIGNS.

CHAPTER XVI.

REGIMENTAL SKETCHES.

CHAPTER XVII.

MITCHELL'S CAMPAIGNS.

CHAPTER XVIII.

BUELL'S CAMPAIGN.

CHAPTER XIX.

STONE RIVER.

CHAPTER XX.

GRIERSON'S RAID.

CHAPTER XXI.

BIOGRAPHICAL.

CHAPTER XXII.

REGIMENTAL.

CHAPTER XXIII.

VICKSBURG.

CHAPTER XXIV.

GEN. SHERMAN'S VICKSBURG CAMPAIGN.

CHAPTER XXV.

ARMY OF THE MISSISSIPPI.

CHAPTER XXVI.

GEN. GRANT'S DESCENT OF THE MISSISSIPPI.

CHAPTER XXVII.

FROM GRAND GULF TO VICKSBURG.

CHAPTER XXVIII.

THE INVESTMENT OF VICKSBURG.

CHAPTER XXIX.

BIOGRAPHICAL SKETCHES OF ILLINOIS GENERALS.

CHAPTER XXX.

THE CAMPAIGNS OF THE ARMY OF THE CUMBERLAND.

CHAPTER XXXI.

TESTIMONIALS.

CHAPTER XXXII.

ILLINOIS ON THE POTOMAC.

CHAPTER XXXIII.

THE POTOMAC—CAMPAIGN AND REGIMENTAL.

CHAPTER XXXIV.

BIOGRAPHICAL.

CHAPTER XXXV.

THE ADJUTANT GENERAL'S OFFICE.

APPENDIX.

LIST OF ILLUSTRATIONS

PATRIOTISM OF ILLINOIS.

CHAPTER I.

INTRODUCTORY.

THE STATE—EXTENT AND BOUNDARIES—DECADES—PRODUCTIONS—CIVIL WAR—FREE AND SLAVE LABOR—DEMANDS OF SLAVERY—LINCOLN AND DOUGLAS—SENATORIAL CONTEST—1860—PRESIDENTIAL CONTEST—THREATS OF DISUNION—NO JUSTIFICATION FOR REVOLUTION—A. H. STEPHENS' SPEECH—MR. LINCOLN'S VIEWS—POWERLESS FOR EVIL—MR. BUCHANAN—CABINET—SCENES IN CONGRESS—SOUTH CAROLINA SECEDES —"COERCION"—LINCOLN'S POLICY FORESHADOWED—MAJOR ANDERSON—FORT MOULTRIE AND FORT SUMTER—COMMISSIONERS—GENERAL SCOTT AND REINFORCEMENTS—A TRUCE—ILLINOIS CONGRESSIONAL DELEGATION—SUMMARY OF IMPORTANT FACTS—TERMINATION OF THE BUCHANAN ADMINISTRATION.

THE STATE OF ILLINOIS stretches from 36° 56′ to 42° 30′ north latitude, and is between 87° 35′ and 91° 40′ longitude. Its extent is truly imperial; its length from north to south being three hundred and eighty-eight, and its extreme breadth from east to west two hundred and twelve miles. Its head is as far north as Lowell, Massachusetts, and its foot farther south than Richmond, Virginia. Its area is 55,405 square miles, or 35,459,200 acres. Its northern boundary is Wisconsin; the north-eastern, Lake Michigan; eastern, Indiana, from which it is, in part, separated by the Wabash River; its southern, Kentucky and the Ohio River, while on its western line is the Mississippi River, across which are the States of Missouri and Iowa. It is divided into one hundred and one counties, which are dotted with villages, towns or cities.

Its growth has been very rapid, as the statement of its decennial periods from 1810 to 1860 shows:

YEAR.	WHITES.	FREE COLORED.	SLAVES,	TOTAL.
1810	11,501	613	168	12,282
1820	53,788	457	917	55,162
1830	155,061	1,637	747	157,445
1840	472,254	3,598	331	476,183
1850	846,034	5,436		851,470
1860	1,704,323	7,628		1,711,951

The development of material prosperity has been proportionate to the increase of population. Broad and beautiful streams open outlets for its products, and supply water-power for its machinery. The Mississippi River, the Illinois River and Canal, and the great Lakes furnish water transportation for its cereals and its beef and pork to southern or eastern tide-water; long lines of railway traverse it in every direction; its prairie soil is of almost exhaustless fertility; vast fields of coal and quarries of stone are hid beneath it; grains and fruits grow in profusion; churches, public schools, academies and colleges give morality and intelligence to its people, and down to the spring of 1861, though there had been disastrous financial revulsions, no serious check had been given to its prosperity.

From 1850 to 1860 the ratio of increase was, of whites, 101.45 per cent; free colored, 40.32 per cent. Judge Fuller, the able and patriotic Adjutant General, says in his report for 1861-2:

> "From a population, in 1850, of 851,470, we had increased to 1,711,951—more than doubling our population in one decade. Our real and personal property, in 1850, valued at $156,265,006, had, in 1860, increased to $871,860,282—being an increase of $715,595,276, or 457.93 per cent. Our improved lands which, in 1850, were but 5,039,545 acres, with an estimated value of $96,133,290, had increased, in 1860, to $13,251,473 acres, with an estimated value of $432,531,072. The two principal staple products of our soil—wheat and corn—had increased in a similar ratio—the former from 9,414,575 bushels, in 1850, to 24,159,500 bushels, in 1860, and the latter from 57,646,984 bushels, in 1850, to 115,296,779 bushels, in 1860. Our magnificent railways, which in 1850 were only 110 miles, costing $1,440,507, had extended in 1860 to 2,867 miles, at a cost of $104,944,561. Nor had the progress of our people been confined to an increase of population and wealth. In every city and town had sprung up, as if by magic, the unmistakable evidences of progress in the arts and sciences. In fact, it could be truly said that, through the enlightened liberality of our citizens, the unfortunate, the poor and the helpless, were provided for and educated, without money and without price."

From its coal mines, which in 1860 had just begun to be fairly worked, were taken 14,158,120 bushels—an aggregate only below the great States of Pennsylvania and Ohio. These are items in a prosperity so great as to be a marvel. A single city had, in thirty years, grown from a small village around an old fort to be the first grain, lumber and beef and pork *entrepot* of the continent, if not of the world.

In this march to greatness Illinois was not alone, but worthy compeers were her near sisters, Michigan, Indiana, Iowa and Wisconsin.

Young Minnesota was whispering her golden promise, and Missouri was waiting until, free from slavery, she, too, could show how States are made.

In 1861, came civil war upon a scale of astounding magnitude, destined, if not to suspend, at least to vary, the direction of its prosperity, and the history of the State through this great war demands our attention.

There had been a struggle between the opposite systems of free and slave labor, which had grown into antagonism, extending into literature, religion, politics. Slavery was outgrown by freedom; its old supremacy was being destroyed by the rapid expansion of the Free States, and their growth in material prosperity. Indeed the rebellion was rather against the revelation of the census tables than against the government of any man or party. The friends of slavery demanded that it should be exempted from free discussion, and not only tolerated but fostered. They claimed for it the right to go, under the Constitution, into the Territories of the United States, setting aside the long established principle that it was the creature of local law and could only exist where covered by positive enactments. Said General Quitman, "Slavery requires for its kind development a fostering government over it. It can scarcely exist without such development." It was to be accepted as good without question, for to question was to irritate. Said Senator Baker, of Oregon, to Senator Benjamin, of Louisiana, "If we, a free people, really, in our hearts and consciences, believing that freedom is better for everything than slavery, do desire the advance of free sentiments, and do endeavor to assist that advance in a constitutional, legal way, is that ground of separation?" Senator Benjamin: "I say, yes."

As early as 1858, Jefferson Davis, the President of the Southern Confederacy, organized by rebellion, said, in a speech, in Jackson, Mississippi, "If an Abolitionist be chosen President of the United States, you will have presented to you the question of whether you will permit the government to pass into the hands of your avowed and implacable enemies? Without pausing for an answer, I will state my own position to be, that such a result would be a species of revolution, by which the purposes of the government would be destroyed, and the observance of its mere forms entitled to no respect. In that event, in such a manner as should be most expedient, I should deem it your duty to provide for your safety outside of the Union with those who have already shown the will, and would have acquired the power to deprive you of your birthright, and to reduce you to worse than the colonial dependence of your fathers."

The simple fact of the constitutional election, by the people, of a President holding that slavery was wrong, should be deemed occasion of revolt. Mr. Davis subsequently said, in conversation with Colonel Jaques, "We seceded to escape the rule of majorities."

In the State of Illinois there was to be a contest which was to have most weighty influence in shaping the pending controversy.

In 1858, Abraham Lincoln was put forward as candidate for the seat in the national Senate about to be vacated by the expiration of the term of Hon. Stephen A. Douglas, who was a candidate for re-election. These distinguished gentlemen canvassed the State and met, for joint discussion, at seven prominent places. Never, in the history of American politics, did a discussion so arrest the public attention, and assume an importance so truly national. Thousands crowded to hear the debates; reporters of the leading newspapers of the Union were in attendance, and the speeches were widely copied. The discussion was termed by a public journal "the battle of the giants." Mr. Douglas secured the State Legislature and his Senatorial seat, and lost the Presidency. Mr. Lincoln, carrying the popular vote of the State, lost, nevertheless, the Legislature, and was defeated for the Senatorship, but the nation had its eye, upon him, and called him to the Presidential chair.

The principal topic of discussion was Slavery and the Territories, Mr. Lincoln insisting that Congress, for the American people, had the right to exclude it, and should do so; Mr. Douglas insisting that each Territory should be left to settle its own domestic institutions in its own way, subject only to the Constitution of the United States. Neither assumed the attitude of hostility to slavery, as existing in States already in the Union. Little did those men know that they were consolidating the forces of the Union and making prominent, and more than ever sacred, the doctrine of the majesty of majorities.

In 1860, four candidates for the Presidential chair were before the American people—Stephen A. Douglas, of Illinois; Abraham Lincoln, of Illinois; John C. Breckinridge, of Kentucky; and John

Bell, of Tennessee. The contest was one of the most exciting of our history, and resulted in the election of Mr. Lincoln, who received one hundred and eighty electoral votes; Mr. Breckinridge, seventy-two; Mr. Bell, thirty-nine; Mr. Douglas, twelve; Mr. Lincoln's electoral majority being fifty-seven. The popular vote was, for Mr. Lincoln, 1,857,610; Mr. Douglas, 1,365,976; Mr. Breckinridge, 847,953; for Mr. Bell, 590,631. The election of Mr. Lincoln was rendered inevitable by the refusal of the Southern States to submit to the nomination of Mr. Douglas, and the factious nomination of Mr. Breckinridge, of Kentucky.

Early in the campaign came threats of disunion, in the event of Mr. Lincoln's election; the Southern States would secede and form an independent confederacy, on the ground that slavery would be imperiled and Southern institutions destroyed by longer union with Free States. The historian who concedes the right of revolution searches in vain for any reason in justification of so grave a step at that time. Up to the election of Mr. Lincoln there had been no change in the Federal Constitution, affecting the rights of either section of the Republic. No statute had been created by Congress in opposition to a united South, or against which its representatives had voted in a body. No change had been made in the status of slavery, but, in fact, the administration, the legislature, the compromises and the patronage of the government had steadily been in its interest. Its area had been broadened by compromise, purchase and conquest. A law, in the judgment of Northern men, of needless severity and downright barbarity, stood unamended and unrepealed upon the statute books, and was everywhere enforced in the rendition of fugitive slaves. There had been no taxation without representation, but on the contrary, a representation had been given, in the South, to what was claimed as property. There had been no interference with the freedom of the press, of education, of speech, of worship, or of the elective franchise. These statements are conceded by Alexander H. Stephens, one of the most acute minds and wisest statesmen of the South, and though he subsequently went with his State, and has been the second officer of the Confederacy, his words have lost none of their significance. In the convention of Georgia, when secession was being discussed, he arose and said:

"This step [the secession of Georgia] once taken, can never be recalled; and all the baleful and withering consequences that must follow (as you will see), will rest on the Convention for all coming time. When we and our posterity shall see our lovely South desolated by the demon of war, which this act of yours will inevitably invite and call forth; when our green fields of waving harvests shall be trodden down by the murderous soldiery and fiery car of war sweeping over our land; our temples of justice laid in ashes; all the horrors and desolations of war upon us; who but this Convention will be held responsible for it? and who but him who shall have given his vote for this unwise and ill-timed measure (as I honestly think and believe) shall be held to strict account for this suicidal act, by the present generation, and, probably, cursed and execrated by posterity for all time to come, for the wide and desolating ruin that will inevitably follow this act you now propose to perpetrate?

"Pause, I entreat you, and consider, for a moment, what reasons you can give that will even satisfy yourselves, in calmer moments; what reasons can you give to your fellow-sufferers in the calamity that it will bring upon us? What reasons can you give to the nations of the earth to justify it? They will be the calm and deliberate judges in the case; and to what cause, or *one* overt act, can you name or point, on which to rest the plea of justification? What right has the North assailed? What interest of the South has been invaded? What justice has been denied? and what claim, founded in justice and right, has been withheld? Can either of you, to-day, name one governmental act of wrong, deliberately and purposely done by the government, of which the South has a right to complain? I challenge the answer! While, on the other hand, let me show the facts (and, believe me, gentlemen, I am not here the advocate of the North, but I am here the friend, the firm friend and lover of the South and her institutions, and for that reason I speak thus plainly and faithfully, for *yours*, *mine*, and every other man's interest, the words of truth and soberness), of which I wish you to judge, and I will only state facts which are clear and undeniable, and which now stand as records authentic in the history of our country.

"When we of the South demanded the slave-trade, or the importation of Africans for the cultivation of our lands, did they not yield the right for twenty years? When we asked a three-fifth representation in Congress for our slaves, was it not granted? When we asked and demanded the return of any fugitive from justice, or the recovery of those persons owing labor or allegiance, was it not incorporated in the constitution? and again ratified and strengthened in the Fugitive Slave Law of 1840?

"But, do you reply, that in many instances they have violated this compact, and have not been faithful to their engagements? As individuals and local communities they may have done so, but not by the sanction of government, for that has always been true to Southern interests. Again, gentlemen, look at another fact: When we have asked that more territory should be added, that we might spread the institution of slavery, have they not yielded to our demands, in giving us Louisiana, Florida and Texas, out of which four States have been carved, and ample territory to be added in due time, if you, by this unwise and impolitic act, do not destroy this hope, and, perhaps, by it lose all, and have your last slave wrenched from you by stern military rule, as South America and Mexico were, or by the vindictive decree of universal emancipation, which may reasonably be expected to follow?

"But, again, gentlemen, what have we to gain by this proposed change of our relation to the general government? We have always had the control of it, and can yet, if we remain in it, and are as united as we have been. We have had a majority of the Presidents chosen from the South, as well as the control and management of most of those chosen from the North. We have had sixty years of Southern Presidents to their twenty-four, thus controlling the executive department. So of the Judges of the Supreme Court, we have had eighteen from the South and but eleven from the North. Although nearly four fifths of the judicial business has arisen in the Free States, yet a majority of the Court has always been from the South. This we have required, so as to guard against any interpretation of the constitution unfavorable to us. In like manner, we have been equally watchful to guard our interests in the Legislative branch of government. In choosing the presiding Presidents (*pro tem.*) of the Senate, we have had twenty-four to their eleven. Speakers of the House, we have had twenty-three and they twelve. While the majority of the Representatives, from their greater population, have always been from the North, yet we have so generally secured the Speaker, because he, to a great extent, shapes and controls the legislation of the country. Nor have we had less control in every other department of the general government.

* * * * * * * * * * * * *

"Leaving out of view, for the present, the countless millions of dollars you must expend in a war with the North, with tens of thousands of your sons and brothers slain in battle, and offered up as sacrifices on the altar of your ambition—and for what, we ask again? Is it for the overthrow of the American Government, established by our common ancestry, cemented and built up by their sweat and blood, and founded on the broad principles of *Right, Justice and Humanity*? And as such, I must declare here, as I have often done before, and which has been repeated by the greatest and wisest of statesmen and patriots, in this and other lands, that *it is the best and freest government; the most equal in its rights; the most just in its decisions; the most lenient in its measures, and the most inspiring in its principles to elevate the race of men, that the sun of heaven ever shone upon.*

"Now, for you to attempt to overthrow such a government as this, under which we have lived for more than three-quarters of a century—in which we have gained our wealth, our standing as a nation, our domestic safety, while elements of peril are around us, with peace and tranquillity accompanied with unbounded prosperity and rights unassailed—is the hight of madness, folly and wickedness, to which I can neither lend my sanction nor my vote."

The President elect stood upon a platform which did not warrant the apprehension that he would interfere, or sanction interference with slavery in the States. It is true he had said, "It is my opinion that this government cannot endure, permanently, half slave and half free," but he had also said, "I now assure you that I neither then had, nor have, nor ever had, any purpose, in any way, of interfering with the institution of slavery where it exists. I believe we have no power, under the Constitution of the United States, or rather under the form of government under which we live, to interfere with the institution of slavery, or any other of the institutions of our sister States, be they Free or Slave States."* If the Southern Senators and Representatives remained in their places, he was without a majority in Congress, and was, indeed, dependent upon the courtesy of his opponents for the confirmation of his cabinet. He was hedged in upon every side, and powerless for evil had it been in his heart.

But madness ruled the hour. Southern conspirators were bent on securing what had long been planned; viz., separation from the Union. Mr. Lincoln's election was made the pretext, and active preparations were made. Unfortunately, the President, Mr. Buchanan, lacked that courage and inflexible purpose which the crisis demanded, and cowered piteously before the coming storm. There was an understanding that, while he remained in power, there should be no open assault upon the government, and the old man seemed to feel with the ancient King, "Good is the word of the Lord, if there be peace in my day." Arch-conspirators were about his council board. They removed southward large stores of heavy ordnance, small arms and ammunition, and then, except where they had reason to believe the commanding officers in sympathy with them, removed the garrisons, leaving only a feeble handful of defenders at each post. The navy was scattered through all distant seas, and made as inefficient as possible. A heavy debt was pressed upon an exhausted treasury.

The Southern press, pulpit and rostrum, were busy "firing the Southern heart," and an excited people was ready for revolt. Union sentiment, where it existed, was suppressed by violence. Proclamations of Governors, Acts of Legislatures, Ordinances of Conventions, followed in rapid succession. Military companies were formed and drilled, Southern Members of Congress resigned and returned to their constituents, and State after State declared itself out of the Union.

* Speech in Cincinnati, September, 1859.

During these days, between the election and inauguration of Mr. Lincoln, it was humiliating to be in the National Capitol. Regularly, for a time, the conspirators arose in their places in the American Congress, and, after the utterance of treasonable sentiments, after defying the government, they would announce their State withdrawn from the Union, and they then said their mock farewells! And all that was borne by the shadow of the government which held the power of this great country!

On the 20th of December, 1860, the Convention of South Carolina declared "The Union now existing between South Carolina and other States of North America is dissolved, and that the State of South Carolina has resumed her position among the nations of the earth, as a free, sovereign and independent State, with full power to levy war and conclude peace, contract alliances, establish commerce, and to do all other acts and things which independent States may of right do."

On the 24th, Governor Pickens issued his proclamation, declaring "South Carolina is, and has a right to be, a free and independent State, and, as such, has a right to levy war, conclude peace, negotiate treaties, leagues and covenants, and to do all acts whatever that rightfully appertain to a free and independent State."

The telegraph carried the news throughout the nation that the chain of the Union was broken, and men said, every where, "What will the government do?" The government did—nothing! In the South, the intelligence excited the people as did the display of the fiery cross the ancient Highland clans. In Congress it produced little apparent excitement. It was announced by Mr. Garnet, of Virginia. The Pacific Railroad was the order of the day, and Mr. G. said that his State would not consent to be held responsible for any financial obligation in its construction. "Sir," said he, "while your Bill is under consideration, one of the sovereign States of this Confederacy has, by the glorious act of her people, withdrawn, in vindication of her rights, from the Union, as the telegraph announced at half-past one to-day." There was applause by a few conspirators, but most of the members manifested utter indifference. Boyce and Ashmore, the only remaining Representatives of the recusant State, left their seats, exchanged salutations with personal friends and fellow malcontents, and retired from the Hall of Representatives. Mr. Buchanan had before him a clearly defined duty, namely, to enforce the authority of the United States, but his blood was thin and ran slowly. He dared not, but contented himself with mumbling dreary platitudes, and prating about "coercion."

The telegraph gave the announcement at Springfield, the home of Mr. Lincoln, giving him an intimation of the unwonted cares and momentous difficulties likely to environ his administration. He had gauged the probabilities long before, and manifested neither surprise nor alarm. The *Journal*, of that city, supposed to reflect his views, said:

> "If South Carolina does not obstruct the collection of the revenue, at her ports, or violate another Federal law, there will be no trouble, and she will not be out of the Union. If she violates the law, then comes the tug of war. The President of the United States, in such an emergency, has an imperative duty to perform. Mr. Buchanan may shirk it, or the emergency may not exist during his administration. If not, then the Union will last through his term of office. If the overt act, on the part of South Carolina, takes place on or after the fourth day of March, then the duty of executing the law will devolve upon Mr. Lincoln."

The influence of the above paragraph can scarcely be estimated. It appeared in a newspaper printed in a little Western city, but it was understood to represent the faith and purpose of the coming Chief Magistrate. It was widely copied, and loyal men, as they read it, took heart and hope. The Union, loved with unutterable love, should not be lost! It would soon have a President who would defend it to the last extremity! "Oh, that the fourth of March were come!" was said by many, both men and women. They felt they had done the South no wrong. They would offer no apologies. The threat of disunion should wring no new abandonment of honor, no new concession to wrong! After the manner prescribed by law, a President had been chosen. If for that, secession was attempted, it should not be permitted. For the present, they would wait and hope that, at the end of the many months of senile incapacity, if nothing worse, the sinewy hand of the Western President should be laid heavily upon treason.

On the 26th Major Anderson evacuated Fort Moultrie and occupied Fort Sumter. His little force was in the greatest peril, but reinforcements were withheld. Two days previously he wrote to Washington, "When I inform you that my garrison consists of only sixty effective men, and we are in a very indifferent work, the walls of which are only fourteen feet high, and that we have, within one hundred and sixty yards of our walls, sand hills which command our works, and which afford admirable sites for batteries, and the finest covers for sharpshooters, and that, besides this, there are numerous houses, some of them within pistol shot, you will at once see that if attacked in force, headed by any one but a simpleton, there is scarcely a possibility of our being able to hold out long enough for our friends to come to our succor."

Fort Sumter was the key to the Charleston harbor; once occupied, from it Moultrie could be knocked to pieces, and reinforcements from the sea prevented. He knew the keen eyes of the Charleston authorities were upon it. He plead for reinforcements—General Scott seconded the appeal. No—the act would be construed as unfriendly, as a menace, and exasperate the South Carolina rebels: must be avoided; and was! Major Anderson went on improving Moultrie, as though he proposed to stay permanently; at the same time he ordered the work being done on Sumter to be pressed to early completion. When notified by Captain Foster that all was ready, he took a responsibility, the announcement of which electrified the nation. Without specific instructions from the President or Secretary of War, on the 26th, he gave orders to prepare for the evacuation of Fort Moultrie. Night came; vessels were loaded with women, children and personal effects. The boats stood off, as if for Fort Johnson, but landed at Fort Sumter. At dawn, all had found the new shelter, except a few who remained to put Fort Moultrie on a peace footing. This was effected by Captain Johnson and eight men, who coolly proceeded to dismount the heavy guns, and burn the gun carriages. Governor Pinckney and the Convention took alarm from the smoke. Drums beat, the militia flew to arms, and soon the wildest rumors were afloat, corrected, however, by the appearance of Captain Johnson, in the streets of Charleston, who, on behalf of Major Anderson, communicated his action to the authorities. It gave great offense and was construed into a threat of "coercion." A communication was sent to Washington, through commissioners, who were instructed to demand of President Buchanan an order remanding Major Anderson to Moultrie, but that was too much, even for him. The State authorities took steps for the immediate occupancy of Castle Pinckney and Fort Moultrie, which Major Anderson was not authorized to prevent. They also sèized the various United States and telegraph buildings. Then, had the word been spoken by the President, Major Anderson could have crushed secession in its nest. His guns could have prevented the erection of those elaborate works which subsequently compelled his surrender, and the dishonor of the flag. It is not the province of the historian to speculate, but it is impossible to resist saying "Ah! what might have been!"

Major Anderson was suddenly the most famous man in the country, and his strategic movement met with hearty approval throughout the loyal States.

Before leaving the record of this first stage of war, for such it was, it is proper to recur to the statement that Lieut.-General Scott urged upon Mr. Buchanan the importance of reinforcing Major Anderson, and of strongly manning the seaboard defenses. Since the above the autobiography of the Lieut.-General has come to hand, and the statements of the venerable hero are overwhelmingly conclusive. On the 29th of October, 1860, he addressed Mr. Buchanan a letter, in which, after alluding to the probable nearness of outbreak to follow Mr. Lincoln's election, he said:

"From a knowledge of our Southern population, it is my solemn conviction that there is some danger of an early act of rashness preliminary to secession; viz., the seizure of some or all of the following forts: Forts Jackson and St. Philip, on the Mississippi, below New Orleans, both without garrisons; Fort Morgan, below Mobile, without a garrison; Forts Pickens and McRae, Pensacola harbor, with an insufficient garrison for one; Fort Pulaski, below Savannah, without a garrison; Forts Moultrie and Sumter, Charleston harbor, the former with an insufficient garrison, the latter without any, and Fort Monroe, Hampton Roads, without a sufficient garrison. In my opinion, all these works should be immediately so garrisoned as to make any attempt to take any one of them by surprise or *coup de main*, ridiculous."

Again, he says:

"OCTOBER 31.—I suggested to the Secretary of War that a circular should be sent at once to such of those forts as had garrisons to be on the alert against surprises and sudden assaults."

A significant foot-note says, "Permission not granted." On the 12th of December he left the bed to which he had been long confined and repaired to Washington. The next day he called upon the Secretary of War and urged upon him—

"The same views; viz., strong garrisons in the Southern forts—those of Charleston and Pensacola harbors at once; those on Mobile Bay and the Mississippi below New Orleans next, etc. * * * The Secretary did not concur in my views, and I begged him to procure me an early interview with the President, that I might make one more effort to save the forts and the Union. By appointment the Secretary accompanied me to the President, Dec. 15th, when the same topics were discussed. * * * The President, in reply to my arguments for immediately reinforcing Fort Moultrie and sending a garrison to Fort Sumter, said, in substance, the time had not arrived for doing so; that he would wait the action of the convention of South Carolina, in the expectation that a commission would be appointed and sent to negotiate with him and Congress respecting the secession of the State and the property of the United States held within its limits; and that if Congress should decide against the secession then he would send a reinforcement and telegraph the commander (Major Anderson) of Fort Moultrie to hold the forts (Moultrie and Sumter) against attack. And the Secretary, with animation, added, 'We have a vessel of war (the Brooklyn) held in readiness at Norfolk, and he would then send three hundred men in her from Fort Monroe to Charleston.' To which I replied, first, that so many men could not be withdrawn from that garrison but could be taken from New York; next, that it would then be too late, as the South Carolina commissioners would have the game in their hands, by first using and then cutting the wires; that as there was not a soldier in Fort Sumter any handful of armed secessionists might seize and occupy it.

"Here the remark may be permitted, that if the Secretary's three hundred men had then, or some time later, been sent to Forts Moultrie and Sumter, both would now have been in the possession of the United States, and not a battery below could have been erected by the secessionists; consequently the access to these forts from the sea would now (the end of March, 1861,) be unobstructed and free.

"Dec. 30.—Will the President permit Gen. Scott, without reference to the War Department [foot-note—'The Secretary was already suspected'] and otherwise, as secretly as possible, to send two hundred and fifty recruits from New York harbor, to reinforce Fort Sumter? etc. * * * It would have been easy to reinforce this fort down to about the 12th of February. In this long delay, Fort Moultrie had been rearmed and greatly strengthened, etc. * * * The difficulty of reinforcing had thus been increased ten or twelvefold. First, the late President (Buchanan) *refused to allow any attempt to be made because he was holding negotiations with the South Carolina commissioners*," etc.—*Aut. Vol. II.*

There is another quotation from the same authority, which is highly significant:

"Before any resolution was taken, the late Secretary of the Navy making difficulties about the want of suitable war vessels, another commissioner from South

Carolina arrived, causing further delay. When all this had passed away, Secretaries Holt and Toucey, Capt. Ward of the navy, and myself, with the knowledge of the President (Buchanan), settled upon the employment, under the Captain (who was eager for the expedition) of three or four small steamers belonging to the coast survey. At that time (late in January) I have no doubt Capt. Ward would have reached Fort Sumter with all his vessels. But he was kept back by something like a *truce* or armistice made [here] embracing Charleston and Pensacola harbors, agreed upon between the late President and certain principal seceders of South Carolina, Florida, Louisiana, etc., and that truce lasted to the end of that administration."

Alas! that the evidence should be so conclusive! Alas! that such a record must be written! Yet we may even now see the finger of Providence. Great events were shaping. By the Calvaries, and through the Gethsemanes of sorrow and purification was the nation to march reverently and penitently to the Bethany of its ascension!

Of course events so momentous caused great anxiety and produced exciting discussions, which cannot be reproduced in a work so specific in its character as this one. How did the Representatives and Senators of Illinois meet the crisis? In the Senate were Mr. Douglas and Mr. Trumbull. The former was disposed to go as far as possible towards conciliation, farther than his colleague would have deemed proper, but they united in condemning secession. Mr. Douglas, on Tuesday, Dec. 18th, promptly moved to "lay over" a scheme proposed by Senator Joseph Lane of Oregon, which declared the government unfitted for the exigences of the times, and proposing the appointment of commissioners to suggest remedies! January 7th, in reviewing the speech of Senator Baker, after criticising the views of the Republican party, he said: "I feel bound, however, and take pleasure in saying, that I don't believe the Southern States are in any danger, or ought to have any apprehension, that Mr. Lincoln, or his party can do any harm or render insecure their rights to persons or property anywhere in this country." In that speech he used the words subsequently so often quoted—"War is disunion, certain, inevitable, final and irreversible." He made a point of keen, telling, illustrated logic, in these words: "The President in his message first said we could not coerce a state to remain in the Union, but in a few sentences he advised the acquisition of Cuba. As if we should pay $300,000,000 for Cuba, and the next day she might secede and re-annex herself to Spain, and

Spain sell her again." He (Mr. Buchanan) had admitted that Texas cost us a war with Mexico, and 10,000 lives, and besides, we had paid Texas $10,000,000 for land which she never owned." Again, speaking of war: "The atmosphere is full of it. I have determined that I will do all that is in my power to rescue the country from such a dreadful fate. But I will not consider this question of war till all hope of peaceable adjustment fails. Better, a thousand times better, that all political parties be disbanded and dissolved. Better that every public man now in existence be consigned to retirement and political martyrdom, than this government should be dissolved, and this country plunged in civil war. I trust we are to have no war for a platform. I can fight for my country, but there never was a political platform that I would go to war for. I fear if this country is to be wrecked it is to be done by those who prefer party to their country." Later, in reply to Mr. Wigfall, of Texas, he said: "The senator (Wigfall) had better read the Constitution again, then let him tell me where he finds the power given to this government to protect horses, or cattle, or merchandise, or slaves, or any species of property in any state or territory of this Union?" Until the close of Congress he earnestly sought to secure peace, by such amendments to the Constitution as would forever place slavery without the bar of Congressional action or Federal controversy.

Mr. Trumbull, his colleague, was an able and ardent advocate of the policy of the party which had elected Mr. Lincoln, yet he was conciliatory, though bating not one jot of Federal authority. He said in a speech on the night of March 3d, that there would have been no triumphant secession but for complicity with treason in the very cabinet of the government. The President received commissioners who, under any other government would have been hung for treason, and that, not until the last moment, when forced to take sides, and either join the secessionists and let Major Anderson perish, or to meet the anger of his countrymen, did the President declare for the Union. Speaking of compromise he said, if they wanted anything let them go back to the Missouri Compromise and stand to it. All agreed that Congress had not the right to interfere with slavery in the States. But he would never, by his vote, make one slave, and the people of the great Northwest would never consent by their act, to establish slavery anywhere. He did not believe the Constitution needed amending, but was willing to vote a recommendation to the States to make a proposal to call a convention to consider amendments. His position was clearly defined; viz., peace, if possible; government in the Union at all hazards.

In the popular branch were several members of prominence. There was Owen Lovejoy, a primitive anti-slavery man, who had been bereaved of a brother by a pro-slavery mob. John A. Logan and Mr. McClernand, both of whom became Major Generals of U. S. Volunteers, were in opposition to the Republican party, both conservative, and Mr. Logan opposed to coercion. Mr. Morris, Mr. Kellogg and Mr. Washburne were also prominent. Mr. Lovejoy, considered one of the most radical of the extreme abolitionists, on the 17th of December, offered, and pressed to a vote, the following:

"WHEREAS, the Constitution of the United States is the supreme law of the land, and its ready and faithful obedience a duty of all good and law-abiding citizens; therefore,

"*Resolved*, that we deprecate the spirit of disobedience to the Constitution, wherever manifested, and that we earnestly recommend the repeal of all nullification laws; and that it is the duty of the President to protect and defend the property of the United States."

The conspirators were much annoyed by this flank movement of "an extremist" and generally refused to vote, but without them it was passed by an affirmative vote of 124, none voting nay. On the same day Mr. Morris, for the third time, brought forward his Union resolution declaring "the immense value of the national Union," that "we will frown upon the first dawning of every attempt to alienate any portion of our country from the rest, or enfeeble the sacred ties which now link together the various parts," and added, "nor do we see anything in the election of Abraham Lincoln to the Presidency of the United States, or from any other existing cause to justify its dissolution," &c., which was adopted by a vote of 115 to 44. It is singular to find among the nays that of Daniel Sickles, subsequently a gallant and able Major-General of the Union army. Later, Mr. Lovejoy made a remark in caucus which has become famous among the memorable sayings which the war has occasioned. He was speaking of a proposition to divide the country to the Pacific between freedom and slavery, and in his own peculiar way said, "There never was a more causeless revolt since Lucifer led his cohorts of apostate angels against the throne of God; but I never heard that the Almighty proposed to compromise the matter by allowing the rebels to kindle the fires of hell south of the celestial meridian of 36° 30′!" Mr. Logan has been spoken of as opposed to coercive measures at the outset, but when the vote was called upon a resolution approving the act of Major Anderson in removing from Fort Moultrie and also pledging to "support the President in all constitutional measures to enforce the laws, and preserve the Union," he said in answering to his name, "As the resolution merits my unqualified approval, I vote aye."

The record of Kellogg, McClernand, Washburne, &c., during that memorable session, the last of the XXXVI. Congress, need not be transcribed. Whatever theoretical differences may have divided them, when war really came they were found unflinching on the side of the Union.

The position of the Governor and other state authorities, will be seen in a subsequent chapter. It is enough to say that there was no doubt in what direction the hearty influence of the Illinois Executive would be thrown. This introductory chapter will be fitly closed with a statement of the principal events down to the close of Mr. Buchanan's administration.

On the 28th of December South Carolina troops occupied Fort Moultrie and Castle Pinckney, and the Palmetto flag was hoisted on the ramparts, instead of the honored national colors. The ensuing day John B. Floyd resigned his place in the cabinet, as Secretary of War, charging, with an impudence unparalleled, that the President, by declining to remove Major Anderson, and to withdraw the Federal troops from Charleston Harbor, designed to plunge the country into civil war! He said, "I cannot consent to be the agent of such a calamity." On the same day the South Carolina Commissioners presented their official credentials which, on the next day were declined. On the 1st day of January, 1861, the loyal press rang with warning that the Capital was in danger of seizure by armed rebels, and called for instant and efficient measures for its protection. On the 2d it was announced that Lieut.-General Scott had taken steps to organize the militia of the District of Columbia, and that regulars had been placed in the navy yard and other precautions taken against surprise or revolution. On the same day came telegraphic information that Georgia had declared for secession, and that Georgia troops had taken possession of the U. S. Arsenal in Augusta, and Forts Pulaski and Jackson. Governor Ellis, of North Carolina, seized the forts at Beaufort and Wilmington, and the arsenal at Fayetteville, stating with Floyd-like truthfulness that he did so to protect them from mobs! On the 3d the South Carolina Commissioners departed from the Capitol. On the 5th it was announced that enrollments of men to aid the government in enforcing the laws and maintaining the union of the States were progressing in the Northern cities. The Alabama and Mississippi delegations in Congress, who had met the preceding evening, telegraphed the conventions of their respective states, advising them to secede, stating there was no prospect of satisfactory adjustment. The steamer "Star of the West," sailed secretly from New York with supplies and reinforcements for Fort Sumter. Companies of Federal troops were being concentrated in and about Washington, and the public began to hope that at last Mr. Buchanan would prove himself worthy of honorable mention in American history. On the 7th the conventions of Alabama, Mississippi and Tennessee met. On the 8th Secretary Thompson resigned his seat in the Cabinet, on the ground that, contrary to promise, troops had been sent to Major Anderson. On the next day the "Star of the West" was fired into from Fort Moultrie and Morris Island, and turned homeward, leaving Sumter and its gallant defenders. Henceforward events crowd with fearful rapidity, of which only a few can be recorded. The ordinance of secession passed the Mississippi convention on the 9th, that of Florida, purchased with Union gold, on the 10th, and that of Alabama on the 11th. The same day witnessed the resignation of Mr. Thomas, Secretary of the Treasury, and the seizure by the rebels of the arsenal at Baton Rouge, and Forts Jackson and St. Philip at the mouth of the Mississippi River, and Fort Pike at the Lake Ponchartrain entrance. On the 13th the Pensacola Navy Yard and Fort Barrancas were surrendered to rebel troops by Col. Armstrong. Lieut. Slemmer, who had withdrawn his command from Fort McRae to Fort Pickens defied Armstrong's orders, and announced his intention to hold his post at all hazards. On the 16th

Major-General Sandford, of New York, tendered the President and General Scott the service of the first division of N. Y. Militia, well armed and disciplined, and numbering seven thousand. On the 18th came a voice from Massachusetts, her Legislature unanimously tendering the President all the men and money required to maintain the authority of the Federal Government, and declaring that South Carolina, in seizing the national fortifications with the Post Office and Custom House, and in firing upon a vessel in the U. S. service, had been guilty of an act of war. And so it had as truly as when, later, fire was opened upon Fort Sumter. The Georgia Convention voted the secession ordinance on the 19th. On the 20th it was announced in Washington that a "thousand allied troops" were besieging Lieut. Slemmer and his command in Fort Pickens. On the 24th the Augusta Arsenal was seized by Georgia authorities. The next day the Louisiana ordinance of secession passed the convention. On the 30th the revenue cutters, Cass and McClelland, were betrayed by their commanders into the hands of Louisiana and Alabama rebel officers. On the 1st of February the U. S. Mint and Custom House at New Orleans were seized, and the same day the Texas Convention voted that state out of the Union. On the 4th the "Peace Convention" assembled in Washington, and the Congress of seceded States met in Montgomery, Ala., and John Tyler was chosen President of the former. On the 9th a provisional Constitution was adopted at Montgomery, it being the U. S. constitution varied to suit the purposes of treason. Jefferson Davis, of Mississippi, was chosen President, and Alexander H. Stephens, despite the sentiments of his speech already quoted, Vice-President of the "Confederate States of North America." And yet the President of the United States saw no occasion to employ the troops tendered him! The government was going to pieces, and he was trembling with fear, not daring to strike, when a single blow might have crushed rebellion and saved the nation its terrible ordeal of blood. On the 11th Mr. Lincoln left his home for Washington; of his journey the next chapter will speak. On the 18th Jefferson Davis was inaugurated President of the C. S. A. On the 25th it was ascertained that General Twiggs, commanding the department of Texas, had basely betrayed his trust and given up all the military posts, munitions, arms, &c., to the authorities of Texas. On the 3d of

March, at midnight, the term of James Buchanan expired. His administration commenced with a prosperous country, a full treasury, and a triumphant party. He went out with the latter beaten, the treasury empty, the nation in debt, and the country tossing in the agony of disruption. He sacrificed Mr. Douglas and was in turn sacrificed by his Southern allies. It, perhaps, remains to be seen whether his closing months of power gave the country an administration controlled by fear of the solemn responsibilities of the crisis or something worse. Be this as it may, the nation thanked God and took courage at twelve o'clock on the night of March 3, 1861.

CHAPTER II.

THE ILLINOIS PRESIDENT.

ABRAHAM LINCOLN—EARLY HISTORY—REMOVALS—TASTE OF WAR—CANDIDACY—A SURVEYOR—MEMBER OF ILLINOIS LEGISLATURE—INTERNAL IMPROVEMENT—PRIVATE LIFE—IN CONGRESS—WILMOT PROVISO—NEBRASKA BILL—HIS OPPOSITION—MISSOURI COMPROMISE—PEORIA SPEECH—PROPHETIC WORDS—RIGHT AND WRONG—BILL OF EXCEPTIONS TO SLAVERY—THE FATHERS—SENATORIAL ELECTION—CONTEST OF 1858—THE DIVIDED HOUSE SPEECH—THE WAY OF PROVIDENCE—LEADERS FOR CRISES—HIS CHARACTERISTICS—NATIONAL REPUBLICAN CONVENTION—WIGWAM—SEWARD AND LINCOLN—NOMINATION—LEAVING SPRINGFIELD—INVOCATION OF PRAYER—HIS FAREWELL—THE JOURNEY—SPEECHES—AT INDIANAPOLIS—CINCINNATI—NEW YORK—TRENTON—PHILADELPHIA—IN WASHINGTON—INAUGURATION—THE INAUGURAL ADDRESS—CABINET—SUMTER—SURRENDER—A LOWERED FLAG—ONLY A MOMENT.

THE eyes of the Nation had been, from November, turned toward Springfield, the capital of Illinois, where resided the President elect. Illinois had given the Republic the first Northern President who was destined to a re-election. Of necessity our history must make some mention of him who, the nation's chief magistrate and commander-in-chief of its army and navy, is yet of Illinois, whom she received when a young man; who developed into mature strength on her prairies—ABRAHAM LINCOLN.

He was born in Hardin County, Kentucky, February 12, 1809. In 1816 his father removed to what is now Spencer County, Indiana, and cleared his farm from the dense timber of that part of the State. Here the future statesman underwent the discipline of sturdy toil and patient labor. In 1830 his father removed to Illinois, and "located" on new land about ten miles northwest of Decatur on the north bank of the Sangamon, where timber and prairie are blended. His boyhood had few privileges of school or culture in books, and he was emphatically "self-made." In 1832 he volunteered in the noted Black-Hawk war and was captain of a company. He served three months, but was in no engagement with the enemy. Returning home, he became a candidate for a seat in the Legislature only ten days before election, but being an Adams man, he was defeated, though in his own precinct he received more votes than both rival candidates for Congress. He was sometime engaged in surveying, and in 1834 was elected to the Legislature, to which he was subsequently thrice chosen, and devoted himself to the practical work of the people's representative.

Says one of his biographers:

"The period embraced by the eight years in which Lincoln represented Sangamon County, was one of the greatest material activity in Illinois. So early as 1820, the young State was seized with the 'generous rage' for public internal improvements then prevalent in New York, Pennsylvania and Ohio, and in its sessions for a score of succeeding years, the Legislature was occupied by the discussion of various schemes for enhancing the prosperity of the State. The large canal uniting the waters of Lake Michigan and the Illinois River was completed at a cost of more than eight millions. By a Board of Commissioners of Public Works, specially created, provisions were made for expensive improvements of the Wabash, Illinois, Rock, Kaskaskia and the Little Wabash, and the great Western mail route from Vincennes to St. Louis. Under the charge of the same Board, six railroads, connecting principal points, were projected, and appropriations made for their completion at an immense outlay.

"One effect of a policy so wild and extravagant was to sink the State in debt. Another was to attract vast immigration, and fill up her broad prairies with settlers. Individuals were ruined; the corporate State became embarrassed; but benefits have resulted in a far greater degree than could have been hoped when the crash first came. It is not yet time to estimate the ultimate good to be derived from these improvements, though the immediate evil has been tangible enough.

"The name of Abraham Lincoln is not found recorded in favor of the more visionary of these schemes, but he has always favored public improvements, and his voice was for whatever project seemed feasible and practical. During his first term of service, he was a member of the Committee on Public Accounts and Expenditures. He voted for a bill to incorporate agricultural societies; for the improvement of public roads; for the incorporation of various institutions of learning; for the construction of the Illinois and Michigan Canal; he always fostered the interests of public education, and favored low salaries for public officials. In whatever pertained to the local benefit of his own County, he was active and careful; but his record on this subject is of little interest to the general reader.

"Lincoln's voice was ever for measures that relieved the struggling poor man from pecuniary or political difficulties—he had himself experienced these difficulties—he therefore supported resolutions for the removal of the property qualification in franchise, and for the granting of pre-emption rights to settlers on the public lands. He was the author of a measure permitting Revolutionary pensioners to loan their pension money without taxation. He advocated a bill exempting from execution Bibles, school-books, and mechanics' tools.

"His first recorded vote against Stephen A. Douglas, was on the election of that politician to the Attorney Generalship by the Legislature.

"He twice voted for the Whig candidates for the United States Senate. Otherwise than in the election of Senators, State Legislatures were not then occupied with national affairs, and it is difficult to find anything in Mr. Lincoln's legislative history which is of great national interest. There were no exciting questions, and Mr. Lincoln's speeches were few and brief.* He was twice the candidate (in 1838 and 1840) of the Whig minority for Speaker of the House."†

For six years he remained in private life, devoting himself to the practice of law, which he had studied. In 1844 he canvassed his State in behalf of the Whig candidate for the Presidency. In 1847 he took his seat in Congress, the only Whig Representative from Illinois, which then had seven members in the House of Representatives. He was a staunch advocate of the Wilmot Proviso, showing, in 1847, the same care to secure the Territories to freedom which he manifested in the Kansas struggle and in 1860. He declined candidacy for re-election. In 1849 he received the vote of his party in the Legislature for the U. S. Senate.

In 1854 the celebrated Nebraska Bill was passed, rallying anew and into permanent organization the opposition to slavery. In his celebrated "Peoria speech" he went fully into the principles involved in the proposed repeal of the Missouri Compromise. He was replying to Senator Douglas and showing the results of the repeal. The following words there spoken on that 16th of October, 1854, sound now, that ten years have gone, like history written "before the fact."

"In this state of affairs the Genius of Discord himself could scarcely have invented a way of again setting us by the ears, but by turning back and destroying the peace measures of the past. The counsels of that Genius seem to have prevailed; the Missouri Compromise was repealed; and here we are, in the midst of a new slavery agitation, such, I think, as we have never seen before. Who is responsible for this? Is it those who resist the measure? or those who, causelessly, brought it forward, and pressed it through, having reason to know, and, in fact, knowing, it must and would

---

*A protest from Mr. Lincoln appears on the journal of the House, in regard to some resolutions which had passed. In this protest he pronounces distinctly against slavery, and takes the first public step toward what is now Republican doctrine.

† Howell's Life of Lincoln.

be so resisted? It could not but be expected by its author, that it would be looked upon as a measure for the extension of slavery, aggravated by a gross breach of faith.

"Argue as you will, and long as you will, this is the naked FRONT and ASPECT of the measure. And, in this aspect, it could but produce agitation. *Slavery is founded in the selfishness of man's nature—opposition to it, in his love of justice.* These principles are in eternal antagonism; and, when brought into collision so fiercely as slavery extension brings them, shocks, and throes, and convulsions must ceaselessly follow. Repeal the Missouri Compromise—repeal all compromises—repeal the Declaration of Independence—repeal all past history—you still cannot repeal human nature. It still will be the abundance of man's heart that slavery extension is wrong, and, out of the abundance of his heart, his mouth will continue to speak.

* * * * * * * * * * * * *

"And, really, what is the result of this? Each party WITHIN having numerous and determined backers WITHOUT, is it not probable that the contest will come to blows and bloodshed? Could there be a more apt invention to bring about collision and violence, on the slavery question, than this Nebraska project is? I do not charge or believe that such was intended by Congress; but if they had literally formed a ring, and placed champions within it to fight out the controversy, the fight could be no more likely to come off than it is. And if this fight should begin, is it likely to take a very peaceful, Union-saving turn? Will not the first drop of blood, so shed, be the real knell of the Union?

"The Missouri Compromise ought to be restored. For the sake of the Union, it ought to be restored. We ought to elect a House of Representatives which will vote its restoration. If, by any means, we omit to do this, what follows? Slavery may or may not be established in Nebraska. But whether it be or not, we shall have repudiated—discarded from the councils of the nation—the SPIRIT of COMPROMISE, *for who, after this, will ever trust in a national compromise?* The spirit of mutual concession—that spirit which first gave us the Constitution, and which has thrice saved the Union—we shall have strangled and cast from us forever. And what shall we have in lieu of it? The South, flushed with triumph and tempted to excesses; the North, betrayed, as they believe, brooding on wrong and burning for revenge. One side will provoke, the other resent. The one will taunt, the other defy; one aggresses, the other retaliates. Already a few in the North defy all Constitutional restraints, resist the execution of the Fugitive Slave law, and even menace the institution of slavery in the States where it exists. Already a few in the South claim the Constitutional right to take to and hold slaves in the Free States; demand the revival of the slave-trade; and demand a treaty with Great Britain, by which fugitive slaves may be reclaimed from Canada. As yet they are but few on either side. It is a grave question for the lovers of the Union, whether the final destruction of the Missouri Compromise, and with it the spirit of all compromise, will or will not embolden and embitter each of these, and fatally increase the number of both."

In the extract which follows we find, blended with a conservatism so strong that it was not willing to see disturbed the Fugitive Slave Law, because it resulted from a compromise, and, odious as were some of its provisions, he would abide the compact, that honest manly sense of right which has been so marked a characteristic of Mr. Lincoln;—devotion to the right because it *is* right.

"Some men, mostly Whigs, who condemn the repeal of the Missouri Compromise, nevertheless hesitate to go for its restoration, lest they be thrown in company with the Abolitionists. Will they allow me, as an old Whig, to tell them, good-humoredly that I think this is very silly? Stand by anybody that stands RIGHT. Stand with him while he is right, and PART with him when he is WRONG. Stand WITH the Abolitionist in restoring the Missouri Compromise, and stand AGAINST him when he attempts to repeal the Fugitive Slave Law. In the latter case you stand with the Southern disunionist. What of that? you are still right. In both cases you are right. In both cases you oppose the dangerous extremes. In both you stand on middle ground, and hold the ship level and steady. In both you are national, and nothing less than national. This is the good old Whig ground. To desert such ground because of any company, is to be less than a Whig—less than a man—less than an American."

The most ultra enemy of slavery, as interpreted in the red glare of four years of civil war, now scarcely surpasses the sentiments of ten years ago as further expressed:

"I particularly object to the NEW position which the avowed principle of this Nebraska law gives to slavery in the body politic. I object to it because it assumes that there CAN BE A MORAL RIGHT in the enslaving of one man by another. I object to it as a dangerous dalliance for a free people—a sad evidence that, feeling prosperity we forget right—that liberty, as a principle, we have ceased to revere. I object to it, because the fathers of the Republic eschewed and rejected it. The argument of 'necessity,' was the only argument they ever admitted in favor of slavery, and so far, and so far only, as it carried them did they ever go. They found the institution existing among us, which they could not help, and they cast the blame upon the British king for having permitted its introduction. BEFORE the Constitution they prohibited its introduction into the Northwestern Territory, the only country we owned then free from it. AT the framing and adoption of the Constitution, they forebore to so much as mention the word 'slave,' or 'slavery,' in the whole instrument. In the provision for the recovery of fugitives, the slave is spoken of as a 'person held to service or labor.' In that prohibiting the abolition of the African slave-trade for twenty years, that trade is spoken of as 'the migration or importation of such persons as any of the States NOW EXISTING shall think proper to admit,' etc. These are the only provisions alluding to slavery. Thus the thing is hid away in the Constitution, just as an afflicted man hides away a wen or cancer, which he dares not cut out at once, lest he bleed to death, with the promise, nevertheless, that the cutting may begin at the end of a certain time. Less than this our fathers could not do, and more they would not do. Necessity drove them so far, and further they would not go. But this is not all. The earliest Congress under the Constitution took the same view of slavery. They hedged and hemmed it in to the narrowest limits of necessity.

"In 1794, they prohibited an outgoing slave-trade—that is, the taking of slaves from the United States to sell.

"In 1798, they prohibited the bringing of slaves from Africa into the Mississippi Territory—this Territory then comprising what are now the States of Mississippi and Alabama. This was ten years before they had the authority to do the same thing as to the States existing at the adoption of the Constitution.

"In 1800, they prohibited American citizens from trading in slaves between foreign countries, as, for instance, from Africa to Brazil.

"In 1803, they passed a law in aid of one or two Slave State laws, in restraint of the internal slave-trade.

"In 1807, in apparent hot haste, they passed the law, nearly a year in advance, to take effect the first day of 1808—the very first day the Constitution would permit—prohibiting the African slave-trade by heavy pecuniary and corporeal penalties.

"In 1820, finding these provisions ineffectual, they declared the slave-trade piracy, and annexed to it the extreme penalty of death. While all this was passing in the General government, five or six of the original Slave States had adopted systems of gradual emancipation, by which the institution was rapidly becoming extinct within these limits.

"Thus we see the plain, unmistakable spirit of that age, toward slavery, was hostility to the principle, and toleration only by necessity.

"But now it is to be transformed into a "sacred right." Nebraska brings it forth, places it on the high road to extension and perpetuity, and, with a pat on the back, says to it, 'Go, God speed you.' Henceforth, it is to be the chief jewel of the nation—the very figure-head of the ship of state. Little by little, but steadily as man's march to the grave, we have been giving up the old for the new faith. Near eighty years ago we began by declaring that all men are created equal, but now, from that beginning, we have run down to the other declaration, that for some men to enslave others is a 'sacred right of self-government.' These principles cannot stand together. They are as opposite as God and mammon, and whoever holds to the one must despise the other. When Pettit, in connection with his support of the Nebraska bill, called the Declaration of Independence a 'self-evident lie,' he only did what consistency and candor require all other Nebraska men to do. Of the forty odd Nebraska Senators who sat present and heard him, no one rebuked him. Nor am I apprised that any Nebraska newspaper, or any Nebraska orator, in the whole nation has ever yet rebuked him. If this had been said among Marion's men, Southerners though they were, what would have become of the man who said it? If this had been said to the men who captured Andre, the man who said it would probably have been hung sooner than Andre was. If it had been said in old Independence

Hall, seventy-eight years ago, the very door-keeper would have throttled the man, and thrust him into the street.

"Let no one be deceived; the spirit of seventy-six and the spirit of Nebraska are utter antagonisms, and the former is being rapidly displaced by the latter.

"Fellow-countrymen! Americans—South as well as North—shall we make no effort to arrest this? Already the liberal party throughout the world express the apprehension 'that the one retrograde institution in America is undermining the principles of progress, and fatally violating the noblest political system the world ever saw.' This is not the taunt of enemies, but the warning of friends. Is it quite safe to disregard it—to despise it? Is there no danger to liberty itself, in discarding the earliest practice and first precept of our ancient faith? *In our greedy chase to make profit of the negro, let us beware lest we 'cancel and tear in pieces' even the white man's charter of freedom.*

"Our republican robe is soiled and trailed in the dust. Let us repurify it. Let us turn and wash it white, in the spirit, if not in the blood, of the Revolution. Let us turn slavery from its claims of 'moral right' back upon its existing legal rights, and its arguments of 'necessity.' Let us return it to the position our fathers gave it, and there let it rest in peace. Let us readopt the Declaration of Independence, and, with it, the practices and policy which harmonize with it. Let North and South—let all Americans—let all lovers of liberty everywhere—join in the great and good work. If we do this, we shall not only have saved the Union, but we shall have so saved it as to make, and to keep it, forever worthy of the saving. We shall have so saved it, that the succeeding millions of free, happy people, the world over, shall rise up and call us blessed, to the latest generations."

He then saw, with eagle eye and prophetic foresight, the beginning of the end. The State voted anti-Nebraska, and Mr. Lincoln was the prominent man for the seat in the national Senate to be vacated by General Shields, and was voted for on several ballots, but fearing division might result in the election of some man of doubtful policy he used his influence to harmonize his friends in the support of Lyman Trumbull, who was elected. Mr. Lincoln was in training for a higher post, though he knew it not.

In a former chapter there has been mention made of the great contest of 1858 between himself and Mr. Douglas—"the battle of the giants." It is only adverted to here to complete the links of the historic chain, and for the purpose of quoting from his Springfield speech of June 17, 1858, the sentences so often quoted by friends and foes:

"A house divided against itself cannot stand. I believe this government cannot endure permanently half slave and half free. I do not expect the Union to be dissolved, I do not expect the house to fall, but I do expect it will cease to be divided. It will become all one thing or all the other."

The result of the contest has been noticed. Mr. Lincoln did not enter the Senate. Providence hath its own hour and its own way of raising up the leaders for great crises, and one of these was upon the country. Mr. Lincoln had grown up among the people and not in a political hot-bed. He had a native, vigorous logic, not inaptly symbolled by his physique. He was one of the people. He came not from titled or moneyed aristocracy, but was of the hard-handed nobility of toil. He knew at once the dignity and the value of a freeman's labor, and God raised up this man, this vigorous, cool-brained, warm-hearted, strong-handed laborer, to be the leader of free men in the battle between freedom and slavery. On that rugged homely face was written an honest character. In him was a simplicity which more than matched the subtilty of his opponents. He was written as the Moses who should lead the children of this Israel through a deep Red Sea into the promised land of freedom.

THE NOMINATION.

The Republican National Convention of 1860 met in Chicago on the 16th of May. A huge building, called "the wigwam," had been erected by the citizens for the occasion. The names of Gov. Chase, Mr. Bates, and Mr. Cameron had been pressed, but it was evident from the first hour that the contest was between W. H. Seward, of New York, and Abraham Lincoln, of Illinois.

The one had spoken of the "irresistible conflict," the other of the "divided house." Their names now connected were to be written together in succeeding chapters of pregnant history. These men were to stand shoulder to shoulder through the most momentous struggle of the world's annals. On the third ballot Mr. Lincoln received 354 votes and was nominated. On motion of Mr. Evarts, of New York, the nomination was made unanimous. The contest came and Abraham Lincoln was elected President of the United States.

FOR WASHINGTON.

On the 11th of February the President elect left his Illinois home for Washington, there to meet such difficulties as had never confronted a Chief Magistrate. An organized conspiracy, ripened into an extensive secession, sought to prevent him in the exercise of the functions of the high office to which he had been chosen as President of the *whole country*. War rolled up in the near future, and how long, how terrible, and with what results none could prophesy with surety. At the Springfield depot he thus bade farewell to his neighbors:

"MY FRIENDS:—No one not in my position can appreciate the sadness I feel at this parting. To this people I owe all that I am. Here I have lived more than a quarter of a century; here my children were born, and here one of them lies buried. I know not how soon I shall see you again. A duty devolves upon me which is, perhaps, greater than that which has devolved upon any other man since the days of WASHINGTON. He never would have succeeded except for the aid of Divine Providence, upon which he at all times relied. I feel that I cannot succeed without the same Divine aid which sustained him; on the same Almighty Being I place my reliance for support, and I hope you, my friends, will all pray that I may receive that Divine assistance, without which I cannot succeed, but with which success is certain. Again, I bid you all an affectionate farewell."

These few, simple words thrilled the country through. The recognition of Divine aid made so honestly, and his desire to be remembered in the prayers of the people so expressive of a childlike faith in God, at once won the Christian sympathy of the land.

From Springfield to Baltimore was one long ovation. Crowds gathered at the stations and greeted him warmly. He was cautious and guarded in his expressions, as the declaration of a policy upon his part would have been premature and might have been injurious. Yet the policy was foreshadowed in his remarks to the members of the Indiana Legislature, who called upon him at the Bates House, in Indianapolis, on the evening of the 11th:

"FELLOW-CITIZENS OF THE STATE OF INDIANA:—I am here to thank you much for this magnificent welcome, and still more for the generous support given by your State to that political cause which I think is the true and just cause of the whole country and the whole world.

"Solomon says there is 'a time to keep silence,' and when men wrangle by the mouth with no certainty that they *mean* the same *thing* while they use the same *word*, it, perhaps, were as well if they would keep silence.

"The words 'coercion' and 'invasion' are much used in these days, and often with some temper and hot blood. Let us make sure, if we can, that we do not misunderstand the meaning of those who use them. Let us get exact definitions of these words—not from dictionaries, but from the men themselves, who certainly deprecate the *things* they would represent by the use of words. What, then, is 'coercion?' What is 'invasion?' Would the marching of an army into South Carolina, without the consent of her people, and with hostile intent toward them, be 'invasion?' I certainly think it would, and it would be 'coercion,' also, if the South Carolinians were forced to submit. But if the United States should merely hold and retake its own forts and other property, and collect the duties on foreign importations, or even withhold the mails from places where they were habitually violated, would any or all these things be 'invasion' or 'coercion?' Do our professed lovers of the Union, but who spitefully resolve that they will resist coercion and invasion, understand that such things as these on the part of the United Sates, would be coercion or invasion of a State? If so, their idea of means to preserve the object of their affections would seem exceedingly thin and airy. If sick, the little pills of the homeopathist would be much too large for it to swallow. In their view, the Union, as a family relation, would seem to be no regular marriage, but a sort of 'free love' arrangement, to be maintained only on 'passional attraction.'

"By the way, in what consists the special sacredness of a State? I speak not of the position assigned to a State in the Union, by the Constitution; for that, by the bond, we all recognize. That position, however, a State cannot carry out of the Union with it. I speak of that assumed primary right of a State to rule all which is *less* than itself and ruin all which is larger than itself. If a State and a county, in a given case, should be equal in extent of territory, and equal in number of inhabitants, in what, as a matter of principle, is the State better than the county? Would an exchange of names be an exchange of *rights* upon principle? On what rightful principle may a State, being not more than one fiftieth part of the nation, in soil and population, break up the nation and then coerce a proportionally larger subdivision of itself, in the most arbitrary way? What mysterious right to play tyrant is conferred on a district of country, with its people, by merely calling it a State?

Fellow-citizens, I am not asserting any thing; I am merely asking questions for you to consider. And now allow me to bid you farewell.

Again, he thus spoke in Cincinnati on the 12th:

"MR. MAYOR AND FELLOW-CITIZENS:—I have spoken but once before this in Cincinnati. That was a year previous to the late Presidential election. On that occasion, in a playful manner, but with sincere words, I addressed much of what I said to the Kentuckians. I gave my opinion that we, as Republicans, would ultimately beat them, as Democrats, but that they could postpone that result longer by nominating Senator Douglas for the Presidency than they could in any other way. They did not, in any true sense of the word, nominate Mr. Douglas, and the result has come certainly as soon as ever I expected. I also told them how I expected they would be treated after they should have been beaten; and I now wish to call their attention to what I then said upon that subject. I then said, 'When we do as we say, beat you, you perhaps want to know what we will do with you. I will tell you, as far as I am authorized to speak for the opposition, what we mean to do with you. We mean to treat you, as near as we possibly can, as Washington, Jefferson, and Madison treated you. We mean to leave you alone, and in no way to interfere with your institutions; to abide by all and every compromise of the Constitution; and, in a word, coming back to the original proposition, to treat you so far as degenerate men, if we have degenerated, may, according to the example of those noble fathers, WASHINGTON, JEFFERSON, and MADISON. We mean to remember that you are as good as we; that there is no difference between us, other than the difference of circumstances. We mean to recognize and bear in mind always that you have as good hearts in your bosoms as other people, or as we claim to have, and treat you accordingly.'

"Fellow-citizens of Kentucky! friends! brethren, may I call you in my new position? I see no occasion, and feel no inclination to retract a word of this. If it shall not be made good, be assured the fault shall not be mine."

Passing several short speeches we quote his remarks in New York in response to the reception by Mayor Wood:

"MR. MAYOR:—It is with feelings of deep gratitude that I make my acknowledgments for the reception that has been given me in the great commercial city of New York. I cannot but remember that it is done by the people, who do not, by a large majority, agree with me in political sentiment. It is the more grateful to me, because in this I see that for the great principles of our Government the people are pretty nearly or quite unanimous. In regard to the difficulties that confront us at this time, and of which you have seen fit to speak so becomingly and so justly, I can only say that I agree with the sentiments expressed. In my devotion to the Union I hope I am behind no man in the nation. As to my wisdom in conducting affairs so as to tend to the preservation of the Union, I fear too great confidence may have been placed in me. I am sure I bring a heart devoted to the work. There is nothing that could ever bring me to consent--willingly to consent—to the destruction of this Union (in which not only the great city of New York, but the whole country, has acquired its greatness), unless it would be that thing for which the Union itself was made. I understand that the ship is made for the carrying and preservation of the cargo; and so long as the ship is safe with the cargo, it shall not be abandoned. This Union shall never be abandoned, unless the possibility of its existence shall cease to exist, without the necessity of throwing passengers and cargo overboard. So long, then, as it is possible that the prosperity and liberties of this people can be preserved within this Union, it shall be my purpose at all times to preserve it. And now, Mr. Mayor, renewing my thanks for this cordial reception, allow me to come to a close. [Applause.]"

At Trenton, after briefly addressing the Senate, he repaired to the Assembly Chamber, where, in reply to the Speaker, he said:

"MR. SPEAKER AND GENTLEMEN:—I have just enjoyed the honor of a reception by the other branch of this Legislature, and I return to you and them my thanks for the reception which the people of New Jersey have given through their chosen representatives to me as the representative, for the time being, of the majesty of the United States. I appropriate to myself very little of the demonstrations of respect with which I have been greeted. I think little should be given to any *man*, but that it should be a manifestation of adherence to the Union and the Constitution. I understand myself to be received by the representatives of the people of New Jersey, a majority of whom differ in opinion from those with whom I have acted. This manifestation is, therefore, to be regarded by me as expressing their devotion to the Union, the Constitution, and the liberties of the people. You, Mr. Speaker, have well said that this is a time when the bravest and wisest look with doubt and awe upon the aspect presented by our national affairs. Under these circumstances, you will readily see why I should not speak in detail of the course I shall deem it best to pursue. It is proper that I should avail myself of all the information and all the time at my command, in order that when the time arrives in which I must speak officially, I shall be able to take the ground which I deem the best and safest, and from which I may have no occasion to swerve. I shall endeavor to take the ground I deem most just to the North, the East, the West, the South, and the whole country. I take it, I hope, in good temper, certainly with no malice towards any section. I shall do all that may be in my power to promote a peaceful settlement of all our difficulties. The man does not live who is more devoted to peace than I am. [Cheers.] None who would do more to preserve it, but it may be necessary to put the foot down firmly. [Here the audience broke out into cheers so loud and long, that for some moments it was impossible to hear Mr. LINCOLN'S voice.] And if I do my duty and do right you will sustain me, will you not? [Loud cheers, and cries of 'Yes, yes, we will.'] Received, as I am, by the members of a Legislature, the majority of whom do not agree with me in political sentiments, I trust that I may have their assistance in piloting the ship of State through this voyage, surrounded by perils as it is, for if it should suffer wreck now, there will be no pilot ever needed for another voyage. Gentlemen, I have already spoken longer than I intended, and must beg leave to stop here."

The party arrived at Philadelphia, and the President-elect, proceeding immediately to the Continental Hotel, was welcomed in a brief speech from Mayor Henry, to which he replied as follows:

"MR. MAYOR AND FELLOW-CITIZENS OF PHILADELPHIA:—I appear before you to make no lengthy speech, but to thank you for this reception. The reception you have given me to-night is not to me, the man, the individual, but to the man who temporarily represents, or should represent, the majesty of the nation. [Cheers] It is true, as your worthy Mayor has said, that there is anxiety amongst the citizens of the United States at this time. I deem it a happy circumstance that this dissatisfied position of our fellow-citizens does not point us to any thing in which they are being injured, or about to be injured, for which reason I have felt all the while justified in concluding that the crisis, the panic, the anxiety of the country at this time, is artificial. If there be those who differ with me upon this subject, they have not pointed out the substantial difficulty that exists. I do not mean to say that an artificial panic may not do considerable harm: that it has done such I do not deny. The hope that has been expressed by your Mayor, that I may be able to restore peace, harmony, and prosperity to the country, is most worthy of him; and happy, indeed, will I be if I shall be able to verify and fulfill that hope. [Tremendous cheering.] I promise you, in all sincerity, that I bring to the work a sincere heart. Whether I will bring a head equal to that heart will be for future times to determine. It were useless for me to speak of details of plans now; I shall speak officially next Monday week, if ever. If I should not speak then it were useless for me to do so now. If I do speak then it is useless for me to do so now. When I do speak I shall take such ground as I deem best calculated to restore peace, harmony, and prosperity to the country, and tend to the perpetuity of the nation and the liberty of these States and these people. Your worthy Mayor has expressed the wish, in which I join with him, that it were convenient for me to remain in your city long enough to consult your merchants and manufacturers; or, as it were, to listen to those breathings rising within the consecrated walls wherein the Constitution of the United States, and I will add, the Declaration of Independence, were originally framed and adopted. [Enthusiastic applause.] I assure you and your Mayor that I had hoped on this occasion, and upon all occasions during my life, that I shall do nothing inconsistent with the teachings of these holy and most sacred walls. I never asked any thing that does not breathe from those walls. All my political warfare has been in favor of the teachings that came forth from these sacred walls. May my right hand forget its cunning, and my tongue cleave to the roof of my mouth, if ever I prove false to those teachings. Fellow-citizens, I have addressed you longer than I expected to do, and now allow me to bid you good night."

These brief addresses indicated his strong desire to avoid bloodshed, to restore peace and quietness but at the same time to maintain the unity of the States at every cost. Disappointing the schemes of conspirators he reached Washington on Saturday morning of Feb. 23d, in advance of all expectation, and of hospitable preparations for his reception. Threats had been made of a forcible prevention of the inauguration, but the thorough preparations of Lieut.-Gen. Scott prevented any outbreak and secured the utmost quiet.

The ceremony of inauguration took place as usual in front of the Capitol, and in the presence of a vast number of witnesses. Before taking the oath, Mr. Lincoln, in a clear ringing voice delivered his inaugural address, to hear which there was intense solicitude; to read which the nation and the world waited. The intimate relation of the President to Illinois warrants the reproduction of the entire address.

INAUGURAL ADDRESS.

"*Fellow-citizens of the United States :*

"In compliance with a custom as old as the government itself, I appear before you to address you briefly, and to take in your presence the oath prescribed by the Constitution of the United States to be taken by the President 'before he enters on the execution of his office.'

"I do not consider it necessary at present for me to discuss those matters of administration about which there is no special anxiety or excitement.

"Apprehension seems to exist among the people of the Southern States that by the accession of a Republican Administration their property and their peace and personal security are to be endangered. There has never been any reasonable cause for such apprehension. Indeed, the most ample evidence to the contrary has all the while existed and been open to their inspection. It is found in nearly all the published speeches of him who now addresses you. I do but quote from one of those speeches when I declare that 'I have no purpose, directly or indirectly, to interfere with the institution of slavery in the States where it exists. I believe I have no lawful right to do so, and I have no inclination to do so.' Those who nominated and elected me did so with full knowledge that I had made this and many similar declarations, and had never recanted them. And more than this, they placed in the platform for my acceptance, and as a law to themselves and to me, the clear and emphatic resolution which I now read:

"'*Resolved*, That the maintenance inviolate of the rights of the States, and especially the right of each State, to order and control its own domestic institutions according to its own judgment exclusively, is essential to the balance of power on which the perfection and endurance of our political fabric depend, and we denounce the lawless invasion by armed force of the soil of any state or territory, no matter under what pretext, as among the gravest of crimes.'

"I now reiterate these sentiments; and, in doing so, I only press upon the public attention the most conclusive evidence of which the case is susceptible, that the property, peace, and security of no section are to be in any wise endangered by the now incoming Administration. I add, too, that all the protection which, consistently with the Constitution and laws, can be given, will be cheerfully given to all the States, when lawfully demanded, for whatever cause—as cheerfully to one section as to another.

"There is much controversy about the delivering up of fugitives from service or labor. The clause I now read is as plainly written in the Constitution as any other of its provisions:

"'No person held to service or labor in one state, under the laws thereof, escaping into another, shall, in consequence of any law or regulation therein, be discharged from such service or labor, but shall be delivered up on claim of the party to whom such service or labor may be due.'

"It is scarcely questioned that this provision was intended by those who made it for the reclaiming of what we call fugitive slaves; and the intention of the lawgiver is the law. All members of Congress swear their support to the whole Constitution—to this provision as much as any other. To the proposition then, that slaves, whose cases come within the terms of this clause, 'shall be delivered up,' their oaths are unanimous. Now, if they would make the effort in good temper, could they not, with nearly equal unanimity, frame and pass a law by means of which to keep good that unanimous oath ?

"There is some difference of opinion whether this law clause should be enforced by national or by state authority; but surely that difference is not a very material one. If the slave is to be surrendered, it can be of but little consequence to him, or to others, by which authority it is done. And should any one, in any case, be content that his oath shall go unkept, on a mere unsubstantial controversy as to how it shall be kept ?

"Again, in any law upon this subject, ought not all the safeguards of liberty known in civilized and humane jurisprudence to be introduced, so that a free man be not, in any case, surrendered as a slave ? And might it not be well, at the same time, to provide by law for the enforcement of that clause in the Constitution which guarantees that 'the citizens of each State shall be entitled to all privileges and immunities of citizens in the several States ?'

"I take the official oath to-day with no mental reservations, and with no purpose to construe the Constitution or laws by any hypercritical rules. And while I do not choose now to specify particular acts of Congress as proper to be enforced, I do suggest that it will be much safer for all, both in official and private stations, to conform to and abide by all those acts which stand unrepealed, than to violate any of them, trusting to find impunity in having them held to be unconstitutional.

"It is seventy-two years since the first inauguration of a President under our national Constitution. During that period, fifteen different and greatly distinguished citizens have, in succession, administered the Executive branch of the government. They have conducted it through many perils, and generally with great success. Yet, with all this scope for precedent, I now enter upon the same task for the brief constitutional term of four years, under great and peculiar difficulty. A disruption of the Federal Union, heretofore only menaced, is now formidably attempted.

"I hold, that, in contemplation of universal law, and of the Constitution, *the Union of these States is perpetual.* Perpetuity is implied, if not expressed, in the fundamental law of all national governments. It is safe to assert that no government proper ever had a provision in its organic law for its own termination. Continue to execute all the express provisions of our national Constitution, and the Union will endure forever—it being impossible to destroy it, except by some action not provided for in the instrument itself.

"Again, if the United States be not a government proper, but an association of States in the nature of contract merely, can it, as a contract, be peaceably unmade by less than all the parties who made it ? One party to a contract may violate it—break it, so to speak; but does it not require all to lawfully rescind it ?

"Descending from these general principles, we find the proposition that, in legal contemplation, the Union is perpetual, confirmed by the history of the Union itself.

The Union is much older than the Constitution. It was formed, in fact, by the Articles of Association in 1774. It was matured and continued by the Declaration of Independence in 1776. It was further matured, and the faith of all the then Thirteen States expressly plighted and engaged that it should be perpetual, by the Articles of Confederation in 1778. And, finally, in 1787, one of the declared objects for ordaining and establishing the Constitution was 'to form a more perfect union.'

"But if destruction of the Union, by one, or by a part only, of the States, be lawfully possible, the Union is less perfect than before, the Constitution having lost the vital element of perpetuity.

"It follows, from these views, that no State, upon its own mere motion, can lawfully get out of the Union; that resolves and ordinances to that effect are legally void; and that acts of violence within any State or States, against the authority of the United States, are insurrectionary or revolutionary, according to circumstances.

"I, therefore consider that, in view of the Constitution and the laws, the Union is unbroken, and to the extent of my ability I shall take care, as the Constitution itself expressly enjoins upon me, that the laws of the Union be faithfully executed in all the States. Doing this I deem to be only a simple duty on my part; and I shall perform it, so far as practicable, unless my rightful masters the American people, shall withhold the requisite means, or, in some authoritative manner, direct the contrary. I trust this will not be granted as a menace, but only as the declared purpose of the Union that it will constitutionally defend and maintain itself.

"In doing this there need be no bloodshed or violence; and there shall be none, unless it be forced upon the national authority. The power confided to me will be used to hold, occupy, and possess the property and places belonging to the government, and to collect the duties and imposts; but beyond what may be but necessary for these objects, there will be no invasion, no using of force against or among the people anywhere. Where hostility to the United States, in any interior locality, shall be so great and universal as to prevent competent resident citizens from holding the Federal offices, there will be no attempt to force obnoxious strangers among the people for that object. While the strict legal right may exist in the government to enforce the exercise of these offices, the attempt to do so would be so irritating, and so nearly impracticable withal, I deem it better to forego, for the time, the uses of such offices.

"The mails, unless repelled, will continue to be furnished in all parts of the Union. So far as possible, the people everywhere shall have that sense of perfect security which is most favorable to calm thought and reflection. The course here indicated will be followed, unless current events and experience shall show a modification or change to be proper, and in every case and exigency my best discretion will be exercised, according to circumstances actually existing, and with a view and a hope of a peaceful solution of the national troubles, and the restoration of fraternal sympathies and affections.

"That there are persons in one section or another who seek to destroy the Union at all events, and are glad of any pretext to do it, I will neither affirm nor deny; but if there be such, I need address no word to them. To those, however, who really love the Union, may I not speak?

"Before entering upon so grave a matter as the destruction of our national fabric, with all its benefits, its memories, and its hopes, would it not be wise to ascertain precisely why we do it? Will you hazard so desperate a step while there is any possibility that any portion of the ills you fly from have no real existence? Will you, while the certain ills you fly to are greater than all the real ones you fly from—will you risk the commission of so fearful a mistake?

"All profess to be content in the Union, if all constitutional rights can be maintained. Is it true, then, that any right, plainly written in the Constitution, has been denied? I think not. Happily the human mind is so constituted that no party can reach to the audacity of doing this. Think, if you can, of a single instance in which a plainly written provision of the Constitution has ever been denied. If, by the mere force of numbers, a majority should deprive a minority of any clearly written constitutional right, it might, in a moral point of view, justify revolution—certainly would if such right were a vital one. But such is not our case. All the vital rights of minorities and of individuals are so plainly assured to them by affirmations and negations, guarantees and prohibitions in the Constitution, that controversies never arise concerning them. But no organic law can ever be framed with a provision specifically applicable to every question which may occur in practical administration. No foresight can anticipate, nor any document of reasonable length contain, express provisions for all possible questions. Shall fugitives from labor be surrendered by national or by State authority? The Constitution does not expressly say. May Congress prohibit slavery in the territories? The Constitution does not expressly say. Must Congress protect slavery in the territories? The Constitution does not expressly say.

"From questions of this class spring all our constitutional controversies, and we divide upon them into majorities or minorities. If the minority will not acquiesce the majority must, or the government must cease. There is no other alternative; for continuing the government is acquiescence on one side or the other. If a minority in such case will secede rather than acquiesce, they make a precedent which, in turn, will divide and ruin them; for a minority of their own will secede from them whenever a majority refuses to be controlled by such minority. For instance, why may not any portion of a new Confederacy, a year or two hence, arbitrarily secede again, precisely as portions of the present Union now claim to secede from it? All who cherish disunion sentiments are now being educated to the exact temper of doing this.

"Is there such perfect identity of interests among the States to compose a new Union, as to produce harmony only, and prevent renewed secession?

"Plainly, the central idea of secession is the essence of anarchy. A majority held in restraint by constitutional checks and limitations, and always changing easily with deliberate changes of popular opinions and sentiments, is the only true sovereign of a free people. Whoever rejects it, does, of necessity, fly to anarchy or to despotism. Unanimity is impossible; the rule of a minority, as a permanent arrangement, is wholly inadmissible; so that, rejecting the majority principle, anarchy or despotism in some form is all that is left.

"I do not forget the position assumed by some, that constitutional questions are to be decided by the Supreme Court; nor do I deny that such decisions must be binding, in any case, upon the parties to a suit as to the object of that suit, while they are also entitled to very high respect and consideration in all parallel cases by all other departments of the government. And while it is obviously possible that such decisions may be erroneous in any given case, still the evil effect following it being limited to that particular case, with the chance that it may be overruled, and never become a precedent for other cases, can better be borne than could the evils of a different practice. At the same time the candid citizen must confess that if the policy of the government upon vital questions affecting the whole people, is to be irrevocably fixed by decisions of the Supreme Court, the instant they are made in ordinary litigation between parties in personal actions the people will have ceased to be their own rulers, having to that extent practically resigned their government into the hands of that eminent tribunal.

"Nor is there in this view any assault upon the Court of the Judges. It is a duty from which they may not shrink to decide cases properly brought before them, and it is no fault of theirs if others seek to turn their decisions to political purposes. One section of our country believes slavery is right, and ought to be extended, while the other believes it is wrong, and ought not to be extended. This is the only substantial dispute. The fugitive-slave clause of the Constitution, and the law for the suppression of the foreign slave-trade, are each as well enforced, perhaps, as any law can ever be in a community where the moral sense of the people imperfectly supports the law itself. The great body of the people abide by the dry legal obligation in both cases, and a few break over in each. This, I think, cannot be perfectly cured; and it would be worse in both cases after the separation of the sections than before. The foreign slave-trade, now imperfectly suppressed, would be ultimately revived without restriction in one section, while fugitive slaves, now only partially surrendered, would not be surrendered at all by the other.

"Physically speaking, we cannot separate. We cannot remove our respective sections from each other, nor build an impassable wall between them. A husband and wife may be divorced, and go out of the presence and beyond the reach of each other, but the different parts of our country cannot do this. They cannot but remain face to face; and intercourse, either amicable or hostile, must continue between them. Is it impossible, then, to make that intercourse more advantageous or more satisfactory after separation than before? Can aliens make treaties easier than friends can make laws? Can treaties be more faithfully enforced between aliens than laws can among friends? Suppose you go to war, you cannot fight always; and when, after much loss on both sides, and no gain on either, you cease fighting, the identical old questions, as to terms of intercourse, are again upon you.

"This country, with its institutions, belongs to the people who inhabit it. Whenever they shall grow weary of the existing government, they can exercise their constitutional right of amending it, or their revolutionary right to dismember or overthrow it. I cannot be ignorant of the fact that many worthy and patriotic citizens are desirous of having the national Constitution amended. While I make no recommendation of amendments, I fully recognize the rightful authority of the people over the whole subject, to be exercised in either of the modes prescribed in the instrument itself; and I should, under existing circumstances, favor rather than oppose a fair opportunity being afforded the people to act upon it. I will venture to add, that to me the convention mode seems preferable, in that it allows amendments to originate with the people themselves, instead of only permitting them to take or reject propositions originated by others not especially chosen for the purpose, which might not be precisely such as they would wish either to accept or refuse. I understand a proposed amendment to the Constitution—which amendment, however, I have not seen—has passed Congress, to the effect that the Federal Government shall never interfere with the domestic institutions of the States, including that of persons held to service. To avoid misconstruction of what I have said, I depart from my purpose not to speak of particular amendments so far as to say that, holding such a provision now to be implied constitutional law, I have no objections to its being made express and irrevocable.

"The Chief Magistrate derives all his authority from the people, and they have conferred none upon him to fix terms for the separation of the States. The people themselves can do this also if they choose; but the Executive, as such, has nothing to do with it. His duty is to administer the present government as it came to his hands, and to transmit it, unimpaired by him, to his successor.

"Why should there not be a patient confidence in the ultimate justice of the people? Is there any better or equal hope in the world? In our present differences, is either party without faith of being in the right? If the Almighty Ruler of nations, with his eternal truth and justice, be on your side of the North, or on yours of the South, that truth and that justice will surely prevail, by the judgment of this great tribunal of the American people.

"By the form of the government under which we live, the same people have wisely given their public servants but little power for mischief; and have, with equal wisdom, provided for the return of that little to their own hands at very short intervals. While the people retain their virtue and vigilance, no administration by any extreme of wickedness or folly, can very seriously injure the government in the short space of four years.

" My countrymen, one and all, think calmly and well upon this whole subject. Nothing valuable can be lost by taking time. If there be an object to hurry any of you in hot haste to a step which you would never take deliberately, that object will be frustrated by taking time; but no good object can be frustrated by it. Such of you as are now dissatisfied still have the old Constitution unimpaired, and, on the sensitive point, the laws of your own framing under it; while the new administration will have no immediate power, if it would, to change either. If it were admitted that you who are dissatisfied hold the right side in the dispute, there still is no single good reason for precipitate action. Intelligence, patriotism, Christianity, and a firm reliance on Him who has never yet forsaken this favored land, are still competent to adjust, in the best way, all our present difficulty

"In your hands, my dissatisfied fellow-countrymen, and not in mine, is the momentous issue of civil war. The government will not assail you.

"You can have no conflict without being yourselves the aggressors. You have no oath registered in heaven to destroy the government; while I shall have the most solemn one to 'preserve, protect, and defend' it.

"I am loth to close. We are not enemies, but friends. We must not be enemies. Though passion may have strained, it must not break our bonds of affection.

"The mystic cords of memory, stretching from every battle-field and patriot grave to every living heart and hearthstone all over this broad land, will yet swell the chorus of the Union, when again touched, as surely they will be, by the better angels of our nature."

He had come into power at a dark and stormy hour. Several States had seceded, and others were consummating their arrangements to do so. There was treason in army and navy. He was almost without means of offence or defence.

The President's first act was to construct his Cabinet, which was done by the appointment of William H. Seward, of New York, Secretary of State; Salmon P. Chase, of Ohio, Secretary of the Treasury; Simon Cameron, of Pennsylvania, Secretary of War; Gideon Welles, of Connecticut, Secretary of the Navy; Caleb B. Smith, of Indiana, Secretary of the Interior; Montgomery Blair, of Maryland, Postmaster General; and Edward Bates, of Missouri, Attorney General. These nominations were all confirmed by the Senate, and these gentlemen entered upon the discharge of the duties of their several offices. Hereafter Mr. Lincoln's administration will only come incidentally under review.

Meanwhile the works upon which Major Anderson might not open fire were progressing and were finally completed, and were soon to hurl shot and shell upon its doomed defences. On the 11th of April came the demand for surrender which Major Anderson declined, but admitted that unless supplies reached him before the 15th, hunger would compel surrender. On the morning of the 12th, at four o'clock, fire was opened upon some threescore men from about three thousand, though they knew the threescore were cooped for hopeless starvation. The story has been often told. The garrison did what it could, and then surrendered, and the national flag was struck before the assaulting hands of men born and reared under its protecting folds. It was the first act in the drama of stern, terrible war, and the awe-struck nation stood for a moment and confronted it—only a moment.

S. A. Douglas

HON. STEPHEN A. DOUGLAS.

ENGRAVED EXPRESSLY FOR PATRIOTISM OF ILLINOIS. CLARKE & CO. PUBLISHERS.

CHAPTER III.

THE GREAT UPRISING.

Sabbath and Sumter—Pulpits—Excitement—How Could it be?—Reasons for Surrender—Watchwords of Loyalty—The Flag—The Churches—The Press—Oratory—The Children—Woman—Voice of Providence—President's Proclamation—Blockading Proclamation—Springfield—Governor Yates's Proclamation—Six Regiments—Senator Douglas's Springfield Speech—Interview with Governor Yates—Wigwam Speech—Its Influence—His Death—Speech quoted—Baltimore Riot—A Minister's Expression—Popular demand to take Troops through Baltimore—Object of mob Defeated—Men and Money tendered—People demand short, earnest War—Influence of the "Great Uprising" on the Secessionists.

"Throughout the land there goes a cry;
A sudden splendor fills the sky;
From every hill the banners burst,
Like buds by April breezes nurst;
In every hamlet, home and mart,
The firebeat of a single heart
Keeps time to strains whose pulses mix
Our blood with that of Seventy-Six!

"The shot whereby the old flag fell
From Sumter's battered citadel,
Struck down the lines of party creed,
And made ye One in soul and deed,—
One mighty people, stern and strong,
To crush the consummated wrong;
Indignant with the wrath whose rod
Smites as the awful sword of God!"

[Bayard Taylor, April 30, 1861.

THE morning of Sabbath, April 14th, brought to the principal cities of the Union the announcement that the flag had been struck, and that, overborne by superior strength, Major Anderson had capitulated. That was all, but that was enough! Pulpits rang that Sabbath with extemporized sermons, yet none more eloquent were ever preached. Strong men bowed their heads and wept as children. Along the streets trod hosts of excited men; martial music was heard on every side, and active measures were taken to organize military companies.

The next day brought more definite intelligence, and the whole land rocked with excitement. At first there was surprise bordering on incredulity. How could it be so? How could the strong walls of Sumter give way? They forgot, in the hurry of the moment, that the most elaborate and extensive preparations had been made, and that Major Anderson had been compelled to see them completed before his eyes, while he knew that, if permitted to do so, he could easily prevent the finishing of a single battery. They forgot, for the moment, that a handful of men was no match for eager thousands, and that sheer exhaustion would soon cause them to succumb. They did not think, for the moment, of the "hell of fire" to which they were subjected.

But they soon remembered it all, and did full justice to the heroic commandant and his garrison. And then came the terrible consciousness that war was upon them. The Union was assailed; the right of the constitutional majority to rule was denied; and war had begun! Perhaps no single thought proved more intensely exciting than the dishonor of the flag. It was the representative of Government; it was the symbol of national majesty; it was the emblem of authority and protection. It had been honored on all seas, had afforded sanctuary in all lands, and now it was insulted and hauled down before home conspirators! "For the Flag!" "Defend the Flag!" "Rally to the Flag!" "Avenge the Stars and Stripes!" were mottoes seen in all places! The Flag was displayed everywhere, from stores, shops, and printing offices. It floated from church spires, and draped alike orthodox and heteorodox pulpits. It flaunted from private residences and school-rooms, and miniature ones were placed upon the cradles of little ones soon to be left fatherless by "the fortunes of war." It was mounted on almost every locomotive. Copies of the "Star Spangled Banner" and "The Red, White and Blue," were called for until the supply was exhausted, and new editions were demanded. In a day old party lines went down, and for a season we were again one people, united in the determined purpose of National Salvation. Nineteen millions of people were intensely excited; moving like vast waves surging before a great wind.

In the churches, pulpits thundered stern denunciations of Rebellion. The ministers declared that God had set this land midway between the oceans as a great political and religious missionary land. They showed that He marked it as the home of a united people, and that when He aforetime determined the bounds of our habitation, He gave us this land to be made, in its entirety, the land of free speech, free presses, free schools, free pulpits, free men and women. They said He has so built its mountains as to bind together, not divide, the North and the South; and what God hath joined together, let no man or body of men put asunder! He has traced the great rivers of the continent so they cannot be dividing lines between the States of the Cotton, the Rice and the Sugar, and those of the Wheat, the Corn and the Barley, with the beds of coal and the spindles of industry. They said He hath made it one, and never can it be cut in twain. More than one, at the very outset, saw that the contest was between Freedom and Slavery, and putting on the prophet's mantle, said: "Slavery hath taken the sword: it shall perish by the sword." Not in the Crusades was the religious spirit more marked, causative, and controlling than in THE GREAT UPRISING of 1861.

The Press was active. Political, Secular and Religious alike made appeal after appeal. Secular papers teemed with prophecy, sermon and exhortation. Religious papers were crowded with proclamations, general orders and war songs.

Oratory played its part, and from rostrum, from out-door stands, from court-house steps and hotel balconies, speakers addressed masses of people animated with one great purpose.

The children caught the fever, and each school had its play-ground transformed into a parade-ground, while small drums, miniature cannon and harmless small arms, were the playthings of the nursery.

Elsewhere, "Woman's works" remain to be noted, and it is enough to say that, knowing that war meant bereavement of husbands, sons, brothers and plighted lovers, the women said the nation's honor must be preserved, no matter at what cost!

Everywhere, the American people heard the voice of Providence, saying:

"Draw forth your million blades as one;
Complete the battle now begun!
GOD FIGHTS WITH YE, and overhead
Floats the dear banner of your dead.
They and the glories of the Past,
The Future, dawning dim and vast,
And all the holiest hopes of Man
Are beaming triumph in your van.

"Slow to resolve, be swift to do!
Teach ye the False how fight the True!
How bucklered Perfidy shall feel
In her black heart, the Patriot's steel;
How sure the bolt that Justice wings;
How weak the arm a traitor brings;
How mighty they who steadfast stand
For Freedom's Flag and Freedom's Land!"

All eyes were turned toward the National Capital, and the eager question went from lip to lip: "What will the President do?" The question was soon answered. Before nightfall on Monday, the 15th, was transmitted, by telegraph, the following Proclamation:

PROCLAMATION.

By the President of the United States.

"WHEREAS, The laws of the United States have been for some time past and now are opposed, and the execution thereof obstructed, in the States of South Carolina, Georgia, Alabama, Florida, Mississippi, Louisiana, and Texas, by combinations too powerful to be suppressed by the ordinary course of judicial proceedings, or by the powers vested in the marshals by law: now, therefore, I, ABRAHAM LINCOLN, President of the United States, in virtue of the power in me vested by the Constitution and the laws, have thought fit to call forth, and hereby do call forth, the militia of the several States of the Union to the aggregate number of 75,000, in order to suppress said combinations, and to cause the laws to be duly executed.

"The details for this object will be immediately communicated to the State authorities through the War Department. I appeal to all loyal citizens to favor, facilitate, and aid this effort to maintain the honor, the integrity, and existence of our national Union, and the perpetuity of popular government, and to redress wrongs already long enough endured. I deem it proper to say that the first service assigned to the forces hereby called forth, will probably be to re-possess the forts, places and property which have been seized from the Union; and in every event the utmost care will be observed, consistently with the objects aforesaid, to avoid any devastation, any destruction of, or interference with, property, or any disturbance of peaceful citizens of any part of the country; and I hereby command the persons composing the combinations aforesaid, to disperse and retire peaceably to their respective abodes, within twenty days from this date.

"Deeming that the present condition of public affairs presents an extraordinary occasion, I do hereby, in virtue of the power in me vested by the Constitution, convene both houses of Congress. The Senators and Representatives are, therefore, summoned to assemble at their respective Chambers at twelve o'clock, noon, on Thursday, the fourth day of July next, then and there to consider and determine such measures as, in their wisdom, the public safety and interest may seem to demand.

"In witness whereof, I have hereunto set my hand, and caused the seal of the United States to be affixed.

"Done at the City of Washington, this fifteenth day of April, in the year of our Lord one thousand eight hundred and sixty-one, and of the independence of the United States the eighty-fifth.

"ABRAHAM LINCOLN.

"By the President,
"WILLIAM H. SEWARD, Secretary of State."

This was followed, on the 19th, by the celebrated Blockading Proclamation, which is here appended:

A PROCLAMATION,

By the President of the United States.

"WHEREAS, An insurrection against the government of the United States has broken out in the States of South Carolina, Georgia, Alabama, Florida, Mississippi, Louisiana and Texas, and the laws of the United States for the collection of the revenue cannot be efficiently executed therein conformable to that provision of the Constitution which requires duties to be uniform throughout the United States;

"And, *whereas*, a combination of persons, engaged in such insurrection, have threatened to grant pretended letters of marque, to authorize the bearers thereof to commit assaults on the lives, vessels, and property of the good citizens of the country, lawfully engaged in commerce on the high seas, and in waters of the United States;

"And, *whereas*, an Executive Proclamation has already issued, requiring the persons engaged in these disorderly proceedings to desist therefrom, calling out a militia force for the purpose of repressing the same, and convening Congress in extraordinary session to deliberate and determine thereon;

"Now, therefore, I, ABRAHAM LINCOLN, President of the United States, with a view to the same purposes before mentioned, and to the protection of the public peace, and the lives and property of quiet and orderly citizens pursuing their lawful occupations, until Congress shall have assembled and deliberated on the said unlawful proceedings, or until the same shall have ceased, have further deemed it advisable to set on foot a blockade of the ports within the States aforesaid, in pursuance of the laws of the United States and of the laws of nations, in such cases provided. For this purpose, a competent force will be posted so as to prevent entrance and exit of vessels from the ports aforesaid. If, therefore, with a view to violate such blockade, a vessel shall approach, or shall attempt to leave any of the said ports, she will be duly warned by the commander of one of the blockading vessels, who will endorse on her register the fact and date of such warning; and if the same vessel shall again attempt to enter or leave the blockaded port, she will be captured and sent to the nearest convenient port, for such proceedings against her and her cargo, as prizes, as may be deemed advisable.

"And I hereby proclaim and declare, that if any person, under the pretended authority of such States, or under any other pretence, shall molest a vessel of the United States, or the persons or cargo on board of her, such persons will be held amenable to the laws of the United States for the prevention and punishment of piracy.

"By the President. ABRAHAM LINCOLN.

"WILLIAM H. SEWARD, Secretary of State.

"WASHINGTON, April 19, 1861."

These documents convinced all that war would be waged until rebellion should be suppressed, and they intensified the popular enthusiasm.

In this State all eyes were turned toward Springfield. It was known that Governor Yates had expressed himself determined to use every means to maintain the unity of the States, and none doubted that his measures would be promptly taken. It was known that, in view of possible war, Judge Allen C. Fuller had accepted the position of Adjutant General of the State, and there was confidence in his integrity and executive ability.

On Tuesday morning, it was ascertained that the following dispatch had been received at Springfield:

"WASHINGTON, April 15, 1861.

"*His Excellency, Richard Yates:*

"Call made on you by to-night's mail for six regiments for immediate service.

"SIMON CAMERON, Secretary of War."

On the same date Governor Yates issued the following Proclamation:

"SPRINGFIELD, Ill., April 15, 1861.

"I, RICHARD YATES, Governor of the State of Illinois, by virtue of the authority vested in me by the Constitution, hereby convene the Legislature of the State, and the members of the twenty-second session of the General Assembly are hereby required to be and appear in their respective places, at the Capitol, on TUESDAY, the *twenty-third day of April, A. D.* 1861, for the purpose of enacting such laws and adopting such measures as may be deemed necessary, upon the following subjects: The more perfect organization and equipment of the militia of the State, and placing the same upon the best footing to render assistance to the General Government in preserving the Union, enforcing the laws and protecting the property and rights of the people; also, the raising of such money and other means as may be required to carry out the foregoing object; and also to provide for the expenses of such session.

"In testimony whereof, I hereunto set my hand, and have caused the Great Seal of the State to be hereunto affixed at the City of Springfield, the 15th day of April, A. D. 1861.

"RICHARD YATES.

"By order of the Governor:
"O. M. HATCH, Secretary of State."

General Order No. 1 was issued on the 15th, from the headquarters at Springfield, directing all commandants of divisions, brigades, regiments and companies to hold themselves ready for actual service; and on the 16th, Order No. 2 provided for the immediate organization of the six regiments, and within ten days, more than ten thousand men had offered their services; and in addition to the force dispatched to Cairo, more than the full quota was in camp at Springfield.

A little later two other circumstances increased the intensity of public feeling. The first, the news of the assault on the Massachusetts sixth and Pennsylvania troops by the Baltimore mob. Nobly has that city redeemed itself from that disgrace, but when the news was read in Chicago, on the morning of the 20th, that on the day preceding, brave men, rushing to the defense of the Capital, were murdered in the streets of Baltimore, there was a demand for the sternest measures. Excited groups, pale with indignation, gathered on the corners and asked to be armed and led to Washington *through* Baltimore. Said a minister of eminence, in his sacred calling: "I was born in Baltimore; I have loved its name; my kindred are there, but I should rejoice to know that it was laid in ashes." The State was agitated beyond description when it was learned that the route to Washington was thus closed by violence. In common with sister States, it demanded that the way should be opened, not around the city, as alarmists suggested, but *through it.*

The policy which consented temporarily to another route was condemned as an unwise and undignified concession to a brutal mob, itself the tool of the secession leaders. That mob was expected to stay the march of Union troops until Washington should be captured. Its failure was felt to be the first rebel defeat of the campaign.

The other was the course of Senator Stephen A. Douglas, Mr. Lincoln's competitor for the Presidency. They had been political antagonists, and, as we have seen, had represented opposing policies. Mr. Douglas possessed great popular power. He had a commanding will—was bold to audacity; as an orator, he had few equals, whether he spoke to the American Senate, or to the masses who gathered on the prairies of his own State. In the great uprising, there were whispers that there were parts of the State whose sympathies, from ancestry, trade and political affinities were with the South, and that they would not go with Mr. Lincoln in the coercion of sovereign States. It was said they would range themselves under another banner, and that the southern counties of Indiana were with them.

These localities had been devoted to Mr. Douglas, and had steadily and enthusiastically supported him. He waited on the President, and expressed his concurrence in the policy of calling out the troops and maintaining the national honor at all hazards, and on the 18th set his face toward the West.

Reaching Springfield, on the 25th he addressed the two houses of the Illinois Legislature in a style of magical power. He said:

"For the first time since the adoption of the Federal Constitution, a wide-spread conspiracy exists to overthrow the best government the sun of heaven ever shone upon. An invading army is marching upon Washington. The boast has gone forth from the Secretary of War of the so-called Confederate States, that by the first of May the rebel army will be in possession of the National Capital, and, by the first of July, its headquarters will be in old Independence Hall.

"The only question for us is, whether we shall wait supinely for the invaders, or rush, as one man, to the defence of that we hold most dear. Piratical flags are afloat on the ocean, under pretended letters of *marque*. Our Great River has been closed to the commerce of the Northwest. * * * * * * * So long as a hope remained of peace, I plead and implored for compromise. Now, that all else has failed, there is but one course left, and that is to rally, as one man, under the flag of Washington, Jefferson, Hamilton, Madison and Franklin. At what time since the government was organized, have the constitutional rights of the South been more secure than now? For the first time since the Constitution was adopted, there is no legal restriction against the spread of slavery in the territories. When was the Fugitive Slave Law more faithfully executed? What single act has been done to justify this mad attempt to overthrow the Republic? We are told that because a certain party has carried a Presidential election, therefore the South chose to consider their liberties insecure! I had supposed it was a fundamental principle of American institutions, that the will of the majority, constitutionally expressed, should govern! [Applause.] If a defeat at the ballot-box is to justify rebellion, the future history of the United States may be read in the past history of Mexico.

* * * * * * * * * * * * * *

"It is a prodigious crime against the freedom of the world, to attempt to blot the United States out of the map of Christendom. * * * * * * How long do you think it will be ere the guillotine is in operation? Allow me to say to my former political enemies, you will not be true to your country if you seek to make political capital out of these disasters [applause]; and to my old friends, you will be false and unworthy of your principles if you allow political defeat to convert you into traitors to your national land. [Prolonged applause.] The shortest way now to peace is the most stupendous and unanimous preparations for war. [Storms of applause.]

"Gentlemen, it is our duty to defend our Constitution and protect our flag."

While in Springfield, he and Governor Yates met. Between these two gentlemen there had been bitter feelings, growing out of political contests. But what were past party conflicts to them now, as they stood face to face, each bent on the salvation of his country? Nothing and less than nothing.

The Senator next proceeded to Chicago, where men of all parties hailed his coming with a grand ovation. He again spoke; this time—and the last—in the "Republican Wigwam," the building in which was held the Convention which nominated his successful rival, Abraham Lincoln. It was an effort worthy the last public hours of the statesman's life. Its arguments were unanswerable—its appeals irresistible. He closed, returned to his rooms at the Tremont House, to die!

It is scarcely too much to say that those two speeches united the West, and prevented the horrors of civil war on this side of the Mississippi River. They were as the word of the prophets of old, falling upon the public conscience and the public heart. His voice had such power as had no other.

"One blast upon his bugle horn
Was worth a thousand men."

His speeches were transmitted by telegraph; they were copied into newspapers; they were read in all homes, and the cry sped from lip to lip—"Douglas sustains Lincoln!" In vain did the emissaries of Davis cry "No coercion." "Douglas sustains Lincoln," not as Lincoln, but as President of an assailed Republic," was too strong for their piping treason.

Lying in his sick-room, he dictated his last letter, on the 10th of May. It was addressed to Virgil Hickox, Chairman of the State Central Democratic Committee. In that he said: "*It seems that some of my friends are unable to comprehend the difference between arguments used in favor of an equitable compromise, with the hope of averting the horrors of war,* and those urged in support of the government and flag of our country, *when war is being waged against the United States, with the avowed purpose of producing a permanent disruption of the Union and a total destruction of its government.* * * * * * * * * *
In this view of the state of facts, *there was but one path of duty left to patriotic men.* It was not a party question, nor a question involving partisan policy; it was *a question of government or no government; country or no country;* and hence it became the imperative duty of every union man, every friend of constitutional liberty, *to rally to the support of our common country, its government and flag,* as the only means of checking the progress of revolution and preserving the Union. * * * * * *
I trust the time will never come when I shall not be willing to make any needful sacrifice of personal feeling and party policy for the honor and integrity of the country."

And when the word "Douglas is dead," was flashed along the wires, men of all parties wept. They came from almost every county in Illinois, to look upon his remains as they lay in state in Bryan Hall; and as they passed the pile on which they rested, few looked upon them who did not feel that the last days of his life were incomparably the most glorious. He had crowned his pyramid with a capital of stars! The long procession which followed his body to the quiet grave on the western shore of the grand lake he so much loved, followed not the partisan—not the eloquent Senator—but Stephen A. Douglas, THE PATRIOT! Old strifes were forgotten; old blows forgiven; old feuds buried.

His words completed the majesty of the "Great Uprising;" they completed the prostration of party lines, and the unity of the people.

It is due to his memory that we place in this chapter some extracts from his last speech:

"I beg you to believe that I will not do you or myself the injustice to think that this magnificent ovation is personal to myself. I rejoice to know that it expresses your devotion to the Constitution, the Union, and the flag of our country. I will not conceal gratification at the uncontrovertible test this vast audience presents—that, what political differences or party questions may have divided us, yet you all had a conviction that, when the country should be in danger, my loyalty could be relied on. That the present danger is imminent, no man can conceal. If war must come—if the bayonet must be used to maintain the Constitution—I say before God, my conscience is clean. I have struggled long for a peaceful solution of the difficulty. I have not only tendered those States what was theirs of right, but I have gone to the very extreme of magnanimity.

"The return we receive is war; armies marched upon our Capital; obstructions and dangers to our navigation; letters of marque, to invite pirates to prey upon our commerce; a concerted movement to blot out the United States of America from the map of the globe. The question is, Are we to maintain the country of our fathers, or allow it to be stricken down by those who, when they can no longer govern, threaten to destroy?

"What cause, what excuse do disunionists give us, for breaking up the best Government on which the sun of heaven ever shed its rays? They are dissatisfied with the result of the Presidential election. Did they never get beaten before? Are we to resort to the sword when we get defeated at the ballot box? I understand it that the voice of the people expressed in the mode appointed by the Constitution, must command the obedience of every citizen. They assume, on the election of a particular candidate, that their rights are not safe in the Union. What evidence do they present of this? I defy any man to show any act on which it is based. What act has been omitted to be done? I appeal to these assembled thousands, that so far as the constitutional rights of slaveholders are concerned, nothing has been done, and nothing omitted, of which they can complain.

"There has never been a time from the day that Washington was inaugurated first President of the United States, when the rights of the Southern States stood firmer under the laws of the land than they do now; there never was a time when they had not as good cause for disunion as they have to-day. What good cause have they now that has not existed under every administration?

"If they say the Territorial question—now, for the first time, there is no act of Congress prohibiting slavery anywhere. If it be the non-enforcement of the laws, the only complaints, that I have heard, have been of the too vigorous and faithful fulfillment of the Fugitive Slave Law? Then what reason have they?

"The slavery question is a mere excuse. The election of Lincoln is a mere pretext. The present secession movement is the result of an enormous conspiracy formed more than a year since, formed by leaders in the Southern Confederacy more than twelve months ago.

"But this is no time for the detail of causes. The conspiracy is now known.

Armies have been raised, war is levied to accomplish it. There are only two sides to the question. Every man must be for the United States or against it. There can be no neutrals in this war; *only patriots—or traitors.*

"Thank God, Illinois is not divided on this question. I know they expected to present a united South against a divided North. They hoped in the Northern States party questions would bring civil war between Democrats and Republicans, when the South would step in with her cohorts, aid one party to conquer the other, and then make easy prey of the victors. Their scheme was carnage and civil war in the North.

"There is but one way to defeat this. In Illinois it is being so defeated by closing up the ranks. War will thus be prevented on our own soil. While there was a hope for peace, I was ready for any reasonable sacrifice or compromise to maintain it. But when the question comes of war in the cotton fields of the South, or the corn fields of Illinois, I say the further off the better.

"I have said more than I intended to say. It is a sad task to discuss questions so fearful as civil war; but sad as it is, bloody and disastrous as I expect it will be, I express it as my conviction before God, that it is the duty of every American citizen to rally around the flag of his country.

"I thank you again for this magnificent demonstration. By it you show you have laid aside party strife. Illinois has a proud position—united, firm, determined never to permit the government to be destroyed."

The uprising of the people tendered to the Government all it wanted of men and means, only asking that there should be a short, sharp, earnest campaign, the speedy suppression of rebellion and the restoration of the Union.

From the outset the people were in advance of the calls of the government. They asked the privilege of going into war. They tendered brigades where the administration only asked for regiments. This uprising, on a scale of such grandeur, and with spirit so intense, was evidently unexpected to secessionists. They had so long vaunted themselves the masters of "Northern mudsills," that they had ended, greatly to their cost, in believing it themselves, and thought they had but to frown and Northern men would fly trembling to their retreats. They further expected Northern divisions to so weaken us as to counterbalance our numerical supremacy.

But instead of these things, they saw an outburst of military enthusiasm. They saw the nation of tradesmen suddenly a nation of soldiers, and a UNITED NORTH ready to do them battle for right of constitutional authority and for the majesty of law. And seeing that, they knew war awaited them, stern and uncompromising war, and they girded themselves to meet it.

HON. RICHARD YATES.

ENGRAVED EXPRESSLY FOR "PATRIOTISM OF ILLINOIS" CLARKE & CO. PUBLISHERS.

CHAPTER IV.

EARLY WAR MEASURES.

Patriotic Governors—Richard Yates—Parentage and Education—State Legislature—In Congress—Elected Governor—Inaugural—What shall be done?—Adjutant-General Fuller—First call for Troops—The Situation—The Militia—Proclamation—Special Message—Aid—General Orders Nos. 1, 2—Character of the First Call—Why was it so?—Perhaps—Hopes of Peace—Awaiting Congress—Mr. Cameron on the Situation—Richmond Enquirer—The Navy—After the Event—Egypt and Israel.

IT was surely providential that in the loyal States there were so many Governors who proved to be, emphatically, men for the hour. There was Andrews of Massachusetts, Dennison and Tod of Ohio, Curtin of Pennsylvania, Morton of Indiana, with the noble of executives of Michigan, Iowa, Wisconsin and Minnesota. With these, as the earnest patriot, the stirring orator, the efficient administrator, the active and prudent Commander-in-Chief, Illinois writes the name of her citizen-Governor, Richard Yates.

He was born at Warsaw, Gallatin county, Kentucky. In 1831 his father removed to Illinois and settled at Springfield. He graduated at Illinois College, Jacksonville, and subsequently studied the profession of law with Col. J. J. Hardin, who fell in the Mexican war. He represented his country three times in the State Legislature. In 1850, he was nominated, by a Whig Convention, to represent his district in Congress, and was elected, and found himself the youngest member of the body. In spite of a change in the district, which, it was supposed, secured it to the opposite party, he was elected over Mr. John Calhoun, a popular leader of the other party. At the next election he was defeated, the district sustaining, by its vote, the "Nebraska Bill" measure of Senator Douglas.

While in Congress he made his mark as an able member, and an able opponent of the extension of the area of slavery. His opposition to the repeal of the Missouri Compromise and its associate legislation was stern and persistent. In 1860 he received the nomination of the Republican State Convention as its candidate for Governor, and after a spirited and exciting canvass was elected.

On the 14th of January he delivered his inaugural message to the General Assembly, and in discussing national affairs, showed that, while disposed to tender every lawful measure of pacification, the State of Illinois, as represented by its executive chief officer would maintain the Union and vindicate the right of constitutional majorities. He said:

"Whatever may have been the divisions of parties hitherto, the people of Illinois will, with one accord, give their assent and firm support to two propositions:

"FIRST—That obedience to the Constitution and the laws must be insisted upon, and enforced as necessary to the existence of the government.

"SECOND—That the election of a chief magistrate of the nation in strict conformity with the constitution, is no sufficient cause for the release of any State from any of its obligations to the Union.

"A minority of the people may be persuaded that a great error has been committed by such election, but for relief in such a contingency, the Constitution looks to the efficacy of frequent elections, and has placed it in the power of the people to remove their agents and servants at will. The working of our government is based upon the principles of the indisputable rights of majorities. To deny the right of those, who have constitutionally succeeded by ballot to stations only to be so occupied, is not merely unfair and unjust, but revolutionary; and for a party which has constitutionally triumphed, to surrender the powers it has won, would be an ignoble submission, a degradation of manhood, a base desertion of the people's service, which should inevitably consign it to the scorn of Christendom and the infamy of history.

"The American people need no assurance that the Republican party, valuing as it ought the triumph it has won, will never be disposed to yield its honors or avoid its duties. They not only claim, but intend to have the administration for the period of time allotted to them by the Constitution.

"To give shape and form to their purpose of resistance, the dissatisfied leaders of the South Carolina movement have revived the doctrine, long since exploded, that a State may nullify a law of Congress and secede from the Union at pleasure. Such a doctrine can never for a moment be permitted. Its admission would be fatal to the existence of government, would dissolve all the relations which bind the people together, and reduce to anarchy the order of the Republic.

"This is a government entered into by the people of the whole country in their sovereign capacity, and although it have the sanction also, of a compact between sovereign States, does not receive its chief support from that circumstance, but from the original and higher action of the people themselves.

"This Union cannot be dissolved by one State, nor by the people of one State or of a dozen States. This government was designed to be perpetual and can be dissolved only by revolution.

"Secession is disunion. Concede to South Carolina the right to release her people from the duties and obligations belonging to their citizenship and you annihilate the sovereignty of the Union by prostrating its ability to secure allegiance. Could a government which could not vindicate itself, and which had exhibited such a sign of weakness, command respect or long maintain itself? If that State secede, why may not California and Oregon, and with better reason, because they are remote from the Capital, and separated by uninhabited wildernesses and vast mountain ranges, and may have an independent commerce with the shores and islands of the Pacific and the marts of the Indies? Why may not Pennsylvania secede and dispute our passage to the seaboard through her territory? Why may not Louisiana constitute herself an independent nation, and dictate to the people of the great Northwest the onerous terms upon which her millions of agricultural and industrial products might find a transit through the Mississippi and be delivered to the commerce of the world.

"It will be admitted that the territory of Louisiana, acquired in 1803, for the purpose of securing to the people of the United States the free navigation of the Mississippi, could never have seceded; yet it is pretended, that when that territory has so perfected its municipal organization as to be admitted into the Union *as a State*, with the powers and privileges equal to the other States, she may at pleasure repudiate the union and forbid to the other States the free navigation which was purchased at the cost of all, not for Louisiana, but for all the people of the United States. A claim so presumptuous and absurd could never be acquiesced in. The blood of the gallant sons of Kentucky and Tennessee was freely shed to defend New Orleans and the Mississippi river from a foreign foe; and it is memorable that the chieftain who rescued that city from sack and siege, was the same who, at a later date, by his stern and patriotic rebuke, dispersed the ranks of disunionists in the borders of South Carolina.

"Can it be for a moment supposed, that the people of the Valley of the Mississippi will ever consent that the great river shall flow for hundreds of miles through a foreign jurisdiction, and they be compelled—if not to fight their way in the face of the forts frowning upon its banks—to submit to the imposition and annoyance of arbitrary taxes and exorbitant duties to be levied upon their commerce? I believe that before that day shall come, either shore of the "Father of Waters" will be a continuous sepulcher of the slain, and, with all its cities in ruins, and the cultivated fields upon its sloping sides laid waste, it shall roll its foaming tide in solitary grandeur, as at the dawn of creation. I know I speak for Illinois, and I believe for the Northwest, when I declare them a unit in the unalterable determination of her millions, occupying the great basin drained by the Mississippi, to permit no portion of that stream to be controlled by a foreign jurisdiction.

"If, wearied by the persistent clamors and panics accompanying these ceaseless threats of secession, any good citizen has suffered himself to entertain a thought that the peace and unity of the nation might be promoted by the withdrawal of the dissatisfied State or States, let him remember that this Union is an inheritance from our fathers, to be transmitted by us to our posterity, and that the great hope of down-trodden humanity throughout the world is in its permanence. Let us never forget the solemn warnings of the Father of his Country, that 'we should accustom ourselves to think and speak of the Union as the palladium of our political safety and prosperity, discountenancing whatever may suggest even a suspicion that it can, in any event, be abandoned.'

"So deeply impressed were Jackson, Webster and Clay, with the conviction that the durability and efficiency of our free institutions depended upon a perpetual, unbroken Union, that they have left, upon many a page of the national history, most eloquent warnings that the thought, even, that the Union could be dissolved, was never to be entertained. The veteran Cass has said that the man 'who believed this Union could be broken up without bloodshed, has read history to little purpose.' As we love our common country in all its parts, and with all its blessings of climates and cultures, its mountains, valleys and streams; as we cherish its history, and the memory of the world's only Washington; as we love the grand old flag, 'sign of the free heart's only home,' that is cheered and hailed on every sea and haven of the world, let us swear that its glories shall never be dimmed—that there shall be no secession, no disunion—and that the American people shall be one and united, now and forever.

"I believe and trust it is to be the mission of those to whom the people have lately committed, for a period, the interests of this nation, to administer public affairs upon the theory of THE PERPETUITY OF THE CONSTITUTION AND THE GOVERNMENT ORGANIZED UNDER IT.

"No matter how vociferously South Carolina may declare that the Union is dissolved, and that she and other States are out of the confederacy, no recognition whatever is due to her self-assumed independence in this regard. It took seven years to establish our independence. The precious boon purchased by patriot blood and treasure was committed to us for enjoyment, and to be transmitted to our posterity, with the most solemn injunctions that man has the power to lay on man. By the grace of God, we will be faithful to the trust. For seven years yet to come, at least, will we struggle to maintain a perfect union—a government of one people, in one nation, under one Constitution."

He then asked, "What is to be done?" and suggested that if any grievances had been wrought by Northern States, they should be redressed, even though the complaint comes from States which have ignored the rights of Northern citizens. The Fugitive Slave Law, with all its errors, must be enforced while it stands unrepealed; if any State laws exist which contravene the letter or spirit of the Constitution they should be repealed, and "let all parties cordially unite and assure the South that the North has no design or purpose to interfere with slavery in the States, and entertain no hostility to the people of the slave States." But if lawless resistance should not willingly yield to constitutional authority, then it must be compelled to do so. He said:

"I know not what the exigencies of the future may be, nor what remedies it may be necessary to use, but the administration of the incoming President, I have no doubt, will be characterized by wisdom as well as firmness. He certainly will not forget that the people of all the United States, whether loyal or not, are citizens of the same Republic, component parts of the same integral Union. He never will forget, so long as he remembers his official oath, that the whole material of the government, moral, political, and physical, if need be, must be employed to preserve, protect and defend the Constitution of the United States. In such an event as this I hesitate not to say, that the General Assembly, without a dissenting voice, and the people of Illinois, would unanimously pledge the men and means of the State to uphold the Constitution and preserve the Union. To those who would distrust the loyalty of the American people to the Union, let the spontaneous response of the national heart, borne upon ten thousand streams of lightning to the heroic Anderson, answer.

"It is, perhaps, impossible to tell what may be the exact result of this South Carolina nullification, but do what she will, conspire with many or few, I am confident that this Union of our fathers—a Union of intelligence, of freedom, of justice, of industry, of religion, of science and art, will, in the end, be stronger and richer and more glorious, renowned and free, than it has ever been heretofore, by the necessary reaction of the crisis through which we are passing.

"As to our own State, we are closely allied in origin, in kindred, in sympathy, in interest, in civilization and in destiny, with many of the best of both the slave and the free states, and though young in years, we have learned to be proud of our origin, and of our neighbors, and of our sister States. No State has entered into the recent political campaign with more intense partisan prejudices and zeal than our own. Each opposing party nominated for the Presidency the favorite son not only of the State, but of the Northwest. We fought the canvass through to the hilt; but the moment the contest was decided, the world was at a loss to know which most to admire, the exuberant joy of the victors, or the admirable gallantry, grace and dignity of the unsuccessful party. We have put one of our champions into the Presidency, the other still stands in the Senate, places almost equal for usefulness; which will achieve most honor to himself and good to his country and the world, time will decide. We will believe that neither will prove coward in the fight, or traitor to the cause. On the question of the union of these States they, and all our people, will be a unit. The foot of the traitor has never yet blasted the green sward of the State of Illinois. All the running waters of the Northwest are waters of freedom and union, and come what will, as they glide to the great gulf, they will ever, by the ordinance of '87, and by the higher ordinance of Almighty God, bear only free men and free trade upon their bosoms, or their channels will be filled with the commingled blood of traitors, cowards and slaves."

The first call for troops was made on the 15th of April, 1861, by Hon. Simon Cameron, Secretary of War, requiring the Governor to detach from the State militia 225 officers and 4,458 men, to compose six regiments. The order, "to detach," supposed the previous existence of an efficient, organized militia force, properly officered and equipped, capable of being called at once into active service. Such was not the case. In the long sway of peace, the people had neglected the "mimic show of war;" few companies were organized; fewer still were drilled and supplied with arms. Plowshares instead of swords, pruning-hooks instead of spears or bayonets, was the order from Lake Michigan to the Great River.

Adjutant-General Fuller, in his Report for 1861–2, gives the situation:

"From papers turned over to me by my predecessor, I find but twenty-five bonds for the return of arms issued to militia companies in 1857–8–9 and '60, and during that time but thirty-seven certificates of the election of company officers. It will furthermore appear from the report of the Quartermaster-General, who, until about the first of April, 1862, had charge of the Ordnance Department, there were but three hundred and sixty-two United States altered muskets, one hundred and five Harper's Ferry and Deniger's rifles, one hundred and thirty-three musketoons and two hundred and ninety-seven horse pistols in the arsenal. A few hundred unserviceable arms and accoutrements were scattered through the State, principally in possession of the militia companies. In fact, there were no available, efficient, armed and organized militia in the State, and it is doubted whether there were thirty companies with any regular organization. It is true there were in our principal cities and towns several independent militia companies whose occasional meetings for drill were held more for exercise and amusement than from any sense of duty to the State. Many of these formed the nucleus of splendid companies, which came promptly forward, and who have rendered excellent service to their State and country."

The day the Governor received the call of the War Department, he issued a proclamation for a special session of the Legislature to meet on the 23d of April. As part of the history of the beginning of the war some extracts from the message are appended:

THE OCCASION.

"The Constitution authorizes me on extraordinary occasions to convene the Legislature in special sessions. Certainly no occasion could have arisen more extraordinary than the one which is now presented to us. A plan conceived and cherished by some able but misguided statesman of the Southern States for many years past, founded upon an inadmissible and destructive interpretation of our national constitution, considered until very recently as merely visionary, has been partially carried into practical execution by ambitious and restless leaders, to the great peril of our noble Union, of our Democratic institutions and of our public and private prosperity.

"The popular discontent, consequent inevitably upon a warmly-contested Presidential election, which heretofore has always soon subsided amongst a people having the profoundest respect for their self-imposed laws, and bowing respectfully before the majesty of the popular will, constitutionally expressed; this discontent was in this instance artfully seized upon, and before there was time for the angry passions to subside, one State after another was precipitated out of the Union by a machinery, wanting in most instances, the sanction of the people in the seceding States.

"No previous effort was made by the disloyal States to procure redress for supposed grievances. Impelled by bold and sagacious leaders, disunionists at heart, they spurned in advance all proffers of compromise. The property of the Union, its forts and arsenals, costing the people of all the States enormous sums of money, were seized with a strong hand. Our noble flag, which had protected the now seceding portions of the Confederacy within its ample folds in their infancy, and which is the pride of every true and loyal American heart, and which had become respected and revered throughout the world as the symbol of democracy and liberty, was insulted and trampled in the dust. * * * * * * * * *

"A conference of Commissioners, at the instance of the Commonwealth of Virginia, was held at the Capital, attended by nearly all the border States and all the free States, with but one or two exceptions. Propositions of a highly conciliatory character were adopted by a majority of the free States represented in said conference; but before Congress had even time to consider them, they were denounced by leading men in the border States, and by almost every one of their members of Congress, as unsatisfactory and inadmissible, though they met the approval of the best patriots and of the mass of the people in the border States. The seceded States treated them with the utmost contempt. That, under such circumstances, and when no practical object could be obtained, the representatives of the free States declined to adopt them, is no matter of surprise.

"A proposition, first made by the Legislature of Kentucky, for the call of a National Constitutional Convention, as provided in the Constitution, for the redress of all grievances, undoubtedly the best and surest mode of settling all difficulties, was responded to by Illinois, and by many other free States, and such a convention was definitely recommended by the present administration on its advent to the government. Enough had been done by the border and free States to satisfy every rational mind that the South would have nothing to fear from any measures to be passed by Congress, or by any of the State Legislatures.

"Public sentiment was everywhere, in the free States, for peace and compromise. No better proof could be required, that the conspiracy, which has now assumed such formidable dimensions, and which is threatening the destruction of the fairest fabric of human wisdom and human liberty, is of long standing, and is wholly independent of the election of a particular person to the Presidential office, than the manner in which the seceded States have acted toward their loyal brethren of the South and North since they have entered upon their criminal enterprise. We must do them, however, the justice to say, that all their public documents, and all the speeches of their controlling leaders, candidly admit that the Presidential election has not been the cause for their action, and that they were impelled by far different motives. * * * * * * * * * * * * *

"The spirit of a free and brave people is aroused at last. Upon the first call of the constitutional government they are rushing to arms. Fully justified in the eyes of the world and in the light of history, they have resolved to save the government of our fathers, to preserve the Union so dear by a thousand memories and promising so much of happiness to them and their children, and to bear aloft the flag which for eighty-five years has gladdened the hearts of the struggling free on every continent, island and sea under the whole heavens. Our own noble State, as of yore, has responded in a voice of thunder. The entire mass is alive to the crisis. If, in Mexico, our Hardin and Shields, and Bissell and Baker, and their gallant comrades, were found closest to their colors, and in the thickest of the fight, and shed imperishable luster upon the fame and glory of Illinois, now that the struggle is for our very Nationality, and for the Stars and Stripes, her every son will be a soldier and bare his breast to the storm of battle.

"The attack upon Fort Sumter produced a most startling transformation on the Northern mind, and awakened a sleeping giant, and served to show, as no other event in all the history of the past ever did, the deep-seated fervor and affection with which our whole people regard our glorious Union. Party distinctions vanished as a mist, in a single night, as if by magic; and parties and party platforms were swept as a morning dream from the minds of men; and now men of all parties, by thousands, are begging for places in the ranks. The blood of twenty millions of freemen boils, with cauldron heat, to replace our national flag upon the very walls whence it was insulted and by traitor hands pulled down. Every village and hamlet resounds with beat of drum and clangor of arms. Three hundred thousand men wait the click of the wires for marching orders, and all the giant energies of the Northwest are at the command of the government. Those who have supposed that the people of the free States will not fight for the integrity of the Union, and that they will suffer another government to be carved out of the boundaries of this Union, have hugged a fatal delusion to their bosoms, for our people will wade through seas of blood before they will see a single star or a solitary stripe erased from the glorious flag of our Union.

ASSISTANCE RENDERED.

The Governor thus refers to aid rendered him by gentlemen of adverse political sentiments, and by the citizens of various portions of the State:

"The services already rendered me, in my effort to organize troops, provide means, arms and provisions, by distinguished members of the party, hitherto opposed to me in political sentiments, are beyond all praise, and are by me, in behalf of the State, most cheerfully acknowledged. There are now more companies received than are needed under the Presidential call, and almost unlimited numbers have formed and are forming, awaiting further orders. A single inland county (La Salle) tenders nine full companies, and our principal city (Chicago) has responded with contributions of men and money worthy of her fame for public spirit and patriotic devotion. Nearly a million of money has been offered to the State, as a loan, by our patriotic capitalists and other private citizens, to pay the expenses connected with the raising of our State troops and temporarily providing for them."

NEEDED LEGISLATION.

In this sudden emergency, when the call was made by the National Government, I found myself greatly embarrassed, by what still remains on our statute book, as a militia law, and by the entire want of organization of our military force. A great portion of this law has grown entirely obsolete, and cannot be carried out, and moreover is in conflict with the instructions of the war department, which latter are based on the various military laws of the United States now in force. But as far as possible, I have made an effort to keep within the provisions of our law.

"I have to call your attention most emphatically to the enactment of a practicable militia law, as recommended in my Inaugural Address, which should recognize the principle of volunteering as one of its most prominent features. It ought to be plain and intelligible as well as concise and comprehensive. It ought to provide for many emergencies and future contingencies, and not for the present moment alone. I trust that our conflict will not be a protracted one; but if it unfortunately should be, we may well expect that what is now done by enthusiasm, and in the first effervescence of popular excitement, may hereafter have to be done by a stern sense of duty, to be regulated by an equally stern law. Trials may come, which can only be met by endurance and patient performance of prescribed duty.

"I deem the passage of a well digested militia law the more necessary, as it seems to me, that the present levy of troops, which will soon pass under the control of the General Government, is insufficient to protect our State against threatened invasion, and such commotions as frequently follow in the train of war: I would recommend to keep an active militia force, consisting of infantry, cavalry and artillery, for some time to come, at least; also a reserve force for protection against dangers of any kind, and for the purpose of readily complying from time to time, with the requisitions of the General Government.

"It is for you, representatives of the people, if you coincide with my views in this respect, to pass the proper laws to accomplish the objects recommended to your most earnest consideration. * * * * * * * * *

"I recommend the appropriation by the Legislature of a sum not exceeding three millions of dollars, so much of which only is to be expended as the public exigences may require; and I would further recommend that the law be passed authorizing the Governor to accept the services of ten regiments, in addition to those already called out by the general government.

"Though the Constitution has very properly restricted the contracting of a public debt in all ordinary cases, it has, with commendable foresight, provided for cases of emergency such as the present, in allowing loans to be made 'for the purpose of repelling invasion, suppressing insurrection, or defending the State in war,' I invite you to a prompt action on this all important subject, and feel no hesitation that you will come forward with a zeal and alacrity, in providing ample means for the present emergency, corresponding to the devotion of our people to their sacred honor and their glorious flag.

"It has come to my knowledge that there are several thousand stand of arms scattered over the State, which are, however, not of the most approved construction, and need to be exchanged for others, or to be provided with the more modern appliance, to make them serviceable. I have already instituted means to have these collected at the State Armory at the Capital, and what disposition shall be made of them is respectfully submitted to your consideration.

"Other measures may be necessary by you for the purpose of lending efficient assistance to the General Government in preserving the Union, enforcing the laws, and protecting the rights and property of the people, which I must leave to your judgment and wisdom. As one of such measures, however, I recommend the propriety of passing a law restraining the telegraph in our State from receiving and transmitting any messages, the object of which shall be to encourage a violation of the laws in this State or the United States, and to refuse all messages in cipher, except when they are sent by the State or national authorities, or citizens known to be loyal.

"And now, as we love our common country, in all its parts, with all its blessings of climate and culture; its mountains, valleys and streams; as we cherish its history and the memory of the world's only Washington; as we love our free civilization, striking its roots deep down into those principles of truth and justice eternal as God; as we love our government so free, our institutions so noble, our boundaries so broad; as we love our grand old flag, 'sign of the free heart's only home,' that is cheered and hailed in every sea and haven of the world, let us resolve that we will preserve that Union and those institutions, and that there shall be no peace till the traitorous and bloodless palmetto shall be hurled from the battlements of Sumter, and the star-spangled banner in its stead wave defiantly in the face of traitors, with every star and every stripe flaming from all its ample folds."

On reception of the call, General Order No. 1 was issued from headquarters, requiring all commandants of divisions, brigades, regiments and companies, to hold themselves in readiness for actual service, and on the 15th, General Order No. 2 directed the immediate organization of the six regiments.

In reviewing the war, and looking back upon the formidable

preparations made by the secessionists, it is at once matter of surprise and regret that the first call was for 75,000 instead of 500,000 men, and for the brief term of ninety days instead of three or five years. Perhaps, trusting to that love of country which had been so prominent a characteristic to the American people, the President had faith that the sober second thought would rescue the Southern people from the mælstrom of treason, and that, when the misguided leaders should see that the Government would preserve its authority, integrity and existence at every price, and that a separate confederacy could only be established by a costly war, extending almost indefinitely, they would recoil from the opening gulf, would decline to lay down the crimson consideration. Perhaps there was an over-confidence in the existence of Union sentiment in the revolted States, and yet a comprehensive view of the whole subject would have suggested that the Union sentiment in South Carolina, Georgia or Alabama needed large armies to give it assurance.

The President was reluctant to concede the existence of *war*, hence his proclamation summoned the militia of the States to "suppress combinations too powerful to be suppressed by the ordinary course of judicial proceedings or by the powers vested in marshals by law," and with this, he would be content to await the action of Congress, which, by the same proclamation, he convened in special session on the 4th of July following, leaving it to decide, after it should be seen that the States in rebellion should refuse to recognize the demands of the government and to bow to its authority, what further "measures the public safety and interests may seem to demand."

It is also true that the President found the government almost destitute of the arms and munitions of war. Said Mr. Secretary Cameron: "Upon my appointment to the position, I found the department destitute of all the means of defence—without guns, and with little prospect of purchasing the *material* of war; I found the nation without an army, and I found scarcely a man throughout the whole War Department in whom I could put my trust. The Adjutant-General deserted. The Quartermaster-General ran off. The Commissary-General was on his death-bed. More than half the clerks were disloyal."

That the Secretary did not overstate the appalling difficulties we have the confirmatory evidence of rebel authorities. Said the Richmond Enquirer:

"The facts we are about to state are official and indisputable. Under a single order of the Secretary of War, the Hon. Mr. Floyd, made during the last year, there were 115,000 improved muskets and rifles sent from the Springfield Armory, Mass., and Watervliet Arsenal, N. Y., to different arsenals at the South. The total number of improved arms, thus supplied to five depositories in the South, by a single order of the late Secretary of War, was 114,868."

Another secession organ (Memphis Appeal), stated that there had been distributed at different convenient points in the South, 707,000 stand of arms, and 200,000 revolvers. Not less discouraging was the state of the Navy. Demoralization prevailed among its officers, and the Secretary, Mr. Welles, said in his official report, "Many of whom (the officers) occupying the most responsible positions, betrayed symptoms of that infidelity which has dishonored the service." "The Home Squadron consisted of twelve vessels carrying 187 guns and about 2,000 men. Of this squadron *only four small vessels*, carrying 25 guns and about 280 men were in Northern ports."

The people have since shown that they can create armies and improvise navies, and had they been trusted, half a million might have been in the field or in camps of instruction before the meeting of Congress.

We must remember that all this is written *after the events*, and in the light of history, rather than in the dim twilight of uncertainty and the haze of doubt in which were Lincoln and his advisers. And in our very delays are seen the developing plans of the Infinite, who was leading our nation out of its Egypt of bondage into an Israel of freedom.

CHAPTER V.

EARLY STATE MOVEMENTS—ORGANIZATION.

TEN DAYS' WORK—TEN THOUSAND—WITHOUT ARMS—STATE MESSENGER IN BALTIMORE—IMPORTANCE OF CAIRO—RIVER AND RAILWAY KEY—YATES'S ORDER TO GEN. SWIFT—MEANS BUSINESS—CAIRO EXPEDITION—EQUIPMENT—BIG MUDDY—AT CAIRO—ARTILLERY AMUNITION—A TRIO OF BORDER GOVERNORS—IMPERTINENCE—KENTUCKY NEUTRALITY—PIOUS BERIAH—GOVERNOR'S SPECIAL MESSAGE—GRIM ROMANCE—BRASS MISSIONARIES—CAIRO IN KENTUCKY—COL. PRENTISS IN COMMAND—CONTRABAND TRADE—SEIZURE OF STEAMERS—CARGO—LEGISLATIVE ACTION—WAR-FOOTING—NUMBERING REGIMENTS—TEN REGIMENT BILL—DISTRICT HEADQUARTERS—PRESIDENT'S SECOND CALL—CAPTAIN STOKES—ST. LOUIS ARSENAL—SECESSIONIST DIFFICULTIES—TACT AND COURAGE—SUCCESS—"STRAIGHT FOR ALTON."

Within ten days after the proclamation of Governor Yates was published, more than ten thousand men had offered their services. On all sides, enlistments went rapidly forward, and there was earnest competition for the perilous honor of acceptance.

But the State was without arms. In addition to the former extracts from the Adjutant-General's report, the following paragraphs show how deplorable was the condition of a State "on the border," and liable to immediate invasion:

There being no serviceable arms in the arsenal at Springfield, an unsuccessful application was made to Brigadier-General Harney, at the arsenal in St. Louis. Application was also made, on the 19th, at the arsenal at New York and a messenger dispatched to Washington to obtain them. As these troops were to be mustered into the service of the United States, on the 19th, more than our full quota having been tendered, application was made for a mustering officer, and on the 22d Captain Pope arrived to perform that service. There were volunteers enough, and a surplus, on that eventful 19th of April, 1861, but the want of arms had become painful and alarming. It was on that day that Union soldiers from a sister State, hastening to the defence of the National Capitol were shot down in the streets of Baltimore; and on that, and following days, that your messenger, returning from that Capitol, and bearing concealed orders from the President to the commanding officer at St.

Louis for arms, was obliged to deny the principles of his manhood, and avow disloyal sentiments, to escape the vengeance of an infuriated mob in that city."

The unprofessional common sense of the people, as well as the judgment of military authorities, pronounced Cairo a point of strategic importance, valuable for defence, and as a depot for supplies. It is situated at the confluence of the Ohio and Mississippi Rivers, and is the key to the navigation of both. It is also the southern terminus of the Illinois Central Railroad, which runs thence to Centralia, where, dividing, one line tends northward to Chicago, there striking Lake Michigan, thus connecting the river and chain of great lakes; the other reaches northwestwardly striking the Mississippi River again at Dunleith, opposite the flourishing city of Dubuque, Iowa. These lines have connection with other roads, and their importance for furnishing transportation of troops and subsistence for operations in the Southwest, can scarcely be overestimated. The seizure of Cairo would have given the rebels control of the railway combinations of the West, and would have closed the navigation of its two chief water lines. It was, therefore, no matter of surprise to Governor Yates that he received, on the 29th of April, the following dispatch from the Secretary of War: "As soon as enough of your troops are mustered into service, send a Brigadier General at or near Grand* Cairo." The Governor at once sent the following dispatch:

"SPRINGFIELD, April 19, 1861.

"*General Swift:*

"As quick as possible have as strong a force as you can raise, armed and equipped with amunition and accoutrements, and a company of artillery, ready to march at a moment's warning. A messenger will start to Chicago to-night.

"RICHARD YATES,
"Commander in Chief."

"That means business," was the response when this dispatch appeared in the newspapers, and business it was, for on the 21st, or only forty-eight hours after its reception, General Swift left Chicago with four six-pounders, and 495 men. His artillery was strengthened, however, by Captain Houghtaling's battery, of Ottawa, Captain Hawley's, of Lockport, Captain McAllister's, of Plainfield, and Captain Carr's, of Sandwich, which went forward on the 23d.

*The Hon. Secretary knew Cairo was in "Egypt," hence some confusion of prefix.

The expedition consisted of the following force:

Brig. Gen. Swift and Staff	14
Chicago Light Artillery, Capt. Smith	150
Ottawa Light Artillery, Capt. Houghtaling	86
Lockport Light Artillery, Capt. Hawley	52
Plainfield Light Artillery, Capt. McAllister	72
Co. A, Chicago Zouaves, Capt. Hayden	89
Co. B, Chicago Zouaves, Capt. Clybourne	83
Capt. Harding's company	80
Turner Union Cadets, Capt. Kowald	97
Lincoln Rifles, Capt. Miholotzy	66
Sandwich company, Capt. Carr	102
Drum Corps	17
Total	908

To which was added Captain Campbell's Ottawa Independent Artillery, with about twenty men and two six-pounder cannon, which reported to the commanding General on the 28th.

This advance "army of occupation" and defence was equipped after a fashion not specified in the Regulations, nor described in the "Tactics." It was a citizen-corps, made up largely of the youth of the best families of the State, and many of them were armed by a requisition on their homes and friends, and Chicago stores.

The expedition reached Big Muddy Bridge, on the Illinois Central road, at 5 P.M., on the 22d. Here Captain Hayden's company was detached to guard the bridge, and protect the road from straggling traitors.* The rest went forward, arriving at Cairo the next morning at 8 o'clock. The batteries, for which they had neither shot, shell, nor canister, were provided with slugs hurriedly made, and destined to do deadly work among the rebel squadrons at Fort Donelson.

The occupation was not effected a day too soon. Hard by were the disloyal Governors, Claibourn M. Jackson, of Missouri, Isham Harris, of Tennessee, and Beriah McGoffin, of Kentucky, who prated of neutrality. Jackson responded to the President's call for troops by saying, "Your requisition, in my judgment, is illegal, unconstitutional and revolutionary in its objects, inhuman and diaboli-

* Information having been received of an attempt to burn the bridge at Big Muddy, Gen. Swift detached part of Company B Chicago Zouaves, under command of Lieut. P. N. Guthrie, and one section of Capt. Smith's Chicago Light Artillery, under command of Lieut Willard, with instructions to report to Capt. Hayden. A section of Capt. Houghtaling's Ottawa Light Artillery, was also ordered to this bridge.

cal and cannot be complied with. Not one man will the State of Missouri furnish to carry on such an unholy crusade." Harris flung into the face of the chief magistrate this defiant answer, "Tennessee will not furnish a single man for coercion, but fifty thousand, if necessary, for the defence of our rights, and those of our brethren." The answer of Beriah McGoffin, who has the questionable fame of having invented a novel style of neutrality, bristling northward with bayonets and looking southward with men and means, said: "In answer, I say, emphatically, that Kentucky will furnish no troops for the wicked purpose of subduing Southern States!" The conscientious care of Beriah, lest the President "should put forth his hand into iniquity," would savor much of hopeful sanctity, did it not so strongly suggest the ancient, but unseemly *role* of Satan as a reprover! The precious trio of Border State statesmen, had their emissaries watching this important river and railway center, with eagle and evil eyes, and were almost ready to seize it, but the commander of the Union forces, was swift to forestall them, and Cairo became, and has remained, a military post of the United States.

In his message to the Legislature in extraordinary session, Gov. Yates states the reasons for the immediate occupancy of this point:

"The transfer of part of the volunteer forces of this State was made in compliance with an order of the War Department, directing a force to be stationed at Cairo. Simultaneously with the receipt of the order, reliable information reached me of the existence of a conspiracy by disaffected persons in other States to seize upon Cairo and the southern portion of the Illinois Central Railroad and cut off communication with the interior of the State. It was my desire that the honor of this service should have been given to the patriotic citizens of the counties in the immediate vicinity. But as these were not at that time organized and armed for patriotic duty, and the necessity for speedy action was imperative, the requisition was filled from companies previously tendered from other portions of the State."

The arrival of the troops had its grim poetry and romance. The loyalty of all the residents of the city was not above suspicion, but they met a sudden change of expression, if not of heart. The *rationale* of their conversion was well stated by a plain farmer of the vicinity: "I tell you what it is, them brass missionaries has converted a heap of folks that was on the anxious seat!" Even so, and the government was to learn that "brass pieces," ball and bayonet, were the true evangels of peace and the *avant couriers* of a restored Union!

An aggrieved Kentucky Congressman wrote Mr. Lincoln a note complaining that Cairo was occupied by armed troops, and that Kentucky regarded the act as a usurpation and offensive. The President replied by assuring the honorable member that when he ordered the troops to Cairo, *Illinois*, he did not suspect that it was included in a *Kentucky* Congressional District or he surely would not have done so! But he did not soothe the ruffled representative by an order to remove the forces.

On the 24th the seven companies arrived from Springfield, commanded by Colonel, afterward Major-General B. M. Prentiss, who relieved General Swift, and assumed command. The companies of of Harding, Hayden and Clyborne proceeded to Springfield to join a regiment then organizing, but were too late and were mustered out of service, receiving one month's pay, allowed them by act of the Legislature then in extraordinary session.

Under the provisions of the Legislature, six regiments were organized, and called the "First Brigade of Illinois Volunteers." These regiments were numbered, seven, eight, nine, ten, eleven and twelve, in respect to the regiments of Illinois volunteers, that had served in the Mexican war. As soon as these forces were mustered, they were ordered to duty. The Seventh, commanded by Colonel Cook, was mustered into service at Springfield, April 25th and ordered to Alton, Ill., on the 27th inst.

The Eighth, commanded by Colonel Oglesby, was mustered into service, the same day, and ordered to Cairo on the 27th inst.

The Ninth, commanded by Colonel Paine, was mustered into service, at Springfield, April 26th, and was ordered to Cairo, May 1st.

The Tenth, commanded by Colonel Prentiss, with part of his command, was ordered to Cairo, April 22d, and on the 29th was mustered into service at Cairo.

The Eleventh, commanded by Colonel Wallace, was mustered into service at Springfield, April 30th, and ordered to Villa Ridge, May 5th.

The Twelfth, commanded by Colonel McArthur, was mustered at Springfield, May 2d, and ordered to Cairo, May 10th.

In relation to the formation of this brigade, Adjutant-General Fuller, makes the following interesting remarks: "On the completion of the organization of these regiments several hundred volunteers were left unprovided for. Most of the companies arrived in camp with over one hundred men. Seven hundred and eighty, rank and file, was the maximum allowed by the War Department, and among the most touching and painful incidents, indicating the patriotic fervor of our people, at that time, noticed in the preparation of these troops for the field, was the rejection of these surplus volunteers. Strong men, who had left their homes at an hour's notice to enter the service of their country, wept at the disappointment of being refused admission to companies on muster day. Provision was made for them of one month's pay, and they filed their rolls and were mustered out of the service of the State!"

The service rendered by these forces to the Government, while posted at Cairo, can not be too highly prized.

One of the early doings of the Cairo garrison was the stoppage of the river trade in Galena lead and Cincinnati and Louisville dry goods. Boats were passing daily with such stores, designed for "Southern trade." In advance of orders from Washington, Governor Yates sent the following order:

"SPRINGFIELD, April 24, 1861.

"*Col. B. M. Prentiss, Cairo:*

"The steamers C E Hillman and John D. Perry are about to leave St. Louis with arms and munitions. Stop said boats and seize all the arms and munitions.

"RICHARD YATES,
"Commander-in-Chief."

On the evening of the 24th and morning of the 25th the steamers came on, not suspecting stoppage. Col. Prentiss had given orders to Capt. Smith, of Chicago Light Artillery, and Capt. Scott, of the Chicago Zouaves to board and seize them, and those gallant young officers performed the work with a relish, and the arms and munitions, of which there were large quantities, were seized, and their confiscation was subsequently approved at Washington, and on the 7th of May Secretary Chase, of the Treasury, issued a circular forbidding shipments to ports under insurrectionary control, and directing that all such shipments should be stopped at Cairo.

The Legislature passed liberal appropriation bills, that the State might be placed on a war footing, and authorized the creation of ten regiments of infantry, one regiment of cavalry and one battalion of light artillery, for State service. One of these might be organized from volunteer companies then at Springfield, and one from each of the then existing nine Congressional districts. Volunteers accepted in these regiments were required to give pledge to tender their services to the War Department, if called for. As soon as arms could be furnished, each regiment was to be placed in encampments at Regimental Headquarters, in the Congressional district where it was raised, and remain in camp thirty days for drill and instruction, unless sooner demanded by the General Government. This act took effect May 2d, but the next day a new phase was given.

The President, without awaiting the assembling of Congress, made another call, this time for three years unless sooner discharged, but only for 42,032 men, of whom Illinois was to furnish six regiments. For some time the history is that of a persistent effort by the people to place enough men at once in the field, to march over all opposition to Richmond, Montgomery, and Charleston, and on the part of the War Department to carry on the "suppression of disturbances" with as little military array as possible, with the fewest number of men, and least possible *war materiël.* That there was loyal determination, we do not doubt, but the General-in-Chief was aged, and Mr. Stanton was not yet Secretary of War.

At this point the reader will excuse the insertion of an interesting episode which merits a place in history, both in view of the daring and tact of its performance and the advantages resulting.

We have heretofore spoken of the difficulty of arming the Cairo expedition, and the same difficulty was anticipated in reference to the ten regiments called, at first, into the State service. A messenger was sent to Washington City to procure arms, who returned, in the latter part of April, with an order from the Secretary of War for 10,000 of the muskets in the arsenal at St. Louis. At that time the arsenal at St. Louis was closely watched by secession spies, and a mob of secessionists were ready to seize the arms the moment an attempt should be made to remove them. The question was, who will undertake the hazardous enterprise, and how can it be made successful? Captain James H. Stokes, of Chicago, volunteered to undertake the perilous mission. Gov. Yates placed in his hands the requisition of the Secretary of War for 10,000 muskets. Captain Stokes proceeded to St. Louis, and made his way as rapidly as possible to the arsenal. He found it surrounded by an immense mob, and the postern gates closed. His utmost efforts to penetrate the crowd were for a long time unavailing. The requisition was shown to the commander of the arsenal. Captain Lyon doubted the possibility of executing it. He said the arsenal was surrounded by a thousand spies, and every movement was watched and reported to the headquarters of the Secessionists, who could throw an overpowering force upon them at any moment. Captain Stokes stated that every hour's delay was rendering the capture of the arsenal more certain, and that the arms must be moved to Illinois now or never. Major Callender agreed with him, and told him to take them at his own time and in his own way. This was Wednesday night, 24th of April.

Captain Stokes had a spy in the camp whom he met at intervals in the city. On Thursday he received information that Gov. Jackson had ordered two thousand armed men down from Jefferson City, whose movements could only contemplate a seizure of the arsenal by occupying the heights around it, and planting batteries thereon. The undertaking would have been an easy one. His friends had already planted one battery on the St. Louis levee, and another at Powder Point, a short distance below the arsenal. Captain Stokes immediately telegraphed to Alton to have the steamer *City of Alton* drop down the river to the arsenal, and to land there about midnight. He then returned to the arsenal, and commenced moving the boxes of guns, weighing some three hundred pounds each, down to the lower floor.

About 700 men were employed in the work. He then took 500 Kentucky flint-lock muskets, brought there to be altered, and sent them to be placed on a steamer as a blind to cover his real movements. The Secessionists seized the muskets at once, and raised a perfect shout of joy over the capture. A large portion of the outside crowd left the arsenal when this movement was executed; and Captain Lyon took the remainder, who were lying around as spies, and locked them up in the guard-house. About 11 o'clock the steamer *City of Alton* came along side, planks were run from the windows to the main deck, and the boxes were shoved down into the boat. When 10,000 were safely on board, Captain Stokes went to Captain Lyon and Major Callender, and urged them, by the most pressing appeals, to let him empty the arsenal. They told him to go ahead and take whatever he wanted. Accordingly, he took 10,000 more muskets, 500 new rifle carbines, 500 revolvers, 110,000 musket cartridges, to say nothing of the cannon, and a large quantity of miscellaneous accoutrements, leaving only 7,000 muskets in the arsenal to arm the St. Louis volunteers.

When the whole were on board, about two o'clock on Friday morning, the order was given by the captain of the steamer to cast off. Judge of the consternation of all hands when it was found that the boat could not be moved. The arms had been piled in great quantities around the engines to protect them against the battery on the levee, and the great weight had fastened the bow of the boat firmly on a rock, which was crushing through the bottom at every turn of the wheels. A man of less nerve than Captain Stokes would have despaired. He called the men from the arsenal on board, and commenced moving the boxes to the stern. Fortunately, when about two hundred had been shifted, the boat fell away from the shore and floated in deep water.

"Which way?" said Captain Mitchell, of the steamer. "Straight to Alton, in the regular channel," replied Captain Stokes. "What if we are attacked?" said Captain Mitchell. "Then we will fight," was the reply of Captain Stokes. "What if we are overpowered?" said Mitchell. "Run the boat to the deepest part of the river and sink her," replied Stokes. "I'll do it," was the heroic answer of Mitchell; and away they went past the secession battery, past the entire St. Louis levee, and in the regular channel on to Alton, where they arrived at five o'clock in the morning.

When the boat touched the landing, Captain Stokes, fearing pursuit by some of the secession military companies by which the city of St. Louis was disgraced, ran to the market house and rang the fire-bell. The citizens came flocking pell-mell to the river, in all sorts of habiliments. Captain Stokes informed them as to the state of affairs, and pointed out the freight cars. Instantly, men, women, and children boarded the steamer, seized the freight, and clambered up the levee to the cars. Rich and poor tugged together with "might and main" for two hours, when the cargo was all deposited in the cars, and then the train moved off for Springfield amid the most enthusiastic cheers!

CHAPTER VI.

THE STATE AUTHORITIES AND WAR DEPARTMENT.

Six Regiments Wanted—Two Hundred Companies Offered—Selection—Regimental Head-Quarters—Cavalry Declined—Secretarial Wet Blanket—Messenger to Washington—Four Additional Regiments Accepted—Reclaiming Enlisted Men—The Colonels—"Foraging Stopped"—"Go to your Consul"—Correspondence Between Governor Yates and Mr. Cameron—After Bull Run and Wilson's Creek—At Last—Cavalry—Ten Companies—Thirteen Regiments—Artillery—Infantry Regiments—Enlisting again Stopped—Illinois and Sister States.

ILLINOIS was permitted only to furnish six regiments, and two hundred companies were contending for acceptance, as zealously as ever knightly chieftains pressed for the privilege of leading the van. The task of selection was delicate and painful, but was promptly performed by the sixth of May, and the regiments ordered into camp in their respective Congressional districts, at the dates and places given below:

1st District, at Freeport, May 11th; 2d, at Dixon, May 9th; 3d, at Joliet, May 11th; 4th, at Peoria, May 13th; 5th, at Quincy, May 9th; 6th, at Jacksonville, May 11th; 7th, at Mattoon, May 9th; 8th, at Belleville, May 11th; 9th, at Anna, May 16th; and the regiment from the State at large, made up in part of regiments at Springfield, was ordered to rendezvous at Chicago June 13th.

The State authorities then tendered the War Department ten regiments of infantry, one of cavalry, and a battalion of artillery, and urged their acceptance. But the War Department was not yet ready to abandon all its ideas of a short and easy campaign, and possibly in some other departments, there was the dream of a war terminated in ninety days by brilliant charges of rhetoric.

The venerable chieftain, Lieut.-Gen. Scott, the hero of many a well-won field, was opposed to the employment of any considerable cavalry force. Its importance was to be demonstrated in the near future.

May 3d the Governor received this dispatch:

"*Governor Yates:*

"In reply to yours of the 2d, I am again obliged, at the solicitation of Lieut.-General Scott, to decline acceptance of cavalry. Adjutant-General Thomas is clear in his opinion that they cannot be of service adequate to the expense incurred in accepting them.

"SIMON CAMERON,
"Secretary of War."

On the 15th, the expectant regiments were tantalized by another dispatch indicating the supremacy of the minifying policy, and the fatal dream, to be broken by the thunders of Bull Run, that there was simply a disturbance to be quieted. This is the dispatch:

"*Governor Yates:*

"The quota of troops from your State for three years, or during the war, under the second call of the President, is six regiments. * * * As soon as the regiments are ready, the mustering officer sent to your State will muster them into service, who has been instructed to do so."

Six only! A few days later came a letter, dated the 16th, from, what the people, heart-sore with their disappointments, began to consider the Peace Department, in which Mr. Cameron more effectually than ever before placed the wet blanket upon the popular enthusiasm. It ran thus:

"It is important to reduce rather than increase this number, and, in no event, to exceed it. Let me earnestly recommend to you, therefore, to call for no more than twelve regiments, of which six only are to serve for three years, or during the war, and if more are called for, to reduce the number by discharge."

A messenger was at once dispatched to Washington to urge upon the Department the importance of accepting the remaining four regiments. They were already in camp, and some of them had acquired much proficiency in drill, and to disband and send them home was to disgust them with the service, and to weaken public confidence in the wisdom and earnestness of the Government. The public saw that more men were needed, and it could see no reason why the same conclusion did not force itself upon the Government when the rebel flag was visible from the Executive Mansion.

The four regiments were finally accepted and an arrangement made by which the seventh, eighth, ninth, tenth, and eleventh, three months' men, might enlist for three years, four-fifths of each regiment concurring, an offer which those regiments, weakened by disease, bad clothing and the vicissitudes of climate, declined, and of 4,680 men only about 2,000 re-enlisted at the expiration of their term the July following.

The policy so long persistently pursued by the War Department began to produce its results. Adjutant-General Fuller thus states them in his report to the Governor:

"The refusal on the part of the Secretary of War to authorize you to accept more troops caused several thousand of our best and impatient volunteers to leave this State in May, June and July, and enlist elsewhere. Denied the privilege of serving their country in regiments from their own State they sought other fields of usefulness. Many whole companies entered Missouri regiments, and are now in the service. From correspondence with many of these so-called Missouri regiments, and from estimates made by those whose opinion is entitled to credit, I have no doubt more than ten thousand Illinoisans left their own State and enlisted in regiments of other States.

"In several cases application has been made to you to have regiments, a large majority of which consisted of Illinoisans, recognized as Illinois regiments. To provide for these cases the War Department, on the 21st of February last, decided that 'whenever a regiment is composed of companies from different states, it will be considered as belonging to the state from which the greatest number of companies was furnished for that regiment.' Under this order the 59th regiment, formerly 9th Missouri, and the 66th, formerly known as 'Birge's Sharp Shooters,' have been reclaimed, and other similar applications are now pending."

As we read the paragraph given below from the same document, we seem to be perusing the records of days long gone by, the annals of another era, so rapidly, and on a scale of such magnitude, has history been made:

"The 13th regiment was mustered at Dixon, July 24th, under Col. Wyman; the 14th, at Jacksonville, on the 25th, under Col. Palmer; the 15th, at Freeport, May 24th, under Col. Turner; the 16th, at Quincy, May 24th, under Col. Smith; the 17th, at Peoria, May 24th, under Col. Ross; the 18th, at Anna, May 28th, under Col. Lawler; the 19th, at Chicago, June 17th, under Col. Turchin; the 20th, at Joliet, June 13th, under Col. Marsh; the 21st, at Mattoon, June 15th, under Col. Grant; and the 22d, at Belleville, June 25th, under Col. Dougherty."

Wyman "sleeps the last sleep" in his soldier-grave; Palmer has bravely won and nobly wears his double stars; Ross received his well merited promotion; Turchin, now out of the service, believing from the outset that his men should be "subsisted" in the enemy's country, in the days when tender-footed surperiors were afraid of "exasperating their Southern brethren," and orders had been issued to stop foraging, came, one day, upon his men busy in a secessionist's potato field. The General raised himself in his stirrups and shouted: "Boys, what does this mean? Foraging is forbidden. If you don't quit, I will put a guard on this potato patch in *just two hours from this time.*" Of course, prior to the set time, the boys had "quit," and foraging had "stopped." Seated, on another occasion, in his tent, a secession Tennesseean approached him and said, "Colonel, some of your men has stole my horse." "Are you a citizen of the United States?" "Wall, no, Colonel, not adzackly. You see—" "Go away with you, and see your Consul then, and get him to attend to your business. I am not out collecting for aliens."

And there, too, was "Col. Grant," a quiet man, who did little talking, but accomplished a great deal of work—he has been heard of elsewhere.

The report of correspondence between the Head-Quarters at Springfield and the War Department, indicates a gradual change in the policy of the latter. We copy from the report of the Governor to the Constitutional Convention on the 6th of February, 1862:

"The number of troops far exceeded the quota which the Government was willing to accept, and, as the character of the rebellion became more formidable, this pressure became so great as to induce me, on the 23d of July, 1861, to send the Secretary of War the following communication:

"'*Hon. Simon Cameron, Secretary of War:*

"'SIR: Being advised that you are receiving tenders of additional troops, I desire to tender you, for Illinois, thirteen additional regiments of infantry, three additional regiments of cavalry, and one additional battalion of light artillery. Illinois demands her right to do her full share in the work of preserving our glorious Union from the assaults of high-handed rebellion, and I insist that you respond favorably to the call which I have made. Respectfully yours,

"'RICHARD YATES.'

"On the 28th of July, 1861, I received the following reply by telegraph:

"'*Governor Yates:*

"'Will accept the thirteen additional infantry regiments, three additional cavalry regiments, and an additional light artillery battalion. If you so desire you can provide for and equip those regiments, if you can do so, at once. Will write to-day.

"'SIMON CAMERON,
"'Secretary of War.'"

[The letter of the Secretary of War is omitted, being merely an expansion of the telegram.]

"About the 12th of August I received the following letter from the War Department in reference to arming and equipping the McClernand Brigade:

"'*His Excellency, Richard Yates, Governor of Illinois:*

"'Please afford to Brigadier-General John A. McClernand all the facilities in your power for arming and equipping his brigade at the earliest date possible.

"'Very respectfully, THOS. A. SCOTT,
"'Acting Secretary of War.'

' The thirteen additional regiments having been filled up, and the people of the State, as one man, humiliated at the disastrous defeat at Bull Run, on the 21st of July, were pressing upon me for acceptance; and on the 7th of August I wrote to the Secretary of War as follows:

"'I would suggest whether it would not be well to receive all the full companies which will report themselves full in the next twenty days.

"'The signs are that we shall need them, as it will stop the application to you for independent regiments.'

"On the 13th of the same month the brave Lyon fell, and on the same day I received the following dispatches:

"'HEAD-QUARTERS WESTERN DEPARTMENT, ST. LOUIS, Aug. 13, 1861.

"'*Governor Yates:*

"'Severe engagement near Springfield reported. Gen. Lyon killed. Sigel retreating in good order on Rolla. Send forthwith all the disposable force you have, arming as you best can for the moment. Use utmost dispatch.

"'JOHN C. FREMONT,
"'Maj.-Gen. Commanding.'

"'WASHINGTON, Aug. 13, 1861.

"'*His Excellency, Gov. Yates:*

"'What number of regiments have you now organized, and what number can be organized ready for marching orders this week? Please advise by telegraph.

"'SIMON CAMERON,
"'Secretary of War.'

"On the same day I telegraphed the Secretary of War as follows:

"'I have had to confine myself, in raising the thirteen regiments you authorized me to raise, to the acceptance of companies first tendered.

"'I have telegraphed your Department repeatedly for authority to accept all the troops offered, but have received no answer to my dispatches. I think you ought to give me authority to accept all the troops willing to enter the service.'

"'WASHINGTON, Aug. 14, 1861.

"'*Governor Yates:*

"'You are authorized to accept all companies of troops willing to enter the service. We shall accept no more independent regiments from Illinois. Many thanks for your promptness and energy.

"'SIMON CAMERON,
"'Secretary of War.'"

At last! After Bull Run and Wilson's Creek, after Lyon has been slain, with the national capital in peril, with Fremont's command confronted with a superior force—at last it realized that something more than the suppression of a disturbance is demanded, and the people have authority to rally to the support and for the salvation of the Government. Thank God for that much! It gave new heart to the people.

These paragraphs have anticipated somewhat the course of events, but have seemed necessary to preserve the unity and completion of the topic of the State policy in enlistments.

We have recorded the unwillingness of the War Department to receive cavalry, a repugnance based on the advice of General Scott, yet the Legislature, in special session, authorized the formation of a cavalry regiment, and it was organized by the acceptance of companies under the provisions of the act. Before the passage of the law, the Chicago Dragoons, commanded by Captain Charles W. Barker, and the Washington Light Cavalry, Captain Fredrick Schombeck, had reported at Camp Yates, and were now mustered into the State service. On the tenth of May three companies were accepted from the counties south of the Ohio and Mississippi Railroad, named and commanded as follows: White County Cavalry, Capt. Orlando Burrell; Gallatin County Cavalry, Capt. James Foster; Centralia Cavalry, Capt. R. D. Noleman.

The State authorities, considering five companies sufficient for State service, declined completing the regiment, though the other companies were ready and were designated in the special order of May 16th; viz., Companies of Capt. John McNulta, of Bloomington; Capt. A. C. Harding, Monmouth; Capt. John Burnap, Springfield; Capt. J. B. Smith, Knoxville; Capt. Paul Walters, Hillsboro.

On the 21st of June the proffer of ten companies of cavalry was accepted by the President, for three years' service, unless sooner discharged, and the companies accepted were assigned by the Governor to make up the "First Regiment of Illinois Cavalry." The Chicago Dragoons had been ordered to Cairo, and from thence were transferred, by order of General McClellan, to his command in Western Virginia, but declining to enlist for three years they were mustered out of service. They were subsequently reorganized under command of Capt. Shearer, and with another company were known as the "McClellan Dragoons." They were for a time attached to a regiment of Regulars, and since then they have been assigned to Col. Voss' 12th Cavalry. Seven companies of this regiment were with Mulligan at Lexington, Mo., and shared the captivity of that officer; they were, by order of the Major-General commanding the Department of the West, mustered out of service Oct. 8, 1861, were reinstated Dec. 21st, by order of the President, and reorganized at Benton Barracks, St. Louis, but continued in service but a short time, in consequence of difficulties arising from irregularity of exchange. Capt. Oscar Huntley's company, raised in Winnebago county, by authority of General Fremont, was assigned to the first regiment at its reorganization at Benton Barracks, but not having been captured was not mustered out. In May, June and July, the 8th, 9th and 11th cavalry were authorized by General Fremont, commanded respectively by Col. Farnsworth, Col. Brackett and Col. Ingersoll; under the call of the President, the 2d, Col. Noble, and the 4th, Col. Dickey, were organized; under the dispatch of July 25th, from Secretary Cameron, the 3d, Col. Carr, 7th, Col. Kellogg, and 6th, Col. Cavanaugh, were raised and accepted. August, the 5th, Col. Updegraff, was accepted, and on the 5th of September the 10th, Col. Barrett, on the 28th, the 12th, Col. Voss, on the 27th of November the 13th, Col. Bell. These last were limited to two battalions of four companies each; and in the last named, a battalion raised by Lt.-Col. Hartman under authority from the War Department was to constitute a part.

In addition to the thirteen regiments of cavalry authorized as above stated, several additional battalions and companies were organized. With the approval of General Smith, Capt. Marx recruited a company for Thielman's battalion, and Thielman was commissioned as Major, with rank from Nov. 1, 1861, his command being his own company, nominally attached to the 1st regiment, commanded by Capt. Marschner, and Capt. Marx's company. By authority of General Fremont, Capt. Warren Stuart recruited a company. Four companies were raised in connection with the 27th, 28th, 29th, 30th, and 31st regiments (Gen. McClernand's brigade), commanded by Captains Hutchens, Carmikel, O'Harnett, and Dollins. These companies, with Captain Stewart's, were subsequently formed into a battalion, and Captain Stewart commissioned as Major, to rank from Feb. 2, 1862, became its commander. Captain McNaughten raised a company under authority from General Fremont, designed to be attached to the 23d regiment, but after the battle of Lexington it was attached to a Missouri regiment known as "The Curtis' Horse." The "Kane County Cavalry," Captain Dodson, was raised for the 2d cavalry, but was ultimately attached to the 15th. Thus it is seen that before the close of 1861 Illinois had placed in the field, almost in spite of the Secretary of War, a small army of cavalry—brave horsemen, ready for active service.

It was soon seen that any number of men could be secured for the artillery service. It has its peculiar perils and hardships, but with all that it has strange fascination. Company A, Chicago Artillery, Capt. Smith (afterwards Willard), Capt. Houghtaling's Ottawa Artillery, and Capt. McCallister's, Plainfield, formed, as we have seen, part of the Cairo expedition under Brig.-Gen. Swift. They all remained in the service, being mustered first into the three months' and then into the three years' service. Also Co. B, Chicago Artillery, Capt. Taylor; Peoria Artillery, Capt. Davidson; Capt. Campbell's Ottawa battery, and Capt. Madison's battery were mustered in under the law of the special session of May, 1861.

Of these more will be heard as we thread the red-line of battles fought for the Republic. In them were such young men as seldom ever before stood by the recoiling piece, all begrimed with powder, amid the thunders of battle or of siege.

May, June and July brought the authorization of the following regiments of infantry, most of whom have since made a brilliant record: 23d, Col. Mulligan; 24th, Col. Hecker; 25th, Col. Coler; 33d, Col. Hovey; 34th, Col. Kirk; 35th, Col. Smith; 36th, Col. Greusel; 37th, Col. White; 39th, Col. Lighte; 40th, Col. Hicks;

41st, Col. Pugh; 42d, Col. Webb; 44th, Col. Knoblesdorf; 45th, Col. Smith; 47th, Col. Bryner; 52d, Col. Wilson; 55th, Col. Stuart. Under the authority of Secretary Cameron's letter of July 25th the the State reported the following infantry regiments: 26th, Col. Loomis; 27th, Col. Buford; 28th, Col. Johnson; 29th, Col. Reardon; 30th, Col. Foulke; 31st, Col. John Logan; 32d, Col. John A. Logan; 38th, Col. Carlin; 43d, Col. Raith; 46th, Col. Davis; 48th, Col. Haynie; 49th, Col. Morrison; 50th, Col. Bane. As has been seen, in response to an application of the Governor, made August 13th, all restriction upon infantry recruiting was removed, and the State was permitted to accept all that offered their services. The following regiments were authorized: 56th, Col. Kirkham; 61st, Col. Fry; 64th, Lt.-Col. Williams;* 65th, Col. Cameron; 51st, Col. Cummings; 53d, Col. Cushman;† 58th, Col. Lynch; 57th, Col. Baldwin; 54th, Col. Harris; 60th, Col. Toler; 62d, Col. True; 63d, Col. Wood.‡

In addition to the above, most of the companies for an additional regiment of artillery had been raised. On the 3d of December the authorities at Washington again became alarmed at the fore-cast shadow of too large an army, and issued the annexed order:

"HEAD-QUARTERS OF THE ARMY, ADJUTANT-GENERAL'S OFFICE,
"Washington, December 3, 1861.

"*General Orders, No.* 105.

"The following orders have been received from the Secretary of War:

"I. No more regiments, batteries, or independent companies will be raised by the Governors of States, except upon the special requisition of the War Department.

"Those now forming in the various States will be completed, under direction of the respective Governors thereof, unless it be deemed more advantageous to the service to assign the men already raised to regiments, batteries or independent companies now in the field, in order to fill up their organizations to the maximum standard prescribed by law.

"II. The recruiting service in the various States for the volunteer forces already in service, and for those that may hereafter be received, is placed under charge of general superintendents for those States, respectively, with general depots for the collection and instruction of recruits."

---

*Battalion of six companies known as Yates' Sharp-Shooters.

†Including squadron of cavalry and battery of artillery.

‡Known as the Kentucky Brigade.

Of course recruiting was suspended, but already the State had made a record. Pressing her claims to replenish the armies of the country upon a slow War Department over discouragements and rebuffs, she had sent to the field, not merely enlisted, more than 43,000 men besides the six months' regiments, and had, at the close of the year, in camps of instruction, 17,000 more. "During the month of December," says the Adjutant-General, "4160 more recruits were enlisted; all squads and parts of regiments were consolidated, and the 45th, 46th, 49th and 57th, were organized and mustered into service. The only incomplete regiments of infantry in the State, December 31st, were the 51st, Col. Cummings, at Camp Douglas; the 53d, Col. Cushman, at Ottawa; the 58th, Col. Lynch, at Camp Douglas; the 23d, Col. Mulligan, at Camp Douglas, reorganizing, and four regiments at Jonesboro', viz., 54th, 60th, 62d and 63d."

The people would have placed one hundred thousand men in the field between the surrender of Fort Sumter and the 31st of December, if the general government would have received them.

It is not claimed that Illinois was in advance of her sister states of the West in devotion to the country, but that she was their worthy compeer, yielding to none in patriotic regard and attesting her faith by her works, by the freely shed blood of her sons.

CHAPTER VII.

THE STATE AND THE ARMY.—61 TO 64.

The New Year—The Situation—Sober Views—The "Cause" to Perish—Carpet Knights—Ahead of All Calls—Other Regiments—To Fill Old Regiments—Special Service—"Washington in Danger"—A Time of Gloom—Tender-footed Commanders—The Inevitable Negro—Fremont and Hunter—War in Earnest—New Call—Governor's Proclamation—Letter to the President—The Old Score—No Draft—A Credit Declined—Two Years' Work—A Shock to State Pride—The Legislature of 1863-4—Its Responsibilities—Governor's Recommendations—Neglect of Grave Business—A Sudden Prorogation—"Profane History"—A Better Record—Governor's Proclamation Feb. 5, 1864—Adjutant-General's Report of Feb. 1, 1864.

EIGHTEEN HUNDRED AND SIXTY-THREE came, and peace was not restored, but seemed farther off than ever. Among the mountains of Virginia, along the Potomac, and the Southern seaboard, the bloody gage of battle had been tendered and accepted. In the West, the Cumberland, Tennessee and Mississippi rivers had been ablaze with camp fires, and their banks had echoed with the reverberations of musketry and artillery. The campaigns of 1861-2 had furnished enough of march, and battle, and incident to swell bulky octavos, but they were only introductory chapters to the real history. With the opening of the New Year the public mind began more clearly to understand that the Rebellion was a thing of gigantic dimensions, and almost infinite resources; that it could not be easily exhausted of men; that to starve it was not practicable; that it could command arms and munitions of war from *neutral* England; that the blockade could not yet prevent the exporting of cotton, and that a protracted and sanguinary war was upon the country. With this revelation there was the strengthened purpose to relax no effort, to spare no expenditure, to shun no sacrifice to maintain the perpetuity and integrity of the National Union, and to uphold the majesty of law. The temporary blockade of the Mississippi river had given the people a conception of the consequences to flow from its permanent occupancy by an unfriendly power. Steadily, too, was strengthening the public conviction that the war, commenced for the restoration of the Union, could only be made successful by the overthrow of its cause; that the real contest was between Freedom and Slavery; that after years of angry peace, they had entered the lists, sword in hand, visor down, with no master of ceremonies empowered to stay the combat, and that their strife was unto the death.

There had been, and at the opening of 1863 there still were, in the Union service, carpet knights, who acted as though their high commission was to keep watch lest slavery should receive damage in the fray, but the voice of an indignant people, and a gallant army, was demanding their displacement, and the employment of men sternly, terribly earnest in this work.

Illinois had, in 1861, placed at the service of the Government 15,000 more men than had been asked at her hands, and there was, at the beginning of January, 1862, but little prospect that others would be required, or, at the farthest, more than sufficient to keep full the decimated regiments already formed. But thousands were coming forward, demanding to be admitted to the honors and dangers of the war for the Union.

"In January the 32d regiment, Col. John Logan; the 45th, Col. John V. Smith; the 64th, Lt. Col. D. Williams, infantry, and the 10th cavalry, Col. J. A. Barrett, were ordered to the field. In February, the 46th, Col. John A. Doris; 49th, Col. Wm. R. Morrison; 57th, Col. Silas D. Baldwin; 58th, Col. Wm. F. Lynch, and 61st, Col. Jacob Fry, infantry; 5th cavalry, Col. Wilson; 9th cavalry, Col. Brackett, and 13th cavalry, Col. Bell, and seven splendid batteries of light artillery followed, commanded by Captains Sparstrow, Stienbeck, Keith, Rogers, Waterhouse, Silversparre and Bouton. The most of these troops reached the field in time to join our old regiments, and with them to participate in the battle of Ft. Donelson on the 15th and 16th of February."—*Adjutant-General's Report.*

On the 16th of February Ft. Donelson was surrendered to the Federal troops, and ten thousand prisoners of war sent to Camp Douglas, Chicago, and Camp Butler, Springfield. To guard those at the former place were detailed the 23d, 53d and 65th infantry, and two or three artillery companies, and for the latter the 12th cavalry, then at Camp Douglas, was ordered to Camp Butler, with two companies of artillery.

In March the 53d, 56th and 60th infantry, and the batteries of Captains Bouton, Cheeney and Coggswell, took the field, and were followed in April by the 62d and 63d infantry, leaving in the State for guard duty only the 65th, now fully organized, the 23d, now completely reorganized, the 12th cavalry and Phillips' battery.

Recruiting was virtually suspended on the 3d of April, 1862, but on the 1st of May the Adjutant-General, at Washington, announced that "upon requisitions made by commanders in the field, authority will be given by the War Department, to the Governors of the respective States, to recruit for regiments now in the service." The ensuing day General Halleck made the following requisition:

"HEAD-QUARTERS DEPARTMENT OF THE MISSISSIPPI,
"PITTSBURG LANDING, TENN., May 2, 1862.

"*His Excellency, Richard Yates, Governor of Illinois, Springfield:*

"GOVERNOR—I am authorized to call upon you for recruits to fill up the volunteer regiments from your State in this army.

"Many of these have been reduced, by disease and recent battles, very far below the minimum standard. A detail from such regiments will soon be sent to you for recruiting service, and it is to be hoped that you will give the matter your immediate attention.

"Very respectfully, your ob't serv't,

"H. W. HALLECK,
"Major-Gen'l Commanding."

Enlisting for old regiments was always difficult compared with the formation of new ones, and the aggregate of such troops from January 1st to December 22, 1862, was only 3,121.

On the 17th of May the State was called upon to furnish one regiment of infantry for special service. On the 25th Governor Yates received a dispatch from Mr. Stanton, Secretary of War, stating that the enemy, in great force, was marching upon Washington, and desiring him to organize and send forward all the volunteer and militia force of the State. Two days subsequently the call was revoked, but under it the following three months' regiments were organized and in camp *in two weeks:* The 67th, Col. Hough; the 68th, Col. Stuart; the 69th, Col. Tucker; the 70th, Col. Reeves; the 71st, Col.

Gilbert, with Phillips' battery. With the exception of the 71st, these remained on guard duty in the State.

The 23d, Col. Mulligan, and Rourke's Battery, left for Annapolis, June 12th; the 65th, Col. Cameron, June 21st; the 12th cavalry, June 27th; the 68th, July 6th; Phillips' Battery, July 12th, and the 71st, for Columbus, July 27th.

The military situation of the country was far from encouraging. There had been magnificent victories in the West, but the Grand Army of the Potomac, after sitting down before Yorktown until the enemy saw fit to evacuate it, had made the memorable James-River-Chickahominy campaign, and fought indomitably at Mechanicsville, Gaines' Hill, Savage Station and Malvern Hill, and had seemed to open the way into Richmond, but to the grief and disappointment of the American people, had fallen back until resting at Harrison's Landing, leaving thousands in their graves, and for what?

Before Corinth the victors of Donelson and Shiloh had waited and waited, until their foemen had evacuated and left them a barren success, and the disappointed people chafed under the vexation.

The course of not a few commanders in our army had added to this feeling. Our soldiers felt all the privations of war, but it appeared to be the purpose of some in high authority that none of its horrors should fall upon rebels. The property of notorious secessionists was carefully guarded; their property was safe. Their slaves were restored by men in the uniform of the country. The slaves, who alone could be depended upon in the enemy's country, and who have never betrayed Union soldiers, were forbidden to come within our lines, and for want of the information they could have given, disaster came. The *status* of the slave confronted each Department commander, and forced itself upon the attention of each victorious General. Here they were cultivating the estates of notorious rebels in arms; there they were captured with their masters. What shall be done with the negro? was the perplexing question, which found various answers. For a time the country floundered on without a manifest policy; meanwhile our brave men were dying in trenches, over-worked, doing what might have been done by freedmen wrested from traitors. This was not to last forever. In spite of passion and party and prejudice, a change was to come.

The proclamations of Fremont and Hunter, liberating the slaves of traitors, had been revoked by the President for prudential reasons, but the act was there, and increased the confusion, the doubt and uncertainty.

There was a demand for *war in earnest*, for leaders who would hurl all the power of the Government upon the rebellion, *and they were to come*, but not yet.

At this juncture came the call of the President, July 6, 1862, for 300,000 volunteers. It was at first intended, says Adjutant-General Fuller, "to credit on this call those States for any surplus which they had furnished. It was not known at the time what our surplus was. On the next day the Secretary of War called upon Illinois for nine more regiments, 'being a part of your (our) quota under the call of the President.' These regiments were immediately called for by General Order No. 42, from this Department, and regulations prescribed for their rendezvous and organization. Before these regiments were filled, however, and on the 17th of July, Congress enacted that whenever the President should 'call forth the militia of the States, to be employed in the service of the United States,' he should specify in his call the period for which said services should be required, not exceeding nine months, and the militia so called should be mustered in and continue to serve during the period so specified. The fourth section of the act authorized the President, for the purpose of filling up old regiments, to accept the services of one hundred thousand volunteers, for a period not exceeding one year.

"Three hundred thousand militia, to serve for a period of nine months, unless sooner discharged, were called for August 5th. The order of the Secretary of War, making the call upon this State, assumed that a draft would be necessary; and, in anticipation that the States would not be able to contribute their quotas of the call in July for three years' service, announced that if any State should not by the 18th of August furnish its quota of the three years' volunteers, the deficiency would be made up by a special draft from the militia."

Immediately after the call for 300,000 for three years, and before the announcement of the quota under the two calls, Governor Yates issued the annexed proclamation:

PROCLAMATION OF GOV. YATES.

"PEOPLE OF ILLINOIS:

"Under a late requisition of the President, I am called upon to furnish, at the earliest practicable period, nine regiments of Infantry, for three years' service, being a part of the quota of the State, under the call of the President for three hundred thousand men. An order of Adjutant-General Fuller, this day published, will give the details as to the mode of raising the troops, subsistence, transportation, place of rendezvous, etc.

"The war has now arrived at the most critical point. A series of splendid successes has crowned our arms. The enemy has been driven from Tennessee, Missouri and Kentucky, from Arkansas, Louisiana and Texas, and from the sea coast at almost all points. The Mississippi has been opened from Cairo to the Gulf. The Potomac has been opened from Washington to the Chesapeake. Beaten, broken, demoralized, bankrupt and scattered, the insurgents have fled before our victorious legions, leaving us a large area of conquered territory, and almost innumerable posts in the enemy's country to garrison with our troops.

"The rebels, whose leaders are bold and sagacious, and with whom it is neck or nothing as to the rebellion, have, with the energy of desperation resolved to cast all upon the hazard of a single battle; and while weak at every other point, they have, by the evacuation of Corinth, and by the rapid concentration of their scattered forces at Richmond, brought together a great and powerful army, far superior in numbers to that of our own at the same point.

"With consummate skill and generalship they have planned so as not only to defend their own capital, but also, should they be succesful in driving back McClellan, to take our's, and raise the rebel flag upon the capitol at Washington, with the expectation that so great a conquest would reanimate the South, revive their fading fortunes, and secure them the immediate co-operation of the two great powers of Europe—England and France.

"This is their last great stake. The desperation with which they have fought has developed the depth, intensity and recklessness of their designs. Their mode of warfare is the most malignant, desperate and savage. Thus we are brought to the very crisis of the rebellion, and all our hopes, and the hopes of this great country, hang upon the issue.

"It is for this reason that the President telegraphs me in a private dispatch, 'Time is everything. Please act in view of this.'

"Illinoisans! In view of the crisis, when the battles soon to be fought will be decisive; when the alliance with foreign powers is not only sought, but confidently relied upon by the rebels; and when our own brave volunteers contending against unequal numbers stretch out their hands for help, I cannot doubt the response you will give. Indeed I am most happy to state, that in response to most active measures already taken, every mail brings me the glad tidings of the rapid enrollment of our volunteers in the nine regiments which are forming.

"Covered all over with glory, with a name honored throughout the earth—shining with the luster of the great achievements of her sons on almost every field, Illinois will not now hold back and tarnish the fame she has so nobly earned. To the timid who suppose that the State will not now respond, I say 'take courage.' They vastly underrate the patriotism and courage of the men of Illinois.

"But I repeat, time is everything. Defeat now would prolong the war for years. Also remember that every argument of public necessity, of patriotism, every emotion of humanity appeals to the people to turn out in overwhelming demonstration, so that the rebellion may be speedily crushed and an end put to this desolating war. Remember the words of Douglas, that the 'shortest road to peace is the most stupendous preparation for war.'

"The crisis is such that every man must feel that the success of our cause depends upon himself, and not upon his neighbor. Whatever his position, his wealth, his rank or condition, he must be ready to devote ALL to the service of the country. Let all, old and young, contribute, work, speak, and in every possible mode further the work of the speedy enrollment of our forces. Let not only every man, but every woman be a soldier, if not to fight, yet to cheer and encourage and to provide comforts and relief for the sick and wounded. The public as yet know but litle how much the country is indebted to the noble women of our State for their assistance to our soldiers in the field. All along the path of our army, upon the banks of our rivers, filling our steamboats and ambulances, in the tent of the soldier far from his home, I have witnessed the bright traces of woman's enduring love and benevolence. When the war shall have closed and its history shall be written, the labors of our Sanitary Associations and Aid Societies will present pages as bright as the loftiest heroism of the camp and field. Let all loyal men and women persevere in the good work.

"Illinoisans! Look at the issue and do not falter. Your all is at stake. What are your beautiful prairies, comfortable mansions and rich harvests?—what is even life worth, if your government is lost?

"Better that the desolation of pestilence and famine should sweep over the State, than that the glorious work of our fathers should now forever fail. Look out upon your country with a government so free, institutions so noble, boundaries so broad—a beautiful sisterhood of States so prosperous and happy, and resolve afresh that as your fathers gave it you, you will hand it down to your children, a glorious inheritance of liberty and union for their enjoyment forever. For seven long years our fathers endured, suffered and fought to build up the fair fabric of American freedom. The precious boon purchased by patriot blood and treasure was committed to us for enjoyment, and to be transmitted to our posterity with the most solemn injunctions that man has the power to lay on man. By the grace of God, we will be faithful to the trust! And if need be, for seven years to come will we struggle to maintain a perfect Union, a government of one people, in one nation, under one Constitution.

"The coming of the brave boys of Illinois will be hailed on the banks of the Potomac and James River with shouts of welcome.

"During my recent visit East, I felt my heart to leap with exultant delight at the praise of Illinois heard from every lip. You will be hailed as the brothers of the men who have faced the storm of battle, and gloriously triumphed at Donelson, Pea Ridge, Shiloh, and other memorable fields.

"Go, then, and doubt not the result. We are sure to triumph. The God of liberty, justice and humanity is on our side.

"Your all and your children's all—all that is worth living or dying for, is at stake. Then rally once again for the old flag, for our country, union and liberty.

"RICHARD YATES, Governor of Illinois."

He also addressed to the President the following letter:

"EXECUTIVE DEPARTMENT, SPRINGFIELD, ILL., July 11, 1862.

"*President Lincoln, Washington, D. C.:*

"The crisis of the war and our national existence is upon us. The time has come for the adoption of more decisive measures. Greater vigor and earnestness must be infused into our military movements. Blows must be struck at the vital parts of the rebellion. The Government should employ every available means compatible with the rules of warfare to subject the traitors. Summon to the standard of the Republic all men willing to fight for the Union. Let loyalty, and that alone, be the dividing line between the nation and its foes. Generals should not be permitted to fritter away the sinews of our brave men in guarding the property of traitors, and in driving back into their hands loyal blacks, who offer us their labor, and seek shelter beneath the Federal flag. Shall we sit supinely by, and see the war sweep off the youth and strength of the land, and refuse aid from that class of men, who are, at least worthy, foes of traitors and the murderers of our Government and of our children?

"Our armies should be directed to forage on the enemy, and to cease paying traitors and their abettors exorbitant exactions for food needed by the sick or hungry soldier. Mild and conciliatory means have been tried in vain to recall the rebels to their allegiance. The conservative policy has utterly failed to reduce traitors to obedience and to restore the supremacy of the laws. They have, by means of sweeping conscriptions, gathered in countless hordes, and threaten to beat back and overwhelm the armies of the Union. With blood and treason in their hearts, they flaunt the black flag of rebellion in the face of the Government, and threaten to butcher our brave and loyal armies with foreign bayonets. They arm negroes and merciless savages in their behalf.

"Mr. Lincoln, the crisis demands greater and sterner measures. Proclaim anew the good old motto of the Republic, 'Liberty and Union, now and forever, one and inseparable,' and accept the services of *all loyal men*, and it will be in your power to stamp armies out of the earth—irresistible armies that will bear our banners to certain victory.

"In any event, Illinois, already alive with beat of drum and resounding with the tramp of new recruits, will respond to your call. Adopt this policy and she will leap like a flaming giant into the fight.

"This policy for the conduct of the war will render foreign intervention impossible, and the arms of the Republic invincible. It will bring the conflict to a speedy close, and secure peace on a permanent basis.

"RICHARD YATES,
"Governor of Illinois."

These calls, and the response of the State Executive, kindled the old enthusiasm, and from all parts of the State came assurances that men should be furnished if time was given for volunteering, and asking that the draft be postponed. This was communicated to the War Department, and it was requested to announce the State quota under the last two calls. "The next day it was announced that our quota, under each call, would be 26,148, but as Illinois had furnished 16,987 in excess of her quota, of those in the field, the total quotas, under both calls, was 35,320. Applications were made hourly from the different counties in the State to ascertain what their quota was, and immediately on ascertaining from the War Department what it was, the announcement was made through the public press. Still, in the minds of some, it was a question whether volunteers for three years would be accepted in lieu of militia. This was quickly settled, however, by a telegram on the 8th, from the War Department, that all volunteers would be accepted until the 15th of August for new regiments, and all after that time, for filling up old regiments, and that all volunteers enlisted before the draft (August 18th) would be credited on those calls."—*Adjutant-General's Report.*

On the 9th General Fuller reported there would be no draft in Illinois, basing his announcement upon the rapid enlistments and the credits for men already in the field, but the same evening he received a telegram from the Assistant Adjutant-General at Washington, stating that it had been decided in fixing the quotas to make no allowance for those in the field prior to the call, and announcing as the Illinois quota to be raised 52,296. This added 16,978 to the needed number. It is due that Adjutant Fuller shall tell how the call was answered, and we quote from the report of 1861–2:

"To raise either 52,296, or 35,320 volunteers (with perhaps the exception of one thousand who had enlisted between July 7th and August 5th) *but thirteen days* were allowed. The floating population of the State who would enlist had already done so. These new volunteers must come, if come at all, from the farmers and mechanics of the State. Farmers were in the midst of their harvests, and it is no exaggeration to say, that inspired by a holy zeal, animated by a common purpose, and firmly resolved on rescuing this Government from the very brink of ruin, and restoring it to the condition our fathers left, over fifty thousand of them left their harvests ungathered—their tools on their benches—the plows in the furrows, and turned their backs upon home and loved ones, AND BEFORE ELEVEN DAYS EXPIRED THE DEMANDS OF THE COUNTRY WERE MET, AND BOTH QUOTAS WERE FILLED!! Proud indeed was the day to all Illinoisans when this extraordinary announcement was made that the enlistment rolls were full. And when the historian shall write the record of these eventful days of August, 1862, no prouder record can be created to the honor and memory of a free people than a plain, full narration of actual facts.

"It is not my province, in this report, to bestow fulsome praise, or write glowing eulogies, but when I remember what we all witnessed in those days—when I remember the unselfish and patriotic impulse which animated every soul—and the universal liberality of those who were either too young or too old to enlist to aid those in the field—when I remember the holy ardor which aged mothers and fair daughters infused into husbands, sons, and brothers—I say when I remember these things, I cannot but feel justified in departing from the dull routine of statistics, and in bestowing upon the subject this passing notice."

Aye, truly, for the raising of more than half a hundred thousand men within one fortnight, in the second year of war, is worthy such a notice. And no words are needed other than the Adjutant-General has so well employed.

The appended extract, from the same document, will enable the reader to see what the State had done toward filling up the army of the Union:

"Immediately after the call for nine regiments, in July, nine camps were estabtablished, one in each of the old congressional districts of the State, for the temporary rendezvous of those regiments, but with the intention of removing them, as soon as they should be full, into the principal camps of instruction at Chicago and Springfield, for permanent organization and instruction.

"There was, however, in the State barely enough camp and garrison equipage for these regiments, and consequently an additional embarrassment presented itself to provide for those called August 5th. The State was soon full of volunteers. All had left their business, and some of them were without homes. The General Government was unable to supply tents, and there was not time to erect barracks to accommodate half of them. Such, therefore, as were not supplied were directed to remain at home or seek temporary quarters, as best they could, and await orders.

"And still another difficulty grew out of the want of clothing, and especially blankets. All the resources of the Government were taxed to supply the immense army organizing throughout the country, and, considering the immense amount of supplies required, and the suddenness of the emergency which had called out these volunteers, their wants were met with very commendable promptness. In most of the counties of the State there were fair grounds at the county seats. In many counties the sheds on these county fair grounds were repaired and occupied by companies and regiments until quarters could be prepared for them at the general camps of instruction. Several regiments, however, which were unable to obtain quarters at the principal camps, moved from these neighborhood rendezvous directly to the field.

"Six of these new regiments were organized, mustered, armed, and clothed, and sent into the field in August; twenty-two and Board of Trade Battery, Capt. Stokes, and Miller's Battery, in September; thirteen in October; fifteen, besides the Springfield Light Artillery, Capt. Vaughn, and Mercantile Battery, Capt. Cooley, in November, and three in December, making an aggregate of fifty-nine regiments of infantry and four batteries, consisting of fifty three thousand eight hundred and nineteen (53,819) officers and enlisted men. Besides this, twenty-seven hundred and fifty-three (2,753) were, during about the same time, enlisted and sent to old regiments, under the direction of Col. Morrison, State Superintendent. Add to these 1,083, 14th cavalry, now organizing at Peoria: 386 in Camp Butler; 156, Elgin Battery, Capt. Renwick, at Camp Douglas, now under marching orders; 135, Henshaw's Battery, at Ottawa, and 83, Capt. Adams' cavalry company of the 15th regiment, makes the grand total, under the last calls, fifty-eight thousand four hundred and sixteen (58,416), or six thousand one hundred and nineteen (6,119) more than our quotas under the last calls. The excess furnished by this State, as reported by the Secretary of War, August 8th, was sixteen thousand nine hundred and seventy-eight (16,978), which, added to the surplus under the last calls of six thousand one hundred and nineteen (6,119), makes the total excess, as officially ascertained, *twenty-three thousand ninety-seven* (23,097). That the real excess is much greater there can be no doubt whatever. The reasons for this conclusion have been heretofore stated.

"Since the call of August 5th, the Secretary of War has authorized the acceptance of several regiments of cavalry and six batteries of light artillery. But two of these regiments will probably be raised by enlistments, the 14th, Col. Capron, at Peoria, and the 16th, now known as the 17th, Col. Thieleman, at Camp Butler. The 15th, Col. Stewart, was organized on the 25th ultimo, by assigning to his battalion of six companies, two companies, Capts. Willis and Shearer, attached to the 36th infantry; one, Capt. Gilbert, formerly attached to the 52d, and afterwards nominally assigned to the 12th cavalry; one, Capt. Ford, attached to the 53d infantry; one, Capt. Huntley, formerly of the 1st cavalry, and one, Capt. Wilder, known as the 'Kane County Cavalry.'

"Four of the six batteries have already been raised. Three of them—Board of Trade Battery, Capt. Stokes; Mercantile Battery, Capt. Cooley; Springfield Battery, Capt. Vaughn—are in the field. The Elgin Battery, Capt. Renwick, is ready and under orders. Capt. Henshaw is nearly full, and Capt. Hawthorne will probably be full the present month."

Within two years the State of Illinois placed one hundred and thirty-five thousand four hundred and forty men in the field, and they had been heard from in the midst of battle. The list of promotions for gallant conduct and superior courage had already become large, and not a few were wearing the insignia of Brigadier and Major Generals, while one of the most modest was steadily making his way to the command of all the forces of the Union.

It breaks the sentiment of State pride which inspires one in reviewing the war record of Illinois, when compelled to read the legislative history of the General Assembly of 1863–4. Assembled at a time of profound anxiety, with the Nation in its struggle for life, with nearly one hundred and thirty-five thousand citizens under arms, surely the solemnity and magnitude of the issues should have elevated those representatives of the people to the dignity of statesmanship, and to a comprehension of the supreme importance of the hour. Alas, that it was not so. The Governor delivered an able and patriotic message, giving full information of the military condition of the State, and recommending needed legislation. Among the topics were, that provision should be made for the payment of expenses incurred in relieving the pressing wants of the soldiers in the field; for compensation to the allotment commissioners, appointed to visit the volunteers in the field and receive and send forward from time to time to their families or friends their respective allotments of pay; to the proper organization of the militia for home service; that provision be made for drafting in all cases where it should become necessary to suppress insurrection and supply any deficiency in the ordinary militia organization, that in the event of sudden danger the entire population, capable of bearing arms, might be called out on the shortest notice; that suitable legislation should provide facilities for military education; that a memorial to the President and Congress be sent from the General Assembly, seeking the brigading of State troops together, instead of scattering them, and that volunteers from the State who had enlisted elsewhere, when the War Department refused their services, might be reorganized as Illinois troops; that Congress should be asked to give the election of officers into the hands of soldiers themselves; and that provision be made for the taking of the votes of volunteers in the field. Said he:

"I desire to call especial attention to the importance of an enactment, making provision for taking the votes of the volunteers of the State in actual service. The fact that a man is fighting to sustain his country's flag should not deprive him of the highest privilege of citizenship; viz., the right to take a part in the selection of his rulers. The soldier should be allowed a voice in the nation for the existence of which he is placing his life in peril. The reason which has excluded the soldier in the regular army does not apply to the soldier in the volunteer service. The regular, loses his State identity, and, to a certain extent, local citizenship. The volunteer, on the other hand, does not. He still continues to be a son of Illinois, fighting under his State flag as well as the stars and stripes. A force of one hundred and thirty-five thousand volunteered to the field from our State. Of this number it is safe to say one hundred thousand are voters. And if they were not legally voters previous to enlistment, that act ought certainly to make them so. No man more justly owns the rights of citizenship than he who voluntarily takes up arms in defense of his country and its dearest rights. These men have as deep an interest in the selection of the representatives who are to a great extent to control and direct the destinies of the country, as any other class of persons. The Secretary of War most justly decided that he who votes must bear arms. Shall not the Legislatures of the different States respond by saying: 'And who bears arms must vote?' I see nothing in our constitution which prohibits the enactment of such law. On the contrary, Section 5, of Article III. of that instrument, provides that 'no elector shall be deemed to have lost his residence in this State by reason of his absence on business of the United States or of this State.' Justice demands that this provision should be carried out in its letter and spirit. Past legislatures, not anticipating the present anomalous condition of national affairs, passed no enactment by which it can be legally carried into effect. A law can be framed without difficulty, providing for taking the votes of the soldiers in active service, at least for the most important officers; viz., State officers, representatives in Congress, and members of the Legislature. In the election of these officers, the soldier, although away from home, takes as much, if not more, interest than the citizen actually on the spot. He reads the newspapers, receives letters from his friends, and in fact understands the issues of the day as well, if not better, than the man for the defense of whose home he has taken up arms.

"It may be objected, that great difficulty and expense would necessarily be created in taking the vote of the army in the field. But I submit that nearly all the difficulty and expense would be obviated by the following simple and effective plan: The three field officers, or in their absence, the three ranking officers of each regi ment of infantry or cavalry, and three highest commissioned officers, or those acting in their places, of each battery of artillery, or each company or squadron of infantry or cavalry on detached service, might be made the inspectors of the election, with power to appoint the proper person clerk of the election, so that the vote may be taken on the day fixed by the Constitution."

The message also asked the attention of the Legislature to the Sanitary Bureau; to the erection of a hospital or soldiers' home; to the question of liberal bounties to volunteers, especially that some measures be adopted "to refund to the counties the bounties which they so generously paid to their soldiers, or in some equitable mode to relieve them, *pro tanto*, of the amount required to be raised towards this object," and that the General assembly should, to quote from the message, "send its potent voice to Congress, demanding an increase of pay to the private soldier. His present pay is only $13 per month, or $156 per year, a sum totally insufficient to support him and his family at the present high rate of every article of family consumption, at least fifty per cent. higher now than when the war commenced. Thirteen dollars per month is no better pay now than seven dollars would have been two years since. It will be economy to the Government to increase the pay, or desertions, already numerous, will become still more so. No soldier can bear the thought that his wife and children are in destitution and suffering. I recommend a strong appeal by this General Assembly to Congress, for this important and humane object."

But other topics engrossed the majority. There were other objects to be secured. Extreme parliamentary stratagems were required to prevent the adoption of legislation which, had it been formerly enacted, would have blasted the fair fame of the State forever.

In June, 1863, a disagreement having occurred between the two Houses, as to the time of final adjournment, the Governor availed himself of a power, lodged in his hands by the Constitution, and prorogued the General Assembly to the 31st day of December, 1864, the day when its legal existence would terminate by law. The blow fell like a thunderbolt, and the startled representatives found themselves adrift. We sadly fear that the army in Flanders was completely outdone in the use of explosives. To write literally the remarks of some of the honorables, were to render this a very "profane history."

But there is a State record for 1863–4 of honor, namely that of the people and the gallantry of the citizen soldiery. We present the Governor's Proclamation of February 5, 1864, with copious extracts from the report of Adjutant-General Fuller of February 1, 1864, bringing down the history of the State responses to the calls of Government, to October 1, 1863, and it will be seen that all that was asked had been freely given:

PROCLAMATION.

"Executive Department,
"Springfield, Ill., February 4, 1864.

"*To the People of Illinois:*

"It is with feelings of the profoundest satisfaction that I announce to you the number of men which Illinois has contributed to the armies of the Union from the commencement of the rebellion to the present time.

"Our contingent of volunteers under the calls of the President:

"In 1861 was	47,785
"In 1862 was	32,685
"In 1863 was	64,630
"Total quotas under all calls	145,100

"The last call was made October 17, 1863, and the State had furnished and been credited one hundred and twenty-five thousand three hundred and twenty-one (125,321) men—a surplus of eight thousand one hundred and fifty-one (8,151), over all other calls to be credited to our contingent for that call, and which reduced it to 19,779 men, with still other credits claimed, but not fully adjusted because of imperfect record in case of citizens, and in some instances whole companies of Illinoisans, who had entered the regiments of other States at times when our quotas under given calls were entirely full, and because of which, their services I was reluctantly compelled to decline.

"In the volunteer regiments from the State of Missouri 6,032 citizens of Illinois, were enrolled and mustered, and in Illinois regiments there have been 1,659 residents of the State of Missouri enlisted; which leaves, as between the States, a credit of 4,273 in favor of Illinois.

"After an adjustment of credit of 125,321 at and prior to October last, from more careful examination of the rolls and returns from the field, it was ascertained that we were entitled to an additional credit of 10,947, which increased the number enrolled *in our own regiments*, and for which we were entitled to credit prior to last call, to 136,238, leaving the whole account thus:

"Quotas under all calls		145,100
"Credits for enlistments in Illinois regiments	136,268	
"Balance in Missouri regiments	4,373—	140,641
"Total Balance due the Government under last call		4,459

"Besides the foregoing, the State claims an unadjusted balance of 3,264 for volunteers furnished prior to October 1, 1863, which I doubt not will soon be credited by the War Department.

"Independent of the last mentioned figures, and *exclusive of old regiments re-enlisting as veterans*, our quota *on the first day of January was more than filled*, as evidenced by rolls returned since the last call.

"In other words, *the State of Illinois, having under every call exceeded her quota by the voluntarily demonstrated patriotism of her people, was not, on the first day of January last, or at any other time, liable to* DRAFT.

"That this information has not been communicated to the public sooner is fully explained in the uncertainty which has existed as to the credits which would be allowed by the War Department, the unadjusted account between our own and neighboring States of the volunteers of the one enlisted in the regiments of the other, and the incomplete returns of the new recruits enlisted just prior to and about the first day of January, 1864.

"Thus it will be seen that Illinois alone, of all the loyal States of the Union, furnishes the proud record of not only having escaped the draft, without credit for her old regiments, but of starting under the new call with her quota largely diminished, by the credit to which she is entitled by thousands of veterans already re-enlisted.

"This is only an additional chapter to the fame of our noble State, promptly and patriotically responding to every call of the Government for men—and men, too, whose valor, endurance, prompt obedience, noble daring and brilliant achievements are unsurpassed by those of any State in the Union.

"I cannot forbear to refer specially to the cheerful re-enlistment of our old regiments. Those so designated are the regiments of infantry numbered the 7th, 8th, 9th, 10th, 11th and 12th—organized under the call of the President, of April 15, 1861, for 75,000 three months' volunteers, and were the first in the field—and reorganized in July and August, 1861, for three years' service—the 13th, 14th, 15th, 16th, 17th and 18th regiments, which were first organized under provisions of an act passed by an extraordinary session of the General Assembly of Illinois, convened April 23, 1861, in anticipation of future calls of the Government for troops, and which organizations were preserved intact in State camps until the latter part of that month, and mustered into the United States service as organized under the law referred to. All the other mentioned regiments were organized in pursuance of the calls of the President and orders of the War Department, based on the laws of Congress of that year.

"The infantry regiments at the the time of organization, and since, have contained 38,173, and the cavalry 7,477; aggregate 45,650 men, and now comprise:

"THE VETERAN ROLL OF HONOR OF ILLINOIS.

"The 7th, 8th, 9th, 10th, 11th, 12th, 13th, 14th, 15th, 16th, 17th, 18th, 26th, 29th, 30th, 31st, 32d, 33d, 34th, 36th, 39th, 40th, 41st, 43d, 44th, 45th, 46th, 48th, 49th, 50th, 52d, 53d, 54th, 57th, 58th, 62d, 64th and 66th infantry; 2d, 4th, 8th, 9th, 10th and 12th cavalry.

"The old regiments not yet reported as having re-enlisted are the 19th, 20th, 21st, 22d, 23d, 24th, 25th, 27th, 35th, 37th, 38th, 42d, 47th, 51st, 55th, 56th, 59th, 60th, 61st, 63d, 65th regiments of infantry, and the 3d, 5th, 6th, 7th and 11th regiments of cavalry, and the 1st and 2d regiments of artillery.

"Total number of old regiments organized for three years' service:

"Infantry	59
"Cavalry	10
"Artillery	2
"Aggregate	71

"Number of regiments re-enlisted as veterans:

"Infantry	38
"Cavalry	6
"Aggregate	44

"The order for re-enlistment of veteran volunteers, issued on the 11th day of September, 1863, and the rapidity with which they have responded, is a striking evidence of the attachment to the service, and the esteem and respect which our general, field, staff and line officers have inspired in the ranks of our invincible armies, and above all, the appreciation they have of the magnitude of the issue at stake. The most cheering intelligence is also received from the regiments not officially reported as re-enlisted. They are all made of the same invincible material, and I doubt not, *that every regiment will retain its number*, and soon wheel gloriously into the *veteran line*.

"Though absent for years from their homes and everything held most sacred and dear, and exposed to untried, rigid discipline, and dangers of every kind, decimated by disease and death on the battle field, these veterans return with their old banners, which they have borne aloft amid shot and shell, and the cloud and smoke of many victorious battle fields, to receive the welcome and congratulations of their loyal countrymen, and for only a brief furlough to enjoy the sweets of home and friends, again to return to meet the foe and fight on until the last rebel shall have laid down his arms, and the rightful authority of the Government shall be restored over every inch of American soil. They have come in contact with the enemy, and know better than the philosopher at home that the rights of man and the power of the Government can now only be secured by sword and cannon. Their devotion to country is full of sublimity, not surpassed by that of the veterans of the ancient Republics, whose patriotism and deeds of valor have been the themes for song and eloquence for over a thousand years. Can the proudest page of history point to a nation whose army has participated in more battle fields than the veteran soldiers of Illinois? At Boonville, Carthage, Wilson's Creek, Fredericktown, Lexington, Belmont, Fort Henry, Fort Donelson, Pea Ridge, New Madrid, Island No. 10, Shiloh, Farmington, Britton's Lane, Iuka, Corinth, Hatchie, Parker's Cross Roads, Prairie Grove, Coffeeville, Chicksaw Bayou, Arkansas Post, Port Gibson, Raymond, Jackson, Champion Hills, Big Black, Siege of Vicksburg, Helena, Port Hudson, Jackson, Little Rock, Pine Bluffs, Perryville, Stone River, Chickamauga, Lookout Valley, Tuscumbia, Mission Ridge, Ringgold and Knoxville, in the West—the battles of the Peninsular campaign, Antietam, Gettysburg, Fredericksburg, Chancellorsville, Siege of Charleston, on the Eastern coast, and other engagements in the Department of the Gulf and in innumerable skirmishes have these same returned veterans of Illinois participated and borne conspicuous parts. All honor to them that have so proudly borne themselves; all honor to them that they still swear fresh allegiance to their country, and with unconquered spirit resolve never to sheath their swords except over the grave of treason, and the vindicated authority of the Government, and our glorious Union restored.

"The quota of the State under the new call will soon be announced, and each county definitely informed of the number required, and I have no fears that a single county will fail to fill its quota. Recruiting will go on. At the roll call of the State for their quota on the first day of March, Illinois will answer '*Here*,' and should the Government, as in my judgment it ought, call out full 500,000 more men, and, with demonstrated and overwhelming power crush out the last vestige of the rebellion, in such an event Illinois would again respond with her full quota of as brave, patriotic and loyal men as those who have reflected such resplendent luster upon her arms.

"I express my gratitude for the aid and counsel the old and wise men and loyal women have given me in organizing troops, and caring for the sick and wounded of our State through the trying months we have passed, and I now appeal to the young men of Illinois to join our veteran heroes, who, on weary march and battle plain, call you to their side. You have the renown of forefathers to sustain you, and the consecrated memories of the noble dead, to write upon the annals of the Republic, to be saved by its citizens in arms. Between you and them there is a covenant, and you are pledged by every sentiment of loyalty and honor to God and country, to sustain them in the hour of conflict. 'Tis yours to accomplish the mission of the century, to inspire new faith in the capacity of man for self-government, to preserve the dignity of labor, and to transmit to posterity the free government of Benjamin Franklin and George Washington. If you desire your names associated with the glories of this war, *enlist now*, for the signs are that the end is near at hand.

"The South is fast becoming convinced that the cool determined bravery of *one* Northern man is equal to the fiery, impetuous valor and bravado of *one* Southern man; and that while, day by day, the resources of the South in men, money and munitions of war and supplies are nearing the point of final exhaustion, the arm of the loyal States is daily being strengthened, the credit of the Government is unimpaired, the preparations for prosecuting the war on the land and on the sea are constantly increasing, and scarcely any limit can be assigned to the number of men which the Government may call to its aid. The doom of the rebellion is inevitable. It can, to say the least, only be a question of time.

"Then fill up the ranks—reinforce the column still advancing—and by strength of strong arms in the field, and patriotic sentiments at home, fill every village and hamlet, claimed by traitors, with the old flag and anthems of VICTORY, FREEDOM, and NATIONAL UNION.

"I submit herewith the Report of Adjutant-General Allen C. Fuller, who, in the organization of our regiments, has labored faithfully, and brought great energy, efficiency and ability in the discharge of all the varied and complicated duties of the Adjutant-General's office. To him, and assistants in office, and to my own staff, am I much indebted for the success which has crowned my labors in raising, organizing and responding to all the demands of the large number of troops which Illinois has sent to the field.

"RICHARD YATES, Governor."

ADJUTANT-GENERAL'S REPORT.

"ADJUTANT-GENERAL'S OFFICE,
"Springfield, February 1, 1864.

"HIS EXCELLENCY, GOVERNOR YATES:

"I have the honor to submit herewith copies of communications from the War Department, showing the quotas of this State for three years' volunteers, under all calls of the Federal Government, to be as follows:

"Total quotas under calls of 1861		47,875
"Quota under call of July, 1862	26,148	
"Quota under call of August 1862, of 126,148 nine months' men, equivalent to	6,537	
		32,681
"Quota under draft call of 1863	36,700	
"Quota under call for 300,000, October 17, 1863	27,930	
		64,000
"Grand total		145,100

"The calls of 1861 and 1862 were based upon population. The calls of 1863 were based upon first-class enrollment.

"When the last call was made, in October last, the State had been credited one hundred and twenty-five thousand three hundred and twenty-one (125,321), being a surplus of eight thousand one hundred and fifty-one (8,151) over previous calls, and leaving the balance of our quota, under that call, of nineteen thousand seven hundred and seventy-nine (19,779), but subject to a further reduction to the extent of all volunteers furnished, but not therefore credited.

"To ascertain what this further reduction should be, by showing the number who had entered the service and had not been included in the above general credit of one hundred and twenty-five thousand three hundred and twenty-one (125,321), became a duty of grave importance to the people of the State, and, on account of defective and irregular returns from mustering officers, one of considerable difficulty.

"In my report of January 1, 1863, the number of *three years' volunteers* furnished by the State prior to that time, and of which returns were then on file, was stated at one hundred and thirty thousand five hundred and thirty-nine (130,539). In addition to this it was believed that several thousand had joined our old regiments in the field, from which no satisfactory returns have been received, and it was known that between the first of January and the first of October several hundred had been mustered in the State.

"A thorough revision of rolls, which had been commenced in June last, has been completed; additional returns from regiments in the field have been sent for and received; a re-examination of the rolls and returns of volunteers furnished by the State has been made by the War Department, and the result is an additional credit for volunteers, furnished by this State prior to the last call of ten thousand nine hundred and forty-seven (10,947) secured, making a total credit IN OUR OWN REGIMENTS of one hundred and thirty-six thousand two hundred and sixty-eight (136,268).

"In July last, I made an arrangement with Gen. John B. Gray, Adjutant-General of Missouri, to ascertain the number of citizens of Illinois who had enlisted in Missouri regiments, and the number of citizens of Missouri who had enlisted in Illinois regiments, with the agreement, that when the same should be ascertained, that, with the approval of the War Department, each State should be credited with its own volunteers.

"On the 10th day of August last, a partial settlement was made, which showed a balance in favor of this State of three thousand one hundred and twenty-nine (3,129). This was placed to the credit of this State by the War Department on the 27th of last November. During the month of December, the rolls of Illinoisans in Missouri regiments, through the courtesy of the Adjutant-General of Missouri, were copied by employees of this Department. The result of that examination shows that six thousand and thirty-two (6,032) citizens of this State have enlisted in Missouri regiments, and sixteen hundred and fifty-nine (1,659) citizens of Missouri have enlisted in Illinois regiments; giving the State of Illinois an additional credit from this source of twelve hundred and forty-four (1,244), making a total on this account of four thousand three hundred and seventy-three (4,373), and which has been credited to this State.

"From the foregoing it will be seen that our quota, under all calls, is one hundred and forty-five thousand one hundred (145,100).

"Amount of credits for enlistments in our regiments, 136,268; balance in Missouri regiments prior to last call, 4,373—140,641; leaving a balance under the last call of 4,459, instead of nineteen thousand seven hundred and seventy-nine (19,779).

"There yet remains an unadjusted claim of the State of three thousand two hundred and sixty-four (3,264) for volunteers furnished prior to the first of last October. The officers of the War Department have cordially co-operated with me in arriving at a satisfactory adjustment of differences, and I am under special obligations to Major Thomas M. Vincent, Assistant Adjutant-General at Washington, for his prompt assistance in endeavoring to do full justice to the State. I have, therefore, no doubt but the above three thousand two hundred and sixty-four (3,264) will soon be placed to our credit. *Without, however, including this last number*, and exclusive of re-enlistments of old regiments, most of whom have re-enlisted as veterans, I am happy to inform you that from muster rolls returned to this office since the last call, it is certain, beyond all doubt, *that on the first day of last month our quota was more than filled by enlistments made prior to that date.*

"As you were absent the first time the call was made, and for some time thereafter, I felt very greatly embarrassed concerning the policy which should be adopted under that call. My records showed over fourteen thousand more than the War Department had placed to our credit. An adjustment with Missouri had not been completed, and no reliable estimate could be made with counties until the general balance against the State could be substantially determined. According to my books forty-seven counties had furnished their quotas, and fifty-five were behind. A part of the latter, however, would be relieved from the deficit against them if they could have the credit for such of their citizens as had enlisted in the regiments in other States; but whether such credits could be secured was uncertain. To protect such, however, as far as possible against draft, an equivalent of volunteers from other States in our regiments was reserved until a settlement could be made with such States.

"Under this state of things, to have published my estimates, doubtless would have misled some and might have deceived all. If confidence had been placed in them, officers recruiting in counties which had raised their quotas might have been compelled to close their offices, and in some few counties largely behind, it was feared that a knowledge of the extent of their deficit, unaccompanied by an assurance that a less number might, by saving the State from a draft, protect them, would discourage authorities from making vigorous local efforts to aid enlistments.

"General Order No. 43, was issued October 24th, announcing the quota of this State under the call; and yet only about *five hundred* were mustered during the months of October and November, and recruiting had but slightly improved prior to December 20th. To raise 19,779 by common consent was deemed impossible, and men of all parties seemed, by their inaction, to invite a draft. In fact, many very worthy citizens insisted that a "draft was a good thing to have in this State.

"About the 20th of December, therefore, the public were informed that a part of the deficiency had been satisfactorily adjusted with the War Department, and a part of the credits claimed from Missouri had been placed to our credit. *Counties appearing most behind-hand were notified of their deficit*, and assured that by vigorous efforts in raising a reasonable portion of that number, the State would probably escape a draft. Counties *which applied for information* on the subject, were informed of the probabilities of their situation, but urged to continue their enlistments and aid counties behind in saving the State from a draft. While no information in my possession was *refused*, none was *tendered* to counties which had furnished their quotas, because it seemed probable that the balance of the quota of the State would not be raised unless counties which had furnished their quota aided those who had not.

"I have the honor to submit herewith a tabular statement showing—*

"FIRST—The population of each county in the State according to census of 1860.

"SECOND—The number of persons in each county liable to military duty, according to first class enrollment taken by the Federal authorities in 1863.

"THIRD—The total quotas of each county in the years 1861, 1862 and 1863, inclusive of the call of October 17, 1863.

"FOURTH—The number of three years' volunteers furnished by each county prior to October 1, 1863, *inclusive* of those enlisted in Missouri regiments, and exclusive of those enlisted in regiments of other States than our own and Missouri.

"FIFTH—The number of volunteers in Illinois regiments furnished prior to October 1, 1863, by other States (exclusive of Missouri). This number is believed to be about the same as those furnished by this State to regiments of the same States. A settlement with such States will be made at the earliest practicable period.

"In submitting said tabular statement, it is proper to add that in

* See Appendix A.

reply to a telegram of yours of the 16th ultimo, inquiring whether the War Department proposed to ascertain and determine the number of volunteers furnished by each county *prior to last call*, or whether it would adopt the adjustment with each county made by you, the Provost Marshal General, under date of the 18th ultimo, states, the "War Department does not propose to attempt the ascertainment of the number of volunteers furnished by each county in Illinois prior to the last call," as "no account prior to the last call was kept by the War Department with counties, the record being kept only with the State at large. Expressing the opinion that on account of the hurried manner in which volunteers rushed to arms in the early stages of the rebellion, no State can "ascertain the number furnished by each county and locality prior to the last call," the Provost Marshal General adds, that "there is no doubt that it would be more just and satisfactory if it could be done;" and if the State can show what proportion of all men furnished by it prior to the last call properly belongs to each county, he presumes the "War Department would adopt your report on this subject."

"Prior to the last call, the law did not require the War Department to keep a record of the residence of volunteers at the time of their enlistment. Neither, by any law or regulation except my own was I obliged to keep such a record. Anticipating, however, that this information might be interesting to the people of the State, if not indispensably necessary to protect a portion of them from contributing more than their just proportion of volunteers in prosecuting the war, I have attempted to keep such a record. For more than thirty months I have endeavored to perfect it. Regiments which had taken the field prior to my appointment, and many of which, on account of the hurried manner in which they were ordered away, not even a muster-in roll was on file, I have supplied with descriptive rolls, containing a column of their residence; and our new regiments have been required, when practicable, to furnish such rolls before receiving their commissions. Blanks for men joining our regiments in the field, subsequent to organization, have also been furnished. These blanks have been filled up by inserting, among other things, the name, rank, description of person, occupation, nativity, and RESIDENCE of each man, and returned to this office. I have labored in vain, unless by this means I have succeeded in securing a record of our volunteers which is substantially correct. And I take pleasure in here stating, that I am much indebted to our commanding officers for their cheerful co-operation in completing the record of troops whom they have had the honor to command.

"Since the accompanying statement was prepared, notice has been received that a draft will be made on the 10th proximo for five hundred thousand men, 'crediting and deducting therefrom' so many as may have been enlisted or drafted into the service prior to the first proximo. This is equivalent to a call of two hundred thousand more. As soon as the quota of this State is announced, and the basis upon which the call is made known, I will submit to you a statement of quotas of each county under such call, and, as far as possible, the number of enlistments since the first of October last.

"I have the honor to remain, very respectfully, your obedient servant, ALLEN C. FULLER, Adjutant-General."

CHAPTER VIII.

The Preceding Chapters—Insertion of Documents—Baffled Schemes—Close of First Great Epoch—Administration on Trial—The Issues—The Decision—The Eighth of November—Twenty-seven Years, or from Lovejoy to Lincoln—Oglesby and Bross—Yates—His Final Message—Quotations—Education—Principles—Churches—Benevolent Organizations—Sanitary and Christian Commissions—Freedmen's Aid Societies—Soldiers' Homes—The Hand of Providence—Finance—Implemental Industry—Negro and Machinery—Northern Planters—The Sewing Machine—Achievements of the Year—Prospects.

THE past few chapters have been necessarily fragmentary, and have been broken by the insertion of documents which, in the judgment of the author, are worthy of preservation, and are essential to the understanding of the facts of the history. The *people* speak by their votes; the Government by its official acts. It is due to the men in authority in each great crisis, that after-generations shall know how they bore themselves, how they met its grave responsibilities. "No man liveth unto himself, and no man dieth unto himself," is the teaching of Holy Writ. The patriots of this age and of this war are nerved by the record of the patriots of the past. Thus one generation speaks to another.

It is well that the record of this State stands so fairly. We have seen how adverse legislation, which trifled with destiny, and played disgraceful antics amid throes and upheavals, which insisted upon fiddling during the conflagration, was baffled by the decision and stern promptness of the Executive. Thus were thwarted schemes which threatened mischief, and the people rejoiced that disgrace was wiped from the State's escutcheon.

Before tracing the war path of the men who rallied to the call of the country, it is well to bring this general resume down to the close of 1864, marking, as it does, the termination of the first great epoch of the war, signal in the history of the Republic for the judgment of the Nation upon the Administration, and that of the State, by the close of the official control of Governor Yates.

As to the former, Mr. Lincoln was nominated for re-election upon a platform which endorsed all the debatable points of his administration. A platform which pronounced the war upon the side of the Government just, and declared that it should go forward until the rebellion should be overthrown; approved the Proclamation of Emancipation, and the arming of negroes and their employment as soldiers of the Republic, and pronounced in favor of an amendment to the Constitution of the United States, which should abolish human slavery throughout the States and Territories of the Union. It also denied, in the broadest and most emphatic manner, the right of secession, and insisted upon the paramount authority of the Federal Union.

Nominated at a convention held in Chicago, the opposing candidate was Major-General George B. McClellan, a gentleman who, at one time, had been in chief command of the Union armies, and whose military ability many, both of the army and in civil life claimed to be superior to that of any other leader of our forces. His platform declared for the Union, but intimated that the war had failed; and suggested a "cessation of hostilities" until diplomacy should attempt the restoration of peace. It made its appeal for the freedom of speech and press, and against military despotism. The General, in his letter of acceptance, gave the most patriotic possible construction to the platform, and thus enabled many thousands opposed to the platform to cast their votes for its candidate. Thus went the war policy of the President to the court of last resort, *the ballot-box*, and on the 8th day of November, 1864, the decision was given, and Abraham Lincoln was re-elected President of the United States. It was an emphatic endorsement of his policy, including Emancipation and the arming of Freedmen!

As an evidence of the growth of a high moral sentiment in Illinois within thirty years, it may be stated that on the 8th day of November, 1837, the Rev. E. P. Lovejoy, editor of an anti-slavery journal, was shot to death in the city of Alton, nor were his murderers harmed by the process of law. Twenty-seven years later to a day, Abraham Lincoln was re-elected President of the United

States on a radical anti-slavery platform, with an endorsement of military emancipation and the arming of freedmen; and Illinois, whose soil had been watered by the blood of Lovejoy, gave him a majority of more than 30,000! One must think of the words of poor Galileo, manacled, and humiliated as he paced his way to his cell, "*the world does move though.*"

At the same time, and by about the same majority, Richard J. Oglesby, late a gallant Major-General of volunteers, and who had been scarred on more than one hotly-fought battle field, was chosen Governor, as the successor of Richard Yates, and Wm. Bross, one of the editors of a radically anti-slavery sheet, was elected Lieutenant-Governor, with a General Assembly which should choose Richard Yates to occupy the seat in the United States Senate, so long filled by Stephen A. Douglas.

Verily, time is an inexorable Nemesis. From Lovejoy dead to Lincoln and Oglesby, only twenty-seven years!

The final message of Governor Yates was delivered to the General Assembly on the 3d of January, 1865, and reviewed the two years preceding. It summed the State resources and liabilities; gave the evidence that through the war the State had steadily advanced in the great material and educational interests essential to her prosperity.

He thus aggregates the State contributions of men to the national armies:

"The following exhibits the quotas of the States under respective calls since the commencement of the war, and the number of men furnished to the national armies up to the present time:

"Our quota, under calls of the President

"In 1861, was	47,785
"In 1862, "	32,685
"In 1863, "	64,630
"In 1864, "	52,260
"Total quotas under all calls prior to Dec. 1, 1864	197,360

"During the years 1861, 1862, and to the 18th day of October, 1863, the State, by voluntary enlistment, had exceeded its quota under all calls. Prior to that date settlements had not been made with the War Department, because of the voluntary action of our people in meeting the requirements of the country and their per. istence in organizing, with unparalleled enthusiasm and determination, a larger number of regiments and batteries than the actual quotas under each levy called for. Prior to 17th October, 1863, the State had furnished and been credited with one hundred and twenty-five thousand three hundred and twenty-one (125,321) men—a surplus of eight thousand one hundred and fifty-one (8,151) over all other calls, to be credited to our quota for that call, and which reduced it to 19,779 men; and we claimed, besides, other credits, which could not be fully adjusted because of imperfect record of citizens (and in some cases whole companies of Illinoisans) who had entered the service in regiments of other States, at times when our quotas on special calls were full, and because of which I was compelled to decline their services. Six thousand and thirty-two (6,032) citizens of Illinois prior to that date had been enlisted in Missouri regiments, and residents of Missouri had enlisted and been mustered into Illinois regiments, which left a credit, as between the States, in favor of Illinois of 4,373 men.

"After adjustment of credit of 125,321, at and prior to October, 1863, it was ascertained we were entitled to an additional credit of 10,947, which increased the number enrolled *in our own regiments*, and for which we were entitled to credit prior to that call, to 136,-268—leaving the whole account, at that date, thus:

"Quotas under calls to October, 1863		145,100
"Credits for enlistments in Illinois regiments	136,268	
"Balance in Missouri regiments	4,373	
		140,000
"Balance due the Government		4,459

"At this time there was a claim made by the State for volunteers previously furnished, which would more than account for the balance against us of 4,459. This adjustment was made in February, 1864, and was *exclusive of old regiments re-enlisting as veterans*, and disclosed the fact that at the time the first draft was ordered, viz., January 1, 1864, under the call of October, 1863, Illinois had exceeded her quota, and, by the voluntarily demonstrated patriotism of her people, was free from draft.

"The unadjusted balances of the State claimed as above were allowed in the settlement made with the War Department in August last.

"Between the first day of October, 1863, and the first day of December, 1864, we have furnished and received additional credits for fifty-five thousand six hundred and nineteen (55,619) men, which, added to credit of 140,641 to October 1, 1863, makes 197,260 men, which leaves our whole account thus:

"Quotas of the State under all calls prior to Dec. 1, 1864..197,362
"Total credits for three years' volunteers, drafted men and substitutes to Dec. 1, 1864..........................197,260

"Balance due the Government Dec. 1, 1864............... 100

"The deficit of *one hundred men* has been more than balanced by enlistments during the month of December, 1864.

"Of the entire quota of one hundred and ninety-seven thousand three hundred and sixty (197,360) men, we have furnished *one hundred and ninety-four thousand one hundred and ninety-eight* (194,198) *volunteers*, and *three thousand and sixty-two* (3,062) *drafted men*—organized as follows:

"138 regiments and one battalion of infantry.

"17 regiments of cavalry.

"2 regiments and 8 batteries of artillery.

"ONE HUNDRED DAY TROOPS.

"In addition to the foregoing the State has furnished thirteen (13) regiments and two companies of one hundred day volunteers, the following being the numerical designation, name of commanding officer and strength of each:

No. Regiment.	Commanding Officer.	Aggregate.
132	Col. Thomas J. Pickett	853
133	Col. Thaddeus Phillips	851
134	Col. Walter W. McChesney	878
135	Col. John S. Wolfe	855
136	Col. Frederick A. Johns	842
137	Col. John Wood	849
138	Col. John W. Goodwin	835
139	Col. Peter Davidson	878

No. of Regiment.	Commanding Officer.	Aggregate.
140	Col. Lorenzo H. Whitney	871
141	Col. Stephen Bronson	842
142	Col. Rollin V. Ankney	851
143	Col. Dudley C. Smith	855
145	Col. George W. Lackey	877
—	Capt. Simon J. Stookey, (Alton bat., 2 co's)	181
Total		11,328

"After the fall of Vicksburg, 1863, and General Sherman's raid into Mississippi, Georgia and Alabama, active military operations were transferred from the Mississippi to Eastern Tennessee and Georgia. The forces of the enemy, during the winter of 1863–4, were being largely increased and carefully prepared for a desperate spring and summer campaign, East and West, and in April he had concentrated his strength for offensive operations in Virginia and Georgia, or, in the event of our advance, for the most determined and bitter resistance. To hold the vast extent of country wrested from the enemy, embracing many States and Territories, many thousand miles of sea coast, the whole length of the Mississippi, and most of her tributaries, and protect our long line of sea and river coast and rail communication, required an immense stationary force. The towns and cities surrounding strongholds, posts and garrisons, situated in the midst of a doubtful and in most part disloyal population, required too great a portion of our large army for their protection and defense. In view of these circumstances, and of the palpable evidence which surrounded us that the battles about to be fought in Virginia by the army under direct supervision of Lieutenant-General Grant, and in Georgia under General Sherman, would doubtless decide the fate of the country, the Governors of the Northwestern States believed that the efficiency of the army and the prospects of crowning victories to the national arms would be greatly increased by a volunteer force, immediately raised, and which should occupy the points already taken and relieve our veteran troops, and send them forward to join the main army, soon to engage the effective forces of the enemy. I, therefore, in connection with Governors Brough of Ohio, Morton of Indiana, and Stone of Iowa, offered the President infantry troops for one hundred days' service, to be organized under regulations of the War Department, and to be clothed, equipped, armed, subsisted, transported and paid as other United States infantry volunteers, and to serve in fortifications wherever their services might be required, within or without the State. There being no law authorizing it, no bounty could be paid or the service credited on any draft. Our quota offered was 20,000 men, which was a fair proportion to the aggregate number (85,000) to be made up by all of said States.

"Our regiments, under this call, performed indispensable and invaluable services in Kentucky, Tennessee and Missouri, relieving garrisons of veteran troops, who were sent to the front, took part in the Atlanta campaign, several of them, also composing a part of that glorious army that has penetrated the very vitals of the rebellion, and plucked some of the brightest laurels that this heroic age has woven for the patriot soldier. Five of our one hundred days' regiment, after their term of service had expired, voluntarily extended their engagements with the Government, and marched to the relief of the gallant and able Rosecrans, who, at the head of an inadequate and poorly appointed army, was contending against fearful odds for the preservation of St. Louis and the safety of Missouri. The officers and soldiers of these regiments evinced the highest soldierly qualities, and fully sustained the proud record our veterans have ever attained in the field—and the State and country owe them lasting gratitude, and we have, in a great degree, to attribute our successes in Virginia and Georgia to the timely organization and efficient services of the one hundred-day volunteers, furnished by all of said States. The President has, by order, returned them the thanks of the Government and the nation for the service thus rendered, and accords the full measure of praise to them, as our supporters and defenders in the rear, to which the regular reserve force of large armies are always entitled."

With a glow of patriotic pride the Governor thus alludes to the State and its men:

"In prompt support of the Government at home, and in response to calls for troops, the State stands pre-eminently in the lead among her loyal sisters; and every click of the telegraph heralds the perseverance of Illinois Generals and the indomitable courage and bravery of Illinois' sons, in every engagement of the war. Our State has furnished a very large contingent to the fighting strength of our National army. In the West, the history of the war is brilliant with recitations of the skill and prowess of our general, field, staff and line officers, and hundreds of Illinois boys in the ranks are specially singled out and commended by Generals Grant, Sherman, and other Generals of this and other States, for their noble deeds and manly daring on hotly contested fields. One gallant Illinois boy is mentioned as being the first to plant the stars and stripes at Donelson; another, at a critical moment, anticipated the commands of a superior officer, in hurrying forward an ammunition train, and supervising hand grenades, by cutting short the fuses of heavy shell, and hurling them, with his own hands, in front of an assaulting column, into a strong redoubt at Vicksburg; and the files of my office and those of the Adjutant-General are full of letters mentioning for promotion hundreds of private soldiers, who have, on every field of the war, distinguished themselves by personal gallantry, at trying and critical periods. The list of promotions from the field and staff of our regiments to Lieutenant and Major-Generals, for gallant conduct, and the prerequisites for efficient and successful command, compare brilliantly with the names supplied by all other States, and is positive proof of the wisdom of the Government in conferring honors and responsibilities; and the patient, vigilant and tenacious record made by our veteran regiments, in the camp, on the march and in the field, is made a subject of praise by the whole country, and will be the theme for poets and historians of all lands, for all time."

During the time which had elapsed since the commencement of hostilities, the people of Illinois, with those of sister States, had been educated in many good things.

They had learned that *principle* is mightier than passion. And down through platforms and old party creeds, through prejudices of long years standing, they had digged to the rock of RIGHT. "Expediency" had lost its old potency, and "Compromise" its cabalistic charm, and RIGHT had become the people's watchword.

The Churches had made a noble record, yet to be written ere these volumes are completed. The ministry had been clothed with new eloquence, and church councils had spoken with a majesty and authority very different from the apologetic and cringing tones of thirty years sooner. They had presented the claims of the country in solemn conclaves, and denounced treason as a deadly sin. They had given, from the most sacred altars, their best and purest gifts, and thus represented on the field, at home they remembered, "without ceasing" in their prayers, their imperiled country.

New forms of organized benevolent action had sprung into existence. The "*Sanitary Commission*," the almoner of the gifts of the people, sent to the field and to the hospitals countless tons of supplies, not furnished by the Government, or furnished but in scanty measure.

The "*Christian Commission*" made herculean efforts to supply the spiritual wants of the soldiers, sending them books, magazines, and the newspapers which had paid them regular visits at their homes, and also dispatched devoted laborers, pastors, lay-preachers and laymen, who gave, unpaid, their services in organizing religious instruction, conducting prayer meetings, and rendering service in the hospital and on the field. A Major-General has been known to dismount amid the storm of battle, and thank the delegates of the Christian Commission for their work among the wounded.

The "Freedmen's Aid Commission" was working steadily for the relief of those made free by the strong arm of Government, supplying them with stores of food, clothing and medicine, teaching them industry and opening schools for their education.

These great organizations will be noted specifically in a subsequent chapter, and are here referred to, that the patriotic devotion of the people may be seen.

Then there were "Soldiers' Homes" and "Soldiers' Rests" at the principal centers of travel, where the defenders of the country were fed and lodged on their journeys. There were "Soldiers Aid Societies" throughout the villages and rural regions, most of which were auxiliary to the Sanitary Commission. The women were active in these movements, and even the children caught the fever, and juvenile fairs reported handsome sums for the "soldiers."

The hand of Providence was clearly seen in the preparation of the State for the burdens to be borne. The financial crash of 1857, and the commotion, drove out the issues of irresponsible banks, making the way smooth for the national currency which succeeded it.

The era of implemental industry came in time to release from the necessity of manual toil, its hardy sons. It was the boast of the South, "We can place in the field every white man, and our slaves at home can grow and harvest the food for his support." It was an idle boast, for well they knew that a strong contingent of white men must remain to drive those slaves to their daily toil, and prevent them throwing off the "paternal system" under which they were placed. It was idle to institute such a comparison, for Northern ingenuity and Northern capital had placed upon the prairies the Planter, the Cultivator, the Reaper, the Mower, the Thresher, each augmenting the power of the laborer, and multiplying the ability of his pair of hands. It was thus the broad prairies could send their stalwart sons to battle, and yet yield the abundant and garnered harvests for their subsistence. The "planter" of the North drinks no whisky and plays no cards; the reaper and mower never forsake the harvest field for the guidance of the North Star, while the cultivator and thresher are in their place without the mediation of rendition laws or bloodhounds. Each laborer became many in the power of production, aud the absence of nearly two hundred thousand "able-bodied men" caused no perceptible shrinkage in the agricultural resources.

It has been a matter of wonder how much has been done in these four years by women. In readiness for these days, the sewing machine was prepared, and woman's fingers, nimble as they were, were multiplied into tenfold activity.

When the year of our Lord one thousand eight hundred and sixty-four closed upon Illinois, it had placed at the service of the General Government one hundred and ninety-seven thousand soldiers, of whom all but three thousand and sixty-two were volunteers; had manifested an unsurpassed liberality in providing for their physical, mental and spiritual wants; had sustained its financial credit; had maintained its system of education; its schools had their teachers, and its pulpits their ministers.

The arms of the Republic had been triumphant under the heroic Sheridan in the valleys of the Luray and Shenandoah. Before Nashville, Thomas had scattered the grand army of Hood as the chaff of the summer threshing-floor, capturing thousands of prisoners and a hundred cannon. Sherman, cutting loose from his base of supplies, had marched his forces from Atlanta through the heart of the Confederacy, "subsisting them" as they went, not upon "hard tack," but upon the fullness of their enemies, and resting them within the fortifications of captured Savannah, which he announced as a "New Year's present" to the President. The army of Lee was held motionless in Richmond, and in the rebel Congress and among its authorities there was dissension.

Worthy were the above triumphs to be recorded on the same page with the capture of Vicksburg, the victory at Chattanooga, and the brilliant charge and carrying of Missionary Ridge, of the preceding year. It was no longer heard that one Southerner was superior in prowess to five Yankees! That miserable bluster had ceased. The world, too, had learned that we so appreciate our Government as to think no price too great for its preservation.

The outward signs warranted the closing paragraphs of Governor Yates' last message.

"Now I am here to-day to say in behalf of the loyal millions of Illinois, and I trust this General Assembly is prepared to say, and to throw in the face of Jeff. Davis and of his minions, and of all traitors who would destroy our Union, the determined response that in the booming thunders of Farragut's cannon, in the terrible onslaught of Sherman's legions, in the flaming sabers of Sheridan's cavalry, and in the red battle glare of Grant's artillery, our voice is still for war—war to the knife—all the dread enginery of war—persistent, unrelenting, stupendous, exterminating war, till the last rebel shall lay down his arms, and our flag float in triumph over the land. * * * * * * * *

"The black wall of slavery, which, like a frightful specter, drove the emigrant from the sunny fields and rich savannas of the South, is, or soon will be, broken down—the process of intermixture, intermarriage, reciprocal business and commercial relations, will assume the place of the unsocial isolations which have heretofore divided the sections. And though the war has been bitter and bloody, yet the history of most nations of Europe teaches that they have survived long and bloody civil wars, and yet afterwards lived in peace and harmony under the same government. Such is the history of France, after her revolution. The civil war of England, in the memorable days of Cromwell, was marked by scenes of violence, of confiscation of property, of devastation of estates and desolation of towns and cities, as intense and terrible as those which have marked the progress of our civil war. Upon the re-establishment of the government, the people became united, and every memory of the rancor of the war soon disappeared. And so, after the vindication of our national authority, each section awarding to the other the credit due to lofty and indomitable prowess, like friends who have fought it out and are better friends ever after, so will the North and the South bury the memory of their wrongs. Massachusetts and Illinois will again reunite with Virginia and Georgia over the grave of treason, and together with the new-born sisters of the Confederacy, will live on in the bonds of a new brotherhood, and with fresh allegiance to the Constitution, and an unfailing faith in the proved strength of our institutions and man's capacity for self-government, strengthened and reassured by the baptism of blood through which the nation has passed, they will move on as one people, united forever.

"Such is to be the end of events passing before us, and I trust that the people of the United States, and their posterity, while they offer up praises and thanksgiving to Almighty God for the deliverance he has brought to our people out of this red sea of blood—they will bless, with a nation's gratitude, from age to age, the memories of the brave men who have perilled all for their country in its dark and trying hour. And when our own Illinois, upon some national holiday, shall meet all our returning soldiers, as they shall pass in serried ranks, with their old battle-scarred banners and shivered cannons, and rusty bayonets and sabers—with rebel flags and rebel trophies of every kind—at this mighty triumphal procession, surpassing the proudest festivals of ancient Rome and Greece, in their palmiest days, then the loud plaudits of a grateful people will go up: All hail to the veterans who have given our flag to the God of storms, the battle and the breeze, and consecrated our country afresh to Union, Liberty and Humanity."

CHAPTER IX.

FREMONT'S ADMINISTRATION.

ILLINOIS TROOPS IN THE WEST—SITUATION OF MISSOURI—ST. LOUIS AND LYON—ATTACK ON BOONEVILLE—CARTHAGE—ARRIVAL OF FREMONT—"WESTERN DEPARTMENT"—A CRITICAL TIME—SOUTHEASTERN MISSOURI—REYNOLD'S PRONUNCIAMENTO—GOV. JACKSON'S PROCLAMATION—WILSON'S CREEK—DEATH OF LYON—PRENTISS TO FREMONT—FREMONT'S STATEMENT—PLAN OF HIS CAMPAIGN—HIS CELEBRATED ORDER—LEXINGTON—COL. MULLIGAN'S FORCE—THE ASSAILANTS—1ST, ESTVAN'S TESTIMONIAL—INDIGNATION—COLFAX AND FREMONT—RETREAT OF PRICE—CROSSING THE OSAGE—FREMONT'S MARCH—ZAGONYI'S CHARGE—PRICE AT PINEVILLE—REMOVAL OF FREMONT—HUNTER'S RETREAT—ITS ADVERSE CONSEQUENCES—FIGHT AT MONROE—GEN. HURLBUT'S ORDER—GEN. POPE'S ORDER—BATTLE OF CHARLESTON—FREMONT'S REPORT—COLONEL DOUGHERTY—THE MARCH—CHARGE—ITS RESULTS—KILLED AND WOUNDED—BATTLE OF FREDERICKTOWN—COL. PLUMMER AND HIS COMMAND—THE ENGAGEMENT—THE VICTORY.

IN the disposition of the armies of the Union, the Illinois troops, with the exception of a few regiments, have been with the armies of the West and Southwest, and not with those of the East; have fought along the Mississippi, the Tennessee, the Cumberland, the White and the Savannah, rather than the Potomac, the James and the Rapidan. This they do not regret, for with occasional disasters the armies of Belmont and Donelson, of Henry and Shiloh, of Corinth and Iuka, of Vicksburg and Stone River, of Chickamauga and Lookout Mountain, of Atlanta and Savannah, may compare their roll of marches and battles with that of the veterans of the famed captains of the past.

The military operations of the West began with the occupying of Cairo, the importance of which has been stated. Missouri, with a disloyal Executive, was plunged into the vortex of secession by his act alone, for not even the pliant, cringing Legislature he assembled would go to the extreme length of voting the State out of the Union, though quite willing to do all lesser acts of treasonable aid and comfort; willing to vote the School Fund, and the money set apart for the payment of the July interest on the State dèbt, and such other funds as they could bring under their control, for military purposes, "that the State might be protected against invasion and insurrection;" willing to give Governor Jackson, as thorough a rebel and as vile a traitor as there was in South Carolina, exclusive military authority, arming him virtually with dictatorial powers, and making merely verbal opposition to his mandates, treason; willing to enact that every citizen, subject to military duty, should be at the traitor Governor's pleasure, subject to draft, and required to take an oath of obedience to the State Executive; all this it could vote, but dared not vote the State out of the Union. The Governor appointed Sterling Price Major-General of the State troops, and divided the State into military districts, under the following named Brigadiers, of his own appointment: viz., Parsons, M. L. Clark, Jno. B. Clark, Slack, Harris, Rains, McBride, Stein and Jeff. Thompson, who were to organize and send their troops to Booneville and Lexington.

The commercial metropolis of Missouri and the Southwest, St. Louis, would have been seized and held but for the intrepid promptness of Captain, afterwards Brigadier-General Lyon. Says Col. Estvan of the Confederate cavalry, "With the permission of the Confederate Government, a body of troops had formed a camp outside of St. Louis. The Captain of the Federal troops stationed there, did not, however, allow this germ of a revolutionary movement to grow under his very eyes. Relying upon the German population of St. Louis, as well as upon the loyalty of their feelings as citizens of the Union, he assembled some battalions of German troops, marched to the revolutionary camp, and after an energetic summons made them surrender. This gave great annoyance to the Confederates at St. Louis. The Germans were received with showers of stones and pistol shots, which unpleasant welcome was responded to by the poor fellows with a volley, which killed some of the ringleaders. The excitement increased, and St. Louis, that beautiful and flourishing city, was on the point of becoming the scene of strife between two contending factions, which it only escaped through the presence of mind of Captain Lyon, of the United States army."

This Captain Lyon was subsequently made Brigadier-General of volunteers, and his characteristic promptness and decision led him to move immediately upon the Confederate forces, which occupied Booneville, on the 18th of June, 1861. Accordingly, with some two thousand men, he left St. Louis on steamers; and after landing at Jefferson City, re-embarked and reached Rockport, nearly opposite Booneville, on the morning of the 17th, and crossing, met the forces of Marmaduke, which came toward the landing to suprise him, but to their own surprise, met him more than half way from the landing to their own encampment. A conflict followed, and the "State troops," under their secession organization, were routed, and fled in wild confusion, leaving their camp equipage, provisions, stores, two iron six-pounders, with horses, and small arms. The loss was small on either side. General Lyon entered the town at half past twelve, and established his head-quarters at the Fair ground, quartering the regiment of Col. Frank. P. Blair in the Thespian Hall.

On the Fourth of July Col. Franz Sigel met the forces of Jackson, and though vastly outnumbered, made a gallant fight, and conducted a masterly retreat to Carthage, and through that town to Sarcoxie. Jackson was reinforced by the command of Price, and Sigel, outnumbered nearly fourfold, was compelled to continue his retreat via Mt. Vernon to Springfield, where he effected a junction with Lyon. This affair was held to reflect great honor upon our arms, both in the engagement and the necessary retreat. The rebel loss far exceeded that of Sigel's force. The latter, a mere handful, after the previous day's march of twenty-two miles, marched more than thirty miles, fought three distinct engagements, besides incessant skirmishing with superior numbers, and when compelled, by lack of ammunition, to fall back, did so, with the enemy hovering on both flanks and pressing his rear, with a loss so small as to excite wonder.

The attention of the War Department appeared, perhaps necessarily, to be directed almost solely to Washington and its defenses. The West, the great rivers and long lines of railway, the cities and immense stores of provisions of the Southwest, were doubtless important, but were left to take care of themselves.

On the 9th of July, 1861, John C. Fremont, who had just arrived from Paris, received the commission of Major-General in the regular army, and with it the following order:

"The State of Illinois, and the States and Territories west of the Mississippi, and on this side of the Rocky Mountains, including New Mexico, will, in future, constitute a separate command, to be known as the Western Department, under the command of Major-General John C. Fremont, of the United States army, head-quarters at St. Louis."

It will be seen by a single glance at the map that his Department was, of itself, an empire in extent, with an armed foe threatening it in various directions. He was expected to raise, organize, arm and discipline his forces, for there could be none spared from the mountains of Virginia or the banks of the Potomac. "He was also expected," says Mr. Abbott, "with his victorious columns, to pierce and divide the Southern Confederacy of rebels, by descending the Mississippi river from the Lakes to the Gulf. No plan for the campaign was afforded him; no special instructions were given. The accomplishment of the object desired was entrusted wholly to his hands."

The appointment was made at a critical time. In Western Missouri Lyon had effected a junction with Sturgis, and with unpaid and poorly armed troops—"Home Guards," three months' men and others, in all not exceeding thirty-five hundred men, and they rapidly melting away—confronted at Springfield by the combined forces of McCulloch, Price and Jackson, whose rapidly increasing forces bade fair to reach the number of twenty-five or thirty thousand, he telegraphed urgently for reinforcements, but "Washington was in danger," and neither Scott nor McClellan could spare any men, and replied by ordering him to send his regulars to Washington! No wonder the wrung heart of Lyon almost despaired, and that on the 15th of July he wrote to a friend: "I must utterly fail if my regulars all go. At Washington, troops from all the Northern, Middle and Eastern States are available for the support of the army in Virginia, and more men are understood to be already there than are wanted, and it seems strange that so many troops must go from the West, and strip us of the means of defense; but if it is the intention to give up the West, let it be so. I can only be the victim of imbecility or malice. Scott will cripple us if he can."—[Letter to Col. Harding.

In southeastern Missouri it was equally gloomy. General Prentiss held Cairo and Bird's Point, with eight regiments, amounting to 6,350 men, of whom six regiments were three-months' troops who, though most of them re-enlisted could not be relied upon for service until after re-organization. Col. Marsh of the 20th Ill. Vols. held Cape Girardeau, an important position between Bird's Point and St. Louis, but had not a single battery for its defence; Col. Bland was stationed at Ironton, seventy-five miles from St. Louis by railroad, and his force was but 850.

At New Madrid Gen. Pillow had a well drilled force of from fifteen to twenty thousand which was daily increasing, while he had also a supply of excellent artillery and cavalry. Hardee was moving on Ironton at the head of three thousand infantry and two thousand cavalry. Another force gathered under Jeff. Thompson at Bloomfield, who wrote vauntingly to a secession friend in St. Louis that the Union forces would be driven north of the Missouri River in thirty days.

Thos. C. Reynolds, Lieut.-Governor, issued a proclamation as acting Governor of Missouri, dated New Madrid, July 31st, stating his return to the State after a two months' absence as Commissioner to the Confederate States, and saying:

"And now I return to the State, to accompany, in my official capacity, one of the armies which the warrior statesman ["one Jefferson Davis"], whose genius now presides over *the affairs of our half of the Union*, has prepared to advance against the common foe. * * *

"I particularly address myself to those who, though Southerners in feeling, have permitted a love of peace to lead them astray from the State cause. You now see the State authorities about to assert with powerful forces, their constitutional rights; you behold the most warlike people on the Globe, the people of the lower Mississippi valley, about to rush with their gleaming bowie-knives and unerring rifles, to aid us in driving out the Abolitionists and their Hessian allies. If you cordially join our Southern friends, the war must soon depart from Missouri's borders; if you still continue, either in apathy, or in indirect support of the Lincoln Government you only bring ruin upon yourselves by fruitlessly prolonging the contest. The road to peace and internal security is only through union with the South. We will receive you as brothers, and let by-gones be by-gones. Rally to the Stars and Bars in union with our glorious ensign of the Grizly Bear!"

"There were two Richmonds in the field." In August, Governor Jackson issued a proclamation designed as a declaration of independence, declaring Missouri out of the Union and in the Confed eracy, though the people of the State had declared to the contrary. An alliance was made with the Richmond usurpation by which a representation in the rebel Congress was secured.

The gloom was to be deepened. The forces of Lyon left Springfield on the 1st of August and encountered a rebel detachment, and by strategem drew them into an engagement and routed them. Movements of the rebel force compelled Lyon to retrace his steps to Springfield. The troops of McCulloch and Price were combined and held a strong position at Oak Hill, or Wilson's Creek. Here they were attacked by Lyon, and a desperate engagement followed, in which the Union troops fought with unsurpassed bravery, but they fought a foe outnumbering them by far, and yet more than once they seemed to, nay they did, snatch victory from the multitude of enemies. Bravely leading a charge Lyon fell—an irreparable loss, and one that threw the land into mourning. General Sigel brought off the troops with marked ability. Says a rebel authority: "The battle lasted full seven hours and our loss of two thousand killed and wounded shows the desperation of this fierce struggle. Our trophies consisted merely of two dismounted cannon and some hundred muskets. The enemy lost in General Lyon a brave defender of the State of Missouri and a good patriot. He fell, whilst encouraging his men by word and deed; two bullets penetrated his heart at the same moment, causing immediate death."

As the troops of this State had no share in these engagements the record of them is necessarily a brief one. The defeat, so-called, at Wilson's Creek, and the death of Lyon gave new boldness to secessionists and added despondency to Unionists.

As Lyon moved his force toward Springfield, telegrams came in swift succession to General Fremont asking aid from various quarters. Marsh was threatened at Cape Girardeau. Col. Stevenson telegraphed on the 27th of July for at least an additional regiment that he might leave a garrison at Booneville and disperse a rebel force at Warsaw, estimated at ten thousand and an encampment at Glasgow of about two thousand. Gen. Prentiss telegraphed on the 28th that Tennessee rebels were concentrating in strong force at New Madrid to move on Bird's Point, or possibly on Cape Girardeau; adding, "Col. Marsh has no battery. I have none to spare." On the first of August, Col. Marsh telegraphed concerning Pillow's force at New Madrid, stating that it was eleven thousand strong and nine thousand moving to reinforce. On the 4th he telegraphed a force of eight to ten thousand at Bloomfield, with a thousand at two other points. The same day he sent information that Thompson was within sixteen miles of him, and asking reinforcements and ammunition. A similar dispatch was sent the next day from Gen. Prentiss, and another on the sixth.

General Fremont thus states the circumstances surrounding him, in his testimony before the Committee on the Conduct of the War:

"A glance at the map will make it apparent that Cairo was the point which first demanded attention. The force under Gen. Lyon could retreat but the position at Cairo could not be abandoned; the question of holding Cairo was one which involved the safety of the whole Northwest. Had the taking of St. Louis followed the defeat of Manassas, the defeat might have been irretrievable; while the loss of Springfield, should our army be compelled to fall back upon Rolla, would only carry with it the loss of a part of Missouri—a loss greatly to be regretted, but not irretrievable.

"Having reinforced Cape Girardeau and Ironton, by the utmost exertion I succeeded in getting together and embarking with a force of 3,800 men five days after my arrival in St. Louis.

"From St. Louis to Cairo was an easy day's journey by water, and transportation abundant. To Springfield was a week's march; and before I could have reached it, Cairo would have been taken, and with it, I believe, St. Louis.

"On my arrival at Cairo, I found the force under Gen. Prentiss reduced to 1,200 men, consisting mainly of a regiment which had agreed to await my arrival. A few miles below, at New Madrid, Gen. Pillow had landed a force estimated at 20,000, which subsequent events showed was not exaggerated.

"Our force, greatly increased to the enemy by rumor, drove him to a hasty retreat, and permanently secured the position. * * *

"I returned to St. Louis on the fourth, having, in the meantime, ordered Col. Stephenson's regiment at Booneville, and Col. Montgomery from Kansas, to march to the relief of Gen. Lyon. Immediately upon my arrival from Cairo, I set myself at work, amid incessant demands upon my time from every quarter, principally to provide reinforcements for Gen. Lyon.

"I do not accept Springfield as a disaster belonging to my administration. Causes, wholly out of my jurisdiction, had already prepared the defeat of Gen. Lyon before my arrival at St. Louis."

The administration of Gen. Fremont and his claim to military distinction belong rather to the general historian than to the annalist who writes the records of a single state included in his Department. But simple justice demands the statement that few of our leaders have been environed with graver difficulties. He had a strong foe and but few men with which to oppose him, and on his right hand and on his left were able and influential opponents. He doubtless committed mistakes, but he moved with energy, and few read the history of the Missouri campaign without saying, "Perhaps the history would have been different, had not Gen. Fremont been removed just at that critical juncture." As to the General's plans Mr. Abbott says: "On the 8th of September Gen. Fremont sent a private note to President Lincoln, communicating his plan for the commencement of the Mississippi River campaign. He had already taken possession of Fort Holt and Paducah, Kentucky, by which movements he was enabled to command the Tennessee River, and thus to prepare the way for the movement down that River, which was afterwards successfully accomplished, at a much later period, by his successor. He proposed also to occupy Smithland, at the mouth of the Cumberland River, and Hopkinsville, a town connected by railroad with Henderson, on the Ohio River, and twenty or twenty-five miles northeast of Fort Donelson; at the same time sending Gen. Nelson with a force of five thousand men to occupy Bowling Green, in southern Kentucky, and Gen. Grant to occupy New Madrid and the western shore of the Mississippi River, opposite Cairo. He then proposed a combined attack on Columbus and Hickman, and an advance from Bowling Green and Hopkinsville on Nashville, with which point they were connected by railroad. These suggestions, which subsequently proved to be so sagacious, were not, however, adopted. The rebels were permitted to occupy Bowling Green, fortify the Tennessee and Cumberland Rivers, and take possession of New Madrid. Months afterward Gen. Fremont's plan was followed to the letter, and the same results which, had he been then sustained, could have been accomplished without a battle, unless probably one at Columbus, were accomplished only after a long delay, and at the expense of millions of treasure and many sanguinary conflicts. The bombardment of Ft. Henry, the terrible battle of Ft. Donelson, the bloody engagement of New Madrid, and the tedious siege of Island No. Ten were among the results of this rejection of Gen. Fremont's strategic plans. To all this we must add the long unmolested occupation of Bowling Green by the rebel army, a source of terror to all Kentucky, of real danger to Louisville and a rallying point for all secessionists in the State."

On the 31st of August he issued his celebrated General Order, which so aroused the Northwest, and brought the question, "What shall be done with the negro?" more directly before the nation. True, the President revoked so much as related to freeing slaves of rebels, but only himself to repeat it in substance at a later day and with a wider scope.

Price was marching northward toward the Missouri River, it was believed, to attack Jefferson City, the Capital, and re-establish Gov. Jackson in authority. He had already reached the Upper Osage with fifteen thousand men, and Fremont was pressing to completion the organization of a force at Jefferson City and Rolla to circumvent or destroy Price, but could not do so as rapidly as he desired for want of transportation, arms and money.

Price moved forward in spite of an effort by Gen. Lane, of Kansas, with a small force to stop him at Dry Wood, occupied, with a detachment of his army, Fort Scott,on the Kansas border. Thence north by east at pleasure, and on the 11th of September sat down before Lexington, a young city of some five thousand inhabitants, situated on the north bank of the Missouri, two hundred and forty miles west of St. Louis. The place was held by Col. Mulligan, of the "Irish brigade," or 23d regiment, Illinois Volunteers. His force consisted of his own regiment, 800; Home Guards, Col. White, 500; 13th Mo., Col. Peabody, 840; 1st Illinois cavalry, Col. Marshall, 500.* The "Home Guards," Col. Mulligan subsequently said, were only too many. He found them, as in other cases—"In peace invincible; in war invisible." The attacking force was far superior in numbers and artillery, of which the Federal commander had but five small brass pieces and two howitzers, the latter contemptible little affairs.

* Lieut. McClure thus states the number: "Of our Brigade (Irish) that are fit for duty, eight hundred and sixty men; Home Guards, six hundred and seventy; artillerymen, seventy; Illinois cavalry (1st), eight hundred; Home Guard cavalry, three hundred men;—making about two thousand seven hundred men all told, to hold one of the most important posts in Missouri."

The round-shot were a few rough-hewn specimens from a neighboring foundery, manufactured by Capt. McNulty, of the cavalry, and the scanty supply of shells were unfilled, and if filled, there was no one who could manufacture fuzes. The assaulting force, was, by the rebel account, composed of the "elite of the Confederate army," with Generals Price, Rains, Slack, Parsons, Harris, Green and Hardee, beside a multitude of Colonels. Such defences were thrown up as the emergency would permit. Says the St. Louis *Democrat:* "The fight really commenced on Monday the 11th, at which time an advance force of three thousand men, under Gen. Harris, advanced upon Lexington from the South. * * * Col. Marshall's cavalry and the 13th Missouri were ordered out to meet them. A sharp, decisive action occurred Wednesday evening at a point some two miles south of the city, and near the Fair Ground, which resulted in considerable loss to the Confederates, owing to their having fallen into an ambuscade prepared for them by the 13th Missouri. The Federal loss was small, only four being killed and a small proportionate number being wounded." A mistaken order to fall back, given by Lt.-Col. Hatcher, prevented the full advantages of this movement. After this, there was little of moment until the 18th; each party anxiously watching for reinforcements, and Col. Mulligan making his position as strong as possible.

"Tuesday evening (the 17th) the aspect of affairs was changed. On the morning of Wednesday, the 18th, the pickets of the Federals were driven in by the overwhelming forces of the enemy, and a battery of two pieces was planted by the Confederates at a distance of six or eight hundred yards, on the street running south from the College grounds, another battery was placed to the southwest across an immense ravine that separates the grounds from the city, another was planted in the northwest, and a fourth on the north, and then at a given signal from Gen. Price, the whole thirteen opened their fiery throats upon the Federals. The latter had one four, one twelve, and three six-pounder pieces,* and getting into position, they too joined the chorus that went thundering over the country."

The great evil apprehended by the garrison was the cutting off of the supply of water, and unfortunately the strong forces of the

* Col. Mulligan says, "we had five six-pounders."

rebels were so disposed on the 17th as to accomplish it. Our brave men were cut off from the river. Providentially a heavy rain fell at intervals, and the soldiers spread their blankets until saturated, and then wrung them in their camp-dishes, and continued to fight, and, with the exception of some of the Home Guards made no murmur or gave no sign of shrinking.

But brave men as they were, they could not contend forever against overwhelming superiority of numbers, with their relentless allies, hunger and thirst, especially when these were aided by the defection of the Home Guards. All could have been borne and the post held but for the demon of thirst. They surrendered at 3 o'clock A. M., the 20th.

Says Col. Estvan, of the rebel service: "Cut off from all help, short of provisions, opposed to a force more than three times* its number, even the bravest might feel discouraged. But Col. Mulligan met our attacks with undaunted bravery, and when we approached too near, he sallied forth and drove us back. It was only after fifty-two hours of uninterrupted fighting, when all its means were exhausted that Mulligan, finding his small garrison worn out by exertions and without a chance of relief, resolved, after holding a council of war, to hoist a white flag as a sign of capitulation. Gen. Price at once ordered the firing to cease, and sent two of his officers to settle the condition of surrender. The stipulations were soon made. The garrison, with their commander, were to lay down their arms, and remain prisoners of war of the Missouri troops, commanded by Major-Gen. Price.

"This surrender does not cast the slightest discredit on Col. Mulligan, his officers and men. After having exhausted all their means against the enemy, of three times their strength, they had no choice left but capitulation. The booty was considerable. In addition to arms, clothing, and ammunition, we took more than a million of dollars in hard cash. These dollars nearly rendered our fellows frantic, for this was the object which had induced the majority of them to take up arms against their former Government.† Gen.

---

* Nearer six times.

† A striking commentary upon the disinterested patriotism of Southern Cavaliers, enlisting, if we may believe rebel papers and speeches, from no motives but love of freedom and fame, leaving to Yankee mudsills all care for dollars! *Vive humbug!*

Price received Col. Mulligan's sword, which he returned to him with a compliment. 'I should be sorry,' he said, 'to see so brave an officer deprived of his sword.' He offered to place Col. Mulligan on parole, but the Colonel declined;" Declined because he would not recognize the right of the Missouri troops to act as lawful belligerents.

The Confederate army had scarcely occupied Lexington when the looked-for reinforcements came, and Col. Sturgis was seen on the opposite side of the river.

The surrender of Mulligan caused a storm to break out against Fremont. Illinois was indignant. Mulligan and Marshall, both wounded, were prisoners. The gallant Col. White was mortally wounded and died, and Missouri asked why was he sacrificed? The daring Capt. Gleeson was badly wounded in the brillant sortie of the 12th, and graves were made for brave private soldiers who died for the right. Why were not reinforcements sent?

On the 14th Hon. Schuyler Colfax was in St. Louis and saw Gen. Fremont and told him that the public were clamoring because troops were not sent to interrupt and destroy the army of Price, then supposed to be closing on Mulligan.

"Mr. Colfax," said the General, "I will tell you confidentially how many men we have in St. Louis, though I would not have it published on the streets for my life. The opinion in the city is that we have twenty thousand men here, and this gives us strength. If it were known what is the actual number, our enemies would be promptly informed. But I will show you how many there are." The muster-rolls were brought in and gave an aggregate for the city, including Home Guards, of but eight thousand men. There were but two full regiments, the rest being fragments. He had just received orders from Secretary Cameron and Gen. Scott to detach 5,000 infantry from his command and send them without a moment's delay to Washington. The "anaconda" demanded another gorge. He sent two regiments in response, and succeeded, though too late to save Lexington, in securing permission to retain the three regiments. He telegraphed Col. Jeff. C. Davis to send two regiments to Lexington. He telegraphed Sturgis to proceed thither with his entire force, and take command. He ordered Gen. Lane to co-operate with Sturgis. On the 16th he received a telegram from Gen. Pope that two regiments of infantry, four pieces of artillery, and one hundred and fifty cavalry would arrive at Lexington, and by the day following additional reinforcements, amounting to four thousand men. He had a right to suppose Mulligan would be relieved and that the Federal forces would be sufficient to assume the offensive against Price.

Gen. Fremont left St. Louis on the 27th for Jefferson city, expecting to confront Price at some point on the Missouri River, but his crafty foe moved southward and southwestward the same day. With his superior cavalry force he made offensive feints, and succeeded in crossing the Osage. Pollard, a Confederate authority, says, "in two days he put over it 15,000 men in two flat boats." "In the southwestern part of the State," says Estvan, "the Confederate Generals sustained a series of defeats. Generals Pillow, Hardee and McCulloch were driven out of the field." Price was hated by McCulloch, and seeing the Federal troops too cautious in their movements, he would not venture to undertake anything until the three divisions had approached closer to each other. Taking advantage of the slowness of the enemy, Gen. Price made a rapid movement southward, leaving orders for his cavalry to follow him and cover his retreat. He reached the Osage without any obstruction, and crossed that river in boats with his infantry, the cavalry swimming across; without any loss either in time or men, he reached the other bank in safety. In military annals, this passage of a river by 13,000 men will figure conspicuously, as it was performed without pontoons, or any other facilities. * * * Gen. Price allowed his men a respite to recover themselves from the fatigue they had undergone and remained here fourteen days, when he resumed his march toward Pineville, in McDonald county, there to reorganize his men.

"Meantime Generals Sigel and Fremont concentrated their troops at Springfield, with the intention of putting an end to the war in Missouri. Sigel having proceeded from thence with the advanced guard to Wilson Creek, Gen. Price ordered our troops to retire on the appearance of the enemy; but whilst about to carry out this order, our rear was attacked by Fremont's body-guard, under the command of Major Zagonyi, formerly in the Hungarian service, doing us a good deal of damage, and compelling us to accelerate our retreat. On reaching Pineville, Gen. Price made arrangements to await Gen. Fremont's attack, and then to leave Missouri without once more trying the chances of a battle. He well knew how to inspire his men with confidence in his plans.

"And now Gen. Fremont had caught us, as it were in a net, what saved us? A battle? No; *the Government at Washington, at this juncture, deprived Fremont of his command.* This caused a complete change in the enemy's plans, and allowed our Generals full scope to alter their position. The Federal army was now compelled to beat a retreat, abandoning the rich district of Springfield to Gen. Price. The latter at once took possession of it, and settled himself down comfortably for a time in the position abandoned by our enemies."

That Gen. Fremont erred in some things may be conceded, for he was surrounded by fearful difficulties. But it is impossible not to regret his removal at that juncture. Mr. Greeley well says in his "American Conflict:" "But none of his errors, if errors they were, can compare in magnitude with that which dictated a second abandonment of Springfield and retreat to Rolla by our army five days after Hunter had assumed command. No doubt, this was ordered from Washington; but that order was most mistaken and disastrous. We had already once abandoned southwestern Missouri, and, even then, Lyon had wisely and nobly decided that it was better to risk a probable defeat than to give up a Union loving people to the mercies of their enemies without making a determined effort to save them. But now there was no such exigency. We were too strong to be beaten, and might have routed Price near Pineville, chasing the wreck of his army into Arkansas, thus insuring a dispersion of large numbers of the defeated Missourians to their homes; and then 5,000 men, well intrenched, could have held Springfield against all gainsayers, until the next spring. But our second retreat, so clearly wanton and unnecessary, disheartened the Unionists and elated the secessionists of all southern Missouri. It made our predominance in any part of the State appear exotic and casual, not natural and permanent. It revived all the elements of turbulence, anarchy, and rapine which the uncontested supremacy of our cause, under Fremont, had temporarily stilled.

"The secessionists along and even above the Missouri River were galvanized into fresh activity in guerrilla outrages and murders, by the unexpected tidings that we had abandoned southern Missouri without a blow, and were sneaking back to our fastnesses along the lines of completed railroads, and within striking distance of St. Louis."

During Fremont's administration occurred some minor engagements in which troops from Illinois bore a conspicuous part. Col. R. F. Smith, of the 16th Regiment, was in charge of the Camp near Monroe Station, thirty miles west of Hannibal, Mo., having under him, in addition to a detachment of his own regiment, one from the Iowa Third, with about 100 of the Hannibal Home Guards, in all about 600 men. Hearing that Gen. Harris, with a Confederate force, was encamped at Florida, he took 500 men and went forward to disperse them. Passing Florida, when a short distance north of one of the fords of the Salt River, he was suddenly fired upon from an ambush, and Capt. McAllister, of his own regiment, was mortally wounded. The fire was returned, and the Federals fell back. There was a skirmish on the way, but Col. Smith reached Monroe in safety and threw his entire force into an academy. Harris' command, numbering 2,500,* surrounded it and fired *at*, rather than upon it. Reinforcements under ex-Governor Wood arrived from Quincy and falling upon the enemy's rear, completely routed them, capturing seventy prisoners, one gun, and a large number of horses.

On the 15th of July, Brigadier-General Hurlbut issued a stirring proclamation to the people of Northeastern Missouri, assuring them that the time for treating treason with leniency had passed away and that sterner measures would be adopted.

On the 31st of July, Brigadier-General Pope issued a special order assigning Brigadier-General Hurlbut to the command of the U. S. forces along the Hannibal & St. Joseph Railroad; Col. Grant to command at Mexico, on the North Missouri road; Col. Ross to occupy Mounton, and Col. Palmer to post his regiment at Renick and Sturgeon with head-quarters at Renick.

* Another statement says 1,200.

On the 19th of August there was an engagement which, at that early stage of the war, before battles had become so stupendous in dimension and so frequent as to stale curiosity, caused no little excitement. Gen. Fremont's official dispatch is as follows:

"St. Louis, August 20, 1861,

"*To Colonel E. D. Townsend:*

"Report from commanding officer at Cairo says that Colonel Dougherty, with three hundred men, sent out yesterday at seven o'clock from Bird's Point, attacked the enemy at Charleston, one thousand two hundred strong, drove him back, killed forty, took seventeen prisoners, fifteen horses, and returned at two o'clock this morning to Bird's Point with a loss of one killed and six wounded. Col. Dougherty, Capt. Johnson and Lieutenant-Colonel Ransom are among the wounded.

"Our forces under General Prentiss are operating from Ironton in the direction of Hardee.

J. C. Fremont,
"Maj.-Gen. Commanding."

A reconnoissance by Capt. Abbott having ascertained the strength of the foe occupying Charleston, reported it to Colonel Dougherty as one thousand and that an attack on the Union forces was appointed that very night. The St. Louis Democrat thus reports it:

"'We are going to take Charleston to-night' said Colonel Dougherty. 'You stay here, and engage the enemy until we come back—we shall not be gone long. Battalion, right face, forward, march!' and on we went, company E ahead, company A next, and so on. 'Double quick' was given, and the two front companies only responded. Arriving at the town, we ascertained for the first time, that the four rear companies were detached. A few minutes' delay and we were ordered forward without them. The pickets fired upon us, and we followed them in. We dispersed the cavalry, capturing twenty-one horses and rushed on, the bullets whistling around our heads like hail, but we shooting down and dispersing the enemy. We charged furiously on, carrying everything before us. Colonel Dougherty, Capt. McAdams and Capt. Johnson, and leaders of companies A and E, one hundred and twenty-five men, alone engaged the whole force. At the court-house the enemy made a stand. Here Lieutenant-Colonel Ransom of the 11th Ills. who had volunteered to accompany the expedition, inquired of Colonel Dougherty what should be done next. 'Take the court-house or bust,' was the emphatic answer—and we did take it.

"The volleys from the windows passed over our heads, or fell at our feet. Those who did not escape from the windows, were killed or taken prisoners, and when we emerged from the house, the enemy were to be seen fleeing in the distance. We leisurely retraced our steps. At the railroad track we met the detached portions of our regiment, under Lieutenant-Colonel Hart. * * * * They had fallen in with the flying enemy and killed sixteen of them. All returned to Capt.

Abbott's encampment, with twenty-one horses and eighteen prisoners, having been less than two hours absent. * * * We killed about sixty or seventy of the enemy and probably wounded twice that number. There were some fearful contests—some hand-to-hand fighting. The enemy were impaled upon the bayonet, pulled from their horses, knocked over with the butt of the gun, or of the pistol, and so bold and impetuous was every movement, that the enemy fled in confusion. Before morning, our cavalry succeeded in capturing a camp of rebel cavalry above town, and brought in forty horses and thirty-three prisoners."

Capt. William Sharp, of company A, was killed. A correspondent of the N. Y. *Tribune* relates the following of Lieutenant-Colonel Ransom! "He was urging his men to the charge, when a man rode up, and called out, 'What do you mean? You are killing our own men.' Ransom replied, 'I know what I am doing; who are you?' The reply was, 'I am for Jeff. Davis.' Ransom replied, 'You are the man I am after,' and instantly two pistols were drawn, the rebel fired first, taking effect in Colonel Ransom's arm near the shoulder. The Colonel fired, killing his antagonist instantly." This was a single instance of the courage which made that gallant young officer so great a favorite, and inspired his men when he came to command a brigade or division with such admiration for his personal courage as made them ready to follow anywhere that he should lead.

Another spirited engagement between the Union forces commanded by Colonel J. B. Plummer of the 11th Missouri and the Confederate troops under Brigadier-General Jeff. Thompson occurred near Fredricktown, Mo., on the 21st of October. Colonel Plummer received orders, on the 17th from General Grant, commanding the district of Southeast Missouri, with head-quarters at Cairo, to move out and cut off Thompson, and on the following morning marched with about fifteen hundred men composed of the 17th Illinois, Colonel Leonard F. Ross; the 20th, Colonel C. C. Marsh; the 11th Missouri, Colonel Pennabaker; Lieut. White's section of Taylor's Battery, and Captain Steward's and Lansden's companies of cavalry. Arriving at Fredericktown on Monday the 21st at 12 M. he found the foe gone and the town in possession of Colonel W. P. Carlin (called Carlile in Greely's History) of the 38th Illinois. Colonel Carlin waved his seniority and gracefully reported to Colonel Plummer for orders. With his force were the 21st and 33d Illinois regiments commanded by Colonels

Alexander and Hovey, six companies of the 1st Indiana Cavalry, commanded by Colonel Baker, and the 11th Wisconsin, Colonel Murphy, and one section of Major Schofield's battery. A rapid march of half a mile from the village and the enemy was discovered by Captain Stewart. Colonel Ross threw forward two companies as skirmishers, and then advanced his regiment into a cornfield to support them. The artillery of Taylor's battery, under White, which had been masked upon the slope of a hill opened with effectiveness. The 17th Illinois was soon engaged with the main body of rebel infantry, commanded by Colonel Lowe. The other regiments deployed to the right and left of the road as they came up, and the 38th came promptly on the field as soon as permitted. Under the steady advancing fire of the Illinois 17th and 20th, and Wisconsin 11th, the enemy was falling back, and soon broke and fled in disorder, the retreat having become a rout. On the right the rebel force under Thompson in person, which had also been retreating was rallied, and made a stand with a gun in battery. With a wild shout and ringing sabers the Indiana cavalry charged the battery and carried it, but not being duly supported, the enemy carried off the gun. Here fell the brave Major Gavitt, and Captain Highman. The rout soon became general, and they were pursued some twenty-two miles. The rebel Colonel Lowe was killed with nearly two hundred others, and eighty prisoners captured—the number of their wounded is not stated. The Union loss was six killed and sixty wounded.

U. S. Grant

LIEUT. GEN. U. S. GRANT.

ENGRAVED EXPRESSLY FOR "PATRIOTISM OF ILLINOIS." CLARKE & CO. PUBLISHERS.

CHAPTER X.

U. S. GRANT.

THE LIEUTENANT-GENERAL—BIRTH—AT WEST POINT—HIS ACADEMIC COURSE—GRADUATION—HIS CLASS-MATES—BREVET 2D LIEUTENANT—TO MEXICAN BORDER—FULL COMMISSION AS 2D LIEUTENANT—PALO ALTO—RESECA DE LA PALMA—ALONG THE RIO GRANDE—MONTEREY—MOLINO DEL REY—PROMOTED—BREVET DECLINED—CHEPULTEPEC—NOTICED IN REPORTS—CAPTAIN'S BREVET—FULL COMMISSION AS 1ST LIEUTENANT—TO OREGON—COMMISSIONED CAPTAIN—RESIGNATION—ST. LOUIS—GALENA—CONVERSATION WITH REV. MR. VINCENT—GOVERNOR YATES' ACCOUNT—IN COMMAND AT MEXICO—AT CAIRO—SEIZES PADUCAH AND SMITHLAND—THE BATTLE OF BELMONT—LOSS—FOUKE AND WRIGHT—ILLINOIS REGIMENTS—GUNBOATS—HALLECK—GRANT'S DISTRICT—NEW CAMPAIGN—MAJOR-GENERAL—PROMOTION—ELEMENTS OF SUCCESS.

HENCEFORWARD, through two years, the soldiers of Illinois are so intimately associated with one man, about whom they group as a center, that a brief sketch of his life and military career will enable the reader better to understand their shifting movements.

It is the fortune of Illinois to have given the nation its chief magistrate, and also to see one of its quiet, unobtrusive citizens rise from Colonel commanding the 21st Regiment to the high grade of Lieutenant-General, commanding all the armies of the United States.

Ulysses S. Grant was born in Clermont Co., Ohio, April 27, 1822. In 1839, at the age of seventeen, through the kindness of Gen. T. L. Hamer, he was admitted to the Military Academy at West Point, passing a thorough examination, and was admitted into the fourth class, his studies consisting of mathematics, English grammar, including etymological and rhetorical exercises, composition, declamation, the geography of the United States, the French language and the use of small arms. In 1840 he was advanced to the third class, ranking as corporal in the cadet battalion, studying the higher mathematics, French, drawing, and for sixteen weeks the duties of a cavalry soldier. In 1841 he passed into the 2d class with the rank of sergeant of cadets, with a higher and more laborious range of studies, gaining steadily, if not rapidly, and never falling back. In 1842 he entered the first and final class, ranking as a commissioned officer. He pursued the study of civil and military engineering, ethics, constitutional, international and military law, mineralogy, geology and Spanish, these latter extra to the regular curriculum. He also received instruction in ordnance, gunnery and cavalry tactics, and "acquired a practical knowledge of the use of the rifled musket, the field-piece, mortar, seige and sea-coast guns, small-sword and bayonet, as well as of the construction of field works, and the fabrication of all munitions and materiel of war."* He graduated on the 30th of June, 1843, standing No. 21, in a class of thirty-nine. Standing first was William B. Franklin, of Pennsylvania, Major-General U. S. Volunteers, commander of Nineteenth Army Corps, &c.

The names of the next three are not now on the U. S. Army List.

Wm. F. Reynolds graduated fifth. He was appointed an aid on the staff of Gen. Fremont, when that officer commanded the Mountain Department, and held the rank of Colonel.

The sixth, Isaac F. Quinby. He entered the artillery service, and was, for a time, professor at West Point, but had, before the rebellion, gone into civil life. He entered the service for the Union at the head of a New York Regiment, and became a Brigadier in the Army of the Potomac.

Roswell S. Ripley graduated seventh. He entered the rebel service and his name stands henceforth in the dishonored list of traitors.

John James Peck, the eighth, entered the artillery service. He became Major-General of Volunteers, commander of the District of North Carolina, &c.

John P. Johnson, a gallant artillery Lieutenant, who fell bravely at Contreras, Mexico, was ninth.

Major-General Joseph Jones Reynolds, of Indiana, tenth, attained eminence as a Professor of Science. He served with distinction

* Larke's Biography.

through the war in Mexico; became Major-General of Volunteers, and was killed at the battle of Gettysburg, July 1, 1863.

Col. James Allen Hardie, Assistant Adjutant-General of the Army of the Potomac, was eleventh.

Henry F. Clarke graduated twelfth, entered artillery service, gained brevets in Mexico, became Chief Commissary of the Army of the Potomac, and received the rank of Colonel.

The next was Lieutenant Booker, who died in the service at San Antonio, Texas.

The fourteenth was the traitor Samuel G. French, who deserted his country and flag without even the poor apology of Southern birth, being a native of New Jersey. He is Major-General C. S. A.

The fifteenth, Lieutenant Theo. F. Chadbourne, was killed at the battle of Resaca de la Palma, May 9, 1846, bravely distinguishing himself.

The sixteenth was Christopher C. Augar, U. S. Major-General of Volunteers.

The seventeenth was F. Gardner, another northern ingrate, who, born in New York and educated by the Republic, entered the service of the rebels. He became Major-General C. S. A., and won his notoriety by the surrender of Port Hudson.

The next was Lieutenant George Stevens, drowned at the passage of the Rio Grande, May 18, 1846.

The next, Edm. B. Holloway, of Kentucky, breveted at Contreras, Captain in the U. S. A. At the beginning of the rebellion, he resigned his commission and went to the rebels.

The twentieth, Lieutenant Lewis Neill, who died in service at Ft. Croghan, Texas, Jan. 13, 1850.

Twenty-first, Ulysses S. Grant.

Twenty-second, Joseph H. Potter, at the commencement of war was Captain in the Regular Army, and became Colonel of Volunteers, retaining his regular rank.

Twenty-third, Lieutenant Robert Hazlitt, killed at the storming of Monterey, September 21, 1846.

Twenty-fourth, Lieutenant Edw. Howe, died in the service at Fort Leavenworth, March 31, 1850.

Next was Lafayette Boyer Wood, of Virginia, not in service.

Twenty-sixth, Major-General Charles S. Hamilton, U. S. Volunteers.

Next, Wm. K. Van Bokkelen, of New York, cashiered for rebel proclivities May 8, 1861.

The next two were A. St. Armaud Crozet, who had resigned several years before the war; Lieutenant Charles E. James, who died at Sonora, California, June 8, 1849.

Major-General Fred. Steele, U. S. Volunteers, was thirtieth on the list. He was recently relieved from the command of the Army of Arkansas.

The thirty-first was Captain Henry R. Selden, of the Fifth U. S. Infantry.

General Rufus Ingalls, Quartermaster-General of the Army of the Potomac, stood next, followed in order by Major Fred. T. Dent, Fourth U. S. Infantry, and Major J. C. McFarran, Quartermaster's Department.

The thirty-fifth was Brigadier-General Henry Moses Judah, who commanded a division of the 23d Army Corps.

The remaining four are out of the service. They are Norman Elting, Cave J. Houts, Charles G. Merchant and George B. McClellan.

It is not always that brilliancy in early scholarship makes its way to high success in life's practical duties. There are seniors of General Grant who may have been elated with their higher honors at graduation, who are now proud to serve under their slower but persistent junior.

On the first of July, the second day of his graduation, he received the brevet of 2d Lieutenant. The country was happily at peace, and he was attached as supernumerary Lieut. to the Fourth Regiment U. S. Infantry then stationed in Missouri. The trouble with Mexico continuing, his regiment was ordered to join the army of occupation concentrating under General Taylor in the borders of Mexico, and was stationed at Corpus Christi, where he received the grade of full 2d Lieutenant, dated from September 30, 1845, and was assigned to the Seventh U. S. Infantry. Upon personal solicitation he was permitted to remain with the Fourth. The 8th of May 1846, he participated in the Battle of Palo Alto, and on the 9th in that of Resaca de la Palma, and in the subsequent operations of General Taylor along the Rio Grande. On the 23d of September he participated in successful operations against Monterey. The Fourth was transferred to the immediate command of General Scott, and participated in the successful siege of Vera Cruz. The Lieutenant was appointed Quartermaster of his regiment, a position he held until the occupation of the city of Mexico. At the battle of Molino del Rey, September 8, 1857, his bravery was so conspicuous that he was made a 1st Lieutenant on the field. The Senate attempted to ratify this as a mere brevet, which was promptly declined by the young officer. His gallant bearing at Chepultepec is specially noted in the reports of his superiors, and for it he received the brevet of captain in the Regular Army, to date from the 13th day of the battle, which was confirmed. He received his commission as full 1st Lieutenant three days later, which he accepted, holding his prior brevet rank of captain.

Returning to the States his regiment was broken into battalions and he, with one of them, occupied a northern boundary fort. In 1850 or 1851 it was ordered to Oregon with head-quarters for a time at Dallas. While there he received his full promotion to Captain of Infantry, dating from August, 1853. Shortly after he was attached to the army of the West, but subsequently resigned his commission and entered civil life on the 31st of July, 1854. Having married Miss Dent, of St. Louis, he settled near that city and devoted himself to farming.

In 1859 his father, brothers and himself opened a leather store in the city of Galena, Illinois, where he pursued a profitable business life until the rebellion, when he hastened to tender his services to the country from which he had received his education, though fifteen years of service might well be held to have cancelled that obligation.

The Rev. Jno. H. Vincent, at that time pastor of the Methodist Episcopal Church in Galena, the worship of which Captain Grant regularly attended, has given the writer the following incident:

Having occasion to visit Dubuque on an exchange, he breakfasted on Sabbath morning at the Julian House, and found there his parishioner, the captain. Breakfast over, the captain and the pastor were standing near a stove, the former in his old blue army overcoat, when the conversation took a war direction. Says Mr. Vincent, "It then continued so long as to make me nervous lest I should be too late for my engagement, and my unprofessional judgment could not pronounce upon the correctness of his opinions. But now that so much history has been made, I refer with wonder to his comprehensive statements of the magnitude the rebellion would assume; the positions it would assume and the means necessary for its dislodgements. He spoke quietly, but it was with the knowledge of a master. He comprehended the vastness of the coming war."

Governor Yates, in his last annual message, thus narrates the entrance of Captain Grant into the service of the State:

"Prominent among the many distinguished names who have borne their early commissions from Illinois, I refer, with special pride, to the character and priceless services to the country of Ulysses S. Grant. In April, 1861, he tendered his personal services to me, saying 'that he had been the recipient of a military education at West Point, and that now, when the country was involved in a war for its preservation and safety, he thought it his duty to offer his services in defense of the Union, and that he would esteem it a privilege to be assigned to any position where he could be useful.' The plain, straightforward demeanor of the man, and the modesty and earnestness which characterized his offer of assistance, at once awakened a lively interest in him, and impressed me with a desire to secure his counsel for the benefit of volunteer organizations then forming for government service. At first I assigned him a desk in the Executive office; and his familiarity with military organization and regulations made him an invaluable assistant in my own and the office of the Adjutant-General. Soon his admirable qualities as a military commander became apparent, and I assigned him to command of the camps of organization at 'Camp Yates,' Springfield, 'Camp Grant,' Mattoon, and 'Camp Douglas,' at Anna, Union county, at which the 7th, 8th, 9th, 10th, 11th, 12th, 18th, 19th and 21st regiments of Illinois volunteers, raised under the call of the President of the 15th of April, and under the 'Ten Regiment Bill,' of the extraordinary session of the Legislature, convened April 23, 1861, were rendezvoused. His employment had special reference to the organization and muster of these forces—the first six into United States, and the last three into the State service. This was accomplished about the 10th day of May, 1861, at which time he left the State for a brief period, on a visit to his father, at Covington, Kentucky.

"The 21st regiment of Illinois volunteers, raised in Macon, Cumberland, Piatt, Douglass, Moultrie, Edgar, Clay, Clark, Crawford and Jasper counties, for thirty-day State service, organized at the camp at Mattoon, preparatory to three years' service for the government, had become very much demoralized, under the thirty days' experiment, and doubts arose in relation to their acceptance for a longer period. I was much perplexed to find an efficient and experienced officer to assume command of the regiment and take it into the three years' service. I ordered the regiment to Camp Yates, and after consulting Hon. Jesse K. Dubois, who had many friends in the regiment, and Col. John S. Loomis, Assistant Adjutant-General, who was at the time in charge of the Adjutant-General's office, and on terms of personal intimacy with Grant, I decided to offer the command to him, and accordingly telegraphed Captain Grant, at Covington, Kentucky, tendering him the Colonelcy. He immediately reported, accepting the commission, taking rank as Colonel of that regiment from the 15th day of June, 1861. Thirty days previous to that time the regiment numbered over one thousand men, but in consequence of laxity in discipline of the first commanding officer, and other discouraging obstacles connected with the acceptance of troops at that time, but six hundred and three men were found willing to enter the three years' service. In less than ten days Col. Grant filled the regiment to the maximum standard, and brought it to a state of discipline seldom attained in the volunteer service, in so short a time. His was the only regiment that left the camp of organization on foot. He marched from Springfield to the Illinois river, but, in an emergency requiring troops to operate against Missouri rebels, the regiment was transported by rail to Quincy, and Col. Grant was assigned to the command for the protection of the Quincy and Palmyra, and Hannibal and St. Joseph railroads. He soon distinguished himself as a regimental commander in the field, and his claims for increased rank were recognized by his friends in Springfield, and his promotion insisted upon before his merits and services were fairly understood at Washington. His promotion was made upon the ground of his military education, fifteen years' services as a Lieutenant and Captain in the regular army (during which time he was distinguished in the Mexican war), his great success in organizing and disciplining his regiment, and for his energetic and vigorous prosecution of the campaign in North Missouri, and the earnestness with which he entered into the great work of waging war against the traitorous enemies of his country. His first great battle was at Belmont, an engagement which became necessary to protect our Southwestern army in Missouri from overwhelming forces being rapidly consolidated against it from Arkansas, Tennessee, and Columbus Kentucky. The struggle was a desperate one, but the tenacity and soldierly qualities of Grant and his invincible little army, gave us the first practical victory in the West. The balance of his shining record is indelibly written in the history of Henry, Donelson, Shiloh, Corinth, Vicksburg, Chattanooga, The Wilderness, siege of Richmond, and the intricate and difficult command as Lieutenant-General of the armies of the Union—written in the blood and sacrifices of the heroic braves who have fallen, following him to glorious victory—written upon the hearts and memories of the loyal millions who are at the hearth-stones of our gallant and unconquerable "Boys in Blue." The impress of his genius stamps our armies, from one end of the Republic to the other; and the secret of his success in executing his plans, is in the love, enthusiasm and confidence he inspires in the soldier in the ranks, the harmony and respect of his subordinate officers, his own respect for and deference to the wishes and commands of the President, and his sympathy with the government in its war policy.

"As evidence of the materials of the State of Illinois for war purposes, at the beginning of the war, and a pleasing incident of Grant's career, I refer to an article in the Vicksburg paper, the 'Weekly Sun,' of May 13, 1861, which ridicules our enfeebled and unprepared condition, and says: 'An official report made to Governor Yates, of Illinois, by one Captain Grant, says that after examining all the State armories, he finds the muskets amount to just nine hundred and four, and of them only sixty in servicable condition.' Now the name of that man, who was looking up the rusty muskets in Illinois, is glory-crowned with shining victories, and will fill thousands of history's brightest pages to the end of time. I know well the secret of his power, for afterwards, when I saw him at head-quarters, upon the march, and on the battle field, in his plain, thread-bare uniform, modest in his deportment, careful of the wants of the humblest soldier, personally inspecting all the dispositions and divisions of his army, calm and courageous amidst the most destructive fire of the enemy, it was evident that he had the confidence of every man, from the highest officer down to the humblest drummer boy in his whole command. His generalship rivals that of Alexander and Napoleon, and his armies eclipse those of Greece and Rome, in their proudest days of imperial grandeur. He is a gift of the Almighty Father to THE NATION, in its extremity, and he has won his way to the exalted position he occupies through his own great perseverance, skill and indomitable bravery."

The 31st of July, 1861, Col. Grant was placed in command of the troops at Mexico on the North Missouri Railroad in the North Missouri District, commanded by Brigadier Gen. John Pope. The regiment was marched to Pilot Knob, which it garrisoned; then to Ironton, and then to Marble Creek. On the 23d of August he was promoted Brigadier-General with a commission dating from May 17th. He was half way down a list of thirty-four appointed the same day. He was placed in command of the post at Cairo, with his own brigade and that of Brig. Gen. McClernand. His post included within its jurisdiction the Missouri shore of the Mississippi from Cape Girardeau to New Madrid, Kentucky, which was then enjoying its McGoffin neutrality, and rebel bands from Tennessee crossed the dividing line at pleasure, while they were fortifying Columbus and Hickman on the Mississippi, and Bowling Green on the Big Barren River. General Grant perceiving this, at once seized Paducah, a valuable post at the mouth of the Tennessee River, and within nineteen days he occupied Smithland, at the mouth of the Cumberland river, thus blockading the entrance of the rebel States, furnishing bases for future operations and clearing out the pestilent guerrillas who were attempting to close the Ohio River. The "neutral" citizens of Paducah were ready, with ample stores and secession flags, for the reception of the Confederate forces.

On the 7th of November was fought a bloody and sternly contested battle at Belmont, Missouri, and one which has caused much criticism. The object of the movement is stated by General Grant in his official report to have been "to prevent the enemy from sending reinforcements to Price's army in Missouri, and also from cutting off Columbus reinforcements that I had been instructed to send out in pursuit of Jeff. Thompson." The diversion had, it is affirmed, been ordered by his superior, leaving the time and manner optional with Gen. Grant.

The force consisted of two brigades, the first and second; the first consisting of the twenty-seventh, Col. Buford, thirtieth, Col. Fouke, and thirty-first, Col. Jno. A. Logan, Illinois volunteers, to which was added Capt. Dollins' company of Adams county cavalry, 72 men under Lieut. J. R. Collin, and Taylor's battery Chicago light artillery, six guns, and 114 men, under command of Brigadier Gen. McClernand; the second composed of the Illinois twenty-second, Col. Dougherty, and seventh Iowa, Col. Lauman, under command of Col. Dougherty. The whole force numbered 2,850 men of all arms. The Chicago *Evening Journal* thus narrates the battle:

"The design was to reach Belmont just before daylight; but, owing to unavoidable delays in embarking, it was 8 o'clock before the fleet reached Lucas Bend, the point fixed upon for debarkation. This is about three miles north of Columbus, Ky., on the Missouri side.

"The enemy were encamped on the high ground back from the river, and about two and a half miles from the landing. From their position they could easily see our landing, and had ample time to dispose of their forces to receive us, which they did with all dispatch. They also sent a detachment of light artillery and infantry out to retard our march, and annoy us as much as possible.

"A line of battle was formed at once on the levee, Col. Fouke taking command of the center, Col. Buford of the right, and Col. Logan of the left.

"The advance from the river bank to the rebel encampment was a running fight the entire distance, the rebels firing and falling back all the way; while our troops gallantly received their fire without flinching, and bravely held on their course, regardless of the missiles of death that were flying thick and fast about them. The way was of the most indifferent character, lying through woods with thick underbrush, and only here and there a path or a rough country road.

"The three divisions kept within close distance of each other, pressing over all obstacles and overcoming all opposition; each striving for the honor of being first in the enemy's camp. This honor fell to the right division, led by Col. Buford. It was the gallant 57th Illinois, who, with deafening cheers, first waved the Stars and Stripes in the midst of the rebels' camping ground.

"The scene was a terribly exciting one—musketry and cannon dealing death and destruction on all sides; men grappling with men in a fearful death-struggle; column after column rushing eagerly up, ambitious to obtain a post of danger; officers riding hither and thither in the thickest of the fight, urging their men on, and encouraging them to greater exertions; regiments charging into the very jaws of death with frightful yells and shouts, more effective, as they fell upon the ears of the enemy, than a thousand rifle-balls—and, in the midst of all, is heard one long, loud, continuous round of cheering as the Star-Spangled Banner is unfurled in the face of the foe, and defiantly supplants the mongrel colors that had, but a moment before, designated the spot as rebel ground.

"The 22d boys have the honor of having silenced and captured a battery of twelve pieces, which had been dealing destruction with marked success. The 30th had been badly cut up by this battery, and were straining every nerve to capture it. They expressed considerable disappointment that the prize was snatched from them. They turned away in search of new laurels; and, in charging into the very midst of the camp, were drawn into an ambuscade, where they were again suffering terribly, though maintaining their ground unflinchingly, when the 31st came to their assistance.

"An impetuous and irresistible charge was then made, that drove the rebels in all directions, and left the field in possession of the Federal forces. The rebel camps were fired, and, with all their supplies, ammunition, baggage, etc., were totally destroyed.

"The discovery, on the Kentucky side, that we were in possession of their camp, led to an opening of the rebel batteries from that direction upon us. Their fire was very annoying; the more so as we were not in a position to return it.

"Just at this juncture, the report was brought to Gen. Grant, by Lieut. Pittman, of the 30th Illinois, who had, with his company (F), been on a scouting duty, that heavy reinforcements were coming up to the rebels from the opposite side of the river. Indeed, the report was also made that the enemy were pouring over the river in immense numbers, and the danger was imminent that our retreat would be cut off. The order to fall back to the boats was therefore given, but not a moment too soon.

"The way was already filled with rebel troops; and, as we had fought our way up to the encampment, so we were obliged to fight back to our boats, and against desperate odds. But the men were not lacking in courage, and fought like veterans, giving ample evidence of their determination. Every regiment of Federal troops suffered more or less severely in their return march; but the general opinion prevails that the rebels suffered far greater losses than we.

"Wherever they made a stand, we put them to flight; and, although we lost many brave men, either killed, wounded, or taken prisoners, we made at least two of their men bite the dust for every one that fell from our ranks. Our regiments all reached their boats, though with considerably thinned ranks."

In his official report General Grant says: "Our loss was about 84 killed, 150 wounded,—many of them slightly—and about an equal number missing. The Brigade reports show losses as follows:

First Brigade, General McClernand commanding:

	KILLED.	WOUNDED.	MISSING.	TOTAL.
27th Regiment Illinois	11	42	28	81
30th Regiment Illinois	9	27	8	44
31st Regiment Illinois	10	61	18	89
Dollin's cavalry	1	2		3
Taylor's battery		5		5
	31	137	54	222
Second Brigade, Col. Dougherty commanding:				
22d Regiment Illinois	23	74		97
7th Regiment Iowa	26	80		106
	49	154		203
Total	80	391	54	525

The seventh Iowa fought gallantly. Its Colonel was severely wounded and its brave Lieut.-Col. Wentz was killed. The Illinois troops maintained the honor of their State. "Gen. McClernand," says Gen. Grant, "was in the midst of danger throughout the engagement, and displayed both coolness and judgment. His horse was three times shot under him." Col. Dougherty, at the head of his brigade, was three times wounded and taken prisoner. Col. John A. Logan gave promise of the military ability which has made him prominent among the double-starred Generals of the West. Major McCluzken, of the 30th, was mortally wounded. Captains Brolaski and Markle and Lieut. Dougherty were killed. Col. Buford's conduct was unexceptionable and accomplishing a difficult circuit, was the first, says Gen. McClernand, to throw his men within the enemy's defences. Col. Fouke bore himself gallantly. His men were confronted during the engagement with those of Col. John V. Wright, of the 13th Tennessee. The two Colonels had served together in Congress, members of the same political party.

When they separated at the close of the session of 1860–1, Wright said to his friend, "Phil., I expect the next time we meet will be on the battle field." Wright was mortally wounded, and sixty of his men were captured by the regiment of his former friend! Such are the results of civil war! Friend against friend—aye, brother against brother, for among the rebel dead on the field of Belmont a Union surgeon discovered his own brother!

Lieut.-Col. Hart commanded the 22d Illinois, and led his men gallantly and skillfully. Taylor's battery gave both friends and foes prophecy of what it would yet accomplish, and Captain Taylor especially mentions Lieut. P. H. White and his immediate command. Of this battery, 1st Lieut. Charles M. Everett was wounded mortally.

The additional killed and wounded Illinois officers, reported by the brigade commanders are, killed—Captain Thomas G. Markley, Co. D, 30th Regiment. Wounded—Lieut. Wm. Shipley, Co. A, 27th Regiment, mortally; Capt. John W. Rigby, Co. F, 31st Regiment, and Capt. W. A. Looney, Co. C; Captains Challenor, Abbott and Hubbard, with Lieut. Adams, of the 27th Regiment.

Gen. Grant makes the following reference to the gun-boats which were then just beginning to be understood: "The gun-boats Tyler and Lexington, Captains Walker and Stemble, U. S. N., commanding, conveyed the expedition and rendered most efficient service. Immediately upon our landing they engaged the enemy's batteries and protected our transports throughout."

The result of the conflict may be stated as twofold. First, accomplishing the desired diversion, and preventing the marching of a strong rebel force to the reinforcement of Price and Thompson. Second, showing the enemy and our own people the coolness and bravery of our men under circumstances of peril. They fairly won a brilliant victory though compelled by overwhelming numbers to abandon the field they did not purpose to hold.

The rebel loss is conceded by their authorities to have been about one thousand.

Gen. Hunter, who succeeded Gen. Fremont, held the command only temporarily, and Maj.-Gen. H. W. Halleck was assigned to the Department, and organized it into Military Districts. Gen. Grant was appointed commander of the "District of Cairo, including all the southern part of Illinois, that part of Kentucky west of the Cumberland River and the southern part of Missouri, south of Cape Girardeau." He arranged the commands of his subordinates, assigning to Col. T. H. Cavanaugh, of the 6th Ill. cavalry, command of the force at Shawneetown, including troops stationed along the Ohio River on both sides east of Caledonia, and to the mouth of the Cumberland, head-quarters to be at Paducah, Ky. Brig.-Gen. E. A. Paine was assigned to the command of the force at Bird's Point. His men were carefully drilled and distributed in readiness for the grand campaign about to be inaugurated.

On the 10th of January the forces under the direct command of Gen. McClernand left Cairo in transports and disembarked at Fort Jefferson.

And now began the campaign which resulted in the reduction of Forts Henry and Donelson, and rescued the Tennessee and Cumberland Rivers from the enemy, and thus modified the movements of later campaigns and other leaders. These remain for other chapters.

The victory of Fort Henry followed by the capture of Fort Donelson turned the eyes of the nation upon the rising military man of the west. He had been assailed, his private habits had been discussed, but he was successful, and that too under circumstances requiring more than fortune.

On the 14th of February Gen. Halleck issued an order creating the District of West Tennessee, to include the country between the Tennessee and Mississippi Rivers to the Mississippi state line, and Cairo, making head-quarters temporarily at Fort Donelson, or wherever the General might be. Gen. Grant received the rank of Major-General of Volunteers, by act of Congress, his commission fitly dating from the surrender of Donelson.

The fearful three-days' battle of Pittsburg Landing followed; a fight in which, through one dark dreary day, the advantage appeared to be with the rebels, and when the life of the Government hung trembling upon the issue. It was in this that his power to organize victory in the midst of defeat, to retrieve disaster, to conquer by the force of persistent effort came out. The victory was complete and the name of Grant was at once written among those of great captains. Henceforward his sphere of duty was to widen until it should include all the armies of the United States. His promotion was rapid from grade to grade, until, in view of the splendid achievements of Vicksburg, Chattanooga, Lookout Mountain, and Mission Ridge he received the grade of Lieutenant-General, revived by act of Congress.

The characteristics of this eminent soldier can be but seen by the careful study of his campaigns and reports, and that too when they shall be fully developed. But enough has been done to warrant some generalization of character. What has given him success?

I. *A thorough knowledge of military science.* There is much in genius, but for the management of a great campaign, with its different armies, there must be the scientific knowledge of details. Not merely the studies of the academy, but the careful study of military history as made by great leaders. This he has, and, added to this was fifteen years in service with active participation in the triumphal marches in Mexico.

II. *The knowledge of men.* The General must have subordinates. He must be brain, they must be hands. He must *will*, they must *act*. In wielding a hundred thousand men the separate corps are almost distinct armies. Woe to the General who miscalculates the power of his subordinates! The brain may be clear, but the arm palsied; the will may decide quickly and clearly, but they who should concrete that will in heroic acts may fail. Gen. Grant saw at the outset the ability of C. F. Smith, and trusted him in spite of popular clamor. He would trust Sherman, though not a few persisted that he lacked every element of a General. Atlanta and Savannah are sufficient answers. He saw in the lamented McPherson the power to lead, and trusted him. "Give the best man in your army for the Shenandoah Valley," said Secretary Stanton. He gave him Phil. Sheridan, and the result is history.

III. *Clearness of judgment.* He does not become perplexed. His perceptive powers are remarkable and nothing confuses them. He reasons coolly in the most tumultuous excitement, and failing at one point he turns to another, and can scarcely be baffled. With this, is fertile invention never at want for expedients to carry out a purpose.

IV. *Genius.* This is manifested in daring conception. An illustration is stated in Mr. Washburne's speech on the Lieutenant-General bill in Congress; referring to the operations below Vicksburg:

"The expedition by Grenada, the opening of the canal, and the opening of the bayous had not succeeded; the country saw all the attempts to flank that stronghold likely to prove abortive, and there was great anxiety. *But with unshaken confidence in himself General Grant pursued the even tenor of his way*, and with entire reliance upon his success in the plan finally adopted, and which could not be undertaken until the river and bayous should sufficiently recede to enable them to move. Then, sir, was seen that bold and daring conception which I say is without parallel in all military history. It was to send his army and his transportation by land on the Lousiana side from Milliken's Bend to a point below Vicksburg, and then run the frowning batteries of that rebel Gibraltar, with its hundreds of guns, with his transports, and thus enable him to cross the river below Vicksburg, and get on to the shores of the Mississippi. The country was startled at the success which attended the running of those batteries, by the frail Mississippi steamboats used as transports, and the rebels stood aghast when they saw seven or eight transports and all of Porter's gunboats below Vicksburg."

He never boasts of strategy, but his record shows brilliant movements, that could only have emanated from a daring and highly perceptive genius.

V. *Courage.* No one has intimated a lack of personal bravery, that dashing intrepidity which faces peril and without a tremor confronts danger. He is unmoved in peril, and composed in the melee of battle. But above this he has that higher courage which springs from principle, which is immovable in defeat as in victory, which moves steadily to the accomplishment of results, undeterred by the combinations of his enemies.

VI. *Power over men.* His troops believe in him. He impresses, quiet and modest as he is, his confidence upon others. Mighty is faith. He enters into the soldier's life and the soldier's feelings. He shares his rations, endures his privations, hears his complaints, redresses his wrongs. He indulges no hollow display. Mr. Washburne says: "When he left his head-quarters at 'Smith's plantation' below Vicksburg, to enter on that great campaign, he did not take with him the trappings and paraphernalia so common to many military men. As all depended on quickness of movement, and as it was important to be encumbered with as little baggage as possible, he set an example to all under him. He took with him neither a horse, nor an orderly, nor a servant, nor a camp-chest, nor an overcoat, nor a blanket, nor even a clean shirt. His entire baggage for six days—I was with him at that time—*was a tooth-brush.* He fared like the commonest soldier in his command, partaking of his rations and sleeping on the ground with no covering but the canopy of heaven. How could such a General fail to inspire confidence in an army, and to lead it to victory and to glory?"

Such are some of the characteristics of the Lieutenant-General of the American armies. There are other things which may be said, but the time is not yet. The problems of the leader are not wholly solved. His past is his country's. His place in history is however to be decided by events yet unaccomplished.

This much was due to the achieved results of the life and public services of the gallant Colonel of the 21st Regiment of Ills. Vols. Those services, said Mr. Washburne, "Are familiar as household words. Look at what this man has done for his country, for humanity, for civilization—this modest, unpretending General. * * * He has fought more battles, and won more victories than any man living; he has captured more prisoners and taken more guns than any General of modern times. To us in the great valley of the West he has rendered a service in opening our great channel of communication to the ocean so that the great father of waters now goes 'unvexed to the sea.' Sir, when his blue legions crowned the crest at Vicksburg, and the hosts of rebeldom laid their arms at the feet of this great conqueror, the rebel Confederacy was cut in twain and the back-bone of the rebellion broken."

CHAPTER XI.

THE CUMBERLAND AND TENNESSEE.

Reconnoissance—Preparations—Battle of Millford—Mt. Zion—Silver Creek—Columbus—Grant's Brigading Order—Other Forces—Fort Henry—Gunboats—Land Forces—Tennessee Mud—Instructions—The Bombardment—The White Flag—The Surrender—Tighlman and Foote—The Commodore in the Pulpit—Escape of the Camp—Rebels—Iron-clads—Muster of Forces for Donelson—Donelson—Defences—Rebel Commanders—Waiting for the Transports—The Gunboats—They Retire—Grimes on Admiral Foote—Seige—A Sortie—A Terrible Contest—Gen. Smith's Charge—White Flag—Floyd and Pillow—Correspondence—Unconditional Surrender—The Victory—Its Results—Stanton's Letter—Grant's Report—The Tides of War—Kentucky—McGoffin—Better and Truer Men—The Legislature—Gen. Anderson—Buckner's Attempt to Seize Louisville—Gen. Rosseau—Hegira—The Situation—Gen. Anderson Retires—"Crazy Sherman"—A "Bogus Convention"—"Council of Ten"—Broad Farce—A "Strong Ass"—Gen. Buell—Divisions—The Second—The Third—Rowlett's Station—Mill Springs—Defeat of Marshall—Mitchell's March on Bowling Green—Crossing Barren River—Occupation—On to Nashville—Its Occupancy—A Rebel Account—Mitchell's and Buell's Forces.

THE reconnoissance made under orders of General Grant convinced him that the rebel line along the Tennessee and Cumberland could be broken, those rivers opened, the evacuation of Columbus compelled, Nashville captured, and the enemy forced to make his base elsewhere than on those water lines. Preparations were made for a grand movement which was delayed a short time, awaiting the completion of some gunboats.

Meanwhile other stirring events were transpiring. Brigadier-General Pope had charge of Central Missouri, and on the 18th of December, 1861, fought a spirited and successful engagement at Millford, Mo., which resulted, according to Major-General Halleck's report, in taking "thirteen hundred prisoners including three Colonels, and seventeen captains, one thousand stand of arms, one thousand horses, sixty-five wagons and a large quantity of baggage, tents and supplies." General Prentiss had command in North Missouri, and a portion of his force had, on December 28th, a hotly contested fight with the enemy at Mount Zion, Boon county, dispersing and driving them. On the 8th of January, 1862, Major Torrence of the 1st Iowa Cavalry attacked and defeated a rebel force at Silver Creek, Missouri.

Columbus, Kentucky, is situated upon the Mississippi River, about twenty miles below Cairo. It was seized by General Polk, September 4th, and so fortified as to be termed the "Rebel Gibraltar." Naturally strong for defence, it was made almost impregnable by massive works and heavy guns. Of course it closed the Mississippi to navigation as effectually as though its waters had become solid rock. Its possession was indispensable to the Union armies, but it was to be taken by those tactics which since became so unpleasant at Chattanooga and Atlanta. The capture of Fort Henry and Fort Donelson was to uncover its rear, and compel its abandonment by the forces of General Polk. The gunboat fleet was being pressed to completion during the months of November, December and January, and thorough reconnoissances were made toward Columbus, some by water, and one in force by land, causing the Confederates to concentrate their forces for the defences of their Gibraltar.

General Grant had matured his plan for the campaign of the Tennessee and Cumberland, and it is to be remembered that his troops occupied the ports of Paducah and Smithfield at the mouth of those rivers. He issued the following order for brigading them:

"HEAD-QUARTERS, DISTRICT OF CAIRO,
"CAIRO, February 1, 1862.

"[*General Order No.* 5.]

"For temporary government, the forces of this military district will be divided and commanded as follows, to wit:

"The First Brigade will consist of the Eighth, Eighteenth, Twenty-seventh, Twenty-ninth, Thirtieth, and Thirty-first Regiments of Illinois Volunteers, Schwartz's and Dresser's batteries, and Stewart's, Dollin's, O'Harnett's, and Carmichael's cavalry. Colonel R. J. Oglesby, senior colonel of the brigade, commanding.

"The Second Brigade will consist of the Eleventh, Twentieth, Forty-fifth, and

Forty-eighth Illinois Infantry, Fourth Illinois Cavalry, Taylor's and McAllister's Artillery. (The latter with four siege-guns.) Colonel W. H. L. Wallace commanding.

"The First and Second Brigades will constitute the First Division of the District of Cairo, and will be commanded by Brigadier-General John A. McClernand.

"The Third Brigade will consist of the Eighth Wisconsin, Forty-ninth Illinois, Twenty-fifth Indiana, four companies of artillery, and such troops as are yet to arrive. Brigadier-General E. A. Paine commanding.

"The Fourth Brigade will be composed of the Tenth, Sixteenth, Twenty-second, and Thirty-third Illinois, and the Tenth Iowa Infantry; Houtaling's battery of Light Artillery, four companies of the Seventh and two companies of the First Illinois Cavalry. Colonel Morgan commanding.

"General E. A. Paine is assigned to the command of Cairo and Mound City, and Colonel Morgan to the command of Bird's Point.

"By order of U. S. GRANT, *Brig.-Gen. Commanding.*

"JOHN A. RAWLINS, *A. A.-G.*"

This order was published, and no pains taken to prevent its falling into the hands of the rebels, but it was *not* published that there were divisions organizing under Generals C. F. Smith and Lew. Wallace at Paducah and Smithland. Preparations were made for a combined land and naval attack upon Fort Henry, situated on the Tennessee River, near the Kentucky and Tennessee line. It stands on low ground, above high-water mark, just below a bend in the river, and at the head of a straight stretch of about two miles and commands the river for about that distance. It was a bastioned earth-work enclosing about two acres. It mounted seventeen guns including one ten-inch columbiad, throwing a roundshot of one hundred and twenty-eight pounds weight, one breech-loading rifle gun, carrying a sixty-pound elongated shot, twelve thirty-two pounders, one twenty-four pounder, rifled, and two twelve-pounder siege guns. Most of the guns were pivoted, and capable of being played in any direction. It was encompassed by a deep moat, and strongly garrisoned and deemed capable of resisting any assailing force, however formidable.

Late on Saturday night, February 1st, the gunboats St. Louis, Cincinnati, Carondolet, Essex, Tyler and Lexington, left Cairo and proceeded to the mouth of the Tennessee at Paducah, when they were joined by the Conestoga. The fleet was commanded by Commodore, later Rear-Admiral, A. H. Foote, as gallant a seaman as ever trod the quarter-deck, or sailed the deep. Strictly temperate, a God-fearing and God-loving man, he could be trusted with the lives of men and the honor of the flag anywhere. In 1856 he punished a gross insult offered our flag by the Chinese, by attacking and chastising with his three hundred seamen and twenty-two guns, a fort manned by twenty-two guns, and five thousand men. English and French naval officers expressed the warmest admiration for his gallantry. In preparing his Western fleet, his labors had been immense, and at last he took it into the conflict but partially prepared.

The land forces were conveyed from Cairo to Paducah on transports, and from them the whole fleet sailed up the Tennessee, swollen and muddy toward the fort. After suitable reconnoissance, the squadron was moved about four miles below the fort, where the troops landed and encamped for the night. A violent thunder storm burst upon them; the heavens were aglow with lightning and the rain fell in torrents, thoroughly soaking the clay so as to render the next morning's march laborious and difficult. The General commanding ordered the first division, General McClernand's, including the first and second brigades, to take a position on the roads from Fort Henry to Donelson and Dover, to prevent the reinforcement of the fort or the escape of its garrison, and to be in readiness to "charge and take Fort Henry by storm on the receipt of orders." The second division, commanded by General C. F. Smith, was to cross the river and move up the western shore, and occupy a hill overlooking the fort, which the enemy had begun to fortify, and then to send a portion of his force across the river and reinforce General McClernand. The gunboats were to shell the fort and drive the enemy from the guns. The Commodore urged the land forces to start in advance of the gunboats, and when he ascertained they would not, said pleasantly, but prophetically. "I will take the fort before you get there."

The two divisions set out as ordered. The first made every exertion to get up into position to intercept the retreat of the garrison, but the Tennessee mud was too deep. Over slippery hills and through tenacious swamps, the Illinois boys pressed eagerly forward, marching to the music of Foote's deep-mouthed artillery and the reply of the heavy guns from Fort Henry. Suddenly all was still, and the questions ran along the lines, "What does it mean? Is Foote beaten?" They were to learn that the majority of the boasting garrison had fled from their camp and that the remainder had surrendered. In addition to mud, McClernand was obstructed by outer lines of defense, made by felling the timber for several rods in breadth, until the piled trunks and mingled branches made a barrier truly difficult to scale.

The gunboats moved up slowly, firing moderately, until within one mile of the fort, when they opened fire in earnest. The deep thunder of the guns, and the shrieking of the hurtling shells, were echoed by the high hills through which the Tennessee makes its way. The iron hail struck the defenses and fell within them. The artillery of the fort replied, and while most of the balls rattled harmlessly against the mailed side of the vessels, one 24-pound shot pierced the Essex, penetrated the starboard boiler, and disabled it. Volley after volley was fired, more and more deadly became the iron hail, until flesh and blood could endure it no longer, and in one hour and twelve minutes a white flag was raised, which was hidden by the smoke. In a few moments, however, the Commodore discovered that the rebel flag was down and that firing from the fort had ceased.

Captain Phelps, of the Conestoga, with a party, went on shore in a boat and was met by Gen. Tighlman, who surrendered the fort and camp, with about sixty prisoners. The General was taken in the gig to the Commodore's ship and asked what terms would be granted.

"Unconditional surrender," said the old hero. "Well, sir, if I must surrender, it gives me pleasure to surrender to so brave an officer as you." "You do perfectly right to surrender, but I should not have surrendered to you on any condition," was the reply of the Commodore. "Why so? I do not understand you," said the General. "Because I was fully determined to capture the fort or go to the bottom."

Brave veteran, whose brilliant services were to last only long enough to cover the Western gun-boat fleet with imperishable glory, the answer was worthy his lion-hearted courage and supreme conscientiousness. One of the reporters who was at Cairo, relates the following incident: "On the Sabbath before the expedition sailed, the Commodore attended, as usual, worship in the Presbyterian Church. The minister did not make his appearance, and the audience became restless. The Commodore ascended the pulpit, read a portion of scripture, and offered a fervent prayer. He then delivered a brief address* from the text, 'Let not your heart be troubled; ye believe in God; believe also in me.' He specially

* A correspondent of the *Northwestern Christian Advocate*, writing under date of Cairo, Feb. 11, 1862, thus alludes to the address:

"Last Sabbath—the Sabbath after the victory—a congregation assembled at the Presbyterian Church in this place, but the minister expected did not come. As I passed up the street on my way to the Methodist Church, a Presbyterian brother hailed me and informed me of the state of the case, and requested me, if possible, to supply their lack of service. I promised to comply as soon as I could go to my quarters and return. In the meanwhile, the congregation, not seeing any minister present, became restless, and Commodore Foote, seeing the state of affairs, went into the pulpit and remarked, that rather than have such a large congregation disperse without any religious services, he would conduct them himself. On my return to the church, seeing a gentleman in the uniform of a commodore occupying the pulpit and reading from the Scriptures, I took a seat in the body of the church and concluded not to say a word. Unaware of the presence of any minister, the Commodore proceeded with the services. He read the sixth chapter of the Gospel of St. John, offered a brief, earnest prayer, read a hymn, and then, taking as a text the first verse of the chapter he had read, proceeded to address the congregation. The remarks were, like the prayer, brief and earnest, occupying about fifteen minutes time. There was no attempt at sermonizing, but I venture the assertion that few sermons delivered that day were more successful in the accomplishment of the true object of all sermons—the production of a good impression upon the minds of those who hear. Good sense and an honest unfaltering faith in the Word of God characterized all that was uttered. Among other things, the Commodore said that on the morning before he made the attack upon Fort Henry, he prayed and wrestled with God until he was confident of success. He felt that in speaking thus he was exposing himself to ridicule in certain quarters, but feeling, as he did, that we are dependent upon God, as individuals and as a nation, and that without his blessing we must ignominiously fail in the great work before us, he felt it his duty to thus give unpremeditated utterance to his honest convictions—he believed, and therefore spoke. The audience listened with deep and tearful attention, while the veteran Commodore spoke, in plain words and with unaffected earnestness, of our dependence upon God and the obligations we are under to recognize his supremacy in all our ways."

urged his fellow soldiers to constancy in duty and strong trust in the Redeemer. No wonder he was calm in peril and faithful in duty."

The completeness of the victory was marred only by the escape of the rebel force from the camp, which hastily retreated before the force under McClernand came up. The country hailed it, however, with gladness, and saw in it the new power which was henceforth to assert itself in war and to affect so profoundly the question of foreign intervention—iron-armored ships.

The gunboats under Capt. Phelps ascended the river and destroyed the bridge of the Ohio and Mississippi railroad, connecting Bowling Green, Memphis and Columbus, and steamed beyond it to Florence, Ala. Two rebel boats were chased so closely that they were blown up and abandoned by their owners; two steamers loaded with iron, for rebel use, were captured, and three were burned at Florence.

It was understood that Fort Donelson was next to be attacked, and the country waited in breathless suspense. General Grant ordered all available troops in his district to be sent to his command. On the 11th of February, reinforcements left Cairo under orders to join him on the Kentucky strip lying between the Cumberland and Tennessee. The right wing of Buell's army, under Gen. Crittenden, took steamers at Calhoun, on Green River, descended it to the Ohio, down the Ohio and up the Cumberland, where a juncture with Grant was effected. Troops were also sent from St. Louis and Cincinnati, until Grant found himself at the head of a large army, composed of the elite of Western troops. Illinois was well represented; it had present:

Infantry—7th, Col. Jno. Cook, acting Brigadier—Lieutant-Colonel Andrew J. Babcock, commanding; 8th, Col. Richard J. Oglesby, acting Brigadier—Lieut.-Col. Frank L. Rhodes, commanding; 9th, Col. Augustus Mersey; 10th, Col. James D. Morgan; 11th, Col. Thomas E. G. Ransom; 12th, Col. John McArthur; 16th, Col. Robert F. Smith; 18th, Col. Michael Lawler; 20th, Col. C. C. Marsh; 22d, Col. Henry Dougherty (wounded at Belmont)—Lieut.-Col. H. E. Hart, commanding; 27th, Nap. B. Buford; 28th, Col. Armory K. Johnson; 29th, Col. James S. Reardon; 30th, Col. Phil. B. Fouke (absent)—Lieut. Col. E. S. Dennis, commanding; 31st, Col. John A. Logan; 32d, Col. John Logan; 41st, Col. Isaac C. Pugh; 45th. Col. John E. Smith; 46th, Col. John A. Davis; 48th, Col. I. N. Haynie; 49th, Col. W. R. Morrison (wounded)—Lieut.-Col. Thos. G. Allen, commanding; 50th, Col. Moses M. Bane; 52d, Lieut.-Col. John S. Wilcox; 55th, Col. David Stuart; 57th, Col. S. D. Baldwin.

Cavalry Regiments—2d, Col. S. Noble; 3d, Col. E. A. Carr; 4th, Col. T. Lyle Dickey; 7th, Col. Wm. P. Kellogg.

Artillery Batteries—Schwartz's, Dresser's, Taylor's, McAllister's, Richardson's, Willard's, Buell's—in all 34 guns.

The fort was of great strength; the N. Y. *Times* thus described it:

"Fort Henry was thought to be almost a Gibraltar, but its strength is weakness when compared to that of Donelson. Along Dover, the Cumberland river runs nearly North. A half-mile or so below it makes a short bend to the west for some hundred yards and then turns again and pursues its natural course due north. In this bend, on the left bank of the river, and commanding it to the north, are two water-batteries, side by side, and nearly down to the water's edge.

"The main battery has nine guns, all looking straight down the river. The left-hand gun is a 10-inch Columbiad, the rest are 32-pounders. The other battery has three guns—the middle one a formidable rifled 64-Columbiad, the others 64-pound howitzers. All these guns are protected by breast-works of immense thickness, the tops of which are composed of coffee sacks filled with earth. Back of these batteries the shore rises with a pretty steep ascent, until it forms a hill whose top is pretty nearly or quite one hundred feet above the water. On the top of this hill is Fort Donelson, an irregular work, which encloses about one hundred acres. The only guns in the fort are four light siege guns, a 12-pound howitzer, two 24-pound guns, and one 64-pound howitzer. West of the fort, in the direction occupied by General Grant, and south, toward General McClernand's position, the country is a succession of hills. For several hundred yards around the fort the timber has all been cut down, so as to afford a fair sweep for the Confederate guns. Surrounding the whole fort and town, and distant from the former about a mile, is a trench for riflemen, which runs completely around from the river bank, above Dover, almost to a point near the river some distance below the water batteries. Directly west of the fort and within the rifle pit, are formidable abattis, which would render an advance from that direction almost an impossibility."

Within these works were some 20,000 of the fighting men of the Southwest—from Louisiana, Tennessee, Mississippi, Alabama and Kentucky, commanded by Floyd, Pillow, Buckner, and Bushrod R.

Johnson. Floyd, who had proved himself a thief and a perjurer, was here to prove himself a poltroon.

This fort, so strong by nature and art, General Grant and Commodore Foote determined to reduce; that entrenched force they meant to destroy or capture.

On the 12th of February, Gen. Grant began his march from Fort Henry to Fort Donelson, twelve miles, and at noon his troops were in the rear of the rebel batteries. Selecting a position about two miles from the outworks, they extended their lines in a semi-circle, enclosing the fort. This of course brought him into contact with rebel pickets and they moved forward with almost a constant skirmish.

Through Wednesday and Thursday the two divisions awaited the coming of the gunboats and transports with the troops to form the third division, and on Friday, the 14th, they arrived. There were now three divisions, commanded by Generals McClernand, C. F. Smith and Lew. Wallace. The Carondelet arrived on Thursday, and at once engaged the water batteries, receiving one shot through a port-hole, wounding eight men, and throwing one hundred and two shells into the enemy's works. The next day Commodore Foote moved his seven gunboats within range, the four iron-clads leading, the wooden ones following. Gradually they brought on the contest. They showered shell as hail-stones are sifted from the clouds. They came within one hundred and fifty yards of the water-batteries and were silencing them, and here, as at Fort Henry, it seemed the navy was destined to the honor of the capture, when a shot disabled the Louisville, by destroying its steering apparatus. Another shot disabled the flag-ship St. Louis, and both boats rolled in drifting helplessness. The fleet, almost victorious, was compelled to draw off. The Commodore, or Admiral, as we may now term him, was struck in the foot and wounded, and from that wound he never fully recovered.

Senator Grimes, of Iowa, in a speech in the U. S. Senate, said: "Though wounded himself, and his gunboats crippled, yet with the glory of the gallant combat on his brow, he indulged in no repinings, for his personal misfortunes or laudation of his successes; but like a true hero, he thought only of his men. In a letter written the morning after the battle, to a friend, he said: 'While I hope ever to rely on Him who controls all things, and to say from the heart, *Not unto us but unto thee, O Lord, belongs the glory*, yet I feel sadly at the result of our attack upon Fort Donelson. To see the brave officers and men, who say they will go wherever I will lead them, fall by my side, makes me feel sad to lead them almost to certain death.' "

The General Commanding now determined to invest the fort and reduce it by regular seige, or await the repair and co-operation of the gunboats, and accordingly made a change in the disposition of his men. But on the morning of the 15th, a sortie was made by the garrison, falling upon his extreme right in overpowering numbers, causing the Union troops to give way, and capturing two batteries. Reinforcements were brought up, and a terrible and bloody struggle followed resulting in recapturing the lost guns, with three exceptions. Reinforcements swarmed out of the fort, and again the wearied beseigers gave way, while their foe came on with wildest yells, flanking the Union forces, seeming to have victory within their grasp. Other loyal troops came up, but in the confusion friends fired on each other, and still they were pressed back.

The reports were handed to General Grant at his head-quarters, and, comparing them he is said to have remarked to one of his staff, "Good: we have them now exactly where we want them." He ordered General C. F. Smith to make an assault on the left of the line, and carry it, no matter at what sacrifice, and made dispositions on the right to recover the lost ground and gain a position in front from which his men could not be forced.

Smith led his men to the charge. They moved in grim silence, with no roll of fire-arms, and carried the position at the point of the bayonet, and the Stars and Stripes waved from the works, and through the smoke of the battle gleamed the triumphant stars of the Republic!

On the right General Wallace was pressing forward to regain what had been lost earlier in the day, and as the column advanced word was brought that Smith was within the intrenchments! The announcement was greeted with a ringing cheer, and up the hill went those men, with the Zouave regiments, 8th Missouri and 11th

Indiana in advance. No earthly power could stay them. The sullen, angry, beaten foemen were driven within their works; the day went down with our men in better position than before. Success had been won at fearful cost, but it *was* won. That night Floyd, true to his antecedents, *stole* away—the most worthless theft he ever made. He whiningly insisted that, in view of his relations to the Federal government, it would not do for him to be captured, and he surrendered the command to Pillow. This *hero* decided to accompany his *compatriot*, and turned over *his* authority to Buckner, who, with Bushrod Johnson, refused to desert his men. The two seniors, with a few chosen troops, made their way to a steamer and escaped.

Our brave men, with stiffening wounds, slept on their arms meaning, when daylight came, to enter the fort, but daylight found a flag of truce floating from the works. The following correspondence passed between the commanders:

GENERAL BUCKNER TO GENERAL GRANT.

"HEAD-QUARTERS, FORT DONELSON,
"February 16, 1862.

"SIR:—In consideration of all the circumstances governing the present situation of affairs at this station, I propose to the commanding officer of the Federal forces the appointment of commissioners to agree upon terms of capitulation of the forces and fort under my command, and in that view suggest an armistice until twelve o'clock to-day.

"I am, sir, very respectfully, your obedient servant,

"S. B. BUCKNER, Brig.-Gen. C. S. A.

"*To Brigadier-General Grant, commanding the United States forces near Fort Donelson.*

To the bearer of this dispatch General Buckner gave the following orders:

"HEAD-QUARTERS, FORT DONELSON.
"February 16, 1862.

"Major Cashy will take or send by an officer, to the nearest picket of the enemy the accompanying communication to General Grant, and request information of the point where future communication may reach him; also inform him that my headquarters will be, for the present, in Dover.

"S. B. BUCKNER, Brigadier-General.

"Have the white flag hoisted on Fort Donelson, not on the battery.

"S. B. BUCKNER, Brigadier-General.

The answer of General Grant was made at once, and has passed into immortality with the memorable sayings of brave and patriotic men.

"HEAD-QUARTERS, ARMY IN THE FIELD,
"Camp near Donelson, Feb. 16, 1862.

"*To General S. B. Buckner, Confederate Army:*

"Yours of this date, proposing an armistice and appointment of commissioners to settle terms of capitulation, is just received. *No terms, other than an unconditional and immediate surrender, can be accepted. I propose to move immediately upon your works.*

"I am, sir, very respectfully, your obedient servant,
"U. S. GRANT, Brig.-Gen. U. S. A., Commanding."

General Buckner was not pleased, but he saw no escape. The Federal troops were not to be disloged from their positions, and a few hours must bring the carnage of a resistless storming assault. He therefore wrote as follows:

"HEAD-QUARTERS, DOVER, TENNESSEE,
"February 16, 1862.

"*To Brig.-Gen. U. S. Grant, U. S. A.:*

"SIR:—The distribution of the forces under my command, incident to an unexpected change of commanders, and the overwhelming force under your command, compel me, notwithstanding the brilliant success of the Confederate arms yesterday, to accept the ungenerous and unchivalrous terms which you propose.

"I am, sir, your very obedient servant,
"S. B. BUCKNER, Brig.-Gen. C. S. A."

It was a magnificent victory. It gave the Union army nearly 15,000 prisoners of war; it gave it one hundred and forty-six guns, some of the largest caliber; it gave it a fort of almost fabulous strength; it broke the line of rebel defence; compelled the evacuation of Columbus and placed Nashville at the mercy of Federal bayonets. Grant and Foote desired immediately to "move upon its works," but General Halleck refused permission. As the telegraph flashed the news of the surrender the country was wild with excitement. Bells rang, bonfires blazed; strong men embraced each other on the streets and wept and shouted. Mr. Stanton, Secretary of War, said: "We may well rejoice at the recent victories, for they teach us that battles are to be now won, and by us, in the same and only manner that they were ever won by any people, or in any age, since the days of Joshua, by boldly pursuing and striking the foe. What, by the blessing of Providence, I conceive to be the true organization of victory and military combination, to end this war, was declared in a few words by Gen. Grant to Gen. Buckner, '*I propose to move immediately on your works.*'"

There were critics who "smelt the battle from afar," and piled condemnation on its chief, or "damned him with faint praise," but their criticisms little harmed the General who presented 15,000 prisoners of war and a hundred and forty-six cannon as the defence of his strategy.

The following are a few among the many incidents recited of the battle.

On Saturday, a desperate charge was made on one of the guns of Taylor's battery, served, among others, by Lieut. Heartt, of Chicago, and it was temporarily captured. Heartt seized a rope and sprang in among the captors and made it fast to the piece and all hands laid hold and drew off their "speaking trumpet" in triumph.

Another of the battery, who had received a wound in the leg, walked more than a mile to the hospital, had the ball extracted, and desired to go back, but was, of course, refused by the surgeon. "Come," said the artillerist, "put on some of your glue and let me go back."

One of McAllister's howitzer battery met a rebel cannonier, and said to him, "Halloo! where was your battery stationed?" The rebel pointed out the situation. "What! over there," said howitzer; "then you must have been the fellows who were popping us so yesterday. Did you see any little 24-pound shells over your way?" "Well, I guess we did, and plenty of them," and the two stood within the captured works and discussed the comparative merits of six-pound shot and twenty-four-pound shell, from a professional stand-point.

A youth from John A. Logan's Regiment (31st) received a musket-shot wound in the right thigh, passing through the intervening flesh and lodging in the left thigh. He went to the rear, and asked a surgeon to dress his wound at once, and say nothing about it to others, for he was going right back into the fight. The Doctor remonstrated, but the boy told him he had fired twenty-two rounds after receiving his wound, and could fire as many more after it was dressed. It was dressed and he went back, and disposed of his ammunition to the best advantage, and after two or three days came again to have his wound looked after, and continued in duty.

Young Bullard, of the 8th, was shot in the breast by a minie ball, bleeding internally as well as externally. He was carried to a hospital. When he knew he must die in a few hours he clung to life, but said to the lady who cared for him, "If I could only see my mother—if I could only see my mother—before I die, I would be better satisfied." Said she, "You die in a good cause—you die for your country." "Yes," said the brave boy as the gleam of glory lighted up his wan face; "Yes, I am proud to die for my country."

A New Englander, reading the three following dispatches, wrote the accompanying lines:

"McClernand's division, composed of Oglesby's, Wallace's, and McArthur's brigades, suffered terribly. They were composed of the Eighth, Ninth, Eleventh, Eighteenth, Twentieth, Twenty-first, Thirtieth, Thirty-first, Forty-fifth, Forty-eighth and Forty-ninth Regiments."

"The Eighth, Eighteenth, Twentieth, and Thirty-first Illinois regiments occupied a position above the fort."

"The four Illinois regiments held their ground full three hours. Nearly one-third had been killed and wounded. Yet the balance stood firm."

"O gales that dash th' Atlantic's swell
Along our rocky shores!
Whose thunders diapasons well
New England's glad hurrahs—

"Bear to the prairies of the West
The echoes of our joy,
The prayer that springs in every breast:
'God bless thee—Illinois!'

"Oh! awful hours, when grape and shell
Tore through th' unflinching line;
'Stand firm, remove the men who fell,
Close up, and wait the sign.'

"It came at last, 'Now, lads, the steel;'
The rushing hosts deploy;
'Charge, boys!'—the broken traitors reel—
Huzza for Illinois!

"In vain thy rampart, Donelson,
The living torrent bars;
It leaps the wall, the fort is won,
Up go the Stripes and Stars.

"Thy proudest mother's eyelids fill,
As dares her gallant boy,
And Plymouth Rock and Bunker Hill
Yearn to thee—Illinois."

GENERAL GRANT'S REPORT.

"HEAD-QUARTERS, ARMY IN THE FIELD,
"Fort Donelson, February 16, 1862.

"*Gen. G. W. Cullum, Chief of Staff, Department of Missouri:*

"GENERAL:—I am pleased to announce to you the unconditional surrender, this morning, of Fort Donelson, with twelve to fifteen thousand prisoners, at least forty pieces of artillery, and a large amount of stores, horses, mules, and other public property.

"I left Fort Henry on the 12th instant, with a force of about fifteen thousand men, divided into two divisions, under the command of Generals McClernand and Smith. Six regiments were sent around by water the day before, convoyed by a gunboat, or rather started one day later than one of the gunboats, with instructions not to pass it.

"The troops made the march in good order, the head of the column arriving within two miles of the fort at twelve o'clock M. At this point the enemy's pickets were met and driven in.

"The fortifications of the enemy were from this point gradually approached and surrounded, with occasional skirmishing on the line. The following day, owing to the non-arrival of the gunboats and reinforcements sent by water, no attack was made; but the investment was extended on the flanks of the enemy, and drawn closer to his works, with skirmishing all day. The evening of the 13th, the gunboats and reinforcements arrived. On the 14th, a gallant attack was made by Flag-Officer Foote upon the enemy's works with his fleet. The engagement lasted probably one hour and a half, and bid fair to result favorably to the cause of the Union, when two unlucky shots disabled two of the armored gunboats, so that they were carried back by the current. The remaining two were very much disabled also, having received a number of heavy shots about the pilot-house and other parts of the vessels. After these mishaps, I concluded to make the investment of Fort Donelson as perfect as possible, and partially fortify and await repairs to the gunboats.

This plan was frustrated, however, by the enemy making a most vigorous attack upon our right wing, commanded by General J. A. McClernand, with a portion of the force under General Lew. Wallace. The enemy were repelled after a closely contested battle of several hours, in which our loss was heavy. The officers, and particularly field officers, suffered out of proportion. I have not the means yet of determining our loss even approximately, but it cannot fall far short of one thousand two hundred killed, wounded, and missing. Of the latter, I understand through General Buckner, about two hundred and fifty were taken prisoners. I shall retain enough of the enemy to exchange for them, as they were immediately shipped off and not left for recapture.

"About the close of this action the ammunition in the cartridge-boxes gave out, which, with the loss of many of the field officers, produced great confusion in the ranks. Seeing that the enemy did not take advantage of this fact, I ordered a charge upon the left—enemy's right—with the division under General C. F. Smith, which was most brilliantly executed, and gave to our arms full assurance of victory. The battle lasted until dark, giving us possession of part of their intrenchments. An attack was ordered upon their other flank, after the charge of General Smith was commenced, by the divisions under Generals McClernand and Wallace, which, notwithstanding the hours of exposure to a heavy fire in the forepart of the day, was gallantly made, and the enemy further repulsed. At the points thus gained, night having come on, all the troops encamped for the night, feeling that a complete victory would crown their labors at an early hour in the morning. This morning, at an early hour, General S. B. Buckner sent a message to our camp under a flag of truce, proposing an armistice, &c. A copy of the correspondence which ensued is herewith accompanied.

"I cannot mention individuals who specially distinguished themselves, but leave that to division and brigade officers, whose reports will be forwarded as soon as received. To division commanders, however, Generals McClernand, Smith, and Wallace, I must do the justice to say that each of them was with his command in the midst of danger, and was always ready to execute all orders, no matter what the exposure to himself.

"At the hour the attack was made on General McClernand's com mand, I was absent, having received a note from Flag-Officer Foote, requesting me to go and see him, he being unable to call.

"My personal staff—Col. J. D. Webster, Chief of Staff; Colonel J. Riggin, Jr., Volunteer Aid; Captain J. A. Rawlins, A. A. General; Captains C. B. Lagow and W. S. Hillyer, Aids, and Lieutenant-Colonel V. B. McPherson, Chief Engineer—all are deserving of personal mention for their gallantry and services.

"For full details and reports and particulars, reference is made to the reports of the Engineer, Medical Director and commanders of brigades and divisions, to follow.

"I am, General, very respectfully,

"Your obedient servant,

"U. S. Grant, Brigadier-General."

It is proper to answer the question, *What part had Illinois troops in this glory?* In giving in part the answer, there is no disposition to undervalue the heroic achievements of the men of sister States, but simply to speak of Illinois troops from the specific character of this work.

The First Brigade of the First Division was commanded by Colonel W. H. L. Wallace, a gentleman, a brave soldier, a noble leader. It was composed of Lieutenant-Colonel Ransom's (the 11th), Col. Marsh's (the 20th), Col. Jno. E. Smith's (the 45th), Col. Haynie's (the 48th), and Col. Dickey's (the 4th Cavalry) regiments with Captain Taylor's and McAllister's batteries. Col. Haynie's was detached with the 17th and 49th, 3d Brigade, on the 13th, to make an assault on the enemy's middle redoubt, Colonel Haynie, as senior, leading. They marched straight at their works, delivering their fire as coolly as on parade ground. Headley, who criticises the order, says: "They mounted with the coolness of veterans the steep hight on which the redoubt stood. The enemy, screened behind their embankments, poured in a terrible fire of musketry, still the brave Illinoisans steadily advanced. But at this critical juncture it was found that the line was not long enough to envelop the works, and the 45th was ordered to their support. While these movements were carried out, the enemy threw forward strong reinforcements of men and field artillery, which swept the advancing line with murderous effect. But onward pressed those undaunted regiments, leaving their dead and wounded strewing the slope, till they came to the foot of the works where a fringe of long poles and brushwood presented a tangled wall of jagged points, through which no troops under heaven could force their way in such fire. Braver officers never led men to death, but they found they had been sent to accomplish an impossible task and gave the reluctant order to fall back. Col. Morrison commanding the 49th was wounded, and many brave officers fell in this attempt, which is certainly open to criticism." Again and again was this brigade, in whole or in part in the deadly fray, and nobly was upborne the dignity and glory of the State. It reported a loss of 123 killed, 461 wounded and 103 missing.

The first brigade, 1st division, was commanded by Col. Richard J. Oglesby, and included the 8th Ill., Lieutenant-Colonel Rhoades; the 18th, Col. Lawler, the 29th, Col. Reardon; 30th, Lieutenant-Colonel Dennis; 31st, Col. John A. Logan with Swartz's and Dresser's batteries, Stewart's, Dollins', O'Harnett's and Carmichael's cavalry. The 49th was with the third brigade. On Friday these regiments endured a fearful assault and waged terrific battle. The 45th and 12th met the plunging charge of not less than three thousand men. After a time they withdrew, the 8th and 9th coming to their relief. The *Louisville Journal* narrates this incident: "A private in the 9th Illinois was shot in the arm. He went back a short distance to the hospital, had the wound dressed, and returned to his place. Soon a bullet struck his thigh and prostrated him, passing through the fleshy part. His comrades offered to take him to the hospital. 'No,' said he, 'I think I can get along alone.' With his musket for a crutch and the air around him filled with the whistling of bullets, he hobbled to find the surgeon. After his wound was dressed, and he received some refreshment, he said, 'I feel pretty well. I think I will go and join my comrades again. He was soon actively engaged as a skirmisher. As he was stooping to take aim a shot entered his neck, and passed lengthwise through his body, while at the same instant four or five other balls struck his head, and he fell lifeless. The name of such a hero should have been preserved." Oglesby led his brigade wherever there were blows to be given or perils to be braved. Says Mr. Stevenson, author of "Indiana's roll of honor," "Upon Oglesby's division of this (McClernand's) division was first hurled the rebel thunder. Under fire from several batteries, an immense mass of infantry charged upon our lines. Sudden as was the attack, the gallant troops of Illinois were ready to meet it. Into the enemy's teeth they poured a steady and deadly fire. Fresh masses of the enemy advanced, but Taylor's battery, and two of McAllister's guns met them with a storm of grape and shell, and the brigade charging, actually drove four times their number back to their intrenchments. The struggle was hand to hand. The bayonets, the bowie knife, the butt-end of the musket were freely used. McArthur's carried itself nobly. In Col. Cook's brigade, the 7th and 50th participated in General Smith's division. Scarcely a regiment, company or battery from the State failed to distinguish itself, and if there was failure it was from want of opportunity."

Other details will be given in the sketches of officers and regiments, but if Illinois' troops had only participated in the single battle of Donelson only, the record of the State had been made forever glorious.

The tides of war were drifting towards "Pittsburg Landing," where the humble church edifice bearing the name of Shiloh, the Peacemaker, which was to give name to one of the most sanguinary battles. Converging toward that spot were some of the troops of this State, coming via Munfordsville, Mill Spring and Nashville, directly through Kentucky. The insolent reply of Governor McGoffin to the call upon Kentucky for its contingent has been given, and it must be conceded that he did what he could to throw that State into the hands of the Southern conspirators. Fortunately he was not as courageous as he was disloyal. His audacity would not serve as executor of his wishes. Some leading men of the State urged that neutrality was its safest, its only policy. The keen eyes of Holt, and Rosseau, and Breckinridge—not the foresworn traitor who had sunk from the dignified station of Vice-President and Senator in Congress, to that of a traitorous marplot, but the noble old Doctor in Divinity who subsequently said in Baltimore that the nation *must be cemented by the blood of traitors*—saw differently; saw that neutrality was secession, and urged a vigorous policy; urged that troops be raised; that Kentucky should be treated as an imperiled State in the Union. The Legislature broke ground with the Governor; passed loyal resolves over his veto, and called General Robt. Anderson, of Fort Sumter fame, to lead its men, he having been assigned to duty in that district. Colonel T. L. Crittenden, son of the venerable Senator, was placed in command of the State Guard. September 17, 1861, Buckner seized the upward bound passenger train, on the Louisville and Nashville Railroad, embarked his troops, cut the telegraph wires, and started for the occupation of Louisville. Everything moved favorably for him until he neared Elizabethtown, when the train was thrown from the track by the displacement of a rail. Some noble Union man, hearing of Buckner's design, had sought to thwart his purpose and admirably succeeded. This disaster was fatal to the expedition. Night came on before the train was again ready for motion, and then Buckner's heart failed him. He was fearful his coming was known, and that inhospitable prepations were made to welcome him. Meantime Louisville was resting in terrible security, utterly ignorant of the fate which threatened and so nearly overwhelmed it. As the time drew near for the arrival of the Nashville passenger train, the citizens as usual gathered at the depot. The train failed to appear. * * * An attempt to ascertain its whereabouts by telegraph, disclosed the fact that the wires were cut. Suspicion of danger was at once aroused, and rumors of invasion, devastation and ruin, circulated like wild-fire through the city. The most intense excitement prevailed everywhere. Union citizens, fearful of rebel vengeance, crossed the Ohio River into Indiana, or prepared to do so, at the first intimation of actual danger.* When this was known, Kentucky awoke to the fact that war was upon it, and not to be diverted by the missives and jeremiads of the oily Beriah McGoffin.

Rosseau moved with a portion of troops toward the seat of danger and occupied Muldraugh's Hill. Troops from Ohio, Indiana and Illinois were freely offered. Dr. Breckinridge declares that the coming forward of the regiments from those States saved Kentucky. Buckner, John C. Breckinridge, W. B. Preston and other promi-

*Dodge's *Old Second Division.*

nent secessionists went South. John Morgan left Lexington at the head of a company of mounted men. General W. T. Sherman was placed in command of the Federal forces on the line of the L. & N. R. R. General G. H. Thomas was in command at Camp Dick Robinson in the central part of the State. The counsel of Fremont had been neglected and the rebels had seized Bowling Green and were making of it a ·Sebastopol. General Zollicoffer was before Thomas with a large force. Humphrey Marshall the oleaginous Falstaff of the Confederacy was at Big Sandy, and the Confederacy was moving vigorously to secure the State.

Physically worn out, General Anderson proved unfit for his position, and was succeeded by General W. T. Sherman. This officer said 200,000 men were needed to save the State and drive back the Southern armies, and was laughed at as "crazy Sherman," and yet his antics were to give the country Atlanta and Savannah! Had he been heeded, all those border hordes could have been crushed, and the armies of Johnson, Beauregard, Polk, and so on through the catalogue, could have been destroyed. But it was still the days of dress parade on the Potomac.

Meanwhile, a convention, claiming to be the sovereignty of Kentucky, met at Russelville, in November, voted a secession ordinance, elected a Governor and *ten* Councilmen—evidently imagining themselves on the Adriatic—gave them, with the Governor, power to make laws, ordain treaties, enter into State compacts, and to appoint State officers, and consummated the farce by choosing Senators and Representatives to the Confederate Congress, who were, of course, permitted to hold seats, and who gravely mouthed platitudes about their constituents! Their Governor, G. M. Johnson, was solemnly inaugurated; on the 11th of December the rebel Congress formally received the State into the Confederacy!

It is difficult to read those proceedings, so clearly lawless, so transparently devoid of even revolutionary authority, without the sense of the ludicrous, but at the time, they made much trouble. Two governments, two codes of laws, two conflicting authorities—obedience to either being punishable as treason by the other! The early neutrality was supreme folly, and its consequences were upon the State, which was as "a strong ass crouching between two burdens."

November 15th, General Don Carlos Buell arrived at Louisville and took command of the new Department of the Ohio, embracing the States of Ohio, Michigan, Indiana, Tennessee, and that part of Kentucky east of the Cumberland River. He was to oppose a powerful foe from Cumberland Gap to Nashville.

In the 2d Division of his army, commanded by Brig.-Gen. A. McCook, and in the 5th Brigade, was the 34th Illinois, commanded by Col. E. N. Kirk, and in the 3d Division, commanded by General O. M. Mitchell, was Turchin's 19th Zouaves, and Mahalotzy's 24th, the gallant Hecker Regiment. The first named, marched in December, toward Munfordsville, on the north bank of Green River. The railroad bridge had been destroyed, but Willich's artisans provided one which answered all purposes. On the 17th was fought the battle of Rowlett's Station (or Munfordsville), the rebel force commanded by Gen. Hindman and numbering about 2,000, with Col. Terry's Texan Rangers (cavalry), Phifer's cavalry, and four pieces of artillery. Col. Willich's Indiana regiment, the 32d, fought for, and retained, possession of the field. January 19th, General Thomas engaged and defeated the enemy under the rebel Crittenden and Zollicoffer, capturing fourteen pieces of artillery, with large quantities of war *materiël.* This victory turned the right of the rebel offensive line. Humphrey Marshall was beaten at Prestonburg by Garfield and sent flying to Abingdon, Va.

And now came intelligence of the success of Grant and Foote at Henry, and movements on Bowling Green and Nashville began. General Mitchell was ordered to move from Munfordsville on to Bowling Green, and did so on the 13th of Feb., 1862, with Turchin's brigade, consisting of the 37th Indiana, 18th Ohio, 19th and 24th Illinois, Loomis', Edgerton's, and Simonson's batteries and three companies of Kennett's cavalry in advance. The march of forty miles was made in twenty-eight hours, over a frozen, rocky road, obstructed by felled trees. Reaching the Barren River the advance marched rapidly to a ferry on which about fifty infantry could be crossed at once, and in silence and secrecy, were "set over." A writer in the *Providence Journal* says: "The repairs of an old wherry were completed and we crossed the river, protected by artillery. The Nineteenth and Twenty-fourth, Hecker's Illinois, crossed first. We pushed on slowly to within a mile or two of the town, where we halted, waiting for the rest. But the boys, getting almost frozen, declared they would rather be shot than frozen, and we then pushed on, seeing no enemy, but rather fearing a ruse, and that they would return upon us in large force. But no enemy appeared and we were soon surrounding the fires, some of which had been burning for several days." General Buell, in General Orders, thanked Mitchell's Division for its gallantry and celerity.

It has been stated that Grant and Foote desired to move upon Nashville from Fort Donelson, but Gen. Halleck declined consent. That officer doubtless had his reasons, but they have not been divulged. The delay lost some millions of property in destroyed stores, and kept open a door for the retreat of the enemy from Bowling Green.

General Mitchell conveyed his division as promptly as possible, and with the blue flag of the 19th Illinois in advance, took possession of Edgefield, opposite Nashville, which was formally surrendered the next day.

As an episode in the monotony of reading, the account below, written by a rebel, will serve a good purpose. There is in it a good-natured confession, and sad drollery:

"The fight at Fort Donelson, on the 13th, 14th and 15th of February, was of intense concern to us, and each day's work down there wound up with the statement that the fight would be renewed to-morrow. The fears that the fall of Fort Henry were calculated to inspire, had been well-nigh dispelled by the way Fort Donelson was holding out. It was better located, and stronger in men and guns. Pillow, Floyd and Buckner were there. Pillow had said, 'Let come what might, he never would surrender the place,' and Nashville felt that we could not afford to lose that battle. Saturday's work was glorious. Our citizens shouted over it. Many were saying: 'I never liked Pillow, but forgive him now—he is the man for the occasion.' A sober, modest citizen, an old line Whig and Ex-Governor, was heard to say, Saturday afternoon, on being asked how the fight went on: 'First-rate; Pillow is giving them ——, and rubbing it in.'

"The dispatches closed on Saturday as they had for three successive days before—'The enemy are expecting large reinforcements,' but we slept soundly, and expected to have great news on the morrow. About 9 o'clock Sunday morning I rode out into the country seven or eight miles, and leaving the turnpike, dined with a friend in one of the quiet and luxurious farmer-homes of Middle Tennessee. Returning leisurely, I struck the pike about 4 P. M., and as everybody I had met in the morning had asked me the latest news from the city, I asked the first man I met, 'Any news?'—prepared to hear only of victory.

"'News! What's the last you've heard?'

"'Last night's dispatches.'

"'None since? The latest out, and plenty of it. Fort Donelson has fallen, and Nashville is surrendered! They say the white flag is waving now on the capitol, and the gunboats will be up before sundown.'

"I thought he was hoaxing me, but quickened my pace. The next morning confirmed it all and more. I saw there was literally a cloud of witnesses pouring along the turnpike leading to Franklin. Convalescent soldiers, quitting the hospitals, were waddling along with their scanty baggage. Travelers in groups and squads had left the hotels, carrying carpet-bags and satchels, and saddle-bags in hand. The family of the owner of the omnibus line were rolling out in those vehicles. Double and one-horse carriages were full of living freight. On reaching the toll-gate, on the top of the hill overlooking Nashville, I strained my eyes to see the white flag on the capitol. The tall flag-staff was naked. There was no flag of any sort on it.

"Passing down Broad-street by the Nashville and Decatur road, the first man I saw was Gov. Harris, about to leave on a special train, with the Legislature and archives of the State. The town was in commotion. Over the wire bridge that spans the Cumberland, Gen. Johnston's army were passing, taking the direction of the Murfreesboro turnpike. The train of wagons and soldiers reached out of sight, and did not get over that night. The sight of a withdrawing or retreating army is very disheartening.

"My residence is in Edgefield, a little village separated from Nashville by the Cumberland River. For several days Gen. Johnston's headquarters had been established on that side of the river, and near me. The lady with whom he and his staff took their meals is my neighbor and friend, and tells me that the General opened the news to her at table, in these words:

'"Madam, I take you to be a person of firmness, and trust your neighbors are. Don't be alarmed. Last night, my last dispatch, up to 12 o'clock, was favorable, and I lay down expecting a great victory to-day; but this morning, at 4 o'clock, I was waked by a courier, with the news that our forces at Fort Donelson were surrounded and must surrender. They are not made of steel. Our soldiers have fought as bravely as ever soldiers did; but they cannot hold out day after day, against fresh forces and such odds. I cannot make men. Stay at home. Tell all your friends for me to stay at home. I cannot make a fight before Nashville, and, for the good of the city, shall retire. I know Gen. Buell well. He is a gentleman, and will not suffer any violence to peaceable citizens, or disturb private property.'

"It might have been well if the General had issued a proclamation. He and staff crossed the bridge that night at 11 o'clock. Gen. Breckinridge followed, and your correspondent followed soon after.

"The question has often been asked: 'Why didn't the people of Nashville make a stand? What! give up their city without striking a blow?'

"The people were astonished and indignant at the way they were handed over to the enemy's mercy and occupation. But what could they do? When generals, and armed and drilled soldiers give up and retire, what can unarmed and undisciplined citizens do before a foe advancing by land and water?

"'Throw brickbats at them,' said one. Indeed! that would be well enough, if the enemy would deal in the same missiles.

"The bones of Gen. Jackson, the defender of New Orleans, must have turned in his grave at the Hermitage, a few miles away, at such a surrender.

"A few months before, on urgent call, every man who had a rifle or double-barrel gun, had brought it forward and given it up for army service. Not fifty serviceable guns could our citizens have mustered. No, not even pikes, though they had just enrolled themselves and resolved to have them made, and if Gen. Johnston made a stand before the city, they were resolved to stand with him. Such of them as were not willing to be surrendered to the uncovenanted mercies of Lincolndom, with the prospect of having the oath tendered them or the bastile, followed the retiring army.

"After taking my family as far as Decatur, I returned to Nashville on Wednesday. The stores were closed and bolted; the streets deserted, save by a guard here and there, and a press-gang taking up every man they could find, and sending him to load government pork into barges, upon which it was being taken up the river, and put out of the enemy's way. Had a stand been made before the city, or even a feint of a stand, no doubt all the government stores could have been removed safely. As it is, vast amounts have been thrown away, wasted, given out, both from the quartermaster's and commissary's departments. At one time the doors were thrown open to whomsoever would, under the impression that they had better let the poor have these provisions than the enemy, who was expected instantly. A friend said he saw quantities of meat lying on the roadside, where persons, having overloaded their carts, had thrown it out. Barrels of flour, sacks of coffee, tierces of lard and meat, were rolled into private houses and back yards, with hundreds of boxes of candles, bolts of cloth, etc. Afterwards this order was countermanded, as the enemy was not *exactly* at the door, and a guard placed over the stores, and an effort made to get them off by railroad and boat. Private carriages, hacks and carts, were stopped in the street and pressed into service, and some of my friends had to get their baggage to the station in wheel-barrows. Advantage was taken of the confusion and dismay of the hour for private injustice and irresponsible oppression. The selfishness developed in such a crisis is humiliating. * * * * * *

"The opinion prevails there that Nashville will be burnt, first or last—if not when we leave it, then when we drive the enemy out of it. For Tennesseeans are resolved that the enemy shall not rest on their soil. Gen. Floyd and staff left Thursday morning, and it was understood that Capt. John H. Morgan, with his company, would retire slowly, as the enemy in force entered. The Louisiana cavalry, Col. Scott, were near Franklin, on their way to the vicinity of Nashville, where they will act as scouts and hold the enemy closely in bounds.

"As far out as Brentwood, Franklin and Columbia, some people are leaving their homes and sending off their slaves. Others, deeply committed Southerners, stand and risk the consequences. They look for inconveniences and heavy losses, staying or going.

"In reply to the question often asked, whether any Union element has been developed by these events: There was always some of this element in Nashville, but in very inconsiderable proportion to the population. Let Unionists show their hands and heads now; it is hoped they will. We have friends enough left to watch them; and when the tide of war rolls back, the country will finally be purged of them, for they will have to leave with the Lincoln army.

"The great mass of Tennesseeans, especially Middle and West, are sound to the core, and thoroughly aroused for the first time. They chafe under the humiliation and disgrace of the surrender of their capital. Those that can will move their families out of the reach of immediate harm, and return to face the foe on a hundred fields. The great battles of the war are to be fought in the West. This is but the beginning. The people realize now what is at stake, and they will measure out wealth and blood without stint."

From Nashville the division of Mitchell made its way through Tennessee into Alabama, while Gen. Buell was to co-operate with Gen. Grant in the terrible field of Shiloh.

CHAPTER XII.

COLUMBUS: ISLAND No. 10: PEA RIDGE.

Federal Strategy—Results—Columbus—Halleck's Dispatch—Gunboats—"That Flag"—Rebel Strength—General Pope—A Cavalry Skirmish—Capture of New Madrid—Morgan's Gallant Brigade—Evacuation—Pope's Dispatch—"Island No. 10"—Naval Bombardment—Buford's Dash on Union City—Col. Robert's Daring Exploit—Running Batteries—The Surrender—General Presentment—General Pope's Command—Battle of Pea Ridge—Incidents—Major-General Curtis—Brigadier-General Eugene A. Carr—General Julius White—Colonel Greusel—Colonel Post.

THE demonstrations upon Fort Henry and Fort Donelson were really part of the siege of Columbus and Island No. 10, the rebel strongholds, which were relied upon to permanently close the Mississippi River. The Federal strategy pierced the enemy's center, isolated and turned his wings, by the brilliant movements on the Tennessee and Cumberland. Bowling Green and Nashville were the first fruits, and then Columbus and the Island. So much had been said and believed in reference to the strength of Columbus, that a long siege was anticipated, and therefore the country was surprised above measure when it was announced on the 3d of March, 1862, that it had fallen without a struggle!

General Halleck's dispatch of March 4th, modestly said:

"The cavalry from Paducah marched into Columbus, yesterday, at 6 P. M., driving before them the enemy's rear-guard. The flag of the Union is flying over the boasted Gibraltar of the West. Finding himself completely turned on both sides of the Mississippi, the enemy was obliged to evacuate or surrender. Large quantities of artillery and stores were captured."

The naval force under Admiral Foote consisted of six gunboats and four mortar-boats. There were four transports conveying Col. Buford's 27th Ill., a battalion of the 54th and 74th Ohio and 55th

Ill., six companies, of the 55th, commanded by Major Sanger, forming a brigade under Brigader-General Sherman. The expedition moved cautiously to Lucas Bend from which the bluffs of Columbus were visible in the morning light. The fleet was made ready for action, and then doubts arose if there was anything to attack. An examination showed the batteries in position, but where was the foe? On the right-hand side of the river a man was seen in a cornfield, retreating. A boat was sent to him, and he gave the information that Columbus was deserted by the rebels, who had carried with them arms and ammunition as far as possible, and had burnt most of the town. A flag was seen which puzzled the officers of the expedition, for it wore too many stripes for Secessia, and yet had not the appearance of the national bunting. On landing a party the facts were ascertained. On the previous afternoon a detachment of the 2d Illinois' Cavalry, numbering about 600 men, under charge of Lieutenant-Colonel Hogg, had arrived from Paducah and taken possession. The strange flag was one improvised from pieces of calico.

General Polk had with him not less than 20,000 men, and they were within fortifications of great strength, but he deemed it necessary to give up their stronghold and retire without a blow. A singular evil-fortune has attended every effort of the rebels to hold posts on the Mississippi from Paducah to New Orleans. Among the relics was Pillow's great chain, costing forty thousand dollars, designed to obstruct the river against Yankee gunboats. One end was anchored in the bluff, and the other stretching across the river, but alas! it was destined to serve no better purpose than the famous ditch excavated aforetime, within the breast-work by order of the venerable warrior-sage! The chain was broken!

General Pope, with a formidable land force was operating against the enemy. On the 28th of February he moved toward New Madrid, encamping the first night, twelve miles from Commerce. The second day there was a cavalry skirmish near Sykestown, the Union force being under Captain Webster, 7th Ill., resulting in the capture of three small rifled cannon and four rebel prisoners. Approaching New Madrid the command was formed in line of battle including the 7th Illinois Cavalry, and 26th Infantry. The rebel gunboats from Columbus were before the town, and threw shot and shell in the vicinity of the Union forces though with trifling effect, and in the afternoon General Pope gave the order to fall back. He sent a request to Cairo for four siege guns, twenty-four-pounders, and placed General Plummer, 11th Mo., with a battery, three regiments of infantry and three companies of cavalry at Mount Pleasant, *twelve miles below*, thus blockading the river and cutting off supplies and reinforcements. The enemy brought reinforcements from Island No. 10 until he had concentrated some nine thousand infantry, besides artillery, and nine gunboats under Commodore Hollins. The rebel land forces were under Generals McCown, Stewart and Gantt. On the 12th the seige guns arrived from Cairo, at sunset, and that night were placed in a battery within eight hundred yards of the rebel main works, so as to command it and the river above it, and within thirty-six hours from their reception at Cairo, they were thundering against the defences of McCown.

General Pope says in his official report:

"One brigade, consisting of the 10th and 16th Illinois, under Colonel Morgan of the 10th, was detailed to cover the construction of the battery, and to work in the trenches. They were supported by Stanley's division, consisting of the 27th, 39th, 43d and 63d Ohio. Capt. Mower of the 1st U. S. Infantry, with companies A and H of his regiment, was placed in charge of the siege guns.

"The enemy's pickets and grand guards were driven in by Col. Morgan from the ground selected for the battery, without firing a shot, although the enemy fired several volleys of musketry. The work was prosecuted in silence, and with the utmost rapidity until at 3 o'clock, A. M., two small redoubts, connected by a curtain and mounting the four heavy guns which had been sent me, were completed, together with rifle-pits in front and on the flanks, for two regiments of infantry. Our batteries opened as soon as the day dawned and were replied to in front and on the flanks by the whole of the enemy's heavy artillery on land and water."

Through the day the furious cannonading continued. General Paine, supported by General Palmer's division, was ordered to make a demonstration against the rebel entrenchments on the left of our forces, and did so, driving the pickets, his skirmishers forcing their way close to the main ditch.

That night, in a blinding thunder-storm, the rebel forces evacuated in haste, "leaving their dead unburied, their suppers untouched, standing on the tables, candles burning in the tents, and every other evidence of a disgraceful panic."—[Pope's report.] Thirty-three pieces of artillery, with magazines of fixed ammunition, several thousand stand of small arms, hundreds of boxes of cartridges, tents for an army of ten thousand men, with horses, mules, &c., were captured. The fall of New Madrid would "compel the evacuation of Island No. 10, as it could neither be reinforced nor supplied from below." General Pope made the following official notice:

"The 10th and 16th Illinois, commanded respectively by Colonels Morgan and J. R. Smith, were detailed as guards to the proposed trenches and to aid in constructing them. They marched from camp at sunset on the 12th inst., and drove in the pickets and grand guards of the enemy as they were ordered, at shouldered arms, without returning a shot; covered the front of the intrenching parties, and occupied the trenches and rifle pits during the whole day and night of the 13th, under furious and incessant cannonading from sixty pieces of heavy artillery. At the earnest request of their Colonels their regimental flags were kept flying over our trenches, though they offered a conspicuous mark to the enemy. *The coolness, courage and cheerfulness of these troops, exposed for two nights and a day to the furious fire of the enemy at short range, and to the severe storm which raged during the whole night of the thirteenth are beyond all praise*, and delighted and astonished every officer who witnessed it."

Here, as well as elsewhere, wherever brought into conflict, the gallant soldiers of Illinois met danger without flinching, and maintained the honor of the country and the flag.

"Island No. 10" next engrossed public attention. It is situated in the corner of the bend of the Mississippi River, which touches the border of Tennessee, and is *above* though *southwest* of New Madrid; it is 240 miles from St. Louis, and 950 from New Orleans. By the river, it is forty-five miles south of Columbus and about twenty-six from Hickman. The fortifications consisted of eleven earthworks, with seventy heavy cannon, varying from thirty-two to hundred pounders. The operations of General Pope were part of the campaign against this formidable Island, considered by the Confederate officers as of the highest importance to the new line of defence held by them, for on the ability to hold it depended the safety of Memphis and the entire lower Mississippi. The left of this line rested on the Mississippi, the center between Jackson, Tenn., and Corinth, Miss., and the right between Florence and Decatur.

On the 15th of March, Admiral Foote, with several gunboats and part of the mortar fleet left Hickman for the island, and on the next day the bombardment began. On the 18th General Pope's batteries at New Madrid were attacked by the rebel gunboats, but repulsed them. In order to completely isolate the island and cut off retreat it was necessary to throw a portion of Pope's army across the Mississippi River to the Tennessee shore. At the suggestion of Gen. Schuyler Hamilton, a channel was made by Col. Bissel's engineer regiment, twelve miles in length, and six of them through heavy timber requiring to be cut off four feet below the surface of the water. The labor expended upon this work was immense and while it was progressing the bombardment continued.

During the siege Col. Buford, of the 27th, and Col. Roberts, of the 42d Illinois, performed two of those daring acts which make up the romance of war. On the morning of March 31st, Col. Buford taking his own regiment, the 42d Illinois, and 400 hardy Scandinavians of the 15th Wisconsin, Col. Heg, with two companies 2d Ill. cavalry and a battery, proceeded toward Union City by forced marches and surprised a large body of rebels, cavalry and infantry, under Clay King, a notorious desperado. The Union forces entered the town at full speed and the astonished rebels, panic-stricken, fled in all directions. About twenty were killed and one hundred captured, with 200 horses and a large lot of army stores, 500 stand of arms, several officers' swords and flags, and all without the loss of one Union soldier.

Scarcely returned, Col. Roberts was bent on another dash. Col. Buford was ordered to make a reconnoissance, and he selected his Union City associate for the work. On the night of April 1st, Col. Roberts, with forty picked men of his own regiment, took boat from the gunboat Benton, and with muffled oars, made for the island and crept cautiously along the bank. Owing to the violence of the storm and the thick darkness, they passed the bend unperceived, until within a few rods of the upper battery, and then a flash of lightning revealed to the sentinels some dark object approaching the island. They fired at random, the shots passing quite near the boats, but providentially doing no harm. The sentinels fell back to their tents, which were pitched some distance from the battery on a dry ridge, evidently believing the entire Lincoln army was on them. The boats made no answer, but steadily pulled for shore. In two or three minutes they touched the slope of the earthworks, and in less than as many more, the brave lads were over the parapet and among the guns. In less than three minutes all of them were spiked after the most approved and artistic style. There were six of them, two sixty-fours, three eighties, and one of them a superb nine-inch pivot gun, with cushion lock, had the honor of receiving Col. Robert's special attention. This was said to be the "Lady Davis," a boasted and noisy piece, from these, or other considerations, named for the wife of Jefferson Davis. A few moments and all were again on board, rowing through the boiling current and cimmerian darkness for the shelter of the Benton. It was bravely, nobly done.

The beneficial results of this were seen when, on the night of the 3d, the *Carondelet*, having protected her bulwarks with hay, etc., set out upon the hardy mission of running the blockade and going below to Gen. Pope. Had that battery been in condition, the daring boat had been inevitably sunk, but she laughed defiantly at the shower from small arms that pattered about her. She reported to Gen. Pope, and within a few days silenced eleven batteries in the twelve miles between Point Pleasant and New Madrid. The *Pittsburg* followed on the night of the 6th, and the fate of the Island was sealed. On the morning of the 7th, the transports were brought through the canal into the river, and while the division of Col. Paine was embarking, the gun-boats run down the river and silenced the battery. The passage of the river was completed at midnight. As soon as the loyal troops began to cross, the enemy began to evacuate the Island and his batteries along the Kentucky shore. The main-land force retreated disgracefully. Yet four generals, six colonels, with the corresponding number of subordinate officers, with about 5,000 men, one hundred and twenty-five cannon, eleven batteries with vast quantities of small arms and stores fell into our hands. When the forces crossed the river, the advance was led by Gen. Paine.

Thus closed another epoch of the war and the country again breathed more freely.

A paper lying upon the table where these lines are written, dated the 9th of April, says:

"From all accounts the impending battle near Corinth will be the most important of any that has been fought during the war. The fact that the Confederates are drawing their troops from all quarters to the North part of Mississippi and Alabama, where they intend to fall upon the Union advance under Grant is palpable. Beauregard is doubtless directing the effort at concentration. Bragg has already brought up his force from Pensacola, abandoning the siege of Fort Pickens; Van Dorn and Sterling Price are hurrying forward from Western Arkansas; even Virginia is being stripped of rebel soldiers to swell the grand army of the West. The intent evidently is to fall upon our Tennessee army with an immense force gathered from all quarters, and repeat the lessons of Wilson's Creek and Lexington."

This shows the public presentiment in reference to the storm which burst in awful terribleness upon the banks of the Tennessee River on the morning of April 6, 1862, where all was so nearly lost, and yet so bravely won.

Before narrating the events of that terrible field, we must follow a portion of our troops who have been in the thunders of battle under the lead of Curtis, Sigel, Asboth and Davis, where again Iowa, Missouri, Indiana and Illinois were to win imperishable renown.

Gen. S. R. Curtis was in command of "the army of the Southwest," confronted by Price with a superior and augmenting force, and early in March he saw a battle was inevitable. His army was divided into four divisions, commanded, in order, by Generals Sigel, Asboth, Davis and Col. Carr.

Gen. Curtis had been in pursuit of Price, and his winter campaign—from January 20th to March 1, 1862—had been one of much severity and positive hardship, his men skirmishing as they traveled; but he had steadily driven Price until he had chased his force across the Arkansas line, but there the rebel chieftain was reinforced by Van Dorn and McCulloch, increasing this army to more than 30,000 men, of whom Van Dorn assumed chief command, and determined to give the Federal General battle, not doubting but he could turn upon him and crush him by overwhelming superiority of numbers. Gen. Curtis reported his forces in February as 12,095, with fifty pieces of artillery, including four mountain howitzers. Curtis' divisions were separated. He selected Sugar Creek as the most favorable battle-ground to meet

Van Dorn, and dispatched orders for the concentration of his entire force, which, on the 4th of March was located as follows: First and second divisions under Sigel, were four miles southwest of Bentonville; the third, under Gen. Davis, had moved and taken its position at Sugar Creek, while Carr's, the fourth, was at Cross Hollows. Sigel set out at once, on the 6th of March, to obey the order to concentrate, but was compelled to fight his way, a strong force attempting to cut him off. All the divisions being in, the General commanding gave orders to prepare for battle on the morning of the 7th.

It came, and with it the battle-shock in all its terribleness. The right wing of Curtis was worsted, but his left had been successful, and the rebel Generals McCulloch and McIntosh were slain, but the night after the weary day of battle, came with no cheerful prophecy to the Federals. They lay down cold, chilly, without fires, for want of which they suffered, but which could not be kindled with safety. The enemy, during the night, effected a junction of all his forces on the ground held by his successful left wing, intending, with morning, to crush the Federal army by the tactics of massing his forces and beating his enemy in detail. The rising sun brought a renewal of the fight. The Federal troops were skillfully handled. The artillery was so placed as to pour concentrated and almost uninterrupted fire upon the Confederates. The artillery management of Gen. Sigel was most skillful, and not a few openly expressed the opinion that the deliverance of the army was due to him. At length victory crowned the arms of the Union and the foe retreated.

The victory was dearly bought, for the division reports showed a loss in killed, wounded and missing of 1,351. It is not the province of this work to enter controversies which have grown out of the three day's battle of Pea Ridge. There was gallant fighting and a brilliant victory, and in that victory all had a share from the General commanding down to the drummer boy. Of the Illinois troops, the 35th, Col. G. A. Smith, 36th, Col. Greusel, 37th, Col. Julius White, the 59th, Major Post, 3d, cavalry, Col. Carr, a battallion of the 15th cavalry, Capt. Jenks commanding, and Davidson's Peoria battery were in the action and acquitted themselves as elsewhere, bravely. A drummer-boy, Day Ellmore, of the 36th, threw aside his drum, seized a musket and fought in line through the entire battle. McCulloch was killed by Peter Pelican, of the same regiment.

Before going to the grand gathering of our State troops at the plain of Shiloh, some brief notice of officers who have figured in the actions thus far will not be inappropriate.

MAJOR-GENERAL JOHN POPE.

He was born in Kaskaskia, Illinois, March 12, 1823. His father was Hon. Nathaniel Pope, territorial delegate in Congress from Illinois, and district judge. In 1838, John entered the Military Academy at West Point and graduated in 1842, and was commissioned a brevet 2d Lieutenant in the corps of topographical engineers. In the Mexican war he was in General Taylor's army and received his commission as 1st Lieutenant for gallant conduct at Monterey, and for bravery at Buena Vista, was made captain by brevet, his commission being dated February 23, 1846. In 1849 he was in command of the Minnesota exploring expedition, and was entrusted with an expedition to test the practicability of boring Artesian wells on the great Staked Plain which stretches in terrible aridity and sterility between Texas and New Mexico. It is conceded that the experiment yielded more romance than water. In 1853, he had command of one of the Pacific Railroad surveying companies. From 1854 to1859 he spent in the exploration of the Rocky Mountains, and while in this service, received the actual rank of captain in the Topographical Engineering corps. He participated to some extent with the Republicans in the contest of 1860, and having, in a public lecture delivered in Cincinnati, dealt somewhat severely with Mr. Buchanan, the venerable Chief-Magistrate was offended, and the captain was court-martialed, but Mr. Holt had the good sense to see that the President was making himself more than ever ridiculous, and the prosecution was abandoned. He was one of the escort chosen to conduct Mr. Lincoln to Washington.

When the war came he was still captain. When the call was made for four hundred thousand men he was appointed Brigadier-General of volunteers, with commission dating from May 17, 1861, and appointed to a command in Missouri. He was made a Brigadier in the regular army, July 14, 1862, and Major-General of volunteers, March 21, 1862.

In his command in North Missouri he manifested much vigor and ability in checking guerrillas, protecting railways, &c. He broke up predatory bands, hunted them to their places of concealment, and caused a wholesome terror of law and order as interpreted by Federal bayonets to fall upon them. He conducted a successful expedition to Blackwater, where a sharp blow was delivered, numerous rebel prisoners taken and the rebel force dispersed.

How well he did at Commerce, New Madrid and Island No. 10, this chapter has declared. Moving upon Fort Pillow, Gen. Halleck stopped him, sent him to Pittsburgh Landing, and he had charge of a division on Halleck's left. While engaged in the pursuit of Beauregard, he was summoned to Washington to assume command of the Federal forces in the Shenandoah Valley, with Banks, Fremont, and McDowel as subordinates. Here it was his ill-fortune to issue an address which was doubtless well-intended and patriotic, but not modest, and which seemed arrogant and boastful. It was rather the inflated style of the neophyte than the calm dignity of the master, rather the exuberant boasting of the militia Colonel to whom gilt-buttons, eagles, blue and brass, sword and scabbard were intoxicating novelties, rather than the sober dignity of the regular veteran to whom the odor of "villainous saltpeter" is more familiar than that of rose-water.

As was to be expected he gave offence. The newspapers criticised, and masters in rhetoric exhibited his address as a fine specimen of pyrotechnic English. General Fremont regarded the appointment as an affront and resigned his command, being unwilling to serve as General Pope's subordinate.

He fought the battle of Cedar Mountain, fought bravely and claimed a victory, but after all was compelled to find the lines of retreat. He claimed it as a decided success. It is true that Bank's command fought long and nobly, and the enemy retired across the river a few miles toward Gordonsville, but there was no substantial triumph. On the 18th and 19th of August General Pope retired behind the North Fork of the Rappahannock.

His command of the "Army of Virginia" was far from a pleasant one to him. He was active, and could he have had co-operation such as a commanding General should have had, the result would probably have been very different. It may be that when calmer days come, when the smoke of recent events and recent controversies shall have lifted, and men see clearly, that it will be said "Gen. Pope's plans were not visionary, but if the men had been brought him he had a right to ask, and the co-operation been given him which as a commander and a fellow soldier he had the right to demand, the battles of the Antietam and the Wilderness might have been spared."

Under his command were also fought the battles near the Rappahannock and Kettle River, the second battle of Manassas, Groveton and Chantilly. The reverses of the earlier battles threw the country into sadness and brought gloom upon the brave and loyal North. At Chantilly the enemy was driven, but the advantage was gained with the loss of the brave, knightly Kearney, and the gallant Stephens.

Divisions reigned among high Federal officers. Jealousy was one of the household gods of the epauletts of the Potomac. Pope, Burnside, Hooker, each was to be sacrificed, and months of sorrow and blood were to pass,before in Grant and Meade, men should be found of sufficient strength to resist these baleful influences.

Relieved from the command of the army of Virginia at his own suggestion, he was assigned to the Department of the Northwest, including Wisconsin, Iowa and Minnesota, and has had charge of the Indian war, though not personally in the field. Brave, daring, skilful, it seems that a busier field should be found for such a man.

His services may come before us again as we tread the war-path, but this much may be added: General Pope is believed by many of his native State to have the elements of a most successful leader, and to have been sacrificed to jealousy or something worse, by men not so thoroughly in earnest as himself.

GENERAL JULIUS WHITE.

Julius White, son of Lemuel and Emily White, was born at Cazenovia, in the State of New York, September 29, 1816. When the battle of Bull Run was fought, July 22, 1861, Mr. White resided at Chicago, Illinois, and held the honorable and lucrative office of Collector of Customs. He promptly determined to enter the army, and the next day applied to the Secretary of War, and obtained authority to raise a regiment of infantry—the 37th Illinois—to serve for three years or during the war.

This regiment was mustered into the service of the United States on the 18th of September, 1861. Mr. White having been commissioned Colonel, proceeded to Missouri under the orders of Major-General Fremont, was assigned to the Division commanded by Brigadier-General John Pope and accompanied the expedition under General Fremont to Southwestern Missouri, in October, 1861—returned to Otterville, Mo., under the command of Major-General D. Hunter, in November, and remained in winter-quarters, at that post, till January 25, 1862.

In December, 1861, Colonel White was assigned to the command of the 2d Brigade, 3d Division of the army of the Southwest, consisting of his own regiment, the 37th Illinois, the 59th Illinois, and Davidson's Peoria Battery. On the 25th of January, the division under command of Brigadier-General J. C. Davis, marched to Lebanon, Mo., there joining the forces under Major-General Curtis in the pursuit of Price.

The enemy evacuated Springfield and retreated into Arkansas, closely followed by the forces under General Curtis. After being reinforced by Ben. McCulloch, came the battle of Pea Ridge.

The 2d Brigade, Colonel White's command, held a position against the attack of McCulloch's entire force for three-quarters of an hour unsupported, during which time the loss of the brigade in killed and wounded was nearly equal to one-fourth its strength.

On being reinforced by the first brigade, the enemy was driven in great confusion from the field, with the loss among their killed of Generals McCulloch and McIntosh.

The official reports of Brigadier-General Davis and Major-Gen. Curtis, commended the conduct of Colonel White and his command for their bravery and perseverance in this action. The Colonel having been disabled by fracture of the leg, received a leave of absence for thirty days, commencing in the latter part of March, which was subsequently extended thirty days, he being unfit for duty at the expiration of the original term.

On rejoining his regiment he was placed in command of a district comprising several counties in the extreme Southwestern part of Missouri. While in this position he started an expedition into Arkansas, and at Fayetteville captured five rebel officers, and eighty enlisted men, who were engaged in enforcing the conscription of men for the rebel army. The expedition suffered no loss.

Col. White was promoted to Brigadier-General of Volunteers to rank from June 9, 1862, and ordered to report for duty to Major-General Fremont, commanding the Mountain Department in Virginia. That department was, however, immediately merged in the command of Major-General John Pope, known as the army of Virginia, and Gen. White was assigned to the command of a detached brigade of the First Corps, stationed at Winchester, Va. This command was assumed by him, on the 28th day of July, 1862, and held until September 1st, when he was ordered by the General-in-chief to evacuate Winchester and retire to Harper's Ferry. During the occupation of Winchester frequent skirmishes were had with the enemy, with inconsiderable results.

The official report of Major-General Pope contains the following:

"Brigadier-General Julius White with one brigade was in the beginning of the campaign placed in command at Winchester. He was selected for that position because I felt entire confidence in his courage and ability, and during the whole of his service there he performed his duty with the utmost efficiency, and relieved me entirely from any apprehension concerning that region of country."

On reaching Harper's Ferry, September 3, 1862, General White was directed by Major-General Wool, who commanded that department, to turn over his brigade to Colonel Miles, commanding the post, and proceed to, and take command at Martinsburg, Va.

While stationed at that place the enemy's cavalry known as Ashby's regiment, attacked General White's out-posts and were defeated with the loss of twenty-five killed, over fifty wounded, and forty-one prisoners with their horses and arms. For this engagement he received from the Hon. Secretary of War the following dispatch by telegraph:

"Your success this afternoon is very gratifying, and highly creditable to you. Every man must fight as if the safety of the country depended upon his individual exertions. (Signed) E. M. STANTON, Sec'y of War."

On the 10th of September, Stonewall Jackson approached Martinsburg with an overwhelming force, whereupon the place was evacuated and Gen. White with his troops retired to Harper's Ferry. That place was immediately invested by the enemy, and capitulated after four day's siege. On his arrival General White declined to deprive Col. Miles of the command of the post solely on account of superior rank, in-as-much as Col. Miles was familiar with the topography of the place and vicinity and especially because Major-General Wool had in so marked a manner expressed his preference that the Colonel should remain in command. Gen. White volunteered to serve under Colonel Miles, and was assigned to the command of Bolivar Hights. During the siege an attack by the rebel General A. P. Hill on that position was repulsed.

The surrender took place on the 15th of September, and was subsequently made the subject of investigation by a military commission, of which Major-General D. Hunter was President. The report of this commission among other things contains the following:

"Brigadier-General Julius White merits its commendation. He appears from the evidence to have acted with decided courage and capability" (See General Order A. G. O. 183, series of 1862).

In January, 1863, the troops captured at Harper's Ferry were exchanged. Gen. White, who had received leave of absence in November, 1862, "till exchanged," applied immediately for orders, and was directed to report to Maj.-Gen. Wright, commanding the Department of the Ohio, for duty, and was assigned to the command of the Eastern District of Kentucky, a mountainous region, which was overrun by guerrillas. This command was assumed in the latter part of January, 1863. During the six months that ensued Gen. White and his forces were constantly employed in ridding the district of these bands. More than five hundred were killed or captured in small parties during the time. An attack by the rebel Gen. Humphrey Marshall on Louisa, Ky., was repulsed in March.

In June he moved with his troops up the Sandy River, and dividing his force at Pikeville, Ky., into three columns, led the central one in a demonstration upon the salt works, near Abingdon, Va., and sent a detachment on each side under Col. Cameron, of the

65th Ill. infantry, and Major Brown, of the 10th Ky. cavalry, respectively, to the Tug Ford, of the Sandy River, and to Gladesville, Va. The latter place was stormed at daylight on the 6th of July by Major Brown, killing twenty-one of the enemy, and wounding many. Candill, a rebel Colonel, with nineteen other officers, and ninety-nine enlisted men were captured. Colonel Cameron had a running fight with the enemy, killing three and capturing twenty. The enemy directly in front of the central column decamped in the night and retreated to their entrenchments at the salt works, sixty miles distant from Pikeville. The objects of the expedition having been attained, it returned to Louisa, Ky., its total loss being nine wounded, none mortally.

In August, 1863, Gen. White was assigned to command of a brigade of cavalry in the Cavalry Division of the 23d Army Corps. Shortly afterward the command of the 2d Division of that Corps was given to him in consequence of the sickness of Brig.-Gen. Manson, who had been assigned to it.

This Division, consisting of eight regiments of infantry, three batteries of artillery and a detachment of cavalry, marched from Columbia, Ky., as a part of the force under Maj.-Gen. Burnside for East Tennessee, constituting the right wing, and starting from a point sixty miles west of the main body, joined it near the Emory River in Tennessee.

The march was a toilsome one. In crossing the Cumberland Mountains it became necessary to employ from fifty to eighty men to each wagon, and piece of artillery, in order to ascend the hights. In this way the entire train of two hundred and forty wagons, besides the artillery, was moved ten miles in one day, in order that the junction with the main body at the time indicated in General White's orders might be accomplished. On communicating with Maj.-Gen. Hartsuff, commanding the Corps, from Jamestown, Tenn., the latter expressed himself in the following language among other things, by letter:

"You have done wonderfully well, and are a day and a half ahead of all other troops of this army. You will await further orders where you are."

Gen. White's command was stationed at London, on the Tennessee River most of the time for the next two and a half months, during which it was not engaged with the enemy except in some inconsiderable skirmishes.

On November 13, 1863, Gen. Longstreet, of the rebel army crossed a part of his forces over the Tennessee River at a point six miles below London. Maj.-Gen. Burnside directed the retirement of the troops at London in the direction of Knoxville, but on reaching Lennis' Station the order was countermanded and Gen. White's command ordered forward, supported by a part of the 9th Army Corps. The enemy was attacked and driven back to his bridge. Repeated charges were made by Gen. White's command, resulting in each instance in dislodging the enemy from his positions. The 13th Kentucky infantry, comprising less than three hundred men, losing about sixty in killed and wounded in one of these assaults. Gen. White was ordered to assault the bridge during the night, supported by Ferrero's Division of the 9th Corps. The night proving exceedingly dark and stormy, the order for the attack was countermanded by Gen. Burnside, and on the following morning the entire force took up the line of march for Knoxville, with Gen. White's command as rear guard. The enemy immediately following and attacking on the rear and left flank.

Owing to the exhaustion of the horses and the very bad state of the roads, one caisson was abandoned at the foot of a hill where the ground was very unfavorable for fighting.

The enemy were repulsed with heavy loss at the summit of the hill, where he made a furious attack. The pursuit was kept up by him, and light skirmishing was constant. On the next day, Nov. 15th, on approaching Campbell's Station, the junction of the roads leading from Knoxville to London and Kingston respectively, the enemy attacked in great force and vigorously from both roads, on which he was approaching. Gen. White's command was ordered into line of battle, the 9th Corps and the cavalry passing to the rear and forming to support him. Two brigades of the 9th Corps were advanced to positions, respectively on the right and left of the line established by him. The enemy advanced in three lines but was repulsed in two general and one partial attacks. The position was held from 12 o'clock M. till dark, when the retreat was continued, and Knoxville reached the next morning.

The losses of Gen. White's command were less than two hundred in killed, wounded and missing. That of the enemy unknown, as he occupied the ground as fast as Gen. Burnside retired from it.

For the part taken in these engagements Gen. White received for himself and his command, the official commendation of his Corps commander, Brig.-Gen. Manson, as well as frequent verbal approval from Maj.-Gen. Burnside.

During the siege of Knoxville which continued seventeen days, viz., from Nov. 16 to Dec. 4, 1863, he was in command of a work known as Fort Huntington Smith, situated on the right center of the line of entrenchments. His artillery was on several occasions engaged with the enemy's batteries, and the line of skirmishers was almost continually fighting, but no assault was made on that part of the line.

On the raising of the siege his command was, with the remainder of the forces, ordered in pursuit of the enemy, and remained in position at and about Blains' Cross Roads, Tenn., for about four weeks thereafter.

On the 22d day of December, Brig.-Gen. Manson was relieved of the command of the Corps by Brig.-Gen. Cox, by order of Major-General Foster, then in command of the Department. Gen. Manson being the ranking officer was then assigned to the command of the 2d Division.

On being relieved Gen. White, with the concurrence of the Corps and Department commanders, availed himself of a leave of absence for thirty days, (which had been in his possession several weeks). On his way north he was seized with violent illness, and was confined to the house during the entire remaining term of his leave.

On recovering he was ordered to duty at Springfield, Illinois, in command of the general rendezvous for drafted men and volunteers in that State, where he remained until June, 1864, when he was ordered to report for duty to Major-General Meade, commanding the Army of the Potomac, and assigned to the 9th Army Corps under General Burnside. At the request of the latter, he was appointed Chief of Staff and served in that capacity till July. He participated in the battle of July 30th, was assigned to the command of the 1st Division, 9th Corps, July, and with the Division participated in two general engagements for the possession of the Weldon Railroad, August 19th and 21st, 1864, defeating and driving the right of the enemy's line from the field on the 19th, capturing seventy prisoners and over five hundred stand of small arms thrown away by the enemy in his flight.

Subsequently, prostrating and protracted illness compelled Gen. White to tender his resignation which was accepted and he returned to private life.

BRIGADIER GENERAL EUGENE A. CARR.

Col. Carr, of the 3d Illinois cavalry, commanded the Fourth Division of Curtis' army, in the battle of Pea Ridge. He was born in Erie Co., New York, March 30, 1830. His father, Clark M. Carr, removed to Galesburg in 1848, and this State has, since that period, been the General's home. He entered the military academy at West Point at the age of sixteen, and upon his graduation was appointed brevet 2d Lieut. of Mounted Riflemen. He knew it not at that time, but his lot was cast where he was being fitted for the work assigned him, the maintenance of the authority and majesty of the Government.

His first service, and a brief one, was at Jefferson Barracks, Mo., whence he was ordered to Fort Laramie, and was, for several years, actively engaged in suppressing Indian hostilities on the Western plains. One of his frequent skirmishes was in 1854, near the Diabole Mountain, in which as he was pressing upon the rear of a flying expedition, that, in spite of personal illness, he had chased nearly one hundred miles, he was severely wounded by an arrow in the abdomen, and until now he has never recovered fully from its effects. He continued the pursuit, routing the Indians, and inflicting upon them a heavy loss of their bravest warriors. For this he received promotion into the 1st regiment of cavalry.

He was to have another lesson, and to learn the peculiar amiability of slavery and its disregard for law and order. In 1857 he was transferred to Kansas, and assigned as aid to Governor Robert J. Walker. He was there through the Border-Ruffian war, for such it may almost be called, the early stage of the present gigantic strife. In the autumn he accompanied Governor Walker to Washington, and in the spring following (1858) served under Colonel (subsequently General) Sumner in the Utah expedition, where he was privileged by seeing the political workings of the twin abominations of Slavery and Polygamy.

He was promoted Captain in the regular army and placed in command at Fort Washita, and repeatedly warned the War Department of the treasonable movements of the hoary-traitor Twiggs and his younger associates in villainy, but Floyd, the distributor of arms, and, more lately, the retiring hero of Donelson, was in power. He could not order their arrest! Under orders, the Captain moved with his command through the Indian nation to Fort Leavenworth, and thence toward Springfield, Mo., and took part in the bloody battle of Wilson's Creek, and covered Sigel's retreat.

He received permission of the War Department to accept the command of an Illinois regiment of cavalry, two of which were tendered him, and after a short time in camp, took the field at the head of the 3d.

Joining General Curtis, he commanded the Fourth Division and sustained the brunt of the combined assaults of the rebel hordes. Terribly the tide of battle rolled about the handful he commanded. Scarcely 2,500 were with him, and yet the loss of his division was 700 men, more than half the entire loss. He was thrice wounded in the first day's battle, but bandaging his shattered wrist and wearing it in a sling, he continued with his command until victory was gained.

For gallant conduct on this occasion he was promoted Brigadier-General of Volunteers, March 7, 1862, and we may meet him again.

COL. NICHOLAS GREUSEL, Jr.

In the battle of Pea Ridge, Col. Greusel of the 36th Illinois, commanded a brigade, and a brief sketch of him may well follow this first notice of public service. He was the seventh of eight children. His father was a soldier under Murat, and was made sergeant on the field for bravery. The son was trained to understand the duties and appreciate the honor of the soldier. His father's family reached New York June 2, 1833, and the children were notified that each must find a place for himself, which Nicholas was fortunate enough to do in the family of Mrs. N. Fish, mother of Hon. Hamilton Fish, Ex-Governor of New York. Subsequently he was in the employ of Gen. Belnap. In 1835, his father removed to Detroit, Michigan, where the son entered the service of Rice & Co., lumber dealers, where he continued until the breaking out of the war with Mexico. His early teaching had led him into a military organization, "The Scott Guards," of which he had command, and he received the appointment of Captain of Co. G. 1st Regiment Michigan Volunteers, Col. T. B. W. Stockton. This regiment was brigaded with one from Alabama, and four companies of Georgia troops, and did good service from the gates of Vera Cruz to Orizaba. Peace came and the regiment was mustered out of service July 27, 1848, and at sunrise on the 28th the Captain was at his old post in the lumber-yard, as though there had been no bloody episode with marches and weary battles. His scrupulous care for the cleanliness of his command called out, subsequently to his return, expressions of public admiration and official approval.

Captain Greusel continued in the lumber business two years, and was subsequently alderman of the city of Detroit, and was appointed Inspector-General of Lumber for the State of Michigan. Col. Wilson says of him:

"In 1857, Capt. Greusel went to Chicago, Ill., where he entered the service of the Chicago, Burlington and Quincy Railroad Company, and remained in their employ until the bombardment of Fort Sumter, April 13, 1861. On Monday, April 15th, he enrolled himself as a private of a company in the city of Aurora, and arrived at Springfield on Friday, with one hundred and forty-eight privates, and was elected Captain of the same. On the 24th of April, the first regiment was formed—the 7th. John Cook was elected Colonel, and Capt. Greusel Major. The Major being the only man who had ever done military duty, the task of drilling the regiment devolved on him, and it was said by military men to be the best drilled regiment in the service. There are at this writing fifty-eight commissioned officers who were privates on the 24th of July 1861. After the three month's service, Major Gruesel was commissioned Lieut.-Colonel. On the 20th of August, he was promoted to the colonelcy of the Fox River regiment, aftewards called the 36th regiment Illinois volunteers. The regiment was ordered to Rolla, Mo., for drill. On the 14th day of January, 1862, it was ordered to march for Lebanon, Mo., where it arrived on the 25th of January. The regiment was brigaded with the 13th, 3d and 17th Missouri volunteers, Welfley's Missouri and Capt. Hoffman's batteries. Col. Greusel was placed in command by Brig. Gen. Sigel, in which capacity he followed Gen. Price on his retreat to Batesville, Ark. He was in the masterly retreat of Gen. Sigel to Pea Ridge, and fought bravely during that ever memorable battle for three successive days. He was highly complimented by Generals Curtis and Sigel for his coolness and bravery on the field, especially for preventing a stampede, which would have been most disastrous but for the coolness and presence of mind displayed by Col. Greusel.

"The regiment received orders, when fifteen miles beyond White River, Ark., to proceed to Corinth, by forced marches—240 miles distant—which it accomplished in ten days, when it embarked on the steamer *Planet*, and arrived and joined Gen. Pope's command at the trenches in front of Corinth, two days before the evacuation of that place by Gen. Beauregard."

Of the further movements of this gallant regiment notice will be hereafter taken and we may meet him again.

Others who distinguished themselves in the campaigns mentioned in this chapter will be noticed farther on, in connection with regimental histories, campaign or field sketches, or personal biographies.

COLONEL POST OF THE FIFTY-NINTH.

Colonel Philip Sidney Post was born in Florida, Orange Co., New York, in the year 1833, was educated at Union College Schenectady, N. Y., where he graduated with the highest honors in 1855, and immediately entered the law school at Poughkeepsie, N. Y. His father, General Peter Schuyler Post (a soldier of 1812, and a man distinguished for his martial spirit, probity and energy), removed with his family to Galesburg, Illinois, the same year. Upon leaving the law school, Colonel Post followed his family West and spent a year in traveling through the States of Illinois, Iowa, Wisconsin and Minnesota, making the journey through the wilderness between St. Paul to Lake Superior on foot. In 1857, he settled in Wyandotte, Kansas, and was soon engaged in an extensive practice of his profession in the courts of the southern counties of the territory. He also purchased a printing office and established the *Wyandotte Argus* of which he subsequently assumed editorial control without, however, relinquishing the practice of the law.

In the spring of 1861, he rejoined his family in Illinois preparatory to entering the army of the Union. On the 17th of July he was mustered as 2d Lieutenant in a company raised in Knox Co., Illinois. At that time the government would not receive troops from this State, and this company in order to enter the service, proceeded to St. Louis and became Co. A of the 9th Regt. Mo. Vols. The regiment was wholly composed of citizens of Illinois and subsequently, by an order from the War Department, it became the 59th Ills. Vol. Infantry.

It was organized by the appointment of J. C. Kelton, Assistant Adjutant-General, Department of Mississippi, as Colonel, and Lieut. Post as Adjutant. In January, the Adjutant was promoted to Major and took command of the regiment in the stern mid-winter march to join General Curtis on the toilsome and vigorous campaign which preceded the bloody battle of Pea Ridge, Arkansas, at which engagement Major Post was shot through the shoulder, but utterly refused to leave the field until, becoming helpless from loss of blood, he was carried off. His gallantry received especial mention in the official reports, and ten days after the battle, having been unanimously elected by the officers of the regiment, he was commissioned Colonel in place of Colonel Kelton, who had been detached on the staff of Major-General Halleck, and who resigned upon hearing the news of the battle, and recommended the appointment of Major Post.

In May, 1862, though still suffering from the effects of the wound which nearly cost him his life, he reached Hamburg Landing and was assigned to the command of a brigade, which he marched to its place in the line of battle before Corinth four days before the evacuation of that place. The summer of 1862 he spent in Mississippi, actively engaged in military duties. When it was determined to destroy the large factories at Bay Springs, Col. Post was entrusted with the attack on the place, which he entered, surprising the enemy and driving them out in confusion, and completely disabling the mills. One week later he commanded an expedition to Allsborough Ala., for the purpose of capturing a large amount of cotton from the enemy. Starting from Iuka at midnight, driving the enemy before him, he seized and loaded and brought away with him $80,000 worth of cotton, and returned to Iuka in less than twenty hours, having marched thirty-six miles.

On the 18th of August, Col. Post's brigade commenced to cross the Tennessee River at Eastport, en route to assist in expelling Bragg from Tennessee and Kentucky, and from that time he became identified with the Army of the Ohio and of the Cumberland. At Louisville, on the 29th of September, a new brigade was organized for Col. Post consisting of the 22d Indiana infantry, the 59th, 4th, and 5th Illinois infantry and the 5th Wisconsin battery, which became the 1st Brigade, 1st Division, 20th Army Corps, or the right brigade of the entire army.

During thirteen months Col. Post commanded the brigade which Major-General Rosecrans, the Department Commander, especially referred to as "distinguished for drill and discipline."

The separation of the regiments in the re-organization which succeeded the Chickamauga campaign, was the occasion for issuing the following order:

"HEAD-QUARTERS 1ST BRIG., 1ST DIV., 20TH ARMY CORPS,
"Chattanooga, October 16, 1863.

"*General Orders, No.* 51.

"In the re-organization of the army, this brigade will lose its identity, and be transferred to another division and corps.

"Organized on the banks of the Ohio more than a year ago, it has traversed Kentucky and Tennessee, scaled the mountains of Northern Alabama and Georgia, and now terminates its existence on the south bank of the Tennessee. The year during which it has remained intact will ever be remembered as that in which the gallant armies of the West rolled back the advancing hosts of rebellion, and extinguished the Confederacy in the valley of the Mississippi.

"In accomplishing this glorious achievement, you—soldiers of the 1st Brigade—have performed no mean part. On the laborious march you have been patient and energetic, and in the battle and skirmish second to none in stubborn valor and success. In one year you lost upon the battle-field eight hundred and fifty heroic comrades.

"Baptized in blood at Perryville, this brigade led the army in pursuit of the retreating foe, and again attacks him at Lancaster, whence he fled from Kentucky. In the mid-winter campaign it opened the battle at Stone River by attacking and driving the enemy from Nolensville, and on the memorable 31st of December, together with the rest of the 20th Army Corps, valiantly met the attack of the concentrated opposing army. At Liberty Gap and in the late battle of Chickamauga, it performed well the part assigned it, and finishes its honorable career weaker in numbers, but strong in the confidence and discipline of invincible veterans.

"For the able and hearty co-operation its commander has received from the officers, and for the cheerful support yielded by its gallant men, he returns his sincere thanks. No petty jealousies, no intrigue or demoralizing influences have ever disgraced and paralyzed our efforts for the country's cause; and the commander unites in the just pride which all feel in the history of, and in their connection with, the 1st Brigade, 1st Division, 20th Army Corps.

"P. Sidney Post,
"Colonel Commanding Brigade."

On the 12th day of January, 1864, the 59th regiment were remustered as veterans, and are marshaled among the hosts who "strike till the last armed foe expires."

The United States numbers among its officers few as active, resolute and adventurous as Col. P. Sidney Post, and the Division Commander, under whom he served for more than two years, in recommending him for promotion, recounted his services and said: "In all these campaigns and battles, Col. Post has shown himself a commander of rare qualifications and extraordinary energy, and one of the best tacticians of the army. The evidence of his skill was exhibited whenever his brigade maneuvered, whether on drill or on the battle-field."

CHAPTER XIII.

PITTSBURG LANDING—SHILOH.

General Statements—Illinois Interest in the Battle—The New Rebel Line—Union Line—Force at Corinth—Galaxy of Generals—Change of Plan—Savannah—Pittsburg Landing—The Fight Begun—Disposition of our Forces—General Johnston's Address—Rebel Corps—Skirmish of April 2nd—Rebel Design—Rebel Order of Battle—Sunday at Half-past Five—Rebel Mistake—Terrible Charge—Prentiss' and Sherman's Divisions—McClernand's Wallace's—Grant as to a Surprise—Wallace and Hurlbut—Wallace Falls—Disaster—A Lull—Lew. Wallace and Buell—Webster's Gems—Another Conflict—The Enemy Stayed—Sunday Night—Beauregard's Report—Monday Morning—Union Order of Battle—The Fight Opens—Nelson's Advance—Ferrill's Battery—Original Ground Recovered—Battle Ended—Whose the Victory?—A Mourning State—Relief—The Governor—Sanitary Stores—Grant's Official Report—Prentiss' Report—Letter from General Sherman.

THE march of Western events leads to Pittsburg Landing, and to the month of April, where was fought a sanguinary general engagement of such magnitude and persistence as to open the eyes of the world. Europe saw, in a new light, the courage and ability of the contestants. The North anew comprehended the stern and colossal character of the work before it, the strength and resources of the revolted States, and their power to equip, subsist and fight great armies. Anew the insurgents found the earnestness, the power, the intelligent zeal of the armies of the United States, and learned that their dream of military superiority in educated officers and warlike habits *was* a dream from which, though pleasant, there was to be a terrible, gasping, stifling awakening.

In the battle of Shiloh, Illinois had a profound interest. The General in chief command, four division commanders, a large number of brigade commanders and thousands of her gallant sons, not hirelings, not "agrarian mercenaries," but the flower of her young men, were there, some in the long lines of infantry, some moving with masses of cavalry, and others beside caisson or field-piece. There were between thirty and forty regiments from this State on the field.

The situation of the opposing forces on the 1st of March was substantially this: The Confederate line of defense having been broken by the Federal successes, a new one had been formed by the Charleston and Memphis Railroad, the preservation of which was deemed a prime necessity to the preservation of Northern Mississippi, Alabama and Georgia. Along this road are Tuscumbia and Florence, at the foot of Muscle Shoals in the Tennessee River and the junction with the Florence and Nashville Railroad; Decatur, near the head of the lower Muscle Shoals; Huntsville and Bellefontaine; Stevenson, important as the junction with the railroad from Nashville through Murfreesboro and Chattanooga, a strong position. All these points are east of Corinth. On the west of Corinth the railroad runs in nearly a straight line to Memphis, ninety-three miles distant, and northwest runs the road to Jackson, almost in the center of West Tennessee.

"The Union line was the Tennessee River, extending from Paducah, Kentucky, to Eastport in Mississippi. The gunboats Lexington and Tyler, by moving up and down the river, prevented the erection of batteries. Above Eastport, at Chickasaw Bluffs, and at some other points, Confederate batteries were placed to command the navigation of the river."

At Corinth was encamped a vast Confederate force with a galaxy of able generals—Albert Sidney Johnston, Beauregard, Bragg, Polk, Pillow, Hardee, Crittenden and others. Corinth, their center, is at the intersection of the Mobile and Ohio and Memphis and Charleston railroads, in Tishemingo county, Mississippi, forty miles from Grand Junction, fifty-eight from Jackson, Tenn., and about eighteen from Pittsburg, on the Tennessee River.

The original plan, as ordered by Gen. Halleck, contemplated an advance by Buell into Northern Alabama, and accordingly the divisions of Mitchell, Nelson and McCook set out from Nashville the same day by different roads. The new line brought the rebels within the field of Grant's army, made a change in Buell's pro-

16

gramme, who was ordered to turn toward Western Tennessee, cross the river, and co-operate with Gen. Grant. This officer's headquarters were established at Savannah, a small town of about two hundred souls, on the Tennessee River, about one hundred and seventy miles above Fort Henry. Though a large number of troops, brought on transports, concentrated here, they were encamped seven miles above at Pittsburg Landing, a narrow ravine, down which the Corinth wagon-road passed to the river, with overhanging bluffs on either side. It is about equally distant from Owl and Snake creeks. Back from the river lay a rolling country, cut into ravines, partly under cultivation, but mostly thickly wooded and covered with underbrush. A mile or two out, the road forks, one branch being the lower and the other the ridge Corinth road. A little further out, a road leading to the left crosses Lick Creek and returns to the river at Hamburgh some miles further up. On the right, two roads lead to Purdy, and another, more lately cut out, crosses Snake Creek and goes to Crump's Landing on the river below.

On the Sabbath morning the fight began, on and between these roads Grant's divisions were posted. Three divisions formed the advance—Sherman's, Prentiss' and McClernand's. Between these and the Landing were the divisions of Hurlbut and C. F. Smith, the gallant commander of the latter being ill, his place was supplied by Gen. W. H. L. Wallace.

The formation of the advance line was as follows: On the extreme left, near the Lick creek crossing, commanded by the bluffs on the other side was Col. D. Shearl's brigade of Sherman's division. The remaining brigades of this division were three or four miles away, on the lower Corinth road, and between that and the Purdy road. Those brigades formed the advance right. To the left and rather in the rear of these brigades was McClernand's division, and between it and Stuart's brigade was Prentiss', thus completing the front line. Lew. Wallace's division was at Crump's Landing. It seems strange that with a strong rebel force known to be within striking distance and meditating attack, that more vigorous defensive preparations were not taken. A few days' work would have covered the approaches with impassable abattis, and constructed breastworks from which the advancing foe could have been swept by artillery.

General Buell left Nashville on the 28th of March. On the 28th, 29th and 30th, the divisions of this army had crossed Duck River and advanced through Columbia, 82 miles from Savannah. April 3d, the rebel General commanding issued the following order:

"*Soldiers of the Army of the Mississippi:*

"I have put you in motion to offer battle to the invaders of your country, with the resolution and discipline and valor becoming men, fighting, as you are, for all worth living or dying for. You can but march to a decisive victory over agrarian mercenaries, sent to subjugate and despoil you of your liberties, property and honor.

"Remember the precious stake involved; remember the dependence of your mothers, your wives, your sisters, and your children, on the result. Remember the fair, broad, abounding lands, the happy homes, that will be desolated by your defeat. The eyes and hopes of eight million people rest upon you. You are expected to show yourselves worthy of your valor and courage, worthy of the women of the South, whose noble devotion in this war has never been exceeded in any time. With such incentives to brave deeds, and with trust that God is with us, your General will lead you confidently to the combat, assured of success.

"By order of General A. S. JOHNSTON, *Commanding.*"

The rebel army of the Mississippi was then divided into three army corps, and was commanded as follows:

Commanding General, General Albert Sydney Johnston.
Second in Command, General P. G. T. Beauregard.
First Army Corps, Lieutenant-General L. Polk.
Second Army Corps, Lieutenant-General Braxton Bragg
Third Army Corps, Lieutenant-General W. J. Hardee.
Reserves, Major-General G. B. Crittenden.

On the morning of April second, the cavalry of Major-General Lew. Wallace, at Crump's Landing were driven in. On the evening of the fourth, a skirmish occurred between the advance lines, but the Confederates fell back.

It was known to Johnston and Beauregard that Buell was hastening to the relief of Grant, and they determined to crush the latter before the former could arrive. Beauregard says in his official report of April 11th:

"His (General Johnston's) entire force hastened in this direction, and by the first of April our united forces were concentrated along the Mobile and Ohio Railroad from Bethel to Corinth, and on the Memphis and Charleston Railroad from Corinth to Iuka.

"It was then determined to assume the offensive, and strike a sudden blow at the enemy in position under General Grant on the west bank of the Tennessee at Pittsburg and in the direction of Savannah, before he was reinforced by the army under Gen. Buell, then known to be advancing rapidly for that purpose, by forced marches from Nashville, via Columbia. About the same time Gen. Johnston was advised that such an operation conformed to the expectations of the President.

"By a rapid and vigorous attack on Gen. Grant, it was expected he would be beaten back into his transports and the river, or captured in time to enable us to profit by the victory and remove to the rear all the stores and munitions that would fall into our hands in such an event, before the arrival of Gen. Buell on the scene. It was never contemplated, however, to retain the position thus gained, and abandon Corinth, the strategic point of the campaign."

It was surely a Providential interposition which prevented the earlier accomplishment of this plan, for, moving on interior lines of railway, the enemy had massed a force vastly superior to that under General Grant. Beauregard complains in his report, of delays for want of officers, proper organization of brigades and other difficulties, so that they were not fully ready, when, on the evening of the 2d, they ascertained that Buell was dangerously near with his forces and orders were issued at 1 o'clock, A. M., for an immediate advance. But the "chariot wheels drave heavily" and he regrets that the "troops did not reach the intersection of the roads from Pittsburg and Hamburg in the immediate vicinity of the enemy, until late Saturday night." The rebel order of battle is thus stated by Gen. Beauregard:

"It was then decided that the attack should be made on the next morning, at the earliest hour practicable, in accordance with the laws of movement—that is, in three lines of battle: the first and second extending from Owl Creek on the left, to Lick Creek on the right—a distance of about three miles—supported by the third and the reserve. The first line, under Major-General Hardee, was constituted of his corps, augmented on his right by Gladden's brigade of Major-General Bragg's corps, deployed in line of battle, with their respective artillery, following immediately by the main road to Pittsburg, and the cavalry in the rear of the wings. The second line, composed of the other troops of Bragg's corps, followed, the first at a distance of five hundred yards, in the same order as the first. The army corps under General Polk followed the second line, at the distance of about eight hundred yards, in lines of brigades deployed with their batteries, in rear of each brigade, moving by the Pittsburg road, the left wing supported by cavalry; the reserve under General Breckinridge followed closely the third line in the same order, its right wing supported by cavalry.

"These two corps constituted the reserve, and were to support the front lines of battle, by being deployed, when required, on the right and left of the Pittsburg road, or otherwise act according to the exigences of the battle."

At half-past five on Sunday morning, this tremendous force of infantry, cavalry and field artillery was in motion, intending to bear down all opposition and drive Grant into the river. The design was to attack the center, composed of Prentiss' and McClernand's divisions, pierce it, pour in their troops, and attack on each side the wings of our divided army. Here again was a Providential derangement of wisely laid plans. They should have hurled their advancing columns against Sherman's three brigades on our right, and the left of McClernand's. By some miscalculation they assailed only Sherman's left, and that not until after their right had struck Prentiss' division.

As it was, that first charge was lamentably disastrous. It came like an avalanche, driving in the pickets of Prentiss' division and reaching the camp almost as soon as the sentinels. A little later and the same was the case with Hildebrand's brigade, of Sherman's division. The men of this brigade fell back, firing as they retreated, and checked the foe long enough to form an imperfect line of battle. The other two brigades came up on the right to their help, and not a moment too soon, for at once the enemy opened the battle along Sherman's entire line. Hildebrand's brigade fell back; part of it, raw troops, fled—no wonder;—they lived long enough to gloriously redeem the escutcheon of Ohio from that bar sinister. McClernand threw forward his troops to support Hildebrand's brigade. Sherman put forth exertions almost superhuman to rally his mèn and save his division. For a time Buckland's and McDowell's brigade stood as adamant, when they were compelled to give way, and retire from their camps behind a small ravine, when again they made a gallant stand. McClernand's division of tried men, took the place of Hildebrand's brigade and essayed to check the rebel advance.

Prentiss' division did as well as it could, but their line when formed, was in an open space, while their foe was sheltered by the dense scrub-growth from which he directed murderous volleys almost out of danger. The Union men fought doggedly, bravely, obstinately, but they were not made of steel. The enemy poured his fire on either flank, and right on in front came a line of leveled steel—they were compelled to fall back. And yet they fought and seemed at one time about to be saved. McArthur, of W. H. L. Wallace's division, came up to the relief of Stuart's brigade of Sherman's division, and by mistake verged too far to the right and came up on the other side of the rebels assailing Prentiss. His men at once opened fire upon the foe and hope arose among our imperiled men. But McArthur could not hold his position, and was compelled to fall back, the enemy opening a flanking fire on him. By ten o'clock the division of Prentiss had been destroyed or captured, and the General with three regiments was in the hands of an exultant foe. The front line was pierced, and only McArthur's brigade and W. H. L. Wallace's division checked the overwhelming advance.

Grant was at Savannah, his head-quarters, when the fight commenced, and hurried to the field as rapidly as possible, and until his arrival there was no General-in-chief, but each division commander fought according to his own judgment. Much angry criticism was for a time heaped upon him for this absence, and for suffering a surprise. His own answer was, "As to the talk of our being surprised, nothing could be more false. If the enemy had sent us word where and when they would attack, we could not have been better prepared. Skirmishing had been going on for two days between our reconnoitering parties and the enemy's advance. I did not believe, however, that they intended to make a determined attack, but meant simply to make a reconnoissance in force. My head-quarters were at Savannah, though I usually spent the day at Pittsburg. Troops were constantly arriving to be assigned to the different brigades and divisions. All were ordered to report at Savannah, making it necessary to keep an office and some one there. I was also looking for Buell to arrive, and it was important that I should have every arrangement complete for his crossing and transit to this side of the river."

Yet with the facts of the Sunday morning charge on the left and center, it surely is hardly supposable that, if our forces had known the time and place of the attack, they would not have been better prepared for the onset!

Hurlbut and W. H. L. Wallace stood between the army and destruction—stood like ocean-beat rocks. McArthur was reinforced, and the space on the left made vacant by the defeat and capture of Prentiss was filled. The combat raged with fury. Never men fought more bravely. Regiments but a few months from home, and in the first battle, fought with the coolness of battle-stained veterans,

"By the early breaking of Gen. Prentiss's line, the onset of the Confederates had been made to veer chiefly to the Union left. Here the contest continued stubborn. Four times the Confederates attempted to charge on Gen. Wallace's men. Each time the infantry poured in rapid volleys, and the artillery redoubled their efforts. thus compelling them to retreat with heavy slaughter. Farther to the right, Gen. Hurlbut's division, which had taken an advanced position, was compelled to fall back through its camp to a thick wood behind. Here, with open fields before them, they could rake the approach of the Confederates. Three times their heavy masses bravely charged upon the division, and each time they were repulsed with severe loss. The troops from the driven divisions were reorganized so far as available, and re-sent to the field. Thus the right of Gen. Hurlbut, which was almost wholly unprotected, and the weakness of which does not appear to have been discovered by the Confederates, was in a measure patched out. It had been previously determined that in case of an attack at Pittsburg Landing, the division under Gen. Lew. Wallace at Crump's Landing, five miles below, should come up on the right and flank the enemy. But no message was sent to this division until nearly noon, and it missed the way on coming up, and did not arrive until near night. The division of Gen. Hurlbut at length became exhausted, and fell back out of sight of their camps to a point within a mile of the Landing. In consequence of losing his support, the division of Gen. W. H. L. Wallace, thus in isolated advance, was compelled to fall back, the last to leave the field. Just at this moment its brave commander was mortally wounded.

"It was now half past four o'clock. The front line of the divisions had been lost since eleven o'clock, and the reserve line was gone too. The Confederates occupied the camps of every division except Smith's, commanded during his sickness by Gen. Wallace, who had just been wounded. The whole army was crowded in the region of Wallace's camp, and to a circuit of one half to two thirds of a mile around the Landing. The next repulse would put it into the river, and there were not transports enough to cross a single division before the enemy would be upon them. Nearly half the field artillery was lost, nearly all the camps and camp equipage. Prisoners had been taken in great numbers.

"At this time a lull took place in the firing, the first which had occurred since sunrise. It was thought that the enemy were either preparing for the grand final rush that was to crown the day's success, or that they were puzzled by the last retreat, and were moving cautiously. These few minutes were golden ones for that driven and defeated army, and they were improved. Col. Webster, chief of staff, arranged the guns which he could collect of those that remained, in a sort of semicircle to protect the Union center and left, upon which it was thought the enemy were now sure to advance. Corps of artillerists to man them were gathered from all the batteries. Twenty-two guns were thus placed in position, two of which were long 32's. In front was a victorious enemy; behind were the remnants of the repulsed divisions of the army driven within half a mile of the Landing, beyond which was a deep and rapid river. Gen. Wallace's division at Crump's Landing had not been heard from. Across the river now was seen the first glitter of the advance of Gen. Buell, but it could not be brought over in time to do much good. Suddenly a broad flash of light leaped out from the darkening woods, and the whistling leaden hail swiftly followed. The enemy were about to make their crowning effort for the day. Instantly the artillery replied, and as they appoached nearer, the infantry fired volley after volley. At this time the gunboats, Lexington and Tyler, approached the mouth of Lick Creek, and were able with their guns to reach the field occupied by the Confederates near the river. This was a fire in their flank, which disconcerted their plans. Amid this terrible conflict darkness came on. The enemy had been held at bay.

"Meantime Gen. Lew. Wallace had arrived with his division, and Gen. Buell with his forces, a portion of which took part in the battle of the afternoon, and it was decided, after the sounds of battle had ceased, to attack the Confederates as soon as possible after daybreak. Gen. Wallace's division was to take the right and sweep back toward the position from which Gen. Sherman had been driven during the morning, and Gen. Nelson was to take the extreme left. Gen. Crittenden was to take a position during the night next to Gen. Nelson, and Gen. McCook with his division next to Crittenden. The space between Gens. McCook and Wallace was to be filled with the reorganized divisions of Gen. Grant's army. Stealthily the troops crept to their new positions, and lay down in line of battle on their arms. All through the night, Gen. Buell's men were marching up from Savannah to the point opposite Pittsburg Landing, and were ferried across, or were coming up on transports. At nine o'clock, the gunboats commenced a cannonade of the Confederate position, which was kept up all night. It produced little or no effect.

"Gen. Beauregard thus reported his position on Sunday night: 'At six o'clock P. M., we were in possession of all the encampments between Owl and Lick creeks but one. Nearly all of his field artillery, about thirty flags, colors, and standards, over three thousand prisoners, including a division commander (Gen. Prentiss) and several brigade commanders, thousands of small arms, an immense supply of subsistence, forage, and munitions of war, and a large amount of means of transportation—all the substantial fruits of a complete victory—such indeed as rarely have followed the most successful battles; for never was an army so well provided as that of our enemy.

"'The remnant of his army had been driven in utter disorder to the immediate vicinity of Pittsburg, under the shelter of the heavy guns of his iron-clad gunboats, and we remained undisputed masters of his well-selected, admirably provided cantonments, after over twelve hours of obstinate conflict with his forces, who had been beaten from them and the contiguous covert, but only by a sustained onset of all the men we could bring into action.'

"The Federal forces arranged for the battle of the next day were the divisions of Gens. Nelson, Crittenden, McCook, Hurlbut, McClernand and Sherman, including in the three latter the shattered and disorganized commands of Prentiss and W. H. L. Wallace, which were without commanders, and the fresh division of Gen. Lew. Wallace. These divisions were arranged in the order above named, beginning on the left. The change produced in the position of the Confederate forces, by the shells of the gunboats during the night, prevented them from opening the battle at daylight.

"At seven o'clock in the morning, Gen. Nelson, on the extreme left formed his line of battle, and advanced with skirmishers thrown out, for nearly a mile before meeting the enemy in force. They immediately became engaged. There was no straggling, as upon the previous day. Gen. Nelson slowly but steadily advanced, pushing the exhausted enemy before him until half past ten, when, under cover of the timber and a furious cannonading, they made a general rally. Suddenly the masses of the enemy were hurled with tremendous force against the Federal lines, which now halted, wavered, and fell back. At this moment Terrill's battery of 24-pounder howitzers rushed up, and in a few minutes was unlimbered and firing into the compact and advancing ranks of the enemy. Here was the turning point of the battle on the left. The enemy were only checked, not halted; then followed for two hours a contest of artillery and musketry at short range. The enemy began to waver, when Gen. Buell coming up, saw at a glance the chance, and ordered a charge by brigades, at 'double quick.' The Confederates fell back for a quarter of a mile, became more confused, and at half past two that point of the field was cleared. The next divisions, of

Gens. Crittenden and McCook, after an obstinate struggle, were equally successful. The divisions of Gens. McClernand and Hurlbut, nothing daunted by the reverses of the preceding day, fought with much bravery. On the right the contest was more severe, and longer continued. A design was manifested by the enemy to turn the flank of Gen. Wallace's division. This was thwarted, and the enemy steadily driven back until four P. M., when a general retreat took place on the right. Thus the original plan of the enemy was frustrated.

"On the retreat of the Confederate army, the original ground, and even the tents of Gen. Grant's army, were recovered. No regular pursuit was attempted until the next day. The number of the Federal army engaged on Sunday, was estimated by General Beauregard at five divisions of nine thousand men each, or forty-five thousand men. The reinforcements of Sunday night were estimated by him at twenty-five thousand from Gen. Buell's army, and eight thousand under Gen. Wallace, and the entire force on Monday fifty-three thousand. This estimate slightly exceeds the Federal force engaged, especially in the number of reinforcements furnished by Gen. Buell. On the other hand, the Confederate force was estimated at sixty thousand by the Union officers, which was undoubtedly an overestimate. Gen. Grant had a force somewhat less than the enemy on Sunday, but on Monday he outnumbered them. No official statement of numbers has been afforded on either side. The Federal loss was 1,735 killed, 7,882 wounded, and 3,956 taken prisoners. Total, 13,573. The Confederate loss was, killed 1,728, wounded 8,012, missing 959. Total, 10,699."

So began, raged and terminated the battle of Pittsburg Landing or Shiloh. It was terrible in the determination and persistency of the struggles and in the loss of life. And when ended was it victory or defeat? Each General commanding claimed victory, but a few simple facts settle the case.

I. The purpose of the enemy was defeated. General Beauregard states that purpose. It was to fall on Grant before the arrival of Buell, cut off his forces from those of Lew Wallace at Crump's Landing, and drive him into the river or capture him. That Sunday morning not less than sixty thousand Confederates assailed Grant's forty thousand and fought through the day. They did their best. They strained every nerve. Well officered, they fought with desperation and failed. Night came on, and found our forces driven from their camps, and Prentiss's division beaten and prisoners; but they had stayed the columns of Johnson and Beauregard, and *without Buell*, had prevented the accomplishment of the purpose of the foe, and were stronger by the addition of Lew Wallace's division than earlier in the day.

II. The second day's battle was splendidly fought. There was a masterly battle plan and well was it carried out, and steadily backward was pushed the rebel column, until compelled to retreat from the field it came from Corinth to win, and the Union forces held their original lines and rescued their camps. There was a general rebel retreat and Federal pursuit until the weary men were recalled.

III. General Beauregard in his note to General Grant conceded that his "forces were exhausted by the extraordinary length of time in which they were engaged" and that he felt it his duty to *withdraw from the immediate scene of conflict* and asked leave to send a party with a flag of truce to bury their dead.

IV. Thus in every direction the tests of victory were with the Federal troops, they had fought and they had won, and a discomfited foe fell back to his trenches at Corinth, to organize, in watered dispatches, the victory he could not win with his divisions.

But the victory threw our State into mourning. Prentiss and his brave men were in captivity, and were exhibited, rather as captured animals, than as brave soldiers who had fallen by adverse fortune into the hands of the enemy on the field. They were subjected to taunt, scoff, insult and aggravated material misery at the hands "of a brave and chivalric people."

Brigadier-General W. H. L. Wallace with other gallant officers and a host of brave men from the homes of Illinois were slain or wounded.

Governor Yates proceeded in person to the field and cared for the wounded, working with tireless zeal. The Sanitary Commission sent forward vast stores of clothing, bandages, delicacies and nourishing food, while surgeons and nurses volunteered their services until there was no need of them.

It were worth living a hundred years through poverty and sorrow to witness the zeal and unselfish devotion of the people at that hour! It was manifested in gifts, in personal service and in the united demand upon the government to go steadily forward until rebellion should be destroyed! Money for the wounded was lavished like water.

Governor Yates won anew the love of his constituency and the devoted gratitude of the soldier by his activity. He made his calls from the press and then in person saw to the care of the Illinois wounded, himself performing the menial offices of nurse. Returning to Springfield, he dispatched the Adjutant-General with arms and clothing, and again, hearing the wounded were still suffering, he took another corps of surgeons and supply of sanitary stores and ascended the Tennessee. As far and fast as possible his agents secured transportation for the wounded to their houses and to Northern hospitals.

GENERAL GRANT'S REPORT.

"*Major-General Halleck:*

"It becomes my duty again to report another battle fought between two great armies, one contending for the maintenance of the best government ever devised, the other for its destruction. It is pleasant to record the success of the army contending for the former principle.

"On Sunday morning our pickets were driven in by the enemy. Immediately the five divisions stationed at this place were drawn up in line of battle, ready to meet them. The battle soon waxed warm on the left and center, varying at times to all parts of the line.

"The most continuous firing of musketry and artillery ever heard on the continent was kept up until nightfall, the enemy having forced the entire line to fall back nearly half way from their camps to the landing. At a late hour in the afternoon, a desperate effort was made by the enemy to turn our left, and get possession of the landing, transports, etc. This point was guarded by the gunboats Tyler and Lexington, Captains Gwinn and Shirk, U. S. N., commanding, four 29-pounder Parrott guns, and a battery of rifled guns. As there is a deep and impassable ravine for artillery or cavalry, and very difficult for infantry, at this point, no troops were stationed here except the necessary artillerists, and a small infantry force for their support. Just at this moment the advance of Major-General Buell's column (a part of the division of General Nelson) arrived, the two Generals named both being present. An advance was immediately made upon the point of attack, and the enemy soon driven back. In this repulse, much is due to the presence of the gunboats Tyler and Lexington, and their able commanders, Captains Gwinn and Shirk. During the night, the divisions under Generals Crittenden and McCook arrived.

"Gen. Lew. Wallace, at Crump's Landing, six miles below, was ordered at an early hour in the morning to hold his division in readiness to move in any direction to which it might be ordered. At about 11 o'clock the order was delivered to move it up to Pittsburg, but owing to its being led by a circuitous route, did not arrive in time to take part in Sunday's action. During the night all was quiet, and feeling that a great moral advantage would be gained by becoming the attacking party, an advance was ordered as soon as day dawned. The result was a gradual repulse of the enemy at all points of the line, from morning until probably 5 o'clock in the afternoon, when it became evident the enemy was retreating.

"Before the close of the action, the advance of Gen. T. J. Wood's division arrived, in time to take part in the action. My force was too much fatigued from two days' hard fighting, and exposed in the open air to a drenching rain during the intervening night, to pursue immediately. Night closed in cloudy and with heavy rain, making the roads impracticable for artillery by the next morning. General Sherman, however, followed the enemy, finding that the main part of the army had retreated in good order. Hospitals of the enemy's wounded were found all along the road, as far as pursuit was made. Dead bodies of the enemy and many graves were also found. I enclose herewith the report of General Sherman, which will explain more fully the result of the pursuit. Of the part taken by each separate command, I cannot take special notice in this report, but will do so more fully when reports of division commanders are handed in.

"General Buell, coming on the field with a distinct army, long under his command, and which did such efficient service, commanded by himself in person on the field, will be much better able to notice those of his command who particularly distinguished themselves, than I possibly can.

"I feel it a duty, however, to a gallant and able officer, Brigadier-General W. T. Sherman, to make a special mention. He not only was with his command during the entire of the two days' action, but displayed great judgment and skill in the management of his men. Although severely wounded in the hand the first day, his place was never vacant. He was again wounded, and had three horses killed under him.

"In making this mention of a gallant officer, no disparagement is intended to the other division commanders, Major-Generals John A. McClernand and Lew. Wallace, and Brigadier-Generals S. A. Hurlbut, B. M. Prentiss and W. H. L. Wallace, all of whom maintained their places with credit to themselves and the cause.

"Gen. Prentiss was taken prisoner in the first day's action, and Gen. W. H. L. Wallace severely, probably mortally, wounded. His Assistant Adjutant-General, Captain William McMichael, is missing—probably taken prisoner.

"My personal staff are all deserving of particular mention, they having been engaged during the entire two days in carrying orders to every part of the field. It consists of Col. J. D. Webster, chief of Staff; Lieut.-Col. J. B. McPherson, chief engineer; assisted by Lieutenants W. L. B. Jenny and Wm. Kossac, Capt. J. A. Rawlings, A. A.-General, W. S. Hillyer, W. R. Rawley and C. B. Lagow, aids-de-camp, Col. G. G. Pride, volunteer aid, and Capt. J. P. Hawkins, chief commissary, who accompanied me upon the field.

"The medical department, under direction of Surgeon Hewitt, medical director, showed great energy in providing for the wounded, and in getting them from the field, regardless of danger.

"Col. Webster was placed in special charge of all the artillery, and was constantly upon the field. He displayed, as always heretofore, both skill and bravery. At least in one instance he was the means of placing an entire regiment in a position of doing most valuable service, and where it would not have been but for his exertions.

"Lieut.-Col. McPherson, attached to my staff as chief of engineers, deserves more than a passing notice for his activity and courage. The grounds beyond our camps for miles have been reconnoitered by him, and plats carefully prepared under his supervision, giving accurate information of the nature of approaches to our lines. During the two days' battle he was constantly in the saddle, leading troops as they arrived to points where their services were required. During the engagement he had one horse shot under him.

"The country will have to mourn the loss of many brave men who fell at the battle of Pittsburg, or Shiloh, more properly. The exact loss in killed and wounded will be known in a day or two; at present I can only give it approximately at 1,500 killed and 3,500 wounded.

"The loss of artillery was great, many pieces being disabled by the enemy's shots, and some losing all their horses and many men. There were probably not less than two hundred horses killed.

"The loss of the enemy, in killed and left upon the field, was greater than ours. In wounded, the estimate cannot be made, as many of them must have been sent to Corinth and other points. U. S. Grant, Major-General."

After his return from captivity General Prentiss published his official report which claims that all the ordinary and some extraordinary means were employed to guard against surprise. He says:

"Saturday evening, pursuant to instructions, received when I was assigned to duty, * * * the usual advanced guard was posted, and in view of information received from the commandant thereof, I sent forward five companies of the 21st Mo. Infantry, under command of Col. David Moore. I also, after consultation with Col. David Stuart, commanding a brigade of Gen. Sherman's division sent to the left one company of the 18th Wisconsin, under command of Capt. Fiske. At about 7 o'clock the same evening Col. Moore returned and reported some activity in front—an evident reconnoissance by cavalry.

"This information received, I proceeded to strengthen the guard stationed on the Corinth road, extending the picket to the front, a distance of a mile and a half, at the same time extending and doubling the lines of the grand guard.

"*At 3 o'clock on the morning of Sunday, April sixth, Colonel David Moore with five companies of his infantry regiment, proceeded to the front* and at break of day the advance pickets were driven in, whereupon Colonel Moore pushed forward and engaged the enemy's advance, commanded by General Hardee. At this stage a message was sent to my head-quarters calling for the balance of the 21st Mo. which was promptly sent forward."

It seems therefore that in addition to ordinary vigilance, extraordinary precaution had been employed, and at 3 o'clock, two hours and a half before the onset of the foe, a detachment of the 21st Mo. had been sent out to the front, which met and gallantly engaged the rebel advance.

Thus one by one disappear the adverse criticisms upon the Commanding Generals. They were not careless, or reckless. It is true the whole army *might* have been kept up and under arms on Saturday night; and then they might have moved out a few miles and met Johnston and Beauregard, and fought the battle on a different plan, but then the best military authorities recognize the right of a soldier to sleep *occasionally*, and consider the posting of a sufficient picket force as a competent security against surprise. What that force was, General Prentiss states in his report.

Barely in time for insertion at this point comes the annexed letter from Major-General W. T. Sherman, the hero of Atlanta and Savannah. It is written with all the benefit of his mature military experience and is entitled to great consideration. His authority relieves General Grant of no small amount of the criticism heaped upon him for the selection of the battle ground. It also, while giving the army under Buell all due credit, does not admit that Grant, without it, would have been defeated, but rather, as in the preceding pages, holds that the enemy had done his utmost and that Grant, instead of being defeated, was ready, on Monday morning, to assume the offensive, instead of going into the river.

"HEAD-QUARTERS MILITARY DIVISION OF THE MISSISSIPPI.

"*Prof. Henry Coppee, Philadelphia :*

"DEAR SIR:—In the June number of the *United States Service Magazine* I find a brief sketch of Lieutenant-General U. S. Grant, in which I see you are likely to perpetuate an error, which General Grant may not deem of sufficient importance to correct. To Gen. Buell's noble, able and gallant conduct you attribute the fact that the disaster of April 6th, at Pittsburg Landing, was retrieved and made the victory of the following day. As General Taylor is said, in his later days, to have doubted whether he was at the battle of Buena Vista at all, on account of the many things having transpired there, according to the historians, which he did not see, so I begin to doubt whether I was at the battle of Pittsburg Landing of modern description. But I was at the battles of April 6th and 7th, 1862. General Grant visited my division in person about 10 A. M., when the battle raged fiercest. I was then on the right. After some general conversation he remarked that I was doing right in stubbornly opposing the progress of the enemy; and, in answer to my inquiry as to cartridges, told me he had anticipated their want, and given orders accordingly; he then said his presence was more needed over at the left. About two in the afternoon of the 6th, the enemy materially slackened his attack on me, and about four in the afternoon I deliberately made a new line behind McArthur's drill field, placing batteries on chosen ground, repelling easily a cavalry attack, and watched the cautious appoach of the enemy's infantry, that never dislodged me there. I selected that line in advance of a bridge across Snake creek, by which we had all day been expecting the approach of Lew. Wallace's division from Crump's Landing. About five in the evening, before the sun set, General Grant came again to me, and after hearing my report of matters, explained to me the situation of affairs on the left, which were not as favorable; still the enemy had failed to reach the landing of the boats. We agreed that the enemy had expended the *furore* of his attack, and we estimated our loss, and approximated our then strength, including Lew. Wallace's fresh division, expected each minute. He then ordered me to get all things ready, and at daylight the next day to assume the offensive. That was before General Buell had arrived, but he was known to be near at hand. General Buell's troops took no essential part in the first day's fight, and Grant's army, though collected together hastily, green as militia, some regiments arriving without cartridges even, and nearly all hearing the dread sound of battle for the first time, had successfully withstood and repelled the first day's terrific onset of a superior enemy, well commanded and well handled. I know I had orders from General Grant to assume the offensive before I knew General Buell was on the west side of the Tennessee. I think General Buell, Colonel Fry, and others of General Buell's staff, rode up to where I was about sunset, about the time General Grant was leaving me. General Buell asked me many questions, and got of me a small map, which I had made for my own use, and told me that by daylight he could have eighteen thousand fresh men, which I knew would settle the matter.

"I understood Grant's forces were to advance on the right of the Corinth road and Buell's on the left, and accordingly at daylight I advanced my division by the flank, the resistance being trivial, up to the very spot where, the day before, the battle had been most severe, and then waited till near noon for Buell's troops to get up abreast, when the entire line advanced and recovered all the ground we had ever held. I know that, with the exception of one or two severe struggles, the fighting of April 7th was easy as compared with that of April 6th.

"I never was disposed, nor am I now, to question anything done by General Buell and his army, and I know that approaching our field of battle from the rear, he encountered that sickening crowd of laggards and fugitives that excited his contempt and that of his army, who never gave full credit to those in the front line, who did fight hard, and who had, at 4 in the afternoon, checked the enemy, and were prepared the next day to assume the offensive. I remember the fact better from General Grant's anecdote of his Donelson battle, which he told me then for the first time—that at a certain period of the battle, he saw that either side was ready to give way if the other showed a bold front, and he determined to do that very thing, to advance on the enemy, when, as he prognosticated, the enemy surrendered. At four o'clock in the afternoon of April 6th, he thought the appearance the same, and he judged with Lew.

Wallace's fresh division, and such of our startled troops as had recovered their equilibrium, he would be justified in dropping the defensive and assuming the offensive in the morning. And, I repeat, I received such orders before I knew General Buell's troops were at the river. I admit that I was glad that Buell was there, because I knew his troops were older than ours and better systematized and drilled, and his arrival made that certain, which before was uncertain. I have heard this question much discussed, and must say that the officers of Buell's army dwelt too much on the stampede of some of our raw troops, and gave us too little credit for the fact that for one whole day, weakened as we were by the absence of Buell's army, long expected, of Lew. Wallace's division, only four miles off, and of the fugitives from our ranks, we had beaten off our assailants for the time. At the same time, our Army of the Tennessee have indulged in severe criticism at the slow approach of that army which knew the danger that threatened us from the concentrated armies of Johnston, Beauregard and Bragg that lay at Corinth. In a war like this, where opportunities of personal prowess are as plenty as blackberries to those who seek them at the front, all such criminations should be frowned down; and were it not for the military character of your journal I would not venture to offer a correction of a very popular error.

"I will also avail myself of this occasion to correct another very common mistake in attributing to General Grant the selection of that battle-field. It was chosen by that veteran soldier, Major-Gen. Charles F. Smith, who ordered my division to disembark there, and strike for the Charleston Railroad. This order was subsequently modified by his ordering Hurlbut's division to disembark there, and mine higher up the Tennessee to the mouth of Yellow Creek, to strike the railroad at Burnsville. But floods prevented our reaching the railroad, when General Smith ordered me in person also to disembark at Pittsburg, and take post, well out, so as to make plenty of room, with Snake and Lick creeks the flanks of a camp for the grand army of invasion.

"It was General Smith who selected that field of battle, and it was well chosen. On any other we surely would have been overwhelmed, as both Lick and Snake creeks forced the enemy to confine his movements to a direct front attack, which new troops are better qualified to resist than where flanks are exposed to a real or chimerical danger. Even the divisions of that army were arranged in that camp by General Smith's order, my division forming, as it were, the outlying picket, whilst McClernand's and Prentiss' were the real line of battle, with W. H. L. Wallace in support of the right wing, and Hurlbut of the left; Lew. Wallace's division being detached. All these subordinate dispositions were made by the order of General Smith, before General Grant succeeded him to the command of all the forces up the Tennessee—head-quarters Savannah. If there was any error in putting that army on the west side of the Tennessee, exposed to the superior force of the enemy also assembling at Corinth, the mistake was not General Grant's—but there was no mistake. It was necessary that a combat, fierce and bitter, to test the manhood of the two armies, should come off, and that was as good a place as any. It was not then a question of military skill and strategy, but of courage and pluck, and I am convinced that every life lost that day to us was necessary; for otherwise at Corinth, at Memphis, at Vicksburg, we would have found harder resistance, had we not shown our enemies that, rude and untutored as we then were, we could fight as well as they.

"Excuse so long a letter, which is very unusual from me, but of course my life is liable to cease at any moment, and I happen to be a witness to certain truths which are now beginning to pass out of memory, and form what is called history.

"I also take great pleasure in adding that nearly all the new troops that, at Shiloh, drew from me official censure have more than redeemed their good name; among them that very regiment which first broke, the 53d Ohio, Colonel Appen. Under another leader, Colonel Jones, it has shared every campaign and expedition of mine since, is with me now, and can march and bivouac and fight as well as the best regiment in this or any army. Its reputation now is equal to any from the State of Ohio.

"I am, with respect,

"Yours, truly,

"W. T. Sherman, Major-Gen."

Eng[d] by J. C. Buttre.

W. H. L. Wallace

BRIG. GEN. W. H. L. WALLACE.

CHAPTER XIV.

PERSONAL AND INCIDENTAL.

Brigadier-General W. H. L. Wallace—Major-General Benjamin F. Prentiss—General Braymen—General Stuart—Major-General S. A. Hurlbut—Lieut.-Colonel Ellis—Colonel Raith—Major Goddard—Major Eaton—Major Page—Notices of Wounded Officers in Official Reports—The Batteries—The Scout Carson—Our Wounded—Illinois and the Battle of Shiloh!

NOT without the price of costly blood comes the redemption of a nation. It must be the blood of the best, the bravest. And thus has it been in our struggle. The defenders of the Constitution have been as the sons of kings, and freely has been shed their royal gore. The altar of sacrifice has been crimsoned from the veins of the first-born in honor and dignity. Such blood was shed at Shiloh.

William Henry Lamb Wallace was born at Urbana, Ohio, on the 8th of July, 1821. In 1833 his father came to Illinois, and made his residence in Lasalle County, on the south side of the beautiful Illinois river, about four miles southeast of what is now the city of Lasalle. In 1839 another removal placed the family at Mt. Morris, Ogle County, where could be enjoyed the benefits of the young Rock River Seminary, founded by the Methodist Episcopal Church, an institution, the students of which have enriched more than one hotly contested field with their blood.

In this Seminary young Wallace remained until he had completed its course of study. In December, 1844, after some preliminary legal study, he went with Samuel M. H. Hitt, Esq., a member of the General Assembly, to Springfield, with the purpose of entering, as a student, the law-office of Logan & Lincoln—Abraham Lincoln. On the way they fell into company with Hon. T. Lyle Dickey, subsequently judge, and later Colonel, and arriving at the capital the party took rooms together. Judge Dickey says, "Young Wallace assisted me in preparing my cases in Supreme Court and after a few weeks concluded to come to Ottawa and study law in my office, and accordingly did not apply to Logan & Lincoln. In March, 1845, he came and was admitted to the bar soon after."

But war was to delay his professional labors. In 1846 the Mexican war was upon us. The brave and eloquent Hardin was raising the 1st regiment Illinois volunteers, and Judge Dickey recruited and commanded Co. I. His student and prospective son-in-law enlisted as a private, and was made orderly sergeant, and was so mustered June 22, 1846. A few weeks later he was promoted 2d Lieutenant, "and," says the letter of Judge Dickey, "in that capacity he was on duty in his company on the voyage down the Mississippi, across the Gulf to Matagorda Bay, and on the march of 200 miles made in August, over the plains of Texas to San Antonio de Bexar." There Captain Dickey was compelled, by ill health, to resign his command, and 1st Lieut. Ben. M. Prentiss, adjutant of the regiment, succeeded him, and Wallace became adjutant. He fought by the side of his gallant Colonel, and in the thunders of Buena Vista, was near him when he was struck down. Could he dream that a similar fate was to be his own?

With the expiration of his year's enlistment he returned to Ottawa and resumed the profession of law as partner of Hon. John C. Champlin. In 1850, as Deputy U. S. Marshal, he took the census of Lasalle County, discharging his duties promptly and accurately. February 18, 1851, he married Miss Martha Ann Dickey, eldest daughter of Judge Dickey.

In 1852 Mr. Wallace was elected State Attorney for the ninth judicial district, an office he held until the fall of 1856. The duties of such a position are delicate and exacting. There must be firmness; there should not be cruelty. Mr. Wallace met its conflicting and perplexing duties in such manner as to merit approval. He was obliged to measure strength with the ablest talent of the Illinois bar, and his professional brethren saw in him a rising man. From 1852 he was associated in business with his father-in-law, and when the war came the firm was Judge T. Lyle Dickey, Mr. Wallace, and Cyrus E. Dickey. The two junior partners at once volunteered. Wallace did all he could—and with his popularity it was much—to aid the government and arouse the people to the magnitude of the struggle.

In May, 1861, he was chosen Colonel of the 11th three-months' volunteers, rendezvoused at Springfield. He was sent to Villa Ridge, twelve miles north of Cairo, to hold the railroad and watch the river. While here his camp was visited by Major-General Geo. B. McClellan, and that officer pronounced it the best regulated camp, and the regiment the best drilled volunteer regiment, he had seen.

In June (the 20th) he was ordered to Bird's Point and placed in command of the post. The duties at this post were complicated and often dangerous, and tested both his legal and military skill. Here he attracted the notice of General Grant, who read in him the essentials of the commander. About the last of January, 1862, he marched his regiment to Fort Jefferson.

The first of February he was placed in command of a brigade in McClernand's division and marched to Fort Henry. On the 12th his brigade, forming the extreme left of Gen. McClernand's division, marched on Fort Donelson and took part in the severe fighting of the 13th, 14th and 15th. In the account given elsewhere it was shown how well his command bore itself and how it was covered with imperishable honor. In the terrible conflict of Saturday forenoon it was the last to yield to the concentrated attack of the rebel army on the Union right. Wallace proved himself worthy to command such troops as made up his brigade. Their decimated rolls told how sorely they suffered—their comrades tell how nobly they fought. There was no wonder when the rumor came that Col. Wallace was promoted to Brigadier-General of Volunteers for gallant conduct on the field at Fort Donelson.

From Fort Donelson to Pittsburg Landing the troops were moved under the temporary command of Gen. C. F. Smith, and Wallace's brigade went into camp as part of McClernand's division. Here he received the confirmation of his promotion.

General Grant was again at the head of the army of the Tennessee, which he found in six divisions, the first of which was assigned to General C. F. Smith. This brave and able officer was sick, and the command of his division was devolved upon General Wallace, by Major-General Grant's personal direction.

The division was in the heat of battle, and much depended upon the coolness and intrepidity of its chief. He was all they asked. He shunned no danger and neglected no proper caution. From ten to nearly five o'clock that division held its ground. Four times, in massed strength, the foe was beaten back. Wallace's division stood, with Hurlbut's, for a time between the army and ruin. But, without supports, that isolated advance must be abandoned, and a retreat became inevitable. At that critical juncture the brave commander was shot through the head, and fell from his horse insensible, and, as was supposed, dead. His brother-in-law, Lieut. Cyrus E. Dickey, assisted by three orderlies, attempted to carry him from the ground, but, pressed by the pursuing foe, and two of the orderlies being wounded, they sadly laid him down upon the field. The next day the Federal forces regained that ground and he was found, not dead, barely living; the enemy had covered him with a blanket and placed his head upon another folded as a pillow. But his watch and purse were gone. He was removed to Savannah, where he lingered until Thursday, April 10th, when he died. His devoted wife reached Savannah the morning of the battle, and watched him with all of woman's unrecorded tenderness until the spirit had fled.

The remains were conveyed to Ottawa and buried. An immense concourse followed him to the grave, where he was buried with masonic rites. The "acacia sprigs" thrown upon his coffin-lid, not only symboled immortality, but told the undying love in which his memory should be held. Of the military, only his aids, Captain Hotchkiss and Lieut. Dickey, were present, but in the cortege was his own flag, that of the 11th, bullet-torn and rent from the fields of Donelson and Shiloh!

General Wallace was tall and erect, dignified, almost to reserve. As a commander he more than met the highest anticipations of his friends and admirers.

On the 23d of April, the Bar of Illinois, through Judge Purple, presented the following resolutions:

"*Resolved*, That the recent death of our esteemed friend and brother, the late W. H. L. Wallace, from wounds received while gallantly leading a division at the battle of Pittsburg Landing, the Bar of Illinois, in common with the people of the whole State, deplore the loss of a soldier, who, as well in his life as by the manner of his death on the field, has sealed by his blood this new testimony to the ineradicable devotion which the people of Illinois are manifesting in heroic deeds and patriotic sacrifices to that form of free government on this continent which domestic traitors are so wickedly attempting to overthrow.

"*Resolved*, That while, as citizens, the State may regret the loss of the experienced chief who could successfully inspire by his personal daring and valor the troops committed to his charge, and by his example and bravery command success in that desperate charge or assault of battle, and while to the grateful history of his country is now committed that fame which to remote ages will hereafter rank his name with the other heroic defenders of the Republic, yet the Bar of Illinois have a sadder tribute to now render his memory, by an expression of the profound grief which they feel at this parting and loss of a friend and brother.

"*Resolved*, That they knew in the late W. H. L. Wallace one who, while possessing all the virtues which adorn a private life of exemplary excellence; in his professional character he was also a man without a blemish. Of a persevering industry, a very high order of legal attainments, and the very highest order of intellectual capacity—he seemed above all to shine in the very spirit of intellectual, moral and professional rectitude. This was "the daily beauty of his life," which never ceased to distinguish him in that career of professional triumph which had placed him already in the very front rank of eminent professional men, in all his intercourse with his brethren of this Bar and the State. As brethren, therefore, of the profession which he honored in his life, as well as by his glorious death, we may well pause, as we now do, in the midst of our professional and other avocations, to drop a tear upon the tomb, and inscribe this brief tablet by recalling a few of the many virtues of his life.

"*Resolved*, That we tender our deepest sympathies to the widow and family of our departed brother; in their bereavement we are impressed with the conviction that all mere words are inadequate to express that deep sense of affliction which the loss of such a husband must have caused to the bereaved and stricken one. We humbly commend her to the guardianship and care of Him, from whom alone at such a time, can come the only solace for hearts so afflicted. He only can "temper the wind to the shorn lamb."

"*Resolved*, That Hon. Norman H. Purple, the Chairman of this meeting, be appointed to present a copy of these resolutions to the Supreme Court of this State, at its present session, and request that they may be entered on record among the proceedings of said Court.

"*Resolved*, That the Secretary of this meeting furnish a copy of the proceedings of the meeting, and they be presented to the family of deceased."

Judge Purple presented the resolutions accompanied with an

eloquent tribute to the virtues and memory of the deceased, to which his Honor, Chief Justice Caton thus replied:

"The Court received the announcement of the death of Gen. Wallace with emotions, for the expression of which we find no adequate words. In his death the Bar has lost one of its brightest ornaments, the Court one of its safest advisers, and our country one of its ablest defenders. His whole professional life has been passed among us, and we have known him well. All your words of encomium are but simple justice, and we know they proceed from the deepest convictions of their truth. All his instincts were those of a gentleman; all his impulses were of a noble and lofty character—his sensibilities refined and generous. He was certainly a man of a very high order of talent, and he was a very excellent lawyer. By his industry he studied the law closely, and by his clear judgment he applied it properly. He did honor to his profession—it is meet that his professional brethren should honor his memory.

"Scarcely a year ago he was with us, engaged in a lucrative practice—the ornament and the delight of a large circle of friends, and enjoying the quiet endearments of domestic life, loving and beloved by a family worthy of him, now made desolate. At the very first call of his country for defenders, he abandoned his practice, he withdrew from his associates and friends at home, and tore himself from the domestic circle, and pledged his energies and his life to the vindication of his country's flag, which has been torn down and dishonored by rebel hands at Sumter—to the defence of that Constitution and those laws, the maintenance of which is indispensable to material greatness and happiness. For these he fought, for these he died.

"For myself, I may say, he was my near neighbor and my dear friend. He honored me with his confidence, and disclosed to me fully the patriotic impulses which led him to abandon all to defend his native land. If he was an able lawyer, so he was an able commander. If we mourn him as a departed friend and brother, so does the country mourn him as one of her ablest Generals gone.

"With the glad news of victory, comes the sad lament of his death. Our gladness was turned to mourning. So it ever is, and so must it ever be in this sublunary world. With all our joys are mingled strains of sorrow. Happiness unalloyed is reserved for that brighter and better world promised to those who act well their part on earth, into the full fruition of which, those who knew him best, doubt not he is accepted.

"The resolutions which have been adopted by the Bar will be entered upon the records of the Court, as a perpetual memorial of our appreciation of the worth of the late General Wallace, and the Clerk will furnish a copy of them and a copy of this order to the widow and family of the deceased, and out of respect to his memory the Court will now adjourn."

MAJOR-GENERAL B. F. PRENTISS.

The subject of the following sketch was the first in Illinois who wore the insignia of a Brigadier; one of the first placed in command of a division and the first to be carried into captivity, and experience the tender mercies of the Southern chivalry.

BENJAMIN F. PRENTISS was born November 23, 1819 at Bellville, Virginia, subsequently his father removed to Missouri; thus the youth of the future General was spent in the midst of the practical beauties of American slavery. It may be that early recollections had to do with the bitterness with which the General denounced the system and all its appendages in the political campaign in 1864.

In 1841 the family removed to Quincy, Illinois, where he supported and educated himself by working at his trade, rope-making. His first taste of war was in 1844. He was 1st Lieutenant of the Quincy Rifles, of which Captain (Brigadier-General) James D. Morgan was commander. "The Rifles went into Hancock county the infested district and rendered the State some service in the maintenance of order.

At the out-breaking of the Mexican war he promptly volunteered and was made Adjutant of Colonel Hardin's Regiment, 1st Illinois Infantry. On the resignation of Capt. T. L. Dickey, he became Captain of Co. I and was succeeded as Adjutant by W. H. L. Wallace. The companies of James D. Morgan and Prentiss, Morgan the ranking officer, were at the battle of Buena Vista posted at Saltillo, under orders from Gen. Taylor and held it, against a superior force, and these regiments won marked commendation from their perfection in drill, and soldierly efficiency.

Returning to Quincy Captain Prentiss resumed for a time his former trade, and subsequently entered the commission and forwarding business in which he continued until the war began.

In 1860 he was a candidate for Congress against William A. Richardson, but the district was overwhelmingly democratic and he was beaten.

Of course the intelligence of the outrage upon the Flag stirred the blood of one who had carried it beyond the Rio Grande. On Sunday came word of the surrender of Sumter, and in one week, Prentiss, with the reorganized Quincy Rifles and others, amounting in all to two hundred men, was *en route* to Cairo, determined to aid in holding it at all hazards. He was elected Col. of the 7th Regiment, and as soon as there were troops enough to organize a brigade, he was elected Brigadier-General of Illinois troops under the three months' call, his former compatriot, Morgan, succeeding him in command of the 7th. He was active and energetic at Cairo, placing its defences in such order as to promise resistance to any assailing force, drilling his new recruits, who, though since proved to be very brave, were most of them *very raw.*

At the close of the three months' term General Prentiss was made Brigadier-General of volunteers, by Presidential appointment, and very soon was ordered into Southern-Missouri, where he conducted an expedition through Pilot Knob, and the southern part of the State. He was next ordered into North Missouri where, with a handful of troops, whom he multiplied by activity, he subdued for a time the desperate hordes of guerrillas which infested the unfortunate district. From thence he was ordered to report to General Grant at Pittsburg Landing, where he arrived only two or three days before the battle and was ordered at once to take command of the 6th division.

The reader has seen the statement made by the General as to the disposition of troops to prevent surprise and to meet the enemy. Charging with fury came the picked men of Johnston's army, and the gallant sixth division received the attention of its heavy columns. Seeing he was flanked, General Prentiss ordered his division to fall back in order of battle, to the color line of his encampment, at the same time sending word to Wallace and Hurlbut. Again compelled to retire, his division was re-formed on Hurlbut's right and Wallace's left. Again and again came on the foe and his command was greatly reduced by casualties and the escapade of many of his raw troops. At ten A. M., General Grant visited his division and expressed himself gratified with his exertions and plans, and ordered him to maintain his position. He did so, until even Hurlbut's iron division was compelled to give way, when he changed front and attempted to advance upon the enemy, only to find himself encircled by his foe and without supports, and was obliged, with more than two thousand to surrender. He fought desperately to prevent it, but was overpowered. The exultation of the captors was beyond description. As they passed through Southern towns, the population thronged to see a Yankee General, and occasionally the General treated them to a sound stirring Union speech, such as they had not often heard in their "sunny latitudes." In Memphis he made a speech on the 10th, ostensibly to his own troops, but the citizens heard it and some cheered. The Provost Marshal bade him be silent. The General told him that his (Prentiss') friends there, were four to one if they could be heard. He said to the citizens, "Keep quiet a few weeks and you will have an opportunity to cheer the old flag to your hearts' content." His "boys" gave, as musical volunteers, Hail Columbia, Red White and Blue, Happy Land of Canaan, and set to melody the information that

"John Brown's soul is marching on!
Glory, hallelujah!"

They were conveyed to Montgomery, Alabama, where they were paroled, on the 23d of May, 1862. They reached Nashville on the 5th of June. The reason assigned for the parole was the inability to feed them. The rebels had not then reached the savage cruelty of deliberately starving our men taken in battle, as in Libby Prison, Andersonville and Millen!

On the 29th of November his commission as Major-General of volunteers was dated, subsequently to which he rendered comparatively little active service, and within a few months tendered his resignation. In the Presidential canvass of 1863, he was placed upon the Republican electoral ticket for the State at large, and spoke repeatedly in favor of the re-election of Mr. Lincoln and the election of his former companion in arms, General Oglesby, to the gubernatoral chair of Illinois.

Brigadier-General Mason Brayman, was born in Buffalo, New York, May 23, 1813. His farm-life and the common school gave him his early education. He entered the office of the *Buffalo Journal* and learned the printer's trade,and the second year was made foreman. From the types to preparation for the bar was the next step, and at twenty years of age, he was editor of the *Buffalo Bulletin*, a thorough Jackson paper, advocating democracy with all imaginable zeal, and with fair ability to boot. At twenty-two he was admitted to the bar, and the succeeding year he married.

In 1837 he was editor of the *Louisville Advertiser*. In 1842, he removed to Springfield, Illinois, and engaged in the practice of his profession. Three years subsequently, under appointment of Governor Ford, he revised and codified the Statutes of the State. In 1846 he was made a special states' attorney and commissioned to prosecute offences growing out of the Mormon war.

In 1851, he was attorney for the Illinois Central Railway, and as such, had the management of vast pecuniary interests, securing the right of way, protecting its land, &c. He was associated with the late Governor Bissell, and the presence of the latter in Congress devolved most of the care and responsibility on Mr. Brayman.

He was next engaged in a great railway scheme which should connect Cairo with Texas, connecting south and west with Galveston and the Pacific. It was a huge undertaking. Mr. Brayman was president of the two companies engaged in it, and the prospects were flattering until the commencement of the war, which of course laid aside the "Southern route to the Pacific," until peace should return and render Southern travel safe for Northern men with Union principles.

He was an original and thorough Democrat in his convictions and associations, but on the breaking out of the war, he with McClernand and Logan at once offered himself to the country. Governor Yates gave him a commission as Major of the 29th infantry, forming part of General McClernand's brigade. He was appointed chief of staff and Assistant Adjutant, for which position his business habits and decision gave him eminent fitness. Of course his relations to

General McClernand brought him early into action. He was in the battle of Belmont, and Gen. McClernand speaks of him with his other staff officers "as entitled to gratitude for the zeal and alacrity with which they bore orders in the face of danger, and discharged all their duties in the field." He was in the attack on Fort Donelson, and during the battle of Shiloh he manifested gallantry which won admiration from his superiors and the rank and file. At a critical juncture when the enemy came on to carry a battery, and the supporting regiments faltered, the Major seized a flag which had fallen, and passing in front, rallied them, while the enemy's musketry was pouring a shower of balls about him, but escaped unhurt. He believed then and since that God preserved him, for he has faith in Providence.

Colonel Reardon resigning, Major Brayman became Colonel of the 29th infantry April 15, 1862. His service being with our Western armies, will come before the reader with the various campaigns, and is not sketched in detail.

Having, by gallantry and capacity, shown his right to promotion, he was commissioned Brigadier-General of volunteers Sept. 24, 1862.

While Gen. Brayman was commanding the post of Bolivar, Tenn., one Neely, clerk of the Hardeman County Court, was brought before him, and the order in reference to him acquired such a notoriety that the insertion of a part of it will be of interest to our readers:

"SPECIAL ORDER No. 64.

"The General Commanding is advised that Rufus P. Neely, clerk of the Hardeman County Court, late a colonel in the rebel army, and engaged in acts of war against the United States, still persists in treasonable language and acts—giving aid and comfort to armed enemies, and disturbing the peace of this post—he having taken an oath of allegiance to the pretended government of the confederate States, in violation of his oath of office—still adhering to such allegiance, and refusing to take the oath of allegiance to the United States.

"On the night of November 28th, he was arrested and brought within the lines, and on that and the two succeeding nights, a party of mounted men, including two commissioned officers, was detailed to guard his premises and capture guerillas, who were prowling in the neighborhood, and were said to be entertained at his house.

"While there, the party were assailed with abusive epithets, and compelled, while in the performance of duty, to listen to disloyal declarations and threats on the part of the wife and daughters of Mr. Neely. They state in writing that Mrs. Neely acknowledged the fact of harboring Southern soldiers, and declared that she would give the last thing she had to help them—that the federal army 'was a set of murderers and rogues'—that the oath was of no effect for a secessionist to take—that she would go where she pleased and would not take the oath—that 'the Devil had telegraphed to Jeff. Davis not to send him any more Yankees, for hell was already full of them, and he could not accommodate any more until he could dig another pit to put them in,' etc., etc. A daughter is reported as declaring that if she had her way, 'all the Yankees should be put in prison and fed on bread and water thirty days, if they lived so long'—that if 'old Abe Lincoln had been dead, and such a man as Jeff. Davis in his place, this trouble would not have been'—that 'Lincoln and all such men ought to be dead'—that 'old George Washington was a nasty, mean old scamp!'

"The General Commanding regards with great charity, the harmless ebullitions of malevolence and spite, which, so far from being dangerous, only indicate sympathy with a wicked and failing cause. The patriotic officers and soldiers of the American army have been severely tried in this particular, and deserve great credit for the forbearance with which they have listened without resenting. This may, however, be due to the fact that their forbearance has been taxed most severely by those whose gentle sex claimed their homage, and whose social position, education, and supposed refinement of manners would appear to afford a guarantee against intentional and persistent rudeness.

"It is not the desire or duty of officers in command to take account of indecent and treasonable language, unless uttered under such circumstances as to do harm, or to affect the efficiency of the service. In the case under consideration, the officers and soldiers of the United States were on duty—obeying orders, and entitled to protection; not only from molestation, but from insult. The General Commanding will not impose upon his men disagreeable duties, and require of them, in addition, to submit to needless humiliation from public enemies, even though persons called ladies, are the offenders.

"The avowal of treasonable acts and intentions, the coarse and disrespectful terms in which the President of the United States, and the army of which he is Commander-in-Chief, are spoken of, as before recited, are so often heard, and have been so long tolerated under the very shadow of our flag, as to excite no surprise —scarcely rebuke.

"But it is not so—it shall not be so, when the venerated name of WASHINGTON is profaned. Among all nations, civilized and savage—in all languages—by high and low—by the good, the noble, the brave, and gentle—even by the drunkard, the ruffian and the traitor, the memory of Washington is held in reverence. To the men and women of America, his name is expressive of all that is brave and magnanimous in war, and good and wise in statesmanship, and is spoken with something of that reverential awe which is felt when pronouncing that of the Savior of mankind. A case is here presented—the first within memory, in which this universal sentiment of the Christian world has been set at defiance. It affords another striking evidence of the destructive and demoralizing influence of that political heresy which seeks the overthrow of that benignant government, and the dishonor of the sacred flag which the valor and wisdom of Washington gave us. The General Commanding feels no delicate reserve in expressing his abhorrence of such language, whenever and by whomsoever spoken. Let the man who dares to utter it die the death of a traitor, and the roof-tree beneath which, a woman shall revile the memory of Washington, tumble in swift ruin to the ground.

"In consideration of the matters here stated, it is ordered as follows:

"First. The Provost Marshal will release Rufus P. Neely, late colonel in the rebel army, from close custody, and remand him to his plantation outside the picket-lines of this post.

"Second. The Provost Marshal will also revoke any permits heretofore given to said Neely, his wife, and his daughter, Miss Kate Neely, to pass within the picket-lines of this post, and will absolutely exclude them therefrom, until further orders.

"Third. Said Rufus P. Neely is debarred from holding the office, or performing any of the duties of Clerk of Hardeman County."

This was followed by an earnest exhortation to the people of West Tennessee to purge themselves of all complicity with treason *in their homes.*

Gen. Brayman is a Christian patriot who has well served his State. We shall meet him again with our armies.

Brigadier-General David Stuart was the son of Robert Stuart of the old Scotch covenanter type and stock. Mr. Robert Stuart was a prominent trader among the Indians of the Northwest and accompanied the expedition of Clark & Lewis. The General was his second child, and after an academic course at Utica and Oberlin, he graduated at Amherst College. Studying law he became a successful advocate, especially in criminal practice. Popular in his manner and style of oratory, and an ardent democrat, he was early thrown into political life, and in 1852 went into Congress from the first district of Michigan. While in the House, he determined to abandon politics and devote himself arduously to his profession, and seeing in Chicago an inviting field he removed thither in 1855, where he soon took high rank.

He acquired national notoriety from his connection with a celebrated divorce case, the details of which were published in the leading dailies east and west.

Colonel Wilson says of him:

"No sooner had the rebellion broken out, than David Stuart, true to the instincts of his nature and the patriotic blood that flowed in his veins, threw aside his briefs and at once commenced raising a brigade, to be called after Senator Douglas, whose devoted and earnest friend he was. Circumstances* of an unfortunate character had occurred at Chicago which, for a time, cast a cloud over his career; and acting under prejudices very natural, the press, the bar, and even the public, with few exceptions, interposed every obstacle and barrier to his success in raising, equipping and fitting-out the Douglas Brigade. This opposition and these obstacles only served to develop the heroism of the man, and called into play the Scotch persistence of his nature. In spite of the unjust jeers of the press, in spite of the calumnies of the crowd and the taunts of his brethren of the bar, David Stuart, by his own energies, with his own purse, by his talents, persistence and power, raised and put into the field the Douglas Brigade, consisting of two regiments of one thousand men each; and I venture to say, that finer regiments, better equipped or more thoroughly drilled, have not joined the ranks of the armies of the Union.

"July 22, 1861, Stuart was elected Lieutenant-Colonel of the 1st Douglas Regiment, known as the 42d, Colonel Webb, and, October 31st, was elected Colonel of the 2d Douglas (or 55th) Regiment which was sent into the field on the 5th of December. Colonel Stuart was in command of a brigade in Sherman's division at the battle of Shiloh, where he displayed soldierly qualities of the highest order and was severely wounded. General W. T. Sherman, in his report, says: 'My 2d brigade, Colonel Stuart, was detached near two miles from my headquarters. He had to fight his own battle on Sunday, as the enemy interposed between him and Gen. Prentiss early in the day. Colonel Stuart was wounded severely, and yet reported for duty on Monday morning.' Colonel Stuart has been constantly on duty with his regiment or brigade since he first took the field, and, on December 2, 1862, was appointed by the President a Brigadier-General."

It is useless to speculate upon the refusal of the Senate to confirm the nomination, but it did so, and the General retired from the ser-

*The divorce case above mentioned.

vice. He had already won distinction. His bravery and skill promised well to the army, and would have given him eminence among the defenders of the national honor.

MAJOR-GENERAL STEPHEN A. HURLBUT.

General Hurlbut has been from the outset, an officer of ability and terrible earnestness. He has struck hard and telling blows against the foes of his government, but none against its friends. He has won distinction on the field. His division was first to land and hold Pittsburg Landing, and in the long and desperate conflict, the "Fighting Fourth" was as a wall of steel; none of its regiments lost their organization or failed to rally to their colors. It is not claiming too much to say that to him is due the brilliant success of the fight of Hatchie. Subsequently, while in command of the 16th Army Corps, with headquarters at Memphis, there were 79,000 men on its rolls. This leader we simply introduce; he will pass before the reader again as the course of our Illinois legions is marked on the red fields of war, for he is still in the service.

It may be that his fiery earnestness is partially due to his intimate knowledge of the people we have to fight, for he was born in Charleston, S. C., Nov. 29, 1815. The son of a Unitarian clergyman, he received a good education, and then studied law in the office of James L. Pettigrew in Charleston, and in that nest of nullification and treason he practiced law several years.

During the Florida war, he entered the six months' volunteers as sergeant in a company of militia, and came out lieutenant on the staff.

He had the good sense to see that for a man of active temperament and strong convictions, there was ampler scope and better opportunity in the great fields of the free Northwest.

In 1845 he removed to Illinois and settled at Belvidere, Boone County, and engaged in his profession, occasionally mingling in politics, being a prominent member of the State Constitutional Convention in 1847. This fact shows that he soon made his impress upon the people, for as yet he had been resident less than two years. He also represented that constituency in the State Legislature several times and with marked ability.

Mr. Lincoln knew him well and selected him as one of the first generals chosen from civilians. His commission as Brigadier was dated May 17th. He entered the service to help crush the rebellion, and right well he knew the character of the men who led it. He had sounded the depths of pro-slavery hate, and was aware that it meant the destruction of the Union and the enslavement of the North. On the 15th of July, 1861, he issued a proclamation to the people of Northeastern Missouri, where he was in command, in which he taught the restless dupes of Claibourn Jackson, sound doctrine in words of unmistakable import:—"The time for the toleration of treason has passed, and the man, or body of men, who venture to stand in defiance of the supreme authority of the Union, peril their lives in the attempt." He pronounced stern retribution upon the guerrilla mode of warfare invented by secession infamy. He gave fair warning that Missouri courts would not be his resort for justice in such cases, but that it would be sought and administered through the swifter, surer agency of the court-martial.

They soon found that his hand was

"Gauntleted in glove of steel."

In command on the line of the Hannibal & St. Jo. Railroad, and on the 29th of July, 1861, he gave the wealthy secessionists notice of his purpose to keep the road in repair at their expense. That he was not jesting they soon learned. A train was fired upon and a Mr. Wilcox disarmed. Gen. Hurlbut marched his troops into Palmyra, county seat of Marion County, and issued an order requiring the citizens to deliver to Col. Smith, commanding the 16th Illinois, each morning, rations as follows:

"Salt pork or bacon, 412 pounds, or in lieu thereof, 687 pounds fresh beef; corn meal, 687 pounds; beans, 44 quarts, or 55 pounds rice; coffee, 55 pounds; sugar (brown dry), 8⅛ pounds; vinegar, 5½ gallons; soap, 22 pounds; salt, 11 quarts; potatoes, or mixed vegetable diet, 550 pounds; molasses, 2½ gallons; wood, ½ cord; corn in ear, 2 bushels." He farther gave the authorities notice that if these things were not delivered promptly, "they will be taken from the most convenient persons and places and the regiment will be billeted upon the city of Palmyra, in private houses, according to the convenience of the regiment."

In addition the county was notified that it would be required to pay the expenses of the transportation of the regiment. The occupation on the terms of the order to continue until the marauders were given up. There was added a piece of grim humor, that if the county authorities declined to act, or cannot be found, those of the city must "fill the order and render their charges against the county."

This did not prove sufficient to cure the marauding, and he issued, on the 19th of August, an order to the mayor and authorities of Palmyra to "deliver within six days the marauders who fired on the train bound west on the Hannibal & St. Joseph railroad, on the evening of the 16th inst., and broke into the telegraph office. If the guilty persons are not delivered up as required, and within the time herein specified, the whole brigade will be moved into your county and contributions levied to the amount of $10,000 on Marion County, and $5,000 on the city of Palmyra."

It was essential, and it was truly humane, early to teach those "borderers" that treason was costly; that its indulgence was incompatible with both duty and safety. This promptness in settling accounts has marked General Hurlbut's administration wherever he has been charged with the duties of military administrator.

After the capture of Donelson he was temporarily in command at that post. In the battle of Pittsburg Landing he was in charge of the fourth division of General Grant's army, placed across the Corinth road, and which was brought into action early on Sunday, fought through that day with desperate courage, and on Monday morning at eight o'clock was re-formed in line of battle, and after eating a few crackers, again plunged into the sea of fire.

Official and unofficial reports alike concur in honoring the bravery of this division and the gallantry and ability of its commanding General. Mounted on his gray, he rode along the ranks, a prominent target for the enemy's fire. He personally superintended the planting and directing of new batteries, and personally headed his light brigades in the desperate charge. On the second day, his gray which had become a mark for rebel riflemen was killed, greatly to the relief of the General's staff, though to his own grief. It is not proper to re-write what is found in the previous chapter, and which would be necessary to give the details of Hurlbut's division. A member of the staff, says: "The General had several narrow escapes. He was struck by a spent musket ball on his left arm, but save that received no personal injury. The writer saw a rifle-shot strike a tree within a few feet of his head, eliciting from him the remark, 'They have our range pretty well.' At another time a shell burst within ten feet of him, but he was not scratched by it. His courage and coolness under fire, and his entire disregard for his personal safety, were remarked by all under him, and by his bravery and skill in this engagement, he has won the love and confidence of the brave troops under his command."

For bravery on this field, he was promoted Major-General of volunteers, with commission dating from September 17, 1862.

While other troops fought the bloody battle of Corinth, Major-General Hurlbut marching from Bolivar and with Major-General Ord fell upon the enemy's rear at the Hatchie. General Grant says in his official report, these divisions "drove the enemy back and across the Hatchie over ground where it is almost incredible that a superior force should be driven by an inferior, capturing two of his batteries (eight guns) many hundred small arms, and several hundred prisoners. "To these two divisions of the army all praise is due and will be awarded by a grateful country."

The battles of Iuka, Corinth and the Hatchie were part of one grand engagement and will be examined farther on.

It has been the fortune of General Hurlbut to mingle in other battle scenes yet to come in review and also to have command of the important post of Memphis. At present he is in command of the important Department of the Gulf, where his eminent administrative abilities have full scope. None can deny him the meed of the true soldier and the successful commander, for he has been fully tested. We shall meet him in later campaigns.

LIEUTENANT-COLONEL ELLIS.

Among those who fell at Shiloh was Edward F. W. Ellis, Lieutenant-Colonel commanding the 15th Regiment Illinois Volunteers. He was born in Milton, Maine, April 15, 1819. He was a tall, noble looking man of much decision and positiveness. He came to Ohio when nineteen years of age, and was admitted to the bar at twenty-two. In 1849 he went to California, where he was unfortunate in commercial speculation and lost all. He then resumed the profession with marked success. In the year 1851 he was a member of the California Legislature, and fought the effort to shadow the Golden Coast with the curse of slavery. In 1852 he returned to Ohio, and in 1854 removed to Rockford, Illinois, and was associated with a banking firm. When war came he promptly gave himself to his country, and raised for the 15th, a company called the Ellis Rifles. He was chosen Lieutenant-Colonel, but Col. Turner being placed in command of a brigade, he was acting Colonel. At the battle of Pittsburg Landing the 15th, Lieutenant-Colonel Ellis commanding, was in the 2d brigade, Colonel Veatch commanding, of Hurlbut's Division. The line in front, on Monday morning became panic-stricken and stampeded through the lines of the 15th and 46th Illinois—broke without an effort at resistance, General Hurlbut says "without firing a shot." The 15th was left exposed to a terrible fire, which it met and gallantly returned. Lieutenant-Colonel Ellis cheered his men forward, but was struck in the breast by a ball and killed instantly.

The next in command, Major Goddard, a brave soldier and gallant gentleman met a similar fate, falling bravely at his post. The regiment was compelled to fall back.

The city of Rockford mourned the death of Col. Ellis with deep sorrow. His future promised distinction. Major Goddard was worthy of his post and together they went down to the soldier's grave.

Colonel Ransom reports among the names mentioned with honor, that of Captain Henry H. Carter, of Company K, 11th Ill., "who, with his company, so bravely cut his way through the rebel cavalry at Fort Donelson, was among the first to fall on this bloody field, mortally wounded. A good man, a true soldier, his loss is irreparable."

Major Nevieus, of the same regiment, was severely wounded, but rallied sufficiently to assume command when Colonel Ransom was so badly wounded as to be compelled to submit to removal to the rear. "Capt. Coats and Lieut. Walrod were also wounded. Lieut. Freed, commanding Co. A, whose coolness and bravery always made his command invincible, was borne to the rear during the first engagement, severely and, I fear, mortally wounded."

"Acting Quartermaster Goodrich, ever faithful to his trust, a brave soldier, was shot by my side, through the head."

Col. Hare, commanding the first brigade of the first division (W. H. L. Wallace's) says:

"Major Samuel Eaton, of the 18th Illinois, was badly wounded while commanding his regiment. Captain Daniel H. Brush, next in command, was soon after severely wounded. Captain W. Q. Dillon, of Co. C, arrived on the field at this moment and took command, but was almost instantly killed. From that time the regiment was led by Captain Anderson, who did his duty nobly."

General Hurlbut mentions with pride the heroism of Col. John A. Davis, of the 46th, who rallied his regiment in the terrible fire when Ellis went down, and, who, seeing the color-bearer fall, seized and carried off the colors, receiving in so doing a severe wound. He states that Colonel Pugh, of the 41st Illinois was unexpectedly called to command a brigade, "and led it steadily and well through the battle." He says: "Colonel A. K. Johnston, 28th Illinois, was under my eye during both days. I bear willing testimony to the perfect coolness and thorough handling of his regiment throughout the whole time."

Colonel John Logan was severely wounded on Sunday, and the Lieut.-Colonel of the 41st fell about the same time, both in discharge of duty."

General McCook honorably mentions Colonel Kirk, of the 34th Illinois, who commanded a brigade, as a brave and competent officer. When the Major commanding the 34th fell, "the regiment wavered for a moment, when Colonel Kirk seized a flag, rushed forward, and steadied the line again; while doing this he was severely wounded in the shoulder."

Major Levanway, a noble, scholarly gentleman, a popular lawyer, was greatly beloved by the men of the 34th, fell, killed instantly. General McCook said: "The gallant Levanway, foremost in the ranks of danger, was killed instantly by a grape-shot. His name is another bright one added to the list of illustrious Illinois dead, who have dared to do and die in the cause of the Republic. To him and the brave ones who sleep with him, the nation owes the holy debt of remembrance."

Gen. Sherman reports the severe wounding of Col. Julius Raith, of the 43d Illinois, a native of Germany, but who came to this State in 1836, when he was but seventeen years of age. He served as Captain with distinction in Col. Bissell's regiment during the war with Mexico. He entered into the cause of the Union with hearty earnestness and was instrumental in raising the 43d, and entered the service as its Colonel in October, 1861. On that memorable Sunday at Shiloh, he led a brigade made up of the 17th, 29th and 49th Illinois. The brigade was assigned to the immediate defense of Waterhouse's battery. Appler's regiment broke in confusion, and was followed by Munger's, leaving the battery exposed. The enemy rushed forward in overwhelming numbers, but the three regiments stood their ground under the terrific rebel fire, until the commander, Col. Raith, fell from his horse, shot above the knee by a minnie ball, when, to use Gen. Sherman's words, "they manifested disorder" and three of Waterhouse's guns were captured. The brave Colonel lay twenty-four hours on the field, and when picked up was in a feeble and exhausted condition. He was conveyed to the steamer Hannibal, and on the way to the Mound City Hospital his leg was amputated. He never rallied, but died on the 11th of April of tetanus or lock-jaw.

General Sherman says, "Major Sanger's intelligence, quick perception and rapid execution were of great value to me. He also compliments Major Taylor, chief of cavalry, highly.

General Veatch says: "Col. Hall of the 14th Illinois, with his regiment, led that gallant charge on Monday evening, which drove the enemy beyond our lines and closed the struggle on that memorable day. In the heat of the battle he exhibited the skill and firmness of a veteran."

All the reports recognize the efficiency of the Illinois artillery throughout both the eventful days of Shiloh. Waterhouse was left without supports, and with his battery, that scorned to retreat, fought for a terrible half hour with an enemy closing upon each flank and bearing down upon the front, when he retreated, seriously wounded in the thigh by a minnie ball, and his first Lieutenant, Abbott, also wounded, though slightly, bringing off only three guns.

Schwartz fought his guns beside Waterhouse, and under compulsion, shared the retreat, losing most of his guns.

Taylor's battery, commanded by Captain Barrett, supported gallantly by the 22d Illinois infantry, stood firm, sending its terrible fire through the serried lines of Beauregard, until battery and support were outflanked on both sides, when they retired through a heavy cross-fire, the battery losing one man killed, seventeen wounded, twelve horses, the forge and battery wagons.

Waterhouse took a second position with his three guns, supported by McClernand's second brigade, and was again compelled to retreat and again advanced.

The rebels well knew when, on the parade ground of the first division, Taylor's battery took up its second position and engaged in a duel with a rebel battery eight hundred yards in front, which it silenced, and blew up its caisson.

In the Sunday fight Co. A, Chicago Artillery, Captain Wood was so much cut up as to be able to work but three guns.

Matteson's and Silversparre's guns, on Sunday afternoon, effectually stayed the heavy advancing columns of Beauregard's forces.

As to Colonel Webster, all accorded him the meed of the highest skill and coolest decision. Long will be remembered by Southern leaders, that semi-circle of belching cannon he placed to celebrate the vespers of that Sabbath fight, and before which recoiled the hosts dashing forward to "drive Grant into the river."

Col. David Stuart, commanding a brigade, was severely wounded He was commended for bravery and capacity.

In the last bloody effort on our left, the famous scout, Carson from Chicago, was killed instantly by a cannon ball which took off his head. He was a daring and skillful scout, making his way almost at pleasure within and out of the enemy's lines.

The Illinois 57th, Col. Baldwin, lost heavily after exhibiting the most determined bravery. Major N. B. Page, of Malden, was killed, falling in the heroic discharge of duty. He was mourned by comrades and by the community from which he went to war. Five Captains were wounded, one mortally; three Lieutenants were wounded, one mortally.

Captain Lewis Mauss, a noted scientific Chicago occulist, commanding a company in the 43d, was wounded in the side by a fragment of shell and died within twenty-four hours.

Captain E. M. Knapp, of the 52d, was killed on Sunday as he cheered his men on to the battle. But the long roll cannot be perfectly made at this time.

Other cases of merit will be mentioned in the record of regiments and individuals. In the battle of Shiloh, Illinois wrote a glorious historic scroll. Whatever may be hereafter, the memory of that day, with its proud achievements, can never be taken from her. She wrote in blood a chapter that can never be obliterated. In her prairie homes, along her rivers, among her graves, and in her cities, thousands of children will each proudly say, "My father was an Illinois soldier in the battle of Shiloh!"

CHAPTER XV.

Reconnoissance on the Corinth Road—The Movement on Purdy—The Battles at Farmington—Evacuation of Corinth, and its Occupation by the Union Forces—Changes in the Army—Battle of Iuka—The Rebel Defeat at Corinth—Battles of the Hatchie.

GENERAL GRANT, with his customary tenacity of purpose and rapidity of action, did not rest upon the success achieved at Shiloh. On the 8th of April, Gen. Sherman with his cavalry and two brigades of infantry made a reconnoissance on the Corinth road. The rebel cavalry were soon overtaken and a fight immediately occurred. The rebels charged upon our skirmish line and broke through it, putting the Ohio Seventy-seventh to flight, and at the outset throwing Col. Dickey's Fourth Illinois Cavalry into disorder. Gen. Sherman sent orders to the rear for the brigade to form in line of battle. The broken infantry and cavalry rallied on this line and advanced, Col. Dickey's gallant regiment leading off in a dashing charge with their carbines. The rebels broke this time and fled. The troops being wearied out with their three days' hard fighting, privations and exposures, the pursuit was given up, and after caring for the wounded and burying the dead, they returned to camp.

On the 30th of April, another reconnoissance was made by order of Gen. Grant toward Purdy, a small town twenty miles from Corinth, on the Mobile and Ohio Railroad. The force consisting of seven regiments of infantry including the Seventy-eighth and Twentieth Ohio, two batteries of artillery, and the Fourth and Eleventh Illinois and Fifth Ohio Cavalry were commanded by Gen. Wallace, and belonged to his division. At night the infantry and artillery bivouacked in the woods midway between Pittsburg Landing and Purdy, while the cavalry under command of Col. Dickey continued on toward Purdy, reaching its vicinity about midnight. The intense darkness of the night, and a previous storm which set in, rendered operations impossible, and the force returned to the bivouac. The next morning, however, the word was again "Forward," and our cavalry entered Purdy. Col. Dickey sent a small force to skirmish two miles below Purdy, while another force destroyed the railroad bridge two miles above it. The work was accomplished. The bridge was torn up and the connection between Purdy and Corinth completely destroyed. The object of the expedition having been accomplished, the troops returned to camp on the 29th, without the loss of a man by the enemy. Many a brave Illinois soldier however, fell a victim to the exposures of that night in the storm and swamps.

The third reconnoissance developed the battle of Farmington, in which Illinois generals and Illinois soldiers again shone conspicuously. On the 3d of May, our forces had scarcely got into their new camp between Hamburg and Corinth, before the order came for a reconnoissance in force. Generals Paine and Palmer were detailed for the work. The regiments selected were almost entirely from Illinois, comprising the Tenth, Sixteenth, Twenty-second, Twenty-seventh, Forty-second and Fifty-first Illinois, the Yates Sharpshooters (Illinois), Houghteling's Illinois Battery, Hezcock's Ohio Battery, the Sixteenth Michigan Infantry and Second Michigan Cavalry. The column proceeded but five miles on the Farmington road, when a rebel force was encountered and the battle commenced. The rebel pickets were soon driven in. Our forces pushed on and were met with a sharp fire from behind the fallen trees. The gallant riflemen of the Yates Sharpshooters drove them from the abattis, and thus they were pushed from point to point for two miles, until an eminence was reached, from which the rebel artillery commanded the road. The Tenth Illinois and the Yates Sharpshooters, however, flanked them and they retreated under a most galling fire to a second position on the crest of a hill. Houghteling's guns came up on the double quick and opened a murderous fire, and again the rebels fled to a new position, half a mile further on and about a quarter of a mile from Farmington. Houghteling's Battery immediately moved to the rebel left, and Hezcock's Battery to the right. Their concentrated fire was soon too terrible for any troops to endure, and the rebels broke and fled toward Corinth in confusion, pursued by our cavalry. Our loss was only two killed and eleven wounded; the enemy's thirty killed and many wounded.

Farmington was in our possession, but the main battle was yet to come. On the 9th, the enemy twenty thousand strong, drove in our pickets beyond Farmington, and advanced upon the forces under Generals Palmer and Paine evidently with the intention of flanking them and cutting them off from the main army. Gen. Paine at once engaged them, and for five hours the battle was continuous and fiercely waged. Gen. Halleck's orders, however, were peremptory that a general engagement should not be brought on. In accordance with these instructions, Gen. Paine's troops fell back after stubbornly disputing the enemy's advance and finding out their strength. The enemy made a demonstration to pursue, but abandoned the movement. Our loss in the engagement was twenty-one killed, one hundred and forty wounded, and ten missing. Among the killed was the brave Lieut.-Col. Miles of the Forty-seventh Illinois. His leg was crushed by a cannon ball, and he died in a short time from hemorrhage. Major Zenas Applington of the 7th Illinois cavalry also fell mortally wounded while gallantly leading his regiment. The Illinois regiments engaged in this fight were the 42d, Col Roberts; 27th, Lieut.-Colonel Harrington; 22d, Lieut.-Colonel Hart; 51st, Lieut.-Col. Bradley; 26th, Col. Loomis; and 47th, Col. Bryner. It was pre-eminently an Illinois battle, and, although fighting at fearful odds (nearly six to one) the luster of her achievements was in no wise dimmed.

On the 21st of May another armed reconnoissance was made by the 2d division, commanded by Brig.-General Thomas A. Davis, which fought a battle with the enemy's advance line on Phillip's Creek, resulting in their rout and the occupation of a new and advantageous position by our forces. The same day another reconnoissance was made by Col. Sedgwick's brigade, which was successful in ascertaining the position of a part of the enemy's line. During all these reconnoissances and battles between disjointed fragments of either army, the main army of Gen. Halleck was advancing slowly and cautiously, throwing out successive parallels, as if a siege of the works at Corinth were intended. The railroad communication to the northward and southward of Corinth had been destroyed at Purdy and Glendale. To complete the severance of communication and thereby prevent reinforcements reaching the rebels, Gen. Halleck directed that the railroad to the southward of Corinth and in the direction of Mobile should be destroyed. This was effected on the night of the 30th by Col. Elliott. On the 28th, three strong reconnoitering columns advanced on the right, center and left. The rebels hotly contested the ground but were driven at each point. On the 29th, Gen. Pope's heavy batteries opened upon the enemy's entrenchments and drove the rebels from their advanced battery, and at the same time Gen. Sherman established a new battery within a thousand yards of the rebel works.

But while our army was thus slowly and cautiously approaching Corinth, the enemy were rapidly leaving it. The sick and wounded were removed on the 26th. On the 27th, Bragg and Beauregard made their arrangements for falling back, and on the 29th it was safely accomplished. With an army entrenched in successive strong parallels, with heavy siege guns converging upon every part of their works, with the Union army so massed that it could sweep down through Farmington and obtain complete possession of the Mobile and Ohio Railroad, with the Mississippi River open and Fort Pillow evacuated as it must be in a short time, it would have been sheer folly for Beauregard to wait in Corinth and expose his whole army to capture or annihilation. On Friday, the 30th, the Union forces entered Corinth. Desolation and destruction were on every hand. Burned buildings stood on every street. Huge piles of commissary stores were still smoldering in the flames. The only ammunition remaining was damaged and useless. The evacuation was complete—so complete that the rebels not alone successfully withdrew, but took every piece of ordnance with them.

The Illinois troops bore an honorable and conspicuous part in the closing scenes around Corinth. A brigade from Gen. McClernand's division, a brigade from Gen. Hurlbut's division, Gen. John A. Logan's brigade, and two brigades of Gen. Sherman's command were prominent in the fighting of the last two days. Waterhouse's and Silversparre's batteries did magnificent execution. Of Gen. Logan's efforts, Gen. Sherman thus speaks: "I feel under special obligations to this officer, who, during the two days he served under me, held the critical ground on my right, extending down to the railroad. All the time he had in his front a large force of the enemy, but so dense was the foliage that he could not reckon their strength save what he could see on the railroad track." Finally it was reserved for Lieut. Baker, of the Yates sharpshooters, to be the first man in the rebel works, and Col. David Stuart, of the fighting 55th, claims the honor of first raising the Stars and Stripes over Corinth.

The pursuit of the retreating rebels was vigorously kept up. Gen. Pope's cavalry escort pushed after them and had a brisk skirmish, in which several prisoners were captured. A burning bridge obstructed the operations of this force, and another was sent out by Gen. Pope, under Gen. Granger, on the Booneville road. It left Farmington on the 30th, and the same day drove out the rear guard of the enemy posted on Tuscumbia Creek, eight miles south of Corintb. Gen. Granger passed Rienzi only two hours behind the retreating enemy. On the afternoon of June 1st, the rear guard was again overtaken near Boonville. Skirmishing was kept up on the 2d, and on the 3d a reconnoissance was made toward Baldwin and the rebels driven across Twenty Mile Creek. On the 4th, another reconnoissance was made by Col. Elliott, via Blocklands, with similar results, and on the 10th, the occupation of Baldwin and Guntown ended the chase.

During the months of June and July, important changes were made in the army at Corinth. On the 10th, Gen. Buell left with the main body of his army for Chattanooga, to counteract the designs of Bragg, who had massed his army at Chattanooga and Knoxville, by suddenly moving his force from Tupelo, in Mississippi, through the States of Alabama and Georgia, thus reaching Chattanooga in advance of Gen. Buell. On the 27th of the same month, Gen. Pope was assigned to the command of the Army of the Potomac, and on the 23d of July, Gen. Halleck assumed the duties of General-in-Chief of all the armies in the field.

Nothing of interest transpired in Gen. Grant's department until August, when it became apparent that the rebel force south of his position were threatening his line between Corinth in Mississippi and Tuscumbia in Alabama. On the 10th of September, Colonel

Murphy's force fell back from Tuscumbia upon Iuka. Here he was attacked by the rebel cavalry, and after a slight resistance fled and took up a position at Jacinto. Gens. Grant, and Rosecrans who had succeeded Gen. Pope, acted in concert to check the movements of Price, one force moving by way of Brownsville and the other by way of Jacinto. The battle of Iuka was the result of these combinations. It commenced on the 19th with an attack upon Price by Stanley's and Hamilton's divisions of cavalry a short distance south of the village. The advance pickets of the enemy were driven in by the third Michigan cavalry dismounted. Skirmishing was kept up until within two miles of Iuka, when the enemy made a furious attack. Our force took positions under a terrible fire of grape and canister. The 5th Iowa, 26th Missouri and 48th Indiana with the 11th Ohio battery, bore the brunt of the attack until relieved by the 4th Minnesota and 16th Iowa. The attack was renewed with overwhelming numbers and with great fierceness. The 10th Iowa and 12th Wisconsin battery were hurried into position, but still the rebel force vastly outnumbered ours. Our line wavered and rallied. The battery was taken and retaken three times, and the fortune of the fight trembled in the balance. Gen. Stanley threw his forces into the breach. The rebels then massed against the left flank and tried to turn it, but were repulsed. At five P. M., our forces were all in position and from that time until dark the battle was fought with a bravery almost unequaled. The rebels tried, with frantic desperation, but in vain, to break our lines. The 5th Iowa held its ground against four times its numbers, making three desperate charges with the bayonet, driving the rebels every time, and only falling back when every cartridge was exhausted, and night closed in and the Union army held the battle field.

The next morning Gen. Rosecrans ordered the picket line to advance, but they met no opposition. The whole force was then thrown forward and entered Iuka to find it evacuated by Price, who had four miles the start. The cavalry kept up the pursuit until evening, capturing many prisoners. The forces of Gens. Grant and Ord returned to Corinth on the 22d, and the Army of the Mississippi to Jacinto. The 11th Missouri, which did some of the most glorious and desperate fighting in this battle, was in reality an Illinois regiment. At the time of the organization of the regiment the quota of Illinois was full, and rather than not have an opportunity of going into the service they obtained an organization under the laws of Missouri.

On the 26th Gen. Rosecrans proceeded to Corinth and took command of that position, Gen. Grant having been ordered to Jackson and Gen. Ord to Bolivar. In the meantime Price, in his retreat, had been reinforced by Van Dorn and Lovell, and the combined forces moved against Corinth. On the night of the 3d of October, the rebels formed their line within a thousand yards of the Union position and soon after day-break on the 4th opened a furious fire on Corinth. About half past nine the rebels massed their forces and advanced up the Bolivar road in the shape of a wedge, to attack a point completely covered by our artillery. In spite of the hideous rents made in their lines they continued to advance and suddenly extended their force to right and left and approached, covering the whole field. The entire Union line opened fire upon them, but still they advanced. As they approached the crest of a hill where Gen. Davis' division was posted, the division gave way in disorder and the rebels gained possession of Gen. Rosecrans' head-quarters and threatened Fort Richardson. They swarmed up the hill and were swept away. They rallied and again attacked the redoubt and the battery gave way. Then Illinois sprang to the rescue. The 56th Illinois, rising from cover, fired a deadly volley and making the air ring with their battle shout, charged like an avalanche upon the rebels. Nothing could withstand this superhuman effort. The rebels broke and fled. The lost ground was recovered and the whole Union line again advanced to its old position. While Price was there defeated, Van Dorn was attacking on the left the batteries of Williams and Robinett. The fight at these points was fearful. The 11th Missouri (Illinois), the 63d, 27th and 39th Ohio regiments, supported by the 18th U. S. artillery, formed into line and the rebels rushed upon them. A furious hand to hand combat ensued and the carnage was terrible. Bayonets were used, muskets clubbed, and men were felled with the fist, while all the time the guns of Robinett were pouring grape and canister into the rebel ranks with deadly effect. Our forces were again the victors. The rebels fled, howling with rage and despair, Robinett's guns, double-shotted, hurling death and destruction into their ranks, until they tied hàndkerchiefs upon sticks and begged the gunners "for God's sake, to stop." The enemy were defeated, arms were thrown away, and the retreat became a rout. The rebels lost one thousand four hundred and twenty-three officers and men killed, between four and five thousand wounded, two thousand two hundred and sixty-eight prisoners, three thousand three hundred and fifty stands of small arms, fourteen stands of colors, two pieces of artillery and an immense amount of equipments and material. Upon our side General Oglesby was severely wounded, and Gen. Hackleman killed. Our entire loss in officers and soldiers killed was three hundred and fifteen. The Illinois regiments engaged were the 26th, Col. Boomer; the 56th, Col. Kirkham; 7th, Col. Babcock; 9th, Col. Mersey; 12th, Col. Chetlain; 15th, Lieut.-Col. Swartwout; 52d, Col. Sweeney; 57th, Col. Hurlbut; 47th, Col. Bryner, (the Major in command); 26th, Col. Loomis.

The gallantry of Illinois troops was specially manifested in this battle, which was one of the most hotly contested on record. The 7th, 50th, and 57th Illinois regiments held an overwhelming rebel force in check for an hour, and subsequently drove the same force half a mile, recapturing several sections of artillery taken from us before. Col. Mower's brigade made a magnificent charge at Battery Robinett and routed a rebel force in a hand to hand fight. The 52d Illinois was in the hottest of the fight of the two days. On Saturday they made a splendid charge on a fort, which had been taken by the rebels. Lieut.-Col. Wilcox cried out: "Those big guns, boys—forward! double quick, march!" and on they went like an avalanche, and the guns were again ours and the victory ours.

Among the Illinois officers killed in this battle were Lieut.-Col. Thrush, 47th; Adjutant S. A. Brainard, 52d; Lieut. Henry Easterbrook, 17th; and Capt. G. C. Ward, of the 12th.

Among the wounded were Gen. Oglesby, Gen. McArthur, Col. Baldwin, Major Kuhn, of the 9th, Adjutant Klock, of the 9th, Capt. Robinson, of the 50th, and Capt. Wilcox, of the 52d.

The Yates' Sharpshooters lost fearfully. On the morning of the 4th they were two hundred and thirty-three strong; at sunset they were only one hundred and sixty. Seventy-three of their number had fallen in defence of the flag. Capt. Grover fell mortally wounded, while cheering on his command, Cos. B, C and E, who were deployed as skirmishers. Second Lieutenant C. J. Conger, Co. A, commanding Co. E, was wounded in the leg and hip. Capt. J. W. Stewart, Co. D, was shot through the thigh by a minie ball. First Sergeant Henry I. Clark, Co. E, was killed by a wound in the bowels. Co. E suffered most, having lost twenty-one men.

While one division of the army under Gen. Rosecrans was resisting and putting to flight the rebel hosts at Corinth, another from Bolivar, under Gens. Hurlbut and Ord, was marching against their rear. The rebels were retreating by the same route over which they had advanced, which was the Chevalla road. To ensure their safety it was necessary for them to cross the Tuscumbia River near Pocahontas, and a body of troops was sent to guard the Hatchie River bridge, which was two miles from the bridge across the Tuscumbia River. Ord and Hurlbut overtook this force on the 5th, while Rosecrans and McPherson were harassing them in another direction, and constantly capturing prisoners and material of war. The rebels made a stand on the north bank of the river, but so impetuous was the charge of our men, in which the 28th, 32d, 41st and 53d Illinois regiments particularly distinguished themselves, that they were soon driven back and across the Hatchie, losing two batteries of six guns, and several hundred prisoners. The fight was of short duration, but a most gallant one. Gen. Ord, in his official report, says: "Gen. Hurlbut will push forward to-morrow morning, as it is presumed General Rosecrans is harassing the rear of the enemy. My personal staff, Division-Surgeon S. R. Davis, Capt. Sharpe, Lieut. Brown, A. D. C., and Capt. Houghteling, 2d Illinois cavalry, and A. D. C., were by turns Colonels of regiments and Captains of batteries, cheering and leading the men through the thickest of the fight. They always took the shortest line to danger on the field, and were always on hand when wanted." Gen. Lauman, commanding a brigade, in his official report, paid the highest compliments to the gallantry and skill of Col. Johnson, of the 28th Illinois, Col. Logan, of the 32d Illinois, Capt. McClanahan and Capt. Earl, of the 53d Illinois, Lieut.-Col. Ritter and Major Gillem, of the 28th Illinois, Lieut.-Col. Hunter and Major English, of the 32d Illinois, and to Col. Pugh, of the 41st Illinois, to whom was assigned the responsible duty of protecting the rear. Gen. Grant issued an enthusiastic general order thanking and congratulating the army, and President Lincoln telegraphed to General Grant as follows:

WASHINGTON, D. C., Oct. 8, 1862.

Major-General Grant:

I congratulate you and all concerned in your recent battles and victories. How does it all sum up? I especially regret the death of General Hackleman, and am very anxious to know the condition of General Oglesby, who is an intimate personal friend.

A. LINCOLN.

The eulogies were not unworthily bestowed. It was the first instance in the war, of a soldierly pursuit of the enemy—the first time that victory was decidedly and thoroughly followed up.

On the 25th of October, the troops of General Grant had returned to their respective positions, and General Rosecrans reported at Cincinnati, to take charge of a force collecting for a new campaign. But General Grant did not remain idle long. On the 4th of November, he advanced to Lagrange, three miles east of Grand Junction on the Cairo and New Orleans Railroad. On the 29th General Hamilton's corps reached Holly Springs, and on the 18th of December, General Grant's forces encamped at Lumpkin's Mills, seven miles north of the Tallahatchie River, the rebels retiring to the river. The rest of the month was devoted to skirmishing and strategetic moves. General Hovey, with his army, left Helena for the purpose of flanking the rebel forces on the Tallahatchie, but they evacuated their works and retired further South, pursued by our forces, skirmishing taking place at Abbeville and Oxford. The rebels by keeping up a strong rear guard, reached Grenada. In the meantime General Hovey's force crossed the Tallahatchie and cut the Mississippi Central Railroad. His forces kept in the advance and next cut the Mississippi and Tennessee Railroad near Panola. All these movements were carried out with little or no opposition on the part of the rebels, and General Hovey returned to Helena. Their effect was to cause the rebels to evacuate Grenada and fall back to

Canton. On the 20th, the rebels attacked the Union garrison at Holly Springs and captured it, and the same day made an attack at Davis' Mills, which was gallantly repulsed. In the meantime the rebel General Forrest was at work, cutting General Grant's communications. Jackson, Trenton, Humbolt and other stations on the road were captured. Grant was compelled to fall back to Holly Springs, and a detachment of 10,000 men was sent to Gen. Sherman to aid in the capture of Vicksburg, thus virtually ending the campaign of 1862 in Mississippi.

Few campaigns in the war have been marked with so many and desperate battles, or with so much valor and determination upon either side. Few victories have been so complete or so well followed up, certainly none before this campaign. It marked a new epoch in the history of the war, and it is no small honor to the State that Illinois contributed so much to the general result. Nearly all of the prominent Generals—Grant, McClernand, Hurlburt, Logan, Oglesby, McArthur, Pope and others were from Illinois. In every battle Illinois soldiers were engaged and in no instance proved themselves unworthy their name—"*Illini*"—"men."

CHAPTER XVI.

REGIMENTAL SKETCHES.

The Thirteenth Infantry—First Organized for Three Years—Early Services—Battles—Marches—Officers—Colonel Wyman—Chaplain Needham—2d Cavalry—Scattered—Donelson—Marches and Battles—Officers—Col. Mudd—The 22d Infantry—Charleston—Belmont—Shiloh—New Madrid—Marches—Engagements—Col. Dougherty—Lieut.-Col. Swanwick—Major Johnson—The Fortieth—Enlistment—At Paducah—At Shiloh—Corinth—Marches—Officers—Forty-eighth Infantry—Organization—Donelson—Major Stephenson—Mission Ridge—Knoxville—Re-enlisted—Col. Greathouse.

IN chronicling the movements of single regiments there must be some difference in the space allotted. Some regiments have been steadily with certain corps or divisions, and the movements of the army tell the regimental movements. Others have been more frequently detached, or have engaged in a greater variety of service, the recital of which lies outside of the great movements of the army. There is also the difference of accessibility, the material for one being at hand, while for another it is remote.

We here introduce, for the sake of variety, some sketches, and others will follow in due season. The history of Illinois troops is associated with all the great campaigns of the West, and the sketching of these is to chronicle the gallantry of our own men.

THIRTEENTH REGIMENT ILLINOIS VOLUNTEERS.

This regiment has the honor of having been first to organize and enter the field under the President's first call for men for three years, an honor it has not dimmed on the field. It has marched many miles, been in the hottest fire of battle, but has borne an undimmed name.

ORIGINAL ROSTER.

Colonel, John B. Wyman; Lieutenant-Colonel, B. F. Parks; Major, Adam B. Gorgas; Adjutant, H. T. Porter; Surgeon, Samuel C. Plummer; Assistant-Surgeon, David H. Law; Chaplain, J. C. Miller; Quartermaster, W. C. Henderson.

Co. A—Captain, Henry T. Noble; 1st Lieutenant, Henry Dement; 2d Lieutenant, Benjamin Gillman.

Co. B—Captain, D. R. Bushnell; 1st Lieutenant, G. P. Browne; 2d Lieutenant, Wm. W. Kilgour.

Co. C—Captain, H. M. Messenger; 1st Lieutenant, N. Neff; 2d Lieutenant, Geo. B. Sage.

Co. D—Captain, Quincy McNeil; 1st Lieutenant, James M. Beardsley; 2d Lieutenant, A. T. Higby.

Co. E—Captain, F. W. Partridge; 1st Lieutenant, A. J. Brinkerhoff; 2d Lieutenant, G. B. Duvoll.

Co. F—Captain, Z. B. Mayo; 1st Lieutenant, E. F. Dutton; 2d Lieutenant, R. A. Smith.

Co. G—Captain, G. M. Cole; 1st Lieutenant, W. M. Jenks; 2d Lieutenant, S. M. Jackson.

Co. H—Captain, G. H. Gardner; 1st Lieutenant, Edwin Went; 2d Lieutenant, E. A. Pritchard.

Co. I—Captain, S. W. Wadsworth; 1st Lieutenant, J. G. Everest; 2d Lieutenant I. H. Williams.

Co. K—Captain, W. Blanchard; 1st Lieutenant, M. S. Hobson; 2d Lieutenant, J. J. Cole.

It was organized at Camp Dement, Dixon, Ill., May 9, 1861, and two weeks thereafter mustered into the United States service, and was first of the three years' regiments to cross the Mississippi River. During the summer of 1861, it remained at Rolla, Missouri, guarding that post, for it being a depot of supplies, was constantly threatened by the enemy. Here the regiment did excellent service in suppressing many predatory bands that invested that region within a radius of forty miles; and by their zealous protection of the Union people who had suffered from their cruel and relentless foes,inspired this persecuted class with a like attachment and devotion to the cause of their country. While here, Colonel Wyman succeeded in organizing many of the citizens into cavalry companies; and, under Gen. Curtis, these intrepid scouts proved themselves the most daring and efficient cavalry in the Southwestern Army.

In October, 1861, the regiment joined the army under General

Fremont, then forming at Springfield, Mo., and their admirable condition and efficiency in drill being marked by the General, they were assigned the highest post of honor in that "Grand Army;" but on the arrival of Gen. Hunter the plans of Gen. Fremont were entirely changed, and this regiment returned to Rolla.

March 6, 1862, it was sent to join the army of Gen. Curtis, and participated in that terrible march across the country to Helena, Ark., during which journey the most unparalleled suffering was endured from thirst, heat and short rations.

December 26, 1862, the men of this regiment being considered as veterans, were placed in the advance of General Sherman's army in the attack on Chickasaw Bayou, and during the second day's fight lost their brave Colonel, who was shot by the sharpshooters of the enemy. On the 29th, the terrible charge was made on Gen. S. D. Lee's entrenchments, and the regiment lost one hundred and seventy-seven men killed, wounded and missing. They soon thereafter participated in the attack and capture of Arkansas Post. They accompanied Gen. Steele in his Greenville expedition, capturing and destroying immense supplies of the enemy, and subsequently proceeded with Gen. Grant by way of Grand Gulf to the capture of Jackson, siege of Vicksburg, and repossession of the former city.

They accompanied General Sherman in his march from Corinth to Tuscumbia, being for one week daily engaged with the enemy. From the Tennessee to Lookout Valley their division was the rear guard of the 15th Army Corps, and frequently they were engaged with the enemy in his unsuccessful attempts to capture the train.

The 1st division of the 15th army corps, of which they were a part, was temporarily assigned to Gen. Hooker, and participated in the attack and capture of Lookout Mountain, the battles of Mission Ridge and Ringgold Gap. At Mission Ridge the 13th captured more than its own aggregate of the 18th Alabama rebel infantry, carrying the 18th's battle flag in triumph from the field. At Ringgold Gap they were the first to engage the enemy, and, refusing relief, were the last to leave the field. Here their loss was sixty-three killed and wounded.

General Hooker, in speaking of this engagement, says: "Their skirmishers were driven in, and as we had learned the position of the battery, the 13th Illinois regiment, from the right of Wood's line, was thrown forward to seize some houses from which their gunners could be picked off by our men. These were heroically taken and held by that brave regiment." After speaking of the repeated charges of the enemy to drive this regiment back, he continues—"the 13th Illinois all the time maintaining its position with resolution and obstinacy." The General finishes his eulogy on this division in these words, "It has never been my fortune to serve with more zealous and devoted soldiers."

The following is from Gen. Osterhaus' official report:

"Strengthening Col. Cramer by skirmishers from the 12th Missouri infantry, I sent orders to that officer to push the left of his line well forward, and at the same time ordered the 13th Illinois (which held the extreme right) to advance rapidly over an open field to a few houses in front. The 13th Illinois executed the order in magnificent style. They charged through a hail-storm of balls, and gained the position assigned to them, and held it, although the enemy poured a murderous fire into these brave men from the gorge in front, and the hill on the right."

Speaking of the desperate charges repelled by the obstinate bravery of these men, he concludes his allusion to the 13th in the following language: "The 13th Illinois remained undaunted, keeping up a vehement fire."

This regiment was assigned to the post of 1st regiment, 1st brigade, 1st division, 15th army corps; but changed to the 3d division in April as their time had nearly expired. On the 17th inst., they were completely surprised and entirely surrounded by a portion of Roddy's command at Madison Station, Alabama. The surprise was occasioned by the enemy advancing on the pickets clothed in United States uniform. After two hours' hard fighting against immense odds the regiment was compelled to abandon the station, breaking through the enemy's line. The enemy had three pieces of artillery with from 1,000 to 1,500 cavalry and infantry. The regiment at this time only numbered 350 men for duty. Sixty-six pickets and skirmishers were captured by the enemy. The enemy's loss, as reported by flag of truce, was sixty killed, wounded and missing. One out of the four prisoners taken from the enemy has died from his wounds, leaving the killed and wounded of the enemy as high as fifty-seven.

It is due to one officer of the 13th to state a fact or two. The chaplain at the time the regiment went out of service was Rev. Arnold T. Needham. At the breaking out of the war he enlisted as a private. He was subsequently promoted as sergeant for bravery. By his active, yet unobtrusive piety, his zeal in caring for the wounded and dying, he had so won upon the officers of the regiment that they recommended his appointment to that office, although he was not even a licentiate. Leave of absence was granted; he returned to his home in Chicago, was licensed and ordained, and received his commission. Chaplain Needham is a devoted Christian minister, and at the expiration of the time of enlistment, he entered the Rock River Annual Conference of the Methodist Episcopal Church, and was appointed to a pastoral charge, where he gives full proof of his ministry. This regiment entered the service with 1,010 men, since which time it has received fifty-five recruits. The aggregate when mustered out was five hundred, leaving their loss at five hundred and sixty.

In the summer of 1864, worn down with the hardships and hazards of three years' active campaigning, having traveled through seven Southern States, marched more than 3,000 miles, fought for the flag and the Union in twenty battles and skirmishes, the scarred veterans of the 13th came home and were received with a grand welcome. Such men deserve to live in the hearts and affections of the people for whom they have fought.

It is estimated that a majority of the 13th veterans have re-enlisted and are again in the field. Appended is the roster at the time the regiment went out of service:

Colonel, Adam B. Gorgas; Lieutenant-Colonel, Frederick W. Partridge; Major, James M. Beardsley; Adjutant (acting), Joseph M. Patterson; Quartermaster, John S. McClary; Surgeon, Samuel C. Plummer; Assistant Surgeon, Charles A. Thompson; Chaplain, Arnold T. Needham.

Co. A—A. Judson Pinkham, Captain; Mark M. Evans, First Lieutenant.

Co. B—George P. Brown, Captain; Joseph M. Patterson, 1st Lieutenant; John S. Russell, 2d Lieutenant.

Co. C—George B. Sage, Captain; Simeon F. Josselyn, 1st Lieutenant.

Co. D—Matthew McCullough, Captain; Albert T. Higby, First Lieutenant.

Co. E.—George H. Carpenter, Captain; William Wallace, 1st Lieutenant; Benjamin J. Gifford, 2d Lieutenant.

Co. F—Azro A. Buck, Captain; Theodore Loring, 1st Lieutenant.

Co. G—William M. Jenks, Captain; Silas M. Jackson, 1st Lieutenant.

Co. H—Edwin Went, Captain; Ethan A. Pritchard, 1st Lieutenant; Jesse D Pierce, 2d Lieutenant.

Co. I—James G. Everest, Captain; Robert Rutherford, 2d Lieutenant.

Co. K—Jordon J. Cole, Captain; Eli Bailey, 1st Lieutenant.

Among the early slain of much promise was Colonel John B. Wyman, whose blood was offered upon its altar—a costly libation.

Colonel John B. Wyman, of the 13th, was born in Shrewsbury, July 12, 1817. He had an early fondness for military life, and was Lieutenant of the Shrewsbury Rifle Company. Removing to Cincinnati he entered the "Citizens' Guards," remaining with the organization three years, under command of Captain, later Major-General O. M. Mitchell, the gifted astronomer and author. Removing to Worcester, Mass., he became a member and soon thereafter a Lieutenant in the Worcester City Guards, and later he was 1st Lieutenant in the Springfield City Guards (Mass.). In 1848 he held a position on the New York and New Haven Railroad, and residing in the city of New York he served two years in the well known New York Light Guards. In 1850 he was Superintendent of the Connecticut River Railroad, and on the reorganization of the Springfield Light Guards, was chosen their captain, and commanded them two years and a half.

Then he removed to the West, and was appointed Assistant Superintendent of the Illinois Central Railroad, February, 1853. He rendered efficient service in the construction and operation of this great road, built in faith of the future development of the great prairies through which it stretches its way.

The next year the Chicago Light Guards was organized, a band of admirable citizen soldiers, and Superintendent Wyman was chosen captain, and served as such three years, when he resigned. He was, however, re-elected in 1858.

Discontinuing the service of the I. C. R. R. he entered into private business at Amboy, Lee County, Illinois, where he had his home. His neighbors found him a man of activity and industry. They felt his energy.

When war came he at once offered his services to the government. He felt his vocation was war until peace should become honorable, and that one who had so fully made arms his study should now make arms his vocation.

He was commissioned Colonel of the 13th, but was retained for a time in the office of the Adjutant-General, and did not join his regiment until the 14th of June, 1861.

A reference to the movements of the Confederates, and a glance at the map will show the importance of Rolla in the early part of the war. It was the terminus of the southwestern branch of the Pacific Railroad and was the *point d, appui* of southwestern Missouri and Arkansas. On holding it and its approaches, depended questions of subsistence and transportation. There was much to be done, and the military skill and business capacity of the commandant was to be severely tested. Colonel Wyman was ordered to that post and with his regiment arrived there July 7, 1861. For eight months he performed its duties to the satisfaction of government.

The regimental sketch given above shows how much he was called to endure and do, as he led the 13th along its many miles of travel, and into the midst of battle. He became commander of a brigade of picked troops, including his own regiment. As is stated above, he fell at Chickasaw Bayou on the second day of the battle. His remains were brought home for burial. He was a brave man, and competent commander. In battle he was fearless; on the march he was careful for the comfort of his men.

His successor, Colonel Adam B. Gorgas, retained command until the regiment was mustered out of service. The 13th was fortunate in its line officers.

SECOND CAVALRY REGIMENT ILLINOIS VOLUNTEERS.

The following is the original roster of this regiment:

Colonel, Silas Noble, of Dixon; Lieutenant-Colonel, Harvey Hogg, of Bloomington; Major, Quincy McNeil, of Rock Island; 2d Major, John J. Mudd, of Chicago; 3d Major, Daniel B. Bush, jr., of Pittsfield; Adjutant, Wm. Staddin; Adjutant 1st Battalion, John R. Howlett, 2d Battalion, Livander W. Patterson, 3d Battalion, Joshua Rodgers; Quarter-Master, Jerome W. Hollenbeck; Commissary, Lewis Aubere; Surgeon, J. B. Cutts; Assistant-Surgeon, Andrew J. Crane; Chaplain James R. Locke.

Co. A—Captain, John R. Hotaling; 1st Lieutenant, Frank B. Bennett; 2d Lieutenant, Albert J. Jackson.

Co. B—Captain, Thomas J. Larrison; 1st Lieutenant, Alfred U. Stone; 2d Lieutenant, Jerome B. Tenney.

Co. C—Captain, Hugh Fullerton; 1st Lieutenant, Calvin Terry; 2d Lieutenant, David Solenberger.

Co. D—Captain, Franklin B. Moore; 1st Lieutenant, George Lebold; 2d Lieutenant, Thomas Brown.

Co. E—Captain, Samuel P. Tipton; 1st Lieutenant, Edwin F. Babcock; 2d Lieutenant, David H. Porter.

Co. F—Captain, Reuben Bowman; 1st Lieutenant, Mellville H. Musser; 2d Lieutenant, Neil T. Shannon.

Co. G—Captain, Benjamin F. Marsh, jr.; 1st Lieutenant, John G. Fonda; 2d Lieutenant, Thomas Logan.

Co. H—Captain, James D. Walker; 1st Lieutenant, Silas C. Higgins; 2d Lieutenant, John C. Reynolds.

Co. I—Captain, Chas. A. Vieregg; 1st Lieutenant, Henry Bantling; 2d Lieutenant, John H. Cacy.

Co. K—Captain, Presley G. Athey; 1st Lieutenant, Thomas W. Jones; 2d Lieutenant, Benjamin F. Garrett.

Co. L—Captain, Sterling P. Delano; 1st Lieutenant, James K. Catlin; 2d Lieutenant, Joseph L. Lawyer.

Co. M—Captain, David Sollenberger; 1st Lieutenant, Henry B. Crawford; 2d Lieutenant, Wm. A. Mattice.

Company A was enlisted in Ogle County, Company B in Logan County, Company C in Mason County, Company D in Madison County, Company E in St. Clair, Company F in Piatt, Company G in Hancock, Company H in McDonough, Company I in Champaign, Company K in Pike, Company L in Adams, and Company M in Mason County.

The Second Illinois Cavalry rendezvoused at Camp Butler in July, 1861, and was mustered into the service August 12, 1861, numbering eleven companies, and the December following Co. M was added, making the regiment twelve companies strong.

Before leaving Camp Butler the regiment was scattered, and in September we find four companies at Metropolis, Ill., six companies at Cairo, Ill., and one at Fort Holt.

Early in the winter following they commenced active service. Co's. A and B participated in the battle of Fort Donelson and the preliminary engagements. At this memorable battle Major, now

Colonel, Mudd was dangerously wounded. A portion of the regiment, under the gallant Lieut.-Col. Hogg, entered the town of Columbus, Ky., before the enemy had fairly left it, and held it until next day, when the gunboats and Gen. Sherman came in and found it occupied. The Donelson battalion took part in the battle of Shiloh and the advance on Corinth.

During the time intervening between the first of June and the last of August, 1862, the regiment was engaged in many skirmishes and encounters with the guerrillas and bushwhackers of West Tennessee.

At the battle of Merriwether's Ferry, in August, 1862, Lieuts. Terry and Goodheart, of Co. C, were killed, and at the battle of Middleburg, on the 29th of August, Lieut.-Col. Hogg and Lieuts. Shannon and Lieb, of Co. F, met the same sad fate. To Lieut.-Col. Hogg was due to a very large extent the credit for the discipline and efficiency of the regiment, and in his death it suffered an irreparable loss.

In October the regiment routed and broke up Colonel Hayward's band of guerrillas near Woodville, in Hayward County, and participated in the battles of Hatchie and Lagrange. In December it accompanied the advance of Gen. Grant's army as far south as Oxford, Miss., and then returned to Holly Springs to aid in the defence of that place. On the 20th of December, 1862, VanDorn made a descent upon Holly Springs, the infantry, about thirteen hundred strong, surrendering without resistance, the cavalry, five companies from the Second Illinois, made a bold and determined resistance. After many charges and counter charges they broke through the enemy, by whom they were surrounded, and passed out, followed by five times their number.

The regiment lost—Lieut.-Col. McNeil, captured; two Captains and two Lieutenants wounded; thirteen enlisted men killed; forty-one wounded, and ninety-seven prisoners, including sick and wounded. Major, now Colonel, Mudd and Major, now Lieut.-Col., Bush were the only field officers at the post not captured. General Grant complimented the regiment in general orders on this occasion. It joined in the pursuit of VanDorn in his retreat southward.

At the opening of the new year, 1863, we find them at Memphis,

Tenn. They were the first cavalry from the army of the Tennessee to join Gen. Grant in the Vicksburg campaign, and led the advance during the whole of that campaign. They were in the battles of Richmond, Port Gibson, Champion Hills and Black River, and the siege of Vicksburg with its skirmishes, in one of which Col. Mudd received two severe wounds.

After the fall of Vicksburg the regiment led the advance of Gen. Sherman's army in the march to Jackson, Miss., and with the 6th Missouri cavalry, under Major Fullerton, of the 2d Illinois cavalry, made a raid to the south, destroying the railroad for sixty miles towards New Orleans, driving out the rebels and liberating many conscripts.

In August, 1863, they were ordered to the Department of the Gulf and accompanied Gen. Franklin on his grand expedition up the Teche Bayou and back. They were with Gens. Herron and Dana when they made their move on Morganza, and participated in the many battles and skirmishes occurring at that time. After a great deal of the best fighting, without any apparent object or aim, the expedition returned to New Iberia in December, with a loss of more than one thousand men, the regiment worn out with severe duty and being obliged to subsist on damaged food. By extra care it had been kept up to eight hundred, and was now both the oldest and fullest cavalry regiment in the service, and the best mounted in the Western army, if not in the United States.

In the spring of 1864 the regiment asked the War Department to concentrate the companies, and give them a chance to re-enlist as a regiment. But no attention being paid to the request, and the officers and men feeling that it was a reasonable one, determined to make that a condition precedent to re-enlistment. Some efforts were made, but in only one company was the requisite number obtained, and the regiment seemed likely to be lost to the service after the expiration of their term of enlistment. They suffered as did other cavalry regiments from the habit of detailing orderlies and escorts. Their officers were usually powerless to prevent it, as they were in nearly all cases placed under command of infantry officers who knew little of that arm of the service, and were not careful of its wants.

One battalion, commanded alternately by Major Larrison and Captain More, remained for more than a year in Western Tennessee, where they were engaged in guerrilla hunting. They were with Gen. Smith on his celebrated march to Okalona, upon which expedition Lieut. Catlin, of Co. L, fell into the hands of the enemy, supposed to have been mortally wounded. The Second Cavalry deserves much at the hands of a grateful State, for it has wrought well in its service.

Colonel John J. Mudd was born in St. Charles County, Missouri, January 9, 1820. His father died in 1833, and in the same year his mother with her six children moved to Pike County, Illinois, with the object of raising her children free from the curse of slavery.

In 1849 he made the overland journey to California taking the route by the way of Soda Springs, Fort Hall and the Falls of the Cumberland and Truckee River, and home via the Isthmus and New Orleans. And again in 1850 he made a second journey to the "land of gold," via Salt Lake and Carson River, and returned home in 1851 via the Isthmus and New York. In 1854 he moved to St. Louis and entered into the commission business in the firm of Mudd & Hughes, but in the great financial crash of 1857 failed, and shortly after removed to Chicago where he was engaged in a prosperous business at the breaking out of hostilities in 1861.

He was at the St. Charles Hotel, New Orleans, December 1, 1860. The chivalry were then commencing hostilities and were firing the Southern heart by lynching Northern men and driving off their female teachers. To avoid a difficulty he left the hotel having been informed by his room-mates—Southern men—that the vigilance committee had been notified of his presence. He told them that he would return some day when he could tell for whom he voted without fear of being murdered by a drunken mob. And there, at the close of 1863, he witnessed for the first time in his life an abolition meeting.

In September, 1861, he entered the army as 2d Major of the 2d Ills. Cavalry, served at Cairo, Ills., under Gens. Grant and McClernand, at Bird's Point under Cols. Oglesby and Wallace, and Paducah, Ky., under Gen. Smith.

His first encounter with the enemy was on the 9th of February,

1862, at the battle of Tennessee Ridge, where he commanded the cavalry. They routed and dispersed the enemy, pursuing them to within a mile of Fort Donelson, killing and wounding a number of them and capturing twenty-six prisoners, including three officers, with a loss of but six slightly wounded. This virtually opened the battle of Fort Donelson and was characterized by Gen. McClernand as the most brilliant achievement of the war.

Three days subsequently he led the advance of Gen. McClernand's Division in the final movement on Fort Donelson, being the first to meet the enemy's cavalry, driving in their pickets, and holding the main body at bay until Gen. McClernand gained possession of the adjacent hills, and a secure position.

The Major reconnoitered the entire battle grounds and discovered and reported the existence of back water, both above and below the fortifications on which our respective right and left flanks were subsequently formed, rendering the escape of the garrison impossible. Major Mudd was dangerously wounded and sent to St. Louis with but little hopes of recovery. But contrary to all expectation he rejoined the army soon after the battle of Shiloh. Being yet unable to perform cavalry duty in the field, he was attached to the staff of Gen. McClernand during the advance on Corinth, and continued in that position until the last of August when he rejoined his regiment.

On the 29th of August, 1862, Lieutenant-Colonel Hogg fell while leading his men in a gallant charge at Middleburg. Major McNeil being the senior Major succeeded him. In October Major Mudd was sent out by Major-General McPherson with four hundred cavalry in search of the rebel Col. Faulkner between the Hatchie and Forked Deer rivers. They succeeded in getting on Col. Hayward's trail, and after a run of twenty-five miles, overtook, attacked and routed his gang of guerrillas, completely dispersing and breaking up the band. They captured forty prisoners, eighty horses, sixty guns, and all their camp equipage and wagons, and returned after six days absence without the loss of a man killed, wounded, or missing, with the army in the advance south to Holly Springs and Oxford, Miss., in December, 1862.

On the 31st of that month Lieutenant-Colonel McNeil resigned and Major Mudd was promoted to fill the vacancy, and on February,

1863, was promoted to Colonel, and ordered to report to Gen. Grant at Young's Point, opposite Vicksburg.

He participated in the battles of Greenville, Port Gibson, Champion Hills and Black River. His command was the first that skirmished with the enemy over the fields of Champion Hills the day before the great battle. He discovered and suggested to Gen. Lawler the route by which he advanced, and from which he made the heroic and successful charge which decided the fate of the day.

The regiment participated in the siege of Vicksburg and the skirmishes which took place at that time. On the 13th of June the Col. was again dangerously wounded and sent to St. Louis. He returned to the army after an absence of but little over a month, not fully recovered. He went to New Orleans again, at which time he went out with the regiment to Opelousas, Franklin, New Iberia and Vermillion, and also on the expedition under Gen. Franklin towards Texas and back, during which time he was engaged in many petty encounters and some severe skirmishing.

TWENTY-SECOND REGIMENT ILLINOIS VOLUNTEERS.

The 22d Regiment Illinois Volunteer Infantry, one of ten regiments called out by Gov. Yates, was organized at Belleville, St. Clair Co., on the 11th of May, 1861.

The following is the original roster of the regiment:

Colonel, Henry Dougherty; Lieutenant-Colonel, Harrison E. Hart; Major, Enadies Probst; Adjutant, Robert H. Cliff; Quartermaster, Charles M. Hamilton; Surgeon, George Coatsworth; 1st Ass't Surgeon, John Fitzer; 2d Ass't Surgeon, Isaac W. Brown; Chaplain, Thomas F. Houts.

Co. A—Captain, Samuel Johnson; 1st Lieutenant, Theodore Wiseman; 2d Lieutenant, William S. Ford.

Company B—Captain, John Seaton; 1st Lieutenant, Robert H. Clift; 2d Lieutenant, James N. Morgan.

Company C—Captain, Guide W. Stierlin; 1st Lieutenant, Wm. A. Gregory; 2d Lieutenant, George C Stevens.

Company D—Captain, James A. Hubbard; 1st Lieutenant, Elias J. C. Alexander 2d Lieutenant, Lemuel Adams.

Company E—Captain, Samuel G. McAdams; 1st Lieutenant, Charles M. Hamilton; 2d Lieutenant, George Gibson.

Company F—Captain, George Abbott; 1st Lieutenant, Herman Bornemann; 2d Lieutenant, John Frohlich.

Company G—Captain, James S. Jackson; 1st Lieutenant, Solomon Smith; 2d Lieutenant, Edward J. Jackson.

Company H—Captain, Francis Swanwick; 1st Lieutenant, Harvey Nevill; 2d Lieutenant, Cave Montague.

Company I—Captain, John A. Detrich; 1st Lieutenant, Milton A. French; 2d Lieutenant, Robert H. Livingston.

Company K—Captain, Thomas Challener; 1st Lieutenant, Hugh Watson; 2d Lieutenant, William M. Lewis.

From Belleville the regiment removed to Caseyville, and thence to Bird's Point, Mo. Landing on the 12th of July, on the sandy point, without a particle of shade, and under a blazing sun, many of the men suffered severely. The post was then commanded by Col. W. H. L. Wallace, afterwards General. Their duties, in throwing up breastworks, digging trenches, scouting during the excessive heat of that hot summer, standing picket and guarding the bridges over the swamps on the Charleston railroad, together with the unhealthiness of the position, owing to the burning, sandy soil, and the large tract of low, rich bottom land, intersected by swamps and lagoons, a short distance from the river, brought on bilious diseases, diarrhea and dysentery, to such an extent that, at the surgeon's call for sick men one morning, sixty men presented themselves from a single company, and the regiment was soon so reduced as to have less than one half its number for duty. On the night of the 18th of August, Col. Dougherty was ordered to take possession of Charleston, on the Cairo & Fulton Railroad, about twelve miles from the post, which he succeeded in doing, with a loss of one killed and six wounded, the Colonel and Captain Johnson being among the latter, taking some fifty or sixty prisoners. In the month of September, the 8th and 22d regiments, together with a part of Taylor's Battery, took possession of Norfolk, about six miles down the river, and nearer to Columbus, the whole commanded by Col. Richard Oglesby, remaining there about two weeks, during which time continual skirmishing took place.

Nolman's and Burne's companies, of the First Illinois Cavalry, having joined the command, were actively engaged in skirmishing and scouting. Toward the end of September, the enemy approached one of the pickets posted near a bridge over a swamp about a mile from camp. They were handsomely repulsed, with a loss of several killed and wounded. After remaining about two weeks at Norfolk, it was thought prudent to return within the breastworks at Bird's Point.

On the 7th of November was fought the battle of Belmont. The 22d was in the hottest of the fire from first to last. One hundred and twenty-six killed, wounded and prisoners, were its allottment of suffering. Among the wounded were Col. Dougherty, Capt. Abbott, Capt. Hubbard, and Capt. Challener, also Lieut. Adams, of Co. D.

Col Dougherty, who commanded a demi-brigade, was taken prisoner after being wounded and having his horse killed. He was detained some weeks, when he was released, but never returned to the regiment for duty. He remained in service until May, 1863, when he was honorably discharged. Col. D. is still in the very prime of life, has seen much service in the regular army in Mexico, New Mexico, and on the Plains. He possesses the courage and all the natural instincts of a soldier, and had he not been disabled from active service so early in the war, nothing but an adverse Providence could have prevented him from rising in the army.

After the battle it returned to Bird's Point, and there remained until the 10th of March, 1862, when it joined Gen. Pope's army, then moving on New Madrid. During thewinter Major Probst had been compelled to resign from the effects of an injury sustained whilst riding a fiery horse, and Capt. T. Swanwick was commissioned in his place. The regiment was present at the evacuation of New Madrid, crossing the river at that point, and the capture of nearly five thousand prisoners at Tiptonville; landed at Hamburg, on Tennessee River, 22d of April; was present and under fire during the operations around Farmington; was farthest advanced of any regiment on the 8th of May, when fifteen to twenty thousand of the enemy had nearly surrounded the Union forces, consisting of only a few regiments, and narrowly escaped being cut off and captured by holding their advanced position too long, and were only saved by a timely order from Gen. Palmer to retreat. Lost in this affair fifteen in all.

Until the evacuation of Corinth on the night of the 29th of May, the regiment was constantly engaged in skirmishing and throwing up rifle pits, and picketing, and lost two men whilst going out on relief. May 21st it had five or six men sun-struck. It accompanied the army in pursuit of the rebel army as far as Booneville, where want of supplies and water compelled it to go into camp at Big Springs, about four miles southeast of Corinth; there it remained until about the 20th of July, when Roberts' brigade, of which it formed a part, was stationed along the Memphis & Charleston Railroad, the headquarters of the 22d being at Cherokee, Alabama, where, for the first time since leaving Cairo, the men enjoyed a full and comfortable diet, including vegetables, fruit, and fresh meat.

About the last of August it moved to Tuscumbia and from thence accompanied Gen. Palmer from Florence and Decatur to Nashville, Tenn., where it arrived on the 12th of September. This march was one of the most perilous of the war, the wagon train was necessarily very long, and guerrillas and others continually harassed the flanks and rear, firing from covers, picking up all stragglers, and men who fell behind from fatigue. It was made in the hottest time of year and on a McAdamized road without shade. But the sound judgment, firmness, and good management of the able commander, Gen. John M. Palmer, carried his little force through its dangers, losing only a few men. Not a single wagon was taken. On the 15th of September the regiment pitched tents on College Hill, where it remained until the 14th of December, subsisting upon the country &c., fighting for every mouthful of food and forage consumed. Nashville was then cut off from the loyal states so completely that there was no communication until about the 11th or 12th of November. Gen. Negley commanded the post.

The 22d regiment was commanded by Major, now Lieut.-Col., Swanwick, Lieut.-Col. Hart, the courteous gentleman and gallant soldier, having died on the 26th of July. On the morning of the 21st of October a body of about four hundred of Morgan's cavalry surrounded a picket post of thirty-four men and made them prisoners. Major Swanwick mistook them for Union men and ordered the boys not to fire. Many of the rebels wore the blue overcoats of the Union soldiers. The captured men were taken to Murfreesboro, where General Forest then commanded, and there exchanged. About the 1st of December a new organization was made, which separated the 22d regiment from the command of Gen. Palmer, greatly to the regret of both officers and men.

On the 14th of December the regiment moved out to Camp Sheridan, six miles on the Milansville turnpike, and remained there until the 26th. During the stay here another company on picket was surrounded and partly captured. The regiment was now brigaded with the 27th, 42d and 51st Illinois, under the command of Colonel Roberts, attached to the division of Gen. Sheridan. From the 26th to the 30th considerable skirmishing and fighting took place.

Tuesday morning, December 30th, the hard fought, five days' battle of Stone River began, Robert's brigade in advance of Sheridan's division, and the 22d leading the brigade. By command of Col. Roberts the Lieut.-Col. ordered Co. A, commanded by Lieut. W. S. Ford, Co. B, Capt. J. N. Morgan, and Co. C, Capt. W. A. Gregory, to deploy as skirmishers and cover the advance of the right. They did so and advanced rapidly through some open fields into the timber, where they were met and sharply engaged by the enemy's skirmishers. In a short time the right was formed in the edge of the timber and the skirmishers recalled, they having lost ten or twelve men. Towards evening the regiment advanced and was driving the enemy's skirmishers, when, by order of Colonel Roberts, it retired in good order, still covered by several companies deployed as skirmishers. Went into camp for the night about 9 P. M. Wednesday, December 31st, Sheridan's division was soon engaged, and from the fact of the troops on the extreme right being driven back by a furious attack by Hardee, the Division was at once enveloped in a murderous front and flank musketry and artillery fire, from three sides, by which the 22d lost more than half its men in a few hours, and after a determined defence, during which, by a bayonet charge, it took the ground on the Wilkinson pike, over which it had been driven, it was forced from the field and compelled to retreat in haste. It was here about 11 A. M. that Col. Roberts was killed while making a desperate but hopeless effort to stop the advance of an overwhelming force of rebels, with four fragments of regiments numbering all told about six or seven hundred men, and about the same time Lieut.-Col. Swanwick's left arm was broken above the elbow by a rifle bullet, and his horse also received two bullets. After continuing in command for somewhere about half an hour he was compelled to dismount for the purpose of having his wound dressed, but the enemy opened a fire from the rear, and giving up the command to Capt. Johnson, the Lieut.-Colonel lay down behind a log, where he remained three hours, obliged to change position three times to get shelter from the bullets, as the armies advanced or retired. He was then made prisoner and taken to Murfreesboro and there remained two days; from thence to Atlanta, Ga., and thence to Richmond, where, with some sixty or seventy other officers, he arrived March 1st, and remained in Libby prison till May 5th, when he was exchanged and sent home. With his fellow prisoners he suffered greatly, partly from neglect and partly from unavoidable causes. Their food was wretched—the very worst of beef, and in Atlanta the poorest ill-baked corn bread; in Richmond very good bread but only about half enough of it. The Lieut.-Colonel returned to his regiment at Murfreesboro on the 17th of May, without going home, his arm still weak, but went on duty at once. The whole loss of the regiment in the battles of Stone River was one hundred and ninety-nine out of three hundred and forty-one, almost two thirds.

Officers wounded, Capt. Gregory, Co. C; Boonman F. Nevill M. A. French, of Co. I; Lieut. Galloway, Co. D, mortally; Scheener, mann, of Co. F, and Sergeant-Major H. Laraque, mortally wounded. The horses of all the field officers were hit, and Adjutant Clift had his clothes cut.

Thus the regiment was deprived of a fourth field officer within about a year and a half. Captain, now Major, Samuel Johnson, on whom, as senior Captain, the command now devolved, was every way capable of taking command. He had been a soldier in the Mexican war, was present at the night attack on Charleston, Mo., in August, 1861, in command of his Company, A, and was then wounded in the leg. A modest, unpretending man, in the prime of life, and, before his last wound, capable of enduring great fatigue and hardship; of unflinching courage and unyielding firmness. He was again severely wounded at Chickamauga, from which he has not yet (March, 1864,) sufficiently recovered to go on duty. The winter and spring of 1863 were spent in scouting, foraging and picketing around Murfreesboro. On the 24th of June the Army of the Cumberland struck tents and began the memorable campaign of Chickamauga.

For twenty-one days it rained every day, and the men had often to wade streams so deep as to render it necessary to carry their cartridge boxes on their guns to keep the ammunition dry. The boasted fortifications of Tullahoma were evacuated by Gen. Bragg on our approach. The 22d was scarcely under fire from Murfreesboro to Tullahoma. The month of August was passed at Bridgeport, Ala., where Bragg had destroyed the railroad bridge across the Tennessee River. About the 1st of September, the army began the crossing of the river at various points from Stevenson up, and started on the Chickamauga campaign. Friday, September 18th, the regiment had bivouacked when orders came to march, and by dark it was under way, marching until after midnight. Saturday, 19th, broke up camp early in the morning, and soon after heard the first guns of the battle of Chickamauga. About the middle of the afternoon, the 22d, forming a part of the 3d brigade, Sherman's 3d division, went into action, and within ten or twelve minutes after they fired the first gun, *ninety-seven out of less than three hundred men were cut down by a murderous front and flank fire*, the left flank being entirely unprotected, and having advanced within twenty paces of an overwhelming mass of the enemy concealed among the undergrowth, fell back. It rallied in a ditch in an open field and there repulsed a desperate attack. The regiment remained all night in the ditch. Although so early in the season, it was very cold, and all suffered severely. The cries of the wounded were heart-rending; all was done for them that could be, but it was a fearful night. After carrying in all the wounded that could be found, the regiment collected all the guns within reach and loaded them, giving each man from two to five loads, but the night wore away without an attack, and the brigade was withdrawn about daylight under cover of a dense fog. Before noon on Sunday, the 20th, it was again engaged, and after suffering severely, was forced off the field with the loss of the right wing of the army and retreated on Chattanooga, holding the enemy in check all the way, and taking three days to retreat about twelve miles. Total loss of the regiment in the two days' fight, killed, wounded and prisoners (many of the latter wounded) 128 out of less than 300! Among the wounded was Major Johnson, very severely; Captain French, mortally; he had been twice wounded at Stone River, had just returned, still lame, but dragged himself along to meet his fate, like a brave man. He died in the hospital on the 27th. His company (I) had also both Lieutenants, Hood and Wilson, two valuable officers, wounded. Lieut. J. T. Stansifer, of Co. C, had his leg badly shattered below the knee whilst doing his duty manfully with his company in the thickest of the fight. Captain James S. Jackson, acting as Major was made prisoner while pursuing his horse which had broken away from him. The brave old Captain Nevill was again slightly wounded in the leg.

After reaching Chattanooga the troops were constantly at work on the fortifications or engaged in picket duty. Men and officers were on less than half rations; many of both had neither blanket, overcoat or sock, and often went on guard or fatigue without any thing to eat.

It had its share in the glorious events of Lookout Mountain and Missionary Ridge. A little after noon on the 25th, Sheridan's division received orders to drive the enemy from the rifle pits along their front at the foot of Mission Ridge. This was accomplished about 3 P. M., the enemy abandoning them. An officer of the 22d says: "The 22d, among other regiments, moved to the assault on the rifle pits over a perfectly smooth plain, exposed to a terrible artillery fire from the enemy on the top of the mountain, together with a heavy infantry fire, the latter too distant to produce much effect. The line was halted for some time in the rifle pits and a wet ditch at the foot of the mountain, the rebels on top, distant 600 to 800 yards, in full view, with their breastworks and batteries and their red battle flags waving and flourishing in defiance of what they considered a mad attempt. At length the order was given to scale the mountain, and, although it must be confessed, a few held back, the mass of the troops rose up and started on that journey of death without faltering, and almost as far as objects could be distinguished, the glorious old banner of freedom could be seen advancing up the steep mountain side, sometimes one regiment in advance, sometimes another, but all constantly gaining ground. When the 22d reached a point within 150 yards of the summit, it became exposed to a severe cross fire from the head of a ravine on the left, from which many men were hit and the horse of Lieut.-Colonel S. received a third wound, but the line continued to advance. Another shout of 'Forward,' another desperate rush, this time literally 'up to the cannon's mouth,' and the batteries, the forts, the battle, and the whole position were won, and nothing could be seen of our late confident and defiant enemy but their backs, as they fled in wild confusion down the eastern slope of the mountain. This being the first time the 22d had ever had a clear, decided victory on their part of the field, they were much excited and very jubilant, the more so as for the first time the loss of the regiment was proportionately light, although they went up a part of the mountain where they were as much exposed to both artillery and musketry as any other regiment in the whole line."

The whole loss of the 22d regiment, killed and wounded, in this desperate attack, was only twenty-one, out of about one hundred and sixty, all the fighting men that could be found to follow the flag. The night was passed on picket and in pursuit as far as Chickamauga creek, which was reached before daylight, about six miles from the battle-field, but the enemy had crossed and destroyed all the means of crossing.

On the 27th again on the war-path for the relief of Burnside at Knoxville. Then bivouacking on the cold ground without tents or blankets, and with but few overcoats, and living on half rations, some of the men without socks or shoes. Says the writer before quoted:

"They complained, of course, but still did their duty. Went out to Dandridge about the middle of January, retreated from there in a hurry, stopped a day or two at Knoxville, thence went to Louden about the last of January, and built winter quarters—log cabins. Of the campaign from the time of leaving Bridgeport, September 2d, to the end of January it may with truth be said, that for fatigue, exposure, general hardship, with want of clothing and food, it has seldom been equaled, never surpassed, it being a well authenticated fact that the troops never did, and have not yet received at any time a full government ration, and they are not yet, March 6, 1864, fully clothed."

Colonel Dougherty was born in North Carolina, now lives in Carlyle, Ill., has been much of his life in the army, is a civil engineer, a worthy man and good citizen. He proved himself early in the war, a gallant officer and a competent commander. It was only with him to ask "where are the foes," and to order his brave men to follow him in the charge. He retires maimed for life.

Lieutenant-Colonel Hart was born in the city of Philadelphia; his father, still living, is an Englishman; he was a machinist; was in government employ during the Mexican war as a superintendent; was a robust, healthy man at the commencement of his last sickness and was every inch a soldier. He died at his home in Alton, Illinois, July 26, 1862.

Major Abbott, 1st Captain of Co. F, had his thigh badly shattered at the battle of Belmont, he firmly refused to have it amputated and this in all probability saved his life. He has been one of the Provost Marshals of Illinois. Resides at Alton.

Major Samuel Johnson was born in Kentucky, a farmer by occupation, now lives at Collins Station, is slowly recovering from the cruel wound received on the first day's fight at Chickamauga. He is about 33 years of age.

Lieutenant-Colonel Swanwick, the 1st Captain of Co. H, was born in England, in April, 1809, now 55 years of age. Came to Illinois in 1820; now resides in Chester, Randolph County. Miller by occupation. Was out in Black Hawk campaign, 1832. Has been cattle-buyer, merchant and miller—went to California in 1852 over the plains and remained there four years. He has commanded the regiment in every regular battle except Belmont, has been twice a prisoner. In the schools he received a limited education, but the gallant veteran has learned much since the war began.

Company A was commanded at Charleston by Captain Johnson. At Belmont by Lieutenant Malehorn on boat guard; at Farmington, Captain Johnson; Stone River, Lieutenant William S. Ford, now Adjutant; Chickamauga by Lieutenant, now Captain Malehorn. Company B at Belmont and Charleston, Captain Seaton; Farmington and Stone River by Lieutenant, now Captain Morgan; Chickamauga and Mission Ridge, Lieutenant McKinzie.

Company C at Charleston by Captain Starline; at Belmont by

Lieutenant, now Captain Gregory; at Farmington, Capt. Starline; Stone River by Captain Gregory; Chickamauga and Mission Ridge by Lieutenant Welch.

Company D at Charleston, Belmont, Farmington and Stone River by Captain Hubbard; Chickamauga by Captain Phillips; Mission Ridge by Lieutenant File.

Company E at Charleston, Belmont, Farmington, Stone River and Chickamauga by Captain McAdams, at Mission Ridge by Lieutenant, now Captain Gibson.

Company F at Charleston and Belmont by Captain Abbott; Farmington and Stone River by Captain Boonmann; Chickamauga and Mission Ridge by Lieutenant Scheuremann, now prisoner at Richmond; Stone River by Sergeant Gregory; Chickamauga and Mission Ridge by Lieutenant J. R. Smith.

Company H at Belmont, on boat guard, by Captain Swanwick; Farmington, Stone River, Chickamauga and Mission Ridge, Captain Nevill.

Company I, Belmont, on boat guard, Captain Detrick; Farmington, Lieutenant French; Stone River and Chickamauga, Captain French; Mission Ridge, Lieutenant Hood.

Company K, Belmont, Captain Challenor; Farmington, Lieutenant Buchannan; Stone River, Chickamauga and Mission Ridge, Captain Buchannan.

Says our correspondent:

"In addition to the number of killed, wounded and missing reported by the Cos. (496) there has been three field officers severely wounded and Captain Jackson acting as Major made prisoners; two pickets thirty-four and fourteen in number captured by cavalry; four or five men killed by accidental discharge of fire arms, two drowned, and a very considerable number died of disease, and still more discharged on account of disability contracted in the service; the few now left, March 1864, with the flag *fit for duty*, less than two hundred, are equal to Napoleon's, Wellington's, or any other veterans.

"There has always been one remarkable feature in the 22d Regiment, whilst other regiments were divided by jealousy and quarreling among officers, there has scarcely been a serious case of disagreement between any two officers, and promotions have, as a general thing been made harmoniously, and given satisfaction to both officers and prisoners.

THE FORTIETH REGIMENT ILLINOIS VOLUNTEERS.

This regiment was raised by Stephen G. Hicks, Esq., a member of the bar, resident in Salem, Illinois. Its members were from the counties of Fayette, Marion, Clay, Wayne, Edwards, Wabash, White, Hamilton and Franklin. It was accepted by order of the Secretary of War, given July 25, 1861, and was gathered into camp at Sandoval, Aug. 5, 1861.

ORIGINAL ROSTER.

Colonel, Stephen G. Hicks; Lieutenant-Colonel, James W. Boothe; Major, John B Smith; Adjutant, Rigden S. Barnhill; Quartermaster, Albion F. Taylor; Surgeon, Samuel W. Thompson; 1st Assistant Surgeon, William Graham; 2d Assistant Surgeon, Joseph W. Edwards; Chaplain, Richard Massey.

Co. A—Captain, Hiram W. Hall; 1st Lieutenant, Flavius J. Carpenter; 2d Lieutenant, Benjamin W. Herrelson.

Co. B—Captain, William T. Sprouse; 1st Lieutenant, Joshua Goodwin; 2d Lieutenant, Elijah D. Martin.

Co. C—Captain, Elias Stuart; 1st Lieutenant, Samuel S. Emery; 2d Lieutenant, William Merritt.

Co. D—Captain, Samuel Hooper; 1st Lieutenant, William Stuart; 2d Lieutenant, Joseph P. Rider.

Co. E—Captain, Daniel N. Ulm; 1st Lieutenant, Andrew F. Nesbit; 2d Lieutenant William H. Summers.

Co. F—Captain, Tillman Shirley; 1st Lieutenant, William T. Ingram; 2d Lieutenant, Joseph Ing.

Co. G—Captain, William F. Scott; 1st Lieutenant, Carlisle C. Hopkins; 2d Lieutenant, Jonah Morlan.

Co. H—Captain, Samuel D. Stuart; 1st Lieutenant, John G. Lane; 2d Lieutenant, Thomas F. Galvin.

Co. I—Captain, Gamaliel Hoskinson; 1st Lieutenant, George D. Humphries; 2d Lieutenant, Henry Crackel.

Co. K—Captain, Jacob L. Moore; 1st Lieutenant, Woodruff Blacklidge; 2d Lieutenant, Joseph B. Figg.

It was mustered into service August 10th, numbering about seven hundred. On the 12th, though unarmed, it received marching orders, and proceeded by railroad to Illinoistown, and then by river to Jefferson Barracks, where it remained in camp fifteen days. The men were armed with Harper's Ferry rifled muskets, and on the 31st again were on the march. On the next day they were conveyed by transports to Paducah, where they remained some time under the training of General C. F. Smith. The 40th was brigaded with the 23d Indiana, 8th Missouri and 9th Illinois, under Col. W. H. L. Wallace. Early in November they were marched within twelve miles of Columbus, when they were ordered back—a march which seems to have been made not in the best of order. They remained at Paducah until after the surrender of Forts Henry and Donelson.

General W. T. Sherman was placed in command at Paducah, and made all exertion to prepare his troops for field service. The 40th was brigaded with the 48th Indiana and 46th Ohio, Col. Hicks commanding the brigade, Lieut.-Colonel Boothe the regiment.

On the 6th of March, 1862, the troops welcomed the order to strike tents and set out for Savannah, Tenn. A portion of the 40th landed at Savannah, March 8th, and was, with part of the Ohio 46th, the advance of the army of the Union. This place they occupied, awaiting the arrival of the main force. The permanent camps were made at Pittsburg Landing. Sergeant Hart, in his "History of the 40th," says:

"*Monday, March 17th.* At 1 o'clock A. M. all were ordered to go ashore with two days' rations in their haversacks in trim for marching. The 6th Iowa infantry was there attached to our brigade, and their commander, Col. John Adair McDowell, being Col. Hick's senior, took command of the brigade. We moved about four miles from the landing and halted in an open field, where we remained over night, sending out pickets, who were stationed at a meeting-house belonging to the Methodist denomination. Thus the 40th boys were the first Union soldiers that stood picket at the Shiloh church."

Sunday, the 6th, was a bloody day to the 40th. The regiment, in battle line, advanced to meet the enemy, but the line was broken on the left, and McDowell's brigade, which was on the extreme right in front, was compelled to retreat or be cut off and probably captured. A retreat was ordered and the column slowly retired, receiving and returning the enemy's fire. At 2 o'clock Gen. Sherman ordered Col. Hicks to storm, and, if possible, capture a battery, with which the enemy was slaughtering his troops. Immediately the order "Charge," was given, and the regiment went forward in the face of the deadly hail. Many were killed in this fearful charge, and others severely wounded. One-half the regiment was here, in a few moments, placed *hors de combat*. Col. Hicks fell severely wounded, while bravely leading his command. Capt. Hooper, Co. D, was instantly killed. The Colonel was borne from the field and the order was given to retreat, when it was ascertained that the battery was too strongly supported to be stormed by one reduced regiment. The 40th retired a short distance and remained in position during the day, pouring a deadly fire upon the enemy at every opportunity. At night it took a position in support of the line of siege guns in front of Pittsburg Landing, with nothing to eat, tired and hungry, and the cold ground their bed. Forty of their number that day were killed, and a hundred and fifty others were suffering from wounds, some of them yet on the field or in the hands of the enemy. Their Colonel was severely wounded by a musket ball in his left shoulder. It was a dreary night spent near the river, in line and under arms.

Early on the morning of the 7th, the regiment was ordered forward to support a reserve battery in General Nelson's division. It was brought into action twice during the day, once for nearly two hours, and resulting in driving the enemy from his position. The regiment was in front at 2 P. M., on the left of General Nelson's division, when the enemy finally gave way. At night the entire regiment was posted, on picket guard, in front, with orders to keep a sharp look-out in every direction. Forty prisoners were captured and brought in during the night. Major Smith was in command of the regiment, Lieut.-Colonel Boothe being too unwell to take the field on the morning of the 7th. At night Major Smith was taken violently sick and the command devolved upon Capt. Hall, of Co. A. Morning at length dawned, and with it came a detail for the entire regiment for fatigue duty, and all were required to engage in burying the dead. The entire day, April 8th, was spent in burying friend and foe in one common grave-yard. While thus engaged, night again found the regiment on the battle-field. It was the reality of war! On Wednesday morning, April 9th, the regiment was relieved and returned to the former encampment, but found it stripped of every thing that could be carried away. After three days and nights spent in battle, watching, labor and exposure, hungry, weary and worn out, the 40th returned to learn that it was without clothing or subsistence. Regimental and company books and records were all destroyed or carried off. The regiment went into the action with near four hundred and fifty men. The casualties were forty-four killed, one hundred and sixty-six wounded and four missing. It remained in the original camp, drilling and doing guard and fatigue duty during the reorganization of the army for the advance on Corinth. On the 16th of April, while on division drill, General Sherman in person highly complimented the regiment for its bravery and daring on the 6th of April, in charging the enemy and holding its position with the bayonet against the advancing foe for half an hour after its ammunition was exhausted.

April 29th the column moved forward, the 40th forming a part of McDowell's brigade, which occupied the right of General Sherman's division, which was the extreme right in front. It entered Corinth with the division, May 30th, at 9 o'clock A. M. On the morning of June 2d, a complimentary order from General Sherman was read to the regiment on dress parade, commending it highly for the steady, persevering and cheerful manner in which it had performed the duty assigned it. On the evening of the same day it received marching orders, and moved by way of Corinth and down the Memphis and Charleston Railroad four miles, and bivouacked for two days.

June 7th, the regiment moved to Chavialla, when its camp and garrison equipage was ordered to be forwarded. Remained here until June 11th, when it was again ordered forward in the direction of Memphis, on the line of the M. and C. R. R. It arrived at Lagrange, Tenn., June 14th, and rested until the 21st. The weather, during this march, was warm, the roads dusty and water scarce. While at Lagrange, and on the march before reaching there, the men thought it an outrage that they were compelled to act as guards for the residences and property of rank secessionists.

A succession of scouting expeditions occupied the month of July. In one of these, Holly Springs, Mississippi, was captured. They moved in the direction of Memphis, which they reached July 21st, and went into camp at Fort Pickering. Here they were refitted with clothing.

Here Col. Hicks was honorably discharged, on account of disability from his wound, but was reinstated a few months afterward, his commission bearing its former date.

The vacancies in regimental and company offices filled by election, which resulted in the elections of Adjutant R. S. Barnhill, Major, Vice Major Smith resigned May 26th. For company elections see sketch of officers. Wm Elliott of Salem, was duly appointed Surgeon, Vice Dr. Thompson resigned June 3d. James Roy, Sergeant-Major, appointed Adjutant, Vice R. S. Barnhill promoted to Major.

After the elections and appointments, the regiment remained in camp in Fort Pickering four months and four days. It was engaged several weeks as Provost Guard in the city of Memphis. Lieut.-Colonel Boothe's health was poor and Major Barnhill commanded the regiment the greater part of the time. The Major was a favorite in the regiment. In November, General Sherman began organizing the troops concentrated at Memphis for an active campaign. He moved his column from Memphis, November 26th.

The 40th, was still a part of McDowel's brigade of General Denver's division, and moved with the column under the command of Major Barnhill. Lieutenant-Colonel Boothe remained at Memphis. It crossed the Tallahatchie River at Wyatt's Ferry, December 5, and camped at College Hill, Miss. Here General Denver's division was attached to General McPherson's corps, and General Sherman's command returned to Memphis. Before leaving, the General had the division paraded by regiments, and bade each an affectionate farewell. He again complimented the 40th and their battle-scarred Colonel highly, for their gallantry and faithfulness to duty.

The troops moved onward until the 21st, when news of Van Dorn's raid on Holly Springs, cutting off the supplies, was received, and as a necessity on the morning of the 22d, the column reluctantly retracing its steps, arrived at Holly Springs, December 29. The 40th was immediately assigned to duty as Provost Guards in the village. While here on duty Colonel Hicks and Lieutenant-

Colonel Boothe, joined the regiment, January 2d, Colonel Hicks having been restored to his position and rank as Colonel by the Secretary of War. January 6th the column moved by way of Salem and Springhill to Lagrange and Grand Junction.

January 9th, Colonel Hicks with his regiment and Cheney's Battery were detached from the division at Springhill and sent to relieve the garrison at Davis' Mills, five miles south of Lagrange on the Mississippi Central Railroad. The remaining part of General Denver's division was stationed at Grand Junction and Lagrange. The 40th passed the winter pleasantly at Davis' Mills. Lieutenant-Colonel Boothe resigned and left the regiment January 13th. Adjutant Roy also resigned and left the regiment January 26th. Major Barnhill was detached from the regiment January 13th, and appointed Provost Marshal of the District of Corinth. He was soon promoted to Lieutenant-Colonel, Vice Lieutenant-Colonel Boothe resigned, but did not join the regiment until January 15, 1864. Having no field officer to assist him, the double duty of post and regimental commandant devolved upon Colonel Hicks.

On the 7th of April, the regiment under the command of Brigadier-General Smith started in a southwesterly direction on the Mississippi Central road toward Holly Springs. It proceeded by rail to Coldwater bridge, which was swept away, and thence on foot to Lagrange, which it reached on the 25th and remained in active duty until the 3d of June, when it received marching orders and was on the move toward Memphis. On this march the regiment passed through Moscow, Germantown, White's Station, Helena, Council Bend and Milliken's Bend, and arrived at the mouth of the Yazoo River on the 11th of June. It passed up the Yazoo River and encamped at Snyder's Bluff. Here it was set to work fortifying the extensive range of hills surrounding its encampment, digging rifle-pits along the brow of the hills, and erecting strong earthworks, behind which were planted batteries of artillery. On the 23d of June it marched to Oak Ridge sixteen miles from Vicksburg, and about eight miles from Big Black River.

On the fourth of July it set out on the march, camping at night near the "Big Black." It moved early the next morning, but had proceeded but half a mile when it came on the rebel pickets, who fell back across the river and commenced a spirited skirmish. Two companies of the 40th took their position near the bank of the river, while the enemy was on the opposite bank, and kept up a brisk fire all day. At night Colonel Hicks was ordered with his brigade to force a passage across the river, and drive the enemy into their works. The brigade marched at once to the bank of the river. The only mode of crossing was to wade, but on trial the water was found to be too deep. The enemy prevented their crossing until the following morning, when they went over by means of rafts and canoes, but found the foe had retreated.

The 40th was among the foremost in the advance on Jackson, doing its full share in all the preliminary skirmishing, and in the advance of the whole line on the 14th of July.

After marching into the city on the 17th, the 40th went back to the ground it had previously occupied, and thence toward Vicksburg. On the 24th it arrived within five miles of Big Black River. On the following morning crossed the river at Messinger's Ford, and went into camp about one-half mile beyond, where it remained during the remainder of the summer.

On the 25th of September the 40th, together with nearly all the troops then under Gen. Sherman, received marching orders. About two o'clock on the 28th it moved out on the main road to Vicksburg, and the next day marched through the city. On the 30th it embarked on board the steamer Diana and was off for Memphis, where it arrived on the 10th of October. Thence by a series of marches almost incredible, via Corinth, Iuka, Florence, over the mountain, and on by forced marches to take its share in the battle of Missionary Ridge, which it did most gallantly.

Thence there was another series of marches terminating at Scottsboro, Alabama, December 24th, where the regiment went into winter quarters. On the 1st day of January, 1864, the regiment re-enlisted. At that date its aggregate strength was 443. The aggregate re-enlistments were 345. There are reported during the two years and five months' service—deaths, 261; other casualties, 196; discharged, 17; transferred to other commands, 6; missing in action and desertions, 17.

Colonel Stephen G. Hicks was born in Jackson County, Georgia, and was practicing law in Salem, Ill., when he entered the army and took command of the 40th regiment. He was with the regiment in all its marches, and participated with it in camp life, and at the battle of Shiloh was severely wounded. He remained in hospital for some time, and was taken to his home in Salem, Ill., where he remained until the 18th of July, 1862, when he rejoined the regiment.

On the 25th of October, Col. Hicks received an honorable discharge on account of disability caused by his wound, and he, with great reluctance, took leave of the regiment. He returned to his home but soon applied in person to the War Department to be reinstated, which was done on the 13th of December, 1862, allowing his commission to date back to its first issue. He soon after rejoined the regiment. On the 26th of October, 1863, Col. Hicks received orders to report at Paducah, Ky., where he took command of the post. He was in command of the 2d brigade, 15th army corps, for some time, and ever proved himself an efficient officer, never shrinking from duty, and always serving his country faithfully.

Lieutenant-Colonel James W. Boothe, was born at Huntsville, Alabama, and at the breaking out of the rebellion was a resident of Kinmundy, Marion County, Illinois. He was in command of the regiment during the summer campaign through Tennessee. In the fall of 1862 his health became seriously impaired, in consequence of which he was honorably discharged on the 12th day of January, 1863. He returned to his home but died very suddenly on the 17th of February, 1863.

Major John B. Smith was born in Hamilton county, Illinois, and before entering the army resided on a farm near New Baltimore, Wayne county, Illinois. In the battle of Shiloh he exhibited true bravery, commanding the regiment after Colonel Hicks was wounded. On account of ill health he was compelled to resign about the 20th of May, 1862, when he returned to his home.

Chaplain Richard H. Massey was born in Pike County, Indiana, and was a son of the Rev. James Massey. At the time of his entrance into the army, he was an itinerant minister of the Methodist Episcopal Church.

The Chaplain was ever an ardent friend to the Union, and soon after the breaking out of the rebellion, we find him working earnestly for our country's cause.

He commenced his labors by organizing a company of men for the service, in the town where he resided, Mount Erie, Wayne County, Illinois. He was chosen Captain, but when the regiment was organized, was appointed Chaplain by the Colonel, and received a commission accordingly. Says an officer:

"He accompanied the regiment on all its toilsome and dreary marches; was always ready to attend to the wants of the suffering who were confined in the hospitals, and wherever duty called him; always showed himself, by his strict integrity and Christian conduct a true patriot and a staunch friend of the soldier."

FORTY-EIGHTH REGIMENT ILLINOIS VOLUNTEERS.

The following is the original roster of the regiment:

Colonel, Isham N. Haynie; Lieutenant-Colonel, Thomas H. Smith; Major, Wm. W. Sandford; Adjutant, Wm. Prescott; Quarter-Master, Jonathan C. Willis; Surgeon, Wm. Hill; 1st Assistant Surgeon, Henry H. Deshon; 2d Assistant Surgeon, Thomas Williams; Chaplain, Robert H. Manier.

Co. A—Captain, Manning Mayfield; 1st Lieutenant, Malcolm J. Walker; 2d Lieutenant, John F. Johnston.

Co. B—Captain, Wm. J. Stephenson; 1st Lieutenant, Ferdinand D. Stephenson; 2d Lieutenant, Wm. Sneed.

Co. C—Captain, Lucian Greathouse; 1st Lieutenant, Robert P. Randolph; 2d Lieutenant, Jacob G. Stewart.

Co. D—Captain, Wm. H. Reddin; 1st Lieutenant, Hartwell P. Farrar; 2d Lieutenant, Thomas W. Anderson.

Co. E—Captain, Jackson G. Young; 1st Lieutenant, Hiram B. Chadwick; 2d Lieutenant, Abner B. Smith.

Co. F—Captain, Milton H. Lydick; 1st Lieutenant, Alex. L. Willman; 2d Lieutenant, John R. Daily.

Co. G—Captain, Wm. B. Beall; 1st Lieutenant, Edward Adams; 2d Lieutenant, George Ranke.

Co. H—Captain, Asher Goslin; 1st Lieutenant, Sullerd F. Sellers; 2d Lieutenant, George B. Parker.

Co. I—Captain, Ashley T. Galraith; 1st Lieutenant, Elias M. Holmes; 2d Lieutenant, Stephen F. Grimes.

Co. K—Captain, Benjamin F. Reynolds; 1st Lieutenant, Jefferson Farris; 2d Lieutenant, Wm. N. Berkley.

The Forty-eighth Regiment Illinois Infantry was raised in the southern part of the State, and organized at Camp Butler, Illinois, in the month of September, 1861. It left Camp Butler on the 11th of November about nine hundred strong, and arrived at Cairo, Ill., where it went into camp on the 13th, and remained there until January 11, 1862. It then moved with Gen. Grant's command down the Mississippi River to Fort Jefferson, Ky., returning the 21st of March, but soon left camp again with the expedition of Gen. Grant up the Tennessee River to Fort Henry.

Gen. McClernand gave this regiment the credit of being the first Federal regiment that ever formed in line of battle in Tennessee. This was at Camp Halleck, six miles below Fort Henry. It, with the rest of Gen. McClernand's army, moved into Fort Henry February 6th, after Tighlman had surrendered to the gunboats.

On the 11th of that month it moved toward Fort Donelson, and on the following day arrived close under the works. On the 13th, it, together with the 49th and 17th Illinois regiments, made the charge on the works of the enemy.

It was with Gen. W. H. L. Wallace on the 15th of February in his defense against Buckner, when he attempted to leave the Fort. The loss on this occasion was eight killed, thirty-one wounded and three missing. Among the killed was Lieut.-Col. Thomas H. Smith, who had always proved himself a gallant officer and a courteous gentleman.

On the sixth of March the regiment embarked on the Tennessee River, and sailing up that stream arrived at Savannah, Tenn., on the 12th, and on the 21st moved to Pittsburg Landing. It took a gallant part in the battle of Shiloh, as we have seen. It lost in this battle half its numerical strength. Lieut. Holmes, of Co. I, was among the killed, and Col. Haynie and Lieut.-Col. Sandford among the wounded.

It advanced on Corinth with Gen. Halleck's army, frequently changing brigade commanders, Generals Fowler, Logan, Judah, Marsh and Ross taking the command at different times. It arrived at Bethel, Tenn., Corinth having been evacuated, on the 7th of June, 1862. Here it remained, doing its part toward "Unionizing" the inhabitants of that place, until March 9, 1863.

A part of the command participated in the battles of Corinth and Hatchie and also in several scouts after the rebel Forest, upon one of which, an expedition to Lexington, it was absent for several days, capturing—not the rebel leader it had hoped to—but, in the language of Colonel Greathouse, "nothing but the measles and the itch."

Upon leaving Bethel it removed to Germantown, and on the 7th of June to Memphis. In a few days it embarked for the Yazoo River, and was soon in the rear of Vicksburg. During the month of June the men were digging trenches and fighting, until July 4th, when they moved toward Jackson with Sherman, and on the 6th had an engagement with the enemy at Black River and crossed the river in their very face. The regiment arrived at Jackson on the 9th, and was engaged in skirmishing with Johnston's forces until the 16th, at which time it participated in the general charge against the works of the rebels, losing twenty-five in killed and wounded. Among the killed was Major W. J. Stephenson, who fell while gallantly performing his duty with his "back to the heath and his feet to the foe." He was a chivalric, faithful, and efficient officer, ever ready when duty called.

From Jackson by the way of the Black River, where it arrived July 24, 1863. It remained at this place and Oak Ridge until September 28th, when it moved up the Mississippi to Vicksburg. It left the latter place on the first of October and arrived at Memphis on the 9th. On the 11th of the same month we find it on the march toward Corinth, still in Gen. Smith's division, in whose command it had been since March 9, 1863, Gen. Corse now temporarily commanding.

It arrived at Corinth October 18th, and at Iuka, twenty-five miles east, on the 20th. On the 26th it moved to Eastport, and then crossed the Tennessee River, moving with the rest of Sherman's command via Flòrence, Rogersville, Fayetteville and Manchester to Dechard, where it joined the army of the Cumberland. Leaving Dechard November 10th "the boys" went to Stephenson and from there to Bridgeport, where they left every thing they had in their posession, excepting their guns and cartridges, and moved across the Tennessee River south to Trenton, Ga. They dislodged the enemy from this place, and that part of Lookout Mountain, and then went up the Lookout Valley. On the 20th of November, crossed the Tennessee River north to Cumberland, and on the 22d and 23d they obtained a fresh supply of rations and cartridges, and again crossed that river south, in scows, on the morning of the 24th, and on the same day they occupied Mt. Allison before Bragg came up.

They fought their share in the battle of Missionary Ridge, on the 25th of November, pursuing the enemy long before day on the 26th toward Ringgold, and up the railroad. They burned the bridges on the 28th, and on the day following started, *without rations, blankets, or shoes, over the frozen ground*, to the relief of Burnside at Knoxville.

They returned to Chattanooga on the 17th of December, by the way of Lookout and Mount Marrows, and the next day to Bridgeport, thence on foot to Scotsboro, Alabama, where they arrived in January, 1864.

With the exception of thirty-five—out of four hundred and fifty—the regiment re-enlisted as veterans, and left the South for their homes on the 24th of January for the purpose of recruiting. They returned after an absence of two months eight hundred strong, ready to enter the service again, and to battle for the right until the rebellion is no more.

Colonel Lucien Greathouse was born at Carlinville, Illinois, June 7, 1842. He attended the common schools of that place until he arrived at the age of eleven, at which time he entered college at Lebanon, Illinois, where he remained for two years. He then entered the University of Indiana and was graduated at the early age of sixteen. He soon after commenced the study of law and in 1860 was admitted to the bar.

Ere he had reached his nineteenth year, the rebellion broke out, and the cry "To arms!" reached us. Young Greathouse, full of patriotism, could not listen to the appeal for soldiers without any response. He was among the first to leave his home and friends for the glorious cause, and we find him commencing his military career as a private in the Eighth Illinois Infantry, a three months' regiment, but he was soon promoted to corporal for gallantry while in camp.

Having served his time and returned home on September, 1861, he again entered the service as Captain of Company C, Forty-eighth Illinois Regiment, but was soon promoted to Major, and shortly after—November 21—to Lieutenant-Colonel, which rank he held until February 26, 1864. He then received the promotion to the Colonelcy of the regiment, which office he had well earned by faithfulness to his duty. He had accompanied the regiment in all their dreary and toilsome marches, had shared with them their many privations, and had ever shown himself a firm patriot and a true soldier.

CHAPTER XVII.

History of Gen. Mitchell's Campaign—The March Upon Huntsville—Splendid March of Gen. Turchin's Brigade—Illinois in the Advance—Surprise and Capture of Huntsville—Gen. Turchin's Occupation of Tuscumbia—His Retrograde Movement—Occupation of Athens—Refutation of Malicious Charges—The Battle of Bridgeport—Complete Surprise and Rout of the Rebels—Close of the Campaign—Gen. Negley's Expedition—Illinois Again in the Advance—The Shelling of Chattanooga—Life and Character of Gen. Turchin.

THERE was one division of General Buell's army, which, although co-operating with the movements of the main army in its operations at Pittsburg Landing and Corinth, detailed in the 15th chapter, yet occupied a distant part of the field and carried on virtually an independent campaign, sufficiently so to warrant an interruption of chronological sequence, and the devotion of a separate chapter to the development of that campaign. We therefore return to Nashville.

General Mitchell left at the same time with the main army, but took the road to Murfreesboro, at which point he remained until the 4th of April, building bridges, putting roads into repair, and organizing and stripping his army for the impending campaign. Long before this time, the rebel force which had occupied Murfreesboro, had withdrawn and joined Beauregard on the new southern line of defense.

On the 4th, General Mitchell marched to Shelbyville, county seat of Bedford, Tennessee, twenty-six miles distant, and on the 7th advanced to Fayetteville, twenty-seven miles further on, which places he occupied without opposition. On the 8th, fifteen miles beyond Fayetteville, he crossed the state line of Alabama. Huntsville was now the objective point, the occupation of which would sever the main line of communication between the rebel armies in Virginia and Mississippi. It was expected that its occupation would be secured only at fearful cost. It was a railroad point of vital importance to the rebels, and one which it was supposed would be guarded with sleepless vigilance, and defended to the last extremity. Upon that road the rebels had accumulated nearly all the rolling stock of all the railroads from Bowling Green southward, besides what belonged to the road itself, and the rapid transportation and concentration of troops at any given point was therefore a matter of comparative ease. Should reverse happen to either of our armies in Virginia or Mississippi, the destruction of Gen. Mitchell's army was almost certain. But in the midst of all these anxieties, a man stepped forward who was never anxious, who never doubted of success, one bred to arms, and who believed that success—all other things being equal—could always be achieved by celerity of movement, and strength and suddenness of blow. If these are elements of strategy, he was eminently strategetic. That man was General, then Colonel, John Basil Turchin. He conceived that Huntsville might be taken without a struggle, and sought permission of General Mitchell to march thither with his brigade, consisting of the 19th and 24th Illinois, 18th Ohio, 37th Indiana, the 4th Ohio Cavalry, Colonel Kennett, and Captain Simonson's battery. The permission was granted. Taking two days' rations, his brigade, the gallant 19th and 24th Illinois in the advance, left Fayetteville at 6 o'clock, A. M., on the 10th, Colonel Sill's brigade and the Loomis' battery following closely, and the other brigade, General Lytle's, at a greater distance. The weather was cool, but the roads, if by paths can be called roads, were in a frightful condition. Onward the troops toiled through swamps, morasses and almost impenetrable forests, over rocky and precipitous hills, to descend again into swamps, bog holes and thick forests. The progress was slow and painful. The trains were frequently mired. Often it became necessary to hitch the mules of two or three teams to a single wagon, and haul them singly through the swamps and up the steep hills. In some places it was necessary to drag the guns by hand. But the troops made no complaint. The indomitable spirit and untiring energy of Turchin seemed to pervade his troops individually, and still they toiled on though weary and heavy laden.

That night Turchin's brigade rested but little. No tents were pitched. The men threw themselves upon the ground around their camp fires until the moon went down, and then in the darkness, the shrill bugle call summoned them to the march again. The roads became better and progress was more rapid. About six o'clock in the morning, the vicinity of Huntsville was reached, the city being visible behind a beautiful forest of cedars. An advance force of the cavalry, with a section of the battery in charge of Captain Simonson himself, assisted by Lieutenant M. Allen, commanding the section, the whole under charge of Colonel Kennett, first caught sight of the town. Captain Simonson placed his battery in position on the side of one of the hills on the Meridianville road, and the little force moved forward as silently as possible and on the double quick. Two locomotives, with trains attached, made their appearance upon the railroad moving towards Stevenson. The first one crowded on steam and made its escape. The second, however, was brought to by a shot from the battery and captured with one hundred and fifty-nine prisoners. The escaped train was chased ten miles by a squad of the cavalry but the iron horse was too fleet. The infantry had come up while this was going on, and Colonel Mihalotzy of the 24th Illinois sent a detachment to tear up the track in the direction of Decatur, so that the escape of any more trains was effectually prevented.

The word was now " On to the town!" The cavalry force was instantly in motion and an excited race ensued for the honor of the first *entree.* Three troopers gained the honors, rushing into the town far in advance of the rest of the force, and finding a large number of rebel soldiers sleeping about a train, one hundred and seventy of whom they actually captured, including a Major Cavanaugh, six captains and three lieutenants. The rebel Major had been home for recruits and was en route for Virginia to fill up his regiment. It is safe to assume his recruits never reached their destination, and that his chagrin was fully as deep as the merriment of his captors. The surprise was complete. The citizens were asleep, quietly dreaming of future Southern independence or troubled with Yankee nightmares, when our troops entered. The clatter of the cavalry as they swept through the streets, and their triumphant shouts of victory awoke them from their slumbers, and they flocked to the doors and windows, rubbing their eyes and whispering to each other the unwelcome news. Men rushed into the streets half dressed, women fainted, the children screamed, and the negroes were in ecstasies. There was an absolute reign of terror for a short time, the inhabitants uncertain as to what their fate might be at the hands of their sudden and unexpected visitors. Only the cavalry force as yet occupied the town, and the Mayor unaware of the brigades behind, plucked up courage and consoled his demoralized constituents, by assuring them he should send for a rebel cavalry force near by and have the intruders expelled before night. During the forenoon, however, the whole army entered, and the Mayor gave up his design. Colonel Gazley, of the 37th Indiana, was appointed Provost Marshal and his regiment occupied the place as a garrison. Tranquillity was restored, and an examination of the prize which had fallen like overripe fruit into our hands, showed that seventeen fine locomotives, sixteen of them in running order, and one hundred and fifty cars, besides an immense amount of railroad and war material, were the results of General Turchin's well planned and well executed expedition. General Mitchell made good use of his rolling stock. Before the close of the day, our troops had made several railroad excursions into the interior, and one hundred miles of the Memphis and Charleston Railroad, stretching in one direction as far as Stevenson and in the other as far as Decatur, were in our possession.

From Decatur Gen. Turchin pushed on and occupied Tuscumbia. The operations were summed up by Gen. Mitchell in his thanks to his soldiers, as follows: "You have struck blow after blow with a rapidity unparalleled. Stevenson fell, sixty miles to the east of Huntsville. Decatur and Tuscumbia have been in like manner seized and are now occupied. In three days you have extended your front of operations more than one hundred and twenty miles, and your morning gun at Tuscumbia may be heard by your comrades on the battle-field made glorious by their victory before Corinth."

But this very extension of his line, although it made him a Major-General and his force an independent corps, was fraught with great and imminent danger. With the number of troops at his command, it was impossible for him to hold this long line of railroad. The enemy began to gather in force and threaten him. On the right skirmishing was frequent. On the left, at Chattanooga, both his rear and Nashville were threatened. In his front, cavalry were harassing him. No reinforcements came. Supplies were obtained with difficulty, and subsistence forwarded to him by Gen. Halleck had been destroyed to save it from the enemy. Gen. Turchin found his position at Tuscumbia untenable, and although his spirit chafed against it, he reluctantly determined on the 23d to fall back. On the 24th he reached Jonesboro after some severe fighting with the cavalry harassing his rear guard, and on the 26th the bridge at Decatur, the only crossing of the Tennessee river east of Florence above the head of navigation, and west of Bridgeport near Chattanooga. Gen. Turchin continued his retrograde movement to Huntsville, shortly after which occurred the episode at Athens, which has been made the opportunity for much partisan censure and malicious statement concerning the 19th Illinois. When the 19th entered Huntsville, Athens, a small town on the Elk river, a branch of the Tennessee, was occupied by the 18th Ohio, Col. Stanley. They were camped in the race course near the town, but on one occasion neglecting to have pickets out, a squad of rebel cavalry discovered the omission, and, posting themselves in advantageous positions, commenced firing upon our troops. Col. Stanley, thinking that the force was much larger than it really was, evacuated the place and retired upon Huntsville, his *avant couriers* coming in with the most exaggerated stories of the approach of a large rebel force and the annihilation of the regiment. The inhabitants of Athens had made frequent and loud protestations of loyalty, but the departure of the regiment was made the occasion of every indignity. The troops were fired upon from the windows of houses. Women jeered at them with the vilest epithets, spat upon them, and the rabble followed them, throwing filth and garbage. But in the mean time, Gen. Turchin's brigade was ordered to occupy Athens and it was done speedily. No enemy was found there, and the inhabitants were again full of protestations of loyalty. This and the remembrance of the indignities heaped upon their comrades, incensed the troops, and some of the regiments, the 19th in particular, retaliated by the destruction of rebel property. The malicious charge of the ravishing of the inmates of a female seminary near the town by members of the 19th is wholly gratuitous. At the time of the occupation there were but two inmates of the institution within its walls, the landlady and a girl, both of whom were conveyed, at their own request, to a point farther south by one of General Turchin's staff. Undoubtedly excesses were committed, but excesses are the natural and unavoidable concomitants of war, and those at Athens, while the provocation was extreme, were not more glaring than those which marked the early events of the war. After remaining in Athens three or four weeks, the brigade occupied Fayetteville.

The fight at Bridgeport, Ala., virtually closed General Mitchell's campaign. The march to Bridgeport commenced on Tuesday, the 24th of April. The troops pushed eastward along the line of the railroad over roads so bad that the artillery was often dragged by hand. On the afternoon of the 29th the rebel pickets were encountered about three miles from Bridgeport. They were stationed on the bank of a small stream, the bridge across it having been burned, and supported by an infantry and two cavalry regiments, the former of which engaged our advance, the 33d Ohio. After half an hour's fighting, in which the casualties were slight, the 33d fell back unpursued, as the rebels had no means of crossing the stream. Gen. Mitchell, in the mean time, made a wide detour to the left and came upon a road leading to Bridgeport, following which, he reached the rebel fortifications on the bank of the Tennessee and drew up his force in line of battle under cover of a hill which concealed him from the enemy. The whole column then advanced, and reaching the crest of the hill discovered the rebel force with stacked arms at its base, eating supper and lounging about, little dreaming of the enemy so near them. Capt. Loomis quickly and cautiously brought his battery to bear upon the main body of them. They soon had an intimation of what was coming, in the shape of a storm of grape and canister, which went tearing through their ranks. Many of them fled in the wildest confusion without taking their arms. The main body seized their guns and tried to make a stand, but again the pitiless and terrible storm of grape and canister swept through them, scattering death and destruction on every hand. Our columns fixed bayonets and swept down the hill-side like a whirlwind, but before they reached the base the whole rebel force broke and fled with precipitancy, managing to fire the bridge. Capt. Loomis then placed his battery in position to receive the remainder of the force stationed on the railroad. They debouched into an open field, formed their line of battle and came up within three hundred yards of our forces before they discovered their mistake, and then that terrible battery informed them. A terrific fire of canister was poured into them and created another panic. Cavalry and infantry threw down their arms and fled like sheep. Thus the battle of Bridgeport was won, and General Mitchell reported as follows to the Secretary of War: "The campaign is ended, and I now occupy Huntsville in perfect security, while all of Alabama north of the Tennessee River floats no flag but that of the Union."

As an appendix to his campaign, there were many minor expeditions of interest. Gen. Mitchell advanced towards Chattanooga which caused a retreat of the rebels in East Tennessee—a step rendered necessary, as the loss of the single line of railroad running from Chattanooga to Atlanta would compel evacuation above, as in the case of Bowling Green. During May and June, several expeditions were sent out under Gen. Negley against guerrillas and roving bands of cavalry, the results of which may be summed up as follows:

On the 13th of May, Gen. Negley's expedition from Pulaski, supported by Gen. Lytle's expedition from Athens, entered Rogersville, Ala., driving the enemy across the Tennessee and destroying a portion of their ferry boats. On the 29th of May, he again started from Columbia, Tenn., for the purpose of making an expedition into East Tennessee with the intention of threatening Chattanooga and dispersing rebel cavalry. He reached Fayetteville on the 31st, where Gen. Turchin's forces joined the expedition, and thence resumed his march to Salem, which he reached on the following day. The next day he arrived at Winchester. Passing through Winchester, he encamped at Cowan, on the Nashville and Chattanooga Railroad, on a stream called the Burning Fork, a tributary of the Tennessee River, the bridge over which had been burned. The stream was easily forded, however, on the 4th, and the army crossed the Cumberland Mountains, arriving at Jasper, Marion County.

Passing through Jasper, Gen. Negley encamped at the foot of the Waldron Ridge, a spur of the Cumberland Mountains.

The following morning he commenced crossing and first obtained a glimpse of the enemy. At the foot of the mountains the pickets of the rebel General Adams' brigade of cavalry were encountered. After a brisk firing the rebel pickets fell back, and the main body came forward preparatory to a charge. General Negley opened upon them with shell. At the very first fire they fell back in confusion and were hotly pursued by our cavalry under Lieut. Wharton. The enemy were driven two miles before they were reached, but our cavalry at last succeeded in overtaking them, and charged upon them with the saber, killing many and taking many prisoners. The rebels, in their headlong flight, threw away every thing that could impede them, and the woods and roads were strewn for miles with sabers, pistols, haversacks and rations. Gen. Adams, commanding the rebels, lost his hat, horse and sword. His brother was killed. Many of the fugitives did not stop short of Chattanooga, a distance of thirty miles. After pursuing them three miles, the Union forces returned to the foot of the mountains and camped for the night upon a plateau called Sweden's Cove.

On the next day General Negley proceeded towards Chattanooga. He arrived opposite the place on June 7th, and on the afternoon of that day proceeded to reconnoiter. He ascertained that there was a large forçe on the north side of the river, which had crossed to attack the 19th. This regiment had performed a characteristic feat by discovering a shorter path across the mountains than that pursued by the main body, and had, consequently, by striking out for themselves, got to Chattanooga first. The 19th and 24th Illinois were deployed as skirmishers to feel the enemy, and went down the hill as coolly as if on dress parade. The enemy, although in strong force, did not wait to feel the touch of the 19th, but immediately recrossed the river. General Negley at once placed his artillery in a position commanding the town. About 5 o'clock P. M., a brisk fire was kept up between the enemy's riflemen and the 19th and 24th, still acting as skirmishers. General Negley ordered his batteries to open and a fierce cannonading ensued, kept up for two hours, during which time all the enemy's guns were silenced, three of them having been dismantled. The shelling was continued for two or three days, but the place finally had to be abandoned, owing to the difficulty experienced by General Negley in procuring supplies.

On the advance of General Buell, this division, under General Mitchell, was placed under General Rousseau, and General Mitchell was ordered to report at Port Royal, S. C.

A brief sketch of the life and character of one who was so "large a part" of this campaign, whose military genius pervaded all its movements, and whose energy gave to it its success, will fittingly close our narrative.

John Basil Turchin was born in the valley of the Don, Russia, Jan. 18, 1822. At the age of fourteen he attended the military school at St. Petersburg, where he obtained the rudiments of his military education. After his graduation, he received a Lieutenant's commission in the Russian army. His precocious military talent rapidly gained him promotion, and he was soon elevated to the rank of Captain on the general staff, when he again entered the military academy and remained there three years, finishing the theoretical parts of his education. At the outbreak of the Crimean war he received an appointment on the staff of the Crown Prince—the present Emperor of Russia—corresponding in our service to the first assistant adjutant general to a commander of division. The plan adopted for the defenses of the coast of Finland was prepared by him, and to him was entrusted the superintendence of their construction. They are probably among the most elaborate and scientific specimens of military engineering in Europe.

Having imbibed democratic ideas at an early age, he came to the United States in 1856, and was employed in the engineering department of the Illinois Central Railroad, a corporation, by the way, which has furnished four prominent generals to the service in the present war—Banks, Burnside, Turchin and McClellan. When the war broke out for the defense of those same democratic ideas which had led him to abandon his fatherland, he entered heartily into the movement, and in July, 1861, was appointed Colonel of the 19th Illinois, one of the best drilled, most marched, heaviest battle-scarred, and worst abused regiments that ever sustained the honor of Illinois in the field. During its stay in camp in Chicago, it became celebrated for its excellence of drill and *esprit du corps.* General Turchin gave to it his constant personal attention and inspection, and was ever vigilant and unwearied to make it a model regiment. He led it through many hard, wearisome marches and severe battles, that told fearfully upon its numbers, but which made its name the synonym of success, and finally, when court-martialed upon the charges of inferior officers, returned to his home, accompanied by his faithful and gallant lady, who had shared his dangers and privations upon the march and in the field, to be welcomed with princely ovations. While the court martial was pending, he received the commission of a brigadier-general from the President, which was a signal answer to the charges against him.

General Turchin is a man of medium stature and strong frame, slightly inclined to corpulence, with a massive, well formed head, and a face full of intelligence. His countenance is very expressive and genial, and betokens the union of a rare and delicate humor, with great inflexibility of will and decision of purpose. He is impulsive, full of energy, thinks and acts quickly, and is rarely placed in that position where he cannot muster resources to meet its emergencies. In succeeding chapters we shall see more of this General, and find that a lion-like courage was another attribute of his nature.

CHAPTER XVIII.

Gen. Buell's Campaign—Capture of the Union Garrison at Munfordsville—The Battle of Bolivar, Tenn—Splendid Charge of the Second Illinois Cavalry—Death of the Gallant Hero, Lieut.-Col. Hogg—The Last Words of a Brave Man—"For God's Sake, Don't Order Me Back"—The Battle of Perryville—How Illinois Was Represented—Magnificent Charge of Col. Carlin's Brigade—The Heroes of Pea Ridge in Their Glory—The Illinois Regiments Engaged—Closing Scenes of the Campaign—Buell Superseded.

WE have stated in a previous chapter that General Buell left Corinth with the main body of his army about the 10th of June 1862, for the purpose of counteracting the movement of General Bragg upon Chattanooga. Bragg's army was composed of three corps under Maj.-Gens. Hardee, Polk and E. Kirby Smith. The division of Gen. Smith was at Knoxville, where it remained while Chattanooga was occupied by Hardee and Polk. Smith, moving from Knoxville, effected the design of getting into the rear of the Union General G. W. Morgan, at Cumberland Gap, and thence advanced into Kentucky. On the 21st of August, Bragg crossed the Tennessee, and turning General Buell's left, reached Dunlap on the 27th. Thence he moved up the Sequatchie Valley and reached Pikeville on the 30th. On the same day he threw a large force forward to McMinnville, seventy-five miles southeast of Nashville. This force, consisting of cavalry, was driven out however after a severe contest and joined the main army again, which, on the 5th of September, entered Kentucky and moved on towards Bowling Green. On the 13th of September an advance of this force appeared before Munfordsville and captured the place and garrison, composed of five Indiana regiments, a company of cavalry, a part of the 4th Ohio infantry, and a section of an Indiana battery, the whole under

Col. Dunham, who relieved Col. Wilder on the second day, after an obstinate defence of two days.

General Buell deduced from the movements of Bragg that he was aiming at Louisville. While the latter was slowly making his way towards the Cumberland River, the former was on his left flank at Lebanon, protecting Nashville. During all the march, Gen. Buell was harassing his rear, shelled him out of Woodsonville, drove him out of Munfordsville, and followed him closely along the road from Nashville to Louisville. Finally, forced by the need of supplies, Gen. Buell moved directly to the city, around which he encamped.

While these operations were going on, some isolated events of interest occurred in other parts of the field. On the 31st of August Brig.-Gen. Ross, commanding at Jackson, Tenn., received a dispatch from Col. Crocker, commanding at Bolivar, that that post was threatened by a large force advancing from the south, and that Col. Leggett had been sent out to attack the enemy's advance. Colonel Leggett's force consisted of a section of the 9th Indiana battery, two companies of the 11th Illinois cavalry, under Major Puterbaugh, four companies of the 2d Illinois cavalry under the gallant Lieut.-Col. Hogg, and the 20th and 78th Ohio infantry regiments. Col. Leggett engaged the enemy and spendidly held them in check until reinforcements arrived from General Ross. Two companies of the 20th Ohio were deployed to relieve the cavalry, and the artillery was sent a mile to the rear to await reinforcements. About noon, the enemy, in overwhelming numbers, made a desperate attempt to flank on the right and get to our rear. Col. Leggett took the two companies of the 11th Illinois and the mounted infantry and passed over the Middleburgh road, where he found the enemy advancing in strong force. The infantry dismounted and attacked them, and after a struggle of an hour drove them back. Just at the close of the struggle, four companies of the 78th and 20th Ohio came up and engaged the enemy's skirmishers. Leaving a sufficient force to guard his left, Col. Leggett massed the remainder of his force on the Middleburgh road, where it was evident the enemy was attempting to break through the line and gain our rear. At this time Lieut.-Col. Hogg came up with his four companies of the invincible

2d Illinois cavalry. He was asked if he could hold a position on the left against a charge of the rebel cavalry. The gallant hero promptly replied that he could, and asked the honor of taking the position, which was at once assigned him. He had hardly got into position before the rebels charged down the road in overwhelming numbers, but under the deadly infantry fire were compelled to retreat. They twice repeated the charge, but were each time repulsed. They then entered the field upon the left and opened fire upon Lieut.-Col. Hogg's cavalry and the two supporting companies of the 20th Ohio. The infantry and cavalry returned the fire briskly. Col. Leggett then discovered that a full regiment of the enemy's cavalry was forming with a view of charging upon the gallant little band. He sent word to Col. Hogg that if he had any doubts about his ability to hold his position, he had better fall back. Then shone out the splendid bravery of this more than Spartan hero. He sent word back: "FOR GOD'S SAKE, COL. LEGGETT, DON'T ORDER ME BACK." Immortal words, O, dead, gallant hero! Fit epitaph for so brave, so pure, so fearless a spirit. Col. Leggett replied: "Meet them with a charge, Colonel, and may Heaven bless you." He immediately ordered his men to draw their sabers, and placing himself at their head, shouted: "Forward! give them cold steel, boys," and put spurs to his horse. Away they flew like the wind, but their Colonel was flying like the whirlwind far in advance of his men, and a prominent mark for the rebel sharpshooters. Nine balls pierced his body and he fell, and the next minute the line came together with a fearful clash of arms. The enemy wavered and partially gave way, but Col. Hogg had fallen, and there was no other to assume command, and the cavalry became partially disorganized and commenced falling back, when Capt. M. H. Musser, of Co. F took command and restored the line. Thus perished in the defence of liberty one of the bravest of the brave, without fear and without reproach. A more gallant hero never drew sword. Chivalrous, brave and manly, his name is one of the brightest in the annals of Illinois' history. Col. Leggett, in his official report, says: "The 2d Illinois cavalry was on the field so short a time I can only particularize their commander, the lamented Lieut.-Col. Hogg. A braver, truer man never lifted his sword in defence of his country. He was brave to a fault, and fell while leading one of the most gallant cavalry charges of the war."

But in the mean time, infantry reinforcements had come up and formed in line to support the artillery. The enemy came within range, when the battery opened upon them with shell, which caused them to disperse and gave our gallant forces possession of the field. The victory was won, but at a fearful price, for Lieut.-Col. Hogg was no more to lead and inspire his men.

Immediately after the repulse, large bodies of the rebel cavalry attacked the various detachments scattered along the line of the Mississippi Central Railroad. At Medon Station, a barricade of cotton bales had been constructed by Adjutant Frohock, of the 45th Illinois. On the 31st of August this barricade was attacked by a force of rebels numbering 1,500 men, who were gallantly held at bay by one hundred and fifty men of the 45th, until reinforcements from the 7th Missouri arrived and drove the rebels from the town.

Immediately after the demonstration on Bolivar, the force at Estaualga, under command of Col. Dennis, of the 30th Illinois, was ordered to Jackson, Tenn. Col. Dennis' command comprised the 30th Illinois, commanded by Major Warren Shedd, and the 20th Illinois, commanded by Capt. Frisbie, and a section of two pieces of artillery and two companies of cavalry. On the 1st of September his advance guard encountered seven regiments of rebel cavalry numbering 5,000 men, while Col. Dennis' force numbered only eight hundred. Col. Dennis posted his little band in advantageous positions, but the overwhelming force of the enemy enabled them to surround our troops temporarily, and capture the trains. The battle was of four hours' duration, and resulted in leaving Colonel Dennis master of the field, having suffered a loss of only five men, while the total loss of the enemy in killed and wounded was over four hundred. Colonel Dennis, Capt. Frisbie, of the 20th, Major Shedd and Adjutant Peyton, of the 30th, displayed undaunted courage and coolness, the latter, although severely wounded, refusing to leave the field.

But we return to the main operations of General Buell. From Munfordsville, the rebels moved towards the central portion of the State, conscripting as they went and gathering supplies. On the 1st of October, General Buell moved from Louisville, and on the 6th, after slow progress owing to difficulties of the route and skirmishes with the rebel rear guard, arrived at Springfield, sixty-two miles from Louisville. On the 7th, it was reported to General Buell that a large Confederate force was at Perryville, forty-two miles south of Frankfort. General Buell immediately ordered an advance, and the battle of Chaplin's Hills, more generally known as the battle of Perryville, ensued. On the 7th a severe skirmish took place which for the time assumed the dimensions of a battle. On the 8th, the position was as follows: General Sheridan's division had the advance in General Gilbert's corps, Rousseau's and Jackson's divisions having previously advanced by way of Taylorsville and formed a line of battle, Jackson to the rear of Rousseau and forming the extreme left. McCook's brigade was on the right of Lytle's which formed the right wing of Rousseau's division. McCook had moved forward early in the morning with his brigade, accompanied by Barnett's 2d Illinois' battery and occupied his position. The 85th Illinois, Colonel Moore, was deployed upon the right and the 52d Ohio on the left. The 125th Illinois, Colonel Harmon, was placed as a reserve, and the 86th Illinois of this brigade were on picket duty. The rebel pickets opened a sharp fire on the 85th Illinois, and although this was the first fight in which they had ever engaged, they advanced like old veterans up a steep hill side and drove the rebels from the crest, inflicting a severe loss upon them. Irritated at the loss of their position, the rebels massed upon the right and left, and commenced a furious fire of shrapnel upon the brigade. For an hour the firing continued, but the brigade resolutely held its ground. As soon as the position of the rebel battery was discovered, Barnett's battery of two ten-pounder parrotts came into position and silenced it. The rebels rallied to their guns three times, but in vain, and soon the fire of their battery ceased entirely. In the meantime, the right wing of the 125th Illinois was ordered up to support the battery, and did their work splendidly, and the rebels retired leaving the brigade in possession of the ground they had won. A cavalry force advanced in the direction the enemy were retreating and were soon furiously attacked. The situation became critical. The rebels pressed heavily upon our cavalry, but the 2d

Missouri came up gallantly to the rescue, and with deafening shouts advanced steadily upon the rebels who quailed before their unerring and well directed fire, and retreated towards the woods.

As only a division or two had come up, our forces remained in line of battle deeming it imprudent to attack. The enemy in their exasperation determined to overwhelm us before the balance should arrive. At eleven o'clock, A. M., artillery firing commenced. The enemy remained sullenly silent for a long time but, finally opened upon Captain Loomis' and Captain Simonson's batteries. To the extreme left, another of our batteries opened and the enemy replied from at least six different positions. At the foot of the hill just behind the batteries, Rousseau's division was posted, Lytle's brigade on the right, most of it to the east of a narrow lane which opened out into the field where Loomis' battery was at work, the 9th brigade on the left of the lane, and the twenty-eighth brigade still further to the left, supporting the 19th Indiana battery. All of these positions were more or less exposed to the enemy's fire, but not a man flinched. Suddenly the enemy's firing ceased and there was a lull in the battle, but only the lull which precedes the storm. At two o'clock, P. M., the cannonading recommenced with terrific fury all along the line, and the enemy's legions began to emerge from the cover of the woods. At three o'clock, Bragg massed the very flower of the army, artillery, cavalry and infantry, and made a desperate effort, but in vain, to break through our lines to the left of our center. Buckner massed another and an immense force against Jackson's division, and in spite of the desperate resistance offered, by virtue of the disparity of numbers, broke through our line at that point. The partial success of the rebels encouraged them to renew the attack upon Rousseau and a desperate fight ensued. The rebels were in overwhelming numbers and the carnage was terrible. Regiment after regiment was beaten back only to rally again and renew the fight. General Lytle fell in the fiercest of the storm. The 15th Kentucky was decimated almost in a minute. The 10th Ohio was surrounded and cut its way through. While the seventh brigade in spite of its fearful losses was holding the rebels in check, the 9th and 28th brigades came to the rescue and bore down upon the enemy. The combat raged with great fury for half an hour, but in the meantime on the right, Sheridan and Mitchell had repulsed an attack and pursued the rebels beyond Perryville. Upon the disastrous issue of this attack on the right, the attack upon the left was abandoned, and the rebels retired from the field. About sundown, the baffled foe made one last despairing attack upon Rousseau's division, but was repulsed by Loomis' battery, and our men lay upon their arms expecting a renewal of the attack the next morning. During the evening General Crittendon's corps came up, but no movement was made until noon of the next day, when it was found the enemy had retreated in the night. These are the general features of the Perryville battle. We now purpose more particularly to trace the share Illinois had in the combat.

During the afternoon, General Mitchell advanced his brigade in which were the 59th Illinois, Major J. C. Winters; 74th Illinois, Lieutenant-Colonel Keer; 75th Illinois, Lieutenant-Colonel Bennett; 21st Illinois, Colonel Alexander; 38th Illinois, Major Gilmer; 25th Illinois, Colonel McClelland, and the 35th Illinois, Lieutenant-Colonel Chandler, and formed them in position, supporting Gen. Sheridan. Almost immediately on the formation of the line, the rebels advanced against Colonel Carlin's (38th Illinois) brigade, but retired under cover, at the advance of Colonel Carlin's skirmishers. Colonel Carlin was then ordered to advance rapidly to reinforce General Sheridan who was hard pressed. He pushed on through a skirt of timber to the open fields on the right, and upon ascending a hill, discovered the rebels advancing in strong force upon Sheridan's right. Colonel Carlin immediately formed his brigade, and on the double quick charged the advancing foe with such impetuosity that their columns were thrown into confusion and broken. The gallant Carlin completely pierced their center, and chased them for two miles, pressing them closely until they formed under the protection of two powerful batteries on a line of bluffs. Finding that in the impetuosity of his charge and the ardor of his pursuit, he had outstripped all support and isolated himself, he retired in safety before the enemy could recover from their confusion. In Colonel Carlin's advance, the 38th, his own regiment, overtook and captured an ammunition train and the train guard of one hundred and thirty-eight men and three officers. The 75th were fighting their first battle and did their work like veterans, while the 59th added to the laurels they had already gained at Pea Ridge. General Mitchell in his report paid an especial tribute to Major Gilmer of the 38th, for the skill and activity he displayed in capturing the ammunition train, and to his aid de-camp Lieutenant Andrews of the 42d, for the able, gallant, and heroic manner in which he performed his duties. In his division, Surgeon Hazlet of the 59th, Lieutenant Johnson of the 58th, Lieutenant Blean and Lieutenant Eels of the 75th died gallantly in defence of the flag.

General McCook, in his report, honorably mentioned his orderlies, George Richardson, Avery Graham and George P. Jenniss, of the 34th, as behaving with coolness and bravery, and recommended their promotion.

In the 10th division of the 1st corps, the following Illinois regiments participated in the fight with great credit to themselves: 80th, Col. Allen, and 123d, Col. Monroe. The former lost eleven killed, thirty-two wounded, and thirteen missing; the latter, thirty-five killed, one hundred and nineteen wounded and thirty-five missing.

In General Sheridan's division, Barnett's 2d Illinois battery did most excellent service, and, in conjunction with Hezcock's battery, drove the enemy's batteries from every position they took. Colonel Greusel, of the 36th, also behaved with great gallantry, leading his men at all times, and infusing them with a large share of his own coolness and bravery.

In General Rousseau's division, at a critical period of the fight, the old fighting 24th Illinois was ordered up to the support of a weak point, and went into action, deploying as skirmishers in a manner which won universal plaudits. They were repeatedly assailed by overwhelming numbers, but determinedly and firmly held their position. Lieut. William Quinton, of the 19th Illinois, detached for signal duty, was also conspicuous for his bravery, attending General Rousseau voluntarily—although not his place to do so—in the thickest of the fight. Major Winters of the 59th, was highly complimented for his bravery, and Lieut. West of the 39th, A. A. A. G. to Colonel Gooding of the 30th brigade, although wounded in five different places, refused to leave the field until entirely disabled. One hundred and fifty-three out of three hundred and twenty-five of the 59th, and two hundred and twenty-one out of seven hundred of the 75th were lost. In every changing phase of this severe and well-fought contest, Illinois soldiers proved their titles to the laurels they had won at Donelson, Shiloh, Pea Ridge and Corinth.

The remaining events of the campaign we shall trace briefly, to preserve the unity of the narrative, although no great battles were fought. It was expected that General Bragg would make his next stand at Camp Dick Robinson, a place which was defensible in front but easily flanked. Accordingly, General Crittenden was ordered to march to Dick River, as if about to attack in front, and Generals McCook and Gilbert to approach by different roads on the flank and compel Bragg to fight. The rebel general, however, penetrated the plan, owing to the retrograde movement of a division of General Crittenden's corps, and on the night of the 11th the evacuation commenced, the rebel army moving toward Cumberland Gap. There were two lines of retreat converging to that point—one by the way of Richmond and Big Hill, through Madison county, and the other, called the Crab Orchard road, by way of Mt. Vernon and Barboursville, the two roads converging at Pitman's Junction, fifty-eight miles from the Gap. On the night of the 12th, General Buell ordered an advance from Danville, and at 1 o'clock the army was in motion towards Stanford. The advance arrived in time to see the rear of the rebel rear-guard pass out of the town unmolested. Having checked the advance of our army, and gained time for the main body of the rebel army, they retired toward Crab Orchard. On the morning of the 14th, our army was again on the march and soon reached Crab Orchard. The Confederate rear guard again halted and kept up a skirmish with our forces, during which time the rebel army was retreating unmolested. Our advance the next day reached Mt. Vernon, Cook's and Gilbert's corps remaining at Crab Orchard, and the cavalry ordered to the rear in consequence of the difficulty of procuring forage. The Confederate forces rapidly retired and escaped into East Tennessee, laden with the rich spoils they had gathered in Kentucky, and Buell fell back to the line between Louisville and Nashville, where he was superseded in his command by General Rosecrans.

CHAPTER XIX.

GEN. BUELL SUPERSEDED BY GEN. ROSECRANS—REORGANIZATION OF THE ARMY—THE MARCH ON MURFREESBORO—THE BATTLE OF STONE RIVER—THREE DAYS' FIGHTING—PLAN AND DETAILS OF THE BATTLE—THE 89TH ILLINOIS FIGHTING AGAINST FATE—GALLANTRY OF GEN. KIRK'S OLD REGIMENT—WOUNDING OF GEN. KIRK—THE REBEL ATTACK ON OUR LEFT—GEN. NEGLEY COMES UP—ILLINOIS TO THE RESCUE—"WHO WILL SAVE THE LEFT?" "THE 19TH ILLINOIS, SIR"—MAGNIFICENT AND DARING CHARGE OF THE 19TH—COMPLETE ROUT OF THE REBEL RIGHT—CAPTURE OF A BATTERY—THE CHICAGO BOARD OF TRADE BATTERY—CASUALTIES, &c.

GENERAL ROSECRANS assumed command of the army of the Cumberland on the 27th of October. The army was then concentrated at Bowling Green and Glasgow, one hundred and thirteen miles distant from Louisville, whence they moved to Nashville, the advance reaching that place November 7th. From that date until December 26th, the time was occupied in completing the clothing of the army, providing ammunition, and replenishing the depot with necessary supplies and in sufficient amount to ensure against delay or interruption, caused by any breakage of the Louisville & Nashville road, to guard against which, a strong force was posted at Gallatin. The rebels had expected that Rosecrans was going into winter quarters at Nashville, and consequently prepared their winter quarters at Murfreesboro, and sent a large force into West Tennessee to annoy General Grant's communications, and another into Kentucky to break up the railroad. The absence of these forces gave Rosecrans an opportunity for an advance, which he determined to improve without delay. The situation was as follows: Polk's and Kirby Smith's forces at Murfreesboro, Hardee's on the Shelbyville and Nolinsville turnpike, while our troops were in front of Nashville on the Franklin, Nolinsville and Murfreesboro turnpike.

The movement began on the 26th of December. McCook after severe skirmishing gained possession of Nolinsville. Thomas followed on the right and Crittenden advanced to Lavergne. On the 28th, McCook moved to Triune, and Crittenden to Stewart's Creek. Negley's division joined Crittenden, and Rousseau occupied Nolinsville. On the 29th, McCook moved to Wilkinson's Cross Roads, six miles from Murfreesboro. Crittenden and Negley crossed Stewart's Creek to advance upon Murfreesboro. Rousseau remained at Stewart's Creek for his trains to come up. General Palmer led the advance of Crittenden's corps, and about three o'clock in the afternoon sent a message that he was in sight of Murfreesboro, and that the enemy were running. General Crittenden was therefore ordered forward to occupy Murfreesboro, but on moving up, found Breckinridge's main forces on his front, and at dark fell back.

On the morning of the 30th, Rousseau with two brigades was ordered down from Stewart's Creek and took his position in the rear of Palmer's right. McCook moved forward from Wilkinson's Cross Roads and joined Thomas. At nine o'clock that night, the corps commanders met at head-quarters and planned the battle of Stone River. McCook was to occupy the most advantageous position, refusing his right as much as possible and receive the attack; Thomas and Palmer to gain the enemy's center and left, as far as the river; Crittenden to cross Van Cleve's division and advance on Breckinridge; Woods division to move by brigades on Van Cleve's right, and carry everything before them into Murfreesboro. This would give two divisions against one, and as soon as Breckinridge was dislodged, Wood's batteries, taking position east of Stone River, would dislodge the enemy from their works and allow Palmer's division to press them back, while Thomas, sustaining the movement on the center, would advance on Palmer's right, crushing the rebel right. Crittenden's corps advancing would take Murfreesboro, and then moving westward get on their flank and rear and drive them into the country towards Salem, with a good prospect of destroying their army. This combination while it gave us a vast superiority on our left, required for its full success that McCook should hold his position for three hours.

At daylight on the morning of the 31st, the troops stood by their arms. The movement began on the left. Van Cleve crossed the fords of the river, Wood prepared to sustain and follow him. In the meantime the enemy massed against McCook. Willich's and Kirk's brigades were crumbled to pieces. Following them up, the enemy attacked Davis's division and dislodged Post's brigade. Carlin's brigade was compelled to follow, and Johnson's brigade retired. A staff officer from General McCook reported to General Rosecrans that the right wing was heavily pressed. He returned with orders for McCook to dispose of his troops to the best advantage and obstinately hold his ground. Shortly after, a second messenger arrived and announced that the right wing was being driven. General Thomas was dispatched to order Rousseau to the right and rear of Sheridan. General Crittenden was ordered to stop Van Cleve's movement, and Wood was directed to suspend his crossing and hold Haskell in reserve. Fugitives and stragglers commenced pouring in in such numbers that it was soon evident McCook was routed. Crittenden was directed to send Van Cleve to the right of Rousseau and Wood to attack the enemy on Van Cleve's right, the Pioneer brigade in the meantime being in the rear of Palmer's center supporting Stoke's Board of Trade battery. Sheridan swung his right around, repulsing the enemy four times, but getting out of ammunition fell back, and replenished his empty cartridge-boxes. During all this time, Palmer's front had also been in action, the enemy having advanced upon it several times.

At this stage owing to the breakage of our right, it became necessary to form a new line. Rousseau's and Van Cleve's advance having relieved Sheridan, Negley's division and Cruft's brigade of Palmer's division withdrew from their original position and took up a new one in rear of the front line. Hascall supported Hazen, and Rousseau filled the interval to the Pioneer brigade. Negley was in reserve, Van Cleve west of the Pioneer brigade, McCook's corps on his right, and the cavalry further to the rear on the Murfreesboro pike. The enemy attacked with infantry and cavalry on our extreme right, but were repulsed by Van Cleve. After several attempts of the enemy to advance on this new line, which were repulsed as were also the attempts on the left, the day closed. We had lost heavily in killed, wounded and prisoners, and twenty-eight pieces of artillery, but the enemy had been badly damaged and we retained possession of the original ground on the left. At night, the left was retired to more advantageous ground, the extreme left resting on Stone River. Starkweather and Walker's brigades were placed in reserve on McCook's left, and McCook was posted on the left of Sheridan, and next morning relieved Van Cleve who returned to his position on the left wing.

In this position, on the 1st of January, our army awaited attack, but there was no demonstration in the morning. In the afternoon the enemy moved upon our right but were repulsed.

On the 2d, the enemy opened from heavy batteries upon our center, but a well-directed artillery fire silenced his batteries. At three o'clock in the afternoon, a double line of skirmishers emerged from the woods, followed by a heavy column of infantry and three batteries of artillery, and made an attack upon Van Cleve's division. Van Cleve gave way and was closely followed by the enemy, when Crittenden brought his batteries to bear upon them, and ordered up Negley's division and the Pioneer brigade to meet the onset. The firing was terrific, and the determined valor of our men soon caused the rebels to retreat more rapidly than they had advanced. Gen. Davis's division moved to attack the left flank of the rebels, but two brigades of Negley's division, the gallant 19th Illinois in the advance, and Hazen's brigade of Palmer's division had pursued the flying enemy, capturing four guns and a stand of colors. It was now after dark and raining, and the pursuit was discontinued.

On the 3d it rained and no advance was made as the ground was impassable for artillery. Batteries were put in position by which the ground could be swept, and the Parrott guns were in range of Murfreesboro. The heavy picket firing which had been kept up the most of the day, was silenced all along our front by some determined charges, one of which was made in splendid style by the 85th Illinois.

On Sunday morning, the 4th, news reached General Rosecrans that the enemy had fled from Murfreesboro, and cavalry were sent out to reconnoiter. On Monday, General Thomas advanced, driving the rebel rear guard before him seven miles, while McCook's and Crittenden's Corps occupied the town.

We have thus given the bare, lifeless skeleton of the battle of Stone River—a battle full of brave deeds and gallant actions, full of persistent effort and desperate courage, and one in which the tide of battle fluctuated here and there, full of painful uncertainty, until at its flood, under the impulse of northern determination and endurance, it led our forces to victory. It remains to create a soul in that skeleton by the narration of the incidents of exalted patriotism and heroic daring which marked its varying phases, and plucked victory out of the very jaws of defeat. To attempt to enumerate all the splendid performances of Illinois troops on that bloody field would require a volume, and we therefore content ourselves with some of the most prominent.

Few regiments bore thomselves more superbly against an adverse fate than the 34th Illinois, the old regiment of the lamented General Kirk. Not ten minutes after the dawn of the first day, the rebels commenced firing upon General Kirk's line, and soon advanced with a heavy column directly upon the 34th. The regiment, in the face of the overwhelming force, advanced to meet the foe and defend the front. The rebels poured into it a galling fire, but still they stood their ground although suffering terribly. They poured volley after volley into the advancing column, and other regiments came to their support. When within thirty yards of the line the rebel column changed front and moved against the right of Kirk's line, flanking it and rendering it untenable. The 34th were soon engaged in a hand to hand conflict. The strife over its colors was bloody and terrific. Five color bearers fell, but again and again the old flag was raised and flung to the breeze. Santee, Wright and Wendell were dead. Lieut. John Smith, of Company H, rushed to save the colors from the rebels and fell pierced by five balls. Another soldier snatched them from the ground and gave them to a soldier of Edgarton's battery, but he too was shot and the colors were seized by traitors. The column next fell upon Edgarton's battery. Capt. Edgarton was formerly of Barnett's Illinois battery, and displayed the Illinois fire. He told his men to save themselves, and with Lieut. Burwick stood by the guns, mowing huge swaths through the rebel column. But he was wounded and fell across the trail of his gun, while the rebel column swept on.

General Kirk had his horse shot under him, but mounting another, he directed his men. The rebel column was now close upon him, and to remain was either death or capture. Kirk fell back but the foe pressed closely. He had a second horse shot under him, and was severely wounded in the thigh, but still tried to rally his men who were hastening to the cover of some adjacent timber. Kirk followed for a short distance, but his wound exhausted him and he was carried to the rear bleeding and faint, and Colonel Dodge took command. Major Dysart, of the 34th, succeeded in rallying a few of the men, but it was impossible to hold the position and they fell back to the Nashville Pike.

In the mean time, a portion of the 34th had joined the 30th Indiana regiment and were making a stand, supported by the 79th Illinois. Simonson's battery, the 34th and 29th Indiana regiments also came up and formed in line. They had hardly got into position when the rebel column came sweeping on. Our men fought with desperation to stay this advance. Col. Sheridan P. Read, of the 79th Illinois, fell, his head pierced by a rifle ball, while gallantly cheering on his men. Colonel Read was from Paris, Edgar County, and one of the bravest of the brave. He volunteered as a private and was soon appointed Lieutenant-Colonel, and in October, 1862, was commissioned Colonel. He died instantly, and died the death of a hero.

It required more than human endurance to stand up against the repeated attacks of this overwhelming rebel column. It again moved upon the flank and hurled itself against the 79th, which gave way. Regiment after regiment fell back. A new line was formed, but the 79th were again exposed to a terrific artillery fire and retreated to the Nashville turnpike, where the second brigade was rallied. The rebels still swept on, but reinforcements had come up from Van Cleve and their advance was stayed.

We return to the 34th Illinois. When the rebel column advanced to attack this regiment, the reserves of the 32d and 39th Indiana moved up to their support. Under the galling fire General Kirk's pickets gave way, but soon reformed, connecting with the pickets of the 39th. Again they were forced back. The 32d and 39th Indiana also made a gallant stand, but had to fall back to a new position. During this attack the musketry firing was also very severe on the

49th Ohio and 89th Illinois. The latter retired to another locality, and Lieut.-Col. Hotchkiss placed in position the companies of Captains Comstock, Willett, and Whiting, and Lieut. Wells. The enemy advanced upon them and were received with a furious fire which momentarily checked the advance. But it was only for a moment. The enemy pressed on and the 89th was again compelled to fall back. Thus the tide of battle ebbed and flowed until night when the whole brigade bivouacked in rear of Gen. Davis' division. On the next day the 34th Illinois, Capt. Hostetter commanding, was consolidated with the 30th Indiana.

We have incidentally alluded to the 89th Illinois, Lieut.-Col. Hotchkiss, in connection with other regiments. Its movements in this battle are worthy a detailed account. It was in the 1st brigade, 2d division, on the right wing, and left Nashville with the brigade on the morning of December 26th, and arrived on the night of the 30th, at a point about three and a half miles west of Murfreesboro, where the brigade was put in position on the extreme right of the right wing, at right angles with General Kirk's brigade, the regiment being formed in double column in the rear of the 49th Ohio. At half past five on the morning of the 31st heavy firing commenced on Kirk's front. The front gave way and rushed indiscriminately through the ranks of the 89th, closely followed by the rebel column. The 89th could not deploy or change position and the fire was terrible. The gallant fellows laid down until their left was uncovered of fugitives and the rebel column was within fifty yards of their position, when they rose and delivered a well directed fire which lowered the colors of the rebel advance. The other regiments falling back, the order was given to retire, which was done to a lane we have mentioned before where four companies were placed in a good position. Again under their fire the colors of the leading rebel column went down.

The regiment, however, was too closely pressed to hold its position, and was ordered back to a point on a small creek five hundred yards distant, where Capts. Rowen and Blake's companies were placed under the partial cover of a thicket. Their fire checked the rebel advance and gave time for reorganization. Following the creek, the regiment crossed an open field to a point in the woods, where its fire again thinned the rebel ranks and partially checked the advancing column. Under orders, the regiment was retired in line and in good order, making several stands in the woods, and took position in a thicket, but the troops on the right and left of the line having fallen back, and the 89th being exposed to a terrific artillery and musketry fire, retired by the flank to the rear, after having taken and delivered an unceasing fire for five hours. On the night of Friday, the 2d, it held a very responsible position, guarding a ford and supporting Capt. Stoke's Chicago Board of Trade Battery, while Negley made the splendid charge upon the rebel right. The behavior of all the officers through the trying positions in which the regiment was placed and of the men themselves, received many commendations. From morning until night, of the first day's battle, they bore the weight of an overwhelming rebel column and were fighting in the very face of fate itself. No single regiment could have withstood such a force, and few regiments would have made a more determined opposition where success was an impossibility. The total loss in killed, wounded and missing was one hundred and forty-nine. Among the officers killed were Capt. Henry S. Willett and corporal Wm. H. Litsey, of company H.

But no regiment in that bloody fight vindicated its manhood more gloriously than the 19th Illinois. It had been pursued by all the hate and vindictiveness of secession, and stigmatized as thieves and plunderers by partisan malice at home. It had been put under ban, broken up into squads and officially disgraced. It had been marched and counter marched many an unnecessary and weary mile through swamp and forest. Its officers had been hooted at, and its men treated with every soldierly indignity. But at length the day and the hour came when its patriotism, its devotion, its bravery and its discipline were to silence foes at home and abroad, and to achieve for it a name which in history shall illuminate one of the brightest pages of Illinois bravery as developed in the present war.

On the 30th the regiment had but little to do and lost but nine men. The next morning it was up early and in line of battle, although they had scarcely eaten any thing and slept upon the ground without their blankets, which were in the trains, miles to the rear. Soon, by the sound of the musketry, it was evident the rebels had turned our right. Thomas had lost part of his artillery and the veteran troops were retreating. Further back, towards the rear, firing opened. Then the 19th prepared for the fight. They changed front, fixed bayonets, and charged, the foe retiring before their terrible onset. Heavy firing commenced, and a storm of bullets whistled through their ranks. At the first fire corporal Daggy fell mortally wounded. The enemy were repulsed, but the 27th Illinois were hard pressed and needed aid. They faced to the right, and as coolly as if on drill, marched, with the lamented Scott at their head, through a terrific fire of shot and shell and took position by the side of the 18th Ohio. Edgarton's battery had been taken and was turned upon them, and other batteries opened a fearful fire. Word came that they were surrounded and must cut their way out. They faced about again, fixed bayonets, rushed into a cedar swamp, and forced their way out and formed on the left of Sheridan, moved to the front and went into action. They had hardly got into position before portions of the division fell back and the rebels advanced. General Negley ordered the 19th to stand firm until the rest could form, and for half an hour, with the rebels on their front and flanks, they held back the advancing hosts until the 18th Ohio and 42d Illinois were formed, and then they retired to the center as reserves.

On Friday, those who knew the position of VanCleve's division, felt certain that when the assault did come it would come upon the extreme left. At 4 o'clock in the afternoon the fierce cannonading which had prevailed for some time on the left was accompanied by a deafening crash of musketry, and it was evident the battle was renewed in earnest. The enemy massed three of his divisions, Rain's, Anderson's and Breckinridge's, the whole under command of the latter, and hurled them against VanCleve. His men bravely withstood the onset, but were literally overwhelmed by superior numbers and two of the brigades were broken to pieces. The other held its ground manfully, but to save being surrounded had to retreat, and the whole were pushed back in disorder into and across the river. The rebels were preparing to follow when Negley suddenly appeared in compact line of battle. His practised eye at once saw the danger unless an almost superhuman effort was made.

He rode rapidly to their front, and, in his clear voice, shouted: "Who will save the left?" In an instant came back the reply from the gallant Scott: "The 19th Illinois!" "The 19th it is then! By the left flank, march," was the command. Scott put his cap on his sword and shouted, "Forward." The men lay down and fired one volley, then rose, fixed bayonets, and started upon that grand charge which saved the day, immortal as the charge of Balaklava. Into the river they plunged waist deep, although a whole rebel division was disputing the passage, up the precipitous bank, bristling with bayonets, baring their heads to the leaden pitiless rain, against bayonet and shot and shell, careless of the storm that was tearing through their ranks, unmindful of the brave fellows falling in the bloody track they made, they swept on, resistless as a Nemesis. At the top of the hill the rebels try to make a stand but they are shivered like a glass as the 19th strikes them. They hesitate, they stand as if dumb with amazement at this terrible charge Their ranks waver, they break and flee, the 19th, closely followed by the 11th Michigan and 78th Pennsylvania, pouring destruction through their fugitive ranks. Across the open fields they rush to the protection of their batteries beyond, but the march of the 19th is like the march of fate. Regardless of the fact that the field is swept by the battery, they still roll back the rebel foe, vainly trying to seize upon every ridge and clump as a means of defense. Over the corn-fields, up to the very muzzles of the guns in spite of their belching fury and sheeted flame, over the parapet, and the battery belongs to the 19th. The left is saved. The day is ours—the victory is won. Thus the 19th vindicated its good name and made one of the grandest and most glorious charges of the war. Thus the 19th revenged the malice and hatred of secession which had pursued them.

The regiment lost in killed and wounded one hundred and twenty-four out of three hundred and forty men. Col. Scott was seriously wounded in the passage of the river, and died some months after from the effects of the wound. Among the killed were corporal Ira A. Pease, corporal Wm. Leason, corporal W. Ryerson, corporal Robert McCracken, sergeant James Goldsmith, Captain Knowlton, Lieutenant Wellington Wood, and sergeant Daniel Griffin.

On Thursday, the 88th and 36th Illinois regiments made a splendid charge, most important in its developments and destructive to the rebels. They were drawn up in line of battle behind a fence, and in front, over an open field, a heavy column of rebels, three regiments deep, advanced. The 88th lay close to the ground until the enemy were within forty yards of them, when they rose, took deliberate aim and poured a terrible volley into them. The rebels rallied and again advanced, but the 88th had quickly reloaded, and as the enemy came closely up, another volley was fired into them, creating fearful havoc. A charge was ordered, bayonets were fixed, and the 88th and 36th, with a shout, made a furious onset that quickly cleared the field. Major Chandler, of the former regiment, had two horses shot under him, and in every stage of the battle displayed the highest skill and bravery. Among the killed in the 88th were Lieut. Gulick and orderly sergeant Lyford. Several officers were wounded, among them Capt. Geo. W. Smith, Lieut. McDonald, Lieut. Chester, orderly sergeant Griffin and corporal Palmer.

The 35th Illinois, Lieut. Col. Chandler, and 25th Illinois, Col. T. D. Williams, commanding, were in the 14th corps on the right. On the 30th, two companies of these regiments acted as skirmishers, under the command of Major McIlvain, of the 35th, covering the front of General Woodruff. They remained in position until three o'clock P. M., when Major McIlvain sent for another company, and commenced pressing back the enemy's skirmishers to a belt of timber. The rebel advance, however, rapidly caused our skirmishers to fall back. Col. Williams of the 25th, detached another company from his command, and it went forward, deploying as skirmishers while the brigade moved up to their support. The brigade remained in position, receiving a heavy fire for some time, when the batteries came up and did their work so well that the rebel batteries soon were silenced. In the fighting of the succeeding days these regiments bore themselves with determined bravery and heroism. General Woodruff, in his report, says: "I desire to call the attention of the commanding officer to the gallant conduct of Lieut.-Col. Chandler, commanding the 35th Illinois, whose cool, steady courage, admirable deportment and skillful management evinced the soldier true and tried, and who at all times proved himself worthy of the trust he holds. Major McIlvain, of the same regiment, who had the supervision of skirmishers, I cannot praise too much. His good judgment and skillful handling elicited encomiums of well meritèd compliments at all times. He was cool, determined and persevering. Capt. W. Taggert, who succeeded to the command of the 25th Illinois regiment, behaved as a soldier should everywhere—efficient and ever ready to execute orders.

"Amid the glorious results of a battle won, it gives me pain to record the names of the gallant men who offered up their lives on the altar of their country. But we must drop the tear of sorrow over their-resting places and offer our heartfelt sympathies to their relatives and friends, trusting that God will care for them and soothe their afflictions. And while we remember the noble dead, let us pay a tribute of respect to the gallant Colonel T. D. Williams, 25th Illinois regiment, who died in the performance of his duty. He fell with his regimental colors in his hands, exclaiming: 'We will plant it here, boys, and rally the old 25th around it, and here we will die?' Such conduct is above all praise and words can paint no eulogiums worthy of the subject."

The 35th Illinois lost two officers wounded, eight privates killed, forty-nine wounded and thirty-two missing. The 25th, one officer killed and three wounded, fourteen privates killed, sixty-nine wounded and thirty-five missing.

The 110th Illinois, Colonel Thomas S. Casey, were under fire in this battle for the first time, but behaved with the utmost gallantry, and in conjunction with the 41st Ohio, by their unflinching determination and bravery foiled the efforts of an overwhelming force of rebels to break the front of General Hazen. Subsequently they occupied the extreme left against which a heavy attack was directed. This position must be held or the left sacrificed. The ammunition of the 110th was exhausted, but they clubbed their muskets, and coolly as old veterans fought like heroes and held their line unbroken. Later in the fight the 100th Illinois, under command of the gallant and lamented Colonel Bartleson, came up to the support of the 110th and fought side by side with them in generous rivalry.

The 74th Illinois, Colonel Marsh commanding, left Nashville in the advance on the 26th, and came up in the afternoon near Nolinsville, meeting a considerable force of the enemy. The regiment formed in line of battle and advanced, occupying an exposed position. The enemy, however fell back, and the regiment bivouacked for the night. The next day being exceedingly inclement, they marched but five miles and again bivouacked. Resting in camp over the Sabbath, the march was resumed Monday morning, and the next morning the regiment were at their arms at daylight, coming up with the enemy about noon. A slight fire of skirmishers was kept up during the day, but at night a heavy fire opened upon them from a masked battery, making it necessary for the line to fall back. The regiment being within direct and short range of the battery, several casualties occurred. M. O. Felmly and Corporal Cook were killed, and I. B. Caspares, corporal of the same company, was seriously wounded. At four o'clock the next morning the regiment formed in line,. and at day light their skirmishers opened upon an advancing rebel force, emptying many saddles. But the superior numbers of the rebels enabled them to flank, and the regiment fell back in good order. As the rebels came up, the regiment reserved their fire until within short range, when they opened with terrible effect, holding them completely in check until they had delivered ten or fifteen rounds. But the odds were too tremendous, and the regiment had to retreat. At a point about half a mile back they made another stand, where they were joined by three companies of the regiment which had been cut off early in the morning. First Lieutenant Leffingwell came up with the men and helped rally the regiment. After this the regiment had no further share in the fighting of that day, except two companies sent out as skirmishers under command of 1st Lieut. Blakesley, who rendered important service in a skirmish with the rebel cavalry. On Friday the regiment was put in rapid march across Stone River on the left, just after the charge of the 19th Illinois, but the battle had closed by the retreat of the enemy just before their arrival. In the official report of Colonel Marsh, Capt. J. H. Douglass, Major Dutcher and Capt. Nieman were highly commended, and private Charles A. Allen, of Company E, was recommended for promotion for his fearless bravery and enthusiastic zeal.

The 73d and 44th Illinois regiments in Lieut.-Col. Liebold's brigade, also distinguished themselves in this battle. A portion of the 73d supported Hezcock's battery in a gallant manner on the 31st, the balance of the regiment being held in reserve. The 44th Illinois with the 2d Missouri, on the same day made a splendid advance to their position, and, although unsupported, bravely held it until they were attacked on the front and flank at once. The detached battalions of the 73d were attacked several times, but in almost every instance signally repulsed them. Capt. Alsop, of the 73d, and Capt. Hosmer, of the 44th, fell fighting bravely.

The 51st Illinois, Colonel Bradley, was in the thickest of the fight and suffered heavily, but was commended on every hand for its gallant bearing and heroic action.

Although many of the Illinois regiments had to bear the brunt of overwhelming attacks from superior numbers, where success was impossible, there has hardly been a battle in the war where more persistence has been displayed or more heroism evinced. In every part of the field, wherever the fight raged the most fiercely, were the Illinois regiments, and from the overpowering rebel assaults of the first day to the splendid and dashing charge of the 19th Illinois and other regiments which saved the left and the day, there are no words to be used but those of commendation.

CHAPTER XX.

COL. GRIERSON'S RAID—ORGANIZATION OF THE EXPEDITION AND ITS CHARACTER—COL. HATCH LEAVES THE FORCE—ILLINOIS ALONE IN THE FIELD—ON FOR BATON ROUGE—DARING EXPEDITION OF CAPT. FORBES—THREE THOUSAND REBELS SURRENDER TO THIRTY-FIVE UNION TROOPERS—THE CRISIS AT PEARL RIVER BRIDGE—SAVING THE BRIDGE—A PERILOUS MOMENT—CAPTURE OF HAZLEHURST—HOW THEY CROSSED PEARL RIVER—CAPTURE OF BROOKHAVEN—DESTROYING RAILROADS AND TELEGRAPHS—IN THE SWAMPS AND IN AMBUSH—CAPTURE OF STUART'S CAVALRY—ENTERING BATON ROUGE—REJOICINGS AND OVATIONS.

WE now drop the campaign of General Rosecrans for a few chapters, and turn to one of the most thrilling episodes of the war—the raid of General Grierson, which was purely an Illinois operation, conceived and planned by an Illinois officer, and carried out in all its details by Illinois soldiers. Probably no movement in the war so clearly and unmistakably illustrated the dash, courage, hardihood and power of endurance of Illinois soldiers as this raid. Certainly no operation has been more completely carried out or crowned with a greater degree of success. The country traversed by the little force was in many places almost impassable, owing to swamps and bayous, and it swarmed with rebel troops north, south, east and west of them. Not a day passed that they were not in danger of being cut off and annihilated, and oftentimes their fate hung by a single thread. Swinging loose from all communications, destroying every thing behind them, so that return was impossible, scantily provided with food, and riding sometimes fifty miles a day, crossing burning bridges and swollen streams, plunging through swamps and morasses, achieving safety when a minute's delay would have involved destruction, it seemed as if these bold riders and their no less bold and skillful leader bore charmed lives. Poetry and history in time to come will record Grierson's raid as one of the most chivalrous and gallant exploits of a war marked by brave deeds from its commencement to the present time.

In order to facilitate General Grant's operations around Vicksburg, it had been determined to make a cavalry raid in the rear of the doomed city for the purpose of destroying the enemy's railroad communications and preventing his reinforcement. Col. Benjamin H. Grierson, of the first cavalry brigade, had proposed a raid through Mississippi, without meeting the approval of General Grant until April 1st, when he was instructed to prepare for the expedition. His force was stationed at La Grange, about fifty miles east of Memphis and four miles west of the junction of the Mississippi and Charleston Railroad, and consisted of the 6th Illinois cavalry, Colonel Reuben Loomis; 7th Illinois cavalry, Col. Edward Prince; and the 2d Iowa cavalry, Colonel Edward Hatch. On the 17th of April, feints having previously been made from La Grange, Memphis and Corinth, to divert the attention of the enemy from the real objects of the movement, they moved out on the road towards Ripley, the 6th Illinois leading the advance, and at night fall, after riding thirty miles, camped near Ripley, on a plantation owned by one Dr. Ellis. The 6th having taken the wrong road near La Grange were thrown to the westward and did not arrive until night. The 7th, as they were going into camp, made the first capture during the expedition, in the shape of three rebel prisoners who were surprised while crossing a corn-field near the camp.

On the 18th they broke camp at eight o'clock, dividing their forces, the 2d Iowa advancing on the left flank of the column in a southeasterly direction, while the remainder of the column took the direct road south through Ripley towards New Albany. As they neared the bridge across the Tallahatchie, a rebel force was discovered on the opposite bank trying to destroy the bridge. Shouting their old battle cry, Captain Thomas's battalion dashed over the bridge and into the rebel bridge burners with such impetuosity that they fled like sheep without accomplishing much injury to the bridge. The bridge was soon put in good order and the troopers drove into town, lighting their camp fires on the plantation of a Mr. Sloan, four miles south of New Albany. Colonel Hatch's command in the meantime which had been detached, crossed the Tallahatchie some five miles above New Albany, and discovered the whereabouts of two small forces of rebels, and overtook the raiding party the next day. That morning, Captain Trafton at the head of two companies, rode back to New Albany and drove out a rebel force which had occupied the town, and got back to camp before ten o'clock in the forenoon. Two more companies started off into the woods in another direction and brought away all the horses they could lead. Two more started off in still another direction after a rebel cavalry force, but the enemy had decamped, and our boys returned bringing with them a few prisoners. All these movements were made to distract the enemy and conceal from him the real destination of the expedition. Before noon, the whole force were on the march again in a southerly direction, with the 2d Iowa on the left flank and proceeding to Pontotoc, a small rebel force was found there and pursued through the town by the advance, and their entire camp equipage and a large quantity of salt captured which was destroyed before night. They were now sixty miles from their first night's encampment.

On the next day, the 20th, a detachment of the least effective men from the regiments, under command of Major Love of the 2d Iowa, was sent back to Lagrange with one piece of artillery and the prisoners. Colonel Grierson in doing this, secured a double object. First, relief from all encumbrances, and second, the creation of an impression among the rebels that his expedition was retracing its steps. The raiders then moved on and passing around Houston camped that night at Clear Springs, having gone forty miles during the day.

At daylight the next morning they were off again. Col. Hatch, with his brave command, the 2d Iowa, was ordered to move his regiment towards Columbus and destroy as much of the Mobile and Ohio Railroad as possible, attack Columbus, if the rebel force was not too strong, and march thence to Lagrange. Near Okalona, he encountered a large force and a severe fight ensued, in which he himself was wounded and his force badly scattered, but the larger portion of them reached Lagrange. Col. Hatch's movement, although resulting disastrously, had the good effect to mislead the rebel General Chalmers, who was in pursuit of Grierson, and give the latter two or three days' start.

Illinois was now in the field alone, and although the news of the raid had spread over Mississippi like wild fire, and the rebel forces were moving in every direction, trying to intercept the little band, there was no thought of returning. They resolved to escape the toils spread for them on every hand by making a headlong and rapid dash right through the heart of Mississippi to Baton Rouge on the Gulf; and to this end the gallant Colonel gave his clear-headed skill and sagacity, and his troopers their brave hearts and strong hands. To successfully compass this plan it was necessary that the telegraph wires running north along the railroad from Macon should be cut. Col. Prince detailed company B, of the 7th Illinois, under Capt. Forbes, to make the seemingly desperate, if not fatal attempt. He started out with thirty-five men to ride through fifty-miles of the enemy's country and into the vicinity of Macon, one of the most strongly fortified places in the State, and probably occupied by a powerful garrison. Capt. Forbes and his company left the main force, little expecting to return, but good fortune waited upon him at every turn. Macon, the first object of their expedition, was too strong for them to take. Pressing forward, in a southwesterly direction, and seeking for their regiment, they were misled by false information and rode to Enterprise, on the Mobile and Ohio Railroad, where they found three thousand rebel soldiers just disembarking from a train. Capt. Forbes rescued himself from his awkward position by the utmost coolness and presence of mind. Taking a flag of truce, he rode boldly up alone to the rebel force and demanded their surrender to Col. Grierson. The rebels supposing that Grierson's force was close at hand, and believing the exaggerated reports of its numerical strength, concluded discretion was the better part of valor. The rebel commander, Capt. Goodwin, wanted an hour in which to think over the matter, to which Capt. Forbes, after some feigned reluctance, assented and rode back to his handful of men. That hour placed a long distance between his company and Enterprise. It is not known whether the rebel Colonel ever returned to give a final answer on the question of surrendering, but it is certain the little troop were not there to receive it. They escaped successfully after accomplishing their mission, and reported to their colonel on the banks of the Pearl River on the 27th.

Before marching on the 22d, Capt. Graham, with one battalion, was detailed to burn a rebel shoe manufactory near Starkville. He succeeded in destroying several thousand pairs of boots and shoes, a large number of hats and a quantity of leather, besides capturing a rebel quartermaster, who was out foraging for his command at Port Hudson, and then rejoined the main force. During the day of the 22d, and the following night, they made one of the most difficult marches of the raid. At sundown they found themselves in the midst of the overflowed and treacherous swamps of the Okanoxubee River, about seven miles south of Louisville. Eight weary miles they toiled through those swamps. Every stream and creek were swollen by the spring rains, and the swamps were deep lakes without an interval of dry ground. The roads themselves were flooded. Enormous, gloomy trees hung with funeral mosses and parasitic pendants, stood close together three and four feet deep in the water. Every few yards they got into mire holes, in which horses would disappear. They had already marched fifty miles that day and men and beasts alike were jaded and exhausted, but still with brave hearts they pressed on in the darkness, through the raging waters, trusting to Providence to guide and deliver them from the thickly besetting dangers. Not a man was lost, but twenty of the noble animals were drowned. The dismounted men removed their saddles, placed them on some other led beasts, and pushed on. At one o'clock in the morning they emerged and were absolutely compelled to halt for a few hours of rest. At seven o'clock the bugle again sounded the advance. The men were instantly in their saddles and were now pressing forward at top speed for the Pearl River bridge. It was the crisis of the march. Their fate hung trembling in the balance.

The river was too high to be forded and the bridge was the only means of crossing. Rebel scouts had gone before them and given the warning. If they had arrived in time to destroy the bridge, the expedition was over and death or capture was their fate, for the rebel bands were scouring the country in every direction, and delay would have been fatal. They put spurs to their horses and flew along like the wind. Once on the bridge they might achieve safety. On through the swamps and the forests, on without ceasing. It was a fearful race, but they were bold riders and good steeds. The old flag and brave-hearted Grierson, with his kindling eye and solemn, thoughtful face, were at their head. They would follow him to death itself. During the afternoon they neared the stream. They heard the raging of the swollen waters and suspicious sounds as of men at work upon the bridge. Every horse was put at top speed. The 7th was in the advance and rode with all the fury of a charge into the battle-storm. As they got to the bank they discovered a force of rebels working with superhuman energy, tearing up the planks of the bridge flooring and hurling them into the river. Now for the love of home and country, brave hearts within and God overhead, they make one last, grand effort. Rising in their stirrups, driving their spurs into the excited horses, who seem to know and feel the danger, they dash down the river bank like the whirlwind. Shouting the old Illinois battle-cry, they draw their sabers and hurl themselves upon the wonder-stricken bridge destroyers like an avalanche. Who can withstand their resistless fury, their almost superhuman ardor and fierceness?

The skirmish was brief. A few strokes of the saber and the rebels fled, and the gallant Illinois men under the guidance of that Providence who had watched over them, who was their cloud by day and pillar of fire by night, under the indomitable will and never doubting faith of their leader, and the help of their own strong arms and good steeds, reached the other shore in safety. The crisis was over, but even now they must not tarry. On again until night, and all through the night and the next day they rode. They passed through Decatur at four A. M. of the 24th, and captured two trains of cars and two locomotives at Newton Station at eleven. The bridges and trestle work were found burned for six miles each side of the station. Seventy-five prisoners were captured and paroled, two warehouses full of commissary stores were utterly destroyed by fire and four car loads of ammunition for heavy artillery. The bridges on the east side of the station were destroyed by the 2d battalion of the 6th Illinois, Major M. H. Starr. The whole command left Newton at eleven A. M. of the 24th, and marched through

Garlandville to the plantation of a Mr. Bender, where they encamped. They had performed the almost incredible feat of marching eighty miles in two days, after the exhausting and tremendous exertions of the passage through the swamps without rest or halt, except at the place we have mentioned, where they only stayed long enough to destroy such property as would be of benefit to the rebels.

The long march, privations, dangers and exposures began to tell upon the little band. On the 25th, they left camp at 8 A. M., and encamped for the night on Dr. Dore's plantation, eight miles east of Raleigh. At this place they were obliged to leave three of their men, who were utterly exhausted and unable to travel further. Indeed all of the command were so jaded and wearied that they marched but twenty miles that day. On the 26th, they left camp at sunrise, in the midst of a drenching rain, crossed Strong river, near Westville, and took supper at Mrs. Smith's plantation near Strong river bridge, having marched forty miles. On the 27th, at one o'clock in the morning, they resumed their march in the darkness, and reached the Pearl River again, which was now even more formidable than when they made their narrow escape at the bridge. This point on the river was called the Georgetown ferry. There was no bridge and the ferry boat was moored on the other side. To call upon the ferryman was hazardous, but delays were dangerous. Some of the troopers tried to swim over to the boat, but the current of the river was too powerful. At this juncture, the ferryman came along and in the genuine Southern twang, supposing he was addressing the 1st regiment of Alabama cavalry, who were expected in that vicinity about that time, asked them in a careless way if they wanted to cross, to which he got a reply in the same style of twang, that a few of them did want to cross but that it was harder to wake up his negro ferryman than it was to catch conscripts. The ferryman was entirely deceived, woke up his negro, and the whole command were safely ferried over, and did themselves the pleasure of breakfasting at the ferryman's house, the proprietor doing his utmost in lavishing attention upon them, supposing them to be the Alabamians. Not much time was spent over the breakfast, however, and the importance of speed was proven half an hour afterward, when a courier was caught flying to the ferry with dispatches that the Yankees were coming, and with instructions to destroy all the ferries. At Hazelhurst, Colonel Prince of the 7th captured a train of about forty cars, several of which were loaded with shells and ammunition. Another train which had just arrived escaped by backing out before it could be captured. At this point, Captain Forbes, who, it will be remembered, was the hero of the episode at Enterprise, joined the main force.

The command left Hazelhurst at seven P. M., and on the night of the 27th encamped at Gallatin, where they captured fourteen hundred pounds of powder, two wagons, twenty-six yoke of oxen and a 32-pounder Parrott gun, en route for Grand Gulf. The gun was spiked and powder destroyed. They had traveled this day thirty-seven miles. On the 28th they left camp at seven o'clock. Four miles east of Gallatin, at Hardgrove's, companies A, H, F and M, were detailed under command of Captain Grafton, to strike the New Orleans and Jackson station, at Bahala, and destroy the railroad and transportation. This was successfully accomplished and the little force joined the others at sunset, having performed during the day a journey of thirty miles more than the rest. The main force on their march had a skirmish near Union Church, in which two of the enemy were wounded and some prisoners taken. On the 29th, they proceeded towards Brookhaven, on the New Orleans and Jackson road, the 7th in advance. They charged into the place and burned the depot, cars and bridges. Four companies under command of Major Starr took two captains, one lieutenant, one surgeon and nineteen privates prisoners. Two hundred prisoners in all were paroled. They also captured a lot of Mississippi rifles, mules and ox-teams, $5,000 worth of commissary stores and $25,000 worth of army clothing. The people of Brookhaven were wild with terror, supposing that all their property would be consigned to the flames, and their city subjected to murder and rapine. But as soon as they found that the rights of private property were regarded, the delusion created in their minds by their leaders was removed and they crowded around our troops, begging and imploring to be paroled. They were unstinted in their hospitality and often made declarations of their faith in the Union, and their hopes that its integrity would be preserved. On this point Colonel Grierson wrote: "The strength of the rebels has been overestimated. They have neither the armies nor the resources we have given them credit for. Passing through their country, I found thousands of good Union men, who were ready and anxious to return to their allegiance the moment they could do so with safety to themselves and their families. They will rally around the old flag by scores whenever our army advances. I could have brought away a thousand with me, who were anxious to come—men whom I found fugitives from their homes, hidden in the swamps and forests where they were hunted like wild beasts by conscriptive officers with blood-hounds."

On the 30th, at sunrise, the command left camp, the 6th Illinois in the advance. They burned the depot, bridges and cars at Bouge Chito, and following on, burned all the trestle work between that place and Summit, where they arrived at five P. M. At Summit they destroyed a large amount of government sugar and wood, cars and locomotives. The camp of Hughes and Milburn's Partisan Rangers, on Big Sandy Creek, was also destroyed, after which they encamped a short distance southwest of the place, having marched that day twenty-eight miles. On the 18th of May they left camp at daylight, and striking into the woods, moved in a southwesterly direction without regard to roads, until they came to the Clinton and Osyka road, near a bridge four miles northeast of Wall's Post-Office. Here they fell into an ambush. About eighty of the enemy were hidden in a thicket near the bridge. Lieutenant Colonel Blackburn at the head of his scouts, not dreaming of danger, and with more bravery than caution, rode on to the bridge and was immediately struck down by a volley which wounded him severely in the thigh and slightly on the head. Colonel Prince dismounted his men, who charged into the thicket, and after a short fight put the enemy to flight, and the column passed on, reaching the Amite river at ten o'clock at night. Rebel pickets were posted along the bank, but the same watchful Providence that had led them through their thickly besetting dangers, was again present to defend and guard them. The pickets were asleep and the command crossed the river undisturbed within gunshot of the picket lines of the enemy.

On the 2d of May, they were again on the move at sunrise and had marched but a few miles when the 7th Illinois attacked and captured, within a few miles of Baton Rouge, forty-two of Stuart's Mississippi cavalry with their Colonel at their head. At midday of Saturday, May 2d, the toil-worn, jaded, brave-hearted fellows rode into the streets of Baton Rouge, safe at last, and once more under the Stars and Stripes. During the last thirty hours they rode eighty miles, had three skirmishes, destroyed large quantities of camp equipage and military stores, burned bridges, swam one river, took forty-two prisoners and a number of horses, and all this without halting or eating. So exhausted were many of them, that they slept upon their horses as they marched, only to be roused by some pressing danger. The danger over, they slept again and rode forward unconsciously until they met the next shock.

The entrance of the command into Baton Rouge was like the return of an old Roman conqueror. The story of their march and their incredible adventures had preceded them and created a furore of the wildest description. Their story seemed almost improbable, and many would not believe it until they had seen the men and talked with them. On the next day Colonel Grierson, Col. Prince, Major Starr, Adjutant Woodward and one or two privates went to New Orleans, and that evening were serenaded by the band of the 47th Massachusetts regiment. Although no preliminary arrangements had been made, yet at an early hour the hotel and the street were thronged with a rejoicing crowd. The band played on the balcony and in the rotunda. Fireworks were discharged and the cheering was deafening as Colonel Grierson made his appearance on the balcony, introduced to the multitude by Surgeon Smith. The Colonel made a few remarks paying a handsome tribute to the bravery and endurance of his officers and men. Lieut. Woodward, Major Starr and a private of the 7th Illinois made short speeches and were followed by Colonel Prince, of the 6th Illinois, who gave a brief sketch of the expedition and particularly of the ruses by which they deceived the enemy, such as sending out scouts in butternut uniforms, and sending false messages by the telegraph to various places in their vicinity, for the purpose of putting them on a false track. Several short speeches from citizens of New Orleans followed, and the Union flag was unfurled for the first time in the hall of the St. Charles since the capture of the city. The band played all the national airs during the evening, and at the close the officers and leading citizens sat down to a handsome repast. Still later in the evening, a select few adjourned to the parlor, where the gallant Colonel entertained his audience by playing upon the piano and singing, for the Colonel not only can fight but, to use his own words, "can play any instrument from a jew's-harp to an organ." The next night he was presented with a magnificent horse and equipments, and a fine set of equipments was also given to Colonel Prince.

The narrative of this great raid would not be complete without detailing the adventures of Colonel Hatch's command, the 2d Iowa, which originally formed a part of the expedition, and left it near Houston. About twenty-five miles southeast of Houston, they were attacked by eight hundred shot-gun cavalry, whom they easily repulsed. They then turned directly north, crossed a most dismal swamp and swam a deep creek to avoid a battery which was in waiting for them. At sunset of the 22d they went into Okalona and burned the depot, barracks, and hospital buildings. The inhabitants were thoroughly panic stricken and fled in every direction. On the 25th, Colonel Bartow's rebel regiment of cavalry made a dash upon their rear, but was quickly repulsed with a loss of twenty-five men, not one of the 2d Iowa having been injured. On the 26th a most dastardly deed was committed by the guerrillas. While one of Colonel Hatch's orderlies was passing alone from the column to the advance guard with an order, the assassins raised from their hiding place and, without speaking to the orderly, shot him. The rest of the journey was marked with little of incident and the command arrived at their camp in La Grange with a loss of only seven men. They brought in over twenty prisoners, fifty negroes and five hundred head of horses and mules.

It is almost impossible to give a perfect sketch of the sixteen days' march of Grierson's heroes. In all the records of warfare we can scarcely find its parallel. Their endurance under so fatiguing and perilous a march is almost incredible. A large part of the time they were without food and rarely slept more than an hour or two at a time. They were almost constantly in the saddle. Where the roads were good they drove fast and hard to elude the rebels all around them, but more often they were fording or swimming rivers and creeks, dragging their way through almost impassable swamps and plunging into thick, gloomy, roadless forests, trusting only to rude country maps and a little pocket compass to reach their destination. During all these weary eight hundred miles, they lived upon the country both for forage and provisions, and then, although they came into Baton Rouge haggard, hungry, worn out and almost completely exhausted, with only one whole night's rest in the entire ride, they turned over but twelve men to the surgeon. Many of the men suffered from swelling of the legs and erysipelas, from sitting so long in the saddle, but it was only a temporary trouble.

They rode through the entire state of Mississippi from the northeast to the southwest corner. Starting from Lagrange, they first struck Marshall county and then passed through the following counties in succession: Tippah, Pontotoc, Chickasaw, Octebbeha, Winston, Noxubee, Neshoba, Jasper, Smith, Simpson, Copiah, Lawrence, Pike and Amite, and Helena and East Baton Rouge in Louisiana. During this ride they cut three railroads, burned nine bridges, destroyed two locomotives and nearly two hundred cars; broke up three rebel camps, destroyed more than four million dollars worth of rebel governmental property, and brought in with them twelve hundred captured horses and five hundred negroes. Every where the negroes welcomed the adventurers and extended to them the helping hand, and it was only because their presence would have endangered the command by hindering the march that more were not brought in. At several points the enemy tried to catch or surround them but in vain. Thirteen hundred cavalry were sent after them from Mobile, a thousand came south of Port Hudson, some to Pearl River, and two thousand came from the vicinity of Columbia and Grenada, to cut them off, besides the infantry forces of Chalmers and others that were marching and counter marching in every direction. Nearly all of the cavalry forces, after vainly trying to overtake or intercept Grierson, fell back to his rear, expecting to cut him off when he returned. They little dreamed of the Illinois endurance and courage that could hew its way to the Gulf.

The success of this raid was not less important in its physical than in its moral results. It taught the rebels that in spite of the name and fame of their cavalrymen—Stuart, Jackson, Hampton and Forrest—there were Northern troopers who could outride, outfight and outwit them. It disclosed the falseness of their vaunted strength, when seventeen hundred men, without food or rest, could ride from the Union lines in Tennessee to the Gulf, entirely through a State full of rebel forces, and ride through, comparatively unharmed, destroying as they went. It taught the rebels a wholesome respect for the cavalry arm of our service, and an equal respect for the strength of that government of which these men were but a small fragment. The hollowness of the boast that one of the chivalry was the equivalent of five Yankees, was brought home to them by sad experience, and the hollowness of the shell of the Southern Confederacy was none the less apparent to the Southern people who had been so woefully deluded by their military and political leaders.

In history this raid will be one of the most shining spots in the war, whatever event may occur in the future, and one of the proudest boasts in the record of Illinois patriotism, endurance and gallantry. Poetry and history will claim it as their own, and immortalize it as they have the brave deed of Lartius, Herminius and Horatius, who so valiantly kept the bridge "in the brave days of old."

CHAPTER XXI.

LIFE AND CHARACTER OF GEN. KIRK—HIS LAW STUDIES—ENTRANCE UPON THE MILITARY STAGE—ON THE MILITARY BOARD OF EXAMINERS—WOUNDED AT SHILOH—TRIBUTES OF GEN. MCCOOK AND BUELL—IN COMMAND AT LOUISVILLE—WOUNDED AT STONE RIVER—HIS DEATH—CHARACTER OF GEN. KIRK—COL. VON TREBRA—SKETCH OF HIS LIFE—COL. SHERIDAN P. READ—KILLED AT STONE RIVER—COL. GEO. W. ROBERTS—HIS IMPORTANT SERVICES—FELL WITH HIS FACE TO THE FOE—COL. JOSEPH R. SCOTT—THE NATIONAL CADETS—HIS MILITARY KNOWLEDGE—ORGANIZATION OF THE 19TH—THE LEFT WAS SAVED, BUT SCOTT WAS LOST.

EDWARD N. KIRK was born in Jefferson County, Ohio, on the 29th of February, 1828. His parents were Quakers, and in early life he became imbued with the serenity of disposition and steadiness of habit characterizing that sect. He graduated with honor at the Friends' Academy at Mount Pleasant, Ohio, and then taught school at Cadiz; but he had laid out his life-plan deeply and broadly, and urged on by a noble ambition which had for its source a harmoniously formed character, and for its design the most excellent ultimate, the confines of the school room became too narrow for him. He longed to step out into the world among active men and win his place. He gave up the school, chose the profession of the law and entered the office of Gen. Bostwick, a prominent lawyer of Cadiz; continued with him a short time, and completed his studies with Judge Bartol of Baltimore, in which city he was admitted to the bar in 1853. He practiced law in Baltimore for one year, and then removed to and permanently settled in Sterling, Illinois. On the 15th of October, 1858, he married Miss E. M. Cameron, of Philadelphia, an accomplished lady, who sympathized with his aspirations and aided in their accomplishment.

Immediately after the battle of Bull Run, when the demand for men was pressing, he set about raising and organizing a regiment which he tendered to Governor Yates, but at the date of its organization more regiments had been tendered to the Governor than he was authorized to accept. Determined that his regiment should go to the field, he telegraphed to the War Department, and through the influence of friends it was accepted, his commission as Colonel dating from the 15th of August, 1861. Almost instantly he became celebrated not alone for the superiority in drill and bearing which he gave to his regiment, but for his remarkable comprehension of military science, which gained for him a position upon the Military Board of Examiners at Munfordsville, Ky., to pass upon the qualifications of officers. At the battle of Shiloh he was a second Murat. Cool and self-possessed, he led his fine regiment into the very thickest of the fight. Although wounded by a ball which struck him in the right shoulder, partially fracturing the joint, passing below the collar bone and lodging against the breast bone, inflicting a dangerous and painful wound, he refused to leave the field until the issue of the battle was decided. General McCook said of him: "He coolly and judiciously led his men under fire. He has been in command of the fifth brigade for some months, and much of its efficiency is due to the care and labor he bestowed upon it. I respectfully call your attention to his meritorious services upon this day." General Buell in his report commended him "to the favor of the government for his distinguished gallantry and good conduct." In spite of the protestations of the physicians, who knew the character of the wound, he remained at Shiloh for several days, determined to lead his brigade in person in the campaign against Corinth. The result was an inflammatory fever which necessitated his removal to Louisville, where for a long time he hung between life and death.

On the 24th of August, though still suffering from the effects of his wound and from general debility, he started to rejoin his old command but was stopped by an order from General Boyle commanding the army of Kentucky, to take charge of an expedition in defence of Lebanon, Ky., then seriously threatened by Kirby Smith's forces. During the day, however, word came that Lebanon was safe and the expedition was relinquished. He once more determined to rejoin his gallant brigade, but was again impeded by an order from General Boyle, to assume command of all the forces at Louisville, including the new regiments which were rapidly arriving to repel Bragg's invasion. He retained command of these troops until relieved by General Gilbert, when he was assigned to the command of the first brigade, second division, "army of Kentucky," under Major-General Nelson. About this time occurred the defeat of our forces at Richmond, and he was ordered with his brigade and a small cavalry force to cover the retreat of our troops, an operation which he performed with great credit and military success. On the 28th of September, he was ordered to the command of his old brigade and was welcomed with the warmest delight both by officers and men.

On the 29th of November, the government commissioned him a Brigadier-General for his "heroic action, gallantry and ability," and certainly no officer of the State of Illinois ever wore the single star with more credit. He conferred honor upon the star, rather than the star, honor upon him. His splendid conduct upon the field of Stone River, we have already chronicled—how he strove to hold back the overwhelming rebel hordes; how he accomplished, but in vain, all that man could accomplish to save his brigade, and how he was wounded. His wound was a severe one, the ball lodged near the spine, and compelled him to withdraw from the field. He went to Louisville, where he consulted eminent surgical talent, but it was decided not to extract the ball, on the ground that his physical strength would not allow of the operation. He thence went to his home in Sterling where he gained in health and strength, and determined to have the ball extracted that he once more might go to the field. To this end he went to Chicago to undergo an operation at the hands of Dr. Brainard. The ball was successfully taken out and for a short time it seemed as if he were about to entirely recover, but symptoms of an alarming nature set in, and although every attention was bestowed upon him by his devoted wife, his friends and physicians, he died in the most excruciating pain on the 21st of July, 1863.

General Kirk was tall in stature and dignified in bearing, a man born to rule, and while he commanded obedience, none the less to command not only respect but love. He had a broad, intellectual forehead, dark eyes and hair, and a scholarly, genial, thoughtful face. He was mild in his disposition, talented in his conversation, friendly in his intercourse, and unostentatious in his dress. In his presence you knew you were in the presence of a superior man, but at the same time you longed to be familiar with him. As a citizen, he strictly and conscientiously performed all the duties of life; as a lawyer, his place was among the foremost; as a speaker, his power lay in the sincerity and honesty of his character rather than in eloquence; as a politician, he was conservative until treason reared its snaky crest—then he merged the politician in the patriot; as a soldier, he was brave, fearless, chivalrous, skillful and God-fearing, combining the qualities of Murat with the devotion of Havelock, *sans peur et sans reproche.* The officers and men of his old regiment, the 34th Illinois, who loved him almost as a father, have erected a monument to his memory, one side of which bears the following inscription—an extract of one of his letters, written to his uncle, Prof. N. C. Brooks, LL.D., President of the Baltimore Female College, and dated the 7th of April, 1863—"For me, I only hope to have it said, and I ask nothing prouder, 'In the time of peril and darkness he helped to save the commonwealth.'"

We deem this chapter a fitting place to commemorate the life and services of Colonel Von Trebra, an adopted son of Illinois, whose name has not figured in our narrative, as he commanded an Indiana regiment. He was born in Niedor Gorge, near Siejan in Prussia, on the 28th of September, 1830. He attended the gymnasium in Lubin until 1841. From there he went to the military school at Potsdam, where he remained until 1845, when he went to the military academy at Berlin. In 1847, he was promoted to a 1st lieutenancy and joined the 12th infantry. He served with this regiment through the Polish campaign and remained in the Prussian service until 1854, when he came to the United States. When the war broke out, like many others who had come to this country for the sake of its freedom, he took up arms in its defence, and on the 17th of December 1861, fought in the battle of Munfordsville. He served in the battle of Shiloh, the siege of Corinth, and the Alabama and Kentucky campaigns. On the 18th of July, he was commissioned

Colonel of the regiment, Colonel Willich, its former commander, having been promoted to a brigadier-generalship. After the departure of the army from Louisville to check the movement of Bragg, serious illness compelled him to ask for a leave of absence, which was granted. He repaired to his farm at Arcola, Illinois, but never returned to the field. After a long and painful illness, the patriot farmer died on the 6th of August, 1863, and was buried near his home. Death summoned him when his sword was sheathed, but that sword had done good work, and there was no stain of dishonor upon its blade. He died a hero in the service of his country though not upon the bloody field. None the less his memory claims the love and gratitude of those for whom he fought.

Colonel Sheridan P. Read was born in Champaign county, Ohio, in 1829. He was educated at the Ohio University at Athens, Ohio, and graduated at the law school of the Indiana University, at Bloomington, under the instruction of Judges McDonald and Otto. He first commenced the practice of law at Terre Haute, Indiana, but in 1853, he removed to Paris, Illinois. When the call was made for troops in 1862, he volunteered as a private soldier, and was appointed Lieutenant-Colonel of the 79th Illinois, and on the 18th of October following was commissioned Colonel of the regiment. He was a skillful and gallant officer and brought his regiment to a high degree of soldierly bearing and skill. He fell at Stone River, as we have before stated, his head pierced by a musket ball while bravely leading his men, and died instantly. His remains were brought to Paris, and interred near his home. Colonel Read was a lawyer from an ardent attachment to the profession in which he held a high rank. He was always active in everything which pertained to the good of his own community. He was zealous in the cause of education, and for several years the school commissioner of Edgar county. In the mechanical and agricultural interests of his county and the State at large, he took a deep and abiding interest. In politics, he was a Democrat, and was for some time editor of a Democratic paper in Paris. When the war broke out, however, he dropped the pen, took up the sword for his country and died in its defence.

Col. Geo. W. Roberts was born at Chester, Westchester county, in the State of Pennsylvania, October 2, 1833. He completed his school studies at Poughkeepsie, in the State of New York, and entered the sophomore class, of Yale College, graduating with high honors in 1857. He was admitted to the bar and practiced his profession in his native county until 1859, when he removed to Chicago and at once entered the office of E. S. Smith, Esq., where he continued until June, 1861, when, in company with Col. David Stuart, he helped to organize the 42d Illinois regiment. On the 22d of July, he received his commission as Major, on the 17th of September was elected Lieutenant-Colonel, and, upon the death of Col. Webb, in December, 1861, who had succeeded Col. Stuart, he was appointed Colonel. He took part with his regiment in Fremont's march to Springfield, Mo.; afterwards commanded Fort Holt, at Cairo; thence was ordered to Columbus, Ky., after its evacuation by the rebels; thence proceeded to Island No. 10, where he performed one of the most gallant feats of the war by spiking the upper Kentucky battery with four boats' crews of picked men, in a dark, stormy night. He was next ordered to Fort Pillow, and left there with Gen. Pope, to go up the Tennessee River. He participated, with distinguished honors, in the battles at Farmington, was in the advance at the occupation of Corinth, commanding a brigade, his old regiment being the first to plant the flag on the rebel works. Thence he was ordered to Memphis, where he again distinguished himself by breaking up the guerrilla bands infesting that part of Tennessee and capturing many of their most daring and dangerous chiefs. From thence, with his regiment, he was transferred to Gen. Rosecrans' army, and participated with his regiment, in the bloody battle of Stone River. The 42d was attached to Sherman's division, and crowned itself with glory by its magnificent bravery and the desperation with which it strove to repel the terrible onset upon our right wing on Wednesday. The men fought worthy of their fame which they had won at Corinth, Farmington, Island No. 10 and scores of lesser fields. Every man was a hero, and splendidly they fought against fate. Not a man receded although the odds were overwhelming and their numbers were rapidly lessening, until their gallant leader fell mortally wounded with his face to the foe. The heroism, the splendid presence which had inspired them was gone.

The strong arm was powerless, and the brave heart which he had bared to the pitiless storm, was lifeless.

Col. Roberts was a magnificent specimen of a man physically and mentally. His frame was almost herculean and he laughed at toils and privations. His presence was commanding and his deportment dignified. Morally and intellectually he preserved a strict rectitude and never stooped to a low or mean action. He was manly in the broadest and best acceptation of the term. As a lawyer he was eminently successful and had achieved an enviable fame, although comparatively a stranger at the Chicago bar, when he adopted the military profession. As a soldier he was a model for all men. In the language of a speaker at his funeral obsequies, who knew him intimately and well: "When the long catalogue of disasters which this wicked rebellion has entailed upon our country comes to be made up, prominent among these disasters shall be the martyrdom of our friend, and when the record of glorious names who have testified their loyalty and sealed their devotion to their country with their blood comes to be written, high on that record shall his name be inscribed and gather new luster with each succeeding year."

Col. Joseph R. Scott, of the 19th Illinois, was only twenty-seven years of age at the time of his death, and one of the youngest colonels in the service. He was born in Canada, and inherited from his parents the military ardor and impulsive bravery which characterized and so honorably distinguished him. Col. Scott was emphatically a self-made man. Whatever of education, of reputation, or of military knowledge he possessed, was due to his own exertions. Although deprived of the advantages of an early education, he managed in the intervals of labor, from boyhood to manhood, so to perfect himself in his studies, that at the period of his enlistment he was considered an excellent English scholar and a young man of more than ordinary promise. The trait which perhaps peculiarly distinguished him *par excellence* was his military talent. He had a peculiar aptness for military studies and pursued them with enthusiastic assiduity.

There was a remarkable resemblance between Col. Scott and Col. Ellsworth, both in *physique* and in military accomplishments. They were of about the same age, the same height, the same compactness of frame, resembled each other in the face sufficiently to have passed for brothers, and both were apt students of military science, especially as it pertained to drill and soldierly bearing, and both were strict disciplinarians. These qualities combined to make the Zouave Cadets probably the best drilled company that was ever organized in the United States, both in the ordinary school and in the more elaborate and intricate movements of the French Zouave school, designed more for ornament than use. In drill, the company was reduced to the harmony and unity of action of the finest regulated machine and carried off the palm, not alone at home, but even in the large eastern cities that boasted of finely drilled regiments. They created a furore throughout the entire country, and were the originators of scores of Zouave companies that rapidly sprang up, but never reached the excellence of the Zouave Cadets of Chicago. In point of morals the two young officers were equally agreed, and the practice of vice in any of its branches, repulsive or fashionable, was sufficient and immediate cause for dismissal. These stringent notions of discipline, Col. Ellsworth used with great effect in the government of the New York Fire Zouaves, which regiment he organized, and in spite of the wild, ungovernable, almost ferocious material with which he had to deal, he reduced it to a comparatively well disciplined body. He was the earliest victim of the war and died while trampling on the rebel flag against which he had drawn sword. It seems sad that a young officer of so much promise had not been permitted to live and win his way to distinction.

In 1856, while a clerk in a leading dry goods house of Chicago, Scott organized a company of young men called the National Cadets, and for a time commanded them. When Colonel Ellsworth desired them to adopt the drill and practice of the French Zouave school, Col. Scott warmly seconded his effort, and under their joint labors the Cadets were reorganized as the "United States Zouave Cadets." Of this company Col. Ellsworth became the first commander and Col. Scott the 1st Lieutenant. In the brilliant career of the independent command—a command which achieved a national reputation for its splendid drill, nearly every man of which is or has been an officer in the present war, Col. Scott bore a prominent and honorable part, he and his lamented coadjutor little dreaming that they were establishing a nursery of officers who would shortly after be needed in the real din and strife.

In April, 1861, when the whole country was ablaze with indignation at the outrage offered our flag at Sumter, young Scott was one of the first to offer his services to the government. In the hastily improvised expedition to the Big Muddy bridge, at the time Illinois was on the point of being invaded, Col. Scott did most excellent service in guarding the bridge at that place.

When the 19th Illinois was organized, he was elected its first colonel but subsequently resigned in favor of Gen. Turchin and accepted the Lieutenant-Colonelcy. In all the battles in which the 19th participated, up to the time of his decease, he was present. Through all their useless marches and countermarches, put upon them by a regime which was seeking to break them down and impair their usefulness, he accompanied them, sharing their toils and privations and never finding fault with indignities heaped upon them, confident that in its own good time vindication would come. When Col. Turchin was commissioned brigadier-general, he was appointed colonel of the regiment and led them through the bloody and terrific battle of Stone River. We have already detailed the splendid conduct of his regiment and his own heroic bearing; how the regiment vindicated itself and won a name and fame which will be immortal; how they made the fearful charge which saved the left and the day. In that charge he was wounded in the groin and was brought to Chicago, where, under the attentive and devoted care of his wife and excellent surgical aid, he was in a fair way to recover and hoped soon to rejoin his command. That hope, however, was crushed. He was unfortunately thrown from his carriage, and his wound reopened and commenced to bleed. Mortification ensued and he died on the 8th of July, 1863. His funeral obsequies were attended with military honors on the 10th. The officiating clergyman closed the funeral discourse with the following just tribute to his worth: "He was a noble, youthful soldier, calm and dignified, and a resolute defender of the right. A man of his years, who can say to his regiment, 'No spirituous liquors, and not one oath to be used,' it would seem to mortals should be spared to his men. The country, in the hour of her peril, but just as the dark clouds were widely fringed with silvery light, and just closing her festivities appropriate to the national anniversary, has lost a youthful soldier, but a calm and brave leader."

CHAPTER XXII.

The Thirty-fourth and its Officers—The Seventy-ninth—The Tenth Cavalry and its Officers—The Seventy-fourth—The Seventy-fifth—The Twenty-sixth—The Sixtieth—The Seventy-third—Its Officers—Its Colonel in Dixie—Brydges Battery.

THIRTY-FOURTH ILLINOIS VOLUNTEERS.

The following is the original roster of the regiment:

Colonel, Edward N. Kirk; Lieutenant-Colonel, Amos Bosworth; Major, Charles N. Levanway; Adjutant, David Leavitt; Quartermaster, Abram Beeler; Surgeon, Francis A. McNeil; 1st Assistant Surgeon, George W. Hewett; 2d Assistant Surgeon, John L. Hostetter; Chaplain, Michael Decker.

Co. A—Captain, E. Brooks Ward; 1st Lieutenant, Peter Ege; 2d Lieutenant, Jonathan A. Morgan.

Co. B—Captain, Hiram W. Bristol; 1st Lieutenant, Cornelius Quackenbush; 2d Lieutenant, John A. Parrott.

Co. C—Captain, Alexander P. Dysart; 1st Lieutenant, Benson Wood; 2d Lieutenant, Daniel Riley.

Co. D—Captain, Truman L. Pratt; 1st Lieutenant, William S. Wood; 2d Lieutenant, Simon B. Dexter.

Co. E—Captain, Henry Weld; 1st Lieutenant, Samuel L. Patrick; 2d Lieutenant, Thomas Bell.

Co. F—Captain, Oscar Van Tassel; 1st Lieutenant, Uriah G. Galion; 2d Lieutenant, John Slaughter.

Co. G—Captain, Mabry G. Greenwood; 1st Lieutenant, John Hindman; 2d Lieutenant, Samuel R. Cavender.

Co. H—Captain, John M. Miller; 1st Lieutenant, David C. Wagner; 2d Lieutenant Benjamin R. Wagner.

Co. I—Captain, Lewis Heffelfinger; 1st Lieutenant, Amos W. Hostetter; 2d Lieutenant, James Watson.

Co. K—Captain, Orson Q. Herrick; 1st Lieutenant, Stephen Martin; 2d Lieutenant, David A. Zimmerman.

This regiment combined the northern and southern loyalty of the

State, for it was composed of companies from Carroll, Lee, Ogle and Whiteside upon or near the northern line, and Coles and Mòrgan of the southern. It was made of good stuff, as the result has shown. It was organized at Camp Butler, Springfield, and on the 1st of September, 1861, was mustered into the service of the United States. On the 2d of October it was *en route* to Cincinnati, and was among the first to march to the rescue of Kentucky from its apostate sons. On the 4th it entered Covington with hospitable greetings from the citizens. The next day it proceeded to Lexington, and thence on the 9th to Louisville, and thence to Muldraugh's Hill and Nolin or Camp Nevin. Here it was assigned, October 18th, to the 6th brigade, but on the 3d of December was transferred to the 5th, General T. J. Wood commanding.

It marched through Kentucky, enjoyed the evacuation of Bowling Green; thence March 2, 1862, it started with "The Old Second Division" for Nashville. On the 16th of March, this division, with Buell's army moved forward, Colonel Kirk commanding the 5th brigade. The line of march lay along the Alabama and Tennessee Railroad, one of the richest portions of the State, and early as it was, the country was in the beauty of May. Onward it went through Franklin and Spring Hill to Rutherford's Creek, where a halt was made until Kirk's brigade should rebuild a bridge burned by the enemy. This was done under the direction of Lieutenant Colonel Bosworth, of the 34th. On the 25th it was reported to General McCook that at Columbia there was a rebel gun-factory, Lieutenant-Colonel Bosworth was ordered to detail a party to take and hold the factory. Lieutenant S. B. Dexter, of Co. D, took fifteen men, and with the squad, held the town one night. The 34th was detailed to guard the town and Major Levanway was appointed post commandant.

March 31st, the division moved towards Savannah, Tennessee, to effect a juncture with General Grant, and on the 6th of April, after a weary march, came within sound of the cannon of Shiloh. On the morning of the 7th it entered the battle.

There, as has been stated, Major Levanway fell, bravely doing a soldier's duty. Colonel Kirk was severely wounded, and Captains Miller and Patrick, with Lieutenants Wood, Parrott, Wagner and

Hiller were among the wounded. The 34th proved itself a gallant and efficient regiment on that field. In the death of Lieutenant-Colonel Bosworth the regiment and the service sustained a sore loss. He had furnished evidence of rare ability on the field and in the minutie of camp government and instruction. The loss in this conflict was one hundred and two killed and wounded. The death of Lieutenant-Colonel Bosworth followed. Captain Hiram W. Bristol, who commanded after the fall of Levanway, was promoted Lieutenant-Colonel and Captain A. P. Dysart, Major. It moved forward and participated in the siege of Corinth. On the 28th, the 34th participated gallantly in a skirmish with the enemy, the outposts, Cos. B, G and K, being under command of Captain Wagner. He was compelled by a terrific fire to change his line and fall back sufficiently to uncover the enemy's fire, secured by the serpentine formation of the creek. In this case the regiment lost in killed and wounded, seven.

After the surrender it remained with the division in front of Corinth as reserve, until June 6th, when it moved two miles south, and on the 10th with Buell's army moved into East Tennessee. It shared the weary counter-march so famous in Buell's strategy; forced back from his Tennessee and Alabama line by Bragg's generalship, he returned to the Ohio. The 34th shared in the skirmish at Floyd's Fork; at Claysville it poured a murderous fire upon the advancing foe, compelling it to break, and hastening its route. It participated in the affair at "Dog Walk."

Again at Stone River it was in the thunder of real battle, and from December 26, 1862, until January 4, 1863, maintained the honor of the State. We must not re-write the story of the battle. The 34th fought valiantly, and its loss in killed and wounded was one hundred and eighteen. "Here fell Captain M. G. Greenwood and Lieutenant John M. Smith, Captain Van Tassel, acting Major, and H. Riley were wounded—the latter mortally." (Dodge's History.) Here General Kirk was mortally wounded.

In the engagement of Liberty Gap, the regiment lost twenty-five killed and wounded, among whom was "Lieutenant Merrill, a gallant and worthy officer." It is but scanty justice to say with Dodge, "Indeed on all the battle-fields where this regiment has been engaged, it has ever performed its whole duty, and its fearful losses attest the fact more potently than words."

Again at Mission Ridge the 34th participated gloriously in that superb victory, and then marched to relieve the gallant Burnside at Knoxville. It returned to Chattanooga and re-enlisted as a veteran regiment, and after enjoying its well-earned furlough, returned and was placed in the 2d brigade of General Davis's division of the Fourteenth Army Corps, and has participated in the marches and victories of the gallant Sherman, yet to be traced. It was mustered with eight hundred and twenty, increased by muster and transfer to nine hundred and ten. October 10, 1863, it numbered four hundred and ninety-four!

Lieutenant-Colonel Amos Bosworth, was born at Royalton, Vermont, April 12, 1831, and received a common English education. His father removed in 1858 to Grand de Tour, Illinois. Amos formed a business partnership under the style of "Andrews and Bosworth." At the commencement of the war his plowshare was changed for the sword, and with General Kirk and Major Levanway, he aided in raising the 34th and was chosen its second officer. The Colonel being placed over a brigade the Lieutenant-Colonel commanded the regiment, and proved himself an excellent officer. Says Dodge: "His zeal in hastening the completion of the bridge at Rutherford's Creek was doubtless one of the means in the hands of Divine Providence of saving General Grant's army at Shiloh, in the ever memorable battle of Shiloh, on the 6th of April, by the rapid movement of Buell's column marching to his assistance. But this was the Colonel's crowning work. Nearly all one day he worked in the water waist-deep, from which he took a severe cold, ending in a fever. He was borne thence to Savannah, Tennessee, in an ambulance. During the battle of the 7th he lay at Savannah in the delirium of fever, and occasionally hearing the thunder of artillery from the field, he would rouse up and insist upon going to Pittsburg Landing to take command of the regiment. He continued to fail rapidly, and was removed from Savannah, but upon reaching Dixon, Illinois, only a few miles from his home, he was so low that the journey could not be continued longer. He died of typhus fever, at the residence of his friend W. C. Andrus, April 23, 1862. He was buried at Grand de Tour, on the 27th."

His brothers of the ancient order gathered sadly about his open grave. It seemed an untimely death, but God hath his secret ways.

Colonel Hiram W. Bristol was born at Ravenna, Ohio. He was a student in Alleghany College, Meadville, Pa., from 1850 to 1856. He studied law with Judge Day of Ravenna. In 1859 he removed to Morrison, Illinois, where he engaged in the practice of his profession. With the outbreak of rebellion he raised a company of three months' men, but it was before the War Department had learned to accept all the men offered, and it was not accepted. When the gallant 34th was organized, he was mustered as Captain of Company B. When the Major Levanway fell, he found himself in command, and led the regiment through the rest of the fight of Shiloh. He was promoted as Major in the place of Levanway, on the battle-field. April 18, 1862, he was promoted Lieutenant-Colonel, and on the promotion of General Kirk, was made Colonel, his commission dating from December 19, 1862. On the 8th of March following, broken down in health, he resigned his commission. Says Dodge:

"On the 31st of December, the day so fatal to the right wing of the army of the Cumberland, being unable to sit on his horse, he drove to the front in an ambulance, and was twice taken prisoner and twice recaptured—being under fire from daylight until 3 P. M., when he reached the field hospital in the rear of the center of the army, where he was taken out nearly insensible, and on the 4th of January was sent to the hospital at Nashville.

"Colonel Bristol was a good commander, thoroughly versed in the duties of his profession, and as brave an officer as ever led a command on the field. His conduct at Shiloh was the admiration of all who witnessed it, and he will not soon be forgotten by the brave boys he once had the honor to command."

Colonel Alexander P. Dysart, who succeeded Colonel Bristol, was born in Pennsylvania, February 26, 1826, and came into Lee County, Illinois, in 1847, where he resided as a farmer. He raised Company C for the 34th and was chosen its captain. At Shiloh, after Captain Bristol assumed command of the regiment, he acted as Major, and was promoted to that rank on the 18th of the same month.

Upon the resignation of Colonel Bristol, he was promoted

Colonel, his commission dating from November 29, 1862. He continued with the regiment until its arrival at Tullahoma, in July, 1863, when he tendered his resignation, which was accepted, to date from August 7, 1863. As commander he was much beloved by his men.

THE SEVENTY-NINTH ILLINOIS VOLUNTEERS.

This regiment was brigaded, through the campaigns of Kentucky and Tennessee with the 34th, sharing its marches and privations, and should properly find a record with it.

ORIGINAL ROSTER.

Colonel, Lyman Guinnip; Lieutenant Colonel, Sheridan P. Read; Major, Allen Buckner; Adjutant, William H. Lamb; Quartermaster, Charles E. Woodward; Surgeon, ——— ———; 1st Assistant Surgeon, Henry C. McAllister; 2d Assistant Surgeon, Thomas J. Wheeler; Chaplain, Cornelius G. Bradshaw.

Co. A—Captain, Terrance Clark; 1st Lieutenant, James S. Price; 2d Lieutenant, John Mitchell.

Co. B—Captain, Archibald Vanderin; 1st Lieutenant, Seth L. Woodworth; 2d Lieutenant, Horace W. Rideout.

Co. C—Captain, David S. Curtis; 1st Lieutenant, William S. Hendrix; 2d Lieutenant, John H. Patton.

Co. D—Captain, Thomas A. Young; 1st Lieutenant, David B. Elliott; 2d Lieutenant, John P. Vance.

Co. E—Captain, William A. Low; 1st Lieutenant, Harvey J. Bassell; 2d Lieutenant, Henry S. Albin.

Co. F—Captain, Thomas Handy; 1st Lieutenant, David S. Williams; 2d Lieutenant, James R. Patten.

Co. G—Captain, Oliver O. Bagley; 1st Lieutenant, Martin L. Lininger; 2d Lieutenant, Thomas B. Jacobs.

Co. H—Captain, Willis O. Pennil; 1st Lieutenant, James T. Braddock; 2d Lieutenant, Andrew J. Bigelow.

Co. I—Captain, Robert Lacy; 1st Lieutenant, Henry Week; 2d Lieutenant, Samuel Sharp.

Co. K—Captain, Hezekiah D. Martin; 1st Lieutenant, William W. Davis; 2d Lieutenant, Moses Hunter.

It was recruited, by order of Governor Yates, from the counties of Clark, Douglas, Edgar and Vermillion. It was organized at Camp Terry, Mattoon, Coles county, Illinois, and was mustered into the U. S. service Aug. 28, 1862, and in September proceeded to Louisville, Kentucky. It was assigned, on the 13th of September, to the 3d brigade, General Cruft's division, army of Kentucky. On the 29th it was transferred to the 4th brigade of the 2d division, and October 5th, to the 5th, under Gen. Kirk. Col. Guinnip resigned shortly after the regiment entered service, and Lieut.-Col. Sheridan P. Read was commissioned Colonel and Henry E. Rives Lieutenant-Colonel.

The 79th came first into battle at Stone River, and its steadiness and veteran-like coolness elicited commendation from commanding officers. Here its gallant Colonel fell, another costly sacrifice on the altar of freedom.

Thenceforward, for a long time, its history is with the same division and brigade, and wherever it marched it maintained its Stone River fame. In the terrible conflict of Chickamauga it displayed extraordinary bravery. The division with which it had been connected having been disorganized, it was assigned to Col. Harker's brigade of General Sheridan's division, 4th army corps. At the battle of Mission Ridge it charged the rugged hights, and penetrating the enemy's breast-works, captured two heavy guns. It there, as elsewhere, bore itself bravely, and proved itself worthy to be associated with the 34th. It went over the long weary march to Knoxville to the relief of Burnside, threatened by the superior forces of Longstreet. It has subsequently been in East Tennessee, and later participated in the engagements at Dalton and Buzzard's Roost. At the latter the brave Col. Buckner was seriously wounded.

Its record is with campaigns yet to be written, fields remaining to be described. For with the Illinois men who marched southward went honor, and they carried the key which was to unlock the portals of secession and open the way for freedom and Union.

TENTH CAVALRY REGIMENT, ILLINOIS VOLUNTEERS.

The following is the original roster of the regiment:

Colonel, James A. Barrett; Lieutenant-Colonel, Dudley Wickersham; 1st Major, Elin P. Shaw; 2d Major, Joseph S. Smith; 3d Major, Marshal L. Stephenson; Adju tant, James Stuart; Adjutant 1st Battalion, Eli H. Hosea; Adjutant 2d Battalion, Thomas D. Vredenburg Adjutant 3d Battalion, Henry Turney; Quarter-Master, John H. Barrett; Quarter-Master 1st Battalion, Daniel L. Canfield; Quarter-Master 2d Battalion, John P. Cavanaugh; Commissary, Edwin R. Neal; Assistant-Surgeon, Wm. E. Wilson; Chaplain, Francis Springer.

Co. A—Captain, Garrett Elkin; 1st Lieutenant, Alfred A. North; 2d Lieutenant, Thomas H. Anderson.

Co. B—Captain, Samuel N. Hitt; 1st Lieutenant, Augustus A. Shutt; 2d Lieutenant, Joseph B. McCartney.

Co. C—Captain, Hiram E. Barstow; 1st Lieutenant, Hiram C. Walker; 2d Lieutenant, Seth Ingalsbe.

Co. D—Captain, Ephraim Bartle; 1st Lieutenant, Hiram Cady; 2d Lieutenant, Wm. Bennett.

Co E—Captain, Henry Reily; 1st Lieutenant, Columbus Cross; 2d Lieutenant John Mabee.

Co. F—Captain, Isaac H. Ferguson; 1st Lieutenant, Wm. A. Chapin; 2d Lieutenant, Felix Droll.

Co. G—Captain, Wm. S. Hunter; 1st Lieutenant, Zimri B. Bates; 2d Lieutenant, Wm. A. Stinnett.

Co. H—Captain, Thomas S. Crafton; 1st Lieutenant, Herman B. Hoffman; 2d Lieutenant, John W. Crafton.

Co. I—Captain, James Butterfield; 1st Lieutenant, James S. Freeman; 2d Lieutenant, John F. Black.

Co. K—Captain, Cavil K. Wilson; 1st Lieutenant, David H. Wilson; 2d Lieutenant, George W. Curry.

Co. L—Captain, Thomas V. Wilson; 1st Lieutenant, John G. Roberts; 2d Lieutenant, Thomas D. Vredenburg.

Co. M—Captain, Wm. S. Moore; 1st Lieutenant, Elhanen J. Searle; 2d Lieutenant, Wm. H. Watson.

The 10th cavalry regiment, Illinois volunteers, was organized at Springfield, in the fall of 1861, where they remained until April, 1862, when they removed to Springfield, Missouri.

They took a prominent part in the battle of Prairie Grove, Arkansas, Dec. 2, 1862, Col. Wickersham having charge of the following cavalry regiments: 2d Wisconsin, 1st Iowa, 10th Illinois and 8th Missouri. At the battle of Van Buren, Arkansas, Dec. 28th, the cavalry regiments—the 10th among the number—bore a most conspicuous part, and also at the battle of Milliken's Bend, Richmond, Louisiana, Bayou Metre and Little Rock. They participated in the celebrated battle and siege of Vicksburg, and in almost numberless skirmishes, expeditions and reconnoissances. No regiment marched further, surmounted more difficulties, acted in more capacities, or accomplished more in the same length of time than did they. They are not only perfect in cavalry tactics but efficient as infantry soldiers and artillerists. During the first three years of their service they corduroyed miles of swamps, built fortifications, bridged rivers, and always vanquished the enemy whether on foot or mounted.

The regiment re-enlisted as veterans and was attached to Gen. Carr's cavalry division—formerly Gen. Davidson's—at that time serving in the army of the Arkansas, under Major-General Fred. Steel. We subjoin the following extracts from the speech of Governor Yates to the 10th Illinois cavalry:

"*Col. Wickersham, Officers and Soldiers of the* 10*th Illinois Cavalry:*

"I have been requested by the Mayor of the city and many of your numerous friends, to say a word of welcome to you on your arrival home. But not only because I am invited, but prompted by the feelings of my own heart, and because I know it is the desire of the people of the State, of whom I am the humble representative, I bid you welcome to-day, on your return to your homes from the field of duty.

"Some time in January, 1861, two years ago, you left Camp Butler and were stationed for a short time in Missouri. You then, by long and tedious marches, reached Arkansas and Louisiana, and most of you, if not all, have helped to achieve the glorious victories which have been won in these States. It is well known that cavalry regiments cannot be always together, but whether you have been placed on duty as a regiment, in companies, in battalions or in squads, the 10th cavalry was always where danger was nearest, and wherever duty called you, and you are justly entitled to inscribe upon your banner the names of Little Rock, Prairie Grove, Van Buren, Milliken's Bend, Richmond, Louisiana and Vicksburg.

"Many are the instances of bravery reported from Illinois regiments, but I doubt if there is one which has surpassed you in deeds of noble valor. Your record, as soldiers, is glorious enough, but when it is remembered that at the call of your country, disregarding all political and party feeling, you left your homes and friends, and members of all parties went to fight, shoulder to shoulder, for our common cause, and that you have now returned, again to enter the ranks of our army, again to fight for the Union and Constitution, you are doubly entitled to our gratitude.

"You have re-enlisted as veterans, a name which you are truly entitled to; not satisfied with the services which you have rendered to your country, with the dangers you have encountered, the privations and sufferings you have endured—not satisfied with all this—you have come back only to say to your friends, to your country, and to your God: 'We will not now desert the cause for which we have been fighting and for which we have been suffering; that we will not rest until that glorious flag which has been leading us on many a field of battle, will float again over a united and peaceful country.'

"You may say with just pride that you belong to an Illinois regiment. Upon every battle-field from Donelson, Pea Ridge and Shiloh to Gettysburg, there was the never wavering, never faltering flag of Illinois, and in the thickest of the fight the bravest of her sons, always ready when duty called, never quailing before the foe. Illinois has sent one hundred and fifty thousand of her sons to the field; cheerfully has she furnished the flower of the State at the call of the President. I do not forget the cost of this war, nor our noble dead. The graves of many of her bravest boys are scattered along the banks of the Mississippi, the Cumberland, and the Potomac; and many—many of them on all the battle-fields from Chattanooga to Gettysburg—sleep far from their beloved homes. But they have only died a few years before us; their memories will ever be cherished by a grateful people; and, if necessary, I am prepared to say now, we have a hundred thousand more to furnish, as loyal, brave, and patriotic, to help crush this unholy and wicked rebellion.

"I had not intended saying so much, but I have been following you, and every Illinois soldier, from the moment you left the State till you returned. I have been watching you on your marches, in camp and on the battle-field, rejoicing over your victories and mourning over your defeats. I have received your letters out of camp, from the field, and from the sick bed. I have received letters from the dear ones you left at home. They have looked up to me as their protector, and I could hardly say less than I have said. Now, on your return, I can say justly that I am proud of you. You have conducted yourselves as patriots, and you have never disgraced the noble flag under which you have fought.

"In thirty days you will return to the field, and we will have one hundred thousand more bayonets to help you finish this work; and you will then push them forward till the battle-worn veterans of Grant, with the additional hundred thousand will meet the force of Lee. But my confidence in you makes me look forward to this conflict without fear. Fierce as this battle will be, for it is a fight of American against American, and among those on the opposite side, although misguided and fighting for a bad cause, are brave men, as brave as any in our ranks, yet I know that victory will crown our banners.

"And when, at one mighty gathering, the people of Illinois will meet the returning soldiers, and as they pass in serried ranks upon the wide prairie, with their old battle-scarred banners and shivered cannons, rusty bayonets and sabers, with rebel flags and rebel trophies of every kind, at this mighty procession, surpassing the proudest festival of Rome and ancient Greece in their palmiest days; then the mighty shout of a grateful people will go up. All hail to the veterans who have given our flag to the battle and the breeze, and saved our country forever as the asylum for Union, liberty and humanity. Again I say, with all my heart, welcome home!"

COLONEL WICKERSHAM was born in Woodford county, Kentucky, in 1820. He was raised on a farm, and in the fall of 1844 emigrated to Springfield, Illinois, where he engaged in mercantile pursuits. On the breaking out of the Mexican war, he enlisted in the 4th Illinois infantry, and served under the gallant and lamented orator, statesman and patriot, Col. E. D. Baker.

On the 21st of September, 1861, he was appointed Lieutenant-Colonel of the 10th Illinois cavalry, by Governor Yates, and upon the resignation of Col. Barrett, he was selected colonel of the regiment by acclamation.

During his military career in northwest Missouri, and while in command at Fayetteville, Arkansas, Col. Wickersham was particularly successful in his dealings with hundreds of half-decided followers of secession. He was moderate and forbearing almost beyond measure, when that policy was deemed best by the administration and a majority of the people of the country. As the rebellion progressed, and a more vigorous and determined policy was adopted, none was more justly severe than he in laying the hand of military powers upon the neck of the rebellious race.

He was in command of important posts and brigades most of the time, and for some months was the commander of the 2d division of the army of the frontier under Gen. Herron, whilst his regiment was commanded by the Lieut.-Col. Stuart, a brave and accomplished cavalry officer. Col. Wickersham proved himself a brave and efficient officer, esteemed by all those with whom he was associated, and loved and respected by the officers and men of his own regiment.

SEVENTY-FOURTH ILLINOIS VOLUNTEERS.

The 74th regiment was organized at Camp Fuller, in Rockford, Illinois, September 4, 1862, where it remained until September 28th. The following was the original roster:

Colonel, Jason Marsh; Lieutenant-Colonel, James B. Kerr; Major, Edward F. Dutcher; Adjutant, Edward A. Blodgett; Quartermaster, Lewis Williams; Surgeon, Charles N. Ellinwood; 1st Assistant Surgeon, Henry Strong; 2d Assistant Surgeon, Chesseldon Fisher; Chaplain, —— ——.

Co. A—Captain, Thomas J. L. Remington; 1st Lieutenant, Josiah W. Leffingwell; 2d Lieutenant, Alfred Barker.

Co. B—Captain, David O. Buttolph; 1st Lieutenant, Augustus W. Thompson; 2d Lieutenant, Edwin Swift.

Co. C—Captain, Hampton P. Sloan; 1st Lieutenant, Christopher M. Brazee; 2d Lieutenant, Richard P. Blaisdell.

Co. D—Captain, Jonathan H. Douglas; 1st Lieutenant, Hobert H. Hatch; 2d Lieutenant, John H. Nye.

Co. E—Captain, Elias Cosper; 1st Lieutenant, William Powell; 2d Lieutenant, Alpheus M. Blakely.

Co. F—Captain, Henry C. Barker; 1st Lieutenant, Jerome E. Andrews; 2d Lieutenant, Cyrenius N. Woods.

Co. G—Captain, Bowman W. Bacon; 1st Lieutenant, William R. Hoadley; 2d Lieutenant, David McKaig.

Co. H—Captain, Timothy B. Taylor; 1st Lieutenant, Samuel Whitmyer; 2d Lieutenant, Andrew J. Belts.

Co. I—Captain, William Irvin; 1st Lieutenant, Frederick W. Stegner; 2d Lieutenant, Daniel Cronemiller.

Co. K—Captain, Butler Ward; 1st Lieutenant, Henry N. Baker; 2d Lieutenant, Albert G. Lakin.

It reached Louisville, Ky., a little past midnight September 30th, and bivouacked in the streets of that city without shelter, weary and hungry, being the last regiment crossing the Ohio to join the army under General Buell, which, the next morning, October 1st, moved in pursuit of Bragg.

Just at the close of the battle of Perrysville, Ky., October 8th, the 74th having been in reserve, advanced upon the foe at double quick, and within musket range, but the enemy retreating at that point and night closing in, the regiment did but little actual fighting. October 10th it had a sharp skirmish with the rear of Bragg's forces at Lancaster, but only one man in the brigade was killed.

After the army had marched to Crab Orchard and returned to Danville, Ky., the 74th, together with the 22d Indiana Volunteers, and a section of the 5th Wisconsin battery, was sent back on a forced march about thirty miles in the direction of Richmond, Ky., beyond Lowell, on a secret and fruitless expedition, the object of which remains unknown, but the effect of excessive marching and over-working, without shelter or protection through the cold nights, and with scant supply of rations, told most fearfully upon the men, so that by the time they reached Lebanon, Ky., the sick, disabled and broken down were numbered by hundreds. No other service or battle of the 74th has ever equaled, in disabling the men, that unexplained expedition. On the 26th of December, 1862, the army of the Cumberland under command of General Rosecrans, moved from Nashville toward Murfreesboro, Tenn. On the afternoon of that day the brigade to which this regiment belonged overtook the enemy at Nolensville, where it formed in line of battle, and had several hours' skirmishing with infantry and artillery, without any casuality except one wounded. The march was continued from that day, Friday, with daily skirmishing, until Tuesday evening, December 30th, just at dark, when our forces came upon the enemy, who formed in line of battle; our men opened fire upon them, killing one and wounding another.

Early the next morning commenced the battle of Stone River. Without going again into the details of the disasters upon the right, it is simple justice to say this regiment kept its ground in unbroken order, and by a steady, well ordered fire, held the enemy in front in check until the regiments on their right and left had fallen clear back from the line and almost out of sight, and the enemy had nearly flanked it on both sides; and when it retreated, did so in perfect order, and rallied on the reserve.

In the march from Murfreesboro to Winchester, in June, 1863, the regiment was under the command of Lieut.-Col. Kerr, Col. Marsh being obliged to remain in camp on account of illness. During this march it was engaged in several slight skirmishes with the enemy. The brigade, commanded by Colonel Post, was detached from the division on the advance from Stevenson to Chattanooga for the purpose of protecting the rear and the trains, therefore was not engaged in the battle of Chickamauga. But leaving Valley Head the day after the battle, and proceeding along the base of Lookout Mountain towards Chattanooga, its march was attended almost every mile with the most singular incidents, of close approach to the enemy's forces, hair-breadth escapes from capture or destruction, sharp and frequent skirmishes, the whole force of the enemy covering the country all along on their right, and yet it reached Chattanooga with the entire train without the loss of a single man.

On its arrival at Chattanooga, the brigade was placed on outpost duty, guarding and constructing the front line of entrenchments, almost hourly, day and night, exposed to sudden attacks of the enemy, which were, however, successfully repelled. It remained at this duty for six days; in the meantime the 74th, in connection with the 22d Indiana Volunteers, made a pretty thorough reconnoisance upon the enemy's line, for the purpose of ascertaining his position in force in our front. In successfully effecting this purpose the regiment lost one man killed and some severely wounded. The occupation of Chattanooga, followed with the numerous vicissitudes and incidents, hardships, exposures and privations, and the final battles of Lookout Mountain and Mission Ridge, remain to be written. At Mission Ridge the 74th distinguished itself for gallantry, as will be seen hereafter.

Soon after this battle, November 28th, it left Chattanoogo with the entire 4th corps for Knoxville, and went into camp near that place, and remained there during the winter, assisting in guarding the town. In May, 1864, the regiment moved toward Atlanta, and encamped about sixty miles from there, near Kingston, Georgia. On the 17th it had an engagement with the enemy, losing five killed and forty-seven wounded. Among the wounded were Lieutenants Holland and Allen. It left Kingston a few days after and marched thirty miles nearer Atlanta, and went into camp near Dallas, Georgia, May 29th, at which time it again encountered the enemy, losing two killed and four wounded. From this date until June 5th, it was on the skirmish line nearly all the time, and lost five men killed and seven wounded. On the 15th of June the regiment took up the line of march again, this time encamping near Marietta, twenty miles from the much coveted city of Atlanta. It had lost in this campaign thus far, ninety-two killed and wounded. On the 27th of June it made a charge upon the rebel works and was repulsed with the loss of eleven killed and forty wounded.

Soon after the fall of Atlanta the regiment left Georgia for Chattanooga, where it remained until October 31st, when it moved toward Pulaski, Tennessee, which place was reached on the 12th of November. This march proved a very long and severe one; the regiment traveling over 140 miles through mud and rain. On the 25th it built breast-works, and on the 27th fell back across Duck River. On the 29th the division was suddenly ordered to march to Spring Hill. The brigade formed a line of battle, and the 74th and 89th were deployed as skirmishers, with a loss of one man killed and three wounded. The brigade to which the 74th belonged, guarded the rear in the march to Franklin. The enemy were very bold, and made a dash to come upon the train, but a little after noon, the Union troops, with the exception of fifteen or twenty wagons, were all in Franklin. About half-past three o'clock a shell from the enemy burst over our ranks about a mile from where the 74th lay. It was followed by others, and this seemed a signal for an assault along the whole line near them. The men were on their feet in an instant, and were ordered forward to the works.

Among the killed were Captains Stegner and Barker, and Buttolph, who died from his wounds there received. Lieut.-Colonel Kerr was wounded and taken prisoner. Although his wound was not at first thought to be severe, it proved mortal, and the regiment mourns a brave and efficient officer, one who knew no fear, who was ever ready for duty. In the absence of the Colonel, who was at that time sick in hospital, the regiment was put under the command of Captain Bryan.

In the early part of July it moved its camp to within six miles of Atlanta. It was engaged in frequent skirmishes with the enemy, and was employed a part of the time in building breast works On the 2d of August it lost one man killed in the skirmish. Early on the morning of the 25th it again changed camp and this time bivouacked within four miles of Atlanta. On the 1st of September it started on the Macon railroad, and at Battle Station, fourteen miles east of Atlanta, destroyed the track for six miles, and on the evening of the same day encountered the enemy. It captured a hospital and several prisoners, and lost ten or twelve missing. Captains Bryan and Hatch, unarmed, captured four rebels, one of whom carried a loaded rifle.

Colonel Jason Marsh was born at Woodstock, Vermont, March 4, 1808. His father, who was a substantial, industrious farmer, died when his son was ten years old. His mother at the ripe old age of ninety, was yet in the enjoyment of tolerable health, unimpared intellectual faculties, and a calm, placid, loving spirit; a noble specimen of the real woman of olden times.

His education was limited to what was acquired at the common school and academy in Vermont, prior to the age of sixteen. From that time until the year 1832 he was engaged in teaching school and studying the profession of law. In 1832 he was admitted to the bar at Adams, New York. He came to Rockford, Illinois, October, 1839, where he remained until he entered the army.

The military life of Colonel Marsh commenced with the organization of the 74th. At Camp Fuller he had command from August 9th, between which and September 4th, there were organized there four regiments, viz: the 74th, 92d, 95th and 96th. Colonel Marsh left Rockford with his regiment for active service on the 28th of September, 1862, and participated with it in all its skirmishes and battles until after the battle of Mission Ridge, at which time he was severely wounded. He remained in camp at Chattanooga until the 6th of December, when he left for home, in company with several wounded officers and privates of his regiment. Enjoying the benefits of good medical treatment, aided by his vigorous constitution, he rapidly recovered his health and rejoined his gallant regiment hoping to continue wlth them through the war. In this he was disappointed. In the fall of 1864 he resigned his position as Colonel of the regiment, owing to feeble health, and returned to his home.

Major Elis Casper was born in East Union, Wayne county, Ohio, March, 1824. He removed with his family to Chicago, Illinois, in

1851. Here he remained until 1854, when he left that city for Rockford, Illinois, which was his residence until he entered the army. In the fall of 1862, he, with Mr. James B. Kerr, enlisted a company for the war. At the organization of the 74th regiment, Illinois volunteer infantry, Mr. Casper was elected 1st Lieutenant, and the same day (September 4, 1862,) upon the election of Captain Kerr to Lieut.-Colonel, he was promoted to Captain of Company E. Soon after the regiment left Rockford, Capt. Casper was appointed Provost Marshall, and held that position until November, 1864, when he received the appointment of Paymaster. This office he filled with credit to himself and satisfaction to the government.

THE SEVENTY-FIFTH REGIMENT ILLINOIS VOLUNTEERS.

On the 2d of September, 1862, the 75th Regiment Illinois Volunteers was organized and mustered into service by Adjutant-General Fuller.

ORIGINAL ROSTER.

Colonel, George Ryan; Lieutenant-Colonel, John E. Bennett; Major, William M. Kilgour; Adjutant, Jerome W. Hollenbeck; Quartermaster, John E. Remington; Surgeon, George W. Phillips; 1st Assistant Surgeon, John C. Corbus; 2d Assistant Surgeon, Henry Utley; Chaplain, William H. Smith.

Co. A—Captain, James A. Watson; 1st Lieutenant, Ezekiel Giles; 2d Lieutenant, William Parker, jr.

Co. B—Captain, John Whallon; 1st Lieutenant, Albert M. Gillett; 2d Lieutenant, James Blean.

Co. C—Captain, Ernst Altman; 1st Lieutenant, George R. Shaw; 2d Lieutenant, Prentiss S. Bannister.

Co. D—Captain, Andrew McMoore; 1st Lieutenant, Joseph E. Colby; 2d Lieutenant, Edward H. Barlow.

Co. E—Captain, William S. Frost; 1st Lieutenant, Franklin H. Eels; 2d Lieutenant, James H. Blodgett.

Co. F—Captain, Addison S. Vorrey; 1st Lieutenant, James Tourtillott; 2d Lieutenant, Dennis Hannifin.

Co. G—Captain, Joseph Williams; 1st Lieutenant, David Sanford; 2d Lieutenant, Robert L. Irvine.

Co. H—Captain, John G. Price; 1st Lieutenant, Joseph W. R. Stanbaugh; 2d Lieutenant, Abner R. Hurless.

Co. I—Captain, Robert Hale; 1st Lieutenant, Joel A. Fife; 2d Lieutenant, Ezekiel Kilgour.

Co. K—Captain, David M. Roberts; 1st Lieutenant, William H. Thompson; 2d Lieutenant, Isaac L. Hunt.

Having received its outfit of clothing and arms, the regiment left Camp Dixon September 27th, to report at Louisville, Ky. Arrived at Jeffersonville the 29th, crossed the Ohio the next evening in company with the 74th regiment Illinois Volunteers, preparatory to the forward movement the next morning (October 21st) under Gen. Buell. It was their fate to be thrown into the action of Perryville late in the afternoon of the ever memorable 8th of October, only eleven days from home. The arms had been distributed to the regiment only the evening before leaving Camp Dixon, and the men had never been drilled in their use, and several were found in the ranks who had never loaded and fired a gun, until that hour, in the presence of the foe! Colonel George Ryan, the commander of the regiment, having been ordered under arrest, the command devolved upon Colonel Bennett, who, with Major Kilgour, who had seen service in the 13th regiment Illinois Volunteers, and Captain Hale, of Co. I, of the old 12th regiment Illinois Volunteers, led them promptly and gallantly into action!

Just previous to the movement the 74th Illinois, Colonel Marsh, was ordered to another part of the field. In the absence of Colonel Post, of the 59th Illinois, Brigade commander, that duty fell upon Colonel Gooding, of the 22d Indiana. In the midst of the action he fell into the hands of the enemy a prisoner, which left the command to Colonel Bennett. These explanations and facts are justly due to all parties in this connection, as they throw some light upon the results of that terrible scene. The 75th regiment left forty-three dead on the field, nine mortally wounded, one hundred and fifty disabled and twelve prisoners.

Here was a regiment entering a fight for the first time, deployed under a galling fire, exposed front and flank to a force largely outnumbering its own, and yet persistently maintaining its ground for an hour and a half! Veterans could do no more! Said a prisone of the enemy who fought opposite, "We would have whipped you had it not been for them *regulars*,"—meaning the 75th in their comparatively new suits of blue. That experienced officers might have acted differently in that trying hour, should cast no blame upon those whose duty it was to maintain the conflict at that point. The blame, if any, rests upon whoever allowed them to remain unsupported in that exposed condition for that hour and a half of carnage. Such was the undaunted courage of the men that they could not be persuaded to fall back, until the orders had been several times repeated.

Major (now Lieut.-Col.) Kilgour was severely wounded and removed from the field, as were three Captains and four Lieutenants, and two, viz., Lieut. Blean, of B, and Lieut. Eels, of E, were killed. The regiment lost heavily and its dead sleep in graves of heroes!

Colonel Ryan, a surgeon by profession, did efficient service in caring for the wounded during and after the fight. The next day at the personal solicitation of Colonel Bennett, his sword was restored to him and with it the command of the regiment. He was subsequently tried by court martial for his alleged offense, and *honorably acquitted!* The service proving too severe for his health he resigned in consequence, and December 20, 1862, Colonel Bennett succeeded to the command of the regiment.

But the regiment was now reduced to about half its numbers by disease and battle. More than a hundred were sent to the hospital from Camp Edgefield, opposite Nashville, Tenn., within a week of the termination of the march from Crab Orchard, Ky., via Danville and Bowling Green to that place, of whom the larger part never returned to permanent duty in the regiment.

In the reorganization of the army of the Ohio under General Rosecrans, the old 30th brigade, consisting of the 22d Indiana, 74th, 75th and 59th Illinois (old 8th Missouri) and the 5th Wisconsin battery, Captain Pinney, was assigned to be the 1st Brigade of the 1st Division of the right wing under Major-General McD. McCook, with Brig.-Gen. J. C. Davis as division, and Colonel P. Sidney Post as brigade commanders, which organization was retained in the 20th Army Corps from after the battle of Stone River until after the battle of Chickamauga.

In the skirmish and battles of Nolansville, Knob Gap, and Stone River the regiment displayed that efficiency which Colonel Bennett's thorough discipline had given it. Forced steadily back with the right wing all that terrible Wednesday morning of the closing hours of 1862, it rallied under his supervision for the closing up of the new battle-line, and was ready to hurl its remaining strength upon the exasperated foe the Friday following. Recovering its full tone of health and spirits after this depressing campaign, its noble deeds have written its name among the foremost on the scout or march, or in the hour of conflict. We find the regiment next at Liberty Gap, June 25, 1863, and following across the Tennessee over the mountains to Chickamauga, on the 20th of September along the valley road to Chattanooga, and to the front lines on the 22d. Thence across the river, over Waldron's Ridge, recrossing the Tennessee and in camp at Whitesides, ready to lead the charge on "Lookout" under Hooker November 24th, pressing on to Rossville, over Mission Ridge to Ringgold, thence back to camp for a respite, after burying the neglected dead of bloody Chickamauga. Assigned position as a part of 3d Brigade, 1st Division, 4th Army Corps, marched to Camp Blue Springs, Tenn., by February 1, 1864, sharing the reconnoissance in force to Buzzard's Roost, in Rocky Face Valley near Dalton on the 24th and 25th of the same month; returning to camp to await the final "on to Atlanta" under Sherman commencing May 1, 1864, sealing with their best blood their bright record on the fields of Dalton, Resaca, Marietta and Atlanta, where Colonel Bennett and the remnant of the gallant 75th Illinois waited orders to move with the resistless legions of Sherman through the strongholds of the rebellion.

Col. John E. Bennett was born in the town of Bethany, Genesee county, New York, March 18, 1833. During his earlier years he spent his time in the common school of his neighborhood. At the age of thirteen he was sent to the Genesee Wesleyan Seminary, located in Lima, Livingston county, New York, where he remained three sessions.

At the age of sixteen he commenced teaching school. The health of his father failing at this time, he was put in charge of his business, which he continued to manage with uncommon ability for one so young in years, until he was twenty-one years old. In addition, during the winter months he was engaged in teaching school.

In the spring of 1854, he received an invitation from Mr. E. J. Baldwin, a merchant of Cleveland, Ohio, to become his cashier and book-keeper. This situation he accepted, and remained with him about a year and a half. Wishing to engage in business on his own responsibility, he made a tour westward, seeking a suitable locality for that purpose. Through the instrumentality of Wm. H. Van Epps, Esq., a prominent merchant and citizen of Dixon, Lee county, Illinois, he located in Morrison, Whiteside county, Illinois, then only an embryo town, consisting of one house and a few railroad shanties, now the county seat of that county. During his residence in Morrison, he was engaged in business as a merchant, and the proprietor of the Bennett House. He made several trips across the plains to the Pacific coast; in the meantime, however, retaining his business in Morrison.

In politics he was a Democrat of the Jefferson, Jackson and Douglas school. When it became evident that military measures must be taken to crush this rebellion, his patriotism would not permit of his remaining an idle spectator of the scenes about to transpire. He was among the first to advocate the enlistment of troops and a vigorous prosecution of the war. He immediately set to work arranging his affairs so that he might become an active participant in the bloody strife. He applied to Adjutant-General Fuller for permission to raise a company. On the 29th of July, 1862, the permission came, and August 5, 1862, he had enlisted a company of one hundred and eighteen men. He was unanimously elected captain, and went with his company to Dixon, being the first company in rendezvous at that camp.

At the organization of the 75th regiment, Col. Bennett was elected Lieutenant-Colonel. On the resignation of Col. Ryan, December 20, 1862, Col. Bennett succeeded him in command of the regiment. In the battle of Perryville Col. Bennett's horse was shot, but he kept his post to the last. He was never absent from the regiment, save a few days sickness while at Valley Head, and ever shared with it all its duties, greatly endearing himself to his command. The record of his personal service with the 75th Illinois volunteers is upon nearly every battle-field of the department of the Cumberland.

THE TWENTY-SIXTH ILLINOIS VOLUNTEERS.

The following is the original roster of the regiment:

Colonel, John M. Loomis; Lieutenant-Colonel, Charles J. Tinkham; Major, Robert A. Gilmore; Adjutant, Samuel A. Buckmaster, jr.; Quartermaster, Charles A. Nazra; Surgeon, Morse K. Taylor; 1st Assistant Surgeon, Ezra A. Steele; 2d Assistant Surgeon, Charles Woodard; Chaplain, Andrew B. Morrison.

Co. A—Captain, John J. Funkhouser; 1st Lieutenant, Sidney A. Newcomb; 2d Lieutenant, David P. Murphy.

Co. B—Captain, James P. Davis; 1st Lieutenant, George H. Reed; 2d Lieutenant, William Polk.

Co. C—Captain, George U. Keener; 1st Lieutenant, Thomas L. Vest; 2d Lieutenant, James A. Dugger.

Co. D—Captain, John B. Harris; 1st Lieutenant, William W. Foutch; 2d Lieutenant, George W. Kerlin.

Co. E—Captain, Amos F. Jaquis; 1st Lieutenant, Azro C. Putnam; 2d Lieutenant, John S. Lathrop.

Co. F—Captain, Charles J. Tinkham; 1st Lieutenant, George H. Knapp; 2d Lieutenant, Samuel M. Custer.

Co. G—Captain, Thaddeus S. Updegraff; 1st Lieutenant, Bernard Flynn; 2d Lieutenant, Joseph C. Baldwin.

Co. H—Captain, Andrew B. Morrison; 1st Lieutenant, Washington W. Woollard; 2d Lieutenant, Charles F. Wertz.

Co. I—Captain, Washington C. Cassell; 1st Lieutenant, John Archer; 2d Lieutenant, John W. Kelly.

Co. K—Captain, Ira J. Bloomfield; 1st Lieutenant, Allen H. Dillon; 2d Lieutenan, John B. Bruner.

The Twenty-sixth Regiment was enlisted during the summer of 1861, from the counties of Effingham, Stevenson, Lasalle, McLean, Sangamon, Champaign, and one company at large, so that it represented every portion of Illinois. In August 1861, seven companies that were at that time organized, were hurried off to the defence of Quincy, which was then threatened with an attack from Price, Green and their followers. They had no arms, no clothes, no blankets, and went forth to meet the foe. The remaining three companies recruited under the most discouraging auspices, and only by the most strenuous personal exertions, did not join the command until January 1862, up to which time a dreary fall and winter was spent guarding the Hannibal and St. Joseph Railroad, fighting bushwhackers, and kindred occupations.

Finally, Major-General Halleck, after much solicitation, relieved it from this onerous task, and in February, 1862, the regiment, nine hundred and three men and officers, left St. Louis, Missouri, for the field of General Pope's operations. From that date, their career was one of the most active in service and of the most reputable kind.

New Madrid, Island No. Ten., Farmington, Siege of Corinth, Iuka, Corinth October 3d and 4th, Siege of Vicksburg, Jackson, Mississippi, Tunnel Hill and Chattanooga, these are the names which by special order of General Grant, illumine their banners and tell their story more eloquently than tongue or pen. A writer in one of the local papers thus speaks of the Twenty-sixth:

"The characteristic of the regiment is not dash—it is not the *elan* of the Zouave, nor the fiery enthusiasm which sometimes answers as well as a more sterling and enduring courage, but it is an intrepidity, cool, disciplined and tenacious. It was this quality which held them nine long days in the trenches at Tiptonville, in mud and water in midwinter, exposed to rebel sharpshooters, and themselves unable to return a shot; it was this that held them nine *longer hours* under the converging fire of eighteen heavy Napoleon and Parrott guns, and musketry and sharpshooters innumerable, at Tunnel Hill, until Sherman, the war-worn 'regular,' with all his West Point predilections thick upon him, declared they were worthy to fight with his old Thirteenth; and it was this that led them, toil-worn and battle-scarred, barefooted and ragged from the unprecedented march to the relief of Burnside, to take the initiative in their corps in the work of re-enlisting—spreading such a wild fire of enthusiasm, that in one entire division (General Ewing's) there were not more than fifty men eligible for the veteran service who did not re-enlist, and of these fifty, a large majority entered the Invalid Corps."

Colonel John Mason Loomis was born in Windsor, Connecticut. At the early age of eighteen, he was elected captain of the company of militia which held their annual "trainings" in his native place, so that he took with him into the field no mean military reputation. He was captain of a clipper in the East India trade, and coming West in one of the intervals of his occupation, he decided to locate in Milwaukee, and in 1844 he entered into the lumber business in that city.

He removed to Chicago in 1853, and was soon at the head of one of the largest lumber firms in the Northwest. His connection with the old "Light Guard" was but the preparation for the sterner drama in which he bore such a glorious part, and the remaining members of the "Guard" could not but recognize the glory he shed upon the old company.

In speaking of this gallant officer, the Chicago *Tribune* says:

"The same rigidity of discipline, the same enthusiastic devotion to everything which becomes his duty, no matter how trifling the detail, how exacting the observance, which marked him as a train band captain, but when in the army, infused with a living, earnest patriotism, and combined with an almost paternal care and interest in his men, a personal bravery which knows no fear, a coolness and fertility of resource in danger and emergency, characterized him as one of our most successful brigade commanders."

Col. Loomis has greatly distinguished himself in subsequent engagements, not now to be described in detail. His bravery as a soldier, and his skill as a commander, have been fully demonstrated.

SIXTIETH REGIMENT ILLINOIS VOLUNTEERS.

The following is the roster of the regiment:

Colonel, Silas C. Toler; Lieutenant-Colonel, Wm. B. Anderson; Major, Samuel Hess; Adjutant, Thomas G. Barnes; Quartermaster, Cloyd Crouch; Surgeon, Joseph T. Miller; 1st Assistant Surgeon, Ford S. Doods; 2d Assistant Surgeon, John A. Sheriff; Chaplain, Levi S. Walker.

Co. A—Captain, Francis M. Davidson; 1st Lieutenant, Wm. E. Short; 2d Lieutenant, Jerome M. Ingram.

Co. B—Captain, James H. McDonald; 1st Lieutenant, Isaac S. Boswell; 2d Lieutenant, DeWitt Anderson.

Co. C—Captain, John R. Moss; 1st Lieutenant, Thomas J. Rhodes; 2d Lieutenant, Mark Hailes.

Co. D—Captain, Alfred Davis; 1st Lieutenant, Edmund D. Choisser; 2d Lieutenant, James Stull.

Co. E—Captain, Geo. W. Evans; 1st Lieutenant, Hamilton Wiggs; 2d Lieutenant, Wm. Baker.

Co. F—Captain, William May; 1st Lieutenant, Gallatin A. Wood; 2d Lieutenant, Robert B. Stinson.

Co. G—Captain, Andrew J. Alden; 1st Lieutenant, Jehu J. Maxey; 2d Lieutenant, Wm. H. Campbell.

Co. H—Captain, David Ragains; 1st Lieutenant, Joseph F. McKee; 2d Lieutenant, John S. Cochennour.

Co. I—Captain, John Frizell; 1st Lieutenant, John Gibson; 2d Lieutenant, E. W. Hulbert.

Co. K—Captain, Wm. C. Goddard; 1st Lieutenant, James M. Benson; 2d Lieutenant, Wm. E. Goddard.

It was mustered into service on the 17th day of February, 1862, by Captain Watson, at Camp Dubois, Anna, Illinois, and numbered eight hundred and ninety-four men, rank and file.

On the 24th day of February, 1862, it left camp under orders to report to Brigadier-General E. A. Paine, at Cairo, Ill., where it remained until the 14th day of March, when it was ordered by Brigadier-General Strong to move to Island No. 10, and on its arrival there it received orders to report at Columbus, Ky. It remained at Columbus seven days, when orders came to move to Hickman, Ky., and after a stay of five days there it was ordered to return to Cairo, where it remained until the 6th of May, doing garrison and heavy fatigue duty, (except Companies E and K, which were on detached service at Bird's Point and Mound City.) On the 6th of May the eight companies in garrison at Cairo were ordered by General Strong, commanding post, to report to Colonel Noble, at Paducah, Ky., and on the day following the other two companies were ordered to report to the regiment at Paducah, Ky. On the 9th of May, by order of Brig.-Gen. Strong, the regiment went on board the steamer Gladiator to report to Major-General Halleck, at Hamburg Landing, Tenn., which it did on the 12th of May, and was assigned to General Paine's command, 1st division, 2d brigade, Army of the Mississippi. The brigade was composed of the following regiments, 10th, 16th and 60th Illinois, 10th and 14th Michigan regiments, and Captain Houghtaling's battery, Gen. James D. Morgan, brigade commander.

On the 19th of May, at Farmington, Missouri, this regiment was detached from the brigade to support Captain Pile's battery, where it remained until the evacuation of Corinth, Miss., when it rejoined the brigade, and went in pursuit of the enemy, following them five miles south of Booneville, Miss., when the chase was given up and they returned to Booneville. Remained there a few days, then broke up camp and moved within five miles of Corinth, and went into camp at Big Springs, Miss., where it remained until the 21st of July, when it marched for Tuscumbia, Ala., a distance of seventy-five miles, through a beautiful country, arriving at the latter place on the 26th. It there went into camp and remained until the 28th of August, when under command of Brigadier-General James D. Morgan, the entire brigade crossed the Tennessee river and bivouacked in the woods near Florence, Ala.

On the morning of Sept. 2d, they repacked their knapsacks, and took up their line of march for Nashville, Tenn., by way of Athens, Ala., and arrived at Nashville on the 12th of September, having marched a distance of 175 miles, averaging 27 miles per day, and suffering greatly from the scarcity of water. The last 100 miles they were constantly menaced by rebel cavalry and guerrillas; and, although fired upon at different places along the road, they met with no serious loss. They encamped in the city of Nashville, and assisted in garrisoning the city, frequently scouting through the country, having several skirmishes with the enemy, in which they always proved victorious.

On the morning of Nov. 5, 1862, the rebel Gen. Morgan, with a cavalry force of 3,800 men, made a dash on Edgefield, Tenn., but was quickly repulsed by the 16th and 60th Illinois regiments, then stationed at that place. In the early part of November, the 1st division, army of the Mississippi, to which the regiment belonged, was transferred to the army of the Cumberland, and on the 12th of that month they moved to Stone River, Tenn. On the 29th, the regiment, with the 10th Michigan, went on a three days' scout, and returned to camp with fourteen prisoners. On the 12th of December it went back to Nashville.

On the 5th of January, 1863, it was sent to Stone River, as escort to a large ammunition train for the army of the Cumberland. When eight miles from Nashville, the train was furiously attacked by a rebel force under Wheeler, consisting of two brigades of cavalry and six pieces of artillery. A lively skirmish ensued, resulting in the defeat of the enemy, who retreated in double quick, leaving several of their dead. They captured two officers and twelve privates, and lost but one man wounded.

On January 13th, the regiment was sent after a body of rebel cavalry, to prevent their burning the transports on the shoals below

Nashville. It was out three days, marching a distance of sixty-five miles, and capturing thirteen prisoners. They were transferred to the Reserve Army Corps Department of the Cumberland, and engaged in doing garrison duty in the city of Nashville until June 20, 1863.

The 60th took an active part in the battle of Chattanooga, November 25th and 26th. It was in the advance upon Chickamauga, and pursued the enemy to Ringold, continually skirmishing with them until they reached the latter place. They accompanied the grand army of General Sherman in the terrible march to Knoxville preparatory to the raising the siege of that place.

Col. William B. Anderson was born in Jefferson county, Illinois, April 2, 1730. His father, Stinson H. Anderson, served in the State Legislature, was Lieutenant-Governor under Governor Carlin, and also State Marshall during Polk's administration. He served as a private in the Blackhawk war, and was commissioned captain of dragoons by Jackson during the Florida war. His early education was unfortunately neglected. He studied law a short time with Judge Walter B. Scates, who was then a member of the Supreme bench of Illinois. He served as county surveyor for Jefferson county for four years, and soon after was elected member of the State Legislature, and served during the session of 1856–'57, and being re-elected, served again during the next session of 1858–'59. In 1860 he was appointed alternate elector on the Douglas ticket, and here ended his political life.

Upon the commencement of the present war, he entered the service of his country. He raised a company of recruits from his native county, and, with the required number, hastening to the place of rendezvous of the 60th Illinois regiment, Camp Dubois, Anna, Illinois, his company was assigned a place in this regiment, and Mr. Anderson mustered into the service as Lieutenant-Colonel on the 17th of February. He served in that capacity until March 2, 1863, when he was promoted and took his place as Colonel of the regiment.

SEVENTY-THIRD REGIMENT ILLINOIS VOLUNTEERS

The 73d regiment Illinois volunteers was raised from the State at large, and was the first of the new organizations under the call for

300,000, in the year 1862. It was organized at Camp Butler, Ill., and mustered into the United States service for three years or during the war, August 21, 1862, under the following officers, viz.:

Colonel, James F. Jaquess; Lieutenant-Colonel, Benjamin F. Northcutt; Major, William A. Presson; Adjutant, Richard R. Randall; Quartermaster, James W. Slavens; Surgeon, George O. Pond; 1st Assistant Surgeon, Robert E. Stevenson; 2d Assistant Surgeon, Kendall E. Rich; Chaplain, John S. Barger.

Co. A—Captain, William E. Smith; 1st Lieutenant, Edward W. Bennett; 2d Lieutenant, Thomas G. Underwood.

Co. B—Captain, Wilder B. M. Colt; 1st Lieutenant, Harvey Pratt; 2d Lieutenant, Samuel W. McCormack.

Co. C—Captain, Peterson McNabb; 1st Lieutenant, Mark D. Haws; 2d Lieutenant, Richard N. Davis.

Co. D—Captain, Thomas Motherspaw; 1st Lieutenant, Jonas Jones; 2d Lieutenant, Reuben B. Winchester.

Co. E—Captain, Wilson Burroughs; 1st Lieutenant, Charles Tilton; 2d Lieutenant, David Blosser.

Co. F—Captain, George Montgomery; 1st Lieutenant, William Barrick; 2d Lieutenant, Edwin Allsop.

Co. G—Captain, John Sutton; 1st Lieutenant, James F. Bowen; 2d Lieutenant, Uriah Warrington.

Co. H—Captain, James J. Davidson; 1st Lieutenant, Samson Purcell; 2d Lieutenant, Clement S. Shinn.

Co. I—Captain, Peter Wallace; 1st Lieutenant, John L. Barger; 2d Lieutenant, James M. Turpin.

Co. K—Captain, Reuben W. Laughlin; 1st Lieutenant, James Lancaster; 2d Lieutenant, ——— ———.

The regiment thus organized left for Louisville, Ky., on the morning of August 26th, and reached its destination at noon on the following day, and went into its first camp near the Louisville and Nashville depot, called Camp Jaquess, in honor of the Colonel.

It remained in this camp a few days, when it was removed to a new camp—"Dick Yates"—near the Lexington turnpike, eight miles east of Louisville, and was temporarily brigaded with the 79th and 88th Indiana regiments and the 100th Illinois, Gen. Kirk in command. The 73d, however, was soon detached and sent to Cincinnati when that city was threatened by Bragg's army, where it reported for duty on the morning of the 13th September; was ordered to Louisville again, to meet Bragg at that point, and was brigaded with the

2d Missouri, 15th Missouri and 44th Illinois, commanded by Col. Schaefer of the 2d Missouri.

With this brigade the 73d started on the famous march in pursuit of Bragg and his retreating forces. During this campaign the troops engaged in it did severe marching, both by day and night, and many of the new soldiers were unequal to the fatigue. The 73d being composed principally of men innured to toil, stood the test as well as any of their compatriots. Early on the morning of October 12th—one of the most beautiful of Indian Summer days—the firing of musketry near Perryville, Kentucky, indicated an enemy at hand, and by noon the left was in the heat of battle. The right, under Sheridan, was placed in position to await the attack of the rebels. The 35th brigade stood awaiting the shock with the 73d Illinois, and the 15th was in front, supported by the 44th Illinois and 2d Missouri in the rear.

During the interval, while the enemy was approaching, the following disposition was made of the 73d Illinois: Every man was ordered to lie down and conceal himself as perfectly as possible. The position was a good one, on the top of a ridge overlooking an open field over which the enemy must pass. The colors were rolled up and the men ordered to lie upon the ground, to which they consented most unwillingly. The Colonel ordered them to protect themselves and obey orders and he would protect their reputation. "The enemy is approaching," continued the Colonel, "wait till I give you the order to fire. Be calm and deliberate and waste no ammunition; remember that one load in your gun is worth ten in the air. Load quick and fire slow, and be sure and bring a rebel every shot. It is said one wounded man is worth two dead ones on the battle field. I have not so learned war. *War means killing;* therefore let every shot be well directed—aim at the head or the heart and make sure work of it. *Ready! aim! fire!!*" For one hour and thirty minutes did this band of brave young soldiers face the enemy. "The ground in front of the regiment was strewn with the dead," said a wounded officer belonging to a Mississippi regiment—left on the field and captured. "What regiment was that we met just there?" pointing to where the 73d had fought; and being told it was the 73d Illinois, said he, "Every shot you fired seemed to take a man in the head or heart.'

"During this fight we fired no less than forty rounds, and some fired as many as sixty. The men were instructed to lay their extra supply of ammunition on the ground by them, and there was no time lost in using it. The fire from the enemy was terrible, but so well protected was the 73d that only one man was killed, and he was struck in the head while in the act of rising up to shoot."

From Perryville to Murfreesboro, and then into the terrible conflict of Stone River passed the 73d. It was in Sheridan's division and met the shock of the foe. Already was Sheridan winning the laurels which were to brighten in the Valley of the Shenandoah. Says the correspondent from whom we have quoted above: "The brigade, of which the 73d was part, occupied the right of Sheridan's division, and the 73d was on the extreme right of the brigade, and at one time was attacked by overwhelming numbers on the right flank, and changing front in that direction and in a grand charge repulsed the enemy, which gave them their first check. These facts can be substantiated."

After long marches, weary days and nights of picket and guard duty, foraging and skirmishing, the 73d appears on the bloody field of Chickamauga. It was now in the 2d brigade, 3d division, 20th army corps, Sheridan division commander, and McCook corps commander. "The brigade, composed of the same regiments as before, 2d and 15th Missouri, 44th and 73d Illinois, commanded by Colonel Leibold, of the 2d Missouri. At an early hour on the morning of the 20th of September, the brigade was in line of battle, in column of regiments, the 73d Illinois in front. The brigade was held as reserve when it became apparent that the troops on the right and left were being driven back, and that already there was a breach in the line of battle, the 2d brigade was ordered to advance and check the enemy in that direction. The charge was made, but it proved a slaughter pen. Major Smith and Adjutant Wingett were killed instantly, Lieut.-Col. Davidson was wounded, and Colonel Jaquess' horse was struck four times, and he was the only field officer left, and almost the only officer in the regiment. The regiment went into this fight three hundred and eight strong, and numbered next day, of those who had escaped death or wounding, *less than one hundred.*

It also participated brilliantly in the battles of Mission Ridge and Lookout Mountain with credit to its former reputation. It formed part of the 1st brigade, 2d division, 4th army corps. In the charge up Mission Ridge the 73d was in the advance. Said General Sheridan, as the grand charge was commenced, "Go in 73d, you will do your duty, I know!" and most bravely did every officer and man in the regiment execute the command. They captured more prisoners than there were men in the regiment in the three successive charges they made assaulting the enemies' works."

Says our correspondent: "When the 73d Illinois appeared in the field it was called the 'Preachers' Regiment,' its Colonel and several of the officers being ministers, and the question was asked, 'Will such men fight? Can the soldiers be relied on, and will they fight under such commanders?' The world has yet to learn that the Christian hero is God's nobleman, and that the Christian soldier knows no fear. 'Will the preacher regiment fight?' has inquired more than one. Go to the records of Perryville, Ky., Stone River, Tenn., Chickamauga, Ga., and Mission Ridge, above the clouds, and they will tell you."

Colonel James F. Jaquess, of the 73d regiment Illinois volunteer infantry, was born in the state of Indiana, November 18, 1819. He is a graduate of the Indiana Asbury University, from which institution he has received the degrees of A. B., A. M. and D. D. After his graduation he entered upon the study of law, and applied himself closely for two years, during which time he completed the course of study prescribed in Transylvania University, Lexington, Ky., and when about to enter the institution with a view to graduation, he was licensed to preach in the Methodist Episcopal Church. In 1848 he was elected President of the Illinois Female College, at Jacksonville, Ill., and served in that position for seven years. His popularity with the students and friends and patrons of the college was unbounded, and he did much for female education.

His next position of labor was that of President of Quincy College, a regularly chartered institution, located at Quincy, Illinois.

Colonel Jaquess' connection with the army is the result of most earnest solicitation on the part of those prominent in military affairs. His influence among the masses was such as would enable him to render efficient service in the cause. He entered upon the work of recruiting a regiment on the 1st of July, and reported at Camp Butler 1st of August, with a full regiment, and was soon on his way to the field.

When it was known that he was about to enter the army a lady inquired of Governor Yates as to the truth of the rumor, and being informed that such was certainly the case, said she, "Do you think Mr. Jaquess will make a colonel?" The Governor replied: "The best colonel in the United States." Without claiming all that, it is safe to say there have been few better ones.

In addition to leading his gallant regiment in the thickest of many a hard-fought fight, Colonel Jaquess has rendered the government important service not now to be made public. But one episode demands publication, and the more so as it has been given to the public in another form. It was no less than a visit to Jefferson Davis, and a conversation with him in the rebel executive chamber—a journey undertaken from a strong sense of religious duty. The appended account appeared in a weekly newspaper, and the author witnessed its "taking down:"

"A rap at the door of our *sanctum!* Enter—a tall, somewhat slim and altogether impressive form in the uniform of a Union colonel.

"Few men carry more character in their faces than Colonel Jaquess. With classic forehead, large blue eyes, so deep that, as Emerson says, 'one may fall into them,' hair, and neatly trimmed beard, both wearing

"'The silver livery of advised age,'

firm, conscientious and dauntless—he is just the man to hurl his gauntlet at danger—fight his way into, or become a self-appointed embassador at Richmond. Reluctantly he told us his story.

"The incidents of the ride to the city and the formalities which resulted in an interview between Colonel Jaquess, Mr. Gilmore, President Davis and Mr. Benjamin are already recorded by Mr. Gilmore. Colonel Jaquess states that he did not share Mr. Gilmore's fears respecting the important question of a safe deliverance from the rebel capital.

"The evening of the 18th finds the four persons above mentioned seated in a room in the Confederate State Department. After the formal introduction, it was fully agreed upon that in the discussion which was about to follow no personal offense was to be taken, even though it became necessary to employ plain language—and Colonel Jaquess says that he accepted the temporary *status* of affairs, and studiously and politely employed the terms 'Mr. President' and 'Confederacy.' Mr. Benjaman's first and most persistent effort was to secure an admission that the embassy was *official*, and after laboring thus in vain for thirty minutes, he then attempted to brow-beat the Colonel by employing the term 'spy,' and allusions to the ordinary fate of such. These tactics failing, Colonel Jaquess had an opportunity to open a long, serious and exceedingly plain conversation with Mr. Davis, carefully selecting such points as in themselves gave least room for controversy. He emphasized the statement that he was present only in his individual capacity, since he believed that neither of the contending powers would accept commissioners from the other and thus settle existing difficulties, and that negotiation would only end in wrangling, with the more desperate alienation, unless certain points could be previously adjusted by an *unofficial* delegation as a basis for further official discussion. The Colonel therefore remarked, 'Mr. President, I came on my own responsibility to prepare the way, and I hope that we, as Christian gentlemen, may succeed in discussing the question fully, freely and frankly. I have long believed that our troubles were necessary to teach a threefold lesson:

"'1. That the North might believe that the terms 'secession,' 'separation,' and 'independence,' when employed by Southerners, *meant something!*' (At this, the President was manifestly pleased)—

"'2. That the South should learn that one Southerner can *not* whip five Yankees —and

"'3. That foreign nations might learn that the *United* States can never be defeated or insulted with impunity.'

"Mr. Davis then remarked with a degree of satisfaction that 'the South had done its own fighting without foreign aid or sympathy.' Colonel Jaquess replied, with a commendable desire to assure Mr. Davis that the South would not lack further opportunities for display of valor, that 'we in the North have but one sentiment; viz., that of a vigorous prosecution of the war, and that no man could be elected President upon any other platform. We regard you as the aggressor, and if one party must lose its life, we feel not only at liberty, but under obligations, to take yours. We have a 'peace party,' but you cannot afford to trust it, for our masses are against you; and, Mr. Davis, you mistake the spirit of our people. We respect and love you, and in case of the sudden termination of the war, millions of Northern money would flow south to relieve your destitute and suffering. Indeed, we would sustain our President should he in such a case issue his proclamation of universal amnesty.'

"Mr. Davis, with the evident expectation of shaming this speech, replied, 'You have poorly manifested your "*love*" in your conduct of the war.'

"Replied the Colonel promptly, 'Oh, we are *not just now making friends—we are fighting rebellion!*'

"Mr. Davis asserted that he foresaw this struggle, this bloodshed, etc., and while in Congress, strove to avert it. 'Before God,' said he, 'I have not a drop of this blood on my skirts!' The Colonel says he barely escaped the impulse of replying that 'this would be a dangerous appeal to carry before God.' Davis then proceeded with a long description of 'state-rights,' etc., alluding to the Declaration of American Independence and its initial principle that the right to govern depends upon the consent of the governed—and added, 'if we of the South talk of peace and continued union, we will thereby confess that we have blundered in beginning this war.' Colonel Jaquess thinks that Mr. Davis' harangue would compare favorably with the prevailing style of copperhead speeches in the North, and would be fully endorsed by the late peace party.

"The next effort of our worthy Colonel was to change the drift of the conversation and to obtain the rebel *ultimatum.* Mr. Davis asserted that the Southern people have a deep-seated hatred of the Northerners. The Northern reply was, simply, 'I have failed to discover it,' and, the Colonel added, 'we are told that were an armistice for ninety days agreed upon, our people could not be induced to resume hostilities.' 'Oh,' said Mr. D., 'I am in favor of an armistice if you will admit our independence—for we are bound to have separation or annihilation!'

"'Then, Mr. Davis, *you will obtain annihilation*, for our people are determined you shall not establish the doctrine of secession.

"'Would you come back into the Union as a confederacy if we would give constitutional guarantees of your claims in the matter of slavery, etc.?'

"At this point, Mr. Benjamin, who had been writhing for a long time, blurted out with volcanic heat and impatience: 'If the throat of every slave in the confederacy were cut, we would have nothing but separation!' Mr. Davis assented, and reiterated his alternative of 'separation or annihilation,' and again received the emphatic consolation that he would, in that case, inevitably be accommodated with the coveted annihilation. Mr. Gilmore here asked how they would be satisfied with the plan of submitting the question to the people, and allowing them to vote for Mr. Davis as the secession and Mr. Lincoln as the Union candidate? 'Yes,' said the Colonel, 'let the majority decide.' The reply was, from Mr. Davis, with an attempt at severity, 'You can do that in your *consolidated* form, but I have no right to ask my people thus to vote,' and here followed that heretical, despotic, anti-republican sentiment from the arch-rebel—'*We have left you to rid ourselves of the despotism of majorities!*'

"The Colonel suggested to Mr. Davis that he had better not let the Southern people know this, and received the assurance that he was at liberty 'to proclaim it from every house-top,' from the improvement of which invitation the Colonel was 'prevented by *circumstances.*'

"Mr. Benjamin, in his account of the occasion, asserts, for effect, that at this point Mr. Davis wished to close the interview. Colonel J. positively contradicts the statement, and asserts that *he* was the first to indicate such a desire. *Three* times did the Colonel arise, and three times was he detained by a renewal of the conversation! Once Colonel J. asked Mr. D. if they would ever meet again. 'Oh, yes'—was the reply.

"*Col. J.*—My Northern friends say I look like 'Jeff. Davis.'

"*Mr. D.*—You ought not to consider it a compliment.

"*Col. J.*—I do not consider it a left-handed one, by any means.

"*Mr. D.*—Your resemblance to myself occurred to me when you entered the room.

"*Col. J.*—And I had the corresponding thought at the same time.

"Then followed a talk for twenty minutes about ancestry, etc., in which both parties forgot that they were enemies—at the conclusion of which, Colonel J., for the third time, arose, saying, 'When may I come again?' 'When you come to tell me that the North is willing to let us govern ourselves in our own way!' The Colonel extended his hand, which was warmly grasped by both of the President's—and thus closed this remarkable interview.

"We have read Mr. Gilmore's published accounts, and have heard his two subsequent lectures upon the same topic. And now, having talked three or four hours with Colonel Jaquess, we feel that the trip to Richmond was far from a mere romantic expedition, and that the accounts of Mr. Gilmore are far too flippant and superficial, while under the Colonel's grave recounting it rises to the dignity of a Providential mission. Certain it is that the effort of Mr. Benjamin, in his circular, to avert the consequences of the published statements—and his avowal of the designs and wishes, too, of the Southern leaders, went far, oh, *so* far, to gird up the loins of noble Northern freemen for the struggle in which God gave us victory on the 8th of last November."

BRIDGES' BATTERY—ILLINOIS LIGHT ARTILLERY,

Entered camp at Chicago, Illinois, June 21, 1861, as Company G, 19th Illinois Infantry—left Chicago June 12, 1861, with the following officers: Captain, Charles D. C. Williams, 1st Lieutenant, Lyman Bridges, 2d Lieutenant, Charles H. Rolland, and served as such with that regiment in Missouri under Gen. Fremont. Captain Williams having received an appointment in the marine service, and Lieutenant Roland having been appointed Captain in the 51st Illinois Infantry, Lieutenant Bridges was appointed Captain, and Sergeants Wm. Bishop and Morris D. Temple, were appointed Lieutenants in the company, and served in Kentucky, Tennessee and Alabama under Gen. Buell.

It formed a part of Gen. O. M. Mitchell's division in his advance upon Bowling Green, Kentucky, Nashville, Murfreesboro, Shelbyville, Tennessee, and Huntsville, Decatur, Tuscumbia, Alabama, in March and April, 1862. In June of that year, it marched to Chattanooga, Tennessee, as a part of Gen. Turchin's brigade of Gen. Negley's expedition. Returning to Huntsville, Alabama, it marched to Winchester, Tenn. The company was assigned to duty as provost guard, and Capt. Bridges Provost Marshal of the place.

It afterward marched over the Cumberland Mountains, through Point Rock Valley to Bridgeport, Alabama, and returned to Huntsville, Alabama, and was assigned to guard the railroad bridge at Mill Creek on the T. and A. Railroad, when, upon the retreat of Gen. Buell to Louisville, the company was left with the 19th Illinois Infantry as a part of the garrison of Nashville.

The command at that place having a small proportion of artillery, by command of Gen. Negley, commanding post, Capt. L. Bridges commanding the company, was ordered to take his company and fit up a light battery from some captured guns then in the Ordnance Department at Nashville, which was done, and the battery placed in position near the city hospital between the Franklin and G. White Pikes, as a part of the defence of the city. Capt. Bridges having been assigned to duty as Assistant Engineer to Capt. J. St. Clair Morton, Engineer Corps U. S. A., and Chief Engineer of the Department of the Ohio, meanwhile under the direction of Capt. Morton, placed in position nearly or quite all the heavy ordnance for the defence of the city.

Upon the siege being raised by the advance of Major-General Rosecrans, Capt. Bridges was sent to Gallatin with 1,100 pioneers to construct a fort, upon the completion of which, the battery was assigned to and placed in the fort at that place, remaining there in charge of Lieut. Campbell, until December 20th, when, by order of Major-General Rosecrans, the battery turned over the guns to a battery which had lost its guns at Hortonville, a short time previously, returned to Nashville, and drawing muskets, marched before Murfreesboro, and rejoined the 19th Illinois Infantry upon the battlefield on the night of January 2, 1863, remaining with and entering Murfreesboro with that regiment.

January 14, 1863, by order of the War Department, the company was permanently transferred to a battery of light artillery of six guns, and an entire new equipment secured at Nashville, Tenn., and Sergeants Lyman A. White and Franklin Seborn, were promoted to Lieutenants. On February 20th, marched to Murfreesboro, and was assigned to duty with the Pioneer Brigade Department of the Cumberland, marching with that command June 24th to Manchester and Elk River. In July following, Capt. Bridges having applied to have his battery assigned to a more active command, by order of Major-General Rosecrans, it was ordered to report to Major-General Thomas, and was assigned to duty with the 1st brigade, 2d division, 14th Army Corps, and crossed the Cumberland, Sand, and Lookout Mountains, and served through the battles of Dug Gap and Chicamauga with that command.

In the battles of September 19th and 20th at Chickamauga, the battery was warmly engaged each day, losing twenty-six men—six killed, sixteen wounded, and four captured—and forty-six horses.

Second Lieut. Wm. Bishop was killed at his guns on September 20th, while the battery was being charged by the enemy.

Upon the retirement of the army to Chattanooga after the above battles, the battery was placed in position at Fort Negley near the Rossville Pike, and remained in this position until the consolidation of the corps when, on October 12, 1863, it was assigned to the 3d division, 4th army corps, Brig.-Gen. T. J. Wood commanding, and placed in position at Fort Wood, in the northeast defences of Chattanooga, and Sergeant Wm. R. Bite was promoted to a 2d Lieutenantcy.

The battery remained in this position throwing an occasional shot into the enemy's lines daily, until November 23d, when our lines advanced toward Mission Ridge and drove the enemy from and held the Bald Knob, known as Orchard Knob, one and one third miles in advance of our fortified lines and midway between Chattanooga and Mission Ridge.

By order of Maj.-Gen. Granger the battery moved out and was placed in position during the following night upon Orchard Knob. The day following it drove the enemy's guns out of his line of works at the base of the Ridge, and was engaged at intervals. November 25th it was also engaged with the enemy, and by order of Maj.-Gen. Grant at 3 P. M. fired the signal of six guns for the grand charge upon Mission Ridge, the battery retaining its position to the close of the battle. November 28th, the battery received orders to prepare to march to Knoxville, Tenn., and marched with Brig.-Gen. Wood's division to Maryville, Knoxville, Strawberry Plains, Blain's Cross Roads, Clinch Mountains, Danbridge, Knoxville, Maryville, Rutledge, Morristown, etc., being upon a campaign the entire winter of 1863–4. In April, of 1864, it marched to Knoxville, London and

Cleveland, rejoining the corps at that place. On May 2, 1864, marched with Brig.-Gen. Wood's division and 3d division, 4th army corps, to join the grand army of the Middle Division of the Mississippi, under the command of Major-General W. T. Sherman, which was concentrated near Ringgold, Ga.

May 6th, the command marched to Tunnel Hill, Ga., and was engaged at Tunnel Hill and Buzzard Roost. Upon the enemy being driven out of Dalton, the battery marched to Resaca, Ga., and was placed in several positions in reserve during that engagement.

Upon the evacuation of Resaca it marched to Adairsville, where it was thrown into position and engaged the enemy's batteries upon the right of the town. From Adairsville it marched the following day,and May 16 and 18, 1864, shelled the enemy vigorously some two miles south of the town of Kingston, also in front of the town of Cassville. While the army was halted at Cassville a few days for rest and supplies, Captain Bridges was appointed Chief of Artillery of the corps. May 23, 1864, the battery marched in command of Lieut. Morris D. Temple to Enharle and Mount Hope Church, where it was warmly engaged with the enemy's lines and batteries for five days in succession, losing one man killed and several men wounded. June 5th it marched to Morris Hill Church near Ackworth, Ga., where Lieuts. Temple and Bite and all the non-veterans were mustered out of the service and left for Chicago, Illinois. The command of the battery devolved upon 1st Lieut. Lyman A. White. Sergeants C. E. Dodge and L. C. Lawrence received commissions as Lieutenants. The battery marched from Morris Hill Church to Pine Mountain June 10th, and Black Jack Hills June 14th. At each place it was engaged. June 17th it marched to Kenesaw Mountain, and was placed in several positions on the 4th army corps front, engaging the enemy and his batteries daily.

Lieut. F. Seborn was here mortally wounded while working his guns in an artillery duel with a rebel battery. July 3d, the enemy having abandoned his lines at Kenesaw Mountain, the battery marched to Marietta and Neil Dow Station with General Wood's division, and on July 5th marched with General Wood to the Chattahoochee River and engaged the enemy as he was crossing the River, compelling him to abandon his pontoons, and remained in position covering Pace's Ferry several days, until July 12th, when it marched to Powers' Ferry, crossing the Chattahoochee River with General Wood's command. July 16th, it marched to Buck Head and Peach Tree Creek and was warmly engaged with two rebel batteries, one of whom it silenced during the advance of General Wood's lines.

July 19th, it marched to the left of the corps with Gen. Wood's command, and by order of Maj.-Gen. Howard took position upon a knob one-half of a mile in advance of our lines supported by two regiments, and played upon the flank of a column of rebels marching to our right. July 22d, it was placed in position before and within one and one-half miles from the center of the city of Atlanta, and constructed works for the guns. The exact range having been obtained from actual survey, and the points of compass ascertained, the battery opened upon the enemy and city of Atlanta daily. The effect of each shot was observed from a signal station near the battery. July 30th, by the organization of the artillery brigade, 4th army corps, it reported to Captain Bridges, commanding the artillery brigade of the corps. August 25th, it marched with the artillery brigade to Procter's Creek, and on August 26th, to Mt. Gilead Church, and with Brig.-Gen. Wood's division to Rough and Ready, Jonesboro and Lovejoy's Station; at the latter place it was in action three days. On September 4th, it marched with the artillery brigade from Lovejoy's Station to Jonesboro, Rough and Ready and Atlanta, arriving at Atlanta on September 7th. In October, 1864, it marched with the 4th army corps, participated in the pursuit of General Hood's army to Rome, Ga., Galesville, Ala., Chattanooga, Tenn.; Huntsville and Athens, Ala.; and Pulaski, Tenn.; and in November, marched to Columbia, Spring Hill, Franklin and Nashville, being in action at each of the above places except Spring Hill, arriving at Nashville December 1, 1864.

December 21, 1864, the battery was assigned the letter B, 1st Ill. light artillery, and is now known as Battery B, 1st Ill. light artillery, Captain Bridges having been promoted to a Majority in that regiment. The following were the officers January 1, 1865:

Captain, Lyman A. White; 1st Lieutenant, Clark E. Dodge; Junior 1st Lieutenant, Samuel C. Lawrence; 2d Lieutenant, Alphonso W. Potter; Junior 2d Lieutenant, William Peterson.

CHAPTER XXIII.

The Vicksburg Campaign—Original Plan of General Grant's Movement—His Advance on Holly Springs—The Battle Near Coffeeville—Gallantry of Cols. Dickey and Lee's Cavalry—A Retrograde Movement—Col. Dickey's Expedition—His Escape from Van Dorn's Cavalry—Rebel Raids Upon Grant's Communications—The Disgraceful Surrender of Holly Springs—Repulse of the Rebels at Davis' Mills—Forrest's Raid on Humboldt and Trenton—The Battle of Parker's Cross Roads—Gallantry of the First Brigade—A Crisis in the Battle—Its Rescue by the Second Brigade—Gens. I. N. Haynie and Sullivan to the Rescue—The Rebels Defeated—Grant Falls Back to Holly Springs.

WE now approach the persistent and protracted siege of Vicksburg—a siege marked with bloody battles, glorious victories, great loss of life, and the accomplishment of the most valuable results, as it opened the Mississippi River from its source to the Gulf, and divided the armies of the rebels by an effectual barrier. The campaign against Vicksburg really commenced on the 28th of November, 1862, at which time the forces of General Grant were at Lagrange, three miles east of Grand Junction, on the Cairo and New Orleans Railroad, with garrisons at Columbus, Humboldt, Trenton and Jackson in Tennessee, and Bolivar and Corinth in Mississippi. These were known as the Army of West Tennessee. The rebel forces were at Coldwater and Holly Springs, about twenty miles distant.

Large reinforcements having arrived, and ample supplies having been received, General Hamilton's corps, on the 28th of November, moved in the direction of Holly Springs, which was occupied on the 30th. By the 18th of December, all of General Grant's forces had come up and were chiefly encamped at Lumpkins's Mills, north of Holly Springs and seven miles north of the Tallahatchie River. The rebels, under Van Dorn, at once commenced falling back to the river and our cavalry, under Cols. Dickey and Lee, followed them up, harassing their rear-guard. In the pursuit, an attempt was made by our forces to capture Coffeeville, which came near resulting in a serious disaster to our cavalry. The order of march was as follows: Col. Mizener, with the 3d brigade in the advance; Col. Lee, with the 1st brigade, in the center, and Col. Hatch, with the 2d brigade, at the rear. Subsequently, Col. Mizener took a road running parallel to the Coffeeville road, which brought him to the rear of Col. Lee's column when he reached it, thus giving Col. Lee the advance. In this order the column moved forward. When near the river, a large advance guard was sent forward and a company was deployed to right and left as skirmishers. The skirmishing became very heavy, and our forces being unable to move the enemy, Col. Lee brought a 10-pounder and put it into position. This had hardly been done before a full rebel battery opened upon him. While this cannonade was going on, the skirmishers had encountered a heavy force of the rebel infantry which rose from the ground where it had been concealed, and poured volley after volley into our skirmishers, who were obliged to retire after suffering severe loss.

Cols. Dickey and Lee soon found that their position was untenable, and that a retreat must be executed as speedily and as promptly as possible. The flanking parties and skirmishers were called in and two squadrons of the 4th Illinois cavalry, under Capt. Townsend, were left in the rear to delay the enemy's advance. But the movement had hardly commenced when the rear-guard followed, driven before the rebel infantry, who were charging forward in strong force. Two regiments advanced on our right, another on the center, while two more were marching on our left flank. Our forces opened a terrible fire upon them. For a moment they were held in check, when our troops slowly retired up a hill, halting every few rods to pour a volley into the rebel advance, now close upon our rear. At the crest of the hill, Hatch's force which had been in reserve, held their fire until the rebels were within twenty yards of them, and then rose and poured a terrible volley into them. Five times this volley was repeated and the rebels wavered and fell back; but receiving fresh accessions, again renewed the attack, and advanced upon our right and left flanks. To avoid being cut off, our forces fell back through some dense timber, slowly and stubbornly contesting every inch of ground. New lines were formed and fresh troops were brought up, but the rebels were equally fortunate in this respect, and constantly opposed new and fresh troops to ours. The danger of being flanked and cut off was still imminent, and a hasty retreat was ordered. For three miles this style of warfare was continued, when the enemy gave up the pursuit and our forces arrived at their camping grounds. The fight, while it lasted, was most obstinate, although the odds against our forces were nearly three to one. Both officers and men did nobly. Cols. Dickey, Lee and Mizener, Lieut.-Colonels Prince and McCullough, and Majors Coon, Rickards and Love were constantly exposed to a most galling fire and were everywhere in the fiercest of the strife. One of Col. Lee's best officers was killed and five of Col. Hatch's were wounded. Lieut.-Colonel McCullough, of the 4th Illinois cavalry fell bravely at the head of his column, shot in the breast. The casualties among Illinois troops in this fight and retreat were as follows: 4th Illinois, one killed, thirteen wounded and three missing; 7th Illinois, three killed, eleven wounded and twenty missing. The total of casualties in killed, wounded and missing, of all the troops engaged, summed up ninety-nine.

But our cavalry had little rest. They were constantly on the alert and in the advance, engaged in harassing the enemy or upon important expeditions. On the 13th of December, Colonel Dickey received an order from General Grant, commanding him to take a part of his division of cavalry and strike the Mobile and Ohio Railroad as far south as practicable, and destroy it as much as possible. On the 14th Col. Hatch reported to Col. Dickey with eight hundred picked men, ready for his share of the expedition. Major Rickards, with a battalion of the 5th Ohio cavalry, was sent to make a demonstration toward Grenada, and the remainder of the 2d brigade went with the train to the rear. Col. Mizener was ordered to the command of the 1st and 3d brigades to make a reconnoissance towards Grenada.

On the 14th, with a small escort from company F, of the 4th Illinois cavalry, under Lieut. Carter, Col. Hatch's detachment and the

7th Illinois cavalry, Col. Dickey, took the road towards Okolona, and reached Pontotoc on the next morning, after a march of forty-five miles. Several scouting parties of the rebels were captured, who gave the information that a body of rebel infantry from Bragg's army was encamped near Pontotoc and another near Tupelo, and that there was a strong rebel force at Okolona. At Pontotoc a violent storm set in and the roads became very heavy, obliging Col. Dickey to send back the prisoners, ambulances, and some wagons laden with spoils found at that place. Major Coon, of the 2d Iowa, with one hundred men, was sent forward to strike the railroad at Coonawa Station, with orders to destroy the telegraph line and railroad and the railroad bridge near Okolona.

On the 15th, with the rest of the command, Colonel Dickey took the road for Tupelo in the midst of a terrific rain storm, but they moved steadily forward over the low muddy ground, and through swamps and creeks until within two miles of Tupelo, when it was found that a Union force from Corinth had arrived at Saltillo, eight miles north of Tupelo that day, and that the rebels had retreated. Lieutenant-Colonel Prince of the 7th Illinois Cavalry, with one hundred men, pushed forward and occupied Tupelo, while the rest of the force fell back seven miles to render aid to Major Coon if necessary. The Major, however, had thoroughly and successfully performed his work. Lieutenant-Colonel Prince returned to the camp on the 16th, having found no enemy at Tupelo and having destroyed some important trestle-work north of the town. On the 16th and 17th, all the trestle-work and bridges from Saltillo to Okolona, a distance of thirty-four miles, were destroyed, as well as a large amount of timber for repairing purposes. At Verona, Lieutenant-Colonel Prince captured eighteen large boxes of infantry equipments marked, "Colonel S. D. Roddy," several boxes of canteens, a large quantity of clothing and tents, some commissary stores, small arms and ammunition, all of which was destroyed.

On the night of the 17th, the force camped at Harrisburgh, a deserted village about two miles from Tupelo and on the morning of the 18th took up their line of march on the return. About noon Colonel Dickey ascertained that a large rebel force of cavalry was in Pontotoc. Closing up his column, he moved to the northwest with a view of passing some four miles north of Pontotoc. Some stragglers from the rebel columns were captured, and from them it was learned that the rebel force was moving out from Pontotoc and passing across his track a mile ahead of them. The enemy was over whelming in point of numbers and our troops worn out. It was therefore not deemed prudent to attack. Throwing out a small guard at a strong position, the column was moved towards Pontotoc on the road leading to Tuscumbia. Passing down this road, the rebel force was in full view about three-quarters of a mile distant, moving in another direction. Couriers were dispatched to Gen. Grant informing him of this cavalry movement, and the column moved on from Pontotoc in a northwest direction for a few miles, and then turned southwest across the country to the road from Pontotoc to Oxford. Following this a few miles it again turned south and crossed the Yockna River. Early on the morning of the 19th, it again took up the line of march, and after a day's march reported at Oxford to which place General Grant had in the meantime advanced. The expedition had been absent six days, and in that time had marched two hundred miles, worked two days at the railroad, captured one hundred and fifty prisoners, destroyed thirty-four miles of railroad and a large amount of the enemy's stores and returned, passing round our enemy, nine to their one, and reached camp without having a man killed, wounded or captured.

The force of rebel cavalry passing northward which Col. Dickey had seen, was closely followed by Gen. Grant's scouts. So well had Gen. Grant divined Van Dorn's purpose and timed his march, that on the 19th he telegraphed to the commandant of the garrison at Holly Springs that the enemy would attack him next day, but that he had sent him sufficient reinforcements to repel the attack, but unfortunately they arrived too late owing to obstructions in the road. The rebel force consisting of twenty-two regiments of Van Dorn's cavalry dashed into the town, which was surrendered with all its valuable stores without resistance. A guard of a hundred infantry around the government stores made a brief fight, but were soon overwhelmed. Six companies of the 2d Illinois Cavalry were completely surrounded in the town by as many thousands, and were called upon to surrender, to which demand they made reply by dashing upon the enemy in splendid style and cutting their way out. It was one of the most gallant deeds of the war—a little band of six hundred men against over eight thousand, and still they mowed their way through them, made a path for themselves and escaped. Van Dorn remained in the town from seven o'clock in the morning until five in the evening, during which time he destroyed government property to the value of over three millions of dollars, besides an immense amount of private property, and then left, his rear guard marching out of the place about an hour before the reinforcements arrived. General Grant issued a severe order reflecting upon this disgraceful surrender, both on account of the absence of any resistance, and the fact that the prisoners had taken parole. He excepted one regiment from censure, however, in the following terms: "It is gratifying to notice in contrast with this, the conduct of a portion of the command, conspicuous among whom was the 2d Illinois Cavalry, who gallantly and successfully resisted being taken prisoners. Their loss was heavy, but the enemy's was much greater. Such conduct as theirs will always insure success."

On the 21st of December, the force which had captured Holly Springs, suddenly appeared at Davis's Mills, a small place on the Wolf River twenty miles north of Holly Springs, garrisoned by six companies of the 25th Indiana infantry and two companies of Ohio cavalry. Although the attack was made in overwhelming numbers and with great fierceness and determination, still the little garrison held them at bay from behind their hastily constructed defences and finally compelled them to retire, leaving their dead and wounded and some prisoners in our hands. Indeed, after leaving Holly Springs, Van Dorn's raid was a humiliating failure. After his defeat he crossed Wolf River, took a look at Bolivar, broke out of our lines at Middleburg and was gone.

But in the meantime the rebel Colonel Forrest was at work upon our communications also. On the 18th of December a report reached General Sullivan commanding at Jackson, that Forrest with a large force had crossed the Tennessee and was rapidly making his way to Jackson via Lexington. He immediately made his preparations to receive the attack, and on the evening of the 18th was reinforced by Brayman's and Fuller's brigades. On the 19th, the enemy was reported within two miles. General Sullivan ordered out the 43d Illinois, Colonel Ingleman, to go to the front and hold back the rebel advance as much as possible. Ingleman ambuscaded his force and waited Forrest's approach. As the rebel advance came on, the 43d fired a terrific volley into the unsuspecting ranks and then commenced falling back slowly, harassing the enemy at every step. In the afternoon more reinforcements arrived at Jackson forwarded from Oxford by General Grant. Forrest, posted as to these reinforcements and constantly harrassed by Colonel Ingleman, feared to attack, and commenced throwing shells into the town hoping to destroy it. Gen. Brayman's brigade was ordered out as skirmishers and did its work so well that it forced back the rebel skirmishers two miles, and then encamped.

On the 20th, leaving eleven hundred men to guard Jackson, Generals Sullivan and Haynie, with the remainder, numbering about seven thousand, set out in pursuit of Forrest, Major Smith of the 45th Illinois being left in command of the town. On the same day cannonading was heard in the direction of Spring Creek and Humboldt, and five hundred men were ordered to reinforce Trenton by way of Humboldt. It was not until late in the afternoon that the news was received that Forrest had destroyed the trestle work on the Mobile & Ohio Railroad, and had captured Humboldt, Trenton, Dyer's, Rutherford, Keaton and other stations on the road.

On the 21st, not finding the rebels, General Sullivan returned to Jackson, where an attack was continually anticipated, and soon after his return, the following troops, by his order, reported to General Haynie: 106th Illinois, Colonel Latham; 119th Illinois, Major Watson; ninety men of the 11th Illinois cavalry; a company of the 18th Illinois; the 39th Iowa, and the Iowa Union Brigade. With these troops he commenced repairing the broken road. Having put the road in running order he moved on to Humboldt, where he remained until the 26th, having been joined in the meantime by the 126th Illinois, Colonel Beardsley, the 122d Illinois, Colonel Rinaker, and the 7th Tennessee. Leaving Colonel Beardsley at Humboldt he moved to Trenton, arriving there at noon of the 26th, and reporting to General Sullivan. Upon sending out his scouts he found that Forrest had changed front, having a portion of his force at Middleburg and the remainder at Dresden, and that the rebel pickets were not over two miles from his own. On the 27th Gen. Sullivan forwarded to him five regiments and two batteries, and at night came up with the remainder of his force.

On the morning of the 28th, General Sullivan camped at Shady Grove, about half a day's march from Huntington. Captain Burbridge, of the 11th Illinois cavalry, was ordered forward on the 29th to occupy Huntington and hold a bridge over a small stream beyond, and prevent the enemy from crossing to the town. They reached the bridge about the same time with the rebel pickets, but the latter fell back and the 11th held the position. The rest of the column rapidly came up and the regiments were placed in position, while another detachment of cavalry was sent out four miles towards Forrest's advance to hold a second bridge on the Dresden road, which was accomplished with small loss.

On the 30th, finding that they were cut off from passing through Huntington, the rebels moved in south and west directions, intending to reach Lexington. General Sullivan learned of the movement and dispatched Colonel Dunham and the 2d brigade to intercept them. Late in the evening the brigade reached Clarksburg, nine miles from Huntington. Thence it moved on towards Lexington. Forrest's force in the meantime had made a detour to the westward and reached the Lexington road at Parker's Cross Roads, intending to strike the road through Lexington for Clifton, the proposed crossing place of the Tennessee River. Colonel Dunham's little force reached the Cross Roads on the morning of the 31st, and to his surprise he found himself confronting Forrest's force drawn up in a field supported by three batteries in front, and the road through which he must pass encircled with rebel cavalry, the whole commanded by Forrest in person. All that was left for Colonel Dunham was to fight it out. Escape was impossible. The enemy made the attack with the batteries. Dunham's brigade formed in solid column south of the batteries, in as good a position as they could find. The enemy poured a terrific storm of shot and shell into and around the column, and for three hours the battle raged fiercely, the little band fighting without hope, but determined to fight on even to the death. But soon all ammunition gave out. It could not be replenished, but each man stood in his place, steadily, coolly, as if on parade, and the rebel cavalry pressing on them and hurled back with the bayonet. There was a sudden movement of the enemy to the right and the brigade was hemmed in, but they never flinched. They still fought on, contesting every inch of ground with the bayonet. Seeing their hopeless condition and perhaps admiring their bravery, Forrest ordered a cessation of hostilities and a parley ensued. A flag of truce came to Colonel Dunham demanding unconditional surrender. The gallant Colonel sent back word: "You will get away with that flag very quickly, and bring me no more such messages. Give my compliments to the General and tell him I never surrender. If he thinks he can take me, come and try." This was at least gaining time. It was noon, and the 1st brigade could not be far away. Forrest had received his answer and was about to resume hostilities, when upon a knoll just in sight appeared Generals Sullivan and Haynie, and behind them the 1st brigade, cavalry, artillery and infantry thundering along on the double quick, which had been kept up for three miles. The scene was an impressive one. The 2d brigade stood in compact form ready to receive anew the attack of the rebel host hemming them in, each man sternly resolved never to surrender. The rebels are preparing to assault the devoted band. Suddenly General Sullivan appears in advance of his brigade. His eye at once catches the situation. He turns on his horse and shouts: "Here they are! Hurry up that artillery." And the artillery did hurry. They rushed to the knoll, unlimbered in an instant, and got the range of a lane in front crowded with rebels. The infantry deployed on the flanks, fixed bayonets, but before artillery could fire or infantry charge, the rebels broke ranks and fled in a panic, stricken with amazement at the almost supernatural appearance of this new force. So suddenly did they make their appearance that even the 1st brigade stood still with wonder. The 2d brigade rapidly dispersed the enemy, and the 1st joined with them. Gun after gun was captured. Every man of the enemy was trying to save himself. The newly arrived artillery did not have an opportunity of firing a single gun. The rebel artillerymen fled with the rest, and could not be driven to their position by the most frantic exertions of their officers. The battle was won and the brigade united in wild cheer upon cheer, and then came the congratulations on one side and the gratitude on the other at relief from peril.

The loss in killed, wounded and prisoners upon the Union side did not exceed one hundred, while upon the rebel side it reached over one thousand. Among the wounded was Colonel Rinaker, who was struck in the leg with a bullet. The principal loss fell upon the members of the 122d Illinois. Lieut. Scott, of the 11th Illinois cavalry, acting as an aid to Colonel Dunham, was taken prisoner. Colonel Dunham, in his official report, paid the following handsome compliment to an Illinois regiment: "The 122d Illinois deserves especial notice. It is comparatively a new regiment, and part of it was at one time more exposed to the enemy's fire than any other; at any rate, it suffered more in killed and wounded. Its gallant Colonel fell severely wounded, yet its courage never flagged, and it met every duty and every danger with unwavering resolution. The detachment of the 18th Illinois acted for the most part with it and deserves the same commendation."

These repeated raids upon Grant's communications, however, so cut off his means of supplies that he was finally compelled to fall back upon Holly Springs until the road from Columbus should be rendered secure. And thus the first co-operative movement against Vicksburg was a comparative failure. We shall see many more failures in the campaign, but shall find a man undaunted by failures, able to wring success almost out of impossibilities.

John A. McClernand

MAJ. GEN. JOHN A. McCLERNAND

CHAPTER XXIV.

Gen. Sherman's Vicksburg Campaign—The Connection of Gen. McClernand with It—Organization of the Expedition—McClernand's Correspondence with the Secretary of War—Letter from the President—Correspondence with Gen. Halleck and Gen. Grant—Gen. McClernand Assigned to a Corps after the Movement of the Expedition—His Voyage Down the River—Assigned to Command the Forces—Letters for Gen. Grant—Gen. Sherman's Failure on the Chickasaw Bayou—Details of the Three Days Battle—Death of Gen. Wyman—Return of the Forces—Gen. McClernand Assumes Command.

WE now come to the second co-operative demonstration against Vicksburg, the expedition of General Sherman. It is due to General McClernand to state that he had labored long and assiduously in organizing this expedition, and in fact had first suggested to the Secretary of War, in an elaborate letter, the extreme importance of reducing Vicksburg, and opening the Mississippi River to the Gulf. A long correspondence passed betwen General McClernand and the Department, the latter mainly adopting his suggestions and urging him to hasten the organization. A dispatch from the Secretary of War, sent on the 29th of October, indicated the importance of moving expeditiously, so as to co-operate with certain movements in the east, and closed as follows:

"You will apprise me of your wants, which will be promptly supplied as far as may be in the power of the Department. For your success, time and diligence, as you know, are important elements. Every confidence is reposed in your skill and zeal, and I long to see you in the field, striking vigorous blows against the rebellion in its most vital point."

The President and Secretary of War coincided with all of Gen. McClernand's plans. They united in drafting a document ordering him to organize the troops remaining in Indiana, Iowa and Illinois, and forward them with all despatch to Memphis and Cairo, to the end that when a sufficient force not required by the operations of General Grant was assembled, an expedition should be organized under his command against Vicksburg. The forces thus organized however, were "subject to the designation of the General-in-Chief," and were to be employed "according to such exigences as the service in his judgment may require." This document was endorsed by the President as follows:

"This order, though marked confidential, may be shown by Gen. McClernand to Governors and even others, when, in his discretion, he believes so doing to be indispensable to the progress of the expedition. I add that I feel deep interest in the success of the expedition, and desire it to be pushed forward with all possible dispatch, consistently with the other parts of the military service."

It was evident that both the President and Secretary of War, in spite of the conditional clauses of this document, expected and intended that General McClernand was to command the expedition, and the General himself so understood it, and acted accordingly. He supposed that he was to command it independently, subject only to the orders of the General in Chief, and with this impression upon his mind, at once visited the Governors of Indiana, Illinois and Iowa, and obtained their hearty cooperation in organizing the troops. In the short space of sixteen days, with the assistance of the Adjutant-General of Illinois, he had completed the organization, mustered and forwarded from the various camps in Illinois, six regiments of infantry and one six gun battery to Columbus, Ky., and six more regiments and one six-gun battery to Memphis, besides five regiments from Indiana and three from Iowa. In addition to these, there was another regiment of infantry in Illinois under marching orders and three others in the same state were ready for muster, and two other regiments of infantry in Iowa. Certain influences were at work, however, which led General McClernand to believe that General Halleck was disposing of the troops in other directions, and that he was about to lose the command. He therefore wrote a strong letter to the Secretary of War, expressing the interest he felt in the enterprise, asking that his connection with it should be severed, and that he might be ordered to other duty in the field at once, if the expedition had become an uncertainty or must be long delayed.

In another communication to the Secretary of War, dated December 1, 1862, he stated that the work of forwarding troops from Indiana, Illinois and Iowa, for the Mississippi River expedition, had been nearly completed, and that a mustering, pay and ordnance officer for each of these states would amply suffice to close up the unfinished business in each of them. He requested therefore to be ordered forward to Memphis, or such other rendezvous as the Secretary should think preferable, that he might organize, drill and discipline his command preparatory to an early and successful movement. On the 12th of December he wrote in a similar strain to the President, and on the 16th to General Halleck, concluding his letter as follows:

"Having substantially accomplished the purpose of the order sending me to the states of Indiana, Illinois and Iowa, by forwarding upwards of 40,000 troops, as was particularly explained in my letter of the 1st inst. to the Secretary of War, and referred by him to you, I beg to be sent forward in accordance with the order of the Secretary of War, on the 21st of October, giving me command of the Mississippi expedition."

Subsequently General McClernand learned that General Sherman had left for Vicksburg in command of the expedition, and at once inquired of the Secretary of War if he had been superseded, and requested to be informed "if it is and shall be so." In answer to this, a dispatch from General Halleck's Assistant Adjutant-General was received on December 22d, informing General McClernand that on the 18th, the following telegram had been transmitted to General Grant, then at Oxford, Miss.:

"The troops in your department, including those from General Curtis's command which join the down river expedition, will be divided into four Corps. It is the wish of the President that Gen. McClernand's Corps shall constitute a part of the river expedition, and that he shall have the immediate command under your directions."

General McClernand did not look upon this dispatch as relieving him from his position at Springfield, and therefore requested of the Secretary of War to order him forward. Mr. Stanton at once relieved him and ordered him to report to General Grant for the purpose specified in the order of the General-in-Chief. This correspondence detained him until the 25th of December, when he left with his staff for Cairo. As reports were rife that the rebels had again obstructed the navigation of the river, he took with him a small company of infantry and left Cairo for the south on the 26th. Upon reaching Memphis, General Hurlbut informed him that Gen. Sherman had left Helena, and that General Grant had fallen back to Holly Springs. Two of his staff officers were immediately despatched across the country to communicate with General Grant. They reached there that night and were informed that orders assigning General McClernand to the immediate command of the expedition had been forwarded on the same day to Memphis by the train sent there under General Quimby. General Grant also remarked that information from rebel sources had been received by General McPherson, stating that Sherman had already attacked and captured Vicksburg.

These orders were received by General McClernand on the 29th, and consisted of two letters, one dated December 18, 1862, informing him of his appointment to the command of an army corps in General Grant's department, giving him command of the Mississippi River expedition, and ordering that the written instructions given General Sherman shall be turned over to McClernand on his arrival at Memphis.

The other letter was dated Holly Springs, December 25th, and was directed to "the commanding officer of the expedition down the river," giving sundry details concerning his own position and some instructions in relation to future plans. Gen. Grant also forwarded the following respecting the delay in sending the letter of the 18th:

"This letter was written the same morning the dispatch from the General-in-Chief was received, and immediately mailed, but when the cars got as far as Jackson, they found they could proceed no further. Since that time there has been no communication with the north prior to the day of Gen. McClernand's arrival."

Leaving Memphis on the 30th, Gen. McClernand and his staff arrived at Helena, Arkansas, and under convoy of a ram, as the river was still seriously obstructed, reached Milliken's Bend. Gen. Sherman, who had abandoned the attack on Vicksburg and descended the Yazoo, came on board the steamer to turn over his instructions to Gen. McClernand and to consult him as to further operations of the army. On the 4th of January, Gen. McClernand assumed command.

We have thus briefly gone over the connection of Gen. McClernand with the Mississippi expedition, simply presenting facts from official sources, leaving the reader to draw his own inferences. The narrative would be incomplete without this presentation and would leave some of the future operations of Gen. McClernand also in an ambiguous light. Gen. McClernand is an able and gallant soldier, and through his personal influence, aided by such a giant as Gen. Logan, did much to secure Southern Illinois against the plots of secessionists and home traitors, and rally it to the defense of the government. This episode, therefore, cannot but prove interesting to Illinois readers, and furthermore, the simple statement of the facts in the case is due to one who has done so much for the service, and who was largely the originator of the campaign against Vicksburg.

We now return to the operations of Gen. Sherman, while this correspondence was going on. Gen. Sherman embarked with a division of troops at Memphis and dropped down to Friar's Point, the place of rendezvous, on the 20th of December. On the next day he was joined by Admiral Porter, in his flag-ship, the main body of the naval force being at the mouth of the Yazoo River. On the same evening the troops from Helena arrived at Friar's Point. On the 22d the fleet got under way and reached the mouth of the White River at sunset. On the next day it descended to Gaines's Landing, to await the arrival of transports in the rear and also a division of troops from Memphis. On the night of the 24th and the evening of the 25th, the fleet arrived at the mouth of the Yazoo. On the 26th, the expedition, under convoy of the gunboats, moved up the Yazoo, and the troops were landed after much difficulty, owing to the character of the ground, but without any opposition on the part of the enemy. The first troops landed were a brigade under Gen. Blair, of Gen. Steele's division, and a brigade from each of the divisions under Gens. M. L. Smith and Morgan. These were ordered out on a reconnoissance, Gen. Blair on the left and the other brigades on the right. The brigade from Smith's division captured some of the enemy's pickets, and the brigade from Morgan's division found the enemy with a battery on the right, two miles from the river. After a slight skirmish they countermarched and returned to the front, as Gen. Sherman had given positive orders that no engagement should be brought on that evening.

It will facilitate the comprehension of this battle to briefly narrate the position. The defenses of Vicksburg consisted of two rivers and a chain of bluffs. The shape of the position may be likened to a horse-shoe, with one side prolonged and a bar joining the extremities of this irregular curve. The curve formed by the Yazoo and Mississippi rivers is the bow, and the chain of bluffs running inland from Vicksburg to Haines's Bluff is the bar. The former was our line of approach, and the latter, the rebel line of defense. The intervening space was low and swampy, and crowded with lagoons, bayous, and quicksands.

On the morning of the 27th the whole army was drawn up in line of battle and ready to assault. Gen. Steele's division was on the left, Gen. A. J. Smith's on the right, Gen. Morgan's on the left center, and Gen. M. L. Smith's on the right center. Gen. M. L. Smith's division took the advance and moved rapidly on the enemy, meeting them about three quarters of a mile from Chickasaw bayou. Skirmishing immediately began and was kept up during the remainder of the day, the enemy making a stout resistance but being gradually pushed back to the bayou.

On the evening before, a part of Gen. Steele's division had been re-embarked on transports and landed on the bayou, for the purpose of attempting to take a battery in the rear which commanded the only point where the bayou could be crossed on the extreme right. While Gen. M. L. Smith's division was skirmishing with the enemy on the right center, Gen. Blair's brigade and Gen. Morgan's division had advanced on the left by different routes, and came into position side by side. Skirmishing took place with the enemy's infantry and at the same time a masked battery opened on Gen. Blair's brigade which was silenced shortly after, the enemy's infantry retreating into a thicket not far off. During the afternoon a dashing charge was made upon the rebel artillerists by the 13th and 16th Illinois infantry, under the lamented Gen. Wyman. By nightfall the enemy had been driven a quarter of a mile from where they were first encountered, and the contest ceased. During the night the rebels strengthened and enlarged their line of defense and also received reinforcements.

On Sunday, the 28th, the enemy commenced the battle at daylight by a heavy cannonade on Gen. Blair's brigade and Gen. Morgan's division. Batteries were brought into position on our side and a sharp exchange of shrapnel and shell ensued. Finding that the rebels were disposed to dispute the possession of the ground, preparations were made for a charge. Gen. Blair, with his brigade, and Gen. Wyman, with the 13th and 16th Illinois regiments were drawn up in readiness for the charge, supported by Morgan L. Smith on the right. Gen. Wyman had just drawn his sword and given the order to advance, when he was struck by a minnie ball and disabled. After a temporary confusion, Lieut.-Col. Gorgas, of the 13th Illinois, took command and Gen. Blair led the brigades in a gallant charge which drove the rebels from their position. Gen. Wyman was mortally wounded and expired in the arms of one of his attendants on the field. He was a gallant and accomplished officer and universally beloved in the army.

At the same time the conflict was pressed by M. L. Smith's division. While riding in the advance, seeking for a place where the bayou might be crossed, he was fired at by a party of the enemy concealed in a neighboring cane-brake and severely wounded. The command then devolved temporarily upon Gen. David Stuart, who kept up during the day a constant skirmishing with the enemy's forces. There seemed to have been no distinct plan of battle that day, the whole operations being a series of skirmishes in which we both gained and lost ground.

On the 29th the rebel batteries opened on Gen. Morgan, the position being as follows: Gen. Morgan on the right of Gen. Blair, next to him Gen. Stuart commanding M. L. Smith's division, and on the extreme right, Gen. A. J. Smith. The day was full of misfortunes.

Gen. Sherman had appointed no hour for the assault, but by order of Gen. Morgan, Gen. Blair advanced, Gen. Thayer coming up to his support. In crossing the ditch and making its way through the abattis, Gen. Blair's brigade was thrown into confusion, but rallied and moved upon the rebel works, carrying two lines of rifle pits. Simultaneously with Gen. Blair's advance, Gen. Thayer was ordered forward. He crossed the same ditch, made his way through the same abattis, and came out to the right of Gen. Blair. As he reached the rifle pits, however, he found he had but one regiment with him. After his movement commenced, the second regiment of his brigade had been sent to the right of Gen. Morgan as a support, and the other regiments had followed this one. Notice of this change of march of the second regiment, although sent to Gen. Thayer, failed to reach him. Bravely pushing forward, however, he occupied the rifle pits and then hurried back for reinforcements. Gen. Blair also vainly waiting for support, descended the hill to hasten up troops. While urging the advance of more troops, his brigade fought desperately to gain the crest of the hill. A short distance above the second line of rifle pits was a cluster of willows into which the rebel riflemen had retired. The 13th Illinois charged into it, and after a gallant hand to hand struggle, drove the rebels out. But the position was too much exposed to the enemy's fire to hold without reinforcements. The latter did not arrive, and Gens. Blair and Thayer were compelled to issue the order to retire. The division of Gen. Morgan was not brought over the bayou in time to engage in the assault. Only one regiment of Gen. Stuart's division got across. No notice of the intended movement on the left had been given to the division commanders on the right. Smith's division was so near Vicksburg and the strength of the enemy before him so great, that an assault would have been fruitless, and thus the day ended in defeat, although our troops had fought with the most desperate gallantry in the face of fearful odds, for the whole assault was made by about three thousand men. The 13th Illinois were the heroes of the day. They fought with magnificent bravery, reckless of all danger, plunging through the most terrific storms of shot and shell, and holding positions like Spartans, when they were exposed to a most pitiless fire from the batteries against which their own was perfectly harmless.

Private F. W. Taylor, of Belleville, Ill., was promoted on the field for bravery.

On Tuesday desultory firing was kept up and on Wednesday a flag of truce was sent in and General Sherman buried his dead. Afterwards an arrangement was made with Admiral Porter to attack Haines' Bluff, but the purpose became known to the enemy and it was abandoned. On Thursday night and Friday morning, January 2, 1863, the troops were embarked and moved down to the mouth of the Yazoo, when General McClernand took command, who ordered the forces to Milliken's Bend. Thus the second great co-operative movement to reduce Vicksburg had failed.

The circumstances of General Wyman's death were as follows: He had placed himself at the head of the 13th Illinois, which was detailed to assist in the charge upon the battery. The entire regiment, officers and all, was moving up an eminence towards the battery. His regiment had succeeded in unmanning two of the guns and had arrived within eighty yards of the battery, when General Wyman raised up, lifting his sword in the air, and was about giving the order to charge on the battery. At that instant, he was struck in the side of the right breast, directly under the sword arm. The ball passed through the body, coming out just below the ribs on the left side. The fall of the General paralyzed the regiment. Lieut.-Colonel Gorgas and others rushed to his assistance. The General raised himself and seeing that his force wavered, said to Lieut.-Col. Gorgas: "For God's sake, Colonel, leave me and attend to these men." The Colonel left him, rallied the men and took the battery. General Wyman for a number of years was at the head of the old Chicago Light Guard, when that organization was at the hight of its fame. He entered the service as Colonel of the 13th Illinois, and was for some time commandant of the post at Rolla, Mo. For meritorious services and bravery in the field, the President commissioned him a Brigadier-General. He was every inch a soldier, and was deeply beloved by his old regiment and all of the army with whom he came in contact.

CHAPTER XXV.

Gen. McClernand Assumes Command of the Army of the Mississippi—The Military Situation—General Order No. 1—Submission of Plan to Gen. Grant—The Movement Against Arkansas Post—Nature of the Position—Illinois Regiments in the Expedition—Preliminary Reconnoissance—The Attack Upon the Fort—Its Surrender—Details of the Battle—Extracts from Gen. McClernand's Report—His Order of Congratulation—The Views of the President—Correspondence Between Gov. Yates and Gen. McClernand.

ON the 4th of January, 1863, Gen. McClernand, in pursuance of orders, assumed the command of the army, styling it the Army of the Mississippi, and issued General Order No. 1, continuing Gens. Sherman and Morgan in command, prohibiting interference with private property, prescribing punishment for straggling, and covering the customary details relative to supplies and reports of corps commanders. The situation at this juncture was substantially as follows: General Grant had failed to carry out his plan of pushing forward from Oxford to Grenada, and had fallen back to Holly Springs. General Sherman's attack on Vicksburg had been repulsed. General Banks was debarred from affording co-operation with the up river movements by the obstinate resistance of the enemy at Port Hudson. In addition, the enemy at Vicksburg had been strongly reinforced and our own army was hardly in condition to move upon the latter place. General McClernand therefore adopted a new plan which he submitted to General Grant by letter, the principal features of which were the following:

General Grant was to make Memphis his base of operations, put the road from Memphis to Grenada in running order, and push forward with his column to the latter place and to Jackson, thence marching upon the rear of Vicksburg, while General Banks' forces and the army of the Mississippi should co-operate as was best found to be practicable. The peculiar military situation of General Grant would render an answer improbable for several weeks. In the meantime, while waiting for orders, General McClernand determined to strike a blow at the enemy near the mouth of the Arkansas river, then seriously threatening communication between Memphis and Vicksburg. Fort Hindman, better known as Arkansas Post, the key to Little Rock and the extensive country drained by the Arkansas river, was the point aimed at. In the two corps which comprised this army were the following Illinois' regiments: 13th, 113th, 116th, 35th, 127th, 77th, 97th, 108th, 131st and 118th regiments of infantry; the 3d Illinois cavalry, one company of the 15th and two companies of Thielman's Illinois battalion; companies A and B, 1st Illinois Light Artillery, and the Mercantile Battery, Captain Cooley. The army safely arrived at the mouth of the White River on the 8th of January and commenced landing, the work of disembarkation being concluded at noon of the 10th.

In the meantime General McClernand had reconnoitered the river road and a part of the levee within a short distance of the fort, and discovered that the enemy was abandoning a line of rifle-pits about half a mile above the levee, under the heavy fire of our gunboats. General Sherman's column was put in motion, and after meeting and dispersing a strong force of the enemy's pickets, the head of the column, General Hovey's brigade, encountered a swamp which was crossed with much difficulty. Witnessing the embarrassment of the troops in crossing, General McClernand reconnoitered to test the practicability of the river road. This road was found not only practicable but good, and the other division of General Sherman's corps, commanded by General Stuart, passed up this road. The rear of General Steel's division, consisting of General Blair's brigade which had crossed the swamp, was obliged to return, as any further approach to the fort could only be gained by a detour of seven miles, and the passage of a bayou by a single narrow bridge. General Sherman then hastened up the river road to General Stuart's division of his corps, the head of which he found resting within half a mile of the fort. General Morgan's corps rapidly advanced in the same direction and General A. J. Smith's division soon made its appearance on the right of Stuart. General Sherman was ordered to move Stuart's division to the right, and General Steele's when it should come up still further to the right, to let in General Smith's and General Osterhaus's divisions on the left so that the investment might be complete. General McClernand then communicated with Admiral Porter, and the gunboats moved forward, opening a furious cannonade upon the fort which was continued until after nightfall, thus diverting the attention of the enemy from the movements of the land forces. During the night General Sherman's corps was pushed forward to the bayou. General Osterhaus took a position covering the landing and the transports, and Colonel Lindsay's brigade had planted a battery on the river bank above the fort, thus cutting off escape or reinforcement of the enemy by water.

At half-past ten o'clock on the morning of the 11th, the two corps were in position. General Steele's division had the extreme right, with General Stuart's and A. J. Smith's division on its left. One brigade of General Osterhaus's division formed the extreme left of the line resting upon the river. Colonel De Courcey's brigade of the same division was held in reserve. The artillery was disposed as follows: Co. A, 1st Regiment Illinois Light Artillery, Captain Wood commanding, to the left of Stuart; Co. B of the same regiment, Captain Barrett commanding, on the center of the same division; the 4th Ohio between Stuart and Steele and the 1st Ohio between Thayer's and Hovey's brigades of Steele's division; the 1st Missouri was in reserve and the 8th Ohio in the rear of the center of the general line. Three pieces of the 17th Ohio battery were in front of Landrum's brigade of General Smith's division and two sections of the Mercantile battery of Chicago were with Colonel Lindsay.

Word was sent to Admiral Porter that General McClernand would advance upon the enemy's works as soon as the gunboats opened fire. At one o'clock they opened fire, which was immediately followed by the fire of artillery along both the right and left wings of the line. At half-past one o'clock, Hovey's and Thayer's brigades of General Sherman's corps, and T. E. Smith's and Giles M. Smith's brigades of the same gained a position near the enemy's rifle pits. Checked for a time by a severe fire of musketry, they afterwards advanced, supported by Blair's brigade as a reserve, until they had approached within short musket range of the enemy's line and found shelter within some ravines. In executing this movement General Hovey was wounded by the fragment of a shell, but continued on the field. Hoffman's battery was advanced within two hundred yards of the enemy's intrenchments and poured in a rapid and effective fire. The artillery of General Morgan's corps opened fire at one o'clock, and kept it up with telling effect—some 20-pounder Parrotts on the river bank, silencing a heavy casemated gun and some lighter barbette guns on one of the bastions. Blount's Parrotts kept up a rapid fire into the enemy's lines until A. J. Smith's division had passed to the front and rear of the enemy's works. Nine regiments detached from this division, and supported by three regiments in reserve, moved forward and drove the enemy's advance toward the open ground in front of his defences, when they sought shelter behind some cabins. The 3d Wisconsin charged and dislodged them, forcing them to flee to their intrenchments. The same regiment then moved forward until within two hundred yards of the fort.

In the meantime Colonel Sheldon under General Osterhaus's direction ordered up the Chicago Mercantile battery within two hundred yards of the enemy's defences and deployed the 118th Illinois on its right and massed the 120th Ohio on its left, the 69th Indiana being in reserve. The enemy poured a galling fire into them, to which our infantry and artillery promptly replied until the rifle-pits in front of the latter were nearly cleared. The 120th Ohio sprang forward to carry the eastern face of the fort, but failed in the attempt. At this juncture Colonel De Courcey's brigade, which had been left to cover the transports, was ordered up. At half-past three o'clock General Sherman was reinforced by the 23d Wisconson, 19th Kentucky, and 97th Illinois from General Smith's division, and took position on the right. The engagement being sharp on both sides General McClernand ordered the assault. Burbridge's brigade and the 12th Ohio dashed forward under a heavy fire to the enemy's intrenchments—the 16th Indiana, 83d and 120th Ohio being the first to enter the fort. Presenting himself at the entrance to the fort, General Burbridge was halted by the guard who denied that the fort had been surrendered, until he called their attention to the white flag, and ordered them to ground arms. Soon after, meeting General Churchill commanding the fort, the latter had an interview with General McClernand and surrendered.

We quote from the elaborate and lucid report of General McClernand, the closing scenes in the reduction of Arkansas Post:

"Further to the enemy's left his intrenchments were stormed by General Sherman's command, who immediately ordered General Steele whose zeal and daring, added to his previous renown, to push forward one of his brigades along the bayou and cut off the enemy's escape in that direction.

Colonel Lindsay, as soon as a gunboat had passed above the fort hastened with his brigade down the opposite shore and opened an oblique fire from Foster's two twenty and Lieutenant Wilson's two ten-pounder Parrotts into the enemy's line of rifle-pits, carrying away his battle flag and killing a number of his men. Eager to do still more, he embarked the 3d Kentucky on board of one of the gunboats to cross the river to the fort, but before it got over, the enemy had surrendered.

"Thus at half-past four o'clock, after three and a half hours' hard fighting, our forces entered and took possession of all the enemy's defences.

"To General Morgan, I assigned the command of the fort, who, as a token of the conspicuous merit of General A. J. Smith, throughout the action, assigned it to that officer. To General Sherman I gave in charge all the other defences and the prisoners outside the fort, who, in like manner, honored General Stuart, by giving them into his charge.

"Seven stands of colors were captured including the garrison flag which was captured by Captain Ennis, one of General Smith's aides-de-camp. General Burbridge planted the American flag upon the fort, which had been placed in his hands as a tribute to his gallantry by General Smith for that purpose. Besides these, five thousand prisoners, seventeen pieces of cannon large and small, ten gun-carriages and eleven limbers, three thousand stand of small arms, exclusive of many lost or destroyed, one hundred and thirty swords, fifty Colt's pistols, forty cans of powder, one thousand six hundred and fifty rounds of shot, shell and canister for 10 and 20-pounder Parrott guns, three hundred and seventy-five shells, grape stands and canister; forty-six thousand rounds of ammunition for small arms; five hundred and sixty-three animals, together with a considerable quantity of quarter-master's and commissary stores, fell into our hands. Of these captures seven pieces of cannon had been destroyed by the fire of our artillery and the gunboats, besides one hundred and seventy wagons which were destroyed for want of means to bring them away.

"Our loss in killed was one hundred and twenty-nine, in wounded eight hundred and thirty-one, in missing, seventeen—in all, killed, wounded and missing, nine hundred and seventy-seven; while that of the enemy, notwithstanding the protection afforded by his defences, proportionately to his numbers, was much larger.

"The prisoners of war I forwarded to the commissioner for the exchange of prisoners at St. Louis; and utterly destroying all of the enemy's defences, together with all the buildings used by him for military purposes, I re-embarked my command and sailed for Milliken's Bend on the 17th inst., in obedience to General Grant's orders.

"Noticing the conduct of the officers and men who took part in the battle of the Arkansas, I must refer to the reports of corps, division, brigade and regimental commanders for particular mention of those who signalized their merit, but in doing so I cannot forbear in justice to add my tribute to the general zeal and capability of the former and the valor and constancy of the latter. Gen. Sherman exhibited his usual activity and enterprise, General Morgan proved his tactical skill and strategic talent, whilst Generals Steele, Smith, Osterhaus and Stuart, and the several brigade commanders displayed the fitting qualities of brave and successful commanders. The members of my staff present, Colonel Stewart, Chief of Cavalry, Lieut.-Col. Schwartz, Inspector-General, Lieut.-Col. Dunlap, Assistant Quartermaster, Major McMiller, Medical Director, Major Ramsey, Capt. Freeman and Lieuts. Jones, Caldwell and Jaynes, aids-de-camp, all rendered valuable assistance. Lieut. Caldwell, who ascended into the top of a lofty tree in full view of the enemy and within range of his fire, and gave me momentary information of the operations both of our land and naval forces and of the enemy, particularly challenged my commendation and thanks. To Colonel Parsons, A. Q. M. and master of transports, I also offer my acknowledgements not only for the successful discharge of arduous duties in his department but also for important services as a volunteer aide in bearing orders in the face of danger on the field, and to Major Williams, Surgeon of the 2d Illinois light artillery, I am also indebted for professional usefulness. * * * * While mourning the loss of the dead, and sympathizing with the bereavement of their kindred and friends and the sufferings of the wounded, we should offer our heart felt gratitude to almighty God for the complete success vouchsafed to our arms in so just a cause."

Following so closely upon the defeat before Vicksburg, which had depressed the whole country, the battle and victory of Arkansas Post were a lifting of the clouds. It proved conclusively that the army was not demoralized by misfortune, that its courage was unshaken and its determination to hew its way through to the Gulf still irresistible. Loyal men breathed more freely and once more augured final success. The army itself began to assume new spirit and moral courage by contrasting the victory just achieved with its recent disaster. The President expressed his thanks to General McClernand and his brave troops for this victory, gained at a time when "disaster after disaster was befalling our arms," closing his letter with these words: "Your success on the Arkansas was both brilliant and valuable, and is fully appreciated by the country and government." Illustrative, also, of the estimation in which General McClernand and his army were held is the following incident with accompanying correspondence: One of the pieces captured, a Parrott gun with its muzzle broken off and the carriage shattered by a shot from our batteries, was sent by Gen. McClernand to Governor Yates, in behalf of the State of Illinois. Accompanying the piece, Governor Yates received the following letter from Gen. McClernand:

"HEADQUARTERS 13th ARMY CORPS,
"Milliken's Bend, March 16, 1863.

"*His Excellency, Richard Yates, Governor of Illinois:*

"I have the honor to send you a broken Parrott piece captured by the force under my command at Post Arkansas. The piece was broken by a shot from one of the guns of my batteries. Please accept it on behalf of the noble State you so worthily represent, as an humble testimonial of the esteem and admiration of the brave men whose valor wrested it as a trophy from the enemy.

"Your obedient servant, JOHN A. MCCLERNAND,
"Major-General Commanding."

To this letter Governor Yates replied as follows:

"STATE OF ILLINOIS, EXECUTIVE DEPARTMENT,
"Springfield, April 2, 1863.

"*Major-General John A. McClernand, Vicksburg, Miss.:*

"MY DEAR GENERAL:—I have the honor to acknowledge the receipt of the broken Parrott gun, captured by the army under your command, at Arkansas Post, and to express my acknowledgments in the name of the people of the State therefor.

"It also gives me great pride and satisfaction to do so, from the fact that I regard the victory at Arkansas Post gained under the able and energetic generalship of a distinguished officer and citizen of Illinois, as second in importance and consequence only to that of Fort Donelson, in which that officer also prominently participated.

"Fort Donelson and Arkansas Post, my dear General, I regard as the two great positive victories of the war in the West. May your participation in the third be equally prominent and attended by as glorious results and substantial advantages.

"With sentiments of respect and esteem, I am, my dear General, your most obedient servant. RICHARD YATES, Governor."

The congratulatory order of Gen. McClernand, on this occasion, which was issued by him the day after the battle, was as follows:

"HEADQUARTERS 13th ARMY CORPS,
"Before Vicksburg, February 13, 1863.

"His Excellency, Abraham Lincoln, President, and Commander-in-Chief of the Army and Navy of the United States, having honored Major-General McClernand and the officers and soldiers of the army of the Mississippi with congratulations upon their success on the Arkansas, Major-General McClernand feels it to be equally a duty and pleasure to publish the fact, together with the encouraging assurance of his Excellency, that 'that success was both brilliant and valuable, and is fully appreciated by the country and government.'"

General Grant and staff arrived at the Post a few days after the battle had been fought and won; and Gen. McClernand, who intended to take advantage of the rise in the river for striking a decisive blow at the rebels at Little Rock, the capital of the State of Arkansas, was peremptorily ordered by Gen. Grant to return with his army to Young's Point, opposite Vicksburg, for the purpose of digging out and enlarging the canal projected and commenced by Gen. Williams and Admiral Farragut in 1862.

CHAPTER XXVI.

GEN. GRANT'S DESCENT OF THE MISSISSIPPI—THE NEW PLAN OF OPERATIONS AGAINST VICKSBURG—CANAL DIGGING—THE WILLIAMS, LAKE PROVIDENCE AND MOON LAKE CANALS—THEIR FAILURES—THE STEELE'S BAYOU EXPEDITION AND ITS FAILURE—GENERAL MCCLERNAND'S MOVEMENT DOWN THE WEST BANK OF THE RIVER—CAPTURE OF RICHMOND—DIFFICULTIES OF THE MARCH—RUNNING THE BATTERIES—THE ILLINOIS VOLUNTEERS—FAILURE OF THE MOVEMENT AGAINST GRAND GULF—RUNNING THE BATTERIES AGAIN—THE ADVANCE ON PORT GIBSON—BATTLE OF PORT GIBSON—GALLANTRY OF THE ILLINOIS TROOPS—GEN. GRANT'S ORDER—EVACUATION OF GRAND GULF—INTERESTING MOVEMENTS OF THE ARMY.

WE have seen the fruitlessness of two movements against Vicksburg. We now come to other movements which after many bloody battles and many weary weeks and months of siege, resulted in final and complete success. Any further attempts to carry Vicksburg from the directions undertaken by Generals Grant and Sherman were abandoned. On the 29th of January, 1863, General Grant descended the Mississippi with gunboats and transports, landing a portion of his army at Milliken's Bend, and the remainder opposite Vicksburg, at Young's Point. Then commenced the stupendous canal operations which were also destined to result in failure. In the attempt upon Vicksburg by Commodore Farragut's fleet, General Williams had attempted to cut a canal across the peninsula opposite Vicksburg, hoping thus to change the course of the river and leave Vicksburg an inland town of no military importance, but the plan was abandoned on account of the low stage of water. General Grant's first attempt on Vicksburg was the renewal of this experiment. For six weeks thousands of men were at work in the trenches, but when the work was almost done, an unfortunate break flooded the canal with water. Before this could be repaired, the season of high water had passed and the work was abandoned.

The Lake Providence canal was the next attempt. Seventy miles north of Vicksburg is Lake Providence, connected with Swan Lake by a bayou full of snags, and winding through a thick, tangled forest. Swan Lake found an outlet in the Tensas River which emptied into the Black River, which last stream flowed sluggishly into the Red River. The attempt was made to cut a canal five miles in length through the morass, dig out the shallows and eradicate the snags and stumps, and was carried out, but the Father of Waters nevertheless refused to change his course. When the spring floods fell, the new channel was nothing but an insignificant creek and thus the Lake Providence canal was a failure.

There was a third plan to be tried. One hundred and fifty miles north of Vicksburg, on the eastern shore of the river, is Moon Lake, from which the Yazoo Pass leads into the Coldwater River. This again enters the Tallahatchie, which in turn empties into the Yazoo, about seventy miles north of Vicksburg It was decided to cut a canal from the river to Moon Lake, clear the obstructions from the Yazoo Pass, and by this series of streams gain a position in the rear of the rebel fortifications at Haines' Bluff. The canal was cut and steamers succeeded after perilous exertions in getting into the Yazoo, but here they were met by formidable batteries unapproachable by land, and against which the wooden gunboats were unable to cope. They could not be reduced and they could not be passed. Thus the third plan failed.

Once more the streams and bayous around Vicksburg were tried. About seven miles up the Yazoo, from its entrance into the Mississippi, there is the mouth of a stream known as Steele's bayou. This bayou is connected with a labyrinthian net-work of creeks called Black Bayou, Rolling Fork and Sunflower River. These sluggish streams have several entrances into the Yazoo, and by them a complete circuit of Haines' Bluff can be made. Admiral Porter with his gunboat fleet attempted to force a passage through them, accompanied by a heavy force of infantry, but by the time they had reached the Sunflower River, their peril became so manifest that the expedition was abandoned.

Failure seemed staring the army in the face whichever way it turned. Sherman's assault had demonstrated that Vicksburg could not be taken by direct attack from the river. The failure of the Yazoo expedition and the expedition through Steele's bayou, proved that it could not be approached from the north. The attempt to convey troops around by the William's canal and by Lake Providence had also failed. It therefore now became a question of the most vital importance whether some point below on the Mississippi might not be reached, and to General McClernand's corps or rather a portion of it, it was given to test the question. That portion embraced the following Illinois troops: The 113th, 77th, 97th, 108th, 120th, 33d, and 99th infantry regiments; Cos. A, E, F, and K, 3d Illinois Cavalry, a detachment of the 2d Illinois Cavalry, the Peoria Light Artillery and Chicago Mercantile Battery, the whole organized into four divisions commanded by Gens. Osterhaus, A. J. Smith, Hovey and Carr.

On the 29th of March, General McClernand ordered General Osterhaus to send forward a detachment and capture Richmond, the capital of Madison parish. This was accomplished on the 30th by the 69th Indiana, a section of artillery and a detachment of the 2d Illinois Cavalry. The road was then seized and guarded, but progress was slow and painful. The road lay through a vast bog, intersected with bayous. Corduroy roads had to be built, outlets cut for the water, and bridges made for the bayous. In fact the army had to build a road as it advanced. As the troops approached New Carthage, they found that the rebels had cut the levee, so that New Carthage was virtually an island. After ineffectual attempts to bridge the floods, it was found necessary to march further down the river. Not discouraged by these obstacles the army pressed on, and after having made seventy miles of road and two thousand feet of bridges they reached their destination.

A considerable part of the army was now south of Vicksburg, but on the wrong side of the river, and without means of crossing. To effect this it was necessary for gunboats and transports from above to run by the rebel batteries. The first passage of the batteries was effected by eight gunboats and three transports, and the second by eight unarmed transports. Only a few hours before the sailing of the latter, their crews declined to accompany them. A recruiting office was immediately opened, and word was sent among the camps that volunteers were wanted to man the boats and carry them past the batteries. The answer was no uncertain one. Men poured in faster than they were wanted. So eager were they, that in less than four hours, over five hundred men had placed their names upon the list. So eager were all to embark that the lists had to be closed, and the lucky ones were chosen by lot. Every man who was chosen, was from the 17th army corps and belonged to General John A. Logan's splendid division. The names of the Illinois soldiers who then sprang forward into the breach when men were wanted, were as follows:

Steamer Tigress—Engineers, E. D. Hunter and Frank Mays of the 81st; Pilot, Lieutenant Smith of the 81st.

Steamer Horizon—Captain, Capt. Geo. W. Kinnard, 20th; mate, Lieut. J. D. Vavney, 11th; engineers, Patrick Vancel, 81st; Lieutenant Roberts, 31st; pilot, John Strong, 8th; firemen, William Walker, J. Roberts, J. Winchester, Wm. Green and E. J. Lewis of the 81st and J. C. Robbins, P. McGrath, J. M. Purriman and John Paul of the 45th.

Steamer J. W. Cheeseman—Firemen, Robert Irwin, C. W. Wengfield, Chas. Checoski, Noah Butler, M. L. Baird, J. St. John and E. Hicksey of the 81st, and A. Mapes, H. Casey and W. H. Harrison of the 30th.

Steamer Anglo-Saxon—Mate, Captain W. B. Short, 31st; engineers, D. B. Franklin, E. Briggs and James R. Clarke of the 20th, and A. Snow, Harrison Hines, and A. J. Esping of the 45th; pilots, John Randall and Charles Evans of the 45th; firemen and crew, James Massey, A. B. Turner, E. B. Cunningham, E. Hamilton and Wm. Winsley of the 8th, J. F. Street of the 20th, Thomas Vancell, J. W. Strickland, David Kesler, Sergeant West and John Reynolds of the 31st.

Steamer Empire City—Captain, Capt. G. W. Lisney, 81st; engineers, C. P. Flint, John Graves, W. H. Tripp and E. W. Fulford of the 45th, John Adams and F. J. Gilbert of the 31st; firemen, H. Cassell, R. Tubbs and H. H. Miller of the 20th.

Steamer Moderator—Captain, Caot. M. M. Twist of the 30th;

mate, Lieutenant Thomas J. McClurg of the 8th; engineers, ——— Mayfield, Wm. Beckman, Lieutenant Sutton, Geo. H. Recker and A. Stahl of the 8th, Wm. T. Roberts and Hugh Oliver of the 81st; pilot, Joseph Forest and Patrick McCarty of the 8th.

On the 29th of April, the 13th corps had reached the Mississippi and the 17th was well on the way. General Grant then embarked so much of the 13th as could be got on the transports and barges, and moved to the front of Grand Gulf, the plan being that the gunboats should silence the fortifications, and under their cover the troops should land and carry the works by storm. The attack was commenced on the morning of the 29th, but the works were too strong and the attack failed after several of the gunboats had been crippled. General Grant, therefore, determined to run the enemy's batteries again and to turn his position by effecting a landing at Bruinsburg from which there was a good road to Port Gibson. The gunboats again engaged the batteries and the transports ran by without material injury.

At daylight on the morning of the 30th, the work of ferrying the troops across the Mississippi was commenced. The 13th corps, Gen. McClernand's, as soon as landed, was pushed on toward Port Gibson. About 1 o'clock on the morning of the 18th of May, when four miles from Port Gibson, Gen. Carr's division leading the advance was met with a light fire of the enemy's infantry and afterwards of artillery. Harris's brigade was drawn up in line of battle and the enemy's fire was speedily silenced. At day-break, General Osterhaus moved his division to the left to relieve a detachment of Gen. Carr's division. In executing this movement, he encountered a strong force of the enemy and a sharp struggle lasting over an hour ensued, resulting in driving the enemy from his position. Gen. Osterhaus then pressed forward until insurmountable objects in the nature of the ground and his exposure to the enemy's fire arrested his progress. What could not be accomplished by an attack in front, however, was easily effected by a flank movement which resulted in the rout of that portion of the enemy and the capture of three cannon. While Gen. Osterhaus was thus pursuing the enemy on the right, Gen. Carr attacked on the left, and a furious battle ensued, and continued for several hours, terminated by a magnificent charge made by Gen. Hovey, which resulted in the capture of four hundred prisoners, two 12-pounder howitzers, three caissons and a large amount of ammunition. Determined to press his advantage, Gen. McClernand ordered Generals Carr and Hovey to push the enemy with the utmost vigor, which they did, beating him back seven miles.

The second position taken by the enemy was a very strong one. It was in a creek bottom covered with trees and underbrush, the approach to which was over open fields and exposed hill slopes. Having advanced until they gained a ridge overlooking the bottom, Generals Carr's and Hovey's divisions were again exposed to the enemy's fire. A hot engagement ensued. The enemy massed a heavy force against our right front with the evident design of forcing it back and turning the right flank. Gen. Smith was sent forward to support that flank, and Gen. Hovey massing his artillery on the right opened a most destructive fire upon the enemy, which forced him back with considerable loss upon his center. Concentrating a large number of troops, the enemy directed another attack against our right center, but the attack was met and returned with great vigor by Gen. Carr. Troops from Generals Smith's and Hovey's divisions came up, and after an obstinate struggle, the enemy was again beaten back until night ended the battle. The next day, the 13th corps entered and occupied Port Gibson, the enemy having hastily fled the night before over the Bayou Pierre, burning the bridge in his rear.

Instances of the daring and valor of Illinois soldiers are not wanting in this well-fought battle. The reports of division and brigade commanders teem with them. On that day so full of heroic deeds, none was more heroic than that of Captain I. C. Dinsmore of the 99th Illinois, who sprang upon one of the enemy's howitzers, in Gen. Hovey's gallant charge, claimed it as his own, turned it upon the enemy and fired at them. Major L. H. Potter, with only four companies of the 33d Illinois, engaged the enemy on the left in the morning, and obstinately held him in check until the arrival of Gen. Osterhaus' division. Gen. Osterhaus having come up, the 33d Illinois commanded by the fearless Col. Lippincott was moved forward along a high ridge, and successfully explored the ravines intervening between our lines and those of the enemy. A brigade was ordered up, the 99th Illinois forming the reserve. After a sharp contest and while the brigade was changing front, the 99th led by "Old Rough and Ready number two," Col. Bailey, came up with cheer upon cheer and on the double quick, and took its place in the line. Three times the rebels charged upon the line and were hurled back by the troops of Indiana and Illinois, fighting side by side in generous emulation. For at least two hours that single brigade held back three brigades of the enemy until reinforcements from Hovey came up, when a charge was made with the wildest enthusiasm, resulting in the rout of the enemy. The 18th Indiana and 99th Illinois were equally gallant in the charge, and are mentioned with equal honors in the official reports. The 118th Illinois in Gen. Garrard's brigade was also mentioned with especial honor for the part they took in the battle, conjointly with the 120th Ohio.

Of so much importance was this victory deemed by Gen. Grant, that he issued the following congratulatory order:

"HEADQUARTERS ARMY OF THE TENNESSEE,
"In the Field, Harkinson's Ferry, May 7.

"*Soldiers of the Army of the Tennessee:*

"Once more I thank you for adding another victory to the long list of those previously won by your valor and endurance. The triumph gained over the enemy near Port Gibson, on the 1st, was one of the most important of the war. The capture of five cannon and more than one thousand prisoners, the possession of Grand Gulf and a firm foothold on the highlands between the Big Black and Bayou Pierre, from which we threaten the whole line of the enemy, are among the fruits of this brilliant achievement.

"The march from Milliken's Bend to the point opposite Grand Gulf was made in stormy weather and the worst of roads. Bridges and ferries had to be constructed. Moving by night as well as by day, with labor incessant and extraordinary privations endured by men and officers, such as have rarely been paralleled in any campaign, not a murmur or complaint has been uttered. A few days' continuance of the same zeal and constancy will secure to this army crowning victories over the rebellion.

"More difficulties and privations are before us; let us endure them manfully. Other battles are to be fought; let us fight them bravely. A grateful country will rejoice at our success, and history will record it with immortal honor.

"U. S. GRANT, Major-General Commanding."

The possession of Grand Gulf, alluded to in General Grant's order, was the result of these movements. Admiral Porter made a movement to attack the works at that place on the 3d, and found them evacuated. General Grant now made the necessary arrangements for changing his base of supplies from Bruinsburg to Grand Gulf. When the enemy moved from Milliken's Bend, the 15th corps, under General Sherman, remained to be the last to follow. General Sherman had also been ordered to make a demonstration on Haines' Bluff, in order to prevent reinforcements leaving Vicksburg to assist the forces at Grand Gulf. General Sherman moved upon Haines' Bluff, but the attack was made chiefly by gunboats. On the 7th the expedition returned and the military part prepared to join General Grant.

It had been General Grant's plan to collect all his forces at Grand Gulf and to get on hand a good supply of provisions and ordnance before moving against Vicksburg from the south. He had also determined to detach an army corps to co-operate with General Banks at Port Hudson and thus effect a junction of the forces. But this plan was given up upon learning that General Banks could not return to Baton Rouge before the 10th of May, and that by the reduction of Port Hudson he could not join General Grant with more than 12,000 men. These delays would be so great that the addition of forces would not make him relatively so strong for the attack upon Vicksburg as if the attack were made at once. Another reason for the change of plan was the expectation of the arrival of reinforcements at Jackson for the rebels.

Meantime, as the army of General Grant lay at Harkinson's Ferry, waiting for supplies and the arrival of General Sherman's corps, demonstrations were made to deceive the enemy, and an elaborate and well ordered system of movements commenced. On the 7th of May an advance was ordered. General McPherson's corps was required to keep the road nearest Black River to Rocky Springs. General McClernand's corps moved on the ridge road running from Willow Springs, and General Sherman followed with his corps divided on the two roads. All the ferries were closely guarded until the troops were well advanced. It was General Grant's plan that Generals McPherson and Sherman's corps should hug the Big Black River as closely as possible, and thus get to the Jackson and Vicksburg Railroad at some point between Edwards's Station and Bolton. General McPherson was ordered to move by way of Utica to Ray mond, and from thence to Jackson, destroying everything of value to the enemy, and then push west to rejoin the main force. General Sherman moved forward on the Edward's Station road, crossing Fourteen Mile Creek at Dillon's plantation. General McClernand moved across the same creek further west, sending one division by the Baldwin's Ferry road as far as the river. At the Fourteen Mile Creek crossing, both Generals McClernand and Sherman had some skirmishing with the enemy, but the latter was easily overcome. That night, May 11th, General McClernand's corps was at the Black River; General Sherman was at and beyond Auburn, and General McPherson a few miles north of Utica.

CHAPTER XXVII.

FROM GRAND GULF TO VICKSBURG—A SERIES OF BATTLES AND VICTORIES—THE BATTLE OF RAYMOND—A SPLENDID CHARGE—GENERAL CROCKER'S CHARGE AT JACKSON—CAPTURE OF THE CITY—THE BATTLE OF CHAMPION HILLS—DESPERATE FIGHTING OF LOGAN'S DIVISION—GALLANTRY OF HIS MEN—THE MARCH ON BIG BLACK RIVER BRIDGE—STORMING THE WORKS—THE REBELS DRIVEN OUT—THE FINAL INVESTMENT OF VICKSBURG—A REVIEW OF THE SITUATION—TRIBUTE TO ILLINOIS VALOR.

THE series of battles which followed each other in rapid succession prior to the final and complete investment of Vicksburg, are of unusual interest, both as illustrating the rapidity and sharpness with which Gen. Grant struck blow after blow, and as developing many instances of the valor of Illinois troops. The first of these which we purpose to notice was that fought on Farnden's Creek near Raymond, May 12th. Skirmishing commenced early in the morning. At nine o'clock in the forenoon, our advanced cavalry reported to Gen. McPherson that a strong body of rebel infantry was ahead of them, which it would be impossible for the cavalry to penetrate. After heavy firing by the cavalry in which the 2d Illinois behaved gallantly, losing a few men, the 20th, 73d and 68th Ohio, and 30th Illinois constituting the second brigade of Gen. Logan's division, were ordered forward. The brigade advanced and held its ground against a superior force. Gen. Logan hurried forward the 1st and 3d brigades of his division. The 8th Michigan battery was also sent to the front, and committed great havoc in spite of the repeated efforts of the rebels to charge upon and capture the battery. Defeated in their efforts, the rebels fell back to a position just in the rear of Farnden's Creek. General McPherson immediately ordered an advance upon the position. General Dennis's and General Smith's brigades moved forward, and a fearful but brief conflict ensued, in which the 20th Illinois fought most desperately and lost heavily, but the rebels were forced from their ground. During this desperate struggle, the rebels attempted to turn our left flank, and very nearly succeeded. The fight on the left was fearful. The 20th Illinois had fired forty rounds of cartridges, and still held the enemy at bay. Their colonel had been mortally wounded while urging on his men, but not one of the heroes faltered. At this critical moment, Gen. Stevenson's brigade came to the rescue. The 8th Illinois, Lieut.-Colonel Sturgis, came on with fixed bayonets and with a wild yell, slowly but steadily as the march of fate. Their old foe, the 7th Texas, who had faced them at Fort Donelson, again stood to receive them, but the 8th dashed them away like chaff. The brigade moved forward, solid and irresistible, and the rebels gave way and fled in disorder, retreating towards Raymond. General Logan, to whose division belongs the honor of the victory, was full of zeal and wild with enthusiasm. Fearless as a lion, he was in every part of the field, and seemed to infuse every man of his command with a part of his own indomitable energy and fiery valor.

On the morning of the 13th, Gen. Crocker's division of the 17th corps was on the move, followed by Gen. Logan's on the road to Clinton. At 6 o'clock on the morning of the 14th, these two divisions, General Crocker's in the advance, moved cautiously along towards Jackson. Rebel cavalry were encountered about three miles from Clinton, but they fell back rapidly. About three miles from Jackson, the main force of the enemy was encountered. Their line was nearly three miles in length, of which the 17th corps engaged one half, Sherman on the right attending to the other half. Learning the situation, Gen. Crocker ordered the 18th Missouri battery into position to test their artillery strength. A reply from three batteries was the result, and an artillery duel commenced, which lasted for half an hour without any decisive results. The infantry were then ordered into action. One of the most magnificent charges of the war followed, in which the 56th Illinois participated with distinguished honor, and won laurels for its bravery. A mile of open space lay between our army and the enemy, every foot of which was swept by the enemy's fire. The 1st brigade under Colonel San-borne, was selected for the bloody work. They formed in line and steadily advanced in spite of the fearful storm of shot and shell which swept through their ranks. They halted for a few moments under cover of a hill-side. Their officers briefly addressed them and then gave the word forward. Onward the column flew on the double quick, their cheers ringing high above the din of musketry. They had hardly struck the rebel front before it was shivered. A long, loud cheer of victory swelled on the air, as the foe fled panic-stricken from the field, and yielded the city of Jackson as the prize of the battle.

On the 16th of May, another glorious and decisive battle was fought. Early in the morning Gen. McClernand's corps was in motion. Gen. Hovey's division was on the main road from Jackson to Vicksburg, but the balance of the corps was a few miles to the southward. On a parallel road Gen. McPherson's corps followed Hovey's division closely. At 9 o'clock, Gen. Hovey discovered the enemy in front, on Champion Hills, to the left of the road near Baker's Creek, apparently in force. Skirmishers were thrown out, and the division advanced cautiously and slowly to give Gen. Logan's advanced division time to come up as a support. General Hovey's division advanced across an open field at the foot of Champion Hills, and commenced battle at eleven o'clock. The rebels, although strongly posted upon a heavily timbered hill covered with almost impenetrable scrub oaks, were deficient in artillery, and opened only with a four-gun battery. Gen. Hovey's division carried the hight in gallant style, and made a dash upon the battery, driving the gunners from their pieces and capturing the latter. At this juncture Mitchell's Ohio battery opened upon another battery about eighty yards from the brow of the hill. The rebels made a desperate charge upon it, and nothing but the fleetness of the horses saved it from capture. After the charge they were reinforced with fresh troops, and redoubled their efforts to hold the position and dislodge our troops on the hill. Hovey's division was slowly forced back, but a brigade from General Quimby's division, hastened to his support, and the ground was re-occupied and the rebels were finally repulsed. In this battle General Logan's splendid division as usual immortalized itself. At the commencement of the battle, he marched past the brow of the hill, and forming in line of battle on the right of Hovey, advanced in magnificent style, sweeping everything before him. At the edge of the woods in front of Logan, the battle was of the most desperate character, but not a man flinched or a line wavered in his division. They bore themselves like veterans, and moved on as if conscious of their invincibility and the certainty of victory.

Driven from his position, and repulsed in his demonstrations upon our right and left, there was no alternative for the enemy but retreat. He moved along the Vicksburg road towards Edwards' Station, under a fearful cannonade and musketry fire from Logan's division. General Stevenson, with a portion of the 13th corps, swung around his left upon the road, cutting off several brigades, which were forced to move across the fields towards the Big Black. The pursuit was given to General McClernand. That General, with his customary vigor, pressed the retreating enemy until he reached a point not more than two miles from Edwards' Station. The column arrived at the Station about dark and bivouacked for the night.

On Sunday morning, March 17th, before daylight, the column was on the march, moving upon the railroad bridge across the Big Black River. General Carr, one of the bravest of brave Illinois officers, had the advance, followed by General Osterhaus, with General Smith as a reserve. General Carr moved up in line of battle with a heavy force of skirmishers in advance. The rebel sharpshooters annoyed him at every turn, so that his advance was frequently delayed, but at 10 o'clock he had reached a belt of timber intervening between the main column and the rebel breastworks. General McClernand, quickly comprehending the situation, ordered General Carr to the right of the road. On the left, General Osterhaus was ordered in line of battle. Just behind the line of skirmishers was posted a battery, which, as the skirmishers advanced, threw shot and shell with great rapidity and effectiveness. The enemy briskly replied, their first shot striking a caisson of the 18th Wisconsin battery, exploding its contents and slightly wounding General Osterhaus. Word was brought to General McClernand that General Osterhaus was wounded and he assigned Brig.-General A. L. Lee to the temporary command of the 9th division. After short skirmishing, the enemy fell back within his entrenchments, so maneuvering as to have an open field between his position and our points of approach. In the meantime the artillery fire was very heavy. General McClernand ordered the works to be stormed, and General Carr prepared to execute the order. The point selected for the charge was upon the extreme left, where, protected by the banks of the river, General Lawler concealed a portion of his brigade. At the word of command, this brigade, with General Benton's on the left, unslung their knapsacks, threw their blankets on the ground and moved forward in gallant style, the troops wading up to their armpits across a bayou. A murderous fire greeted them, but they paid no attention to it, pressed over the entrenchments, presented their muskets and demanded surrender. The arguments were irresistible and the enemy gave up their position.

The enemy had left behind him after constructing a bridge the preceding night, two brigades to defend the works, while the balance of his force passed over and rested on the northern bank of the river. He deemed the position impregnable, but so furious and energetic was the attack that the position was carried with ease. When the enemy retreated, this bridge was burned and it became necessary to construct another. General Lee was entrusted with this order, and in the face of the rebel sharpshooters, by 8 o'clock in the morning, a bridge was thrown across the river over which his command and A. J. Smith's division, followed by McPherson's corps, crossed in safety, Sherman's corps crossing at Bridgeport.

Early on the morning of the 18th, General Sherman commenced his march by the Bridgeport and Vicksburg road, and when within three miles and a half of Vicksburg turned to the right to get possession of Walnut Hills and the Yazoo River. This he successfully accomplished before night. General McPherson crossed the Big Black above the road to Jackson and came into the same road with Sherman, but in his rear. General McClernand moved by the Jackson and Vicksburg road to Mount Albans, in the rear of Vicksburg, and then turned to the left to get into the Baldwin's Ferry Road. By these movements the three corps covered all the ground their strength would admit of, and by the morning of the 19th, the investment of Vicksburg was made as secure and thorough as could be with the forces at General Grant's command.

There probably has never been an instance during the war, of such rapid marching, such powers of endurance, such valor, and such splendid victories, one treading upon the heels of another. In the march from Bruinsburg to Vicksburg, only five days' rations were issued, and three of these were taken in haversacks and soon exhausted. Twenty days elapsed before supplies could be obtained from the government stores. In the meantime the army had to live by foraging upon a country partially exhausted by the rebels and swarming with their troops. The daring passage of the Vicksburg batteries by our soldiers, a large share of them Illinois troops in unarmed transports, poorly protected against the pitiless storm which rained upon them from the rebel batteries—a passage which seemed almost a forlorn hope; the splendid march of the 13th corps from Milliken's Bend to New Carthage, through swamps and bayous, making its roads as it advanced; the second passage of the batteries of Grand Gulf, which only a short time previously had defied our iron-clads; the splendid battles and victories of Port Gibson, Raymond, Jackson, Champion Hills and the Big Black, illustrated with such magnificent charges and brilliant movements; the rapidity and unerring certainty with which each corps performed the work allotted to it in securing the final investment of Vicksburg; all these elements of the campaign may safely challenge comparison in the annals of war. The plan of the capture of Vicksburg commenced with nothing but failures, ended with nothing but the most complete success. Sherman had failed at Chickasaw bayou; Grant had failed in the movement from Grenada; the Lake Providence and Williams canals had failed; the expedition through Steele's bayou had failed and led almost to ruin; the first attack on Grand Gulf failed, but never doubting of ultimate success, never disheartened by failure, our troops moved on. If one plan failed another was tried, and each new movement was worked out with increased courage and determination. While the campaign developed to its utmost the unflinching valor, the exhaustless resources and the determined pertinacity of the ruling spirit—General Grant—it no less developed the abilities and courage of the other Illinois generals in command—McClernand, Logan, Carr, McArthur and their subordinate officers. To chronicle the feats of valor displayed by the Illinois soldiers comprising the commands of these generals would require volumes. It is sufficient that there is no instance of cowardice, not a single occasion where an Illinois soldier faltered, whether he was called upon to run the fearful ordeal of batteries where he could not reply, to hold in check immense odds until reinforcements should come up, or make the final charge in the face of the belching fury of artillery and musketry. The record is clear, and from Memphis to Vicksburg, in every varying phase of the conflict, the ancient valor of Illinois remained unsullied.

CHAPTER XXVIII.

THE INVESTMENT OF VICKSBURG—INCIDENTS OF THE SIEGE—THE CHARGE ON THE 22D OF MAY—GALLANTRY OF RANSOM'S BRIGADE—A TERRIBLE FIRE—GEN. RANSOM LEADS HIS MEN—FAILURE OF THE CHARGE—SPLENDID RETREAT OF THE BRIGADE—GALLANTRY OF THE MERCANTILE BATTERY—GEN. MCCLERNAND PRESENTS THEM WITH TWO NAPOLEON GUNS—DEATH OF DR. STEVENSON AND CAPT. ROGERS—VALOR OF THE 20TH ILLINOIS—ACCURACY OF OUR ARTILLERISTS—A REBEL SORTIE REPULSED—THE ASSAULT ON FORT HILL—THE GLORIOUS LEAD MINE REGIMENT—DEATH OF LIEUT.-COL. MELANCTHON SMITH—CAPITULATION OF VICKSBURG—CORRESPONDENCE BETWEEN GENS. GRANT AND PEMBERTON—BIOGRAPHY OF LIEUT.-COL. WRIGHT OF THE 72D ILLINOIS.

TO present a continuous account of the siege operations around Vicksburg, and the various movements connected therewith, from the 19th of May to its surrender on the 4th of July, or to individualize the instances of patriotism and daring displayed by Illinois soldiers throughout those trying weeks, would require much more extended limits than those of the present work. To enumerate some of the most prominent of these instances will suffice as a sample of the splendid conduct of the officers and men in the great siege of Vicksburg.

Among the brilliant charges upon the rebel works on the 22d inst., that of the lamented General Ransom's brigade shines out conspicuously. In this brigade were the 116th, 11th, 95th and 72d Illinois regiments. General Ransom formed his brigade in line of battle by battalions closed in mass, all under cover of a ravine and within sixty yards of the works. At the signal, the brigade sprang forward with a ringing cheer. He had hardly advanced twenty steps before a most terrible storm of grape and canister swept through his ranks from the rebel earthworks, which, for the instant checked the advancing column. Colonel Humphreys, leading the 95th, fell, stunned by the concussion of a shell. His color-bearer also fell. Colonel Nevins of the 11th was killed. Lieut.-Col. Wright of the 72d, was seriously wounded. While waving his sword over his head, cheering on his men, utterly reckless of danger, he was struck in the arm above the elbow. Lieut. Whittle, acting adjutant of the same regiment, was also among the bravest of the brave. He moved up to the assault with a smile, saying: "Come on, my brave fellows, rebel bullets can not hit us." When wounded, he saluted his general and asked permission to retire. It seemed as if every officer, conspicuous on the field, was either wounded or killed. General Ransom rushed to the head of his brigade, seized the colors of the 95th, and waving them, shouted: "Forward, men! we must and will go into that fort! Who will follow me?" The splendid column again moved up to the impassable ditch and fought desperately across the breast-works for half an hour, when General Ransom, satisfied that the position could not be taken, thus addressed his men: "Men of the 2d brigade! we cannot maintain this position. You must retire to the cover of that ravine, one regiment at a time, and in order. The 17th Wisconsin will remain to cover the movement. The 72d Illinois will move first and move now. Move slowly. The first man who runs or goes beyond the ravine shall be shot on the spot. I will stand here and see how you do it." The movement was executed by every regiment as if upon parade, and the brigade re-formed without confusion or a single straggler.

The Mercantile Battery of Chicago, in the charge of the 22d also added to its previous laurels. The battery was drawn up within twenty feet of the rebel works and fired into their embrasures, using shrapnel as hand grenades and setting on fire the cotton piled around their earth-works. This position they held until relief came. So severe was the fire that they were unable to draw off their guns, but tumbled them down a steep hill into a ravine from which they subsequently removed them. Not a man of the battery was either killed or wounded. As a reward for their bravery, General McClernand presented them with two Napoleon guns, captured at Big Black River Bridge. Lieut. White brought up one of the pieces of the battery by hand almost to the very walls of the fort, and double shotting the piece, poured a most destructive fire into the enemy.

On the 29th, Dr. Stevenson, a gallant surgeon of the 17th Illinois, visited the very front line of skirmishers, and disdaining the advice of the men in the rifle-pits, refused to lie down. Presently a rebel sharpshooter saw him and fired at him, mortally wounding him. On the same day Capt. Rogers, of Co. D, 1st Illinois artillery, better known as McAllister's battery, sighted one of his guns and then leaped upon the parapet to witness the effect of his shot. A rebel bullet struck him directly in the forehead and the gallant officer fell, dying almost instantly.

In the assault of the 22d, but few troops succeeded in reaching the vicinity of the rebel entrenchments. Of the regiments composing the 1st brigade, 3d division, General J. E. Smith, the 20th Illinois alone crossed an open space in front of a formidable fortification, exposed to a furious fire, and planted its colors in close proximity to the rebel works. The 45th Illinois crossed in the afternoon and took position on the right of the 20th, and there the two regiments remained within thirty feet of the rebel fort until the following day, when they were recalled.

As an instance of the accuracy of aim to which our boys attained, it is related that a rebel sharpshooter had taken up a position in a tree, protected by a cotton-bale, from which apparently secure perch he was accustomed severely to annoy our troops. Major Taylor asked the Chicago boys if some of them could not hit that cotton bale. One of the guns was pointed at the tree and the trunk was cleft just below the crotch in which rested the cotton bale, bringing both bale and rebel to the ground.

On the night of the 22d of June, the rebels made a sortie from their works upon our advance in front of General Lauman's division. The 14th Illinois was in the trenches as a working party and support. No videttes were out and the men were surprised and driven from the trenches. The next night the 41st Illinois and some other regiments took possession of the ground from which the 14th had been driven. They were hardly at work before the rebels again sallied out, and approaching the trenches, demanded the immediate surrender of our troops on pain of annihilation. Almost simultaneously with the insolent demand, the Colonel commanding the 41st ordered the artillery to open upon them. A furious fight ensued, resulting in driving the rebels back to their works.

On the 30th of June, McPherson's corps made an assault on the rebel works, for which they had been preparing for several days. A little before 4 o'clock, a heavy cannonading commenced all along the lines, and the whole army was drawn up in battle array. The rebel Fort Hill, in front of General Logan, which he had been steadily approaching, was undermined on the night of the 21st, and the trains were all ready to spring. The 45th Illinois regiment, more familiarly known as the Washburn Lead Mine Regiment, Col. Jasper A. Maltby commanding, was assigned to the post of honor, and ordered to occupy the breach and hold it, cost what it might. The mine was sprung, creating a wide embrasure in the embankment, into which the glorious Lead Mine Regiment plunged. Fighting their way through like Spartan heroes, regardless of the terrible fire which was rapidly thinning their numbers, they planted their flag and there maintained it. Col. Maltby was wounded, and the gallant Lieut.-Colonel, Melancthon Smith, of Rockford, was mortally wounded by a ball which passed through his head, touching the brain. Major Lander B. Fish, who a short time before had been promoted from a captaincy, was killed by a bullet through the heart. Sergeants Breezer and Lewis were killed. Capts. Frohock and Boyce were severely wounded, and eight sergeants, three corporals and forty-one privates were also wounded in the charge through the embrasure. There have been few more gallant actions in the war than this charge, and few if any charges which have been made so desperately and determinedly. The other Illinois regiments which participated in the splendid movement were the 25th, 31st, 124th, 23d and 56th, and over all General Logan, worshiped by his men—a man of iron will and lion-like courage, who seemed under the blasts of war to change into a demi-god.

Vicksburg capitulated on the 4th of July, the anniversary of American independence—a day most appropriate of all to witness the culmination of the great events which had been transpiring around the doomed city. On the 3d, General Grant received a communication, under flag of truce, at the hands of General Bowen, from General Pemberton, proposing an armistice to arrange terms for capitulation. The rebel General desired that three commissioners should be selected from each army to carry out this arrangement and thus "save the further effusion of blood, which must otherwise be shed to a frightful extent." General Grant curtly replied that the effusion of blood could be ended at any time by an unconditional surrender of the city and garrison, and declined the appointment of commissioners, as he had no other terms to propose. General Bowen, the bearer of General Pemberton's letter, was received by General A. J. Smith, and expressed a strong desire to see General Grant. The latter declined, but requested General Smith to say that if General Pemberton desired to see him, an interview would be granted between the lines in General McPherson's front. A message was soon sent back to General Smith appointing 3 o'clock as the hour. At that hour the interview took place. The rebels insisted on being paroled and allowed to march beyond our lines, officers and all, with eight days' rations. General Grant sent in a written reply submitting his proposition, which was to the following effect: He was to march in one division as a guard, and take possession at 8 A. M. on the next day. As soon as paroles could be made out for officers and men, they should be allowed to march out of our lines, the officers taking with them their regimental clothing, and staff, field, and cavalry officers one horse each. Any amount of rations could be taken and thirty wagons for transportation. To these terms General Pemberton replied, accepting them in the main, but proposing the following amendments: That he should be allowed to evacuate the works in and around Vicksburg, and to surrender the city and garrison under his command, by marching out with his colors and arms and stacking them in front of his present lines, after which General Grant was to take possession. Officers were to retain their side arms and personal property, and the rights and property of citizens were to be respected.

To this General Grant immediately replied as follows:

"HEADQUARTERS DEPARTMENT OF TENNESSEE,
"July 4, 1863.

"*Lieut.-Gen. J. C. Pemberton, Commanding forces in Vicksburg:*

"GENERAL:—I have the honor to acknowledge your communication of the 3d of July. The amendments proposed by you cannot be acceded to in full. It will be necessary to furnish every officer and man with a parole signed by myself, which, with the completion of the rolls of prisoners, will necessarily take some time. Again, I can make no stipulation with regard to the treatment of citizens and their private property. While I do not propose to cause any of them any undue annoyance or loss, I cannot consent to leave myself under restraint by stipulation. The property which officers can be allowed to take with them will be as stated in the proposition of last evening. Officers will be allowed their baggage and side arms, and mounted officers one horse each. If you mean by your proposition for each brigade to march to the front of the lines now occupied by it and stack their arms at 10 o'clock A. M., and then return to the inside and remain as prisoners until properly paroled, I will make no objections to it.

"Should no notification be made of your acceptance of my terms by 9 o'clock A. M., I shall regard them as having been rejected and act accordingly. Should these terms be accepted, white flags will be displayed along your lines to prevent such of my troops as may not have been notified from firing upon your men.

"I am, General, very respectfully, your obedient servant,

"U. S. GRANT, Maj.-Gen. U. S. A."

To this General Pemberton returned the following brief but satisfactory answer:

"HEADQUARTERS, VICKSBURG, July 4, 1863.

"*Major-General U. S. Grant, Commanding U. S. forces, &c.:*

"GENERAL:—I have the honor to acknowledge the receipt of your communication of this date, and in reply, say that the terms proposed by you are accepted.

"Very respectfully, your obedient servant,

"J. C. PEMBERTON, Lieut.-General."

As soon as the ceremony of stacking arms was over, General McPherson and staff, accompanied by his division generals, rode into the city and took formal possession. General McPherson proceeded to the court-house, and Col. Coolbaugh and Lieut.-Col. Strong, of his staff, went up, and at 11½ o'clock flung to the breeze the Stars and Stripes on the cupola of the building, gave three cheers, and sang the "Battle Cry of Freedom."

At 12 o'clock Logan's splendid division, with Ransom's brigade, passed High Hill Fort, the scene of their recent gallant actions, and marched into the city. At the head of the column was the heroic Lead Mine Regiment, bravest of the brave, under command of Capt. Seeley. Col. Maltby rode at its head, but too ill to take command. The veteran 20th followed, under Major Bradley, and the Commercial College Regiment, led by Col. Sloan of Chicago, and the gallant 31st, whose chief, Col. Reese, fell at the storming of the fort on the 25th. After General Logan's division came General Ransom's brigade, a noble body of men led by a noble leader, with their banners torn and riddled in many a desperate battle. Then came the veteran 11th Illinois, under Col. Coats, and the 95th, under the fearless Humphreys, and the 72d, a young regiment in organization but old in bravery, under Col. Fred. Starring.

Among the bravest and best of the officers who gave up their lives to attain the possession of Vicksburg, was Joseph C. Wright, Lieut.-Colonel of the 72d Illinois. It will be recollected that he was severely wounded while leading his regiment to the assault on Vicksburg on the 22d of May. His left arm was amputated on the field of battle. He arrived in Chicago about two weeks afterwards among his family and friends, and strong hopes were entertained of his complete recovery. He gradually failed, however, until the 6th of July, when he breathed his last peacefully and calmly.

Lieutenant-Colonel Wright was born in Rome, Oneida County, New York, on the 7th of January, 1821, and was in his forty-third year at the time of his death. He graduated at Capt. Partridge's military school in Norwich, Vermont, and afterwards studied law, and was admitted to the bar of Oswego, New York, at the early age of twenty years. In 1853, he built the Continental Elevator at the latter place, and about that time abandoned the profession of the law and embarked in business. About the year 1857, he came to Chicago, and at once took a prominent place among business men. In all his operations he was bold, persevering, and strictly honest. In the crash of 1857, he found his name on about $40,000 worth of paper, none of it his own, but for all of which he was responsible. Every single dollar of it was paid. He was honest to a fault, for if a doubt existed on which side the beam turned, he always made it a rule to decide against himself. Even in the dark commercial days of 1857, when every creditor was eager and ready to compromise on the first offer, he manfully gave up every dollar he had to pay his debts. As a merchant and a man, his course was always marked by the strictest integrity.

As a member of the Board of Trade of Chicago, he eloquently urged the formation of those regiments which bear its name, and was offered the colonelcy of the first that was raised—the 72d. Being a civilian, he modestly declined the honor, and when offered the lieutenant-colonelcy at once showed his sincerity and patriotic zeal by accepting it, although at great pecuniary loss to himself and family. During the long period from his enlistment, to the investment of Vicksburg, the regiment did not meet the enemy in battle; but on the 22d of May, when General Grant ordered the assault, owing to the illness of Col. Starring, he assumed entire command of the regiment. Not satisfied with the usual position of an officer, sword in hand, he led his men clear up to the rifle-pits, where he received his death wound. He died a true soldier. In his last moments he was continually talking about military movements, giving orders to his regiment, and urging on his men to the charge. We have seen him as a merchant and soldier. As a citizen, he strictly and conscientiously fulfilled all the duties of life. He was not only a professed Christian, but one who practiced his Christianity by carrying it into all the details of every day life. He won hosts of friends among all parties. In the social circle few had such conversational powers, or used those powers in a manner so entirely free from taint or corruption. He was pre-eminently a lover of his family hearth, and the genuineness of his patriotism is no more thoroughly shown, than by the sacrifice it cost him to leave his home. As a speaker, he was fluent, and gifted with an eloquence which has rarely been excelled west of the lakes. For many years he was the leading spokesman of the Chicago Board of Trade, which has boasted many good speakers.

A sincere and humble Christian, an upright and honorable man, a sagacious and enterprising merchant, a gallant and patriotic soldier, a true man—he laid down his life upon the altar of his country, and that country mourning the loss of so many of her sons in this wicked rebellion, has lost none braver, truer or nobler than Joseph C. Wright.

CHAPTER XXIX.

BIOGRAPHICAL SKETCHES OF ILLINOIS GENERALS—LIFE AND CAREER OF GEN. McCLERNAND—HIS YOUTH—ON THE LAW AND IN BUSINESS—ELECTED TO THE LEGISLATURE—ADVOCACY OF GREAT PUBLIC MEASURES—ELECTED TO CONGRESS—BILLS INTRODUCED—ENTERS THE SERVICE—HIS CAREER AS A GENERAL—RESIGNATION—LIFE OF GEN. LOGAN—CONGRESSIONAL CAREER—IN THE SERVICE—PERSONAL SKETCH—HIS INFLUENCE AND EXAMPLE—A NOBLE LETTER—LIFE OF GEN. RANSOM—EARLY DAYS IN CHICAGO—ENTERS THE SERVICE—AT VICKSBURG AND PLEASANT HILLS—HIS HEROISM—LAST ILLNESS—DEATH OF A GALLANT SOLDIER—GRAPHIC DESCRIPTION OF HIS DEATH—SUMMARY OF HIS CHARACTER—GEN. McARTHUR AND HIS LIFE AND CAREER.

JOHN ALEXANDER McCLERNAND was born of Scotch parents, in Kentucky, and, when very young, went with his parents to Shawneetown, Ill. At the early age of twenty he took an honorable position at the bar, in the practice of the legal profession. In 1832, he volunteered as a private in the Black-Hawk war, in which he served until its close, and during which he performed many gallant actions, among them that of bearing a dispatch from General Posey nearly one hundred miles through a wild country infested by hostile Indians.

After the war his health was so impaired that it would not allow him to resume his profession and he consequently engaged in more active pursuits, trading on the Ohio and Mississippi rivers. In 1835 he established the first Democratic press in Shawneetown, and in the same year re-commenced the practice of the law. In 1836 he was elected to the State Legislature from the county of Gallatin. During the session he was appointed on a committee, of which Douglas was a member, to investigate charges preferred by Governor Duncan against President Jackson, and was also an ardent advocate of the "deep-cut plan," for the Illinois and Michigan Canal, of which great

John A. Logan

MAJ. GEN. JOHN A. LOGAN U.S.V.

Engraved expressly for "Patriotism of Illinois" Clarke & Co. Publishers.

work he was soon after elected commissioner and treasurer. In 1838 the office of Lieutenant-Governor was tendered him, which he declined, as he was not yet of the constitutional age—thirty years.

In 1840 he was elected the second time to the Legislature from the county of Gallatin. During the session, Mr. McClernand, in a debate, made a statement, on the authority of Mr. Douglas, impugning the conduct of the Supreme Court, to which Judge Theophilus W. Smith took exception, and sent a challenge, which was promptly accepted. He repaired to the appointed spot but the Judge failed to make his appearance.

In 1839 he was nominated, by a State Convention, as one of the electors to support Van Buren and Johnson. In 1842 he was elected to the Legislature for the third time from Gallatin, during which session he brought forward amendments to the banking system of the State, which were finally adopted. In 1843, while still a member of the Legislature, he was elected a representative to the twenty-eighth Congress. His first speech in Congress was on the bill to refund the fine imposed on General Jackson by Judge Hall. During the same session he made speeches on the Rhode Island controversy and in favor of the repeal of the second section of the apportionment law, requiring the States to elect representatives to Congress by single districts. During this session he also brought forward, as a member of the Committee on Public Lands, a report, accompanied by a bill, for a grant of land to aid in the completion of the Illinois and Michigan Canal. In 1844, owing to a change of the usual time by an act of the Legislature, another election for representatives in Congress came on and Mr. McClernand was elected without opposition. He was one of the members who insisted upon the "fifty-four forty," in the Oregon controversy, and as chairman of the Committee on Public Lands, he introduced a bill to grant to the State of Tennessee the public lands of the United States lying within her borders. During the first session of the twenty-ninth Congress, he introduced the bill to reduce and graduate the price of the public lands. At the ensuing session he took an active part in favor of the bill to bring into market the mineral regions around Lake Superior.

In 1846 he was again elected to Congress for the third time, and again without opposition. In 1848 he was re-elected, but not without opposition. In 1849, as one of the members of a select committee, he submitted a minority report defending the action of President Polk in establishing a tariff of duties in the ports of the Mexican Republic. In 1850 he prepared and offered the first draft of the famous compromise measures of that year, and in the same session drafted the bill granting a quantity of land in aid of the construction of the Illinois Central Railroad and its Chicago branch.

In 1851 he retired from Congress after eight years' service and removed to Jacksonville, Ill. In 1852 he was chosen a second time an elector for President, and voted for Pierce and King. In 1856 he removed to Springfield, Ill. In 1859 he was elected from the capital district to the popular branch of Congress to fill the vacancy caused by the death of Col. T. L. Harris.

In April, 1861, at the instance of Governor Yates, being still a member of Congress, he accompanied an armed volunteer force from Springfield to Cairo and occupied that place. While there he caused the steamers passing from St. Louis to Louisville and other intermediate points in Missouri and Kentucky, to be brought to at Cairo, and thus kept from the rebel agents a considerable quantity of arms and munitions. This was the first time the navigation of the Mississippi had been interfered with by the federal authority. While at Cairo, he informed himself intimately of the condition of affairs in the West and Southwest, and laid them before Governor Yates and the President. In July, 1861, he again took his seat in Congress, but shortly after resigned and returned to Illinois, with written authority to raise a brigade, and before the expiration of August, was ordered to Cairo by General Fremont, assuming command there on the 5th of September.

In the battle of Pittsburg Landing, or Shiloh, Major-General McClernand was conspicuous throughout. His division was engaged through both days of that sanguinary conflict, and bore, without blemish, the honor of the Prairie State.

After the battle he moved his division cautiously forward, protecting it as it advanced.

On the 29th of April he was, by order of Major-General Halleck, assigned to the command of the third division of the Army of the

Tennessee, Major-General Wallace's, the fifth division of the Army of the Ohio, commanded by Brigadier-General Crittenden, with the cavalry and artillery, including the siege trains, attached—these with his own division constituting the Army Corps of the Reserve. A subsequent order assigned the 5th division with one of the siege batteries to Major-General Buell. With this command he moved forward, having some skirmishing, and destroying railroad and telegraphic communication, until the pains-taking strategy of General Halleck gave his magnificent army possession of Corinth, without its army of Confederates, without its munitions or guns. From a providential point of view it is not now difficult to see that such was the best, but from a military, not so easy.

Remaining in the field until September, he was ordered to return to Springfield to assist Governor Yates in organizing the volunteers of this State enlisted under the call for 600,000 men.

Subsequently he commanded the 13th Army Corps in the expedition against Vicksburg and its surroundings. These events will hereafter be considered in their order. In January, 1863, he commanded what he denominated "The Army of the Mississippi," consisting of parts of two Corps d'armee, namely, the 13th, his own, and the 15th, Major-General Sherman's, in the expedition resulting in the reduction and capture of Arkansas Post, with 5,000 prisoners, seventeen pieces of cannon, large and small, with large quantities of small arms, swords, ammunition, etc.

He commanded the 13th Corps at the siege of Vicksburg, and during it, unfortunately, the harmony subsisting between himself and General Grant was disturbed, and on the 18th of June, 1863, he was relieved of his command.

Subsequently General McClernand resigned his commission. In the presidential contest of 1864 he took part for Major-General McClellan in opposition to Mr. Lincoln.

In his address of May 31, 1863, to the 13th Corps, the General thus enumerated the doings of the Corps up to the 22d, when the unsuccessful attack was made on the defences of Vicksburg:

"HEAD-QUARTERS, ARMY CORPS,
BATTLE-FIELD IN REAR OF VICKSBURG, May 31, 1863.

"*General Orders, No.* 72.

"COMRADES: As your commander, I am proud to congratulate you upon your constancy, valor and success. History affords no more brilliant example of soldierly qualities. Your victories have followed in such rapid succession that their echoes have not yet reached the country. They will challenge its grateful and enthusiastic applause. Yourselves striking out a new path, your comrades of the army of Tennessee followed, and a way was thus opened for them to redeem previous disappointments. Your march through Louisiana, from Milliken's Bend to New Carthage and Pekinss' plantation, on the Mississippi River, is one of the most remarkable on record. Bayous and miry roads, threatened with momentary inundations, obstructed your progress. All these were overcome by unceasing labor and unflagging energy. The two thousand feet of bridging which was hastily improvised out of materials created on the spot, and over which you passed, must long be remembered as a marvel.

"Descending the Mississippi still lower, you were the first to cross the river at Bruin's Landing, and to plant our colors in the State of Mississippi, below Warrenton. Resuming the advance the same day, you pushed on until you came up to the enemy near Port Gibson. Only restrained by the darkness of the night, you hastened to attack him on the morning of the 1st of May, and by vigorously pushing him at all points, drove him from his position, taking a large number of prisoners and small arms, and five pieces of cannon. General Logan's division came up in time to gallantly share in consummating the most valuable victory won since the capture of Fort Donelson.

"Taking the lead, on the morning of the 2d, you were the first to enter Port Gibson, and to hasten the retreat of the enemy from the vicinity of that place. During the ensuing night, as a consequence of the victory at Port Gibson, the enemy spiked his guns at Grand Gulf and evacuated that place, retiring upon Vicksburg and Edwards' Station. The fall of Grand Gulf was solely the result of the victory achieved by the land forces at Port Gibson. The armament and public stores captured there are but just trophies of that victory.

"Hastening to bridge the south branch of the Bayou Pierre, at Port Gibson, you crossed on the morning of the 3d, and pushed on to Willow Springs, Big Sandy, and the main crossing of Fourteen Mile Creek, four miles from Edwards' Station. A detachment of the enemy was immediately driven away from the crossing, and you advanced, passed over, and rested during the night of the 12th within three miles of the enemy, in large force at the station.

"On the morning of the 13th, the objective point of the army's movements having been changed from Edwards' Station to Jackson, in pursuance of an order from the commander of the department, you moved on the north side of the Fourteen Mile Creek toward Raymond.

"This delicate and hazardous movement was executed by a portion of your number, under cover of Hovey's division, which made a feint of attack in line of battle upon Edwards' Station. Too late to harm you, the enemy attacked the rear of that division, but was promptly and decisively repulsed.

"Resting near Raymond that night, on the morning of the 14th you entered that place, one division moving on the Mississippi Springs, near Jackson, in support of General Sherman, another to Clinton, in support of General McPherson, a third remaining at Raymond, and a fourth at Old Auburn, to bring up the army trains.

"On the 15th you again led the advance toward Edwards' Station, which once more become the objective point. Expelling the enemy's picket from Bolton the same day, you seized and held that important position.

"On the 16th you led the advance, in three columns, upon three roads against Edwards' Station. Meeting the enemy on the way in strong force, you heavily engaged him near Champion Hill, and after a sanguinary and obstinate battle, with the assistance of General McPherson's corps, beat and routed him, taking many prisoners and small arms, and several pieces of cannon.

"Continuing to lead the advance, you rapidly pursued the enemy to Edwards' Station, capturing that place, a large quantity of public stores, and many prisoners and small arms. Night only stopped you.

"At day-dawn, on the 17th, you resumed the advance, and early coming upon the enemy strongly intrenched in elaborate works, both before and behind Big Black River, immediately opened with artillery upon him, followed by a daring and heroic charge at the point of the bayonet, which put him to rout, leaving eighteen pieces of cannon and more than a thousand prisoners in your hands.

"By an early hour on the morning of the 18th, you had constructed a bridge across the Big Black, and had commenced the attack upon Vicksburg."

On the 14th of February, 1864, General McClernand assumed command of the 13th army corps, then dispersed in detachments from Brownsville, on the Rio Grande, to New Orleans and to Port Hudson, on the Mississippi River, and was dispatched to the coast of Texas. He arrived at Matagorda Island on the 18th of May, and established his headquarters there. Several days were occupied in a thorough inspection of the garrison at various points and in pleasant interviews with Cortinas. On the 18th of April he embarked with a division of the 13th corps for the Red River, in pursuance of General Banks' orders, and on the 24th arrived at Alexandria, upon which place General Banks had retired after the disastrous battle at Sabine Cross Roads. He participated in the battles attending the retreat, ordered a part of his pioneer corps to assist in constructing the dam which relieved the gunboats. He fell sick at Alexandria, arrived at Fort De Russy, and was transferred on stretchers to the hospital boat, carried to New Orleans, and arrived at Alton on the 16th of June. In November, 1865, he tendered his resignation, which was accepted.

While the difficulty between General McClernand and General Grant is to be regretted, it is due to the former to state that he never allowed it to impair his efficiency. We believe he always did his duty manfully and to the extent of his ability. Of his fighting qualities, none, either friend or foe, ever doubted. Although the larger part of his life had been spent in the wordy war of politics, he entered the real theater of war as a trained actor, skilled to carry out his part. He was identified with the war from its very initiation, imbued the southern part of Illinois, where he was a great favorite, with the military spirit, and was never slow, either by advice or by direct physical aid, to encourage and further the cause of the Union. He only resigned when he thought that his services had ceased to be valuable, looking upon his removal to the banks of the Rio Grande as an intimation to that effect.

MAJOR-GENERAL LOGAN.

John A. Logan, the Murat of Illinois bravery, was born in Jackson county, Illinois, February 9, 1826, near the present town of Murphysboro. His father was of Irish descent, and removed to Illinois in 1823. His mother was from Tennessee. During his earlier years he had few educational privileges, as at that early day in Illinois, schools were the exceptions, and their advantages were of the most limited nature. His education was obtained largely at home from his father and from hired teachers, and in 1840 he added to his stock of knowledge by attending an academy in his county, dignified by the name of Shiloh College. His quick perception and tenacious memory enabled him thoroughly to improve his fugitive advantages, and retain and improve what he acquired at the schools.

When the Mexican war broke out, although at that time but a lad of nineteen, he volunteered, and was elected Lieutenant of a company commanded by James Hampton, of Jackson county, in the 1st regiment Illinois volunteers. With these he faithfully served his time, his career being marked especially by coolness and unflinching bravery. In October, 1848, he returned home and entered upon the study of the law in the office of his uncle, Alexander M. Jenkins, formerly Lieutenant-Governor of Illinois, and while thus pursuing his studies, in November, 1849, was elected clerk of his county, which office he held until 1850. During that year he went to Louisville, Ky., to attend law lectures. In 1851 he was admitted to the bar, and returning home, commenced the practice of the law with his uncle. He obtained a prominent position in his profession almost immediately, and was rapidly elevated by his wide-spread popularity. In 1852 he was elected prosecuting attorney of the then 3d judicial circuit, and removed to Benton, Franklin county, Illinois, and in the fall of that year was elected to the Legislature to represent the counties of Franklin and Jackson.

On the 27th of November, 1855, he was married at Shawneetown to Miss Mary S. Cunningham, daughter of John W. Cunningham, formerly register of the land-office at that place. In May, 1856, he was appointed Presidential elector for the 9th Congressional district, and at the November election was re-elected to the Legislature. In 1858 he was nominated and elected to Congress by the Democracy of the 9th district over his Republican opponent by a large majority. In 1860 he was re-elected from the same district. In the winter of 1860, by the action of the Legislature, his county was thrown out of his old district and added to one running northward, and after his return he removed to Marion, Williamson county, that he might still be in his district.

At the outbreak of the war and during the extra session of Congress, in July, 1861, he entered the ranks of Col. Richardson's regiment, and displayed marked bravery at the disastrous battle of Bull Run. He returned home in 1861, fully determined to devote himself, body and soul, to the cause of his country, and on the 3d of September, made a speech to his constituents, in which he declared his intention to enter the service as a "private, or in any manner he could serve his country best in defending and bearing the old blood-stained flag over every foot of soil in the United States." His great popularity and the wide-spread influence he exerted, for in his district he was an idol among the people, at once rallied them to the cause, and on the 16th of September, the 31st regiment was organized at Cairo and immediately recommended him for their Colonel. He was appointed to the post and held his commission from that date. His regiment was attached to General McClernand's brigade, and although only organized for a short time, and having had only six weeks' drill, the heroic part taken by the regiment in the battle of Belmont, on the 7th of November, 1861, proved the qualities of their commander, how active he had been in instruction and how rigid in discipline. He commanded his regiment through the most trying circumstances in the rear of Fort Henry, at the capture of that important post, and in command of 200 cavalry pursued and captured eight of the enemy's guns. During the three days' siege and attack on Fort Donelson, he was constantly engaged and rendered the most valuable service. On the morning of the 15th of February he was wounded while rallying his men when their ammunition was nearly exhausted, although they were hard pressed by a superior force. The bullet entered the fore part of the left arm near the point of the shoulder, passing round and out through the shoulder. Regardless of his wound and despising danger, he kept on the field, and by his magnificent bearing and personal influence, kept his position until reinforcements arrived, when he was forced to retire, weak with the loss of blood and exhausted with fatigue, to have his wounds dressed. He remained prostrated for three weeks with the wound in his shoulder, lameness from being struck in the hip with a spent ball, and disease contracted by exposure.

On the 5th of March, 1862, he was confirmed as Brigadier-General, and reported to General Grant at Pittsburg Landing, who assigned to his command the 8th, 18th, 30th and 31st Illinois and 12th Michigan regiments, of which he retained command during the movement on Corinth. He was a perfect master of the situation before Corinth, and had General John A. Logan commanded, few of the rebel troops would have had an opportunity to escape. He repeatedly insisted on pressing on, but the orders were adverse to bringing on a general engagement, and the Halleckian policy would not allow him to go beyond our lines. From this place he commanded the division engaged in re-building the road to Jackson and Columbus. After the completion of the road he was placed in command of the forces at Jackson, Tenn., from which place, under date of August 26th, he sent a noble and patriotic letter to Hon. O. M. Hatch, Secretary of State, of Illinois, and read at the Union convention in September, 1862, declining to become a candidate for Congress for the State at large. We append some extracts from this letter:

"In making this reply, I feel that it is unnecessary to enlarge as to what were, are, or may hereafter be my political views, but would simply state that politics of every grade and character whatsoever are now ignored by me, since I am convinced that the constitution and life of this republic—which I shall never cease to adore—are in danger. I express all my views and politics when I assert my attachment for the *Union.* I have no other politics now, and consequently no aspirations for civil place and power.

"No! I am to-day a soldier of this Republic, so to remain, changeless and immutable until her last and weakest enemy shall have expired and passed away. Ambitious men, who have not a true love for their country at heart, may bring forth crude and bootless questions to agitate the pulse of our troubled nation and thwart the preservation of this Union, but for none of such am I. I have entered the field—to die if needs be—for this Government, and never expect to return to peaceful pursuits until the object of this war for preservation has become a fact established.

"For the flattering manner in which you have seen fit to allude to my past services; I return you my sincere thanks; but if it has been my fortune to bleed and suffer for my dear country, it is all but too little compared to what I am willing again and again to endure; and should fate so ordain it, I will esteem it as the highest privilege a just Dispenser can award, to shed the last drop of blood in my veins for the honor of that flag whose emblems are justice, liberty and truth, and which has been, and, as I humbly trust in God, ever will be for the right.

"In conclusion, let me request that your desire to associate my name with the high and honorable position you would confer upon me, be at once dismissed, and some more suitable and worthy person substituted. Meanwhile I shall continue to look with unfeigned pride and admiration on the continuance of the present able conduct of our State affairs, and feel that I am sufficiently honored while acknowledged as an humble soldier of our own peerless State."

Fitting words for a hero, and worthy to be framed in gold. That letter may challenge the whole literature of the war to find its equal in sincere patriotism, native manliness and dignity. It is no vain boasting. Every line and letter of it has been more than sustained in the course pursued by General Logan. Of his important service in the battles preliminary to the siege of Vicksburg, and the prominent part he took in the siege of that city, we have already spoken. He nobly sustained the honor of his state and his own fame through those trying months of exposure and battle. The citizens of his State have also followed him with pride through the terrible battles in Northern Georgia, and found that his name was always the signal of success. In the election canvass of 1864, he espoused the cause of the government, and threw himself into it with all the ardor of his fiery nature. The same influence which had rallied the men of Egypt by thousands around the Stars and Stripes, was again brought to bear upon them for what he deemed the best of causes. Former political opinions were laid aside or buried. He worked like a giant, and with his rare and matchless eloquence, and fascinating personal magnetism so won the people of Southern Illinois, that they once more as in old times, hailed him as their leader, and followed his guidance. He advocated the cause of the Union on the stump as vigorously and thoroughly as he had advocated it in the field with more compulsory weapons, and this without any meretricious idea or hope of preferment. He had repeatedly declined offices tendered him, always saying that he was a soldier of the Union, and that he should not leave the service nor lay down the sword as long as there was a rebel in arms against the government. With his promotion to a Major-Generalship, his prowess in the march upon Atlanta, his gallant deeds in the battles around that city, and his participation in the marches through the Carolinas, our readers are familiar. They are appropriate episodes, each taking its place harmoniously in the record of his eventful and patriotic life. Of his personal appearance a writer well says:

"Were one to pass our Generals in review, and endeavor from their countenances to select the man with the most gunpowder in his disposition, he would undoubtedly choose Gen. John A. Logan. He is marked by a square, massive frame of medium hight, a countenance swarthy as that of an Indian, jet black hair, and eyes of the most piercing blackness. The general ferocity of his appearance is not detracted from by a heavy black moustache, whose ends drop below his jaw on either side, and this effect is hightened by a broad, short neck, like that of a bull or gladiator. And yet, when the General's countenance is not lighted by the glow of battle, his swarthy face is sunny with good nature, and his eyes ablaze with fun and good humor. No commander in the army is more popular with his men than he; their love for him as a man is only equaled by their confidence in him as a leader. In all operations he is omnipresent, encouraging his men with advice, urging them on with some funny joke, ever at their head in battle, only happy when moving, and only completely happy when hurling his invincible brigades against the enemy."

BRIG. GEN. T. E. G. RANSOM. U.S. VOLS.

ENGRAVED EXPRESSLY FOR "PATRIOTISM OF ILLINOIS" [illegible] PUBLISHERS.

In his peculiar personal magnetism and the influence he possesses over men, he resembles the lamented Douglas. His eye is commanding and piercing; his voice strong, yet musical and sympathetic and his utterances rapid but distinct. Few men so trouble the fast pens of the phonographers as he. As his nature is passionate and vehement, so is his speech, and when warmed up with the occasion, he is master of all the powers of logic and argument, appeal and invective. There is not a more courageous heart or fearless arm now defending the country than John A. Logan's.

BRIGADIER-GENERAL T. E. G. RANSOM.

Young, heroic and handsome, brave, enthusiastic and manly, courageous as a lion and tender as a woman, no man so completely recalls the best qualities of the days of chivalry as Thomas Edwin Greenfield Ransom. No braver heart has been laid upon the country's altar, no clearer head has bowed before the great destroyer, no more unsullied sword has been hung upon the wall. Yielding up his life in the very flower of his youth, he will remain in memory ever young.

General Ransom was born at Norwich, Madison county, Vermont, on the 29th of November, 1834. His father, Col. Trueman B. Ransom, was born in Woodstock, Vt., in 1803, and was for sometime President of the Norwich University in that State In this school the military element was made prominent. The students were trained in the manual of arms, and during an extended tour in the summer of 1845, in which the cadets attracted great attention, young Ransom accompanied them. The military element of the school made a deep impression upon him. His father at that time was a major-general of militia of the State of Vermont. On the outbreak of the Mexican War, he was appointed colonel of the 9th U. S. Infantry. After participating in several battles and winning for himself a national fame, he fell at the storming of Chepultepec, in September, 1847. His death created a deep impression, for his career had been brilliant and brave. During the Mexican war, young Ransom was taught engineering under the tuition of his cousin, B. F. Marsh, on the Rutland and Burlington Railroad. After his father's death he returned to the military school, and continued there until the spring of 1851, at which time he removed to Peru, Lasalle Co., Illinois, to engage in the practice of the engineering profession. In 1854, he embarked in the real estate business with his uncle, under the name of Gilson, Ransom & Co. In the latter part of 1855, the firm removed to Chicago, and became largely engaged in real estate operations under the name of A. J. Galloway & Co. He afterward carried on the same business in the firm of Bell & Ransom. Mr. Gilson having died in September, 1856, he then removed to Fayette County, Illinois, and while engaged in trade, acted as agent for the Illinois Central Railroad Company. He was there when the war broke out. He threw himself into the Union cause with all the ardor of his nature. He raised a company in that county, and arrived at Camp Yates, April 24, 1861. This company was organized into the 11th Illinois regiment, and on an election for field officers, he was elected Major. The regiment was ordered at once to Villa Ridge near Cairo, and there remained in camp of instruction until June, when it was ordered to Bird's Point, Mo.

On July 30th, the regiment was mustered out of the three months' service and a large majority of the regiment went into the three years' service. On the reorganization, Major Ransom was elected Lieutenant-Colonel. The Colonel of the regiment was most of the time commanding either the post or a brigade, and thus the command and discipline devolved almost entirely upon the young Lieut.-Colonel. He gave his time and attention to his men, and conscientiously and gradually brought them to that pitch of military perfection which subsequently rendered the regiment famous.

On the 22d of August, he led his regiment against a large force of rebels under Major Hunter, concentrated at Charleston, Mo. The regiment made a most gallant fight and captured fifty horses and men. Col. Ransom was wounded in the shoulder by a mounted rebel, who pretended to surrender, but fired upon him as he approached to take his arms. Col. R. immediately fired upon the traitor and killed him. At Fort Donelson the conduct of Col. Ransom was gallant in the extreme. He was again shot in the shoulder but he refused to leave the field until the fight was ended. His clothes were pierced by six or eight bullet holes and his horse was killed under him. Fatigue, cold, wounds and exposures, brought on a long sickness, but still he was devoted to his men, and when they moved from place to place he was carried in an ambulance. For his bravery and skill in this battle he was promoted to the colonelcy of his regiment.

At Shiloh he was the bravest of the brave. He led his regiment through the thickest of the bloody fight, and though wounded in the head, still clung to his regiment. He assisted General McClernand in rallying an Ohio regiment that was falling back, and compelled them to move forward with his own command upon a rebel battery. In the official report of this battle General McClernand spoke of him at a critical moment "performing prodigies of valor, though reeling in his saddle and streaming with blood from a serious wound." The following evidence of the gallantry of his regiment is taken from a private letter:

"It was nearly half a mile from our encampment to the position where the enemy had attacked us. The order for 'double quick' was given, and we were soon on the field of action. We had not to wait long, for soon in front of us was seen—not three hundred yards distant—the enemy, five regiments deep, advancing steadily. It was a glorious but a terrible sight. The order was, 'The whites of their eyes, boys, and then give it to them,' and the 11th was again engaged. Never, *never* in my life have I seen, or in the annals of history have I read of such a death-struggle.

"Our men fought well at Fort Donelson, but never did they fight as they fought on the 6th of April. The enemy were repulsed; they stood for a moment seemingly thunderstruck, and then broke their ranks and started to fly. The officers rallied them, and then, under a most galling fire, commenced retrieving their lost ground. Our regiment being badly cut up—Col. Ransom shot in the head (not mortally), Capt. Carter dead, Capt. Coats mortally wounded, five or six of our lieutenants down, and no reserve coming to our assistance —the order was given to fall back. We gradually, but obstinately, fell back. We were soon cheered by the assistance of several regiments coming up, who filed in our front, and we were for a time relieved. We fell back—and what a sight! Not one hundred men remained in the 11th! It was an awful sight to look at that little band, besmeared with blood and dirt, with their trusty guns in their hands, looking along the line to see how many of their beloved companions were left to them. It was a sight I never wish to see again. But there was little time to lose, and no time to complain. General McClernand came up, and asked if that was all that was left of the 11th. 'Yes,' was the reply. 'Well, my men,' he said, 'we must win this day, or *all* will be lost. Will you try it again?' 'We will, General,' was the response. The boys called on *me* to lead them. I formed the regiment (or company, as it was) on the left of the 70th Ohio regiment, and was again ordered to take our position in front. Ten minutes' time and we were again engaged."

In the spring of 1863 he was promoted to the rank of Brigadier-General, to date from November 29 (his birthday), 1862, for distinguished service on the field of Shiloh and at the siege of Corinth. Many of his gallant actions during the siege of Vicksburg we have already recorded, especially the heroic part he took in the disastrous assaults of May 22d. In the equally disastrous Red River expedition, his coolness and bravery at the battle of Pleasant Hill undoubtedly saved the detachment of the 13th army corps which he commanded from overwhelming defeat and ruin.

Gen. Ransom was four times wounded. At Charleston, Missouri, August 19, 1861; at Fort Donelson, February 15, 1862; at Shiloh, April 6, 1862; and at Pleasant Hill, La., April 8, 1864. His wound at the latter place was very severe, and he returned to Chicago for rest. He had been in continual active service almost from the outbreak of the war without any relaxation; but even before his wound was quite well, feeling that his presence was needed in Georgia, he removed to the front. Through the remainder of the summer he was in good health, and took a prominent part in the campaign which gave us Atlanta.

In the early part of October he was taken sick with dysentery. As his command had been ordered to Rome, he started with it, although his disease was continually weakening him. Sometimes he rode in an ambulance, but always at the head of his troops, and sometimes took the saddle as the advance guard became engaged with the enemy. Generals Sherman and Howard and the medical directors begged him to allow himself to be reported sick, but his decision was unalterable. "*I will stay with my command until I leave in my coffin*," was his final answer. On the 26th of October, still on the move, there was a change for the worse, and his death was hourly expected, but his vigorous constitution and iron will carried him through the relapse. An army chaplain gives the following graphic and mournful picture of his death:

"Late at night of October 7th, our regiment received orders to prepare to march at 5 o'clock next morning as an escort to General Ransom, who, being very sick, was to be sent to Rome. The General was in high favor with Sherman, who sent for him to take an important command, after he had sufficiently recovered from his wounds received on the Red River expedition under Banks. After Atlanta had fallen he had been placed in command of the 17th corps, during the absence of General Blair, who was home on leave. He had been for two or three weeks suffering from a severe attack of dysentery, and for some days it had been necessary to carry him on a bed in an easy spring wagon. Arriving at Galesville he was obliged to give up. He was provided with good quarters in a house, but in spite of the best care he grew worse. And now the army was to move. To leave him behind to the tender mercies of the 'chivalry,' was but to abandon him to robbery and murder. He was very low. Few thought he would get to Rome alive. A comfortable litter was provided, with a little canopy of hoops, etc., as a protection to his head from the sun and wind, and he was to be carried upon the shoulders of four strong men, in relays, relieving each other every fifteen minutes.

"Soon after we had started we passed General Sherman's headquarters. He sent an order to the regiment to halt, and came out to see General R. 'How are you, Ransom?' said he. 'How are you getting on?' 'Oh, finely, thank you.' 'Quite an Oriental style of traveling you are indulging yourself in.' 'It is wonderfully easy and comfortable, General,' said Ransom. 'Well, keep up good heart, my boy, I shall follow you soon, and be near you during the day. I hope the change will restore you.' 'Which way are you going, Colonel?' said he, to the commanding officer. 'Right ahead,' was the reply.

"'Oh, you had better countermarch; take this wagon-path through the brush, here; cross the Chatooga river at a temporary bridge you will find about a half-mile from here and thus save eight miles travel.' I mention this as showing the minuteness of observation for which Sherman is so remarkable. Indeed, close observance of details is a characteristic of all who have become distinguished for great qualities. And it is another peculiarity which distinguishes them that they are apt to be misunderstood. In the first years of the war Sherman was called *crazy*, because he saw so much further than those under whose orders he served, that they could not understand him; therefore he was called insane. Those who stand upon the watch-towers survey a much wider horizon than the multitude below. 'Geniuses are the world's madmen.'

"The day was pleasant and we proceeded on our way at a good rate of speed; those strong men carrying the patient as gently as an infant is rocked in its cradle, and making some twelve or thirteen miles. At night General Ransom appeared better, and the next morning having had refreshing sleep, felt courageous for continuing his journey. Ten miles more were made by noon, when it began to be apparent that his strength was rapidly failing. Reaching a house six miles west of Rome, we halted. He was carried in and placed in a comfortable bed. But it was evident his end was fast approaching. His great fortitude had thus far sustained in him the belief that he might yet survive. But the signs of dissolution were now unmistakable, and it was time to announce to him the inevitable fact. He received it with the same calm courage with which he had so often before stood face to face with death. He sent messages of love and farewell to friends. He said: 'Tell my mother I am not afraid to die. My chief regret is that I cannot be spared to serve my country longer; and, if I must die, that it cannot be with my armor on, confronting her enemies.' He adjusted all his business, and gave directions as to the disposal of his effects and of his mortal remains, to Capt. Cadle and another member of his staff who stood by him with almost womanly tenderness and assiduity in his last hours, as indeed they had all through his sickness. I said to him: 'You have a family, General?' 'A mother and near relatives; but I am not married, nor am I engaged.' 'You are not yet thirty?' I said. 'I should be thirty in November.'

"When very near his end, General Wm. P. Carlin, commanding a division of the 14th corps, which was passing, came up and called to see him. He was almost breathing his last; but rousing himself, with an effort, on hearing his voice, and looking and speaking almost as if his spirit had departed and for a moment returned to make itself again manifest, he greeted General C. with all the courtesy and grace of language for which he was noted. As the General afterwards said: 'He received me with the same dignity and grace as if he were entertaining a distinguished guest in his best estate at his private quarters.' Scarcely had General Carlin retired when he breathed his last. After repeated messages of gratitude to the faithful men who had carried him so far and so gently, and also to Dr. Ormsby and others who had watched by and tended him so long and faithfully, he said he felt like sleeping; and he went to sleep 'among the eternal,' as calmly as the sun went down that mild October evening, amid fleecy clouds of golden glory. Yes, we did escort him home; but arrived there only with his cold remains."

His body was brought to Chicago and interred with impressive ceremonies, and amid the deep grief of thousands who knew him. We cannot better sum up the character of the deceased hero, than in the words of the clergyman who preached the funeral sermon, Rev. W. H. Ryder, D.D.:

"1. General Ransom was retiring and unostentatious. There was no strut about him. He was simple in his manners—quiet, unobtrusive. In a company of gentlemen he would not have been selected as a military man, according to the popular estimate. His power was always in reserve for occasions—and the greater the occasion, the deeper the peril, the more capable did he show himself to be. Ambitious—meaning thereby desire of power or eminence—he was not. His ambition was to honor his country—the service—to quit himself as a man should, acting in such a presence, and such an hour. Whether General Ransom would have arisen to the rank of a *great* leader—*i. e.*, whether he would have gained a still higher grade, and filled it with the same distinguished success which graced all the positions he occupied, is now a question which can never be decisively answered, and which, perhaps, it is not worth while to tarry long to consider. One thing is quite certain: had he been the chief in command of the famous Red River expedition, that blundering campaign, if undertaken at all, would have had a very different issue. And it is a pretty safe rule, that he who does best when most is demanded, is capable of doing more than he has ever yet done.

"2. General Ransom was a kind, pleasant, sympathetic man. He had a sunny face, a clear, cheerful eye. He attached people to him; they loved him, for he was good; they honored him for he was brave. There are those here who knew the kindness of his heart, and who loved him with all the reverence of grateful affection. A dutiful son, an appreciative relative, a faithful friend, a patriot hero, he deserves well of his countrymen, and will long be honored in the sanctuaries of a thousand hearts.

"3. General Ransom's patriotism and high moral tone proceeded from conviction—were the outgrowth of inward stability. The springs of his action were deep. He was true in danger and uniformly prepared for the duty when it came. Hence, also, he did not degenerate into the temptations which beset the service, or lose that strength which comes from Christian integrity. These traits would have served him in any calling. And had he lived to the allotted age of man, it is more than probable he would have held fast to the principles which distinguished his youth, and ended his career in a life of the largest usefulness."

GENERAL McARTHUR.

JOHN MCARTHUR was born in the parish of Erskine, Renfrewshire, Scotland, November 16, 1826. He was sent to school at the usual age, and displayed such proficiency and aptitude in learning his tasks that he attracted the attention of the parish minister, who desired to educate him for the ministry. The boy had a mechanical turn of mind and was fond of working in his father's shop. In his own words at that time, he preferred to be "Jock, the Smith," rather than the "Rev. John McArthur." He remained in his father's shop until the age of twenty-three, when he determined to emigrate to the prairies of Illinois. In due time he arrived in Illinois, and was employed as a foreman in Cobb's boiler foundry, in Chicago. In 1852 he formed a copartnership with his brother-in-law, Carlyle Mason, as blacksmiths and boiler makers, when he laid the foundation of his future brilliant career. He was fortunate in business, and by his integrity and sagacity, placed himself upon a firm footing. Prior to the outbreak of the war he took a deep interest in our citizen soldiery, and on the formation of the Chicago Highland Guards, a Scotch company, he was elected its first lieutenant and soon after captain. When the war broke out he sprang at once into the ranks and devoted himself heart and soul to the service of his adopted country. He was elected Lieut.-Colonel of the Washington Independent Regiment, of which the Highland Guards formed a part, and a few weeks later was elected Colonel of the 12th Illinois regiment. When the troubles commenced in Kentucky, he was stationed with his regiment at Paducah, and from thence was ordered to Fort Henry. At Fort Donelson he was an acting Brigadier, and in that terrible conflict displayed such bravery and coolness as to win his commission. At Shiloh he displayed the same bravery, and was wounded by a ball which passed through his foot, disabling him for more than a month, at the expiration of which time he again joined his brigade in the army of the Tennessee, under General Grant. Since that time he has been almost constantly in the service, without rest or cessation, and has gained for himself an enviable name for all the qualities which should distinguish the model soldier.

CHAPTER XXX.

CAMPAIGNS OF THE ARMY OF THE CUMBERLAND.

Reorganization of the Army of the Cumberland—Second Attack on Fort Donelson—Gallant Defense by the 83d Illinois, Col. Harding—The Rebels Driven off—Col. Colborn's Brigade Captured at Spring Hill—Defeat of John Morgan at Milton—The 123d and 80th Illinois in the Fight—Splendid Conduct of the 80th—Granger Attacked by Van Dorn—Defeat of the Rebels at McMinnsville—Col. Streight's Expedition—The Roll of Honor—Names of Illinois Soldiers Distinguished for Bravery.

IN a preceding chapter we closed the operations of the Army of the Cumberland with the battle of Stone River, which took place on the last days of 1862 and the first of 1863. On the 5th of January, General Rosecrans established his headquarters at Murfreesboro. The army occupied a position in front of the town and a series of formidable earth-works, completely surrounding it, was thrown up to protect it as a base of future operations. On the 9th of January the army was re-organized into three corps, called the 14th, 20th and 21st, and commanded respectively by Generals Thomas, McCook and Crittenden. The collection of supplies occupied considerable time, being somewhat retarded by the rain and the operations of the enemy's cavalry, who were overrunning the country and often captured men and wagons. Many of the transports on the Cumberland River were also captured and burned by gangs of Forrest's and Wheeler's men.

On the 31st of January, General Jeff. C. Davis, at the head of a division of infantry and two brigades of cavalry, moved from camp on an expedition in the direction of Rome and Franklin, and was absent thirteen days, visiting various places, and returned with one hundred and forty-one prisoners.

On the 3d of February an attack was made on Fort Donelson, in another part of the department. On the 2d, the rebel General Forrest, at the head of a large force, had taken a position at Palmyra for the purpose of interrupting the navigation of the Cumberland, and on the next day he advanced upon the fort both from above and below. The garrison consisted of nine companies of the 83d Illinois, under Col. Harding, a battalion of the 5th Iowa cavalry, Flood's battery, and some wounded men. The battery consisted of four rifled guns and one 32-pounder siege gun mounted on a pivot on the northwest corner of the fort. Col. Harding learning that the rebels were approaching, telegraphed to Col. Lowe, at Paducah, and asked for reinforcements. That officer sent word back for Col. Harding to send out scouts and ascertain the exact force of the rebels. This was done. Col. Lowe had nearly all his available force out on scouting expeditions and could not send aid, but learning that the gunboats were coming up the river, he sent word to them of the condition of affairs at Fort Donelson, and telegraphed Col. Harding to hold the place at all hazards, until dark, when help would come. The Colonel promised to do as ordered; with what success, the sequel shows. The rebels made their appearance at 2 o'clock in the afternoon and attacked the fort from the eastward, thinking that the weakest point. The rebel batteries were well placed and poured in a hot fire, which was followed up by several unsuccessful charges upon the works by the infantry and dismounted cavalry, with the intention of carrying them at the point of the bayonet. Ammunition within the fort was scarce, and under Col. Harding's orders his riflemen fired slowly and deliberately, so that each shot was effective. Flood's battery had to be used as a siege battery or series of batteries, as occasion offered, and was worked with most consummate skill. It was the first fight of the 83d, but they stood like veterans, and every shot told with fatal effect upon the thick ranks of the assailants. The fight continued for six hours with small loss to the 83d. Col. Harding was everywhere encouraging and sustaining his men. Wherever the fight was most severe or the danger most imminent, there he was, sword in hand, advising, commanding and urging on his men.

But the rebel force was overpowering, and Col. Harding knew ho could not continue the fight much longer. Nearly all his ammunition was exhausted and his men were worn out with fatigue. Night had come and the battle was still raging but there were no signs of reinforcements. Thus far the enemy had been unable to surround the fort on its three sides unprotected by the river, but now an exultant shout arose. The rebels had completely encircled the fort, and a flag of truce was sent in from General Wheeler demanding the surrender of the fort. Col. Harding sent back an indignant refusal and the battle was renewed with double fury. The rebels charged again and again upon the works, but were each time met and repulsed with the deadly fire of our riflemen or their no less deadly bayonets. The 32-pounder siege gun annoyed the rebels with its fearful fire. A second flag of truce was sent in and rejected, and the rebels then concentrated their efforts to capture the gun. A charge was made, joined in by several mounted men, upon the piece. The gunners discovering the object of the rebels, had double-shotted it with grape and canister. A large force was moving swiftly to the south side of the gun, intending to flank it, get on its rear and cut off the gunners. The assailants advanced and were on the point of seizing it, when the gunners rapidly swung it round and poured its contents full into the faces of the rebels. The havoc was dreadful and the assailing party fled precipitately, and the attempt to capture the gun was not renewed.

Help was now near at hand. The gunboats were heard coming up the river, and at 8 o'clock in the evening Capt. Fitch, with his fleet appeared before the astounded enemy. After the arrival of the reinforcements, Col. Harding ordered his men to cease firing and gather into a protected position out of the reach of the shot and shell from the gunboats. The naval force was divided, half the fleet going above and the other below. The first gun was fired from the Fairplay, which opened with grape and shrapnel. The Lexington followed, with her heavier metal, and the Brilliant, Silver Lake and Robb followed. The St. Clair took an excellent position and did fearful execution. At the opening of the gunboat cannonade the rebel force was formed with the mass of its body below the fort, the right upon the graveyard at the top of the hill, and the left upon the river bank ready to make the final attack upon the fort, which they imagined was to secure victory. The firing of the gunboats, however, disconcerted their plans, and soon after the boats opened they broke ranks and fled in confusion. In twenty minutes after the fleet opened fire there was not an uninjured rebel to be seen.

This, as we have stated, was the first fight of the 83d, and most gallantly they bore themselves. For half a day, with a few rounds of ammunition, they sustained their position against great odds and contemptuously refused the rebel demands for surrender. Few regiments in the service have made a more gallant fight. Their loss was only thirteen killed, fifty-one wounded and twenty taken prisoners, while the rebel loss was two hundred and fifty killed, six hundred wounded and one hundred and five prisoners.

After this battle a period of inactivity ensued, which was broken by the defeat and capture of a Federal brigade at Spring Hill on the 5th of March. On the 4th, an expedition under the command of Col. John Colburn, consisting of part of the 33d and 85th Indiana, 22d Wisconsin and 19th Michigan, numbering 1,589 men, together with the 124th Ohio, six hundred cavalry and one battery of six small guns, was ordered to proceed from Franklin to Spring Hill. After skirmishing, they were attacked on the morning of the 5th by a large force under Van Dorn and Forrest, and a severe struggle ensued which was protracted until Forrest obtained a position in the rear, cutting off retreat, when Col. Colburn, finding his ammunition failing, surrendered.

Meanwhile General Sheridan, with his division, and Col. Minty, with a force of 800 cavalry, made a successful expedition. A portion of the force which had captured Col. Colburn was overtaken and driven from the field, and the force of Van Dorn was followed to Duck River when the expedition returned to Franklin.

On the 18th of March, an expedition consisting of the 105th Ohio 101st Indiana, 80th Illinois, Col. Allen, 123d Illinois, Col. Monroe, forty men of Stoke's Tennessee Cavalry, and two sections of the 19th Indiana battery, numbering about 1,400 men, under command of Col. A. S. Hall, left Murfreesboro and moved in the direction of Liberty. That night Gainesville was occupied, and on the next morning an advance was made, when a slight skirmish ensued. The enemy slowly retired, followed by Col. Hall, until they were overtaken, drawn up in line of battle. Finding that he was greatly out numbered, Col. Hall fell back towards Murfreesboro. That night he encamped at Auburn, seven miles from Liberty, and on the next morning, the 20th, took up a position at Milton, twelve miles north-east of Murfreesboro. Here he was attacked by John Morgan. The rebels made their first attack against the right of the Union force, which was then slowly falling back to obtain a more commanding position half a mile to the rear. The 8th Illinois held the right partially covered by a thicket of cedars. Several rebel regiments were crowding up and deploying into a lane, and had just commenced tearing down fences preparatory to a charge, when the 8th, who were unobserved by the enemy, rose up and poured a most terrible and murderous volley into them. They dropped from their horses by scores and in complete rout they fled from the lane.

By this time the engagement was heavy on the left, the 123d Illinois and the 101st Ohio contending against an overwhelming force who were dismounted and aided by a heavy battery. The two regiments held their ground steadily for a time, but shortly the superior force of the rebels caused a gradual retreat. The retreat, however was of short duration, for the 80th Illinois, relieved on the right, came with a cheer, dashing into the fray. The regiments rallied and charged and drove the rebels from the field. In the meanwhile the rebels had thrown a force completely around the ground occupied by the Union troops, and the 105th Ohio was having heavy skirmishing at the rear. Col. Hall, by his maneuvers, had obtained a commanding position and hurried preparations for defense were made. The foe sent in a flag of truce with a demand for surrender, which was instantly rejected. The rebels had been so severely punished that they did not attempt an enforcement of their demand, and with an occasional artillery duel the time passed until the approach of Union reinforcements. The rebels were quick to discover them and rapidly fell back, quitting the field. A wounded rebel summed up the gallant fight when he said to sergeant Abbott, of the 80th Illinois: "This is the first time Morgan has been out of his hole for some time and he has got most beautifully whipped."

A large number of expeditions similar to the above were constantly on the move. On the 10th of April another attack was made on General Gordan Granger, at Franklin, by Van Dorn. The force of General Granger consisted of Baird's and Gilbert's division, 1,600 men and sixteen guns, and Smith's cavalry brigade of 1,128 men; also a cavalry force of 1,600 men and two guns under Colonel Stanley. The principal defense was an uncompleted fort mounting four guns. General Granger's camp was on the north side of the river about two thirds of a mile from the town. General Baird was ordered to hold in check any force attempting to cross the ford below Franklin, and Gen. Gilbert was in position to meet any attack in front. Gen. Stanley was stationed four miles out on the road to Murfreesboro, and Smith's cavalry was held as a reserve for Stanley. This force, however, under a misapprehension was sent to Brentwood. The attack was made upon Granger's front which was repelled, and was then directed against Stanley, who was driven back by overpowering numbers before help could reach him. After this the enemy withdrew.

On the 20th of April, a force in which were the 123d, 80th, 98th and 24th Illinois, consisting of Major-General Reynolds' division, Col. Wilder's brigade and seventeen hundred cavalry under Colonel Minty, left Murfreesboro to capture or disperse a confederate force at McMinnsville. At night the cavalry encamped between Readyville and Woodbury. Early the next morning the force moved on, and encountered the enemy's pickets. A charge was immediately made and the whole force was driven through, and out of the town. A portion of their wagon train was also captured. Other movements were made by the force which resulted in the destruction of a large amount of property and stores belonging to the rebels.

Simultaneously with this movement, the road leading to Shelbyville was advanced upon by brigades of the 20th corps. The 1st brigade of the 2d division, in which was the 89th Illinois, took the pike going out about eight miles, when the rebel pickets were encountered. The road towards Shelbyville, was occupied by Colonel Frank Sherman's brigade of the 3d division, but no fighting occurred. On the 29th of April, a force of five hundred men under Colonel Watkins, captured a camp of the enemy, taking one hundred and thirty-eight prisoners.

About the same time, the unfortunate expedition under Colonel

A. D. Streight, was fitted out for Northern Georgia. The force numbered about eighteen hundred men, consisting of the 51st Indiana, 80th Illinois and portions of two Ohio regiments. Colonel Streight's instructions from General Garfield were substantially that after equipping his expedition, he should proceed to some good steamboat landing on the Tennessee River not far above Fort Henry, where he was to embark his command and proceed up the river. At Hamburg he was to communicate with General Dodge. If it should then appear unsafe to move farther up the river, he was to debark at Hamburg and join Gen. Dodge's forces in the movement for Iuka, Miss. If safe, he was to land at Eastport and form a junction with General Dodge, and after having marched long enough with him, to create the impression he was a part of the expedition, he was suddenly to push southward and reach Russellville or Moulton. From that point circumstances were to determine the direction in which he should move, but in any event he was to push on to Western Georgia and cut all the railroads which supplied the rebel army by way of Chattanooga.

Under these instructions Colonel Streight proceeded to Fort Donelson and thence marched across the country to the Tennessee River. Thence he moved to Eastport and joined Gen. Dodge's forces, then marching upon Tuscumbia and defeated the rebel troops stationed there with considerable loss to them. Thence he moved to Northern Georgia, aiming to reach Rome and Atlanta. No sooner had he commenced his movements, however, than the rebel Generals Forrest and Roddy were aware of them. By a rapid movement they came upon his rear and commenced a running fight which continued for four days, during which there were two severe battles and several skirmishes, in which the 80th Illinois conducted itself with great coolness and bravery, making some dashing charges. The troops had marched one hundred miles towards the heart of the State and had destroyed bridges, railroads and foundries and large amounts of provisions and war material. The rebel force gradually increased to overwhelming numbers, and Col. Streight, his ammunition expended and his men exhausted, was compelled to surrender at a point fifteen miles from Rome, Georgia. His men were sent to Virginia and exchanged two months afterwards. But the officers were retained and imprisoned by the Governor of Georgia upon a fabricated plea of having violated the State laws by inciting slaves to insurrection. The imprisonment of Col. Streight, led to the stoppage of exchange, and the subsequent imprisonment of Gen. Morgan. Col. Streight was then released from imprisonment as a convict, and Morgan subsequently escaped.

Before coming to the grand movements of the main army which led to the battle of Chickamauga and the end of General Rosecrans' career as commander of the army of the Cumberland, it is due to the brave soldiers from Illinois regiments who were awarded a place in the Roll of Honor that their names be preserved. The Roll was established by Gen. Rosecrans for the purpose of indicating both to the army and to the nation, those officers and soldiers who distinguished themselves by bravery and soldierly conduct. The following is the list as complete as we have been able to obtain it:

FIRST BRIGADE—FIRST DIVISION.

Captains.—Hendrick E. Paine, Co. B, 59th; David O. Battolph, B, 79th; Robert Hale, D, 76th.

Lieutenants.—David W. Henderson, Co. C, 59th; J. W. Leffingwell, A, 74th; Jas. A. Blodgett, E, 75th.

FIFTY-NINTH ILLINOIS VOLUNTEERS.

Sergeants.—James Goodwin, Co. A; Robert S. Sands, B; Geo. R. Stier, C; Benjamin F. Stevens, D; George Kirber, E; William Hill, F; Aaron S. Davis, G; John Goodman, H; Wm. Tierman, I; Daniel Slayton, K.

Corporals.—Wm. B. Camp, Co. A; Francis M. Caldwell, B; Wm. Wilson, C; Jas. H. Williams, D; Chesley Allen, E; Jacob Flint, F; John Simpson, G; Frederick Goring, H; James A. Mitchell, I; Addis Downing, K.

Privates.—Co. A—Geo. H. Castle, John Glendon, Joel B. Holcomb, James H. Patton, Daniel Watkins. Co. B—Lewis C. Dougherty, Michael Kelly, Wm. H. Sankey, Samuel Short, James C. Still. Co. C—George W. Bell, Daniel Nutley, Crist Brinda, John Cheeley, Geo. W. Kerr. Co. D—Joseph Bateman, Nathaniel Daggett, Charles B. Hennason, Charles Shanerstead, Alfred Simerli. Co. E—Wm. Bruck, Joseph A. Cox, Adam Kober, Aaron Faty, James P. Woods. Co. F—Virgil Devore, Alfred Frathoringill, Jeremiah Hagee, John A. G. Kelley, Joseph D. Rader. Co. G—James Cather, Isaac Emly, Wm. Keirn, Abram A. Pruit, James Reed. Co. H—John Carroll, Eugene Gardner, John W. Turen, Jas. E. Reynolds, Benjamin St. Clair. Co I—Charles O. Ingham, John L. Lock, Thomas McCann, Joseph O'Neil, Horatio Foss. Co. K—Wm. A. Paul, Emanuel Herbert, Jacob Neighbour, Frank W. Van Osdel, Walter C. Wyker.

SEVENTY-FOURTH ILLINOIS VOLUNTEERS.

SERGEANTS.—Wm. Leffingwell, Co. A; Edgar Swift, B; Alexander H. Battie, C; John Betson, D; Chas. A. Allen, E; Edward L. Simpson, F; Wm. R. Douglass, G; Chester Weston, H; Geo. Van Valkenberg, I; James Parland, K.

CORPORALS.—Amasa Hutchins, Co. A; Hiram Billich, B; Cyrus Miller, C; James Crane, D; Hiram A. Miles, E; John Hartwell, F; John G. Waldie, G; Samuel A. Carpenter, H; Jacob Wagner, I; Arthur P. Brown, K.

PRIVATES.—Co. A—John Rumelhart, John Rodgers, Edward Black, Gustavus Hastings, Gilbert E. King. Co. B—Daniel M'Gune, John Graham, Daniel G. Kipp, George D. Manuel, Peter Merehart. Co. C—John Woolrey, Henry Miller, John W. Stewart, Harvey W. Kellogg, Wm. T. Robertson. Co. D—Wm. E. Welch, Carver C. Welch, Wm. Gutt, George Smith, Frederick Welch. Co E—Julius Smith, Wm. Weaver, Benjamin Kingsbury, Reuben Banks, Edward Prescott. Co. F—Charles Anderson, Charles C. Errickson, Henry J. Strong, Orlando Woodruff, Levi S. Sanders. Co. G—James King, James Francis, Russell J. Brayton, Levi Butterfield, Charles W. Wood. Co. H—John A. Campbell, George E. Allen, Albert Goodwin, Herrian Campbell, Edwin M. Sherman. Co. I—John Lewards, Joseph Flynn, Robert Burrill, James Elliott, Wm. Bakhaff. Co. K—Thomas Walsh, Henry Tanner, Burl J. Blake, Wesley Anderson, Charles Gorham.

SEVENTY-FIFTH ILLINOIS VOLUNTEERS.

SERGEANTS.—Wm. Coggswell, Co. A; Chauncey B. Hubbard, B; Stephen W. Smith, C; George Newton, Jr., D; Negnella S. Christopher, E; James D. Place, F; Wm Vance, G; Samuel M. Tracy, H; Augustus Johnson, I; Jonathan Hyde, K.

CORPORALS.—Lewis Burkett, Co. A; Asaph C. Demming, B; Oscar A. Seeley, C; Burney McGrady, D; Sylvester S. Nash, E; Charles Gregory, F; James Dysert, G; Frederick Mitchell, H; Jacob Rhodehamer, I; Joshua C. Mills, K.

PRIVATES.—Co. A—Cornelius Vroom, John Beal, Cyrus Inrucker, Charles Croepsey, Joseph Boyer. Co. B—Reuben Feree, Samuel H. Eye, David Hillier, Charles Fellows, Welton D. Strunk. Co. C—Salem H. Town, Wheeler Pratt, Byron Weldon, Wm. Tompkins, George Fairbank. Co D—Joseph W. McDonald, Gustavus Sherman, Theodore Cramphim, Patrick Daily, Henry Potts. Co. F—Thaddeus Spafford, Andrew J. Taylor, Norman Jewett, Chas. D. C. Hubbard, Thomas Dubay. Co. G—Wallace Eastwood, Daniel Spafford, Samuel Bender, Theophilus Gibson, Addison Heekart. Co. H—John Hanprich, Christian Coast, Matthias Schmidt, Paul Hoffman, John G. Seedy. Co. I—John Freek, Cornelius Gerhart, David Molton, David Byron, Robert M'Kinzie. Co. K—John Dilts, Orlando Jones, Oscar M. Town, Frederick Dormoy, James E. Taylor.

NINETEENTH ILLINOIS VOLUNTEERS.

William Inness, Captain, Co. C.

V. Bradford Bell, 2d Lieutenant, Co. K.

SERGEANTS.—John Freeland, Co. A; De Forrest Chamberlain, B; Edmund M.

Sawyer, C; Oliver E. Eames, D; George Steel, E; Stephen M. Porter, F; John Dedrich, H; Harrison Cowden, I; John Stevens, K.

CORPORALS.—James Uttman, Co. A; Henry B. Worth, B; Hiram D. Kellogg, C; Wm. B. Taylor, D; Alexander McL. Frazer, E; William Beck, F; Sumner Herrington, H; Augustus Speck, I; John M'Carthy, K.

PRIVATES.—Co. A—George W. Fitch, George Berry, Wm. Wilson, Robert R. Sampson, John S. S. Smith. Co. B—Wm. Douglass, David Jackson, Wm. Jorday, James G. Turnbull, James Cinnamon. Co. C—Robert Frome, Joseph D. Dobell, Frank Pratt, Frank Applebee, Lyman A. Fowler. Co. D—Richard Lewis, Thos. Mahoney, George Thompson, Thomas Golden, Joseph Smith. Co. E—Edward Cunningham, Thos. Lawler, David M'Arthur, Andrew Innes, Robert F. Fletcher. Co. F—Jacquess Kummel, Thomas A. Hamilton, Wm Walsh, John Russell, David H. Briddlecome. Co. H—John Mercer, John M'Kee, David W. Thompson, Henry C. Mazham, Hiram Rhodes. Co. I—Thomas Craig, Richard C. Walker, Wm. C. Smith, John Morrisey, Conrad Schlosser. Co. K—Abram N. Randolph, Joseph Cobb, Lyman Clark, John M. Hoyt, Charles A. Kent.

SECOND BRIGADE—SECOND DIVISION.

FIELD OFFICERS.—James E. Calloway, Major 21st Illinois.

Henry H. Allen, Major 38th Illinois.

CAPTAINS.—Andrew George, 21st; Thomas Cole, 38th; Lyman Parcher, 101st.

THIRTY-EIGHTH ILLINOIS VOLUNTEERS.

SERGEANTS.—Henry Davis, Co. A; David Blair, B; Samuel Campbell, C; John A. Moore, D; Thomas Fleener, E; Richard W. Adams, F; Alexander McIntyre, G; William H. De Bond, H; James Pettigrew, I; Jonah F. DeBolt, K.

CORPORALS.—Solomon Morris, Co. A; Burton Kile, B; Peter Lynch, C; G. B. Lorance, D; William Morgan, E; Joseph Sollars, F; Ezra Graves, G; James W. Sneedham, H; Lee Woods, I; James D. Devine, K.

PRIVATES.—Co. A—Daniel Ryan, William Welsh, Calvin C. Poppenberger, James Morton, Barnet Peddicoard. Co. B—Aaron Landreth, Hugh M. Hill, John M. Hollis, John Kite, Powell Snelling. Co. C—John Comfort, Alonzo P. Coon, Finaldo Logan, Patrick Gallaher, James Delenty. Co. D—Francis W. VanWinkle, Marion Dean, Jesse Plunkett, Lot Wakst, Robert Watts. Co. E—Robert Bromfield, Nicholas Coy, James G. Hall, William H. Bewee, James G. Morris. Co. F—Wesley F. Skelley, Andrew A. Wright, A. J. Wright, Leonard Waggoner, John F. Bentzley. Co. G—John Howell, James Boggs, Squire W. Peddigo, Wm. F. Hartley, Joseph W. Rowe. Co. H—John S. Richart, Harrison Kibben, John F. Asher, James W. Travis, B. H. Pendleton. Co. I—Dudley McKibben, Joseph Snodle, Geo. W. Michalls, Peter D. McKibben, Henry McKibben. Co. K—William Sutton, John Chestnut, John Allison, Martin Christian, Kennet Newton.

THIRD BRIGADE—FIRST DIVISION.

FIELD OFFICERS—John McIlwaine, Major 35th Illinois.

CAPTAINS.—Joseph Truax, Co. I, 35th; Wesley Taggart, Co. E, 35th.

LIEUTENANTS.—U. J. Fox, 35th; William L. Warning, 35th; T. H. West, 25th.

THIRTY-FIFTH ILLINOIS VOLUNTEERS.

SERGEANTS.—John Hargan, Co. A; Silas Perry, B; Lewis G. Torrence, C; Jackson I. Lister, D; Francis M. Allhands, E; Alexander Hughes, F; Doughty Rightmire, G; John Burgoyne, I; Benjamin F. Markland, K.

CORPORALS.—Albert Gibbs, Co. A; Anthony Cullahan, B; Benjamin W. Jones, C; Daniel C. Deamunde, D; John A. Brothers, E; Alvin H. Miller, F; George Ralston, G; William P. Harrison, H; Charles Caraway, I; William H. Sapp, K.

PRIVATES.—Co. A—N. B. Truax, James Gibson, William Ruskman, John A. Reed, Andrew J. Stewart. Co. B—Adam Young, John E. Sawrey, Curtis Merriman, James M. Minor, William Lees. Co. C—Zeb Smith, A. G. Barrett, Joseph McKee, Charles Hooper, Elbridge A. Oliver. Co. D—John J. Fox, Thomas Arthur, Jeremiah Bull, William Carter, John W. Whetzel. Co. E—George Sprowles, Horace H. Redford, John Gioh, Lewis Dotz, William H. Hennis. Co. F—Enoch Mahony, John Craig, Samuel N. Parker, Reason Howard, Charles Miller. Co. G—James M. Kennedy, John T. Dotson, Nathaniel Gilbreth, Orange R. Drake, Simon Neff. Co. H—Jesse Morris, Madison Vickers, Joel W. Alvord, Jordan R. Murray, Justus R. Farmer. Co. I—Charles Hillman, John T. McBride, David Kinsey, Richard Todd. Co. K—George Bursard, Thomas C. Perry, William Waller, Jesse Gorden, William H. Murray.

TWENTY-FIFTH ILLINOIS VOLUNTEERS.

SERGEANTS.—Aaron Newlan, Co. A; J. K. Wier, B; Abraham Hayes, C; J. K Jenkin, D; H. Cooper, E; John Jordan, F; J. Beard, G; R. S. Robinson, H; Wm. Rothwell, I; Henry Bude, K.

CORPORALS.—John Beecham, Co. A; D. D. Dale, B; J. B. Patton, C; J. B. Shirk, D; William Beaver, E; Giles Dunn, F; L. D. McHenry, G; David Jacobs, H; C. E. Wilson, I; B. Walls, K.

PRIVATES.—Co. A—R. W. Tweedy, Jacob Thompson, George Wilmarth, Robert Joyce, Alexander Baker. Co. B—H. Vandership, John Ingraham, David Claypool, John Schultz, H. Fairchilds. Co. C—George W. Doyle, William Eaton, David Hulick, James Jeffreys, John Bugle. Co. D—William J. Drumkiller, William Aperson, William Bradford, Edmund Betts, W. S. Brown. Co. E—Charles Quich, Daniel McMahon, Samuel Van, Andrew J. West, W. H. Holbrook. Co. F—William Bratton, Benjamin F. Edwards, James Johnson, John Little, William H. Zumwatz. Co. G—Edward Dibble, Robert Walsh, Edward Wilkes, William Rogers, Cyrus L. Wood. Co. H—James H. Isham, George Anderson, John R. Biggs, William F. Sowers, Henry Strenge. Co. I—Edward Phiskey, Philip Smith, John Burham, Moses White, Nehemiah Gerald. Co. K—Pressley W. Glasscock, Thomas Powell, John Hessing, Nicholas Covey, H. Brackendorf.

FIRST BRIGADE—THIRD DIVISION.

FIELD OFFICERS.—George W. Chandler, Major 88th Illinois.

CAPTAINS.—Webster A. Whiting, Co. B, 88th; Albert M. Hobbs, E, 36th.

LIEUTENANTS.—Dean R. Chester, Co. G, 88th; John M. Turnbull, C, 36th.

EIGHTY-EIGHTH ILLINOIS VOLUNTEERS.

SERGEANTS.—Henry L. Sumner, Co. A; Wm. McGregor, B; Chas. Winchell, C; Noah W. Rue, D; William Huntington, E; John Lester, F; David G. White, G; E. S. Rice, H; Marwin M. Chapin, I; James Winship, K.

CORPORALS.—Henry Nicholson, A; Robert Crawford, B; Austin Stebbins, C; Thomas Campbell, D; Ed. Cunningham, E; Stephen Shipman, F; Augustus Young, G; John K. Ely, H; John Segno, I; Solomon Davidson, K.

PRIVATES.—Co. A—David R. Graves, John B. King, Frank Miller, James Maxwell, Henry C. Gallup. Co. B—Benjamin Stofer, Wesley Richard, Samuel Wilcox, Chas. Howard. Co. C—John A. Riley, Simpson Studeven, Thomas Cuddigan, Jacob Wright, Edward Cox. Co. D—John Densmore, Conrad Geis, James Nelson, Wm. J. Russell, George A. Booker. Co. E—Edward James, Robert Stofield, Thomas C. Meil, Martin Kun, Brice Worley. Co. F—Joseph Jackson, Mark Esgar, Alexander Cassinghan, Henry Whitehouse, Roswell Miller. Co. G—Benjamin Newman, John Frube, John M. Greely, George Codd, George Hast. Co. H—Samuel Robertson, Saleful Eastman, Cornelius Clark, Samuel Bittles, Isaac Wentz. Co. I—Stephen Fields, Eli Hulbertsma, Christopher Saver, Jacob Kregar. Co. K—Thomas Leary, Martin Dock, Phillip Flood, Hiram Corbin, James Weller.

THIRTY-SIXTH ILLINOIS VOLUNTEERS.

SERGEANTS.—Alexander Robertson, Co. A; Henry B. Latham, B; James J. Wilson, C; Clinton Loyd, D; Wm. Willet, E; Wm. Cybond, F; Wm. Rolly, G; Nelson Sherwood, H; Dwight L. Smith, I; John M. Gordon, K.

CORPORALS.—George Peeler, A; George Berger, B; George Mercer, C; John C. Taylor, D; Daniel Darnell, E; John F. Johnson, F; Daniel Kennedy, G; David Hartman, H; George Avery, I; John Johnston, K.

PRIVATES.—Co. A—Leman Bartholomew, Michael S. Saisloff, John O'Connel, Homer Wilcox, George H. Knowles. Co. B—Fritz Warhesian, Robert Logan, Wm. Jackson, Charles Hernse, Wm. L. Campbell. Co C—John McMullen, Wm. Fisher, Isaac Carson, George Monroe, Wm. Allen. Co. D—Seth Darling, Louis P. Boyd, Lyden Benister, Philip Stage, John Page. Co. E—Henry Smith, Walter Ralston, Elisha Loyd, James E. Moss, Herbert Dewey. Co. F—Gunner Gunnerson, Thomas Bowen, Ira Johnson, Louis Beldin, John Roots. Co. G—Isaac Carson, Charles Landon, Sylvester Meecham, Wm. Roseman, Wm. Severns. Co. H—James Perkins, Ebenezer Lamb, Cornelius Van Hess, Wm. Carl, Frederich Smith. Co. I—Dwight Corom, Samuel Hall, Christ Wehtz, Antonie Miller. Co. K—Sidney Wanger, Wm. S. Moore, Edward Mayberry, Romain Smith, Burton Hovey.

SECOND BRIGADE—THIRD DIVISION.

FIELD OFFICERS.—Wm. A. Presson, Lieutenant Colonel 73d Ill.

CAPTAINS.—Gustavus Freysleben, 44th Ill, Wm. E. Smith, 73d Ill.

LIEUTENANTS.—Wm. H. Dodge, 73d Ill.

FORTY-FOURTH ILLINOIS VOLUNTEERS.

SERGEANTS.—Charles Wagner, A; Martin Denin, B; Wm H. Rankin, C; Henry W. Hawes, D; Edward Blind, E; N. Rundall, G; Wm. F. Sickling, H; C. A. Barrett, I; Philip Weber, K.

CORPORALS.—John Kessler, A; F. P. Peckham, B; Milan Barrackman, C; Myron Whitehorn, D; Alfred Siemhaus, E; James D. Campbell, F; N. P. Ramsdell, G; A. Schoomaker, H; Edward R. Bliss, I; Charles Egan, K.

PRIVATES.—Co. A—Fr. Birkenbuel, Jacob Melster, George Vogel, Frederick Bartels, Henry Zimmer. Co. B—Wm. Haymaker, A. H. Limberger, Wm. G. Nickols, Daniel E. Harton, John Weiser. Co. C—Richard Costello, John Williams, James Grahams, Wm H. Mills, John Diggins. Co. D—Joseph C. Skiles, Warren Thomas, Myron Ketchum, Rodney R. Purvis, John N. Russ. Co. E—Christian Heillman, Daniel Groner, Charles Halben, Joseph Pfeffer, Balthazar Gisibel. Co. F—F. M. Faulkner, Wm. Brisbon, Stephen Place, Albert L. Russell, Chas W. Haynes. Co. G—Samuel Vinton, Michael Fuhner, Nathan Rundle, Nathaniel Ramsdell, Isaiah Ferguson. Co. H—Thos. N. Travis, Sidney J. Fletcher, Abraham Loving, Arthur Hamilton, Theodore Bushman. Co. I—John Tiptow, James C. Stark, James Rigsby, Thomas Fisher, Samuel M. Copp. Co. K—Carl Frank, George Essig, Paul Wilker, Florin Zugg, Louis Deusel.

SEVENTY-THIRD ILLINOIS VOLUNTEERS.

SERGEANTS.—T. C. Perry, Co. A; D. W. Dillow, B; W. H. Newlin, C; H. Alroid, D; F. Hendricks, E; John Spindler, F; Wm. Talbert, G; Wm. Cammire, H; Wm. H. Gamble, I; D. M. Davis, K.

CORPORALS.—H. M Cass, A; A. J. Reed, B; A. C. Nickolson, C; Allen Willey, D; John Justice, E; Robert McBride, F; S. P. Goodwin, G; Isaac Lightle, H; Wm. H. Denning, I; E. F. Brown, K.

PRIVATES.—Co. A—Richard Becker, Joseph Baughman, Jeremiah C. Hayne, Piccard Oliver. Co. B—Joel Langley, Cyrus M. Grave, Peter B. Few, Gilbert Harbison, Joseph A. Hunt. Co C—Wesley Bishop, John R. Burk, Chas. M. Cook, Robert J. Halsey, Aaron Willison. Co. D—Elias M. Miller, John Weddles, L. M. McArdle, John M. Albert, Jonas B. Garver. Co. E—B. Kirkley, Charles Harbey, Wm. H. Burk, D. Elliott, S. W. Busby. Co. F—Wm. Vannuter, Henry McBride, Wm. Boyer, George Dudley, Joshua A. Wright. Co. G—Wm. H. Little, J. C Baily, James W. Davis, Wm. Purnell. Co. H—Alphenos Winegar, Archibald Goodwin, David Tunnicliff, George Swackhammer, James Gruns, Edward Penstow. Co. I—Benj. Schaffner, Hiram Hauptmann, James B. Hurds, James Oliver Weis, Calvin A. Heumann. Co. K—James Murrey, Henry Nosley, Elijah Stacy, George Kalb.

THIRD BRIGADE—THIRD DIVISION.

FIELD OFFICERS.—F. A. Swanwick, Lieutenant Colonel 22d Illinois; John A. Hottenstein, Lieutenant Col. 42d.

CAPTAINS.—L. G. McAdams, Co. E, 22d Ill.; Robert P. Lytle, B, 27th; E. D. Swain, I, 42d; Chas. C. Merrick, G, 51st.

LIEUTENANTS.—S. B. Hood, Co. I, 22d Ill.; Hugh M. Love, G, 27th; A. O. Johnson, G, 42d; Albert Eads, C, 51st.

TWENTY-SECOND ILLINOIS INFANTRY.

SERGEANTS.—Wm. M. Austin, Co. A; W. H. Edsall, B; John W. Young, C; Wm. Scott, D; Wm. Kershem, E; C. Hunnewell, F; John G. Beashy, G; Wm. C. M. Kerr, H; Wm. A. M. Clinton, I; C. Kern, K.

CORPORALS.—Samuel Smith, Co. A; John W. Jones, B; A. J. Hoffman, C; J. W. Tabor, D; James Collier, E; P. Romeiser, F; James W. Butt, G; James B. Couch, H; Wm. Gray, I; R. Casey, K.

PRIVATES.—Co. A—F. Dumbeck, John Garber, Wm. Carter, A. H. Sharp, Wm. Hess. Co. B—Chas. Jinks, F. Sackett, W. Asple, John Moore, H. Carpenter. Co. C—L. Cornwell, J. K. Gaston, G. W. Davis, John Puks, G. Armstrong. Co. D—W. V. Rhea, C. Rhea, W. H. White, S. Trammell, W. H. Scott. Co. E—J. Redick, J Keountz, B. Cole, M. Croslie, M. Wood. Co. F—H. Wismarth, P. Hensohn, G. Hockneal, C. Bick, C. Soheiber. Co. G—J. Hensly, Wm. Phillips, J. McRainey, Wm. Boyer, D. Quinn. Co. H—B. McGuire, M. W. Gaston, J. W. Colwell, H. P. Carch, P. Bartliss. Co. I—A. W. West, James Kaley, J. P. Brown, Colin Hodge, B. F. Gillom. Co. K—George Farwell, C. O. Dunnell, B. McAvoy, J. Steintauer, Fred. Feaster.

TWENTY-SEVENTH ILLINOIS INFANTRY.

SERGEANTS.—Adam Fick, Co. A; Wm. F. Hudelson, B; Henry C. Foot, C; G. W. Broden, D; Henry Denver, E; John Richardson, F; Ira Burligim, G; Wm. Hayes, H; W. Blanchard, I; Isaac Nash, K.

CORPORALS.—Frank Consteina, Co. A; Wm. B. Hodges, B; John Keeley, C; A. Fisrheo, D; John C. Conover, E; John Hindman, F; W. B. Fleming, G; John H. Vaught, H; Geo. E Tinker, I; Hansil Burdit, K.

PRIVATES.—Co. A—Henry Frohn, Henry Boschults, R. C. F. Aly, August Boschults, Henry Schwartz. Co. B—Chas. Walker, Lewis Keefner, Andrew Pullin, Wm. Garrison, Wm. Aldrich. Co. C—James Rose, Thomas H. Coomer, John Wood, J. C. Parkhurst, John Y. Winder. Co. D—Wm. Husk, Henry McIntyre, Wm. D. Bell, Jas. W. Page, Frank Mott. Co. E—Shipley W. Lester, John F. Cue, Samuel G. Smith, W. H. Griffin, J. K. Wilson. Co. F—E. Harbetson, Thos. Campbell, Wm. Shiver, John R. Talley, W. H. Ritter. Co. G—John G. Ersley, Samuel Reasoner, Frank A. Wood, Wilson W. Wilcox, Wiley Jackson. Co. H—Wm. Holliday, La. F. Harrington, Jerome Knight, John Romig, Joshua Woolsey. Co. I—Willis Knight,

James McNulty, Joel A. Hall, David A. Hutchinson, Adolphus Godfrey. Co. K—Wilber Dickerson, Jacob Butchle, Henry Ticknor, Willis Brud, Thos. Frashure.

FORTY-SECOND ILLINOIS INFANTRY.

SERGEANTS.—J. Y. Elliott, Co. A; P. Short, B; O. Powell, C; G W. Eells, D; W. H. Colburn, E; C. A. Seaver, F; W. H. Kipsley, G; E. Have, H; J. S. Wilson, I; S. W. King, K.

CORPORALS.—W. W. Norton, Co. A; B. Conrad, B; T. W. Maxwell, C; H. Wells, D; W. H. Clark, E; H. Delong, F; J. Sheeney, G; William Shimp, H; J. Valor, I; J. Beard, K.

PRIVATES.—Co. A—M. Whetstone, L. Mott, L. O. Oliver, A. Isaac, J. Blatzer. Co. B—D. Fishburn, F. Hensey, P. Risedorph, H. E. Teachnot, H. Arnold. Co. C—A. Lamphere, P. McConnell, H. F. Leonard, J. Sharp, G. D. Weir. Co. D—H. Scramlin, A. F. Fuller, R. W. Plummer, G. L. Brown, P. Shuntz. Co. E—E. W. Vaugh, S. Hitsman, J. W. Riley, J. H. Smith, W. Leonard. Co. F—N. Salisbury, W. A. Raymond, Wm. W. Rich, G. Guser. Co. G—J. Gleason, D. Laland, N. B. Collins, S. Magher, S. Freeman. Co. H—E. Wilcox, W. Dittus, J. Woodruff, J. E. Tate, J. Colcomb. Co. I—W. H. Bennett, A. H. Woodale, W. Kellogg, H. Kale, W. H. Carson. Co. K—G. W. Palmer, O. Hendrickson, J. Stitler, W. Mott, W. Wright.

FIFTY-FIRST ILLINOIS INFANTRY.

SERGEANTS.—John R. Parker, Co. A; Thos. Daily, C. H. Thomas, B; Richard Barbour, D; Iven Bailey, C; Barton Bunnel, E; George D. Goldsly, F; Calvin Service, G; N. Kinsman, H; Chas. Hills, K.

CORPORALS.—Chas. Nelson, Chas. H. Merrill, Co. A; Geo. Kirby, B; John D. Rumbo, C; Jerome Mangan, D; George Harris, E; John T. Wright, F; John L. Allen, G; Thomas Gregg, H; M. V. Riley, K.

PRIVATES.—Co. A—Wm. E. Armstrong, James Connell, (No. 1), Presley Guyman, Joseph Jones, Michael Sentell. Co. B—Robert Armstrong, John B. Eldridge, E P. Fredericks, James Gilchrist, Geo. W. White. Co. C—James Brown, Allen Eastbrun, Daniel Flott, Leander Hogle, Oscar Wade. Co. D—Wm. Ainsworth, J. L. McBride, John L. McGuire, Wm. Ruble, John T. Stretch. Co. E—Joseph Gerard, M. W. Romine, George Chambers, James Skidmore, John Smart. Co F—Thos. McCamack, John Hurley, Joseph C. Goodale, John Purkapile, John Williams. Co. G—Thomas Corey, William Duggan, Thomas Chambers, Peter Nolan, Michael Corey. Co. H—Benj. Golden, Willard F. Powker, Alex. W. Jack, Wm. Lindy, David W. Reed. Co. K—Edward Burns, Daniel Ebert, Wm. Patterson, Robert Stack, Frederick Thompson.

Engd by J. C. Buttre.

Jas. A. Mulligan

COL. JAMES A. MULLIGAN.

CHAPTER XXXI.

THE UTTERANCES OF THE PATRIOTISM OF ILLINOIS DURING THE WAR—THE EMANCIPATION PROCLAMATION, THE KEY NOTE OF THE CAMPAIGN—THE GREAT SPEECH OF HONEST FARMER FUNK—A STIRRING LETTER FROM GEN. LOGAN TO HIS SOLDIERS—LETTER FROM COL. FRANK SHERMAN—EXTRACTS FROM SPEECHES OF HON. RICHARD YATES, HON. LYMAN TRUMBULL, HON. OWEN LOVEJOY, GEN. FARNSWORTH, HON. I. N. ARNOLD, &c.—PRESIDENT LINCOLN'S PROCLAMATION, INAUGURAL ADDRESS AND LAST SPEECH—THE NORTH AMERICAN REVIEW AND KENTUCKY LETTER—MR. LINCOLN DEAD.

THE patriotism of Illinois has not only been manifested on tho field, not only proven at the point of the bayonet and the mouth of the cannon, but in the utterances of her sons on the battle-field, in the halls of Congress, and at home. The literature of the war has been enriched with her eloquence, and adorned with the glowing and zealous appeals in behalf of the constitution and the laws. From the President down to the private, for her soldiers have carried the pen with the sword, these utterances have been made in no uncertain manner, and in the present chapter we propose to select extracts here and there from speeches, proclamations and letters, illustrating the general character and sentiment of the people.

First above all other utterances is that edict which sounded the key-note of the war. For thirty years brave men, the pioneers in the van of human progress had built the approaches, cleared away the obstructions, and by slow steps educated the people up to the necessity of removing slavery as an imperative and vital condition to the permanent safety of the Republic. On the first day of January, 1863, Abraham Lincoln made the first assault upon the citadel of slavery; spoke the immortal words that loosened the shackles of the bondmen and let the oppressed go free; that proclaimed to the world this war was not waged by the North for aggrandizement or through malice, but that it had drawn its sword in the interests of religion, humanity, equality, civilization and progress.

That memorable edict which so brightly marks the incoming of the year of our Lord 1863 was as follows:

THE EMANCIPATION PROCLAMATION.

"WASHINGTON, January 1, 1863.

'*By the President of the United States of America.*

"WHEREAS, On the 22d day of September, in the year of our Lord 1862, a proclamation was issued by the President of the United States, containing among other things the following, to wit:

"That, on the first day of January, in the year of our Lord one thousand eight hundred and sixty-three, all persons held as slaves within any State, or designated part of a State, the people whereof shall then be in rebellion against the United States, shall be thenceforth and forever free, and the executive government of the United States, including the military and naval authority thereof, will recognize and maintain the freedom of such persons, and will do no act or acts to repress such persons, or any of them, in any effort they may make for their actual freedom; that the executive will on the first day of January aforesaid, issue a proclamation designating the States and parts of States, if any, in which the people therein respectively shall then be in rebellion against the United States; and the fact that any state, or the people thereof, shall on that day be in good faith represented in the Congress of the United States by members chosen thereto at elections wherein a majority of the qualified voters of such States shall have participated, shall, in the absence of strong countervailing testimony, be deemed conclusive evidence that such State and the people thereof are not in rebellion against the United States.

"Now, therefore, I, Abraham Lincoln, President of the United States, by virtue of the power in me vested as Commander-in-Chief of the Army and Navy, in a time of actual armed rebellion against the authority of the Government of the United States, as a fit and necessary war measure for suppressing said rebellion, do, on this first day of January, in the year of our Lord one thousand eight hundred and sixty-three, and in accordance with my purpose so to do, publicly proclaimed for the full period of one hundred days from the date of the first above mentioned order, designate as the States and parts of States therein, the people whereof respectively are this day in rebellion against the United States, the following, to wit: Arkansas, Texas and Louisiana, (except the Parishes of St. Bernard, Plaquemine, Jefferson, St John, St. Charles, St. James, Ascension, Assumption, Terrebonne, La Fourche, St. Mary, St. Martin, and Orleans, including the city of New Orleans), Mississippi, Alabama, Florida, Georgia, South Carolina, North Carolina and Virginia, (except the forty-eight counties designated as West Virginia, and also the counties of Berkley, Accomac, Northampton, Elizabeth City, York, Princess Ann and Norfolk, including the cities of Norfolk and Portsmouth), which excepted parts are for the present left precisely as if this Proclamation were not issued; and by virtue of the power and for the purpose aforesaid, I do order and declare that all persons held as slaves within the designated States, and parts of States, are and henceforward shall be free, and that the Executive Government of the United States, including the military and naval authorities thereof, will recognize and maintain the freedom of the said persons, and I hereby enjoin upon the people so declared to be free, to abstain from all violence, unless in necessary self-defense, and I recommend to them that in all cases where allowed, they labor faithfully for reasonable wages, and I further declare and make known that such persons of suitable condition, will be received into the armed service of the United States, to garrison forts, positions, stations and other places, and to man vessels of all sorts in said service.

"And upon this sincerely believed to be an act of justice, warranted by the constitution, upon military necessity, I invoke the considerate judgment of mankind and the gracious favor of Almighty God.

"In witness whereof, I have hereunto set my hand and caused the seal of the United States to be affixed.

"Done at the City of Washington, this first day of January, in the year of our Lord one thousand eight hundred and sixty-three, and of the Independence of the United States of America the eighty-seventh.

"(Signed) ABRAHAM LINCOLN.

"By the President:

"WM. H. SEWARD, Secretary of State."

"HONEST FARMER" FUNK.

On the 13th of February, in the same year, a speech was delivered in the Illinois Senate by Hon. Isaac Funk, an old man and one of the wealthiest farmers in the State, which, for brevity, bluntness and energy, has rarely been excelled. Made on the spur of the moment, struck off at white heat, and delivered in indignant response to the efforts of partizans to stave off a vote upon the appropriations for the support of the State government, it gained a wide circulation and achieved a national fame. The Senate was crowded with spectators, when Mr. Funk rose and said:

"MR. SPEAKER:—I can sit in my seat no longer and see such boys' play going on. These men are trifling with the best interests of the country. They should have asses' ears to set off their heads, or they are secessionists and traitors at heart.

"I say that there are traitors and secessionists at heart in this Senate. Their actions prove it. Their speeches prove it. Their gibes and laughter and cheers here nightly, when their speakers get up in this hall and denounce the war and the Administration, prove it.

"I can sit here no longer and not tell these traitors what I think of them. And while so telling them, I am responsible myself for what I say. I stand upon my own bottom. I am ready to meet any man on this floor, in any manner, from a pin's point to the mouth of a cannon, upon this charge against these traitors. [Tremendous applause from the galleries.] I am an old man of sixty-five. I came to Illinois a poor boy. I have made a little something for myself and family. I pay $3,000 a year in taxes. I am willing to pay $6,000, aye $12,000, [great cheering, the old gentleman bringing down his fist upon his desk with a blow that would knock down a bullock, and causing the ink-stand to bound a half dozen inches in the air], aye, I am willing to pay my whole fortune, and then give my life to save my country from these traitors that are seeking to destroy it. [Tremendous cheers and applause, which the Speaker could not subdue.]

Mr. Speaker, you must please excuse me. I could not sit longer in my seat and calmly listen to these traitors. My heart, that feels for my poor country, would not let me. My heart that cries out for the lives of our brave volunteers in the field, that these traitors at home are destroying by thousands, would not let me. My heart, that bleeds for the widows and orphans at home, would not let me. Yes, these villains and traitors and secessionists in this Senate [striking his clenched fist on the desk with a blow that made the house ring again] are killing my neighbors' boys, now fighting in the field. I dare to tell this to these traitors, to their faces, and that I am responsible for what I say to one or all of them. [Cheers.] Let them come on, right here. I am sixty-five years old, and I have made up my mind to risk my life right here, on this floor, for my country.

"These men sneered at Col. Mack, a day or two ago. He is a little man; but I am a large man. I am ready to meet any of them in place of Col. Mack. I am large enough for them, and I hold myself ready for them now, and at any time. [Cheers from the galleries.]

"Mr. Speaker, these traitors on this floor should be provided with hempen collars. They deserve them. They deserve them. They deserve hanging, I say. [Raising his voice and violently striking the desk.] The country would be better off to swing them up. I go for hanging them, and I dare to tell them so, right here, to their traitors' faces. Traitors should be hung. It would be the salvation of the country, to hang them. For that reason, I would rejoice at it. [Tremendous cheering.]

Mr. Speaker: I beg pardon of the gentlemen in the Senate who are not traitors, but true, loyal men, for what I have said. I only intend it and mean it for secessionists at heart. They are here, in this Senate. I see them joke and smirk and grin at a true Union man. But I defy them. I stand here ready for them and dare them to come on. [Great cheering.] What man with the heart of a patriot could stand this treason any longer? I have stood it long enough. I will stand it no more. [Cheers.] I denounce these men and their aiders and abettors as rank traitors and secessionists. Hell itself could not spew out a more traitorous crew than some of the men who disgrace this Legislature, this State and this country. For myself, I protest against and denounce their treasonable acts. I have voted against their measures. I will do so to the end. I will denounce them as long as God gives me breath. And I am ready to meet the traitors themselves here or anywhere, and fight them to the death. [Prolonged cheers and shouts.]

I said I paid three thousand dollars a year taxes. I do not say it to brag of it. It is my duty—yes, Mr. Speaker, my privilege to do it. But some of the traitors here, who are working night and day to get their miserable little bills and claims through the Legislature, to take money out of the pockets of the people, are talking about high taxes. They are hypocrites, as well as traitors. I heard some of them talking about high taxes in this way, who do not pay five dollars to support the Government. I denounce them as hypocrites as well as traitors. [Cheers.]

"The reason that they pretend to be afraid of high taxes is that they do not want to vote money for the relief of the soldiers. They want also to embarass the Government and stop the war. They want to aid the secessionists to conquer our boys in the field. *They* care about taxes? They are picayune men any how. They pay no taxes at all, and never did, and never hope to, unless they can manage to plunder the Government. [Cheers.] This is an excuse of traitors.

"Mr. Speaker: Excuse me. I feel for my country in this her hour of danger; I feel for her from the tips of my toes to the ends of my hair. That is the reason that I speak as I do. I cannot help it. I am bound to tell these men to their teeth what they are, and what the people, the true loyal people, think of them.

"Mr. Speaker: I have said my say. I am no speaker. This is the only speech I have made. And I do not know that it deserves to be called a speech. I could not sit still any longer, and see these scoundrels and traitors work out their selfish schemes to destroy the Union. They have my sentiments. Let them one and all make the most of them. I am ready to back up all I say, and I repeat it, to meet these traitors in any manner they may choose, from a pin's point to the mouth of a cannon."

GENERAL LOGAN.

On the 12th of February 1863, General Logan issued the following stirring appeal to his soldiers. The appeal is dated at Memphis, and created a perfect storm of enthusiasm among his troops who almost worshipped their commander:

"MY FELLOW SOLDIERS:—Debility from recent illness has prevented and still prevents me from appearing amongst you, as has been my custom, and is my desire. It is for this cause I deem it my duty to communicate with you now, and give you the assurance that your General still maintains unshaken confidence in your patriotism, devotion, and in the ultimate success of our glorious cause.

"I am aware that influences of the most discouraging and treasonable character, well calculated and designed to render you dissatisfied, have recently been brought to bear upon some of you by professed friends. Newspapers, containing treasonable articles, artfully falsifying the public sentiment at your homes, have been circulated in your camps. Intriguing political tricksters, demagogues, and time-servers, whose corrupt deeds are but a faint reflex of their more corrupt hearts, seem determined to drive our people on to anarchy and destruction. They have hoped, by magnifiying the reverses of our arms, basely misrepresenting the conduct and slandering the character of our soldiers in the field, and boldly denouncing the acts of the constituted authorities of the government as unconstitutional usurpations, to produce general demoralization in the army, and thereby reap their political reward, weaken the cause we have espoused, and aid those arch traitors of the South to dismember our mighty Republic and trail in the dust the emblem of our national unity, greatness and glory. Let me remind you, my countrymen, that we are soldiers of the Federal Union, armed for the preservation of the Federal Constitution and the maintenance of its laws and authority. Upon your faithfulness and devotion, heroism and gallantry, depend its perpetuity. To us has been committed this sacred inheritance, baptized in the blood of our fathers. We are soldiers of a government that has always blessed us with prosperity and happiness.

"It has given to every American citizen the largest freedom and the most perfect equality of rights and privileges. It has afforded us security in person and property, and blessed us until, under its beneficent influence, we were the proudest nation on earth.

"We should be united in our efforts to put down a rebellion, that now, like an earthquake, rocks the nation from State to State, from center to circumference, and threatens to engulf us all in one common ruin, the horrors of which no pen can portray. We have solemnly sworn to bear true faith to this government, preserve its Constitution, and defend its glorious flag against all its enemies and opposers. To our hands has been committed the liberties, the prosperity and happiness of future generations. Shall we betray such a trust? Shall the brilliancy of your past achievements be dimmed and tarnished by hesitation, discord and dissension, whilst armed traitors menace you in front and unarmed traitors intrigue against you in the rear? We are in no way responsible for any action of the civil authorities. We constitute the military arm of the Government. That the civil power is threatened and attempted to be paralyzed, is the reason for resort to the military power. To aid the civil authorities (not to oppose or obstruct) in the exercise of their authority is our office, and shall we forget this duty, and stop to wrangle and dispute while the country is bleeding at every pore, on this or that political act or measure whilst a fearful wail of anguish, wrung from the heart of a distracted people is borne upon every breeze, and widows and orphans are appealing to us to avenge the loss of their loved ones who have fallen by our side in defence of its old blood-stained banner, and whilst the Temple of Liberty itself is being shaken to the very center by the ruthless blows of traitors, who have desecrated our flag—obstructed our national highways, destroyed our peace, desolated our firesides, and draped thousands of homes in mourning?

"Let us stand firm at our posts of duty and of honor, yielding a cheerful obedience to all orders from our superiors, until by our united efforts, the Stars and

Stripes shall be planted in every city, town and hamlet of the rebellious States. We can then return to our homes and through the ballot-box peacefully redress all our wrongs, if any we have.

"Whilst I rely upon you with confidence and pride, I blush to confess that recently some of those who were once our comrades in arms have so far forgotten their honor, their oaths and their country, as to shamefully desert us, and skulkingly make their way to their homes, where, like culprits, they dare not look an honest man in the face. Disgrace and ignominy (if they escape the penalty of the law) will not only follow them to their dishonored graves, but will stamp their names and lineage with infamy to the latest generation. The scorn and contempt of every true man will ever follow those base men, who, forgetful of their oaths, have, like cowardly spaniels, deserted their comrades in arms in the face of the foe, and their country in the hour of its greatest peril. Every true-hearted mother or father, brother, sister or wife, will spurn the coward who could thus not only disgrace himself, but his name and his kindred. An indelible stamp of infamy should be branded upon his cheek, that all who look upon his vile countenance may feel for him the contempt his cowardice merits. Could I believe that such conduct found either justification or excuse in your hearts, or that you would for a moment falter in our glorious purpose of saving the nation from threatened wreck and hopeless ruin, I would invoke from Deity as the greatest boon, a common grave to save us from such infamy and disgrace.

"The day is not far distant when traitors and cowards, North and South, will cower before the indignation of an outraged people. MARCH BRAVELY ONWARD! Nerve your strong arms to the task of overthrowing every obstacle in the pathway of victory until with shouts of triumph the last gun is fired that proclaims us a united people under the old Flag and one Government! PATRIOT SOLDIERS! This great work accomplished, the reward for such service as yours will be realized; the blessings and honors of a grateful people will be yours.

JOHN A. LOGAN, Brig.-General Commanding.

COL. FRANK SHERMAN.

About the same time Col. Frank Sherman, of the 88th Illinois, son of Hon. Francis Sherman, of Chicago, wrote a letter from which we take the following eloquent extract:

* * * "What can our people be thinking of, when they go so far with their partisan feeling, as to lose sight of the fact that our country is now passing through the darkest hours of her history. With armed rebellion in our front, and insidious foes and traitors in our rear, she needs that all true patriots should step forth, at whatever cost or sacrifice, and crush out traitors at home who are trying to poison the minds of the weak and fearful, whose minds are worked upon by their hellish cunning and damnable sentiments of party, who wish to save the country through dishonorable overtures to rebels in arms, and make us, as a people, a by-word for all time to come.

"The soldiers here, when they look back to their homes and firesides, that they have left for love of country, and to preserve the rich inheritance left us by the fathers of the Revolution, feel that, in the recent political struggle for power and party, they have been ignored by all parties, and left here to contend against disease, death, and an ever vigilant foe alone, whilst the fanatics of the North are giving aid and comfort to rebellion, and revive their broken fortunes by their (the North's) infernal dissensions.

"Let the disunionists of the North take heed. We do not propose quietly to allow them to trample on our rights, and help dig our graves. What we expect and look for is, that men will not long be allowed to utter traitorous sentiments at our homes; that there is true patriotism enough left to save the country, and rub out traitors of all degrees at home, in the guise of loyalty, to whatever party they may belong. The soldiers here, recognize, in the President, one who is constitutionally authorized to administer the laws and direct the operations of the army and navy. As Commander-in-Chief, he has the undoubted right to issue orders and proclamations, whenever the exigencies of the service require it, to suppress armed rebellion against the Government that he, as its Chief Magistrate, has sworn to protect. We, the soldiers of the United States, called forth to save the country, dropped our political differences when we entered its service, and took the oath that we would obey the "orders" of the President of the United States, and we intend to do it; and every officer and soldier that I have talked with, in regard to our duty, agrees with me; *i. e.*, that we will sustain, to the death, our Commander-in-Chief, the President of the United States, in all measures and orders that he may issue for the crushing of the rebellion in the Southern States; and we call on the North to lay aside their bitter feelings, engendered by strife for power, and unite, and come up with a steady front on the war question, and demonstrate that it is the determination of the North, at all hazards, to furnish men and means to prosecute this war to a finality; that traitors shall be punished; and, my word for it, this war will not last one year longer. Those of us who are left, can lay down our arms and return to our homes, and we shall again have a happy and prosperous country, respected and feared by all the nations of the earth. Pursue the mad policy of partisan politics, and we are lost; unhesitatingly yielding to the demands made upon us by the Government, to root out this great wrong that is ruining one of the fairest portions of man's inheritance, all will be well. But, rest assured of one thing: the soldiers are loyal, and will support the Government, and that they would as soon war on traitors in Illinois as in Tennessee. The soldiers must not be ignored, nor must it be forgotten that we yet have rights, and a voice at home, and an interest in our country.

F. T. SHERMAN,

"Colonel Commanding 88th Illinois Volunteers.."

HON. RICHARD YATES.

Few words more eloquent have been spoken or written than are contained in the closing sentences of Governor Yates' message, delivered Jan. 5, 1863. The Governor says:

* * * * "I can think of no peace worth having, short of crushing out the rebellion and the complete restoration of the authority of the Government. The only way to honorable and permanent peace is through war—desolating, exterminating war. We must move on the enemy's works. We must move forward with tremendous energy, with accumulated thousands of men and the most terrible enginery of war. This will be the shortest road to peace and be accompanied with the least cost of life and treasure in the end.

"If our brave boys shall fall in the field, we must bury the dead, take care of and bring home the sick and wounded, and send fresh battalions to fill up the broken ranks and to deal out death, destruction and desolation to the rebels. We might talk of compromise, if it affected us alone, but it would affect our children and our children's children, in all the years of the future. The interests to be affected are far reaching and universal humanity, and lasting as the generations of mankind. I have never had my faith in the perpetual union of these States to falter. I believe this infernal rebellion can be, ought to be, and will be subdued. The land may be left a howling waste, desolated by the bloody footsteps of war from Delaware Bay to the Gulf, but our territory shall remain unmutilated—the country shall be one, and it shall be free in all its broad boundaries, from Maine to the Gulf, and from ocean to ocean.

"In any event, may we be able to act a worthy part in the trying scenes through which we are passing; and should the star of our destiny sink to rise no more, may we feel for ourselves, and may history preserve our record clear before heaven and earth, and hand down the testimony to our children, that we have done all, periled and endured all, to perpetuate the priceless heritage of Liberty and Union unimpaired to our posterity."

The earlier stages of the war were marked with many eloquent appeals to the people at war meetings held for the purpose of filling up the ranks and collecting and forwarding supplies to Illinois troops in the army. From a few of the speeches delivered at that time, we select the following:

HON. LYMAN TRUMBULL.

At a meeting held in Chicago, Oct. 18, 1862, Hon. Lyman Trumbull said:

* * * "I occupied, in the commencement, some time in commenting on this Constitution, the wisdom with which it was framed. I believe it established the best system of government which was ever devised. I know that under its benign influence we have prospered without example in the history of nations. If we can remove this one element, the cause of all the troubles we have had, I know not why this Constitution may not be perpetuated for ages.

"It contains within itself the means of modification in a peaceable way, if in the changing conditions of society any alterations should hereafter be necessary. Under the Constitution every man may be secured in his individual rights. It secures by fundamental law the liberties of the citizen, the very thing which mankind have been struggling to establish for ages. It recognizes the right of the people to rule. It is based, as I said, upon the great idea of equality among men. It repudiates the notion which has prevailed for thousands of years, that any one man or set of men is born with a right to lord it over his fellow man and live upon the earnings of the mass of the people. We desire to restore the Constitution in its original state—to preserve it just as it is. We do not propose to alter it. We want to make it efficient in all its parts and provisions, in all places. We want it to protect a man in South Carolina in saying and publishing what he pleases just as it protects a man in Massachusetts. Practically it has not done that for the last forty years. Do away with the institution of slavery, and a man may talk as freely in Mobile as Chicago.

"This institution can now be got rid of through the folly and crime of the slave owners. [Applause.] In putting down the rebellion it is a legitimate exercise of power, as I have shown, to deprive the rebels of the support of their slaves, a power which we could not exercise but for the existence of the rebellion which the slave owners have inaugurated. What is now our duty as Republicans or as citizens desirous of crushing the rebellion and restoring the authority of the Government? It is to sustain the administration. You have, perhaps, sent your only son to this war —some of you have been yourselves; others are ready to go to maintain constitutional liberty and preserve the Union.

"For this cause you are willing to make these sacrifices. Thousands upon thousands of our fellow citizens are now in the tented field, undergoing all the hardships incident to long marches, to sleeping upon the ground, and also hazarding their lives in the front of battle. Shall we here at home remain inactive and supine, and suffer the Government to fall into the hands of men opposed to the war, who will make peace on humiliating terms, or consent to a dismemberment, when our brethren in the field are undergoing such hardships for a cause which is or ought to be just as dear to us as them? Does it not become us to be up and doing, to exert all the power we have to prevent such a result? If the Congress of the United States falls into the hands of the Peace Democracy, I say to you here to-night that all your sacrifices of blood and treasure will have gone for naught.

"Then let us take hold of this matter; contribute of your substance if it is necessary; devote your time to it; shut up your stores; leave your business; see to it that the civil government of the country sustains your soldiers in the field, or all is gone. What is your business worth? What is your property worth? What is life itself worth, unless you can preserve your liberties? You may be the father of a son, who is down in Alabama or Mississippi, risking his life on the battle field. How can you reconcile it to your conscience to suffer the civil government to fall into the hands of men who will paralyze the whole power of our armies? There never was a greater responsibility resting upon a people from the beginning of time. The redivision of the 14th corps, which was passing, came up and called to see him. He was almost breathing his last; but rousing himself, with an effort, on hearing his voice, and looking and speaking almost as if his spirit had departed and for a moment returned to make itself again manifest, he greeted General C. with all the courtesy and grace of language for which he was noted. As the General afterwards said: 'He received me with the same dignity and grace as if he were entertaining a distinguished guest in his best estate at his private quarters.' Scarcely had General Carlin retired when he breathed his last. After repeated messages of gratitude to the faithful men who had carried him so far and so gently, and also to Dr. Ormsby and others who had watched by and tended him so long and faithfully, he said he felt like sleeping; and he went to sleep 'among the eternal,' as calmly as the sun went down that mild October evening, amid fleecy clouds of golden glory. Yes, we did escort him home; but arrived there only with his cold remains."

His body was brought to Chicago and interred with impressive ceremonies, and amid the deep grief of thousands who knew him. We cannot better sum up the character of the deceased hero, than in the words of the clergyman who preached the funeral sermon, Rev. W. H. Ryder, D.D.:

"1. General Ransom was retiring and unostentatious. There was no strut about him. He was simple in his manners—quiet, unobtrusive. In a company of gentlemen he would not have been selected as a military man, according to the popular estimate. His power was always in reserve for occasions—and the greater the occasion, the deeper the peril, the more capable did he show himself to be. Ambitious—meaning thereby desire of power or eminence—he was not. His ambition was to honor his country—the service—to quit himself as a man should, acting in such a presence, and such an hour. Whether General Ransom would have arisen to the rank of a *great* leader—*i. e.*, whether he would have gained a still higher grade, and filled it with the same distinguished success which graced all the positions he occupied, is now a question which can never be decisively answered, and which, perhaps, it is not worth while to tarry long to consider. One thing is quite certain: had he been the chief in command of the famous Red River expedition, that blundering

Father of Waters? [No!] Then why don't you prevent it? We must preserve our nationality, and for myself I don't want to survive the permanent dismemberment of these United States. I had a thousand times rather lay down my life on the battle field than outlive such a dreadful event. I don't know what God wills, but I have a shrewd suspicion that He wills what *we* will. [Applause.] The maintenance of the Government and the perpetuity of the Union are a necessity. What! consent to a dismemberment? Suppose we allow the confederates to secede, what do we gain? We gain a confederacy more despotic than any monarchy of Europe. With Canada on the north, and this hated Southern Confederacy on the south, with all the power and hate of England to back her, we are ground to powder between the upper and nether mill-stone.

"How is our nationality to be preserved? By every man, woman and child consecrating themselves to the great work till the rebellion is suppressed. This is a matter that cannot be settled by resolutions or meetings, nor ballots; it's got beyond that; it's bayonets and bullets now. War has hardly touched us yet in the great Northwest; it has not yet laid upon us its bloody hand, that we feel its withering, blighting curse. We must buy and sell and conduct our business as usual, but the one grand idea must ever be prominent—the suppression of this rebellion. We must make this war the great business of our lives till it is ended."

HON. J. F. FARNSWORTH.

At the same meeting Hon. J. F. Farnsworth, at that time commanding the gallant 8th Illinois Cavalry, said:

"*Fellow Citizens*:—This call is unexpected. I have but just arrived here and stepped into your public square, interested in everything which has reference to the struggle in which we are engaged. I am gratified at this large audience and the enthusiasm, not only here but all over the country. He was at the great meeting in Union Square, New York. He was satisfied that the time he had been waiting to see, that he enlisted for, was nigh at hand, and that the people were about to put the axe at the root of the tree, and that every agency which the Almighty had provided would be seized upon to put down and end this gigantic rebellion. Such were the sentiments of every man who was not a traitor at heart. He was just from James River. He knew all the sufferings of the army, and all it had gone through. He knew nothing in the wide world which would so inspire our soldiers as to know that the people at home were waking up and taking hold of this war as the rebels are. We've got lessons from the rebels which are profitable examples. They have massed an immense army, and are fighting with a desperation we have not evinced. Until we have the same spirit, we shall not conquer them. When we seize all agencies as they do, we shall conquer, and that right speedily. The rebels have got their last large army. Every man has been compelled to take arms and fight in the front of the rebels. When we do this, rebeldom will be put down. The people of the North are getting over their tender-footed conservatism which has sacrificed too many lives, dear to your firesides. My friends, there is at this moment in the Southern States an army of men equal to our entire army in numbers. They are our friends. They will work for us, and fight for us, if you will but say the word. [Cries: "We will."] You are allowing them now to cultivate corn and wheat to feed your enemy. You are letting them work in the trenches and build fortifications against you. The entire element is ready—and I speak from my knowledge—is ready to act and work and fight for you. *A rebel throat is none too good to be cut by a black man.* I find in Virginia that the only reliable, truthful men from whom we can obtain information about the rebel armies, their roads and their scouts, were in the poor hovels of the negro. Using all the skill and experience I have had as a lawyer, I have questioned white men, and when I had done, some old negro too old to bear arms would nod to me to meet him behind the barn, and would tell me 'massa lied,' and would impart to me information which subsequent experience proved true. *I have never known them to tell an untruth to me.* I want to see an expression go forth from this meeting, lifting up the hands of the President and Cabinet for using every agency we can lay our hands upon. The voice of the people is the voice of God. It is authoritative with statesmen and generals. That voice I trust will be heard. I hope the fruits of this meeting will be felt. I hope it will not be an exodus for the accumulated gas of speeches. Organize your companies and train them at home for any emergency which may occur. I want to see the wealthy merchants who own these large buildings, the well-to do lawyers and thriving physicians, come down with the sinews of war to aid the men who are fighting the battles of the stay-at-homes. I see before me at least two regiments of men. *What are you doing here?* You've all got your little property at stake. Put your names on the muster roll.

"As I may not have another opportunity of addressing you, and may not meet you for a long time, and perhaps never, take my most fervent hopes and prayers that I may meet you and shake hands with you in Richmond."

HON. ISAAC N. ARNOLD.

And at the same meeting Hon. Isaac N. Arnold said:

"This glorious uprising of the people is the highest example of the moral sublime. The days of the crusaders have returned. Starting from the nation's capitol, all along through New York, New Jersey, Pennsylvania, Ohio and Indiana, you see a vast uprising of the people, with a fixed, stern determination, at any cost, to crush out this vast rebellion. But it is in the Northwest, and in this great city of the Northwest, that the zeal and energy of patriotism is most active and all-pervading.

"Illinois is meriting for herself and her children a glorious record. She had won distinguished honors in the Mexican war. Bissell and Hardin had associated their names and the name of Illinois with Palo Alto and Buena Vista; but in this far more glorious war, in which the faithful fights for his country against rebels and traitors far more cruel and barbarous than Mexican guerrillas, Illinois covered herself with glory. The bones of her sons lie scattered on every battle field in the valley of the Mississippi. With more than 60,000 of her gallant sons in the field, the President, whom Illinois has given to the nation, calls for troops.

"Illinois springs to the rescue. Her commercial capital speaks to-day in a voice which will thrill the nation. The Northwest is ready. As a citizen of this city, I claim to-day to express my thanks to the Board of Trade. You have done nobly, and your efforts will tell in all the Northwest, and be felt throughout the loyal States, and I doubt not also the gallant soldiers you raise will be felt among the barbarians in arms against our country.

"There is nothing to discourage us. Our armies during the last six months have achieved great success. When Congress assembled in December last, the capitol was besieged. The rebel flag was visible from the dome of the capitol. Rebel guns could be heard at the White House. The Potomac was blockaded. The Mississippi from Cairo to the Gulf was in possession of the traitors. New Orleans, Norfolk, much of Missouri, Kentucky, and all of Tennessee, were in their hands. Since then Western valor has cleared the Mississippi, driven the enemy out of Missouri, a great part of Arkansas, and Kentucky and Tennessee. On the 4th of July the old flag—God bless and preserve it forever—floated in every State in the Union.

"We have fought and won the great battles of Henry and Donelson, Pea Ridge, Island No. 10, and Shiloh. Butler now holds New Orleans, and is teaching the she traitors of the Crescent City better manners. Norfolk and St. Augustine are ours. We have annihilated the rebel navy, and our gun-boats hold undisputed sway over every harbor, and river, and navigable stream in the enemy's territory. One vigorous, active campaign, and our triumph is achieved.

"*Every great war has underlying it a great idea.* What is the great idea which gives impulse and motive power to this war? It is *our nationality.* The grand idea of a great continental republic, ocean bounded, and extending from the lakes to the Gulf, commanding the respect of the world, is an idea, implanted deeply in the American heart, and it is one for which every American patriot will fight, and if necessary die. Nowhere is this sentiment stronger than in the Northwest. With one hand we *clasp* the East, and with the other the Northwest will *gripe* the South, and we will hold this Union together We will not see this grand Republic split up into contemptible Mexican provinces—always fighting and destroying each other. Incident to this idea of Nationality and becoming every day stronger, is another—that this grand Republic must be all free, filled with one great, free population.

"The suicide of slavery is being enacted before our eyes. Let the cursed, barbarous, traitor-breeding institution die. The slaveholder has himself given to it the mortal wound; let no timid Northern doughface attempt to staunch the blood. *The end of slavery will prove the regeneration of the nation.*

"Liberal bounty is offered to the gallant volunteer. I wish to state a fact which may not be generally known. The Congress just adjourned, provided by law that all our foreign born soldiers should become the adopted children of the Republic; he who fights for the flag shall be immediately a citizen. We could not do less for the gallant Germans, the countrymen of Sigel, and Osterhaus, and Willich. For the brave Irishmen who, under Meagher, and Shields, and Mulligan, are fighting for the old flag. To every Irishman, I would say, remember Corcoran, and rally to his rescue.

"Who shall pay the cost of this war? Let us quarter on the enemy, confiscate the property, and free the slaves of rebels."

THE LAST INAUGURAL ADDRESS.

As this chapter was passing through the press, the nation was startled with the announcement of the President's assassination. The sad story belongs elsewhere. But in view of it the people of Illinois will read with mournful interest the last utterances of Abraham Lincoln before he was struck down by the hand of the assassin. On the 4th of March, 1865, in the presence of a vast concourse of people, he delivered his second inaugural address as follows:

"FELLOW-COUNTRYMEN:—At this second appearing to take the oath of the presidential office, there is less occasion for an extended address than there was at the first. Then a statement, somewhat in detail, of a course to be pursued, seemed very fitting and proper. Now, at the expiration of four years, during which public declarations have been constantly called forth on every point and phase of the great contest which still absorbs the attention and engrosses the energies of the nation, little that is new could be presented. The progress of our arms, upon which all else chiefly depends, is as well known to the public as to myself, and it is, I trust, reasonably encouraging to all.

"With high hope for the future, no prediction in regard to it is ventured. On the occasion corresponding to this, four years ago, all thoughts were anxiously directed to an impending civil war. All dreaded it; all sought to avoid it. While the Inaugural Address was being delivered from this place, devoted altogether to saving the Union without war, insurgent agents were in the city seeking to destroy it, without war—seeking to dissolve the Union and divide the effects by negotiation.

"Both parties deprecated war; but one of them would make war rather than let the nation survive, and the other would accept war rather than let it perish; and the war came. One-eighth of the whole population were colored slaves, not distributed generally over the Union, but localized in the Southern part of it. These slaves constituted a peculiar and powerful interest. All knew that this interest was somehow the cause of the war. To strengthen, perpetuate and extend this interest, was the object for which the insurgents would rend the Union by war, while the Government claimed no right to do more than to restrict the territorial enlargement of it.

"Neither party expected for the war the magnitude or the duration which it has already attained. Neither anticipated that the cause of the conflict might cease even before the conflict itself should cease. Each looked for an easier triumph, and a result less fundamental and astounding. Both read the same Bible and pray to the same God, and each invoke His aid against the other. It may seem strange that any man should dare to ask a just God's assistance in wringing their bread from the sweat of other men's faces.

"But let us judge not, that we be not judged. The prayer of both should not be answered—that of neither has been answered fully. The Almighty has his own purposes. 'Woe unto the world because of offenses, for it must needs be that offenses come, but woe to that man by whom the offense cometh.' If we shall suppose that American slavery is one of the offenses that in the providence of God must needs come, but which, having continued through His appointed time, He now so wills to remove that He gives to both North and South this terrible war as the woe due to those by whom the offense came, shall we discern that there is any departure from those divine attributes which the believers in a living God always ascribe to Him? Fondly do we hope, fervently do we pray, that this mighty scourge of war may speedily pass away; yet, if God wills that it continue until all the wealth piled by the bondman's two hundred and fifty years of unrequited toil shall be sunk, and until every drop of blood drawn with the lash shall be paid by another drawn with the sword, as was said three thousand years ago, so still it must be said that the judgments of the Lord are true and righteous altogether.

"With malice toward none, with charity for all, with firmness in the right, as God gives us to see the right, let us strive on to finish the work we are in, to bind up the nation's wounds, and care for him who shall have borne the battle, and for his widow and his orphans—to do all which may achieve and cherish a just and lasting peace among ourselves and with all nations."

THE LAST SPEECH.

The last speech which President Lincoln ever made in public was delivered in Washington, on the 11th of April, 1865, after his return from Richmond, upon the vexed question of reconstruction, and will forever stand as a monument of the goodness of his heart. The President said:

"We meet this evening not in sorrow, but in gladness of heart. The evacuation of Petersburg and Richmond, and the surrender of the principal insurgent army, give hopes of a righteous and speedy peace, whose joyous expressions cannot be restrained. In the midst of this, however, He from whom all blessings flow must not be forgotton. A call for a national thanksgiving is being prepared, and will be duly promulgated. Nor must those whose harder part gives us the cause of rejoicing, be overlooked. Their honors must not be parceled out with others. I myself was near the front, and had the high pleasure of transmitting much of the good news to you. But no part of the honor for plan or execution is mine. To Gen. Grant, his skillful officers and brave men, all belongs. The gallant navy stood ready, but was not in reach to take active part. By these recent successes the re-inauguration of the national authority—reconstruction, which has had a large share of thought from the first—is pressed much more closely upon our attention. It is fraught with great difficulty. Unlike a war between independent nations, there is no authorized organ for us to treat with. No one man has authority to give up the rebellion for any other man. We must simply begin with and mold from disorganized and discordant elements. Nor is it a small additional embarrassment that we, the loyal people, differ among ourselves as to the mode, manner and measure of reconstruction. As a general rule, I abstain from reading the reports of attacks upon myself, wishing not to be provoked by that to which I cannot properly offer an answer. In spite of this precaution, however, it comes to my knowledge that I am much censured for some supposed agency in setting up and seeking to sustain the new State Government of Louisiana. In this I have done just so much and no more than the public knows. In the annual message of December, 1863, and the accompanying proclamation, I presented a plan of reconstruction, as the phrase goes, which I promised, if adopted by any State, would be acceptable to and sustained by the Executive Government of the nation. I distinctly stated that this was not the only plan which might, possibly, be acceptable; and I also distinctly protested that the Executive claimed no right to say when or whether members should be admitted to seats in Congress from such States. This plan was in advance submitted to the then cabinet, and approved by every member of it. One of them suggested that I should then and in that connection apply the Emancipation Proclamation to the theretofore excepted parts of Virginia and Louisiana, that I should drop the suggestion about apprenticeship for freed people, and that I should omit the protest against my own power in regard to the admission of members of Congress. But even he approved every part and parcel of the plan which has since been employed or touched by the action of Louisiana. The new constitution of Louisiana, declaring emancipation for the whole State, practically applies the proclamation to the part previously excepted. It does not adopt apprenticeship for freed people, and is silent, as it could not well be otherwise, about the admission of members to Congress. So that as it applied to Louisiana every member of the Cabinet fully approved the plan. The message went to Congress, and I received many commendations of the plan, written and verbal, and not a single objection to it, from any professed emancipationist, came to my knowledge until after the news reached Washington that the people of Louisiana had begun to move in accordance with it. From about July, 1862, I had corresponded with different persons supposed to be interested in seeking a reconstruction of a State government for Louisiana. When the message of 1863, with the plan before mentioned, reached New Orleans, Gen. Banks wrote to me that he was confident that the people, with his military co-operation, would reconstruct substantially on that plan. I wrote to him and some of them to try it. They tried it, and the result is known. Such has been my only agency in getting up the Louisiana government. As to sustaining it, my promise is out, as before stated. But as bad promises are better broken than kept, I shall treat this as a bad promise and break it whenever I shall be convinced that keeping it is adverse to the public interest, but I have not yet been so convinced.

"I have been shown a letter on this subject, supposed to be an able one, in which the writer expresses regret that my mind has not seemed to be definitely fixed on the question, whether the seceded States, so called, are in the Union or out of it.

It would, perhaps, add astonishment to his regret, were he to learn that since I have found professed Union men endeavoring to answer that question I have purposely forebore any public expression upon it. As appears to me, that question has not been, nor yet is a practically material one, and that any discussion of it while it thus remains practically immaterial, could have no effect other than the mischievous one of dividing our friends. As yet, whatever it may become, that question is had as a basis of a controversy, and good for nothing at all—a merely pernicious abstraction. We all agree that the seceded States, so called, are out of their proper practical relation with the Union, and that the sole object of the government, civil and military, in regard to those States, is to again get them into their proper practical relation. I believe that it is not only possible, but, in fact, easier to do this without deciding, or even considering, whether those States have ever been out of the Union, than with it. Finding themselves safely at home, it would be utterly immaterial whether they had been abroad. Let us all join in doing the acts necessary to restore the proper practical relations between those States and the nation, and each forever after innocently indulge his own opinion whether in doing the acts he brought the States from without into the Union, or only gave them proper assistance, they never having been out of it. The amount of constituency, so to speak, on which the Louisiana government rests, would be more satisfactory to all if it contained 50,000, or 30,000, or even 20,000, instead of 12,000, as it does. It is also unsatisfactory to some that the elective franchise is not given to the colored man. I would myself prefer that it were now conferred on the very intelligent, and on those who serve our cause as soldiers. Still the question is not whether the Louisiana government, as it stands, is quite all that is desirable. The question is, will it be wiser to take it as it is, and help to improve it, or to reject and disperse ? Can Louisiana be brought into proper practical relation with the Union sooner by sustaining or by discarding her new State government? Some twelve thousand voters in the heretofore slave State of Louisiana have sworn allegiance to the Union, assumed to be the rightful political power of the State, held elections, organized a State government, adopted a Free State constitution, giving the benefit of public schools equally to black and white, and empowering the Legislature to confer the elective franchise upon the colored man. This Legislature has already voted to ratify the constitutional amendment recently passed by Congress, abolishing slavery throughout the nation. These twelve thousand persons are thus fully committed to the Union and to perpetuate freedom in the State; committed to the very things, and nearly all things, the nation wants, and they ask the nation's recognition and its assistance to make good this committal. Now if we reject and spurn them we do our utmost to disorganize and disperse them. We in fact say to the white man, you are worthless or worse; we will neither help you, nor be helped by you. To the blacks, we say: This cup of liberty which these, your old masters, held to your lips, we will dash from you, and leave you to the chances of gathering the spilled and scattered contents in some vague and undefined when, where and how. If this course, discouraging and paralyzing both white and black, has any tendency to bring Louisiana into proper practical relations with the Union, I have so far been unable to perceive it. If, on the contrary, we recognize and sustain the new government of Louisiana, the converse of all this is made true. We encourage the hearts and nerve the arms of 12,000 to adhere to their work, and argue for it, and proselyte for it, and fight for it, and feed it, and grow it, and ripen it to a complete success. The colored man, too, in seeing all united for him, is inspired with vigilance, and energy, and daring to the same end. Grant that he desires the elective franchise, will he not attain it sooner by saving the already advanced steps toward it, than by running backward over them? Concede that the new government of Louisiana is to what it should be as the egg is to the fowl, we shall sooner have the fowl by hatching the egg, than by smashing it. [Laughter.] Again, if we reject Louisiana we also reject one vote in favor of the proposed amendment to the national constitution. To meet this proposition it has been argued that no more than three-fourths of those States which have not attempted secession are necessary to validily ratify the amendment. I do not commit myself against this, further than to say that such a ratification would be questionable, and sure to be persistently questioned, while a ratification by three-fourths of all the States would be unquestioned and unquestionable. I repeat the question. Can Louisiana be brought into proper practical relation with the Union sooner by sustaining, or by discarding her new State Government? What has been said of Louisiana will apply to other States. And yet so great peculiarities pertain to each State, and such important and sudden changes occur in the same State, and withal so new and unprecedented is the whole case, that no exclusive and inflexible plan can safely be prescribed as to details and collaterals. Such exclusive and inflexible plan would surely become a new entanglement. Important principles may and must be inflexible. In the present situation, as the phrase goes, *it may be my duty to make some new announcement to the people of the South.* I am considering and shall not fail to act when satisfied that action will be proper."

The President, during the delivery of the above speech, was frequently interrupted by applause, and on its conclusion, in the midst of the cheering, the band struck up a patriotic air, when he bowed and retired.

THE LAST PROCLAMATION.

The last Proclamation issued by the lamented President, was one claiming that our vessels of war in foreign ports should no longer be subjected to restrictions, but should have the same rights and hospitalities which are extended to foreign vessels of war in the ports of the United States, and declaring that hereafter the cruisers of every nation shall receive the treatment which in their ports they accord to ours. The Proclamation reads as follows:

"*By the President of the United States of America:*

"PROCLAMATION.

"WHEREAS, For some time past vessels of war of the United States have been refused in certain ports privileges and immunities to which they were entitled by treaty, public law, or the comity of nations, at the same time that vessels of war of the country wherein the said privileges and immunities have been withheld, have enjoyed them fully and uninterruptedly in the ports of the United States, which condition of things has not always been forcibly resisted by the United States; although, on the other hand, they have not failed to protest against and declare their dissatisfaction with the same. In the view of the United States, no condition any longer exists which can be claimed to justify the denial to them by any one of said nations of the customary naval rights, such as has heretofore been so unnecessarily persisted in; now, therefore, I, ABRAHAM LINCOLN, President of the United States, do hereby make known that, if, after a resonable time shall have elapsed for the intelligence of this proclamation to have reached any foreign country in whose ports the said privileges and immunities shall have been refused, as aforesaid, they shall continue to be so refused; then and thenceforth the same privileges and immunities shall be refused to the vessels of war of the country in the ports of the United States, and this refusal shall continue until the war vessels of the United States shall have been placed upon an entire equality in the foreign ports aforesaid with similar vessels of other countries. The United States, whatever claim or pretence may have existed heretofore, are now at least entitled to claim and concede an entire and friendly equality of rights and hospitalities with all maritime nations.

"In witness whereof, I have hereunto set my hand and caused the seal of the United States to be affixed. Done at the City of Washington, this eleventh day of April, in the year of our Lord one thousand eight hundred and sixty-five, and of the independence of the United States of America the eighty-ninth.

"By the President: ABRAHAM LINCOLN.

"WM. H. SEWARD, Secretary of State."

In concluding this chapter, there is a letter of President Lincoln's so remarkable for embodying the principles which governed his administration that it is here inserted entire. It shows his long suffering and patience, and that extreme measures with slavery were employed only when milder ones failed. We precede and accompany it with some extracts from the *North American Review*, of January, 1865:

THE KENTUCKY LETTER.

"Unquestionably there is matter for difference in respect to many of the acts of Mr. Lincoln's administration. In the pressure of events of a character utterly novel, and involving consequences of the utmost importance, with the need frequently of prompt decision and immediate action upon them, mistakes have been committed, and errors of judgment have occurred, such as were inevitable in a season of such stress and difficulty. Still further, the period has been one full of instruction to every man of candid and intelligent mind. The whole nation has been at school. It has been taught new ideas in respect to duty and to policy. Old ideas have been rudely shaken, and have given way to others more conformed to the necessities and changes of the time. A policy fit for 1861 is not the policy for 1864. Principles do not change, but their application to events is continually changing. The consistent statesman is not he who never alters his policy, but he who, adapting his policy to shifting exigencies, is true always to the fixed north star of duty and of principle. Above all, in a period of social convulsion, a true and honorable consistency does not consist in adherence to the details of any preconceived plan or system, but in the ready adjustment of its details to the novel demands of the time; and it is this consistency which, in our opinion, Mr. Lincoln has eminently displayed. In his Inaugural Address, he said, 'The power confided to me will be used to hold, occupy, and possess the property and posts belonging to the government, and to collect the duties and imposts; but beyond what may be necessary for these objects, there will be no invasion, no using of force against or among the people anywhere.' But he also said, 'I hold that, in contemplation of universal law and of the Constitution, the union of these States is perpetual.' And in support of this fundamental doctrine, his declaration that 'there will be no using of force against or among the people anywhere' was rightly and consistently disregarded, and the tramp of the soldier in every seceded State was its commentary.

"On no subject have the sentiments of the Northern people undergone a more entire change since 1861, than on the question of the right of the general government to interfere with slavery. Not only is their view of the relation of the Constitution to slavery essentially modified, but within the powers with which the Constitution invested the President, has been found the arm from which slavery has received its death-blow. The idea of being called upon to use this arm had never crossed the mind of Mr. Lincoln up to the time of his inauguration. He, in common with the mass of the people of the North, was ready then to guarantee to the people of the South protection for slavery within its existing limits. His oath as President to support the Constitution was interpreted by him as depriving him of all lawful right to interfere, directly or indirectly, with the institution of slavery in the States where it then existed. But the progress of events taught him, as it taught the people, that slavery, like every other partial interest or relation, was subordinate to the general interest; that it was subject to the Constitution; that if, to preserve the Union, slavery must be destroyed, the Constitution, which formed the bond of the Union, could not be pleaded in its defence. His course on the matter was in accordance with the fundamental principles of his political creed. Other men, no doubt, earlier reached the same conclusions at which he arrived, and urged upon him the adoption of the policy which he at length pursued. But on them the responsibility of decision and action did not rest; and Mr. Lincoln's deep sense of that responsibility caused him to seem to reach slowly the point to which more eager and less considerate men had long before attained.

"Moreover, in Mr. Lincoln's position, the conflicting interests and the contradictory opinions of men of the loyal, and especially of the Border States, have made it a task of extreme difficulty and delicacy to learn the true sentiment of the North. To unite and to keep united the people of the loyal States in the support of the administration, so far as such union was possible, was Mr. Lincoln's arduous task. On this union depended the power to carry on the war. Every delay, every disaster to our arms, every imcompetence, every personal disappointment and private grief, every wounded vanity, all partizan hates and jealousies, every danger, in fine, against which an American statesman could be called on to provide, lay in his path. He could not, if he did his duty, expect either wholly to please his friends or to win his enemies; he could not force compliance with his views, or insist on the adoption of measures which he might esteem desirable or essential. His character was not fitted to secure a strong body of personal supporters. He stood comparatively isolated and alone; and his duty was to save the Union, and to save it with its institutions sound and whole. Popular opinion was changing and developing rapidly. Mr. Lincoln's own views were changing and advancing with it. But it was impossible to make sure of popular opinion, so diverse were the voices of the people. 'I am approached,' said Mr. Lincoln, 'with the most opposite opinions and advice, and that by religious men, who are equally certain that they represent the Divine will. I am sure,' he added, with humorous irony, 'that either one or the other class is mistaken in the belief, and perhaps in some respect both.' The elements in the problem given him to solve were of the most complex and difficult character. He might well be pardoned, if, doing his best, he had failed. But he has not failed. Sagacious beyond most men in his estimate of popular opinion, he has the intuition of a genuine statesman as to the manner and moment of its use. He has not fallen into the common error of politicians, of mistaking a gust of enthusiasm or of passion for the steady wind of conviction, or of fancying a thunder-squall of violence to be a black storm of gathered discontent. He has not sought to control events, but he has known how to turn events, among the most important of which are to be reckoned the moods of a great people in time of trial, to the benefit of the cause of the nation and of mankind.

"In regard to the question of slavery and emancipation, he has, fortunately for the country and for history, given a statement of the principles and motives of his policy in a brief letter, which must take rank as one of the most important documents in the remarkable series of state-papers which he has published since his accession to the Presidency. It is a production of the highest interest, not only as containing the authentic record of his opinions and his action on this great topic, but as exhibiting the frankness, candor, integrity, and sagacity which are the distinguishing traits of his personal character. We cite this letter in full, because, in the crowd of matters of public concern, it has not received the attention it deserves as an exposition of the President's policy, and because it is well fitted to inspire confidence in the wisdom of its author.

"EXECUTIVE MANSION, WASHINGTON, April 4, 1864.

"A. G. HODGES, ESQ., Frankfort, Kentucky.

"MY DEAR SIR:—You ask me to put in writing the substance of what I verbally stated the other day, in your presence, to Governor Bramlette and Senator Dixon. It was about as follows:

"'I am naturally anti-slavery. If slavery is not wrong, nothing is wrong. I cannot remember when I did not so think and feel; and yet I have never understood that the Presidency conferred upon me an un-restricted right to act officially upon this judgment and feeling. It was in the oath I took that I would to the best of my ability preserve, protect, and defend the Constitution of the United States. I could not take the office without taking the oath. Nor was it in my view that I might take the oath to get power, and break the oath in using the power. I understood, too, that in ordinary civil administration this oath even forbade me to practically indulge my primary abstract judgment on the moral question of slavery. I had publicly declared this many times and in many ways; and I aver that, to this day, I have done no official act in mere deference to my abstract judgment and feeling on slavery. I did understand, however, that my oath to preserve the Constitution to the best of my ability imposed upon me the duty of preserving, by every indispensable means, that government, that nation, of which that Constitution was the organic law. Was it possible to lose the nation, and yet preserve the Constitution? By general law, life *and* limb must be protected; yet often a limb must be amputated to save a life, but a life is never wisely given to save a limb. I felt that measures, otherwise unconstitutional, might become lawful by becoming indispensable to the preservation of the nation. Right or wrong, I assumed this ground, and now avow it. I could not feel that to the best of my ability I had even tried to preserve the Constitution, if, to save slavery, or any minor matter, I should permit the wreck of government, country, and Constitution altogether. When, early in the war, Gen. Fremont attempted military emancipation, I forbade it, because I did not then think it an indispensable necessity. When, a little later, General Cameron, then Secretary of War, suggested the arming of the blacks, I objected, because I did not yet think it an indispensable necessity. When, still later, General Hunter attempted military emancipation, I forbade it, because I did not yet think the indispensable necessity had come. When, in March and May and July, 1862, I made earnest and successive appeals to the Border States to favor compensated emancipation, I believed the indispensable necessity for military emancipation and arming the blacks would come, unless averted by that measure. They declined the proposition; and I was, in my best judgment, driven to the alternative of either surrendering the Union, and with it the Constitution, or of laying strong hand upon the colored element. I chose the latter. In choosing it, I hoped for greater gain than loss; but of this I was not entirely confident. More than a year of trial now shows no loss by it in our foreign relations, none in our home popular sentiment, none in our white military force,—no loss by it anyhow or anywhere. On the contrary, it shows a gain of quite a hundred and thirty thousand soldiers, seamen, and laborers. These are palpable facts, about which, as facts, there can be no caviling. We have men, and we could not have had them without the measure.

"'And now let any Union man who complains of the measure test himself by writing down in one line that he is for subduing the rebellion by force of arms; and in the next, that he is for taking three [one?] hundred and thirty thousand men from the Union side, and placing them where they would be but for the measure he condemns. If he cannot face his case so stated, it is only because he cannot face the truth.

"'I add a word which was not in the verbal conversation. In telling this tale, I attempt no compliment to my own sagacity. I claim not to have controlled events, but confess plainly that events have controlled me. Now, at the end of three years' struggle, the nation's condition is not what either party or any man desired or expected. God alone can claim it. Whither it is tending seems plain. If God now wills the removal of a great wrong, and wills also that we of the North, as well as you of the South, shall pay fairly for our complicity in that wrong, impartial history will find therein new causes to attest and revere the justice and goodness of God.

"'Yours, truly,

"'A. LINCOLN."

"This excellent letter, in giving the grounds and explaining the motives of Mr. Lincoln's action, affords a complete vindication from the complaints that have been frequently brought against him by the thoughtless and impatient, by the men of ardent temperament and of limited views, for not advancing more rapidly, for not giving more speedy effect to a supposed popular sentiment, for not adopting what is called a more decisive policy, for being content not to lead the people, but to wait for their progress. These men have desired him to anticipate public opinion, and in doing so they have failed to consider how slow, even in times like these, is the maturing of popular conviction, and how liable to be checked by over-hasty action. The vicissitudes of war produce a frame of mind in which the feelings of the masses of men are likely to oversway their reason, and in which, consequently, there is a constant danger of the rise of reactionary opinions and measures. Political action based on the feeling of a moment is liable to speedy reversal. A policy that is to be lasting must rest on solid and well-formed convictions. The art and the duty of a true statesman in a republic, is not to act on what the people ought to wish and to think, but to adopt the best course practicable in accordance with what they actually do wish and think. It is not to attempt to exercise a despotic leadership, but to divine and to give force to the right will of the nation.

"Above all, in such circumstances as those in which the American nation has been placed by the rebellion, it is of infinite importance that it should learn to conduct its own affairs, trusting to no one man to deliver it from peril, and yielding to no temptation to give up its own power into the hands of any, even the wisest dictator. A Cromwell, if a Cromwell had been possible, would have been an unspeakable calamity to the nation during the past four years. A free and intelligent people have no place for, and no need of, a Cromwell. It must be its own ruler and its own leader. This war has been a war of the people for the people; and in order to reach a successful conclusion—the only conclusion worthy of a self-sustained and self-governed nation, a conclusion which should be a final settlement of the quarrel—it must be fought out by themselves. They are to save themselves, not to look to any man for their salvation. The nation is already lost when it seeks relief from its own duties by shifting them on the shoulders of a leader. And in this view Abraham Lincoln has well fulfilled the duty imposed on him, not seeking to control opinion any more than to control events, but seeking to make use of both in accordance with the laws by which they are governed, so as to secure the working out of the great problem of national salvation. 'I have understood well,' said he, 'that the duty of self-preservation rests solely with the American people.'"

CHAPTER XXXII.

ILLINOIS ON THE POTOMAC.

Campaigns of East and West—Virginia the Battle-ground—Its Natural Divisions—Campaigns of Western Virginia—General Scott—Bull Run—General McClellan—Waiting—"On to Richmond"—Yorktown—Battles of the Chickahominy—Pope—McClellan—Burnside—Fredericksburg—"No. 8"—Hooker—Chancellorsville—Lee's Strategy—His Advance on Pennsylvania—New Call—Lee's Ultimate Advance—Meade—Advance of His Army—Gettysburg—Battles—Lost Opportunity—More Waiting—Lee's Army Escapes, and Gen. Meade Escapes the Highest Honor—Gettysburg and Vicksburg—Shenandoah Valley—The Coast—Lieut.-General Grant—Into the Wilderness—Its Battles—Before Petersburg.

UNTIL since the battles of Franklin and Nashville, few Illinois troops have been with the armies of Virginia. Consequently in such a work as this, the Eastern campaigns must receive much less attention than Western, where Illinois battle-flags were in almost every brigade, and Illinois blood made sacred every battle-field. Not meaning to make this a history of the war, it was yet impossible to give a shadow of Illinois patriotism without marching with the campaigns of the West. In every Western conflict, our men were there—there in the dim smoke of battle, in the wild charge—there for the desperate charge or the stern resistance. In the campaigns of the East you may count upon your fingers all the Illinois regiments or squadrons engaged, and that before you have counted both hands.

Virginia has been the great Eastern battle-field. It is true the sea-board generally has been contested and won. In North Carolina there were early and important movements, but in Virginia have been massed the grand armies of the contestants, and on its "sacred soil" has blood been poured out as water.

The old dominion is divided naturally into three sections: The Eastern, extending from salt-water to the Blue Ridge; the Middle or Valley, lying between the Blue Ridge and the Alleghanies, and the Western reaching from the Alleghanies to the Ohio River. The Middle and Western had their own grounds of quarrel with the Eastern, and there were bitter strifes to be intensified by civil war.

In May, 1861, Brigadier-General George B. McClellan was assigned to the department of the Ohio, including Western Virginia. With him were Rosecrans, Morris, Reynolds, Milroy and others who have won distinction. The contest really opened at Philippi. The engagements of Laurel Hill, Rich Mountain, and Carrick's Ford followed. The campaign was short and successful.

Before Washington the enemy was concentrating in threatening strength. The armory and public store-houses at Harper's Ferry were burned to prevent their seizure; Massachusetts and Pennsylvania troops were fired upon in Baltimore, navy yards were burned, and all this time General Scott was busy devising grand schemes for great campaigns. He projected a movement of three columns on Baltimore, but General Butler quietly moved on the Relay House and took Baltimore as a matter of course.

July 21st came the disaster of Bull Run. Patterson suffered Johnson to escape from Winchester, and his coming turned the day almost won against the Federal troops.

On the 25th, General McClellan, (after Major-General, U. S. A.) arrived in Washington to assume command of the Army of the Potomac. He gathered, equipped and disciplined one of the mightiest armies ever led by a commander. In *materiel* none had ever equaled it. It had unbounded confidence in the loyalty, skill and courage of its leader—ready to follow him anywhere. The nation believed the army would be unconquerable and resistless. It waited for it to move. In sight of that magnificent army floated the rebel flag. The people waited.

It is no purpose of this work to enter a discussion of the questions concerning that army, or to arbitrate those which have arisen concerning its different leaders. After waiting, the country heard that Manassas was evacuated, but the enemy was gone. With rare magnanimity he left his wooden guns!

The cry, "On to Richmond!" was everywhere, and the grand army moved and sat down before Yorktown, which in due time was also evacuated, and another bootless victory won. Then came Williamsburg and West-Point. Then followed the terrible battles of the Chickahominy, Fair Oaks, Mechanicsville, Gaines' Mills, Peach Orchard, and Savage Station, White Oak Swamp and Glendale, and Malvern Hill—names never to be forgotten, forever linked with the memories of May 31st to July 2, 1862. They were horrible for their slaughter. Never army fought better than ours, and victories were won, but the commander found it necessary to command retreat, and back, still back, until the broken remnants of that proud army were at Harrison's Landing.

Pope took command of the Army of Virginia. He had been crowned with glory in the campaign of the Mississippi, and had shown himself possessed of military ability. He was sacrificed by jealousies and the refusal of co-operation. It might have been different.

Again General McClellan wields the Marshals' baton. Lee crosses the mountains, and then follow the battles of South Mountain, Crampton's Gap and Antietam. At the latter place, as at Malvern Hill, it seemed that a bold onward push would have given us the army of Lee, and virtually have ended the war. But it was not so to be. We were to be more severely disciplined and to learn that God was teaching us high moral duties in the red flames of war.

With Antietam, closed General McClellan's military career. It has been discussed fully by his admirers and opponents. Virtually the questions at issue between him and the President were carried before the Supreme Court of the popular ballot, on the 8th of November, 1864, and the decision was given. Let the controversy rest. And yet, a calm examination seems to show the lack of that deep, stern, terrible earnestness which a man must have who would successfully wield vast masses of men.

Next came Burnside. He had won eclat at Roanoake, Eden, Plymouth, and Hatteras. A braver General and a more successful corps commander had rarely worn the double star. He was modest and distrustful of his ability. The battle of Fredricksburg came on. It was the old story. As with Pope, so with Burnside. The want of co-operation, and from that, disaster. The army fell back across the river. Before he would make another advance the General issued the celebrated "Order No. eight," dismissing from the service, subject to the President's approval, several officers high in rank, and ordering others, with the same condition, to report to the Adjutant-General of the United States' Army. The measure was a bold one, but General Burnside knew that only with unity could he hope for success. He erred in making that order so sweeping, for it included some who may have used unsoldierly freedom of criticism, but who were, nevertheless, brave and loyal.

That order was forwarded to the President, with General Burnside's resignation of his commission, if the President preferred to accept it. After mature deliberation, Mr. Lincoln decided not to approve the order, but to relieve him of his command and appoint General Hooker as his successor. General Burnside was assigned to the department of the Ohio.

On the 26th of January, 1863, General Hooker assumed command. After preliminary movements, the battle of Chancellorsville occurred last of April and early in May. General Hooker claimed the capture of 5,000 prisoners, fifteen colors, seven pieces of artillery, and to have "placed *hors de combat* 18,000 of Lee's chosen troops; destroyed his depots filled with vast amounts of stores; deranged his communications; captured prisoners within the fortifications of his capital and filled his country with fear and consternation." On the other hand General Lee called for a day of special thanksgiving for the "glorious victory" won over an "enemy strongly entrenched in the tangled depths of a wilderness."

The Secretary of War took a sober view in his dispatches to the Governors. He conceded the failure of General Hooker's principal operations, but that there had been "no serious disaster to the organization and efficiency of the army. It is now occupying its former position on the Rappahannock, having recrossed the river without any loss in the movement. Not more than one-third of General Hooker's force was engaged. General Stoneman's operations have been a brilliant success. Part of his force advanced to within two miles of Richmond, and the enemy's communications have been cut in every direction." It was in this engagement that the ablest field-marshal of the Confederate service, General "Stonewall" Jackson—a tower of strength to the rebellion—fell.

In June, General Lee moved with masterly strategy. He concentrated his forces for a decisive campaign, which should place at his mercy either Washington, or the rich towns and cities of Pennsylvania. At the same time, as parts of one grand scheme, the disaffected population of New York was to rise *en masse;* Morgan was to cross the Ohio and pass on a grand raid through Indiana and Ohio, rallying to his standard the peace-men of the Northwest, while secret leagues with their chief officers in Canada were to order their uprising. Loyal Governors were to be assassinated; camps of rebel prisoners were to be opened, Northern cities were to be given to the flames. Never did the country stand in graver peril —never was it nearer signal deliverance. In God's good Providence each of these schemes was to be baffled.

General Ewell with the divisions of Johnson and Early moved up the Shenandoah valley through Snicker's Gap, and overwhelmed the force of General Milroy at Winchester, compelling him to retreat with much loss to Harper's Ferry. The capture of Martinsburg followed, and on to Chambersburg, McConnelsville, &c.

It was now evident that grave perils were upon our cause. The President issued a proclamation on the 15th of June, calling for one hundred thousand six-months' militia from the States of Maryland, Pennsylvania, Ohio and Western Virginia. The Governors issued earnest calls, and troops poured in for the defense of Northern soil and the nation's capital.

General Hooker hurried forward the forces under his command, his first care being Washington, and his rapid movements left Lee at the choice between attacking him in the strong defences of that city, to fall back, or move into Maryland and Pennsylvania. He held Winchester, and Ewell was in Pennsylvania, but could not draw Hooker from Virginia. The fords of the Potomac between Harper's Ferry and Williamsport were seized. On the 21st of June, Lee issued his orders regulating the troops on the march. Correspondence of an important character was intercepted by General Hooker, disclosing the plan of the enemy. Ewell's corps, the rebel advance, passed from Williamsport to Hagerstown, on the 22d entered Greencastle, Pennsylvania, and on the 23d Chambersburg was re-occupied by his force.

General Lee crossed into Maryland on the 24th. At the same time his main army crossed the fords at Shepherdstown and Williamsport. The movement continued up the Cumberland Valley, on the west side of the Catoctin Mountains, the advance moving in two columns; one by way of the Harrisburg and Chambersburg Railroad toward Harrisburg, and the other from Gettysburg eastward to the Northern Central Railroad, connecting Baltimore and Harrisburg, and thence extending to York and Lancaster. On the 27th Carlisle was occupied, and the same day the rebel cavalry was within four miles of Harrisburg, the capital of the great State of Pennsylvania. On the 27th General Lee issued orders from the "Headquarters Army of Northern Virginia, Chambersburg, Penn." The rebel army was then distributed as follows: The main body, with the corps of Longstreet and Hill, were at or near Chambersburg; the divisions of Rhodes and Johnson, Early's corps, were in the vicinity of Carlisle and Harrisburg, while Early's own division with Gordon's brigade, was at York—Harrisburg, Philadelphia, and then on to New York!

It was not so written. No Union capital or principal city was to be occupied by the rebel army! In the midst of disloyal exultation, the "dream of the barley-cake" fell upon their leaders, and on the 28th orders were issued for both lines to fall back on Gettysburg. The army of the Union had crossed the Potomac, and its head was at South Mountain. Lee must protect his threatened communications, must assume the defensive.

On the 22d the Union army occupied the line of the Potomac on the Virginia side of the river, extending beyond Leesburg, and held all the gaps of the Bull Run range. Saturday, the 27th, it was at Frederick, Md. That day the order came relieving Hooker, and transferring the command to Major-General Meade. Hooker, too, found the demon of in-co-operation too hard for him, and desired to be relieved. The change took the army, as it did the country, by surprise. A forward movement was ordered by the new commander. The sixth and eleventh corps, which were at Middletown, in the valley between the Catoctin and the Blue Ridge, were moved east to Frederick, then up the Monocacy Valley through Mechanicsburg and Emmitsburg toward Gettysburg. The second and fifth corps crossed the Monocacy east of Frederick, and marched northeast through Union to Frizelburg, near the State line. The sixth moved to Westminster. The routes were so selected that Washington and Baltimore could be covered. Harper's Ferry was ordered to be evacuated, under the impression that it was without provisions, but the order was recalled. On the 30th General Meade changed the line of march of all his corps except the first and eleventh, toward Gettysburg. Those already were moving thither.

On the morning of July 1st the armies joined battle, and the brave Major-General Reynolds fell. Through the day the conflict raged, and night came on with results not favorable to our cause, for only our advance was brought into action. Thursday afternoon there was another desperate struggle, which closed without decisive results. On Friday, the 3d, the storm of battle was almost without precedent. The massed artillery of the enemy was directed against the left center of General Meade, and continued three hours. Twice the enemy rushed forward with desperate fury, charging up to our guns only to be broken and thrown back with fearful slaughter, the dead and wounded lying in windrows.

The Battles of Gettysburg were ended, and the defeated army of Lee began its retreat. Congratulations danced along the wires. General Meade was the hero of the hour.

That same "Fourth," the stronghold of the Mississippi was surrendered, to be followed by the surrender of Port Hudson, thus opening the Great River. And so Vicksburg and Gettysburg shouted their glad triumph across the mountains, the plains and the rivers! The national heart grew strong; the national faith took new life. Henceforward the Fourth of July was to have a new and grander meaning than ever.

The country expected confidently to hear of the capture of Lee and his whole army. The Potomac was behind him, and, as if to render his escape impossible, heavy rains swelled it to flood-tide. Not more manifestly fought the stars in their courses against Sisera than fought the elements against Lee, and Providence seemed to have given him into our hands. But there was delay in pursuit, halting, and "caution." On the 14th came the word from General Meade himself, "the enemy are all across the Potomac." The war, which seemed so near its completion, was to be indefinitely extended, and General Meade missed the glory which seemed his inevitably.

It was a well-fought series of battles at Gettysburg, and should be wisely estimated; there were bravery and skill, but again a victorious army was halted within sight of grand results.

The valley of the Shenandoah, until the later days of Grant and Sheridan, was our valley of Hinnom. Banks, Hunter, Fremont, Milroy, Sigel, all failed to clear it of the foe, and there we seemed destined to defeat. Yet some of the most brilliant heroism was displayed, and by none more than by Illinois troops which chanced to be there. In the operations on the coast of North Carolina and before Charleston, Illinois had so few men engaged as to not warrant extended notice. The 39th was with General Gilmore in the early stages of the siege of Charleston and distinguished itself by gallantry in an assault, which will be hereafter noticed.

On the 1st of March, 1864, the President gave his signature to the bill establishing the grade of Lieutenant-General, and, as Congress, the people and the army expected, nominated to receive it, Major-General U. S. Grant, the hero of Vicksburg and Mission Ridge, and on the 8th the commission was handed to the former Colonel of the "21st Regiment Illinois Infantry," by the President in person, in presence of the Cabinet, and he became commander of the armies of the United States. He framed a vast and comprehensive plan, the outworking of which we begin to see. It included the movements of Sherman through the Confederacy, of Thomas before Nashville, Sheridan in the Shenandoah, and Meade upon Petersburg and Richmond. The army of Lee was to be broken or driven within the defenses of Richmond, and held there, while Sherman, Thomas and Sheridan should operate elsewhere, and then, like the iron-chamber of the inquisition, the walls of steel should close in upon Lee's army on every side. On the 17th he formally assumed command. The fears freely expressed that he would be buried in Washington, and possibly come to manage the armies after the fashion of his predecessors, was relieved by the announcement that his "headquarters would be in the field"—where they remain.

The army of the Potomac had been concentrated in great strength at Culpepper, while that of Lee was at Orange Court House. Grant's army, under the immediate command of General Meade, moved, with six days' rations, on the 3d of May, 1864, and crossed the Rapidan on pontoon bridges at Germania and Ely's fords. It approached the Wilderness without opposition, avoiding the heavy works at Mine Run. The 5th corps was commanded by Warren; the 6th by the brave and accomplished Sedgwick; the 2d by Hancock, and the 9th by Burnside, as reserve, holding the north bank.

On the 5th the armies met in the tangled brush and undergrowth of that Spottsylvania Wilderness, and joined battle. There was obstinate bravery on both sides. Lee adopted his tactics of massing his forces and inflicted great loss upon us. Subsequently our forces inflicted severe punishment upon his columns. The loss of the two armies in that day's fighting is estimated at more than 12,000 men. It was no artillery duel, for the undergrowth was too dense for its use, but the stern hand-to-hand fighting of infantry and cavalry. No decisive results were reached, but General Grant selected a more advantageous position.

On the 6th Lee's army began the melee. His force was thrown now against one wing and now another, and the loss of Shaler's and Seymour's brigades periled our right. The gallantry of Sedgwick saved the day for us.

The next day our guns were in position and all ready for battle, but Lee was moving southward to interpose between Grant and Richmond at some other point. The army of the Union advanced to Spottsylvania Court House where the enemy was strongly intrenched. A cavalry fight for certain points along the line of march cost us 300 men.

On the 9th General Sedgwick, himself equal to a division, was killed by a sharpshooter. Generals Hays and Wadsworth had previously fallen. On the 10th the fighting was of the most desperate and sanguinary character. The line of battle was six miles, and for this length our brave men stood before the breastworks of the enemy. The corps of Burnside, Hancock, Warren and Wright were all engaged, and for the first time in the battles of the Wilderness our artillery came into deadly play. The carnage was frightful. It is said we lost 4,000 men killed, and that 8,000 wounded were left on the field! Generals Stevenson and Rice fell. There was constant skirmishing. On the 11th Sheridan made his great raid, in which General J. E. B. Stuart, one of the most efficient rebel cavalry officers, was killed. Up to this date we had captured some 5,000 prisoners. The 12th witnessed fifteen hours' terrible strife. Hancock threw his corps upon the rebel entrenchments and captured a division of 3,000. Thirty rebel guns were also captured. Five times did the forces of Lee, with bravery and audacity unsurpassed, attempt the re-capture of their works, but they beat hopelessly against the granite corps of Burnside and Warren. At another point our troops put forth most heroic courage and desperate daring in an unsuccessful effort to carry the rebel entrenchments. The Union loss of this day is estimated by some at 11,000. Four thousand prisoners were captured. Through that night was the incessant roar of artillery.

It became evident to the enemy that they were dealing with such persistence and dogged resolution, and with such masterly combinations as they had not before met on the Potomac. They claimed victory but had found themselves compelled to fall back before a beaten foe who steadily followed them. The "Colonel of the 21st Illinois" meant war, and knew how to wage it. There was constant skirmishing for some days, but no general engagement.

On the night of the 21st Grant moved his forces quietly southward, on toward Richmond, and it became a question who should sooner reach it, he or Lee! "Grant is in full retreat" was the rebel news, but strange to say it was by a flank movement directly toward the rebel capital! The defences at the North Anna were stormed on the 23d, and on the next day our army crossed that river, having to fight their way at every ford. At the South Anna the enemy had constructed defences almost impregnable.

Another flank movement threw our forces across the Pamunkey, and it was apparent that the Federal leader was maneuvering to approach Richmond from the North. There was constant fighting in some direction. On the 1st of June there was a desperate engagement at Cold Water. On the 3d was fought a desperate battle at Cold Harbor, where our loss was nearly 6,000.

The line of the Chickahominy was abandoned, and the Federal

army led to the south side of the James, and on the 16th operations were commenced before Petersburg. It may be conceded that General Grant did not in the campaign of the Wilderness accomplish all he wished, for he did not destroy the army of Lee. But it was shown that ours could march from Washington to the defences of Richmond in spite of it, clearing the way with ball and bayonet and breaking both the power and prestige of the grand army of the Confederacy.

The events of the siege can be adverted too only incidentally in the present volume. The iron-hand closed upon that great army compelling it to remain inactive, while in other directions the armies of the Republic were winning glorious victories. Sherman had occupied Savannah, Charleston and Columbia. Wilmington had fallen, and the coast was sealed to the importation of supplies. Sheridan had swept the valley of the Shenandoah, repeatedly defeating Early, capturing large numbers of cannon and prisoners, and cutting railway and canal at his pleasure. All looked well, and in calm trust the people were content to wait, for waiting had come to mean victory instead of defeat.

CHAPTER XXXIII.

THE POTOMAC—CAMPAIGN AND REGIMENTAL.

MAJOR-GENERAL HUNTER—THEN AND NOW—THE 8TH CAVALRY—GENERAL FARNSWORTH—GENERAL GAMBLE—COL. CLENDENIN—GENERAL BEVERIDGE—MAJOR MEDILL—THE CHAPLAINS—THE 12th CAVALRY—COL. VOSS—COL. DAVIS—BARKER'S DRAGOONS—THE 23D INFANTRY—GENERAL MULLIGAN—THE 39TH INFANTRY—COL. OSBORN—LIEUT.-COLONEL MANN—THE STURGIS RIFLES.

MAJOR-GENERAL DAVID HUNTER has been conspicuous in the earlier campaigns of our army. His birth-place was the District of Columbia. In 1822 he graduated at West Point, and was appointed Second Lieutenant in the infantry, his commission dating July 1, 1822. He was then twenty years of age. He early became identified with Illinois, being placed in command of Fort Dearborn, Chicago, in 1830, where he remained about one year, marrying, meanwhile, Miss Kinzie, "daughter of the first permanent resident of the city." He was regularly promoted 1st Lieutenant of Dragoons, and in 1832 was made Captain of Dragoons, and twice crossed the plains to the Rocky Mountains. In 1836 he resigned his commission and entered business. In 1842 he re-entered the army as paymaster with the rank of Major, which he held when the war began. He was made Colonel of the 3d Regiment U. S. Cavalry, and came prominently into notice at the first battle of Bull Rnn. He was placed in command in the 2d division, and while leading his command was, early in the action, severely wounded. On the 13th of August, 1861, he was commissioned Major-General of volunteers, and in November following superseded General Fremont in command of the Department of Missouri. His failure to push Price to the wall on assuming command, has subjected him to criticism. Subsequently, General Hunter commanded the Department of Kansas with headquarters at Fort Leavenworth. General Halleck sent him the following dispatch recognizing his services at an hour of need. "To you, more than any other man out of this department, are we indebted for our success at Fort Donelson. In my strait for troops to reinforce General Grant, I applied to you. You responded nobly placing your forces at my disposal. This enabled us to win the victory. Accept my hearty thanks."

In March, 1862, he took command of the Department of the South, comprising South Carolina, Georgia and Florida, with headquarters at Hilton Head. The problem of slavery and the war had been early forced upon his attention. He was born amid slavery, and was of the stock of Virginia Hunters, and had been educated in all the conservative teachings of West Point, yet he soon saw that the way to peace was over the grave of slavery, and that never could the country receive the olive branch except from the hands of Victory and Freedom. Undeterred by the experience of his predecessor in Missouri, on the 9th of May, 1862, General Hunter issued a proclamation declaring *free* all the slaves of rebels within his department. The President, reserving to himself the right to determine the time for such a measure and the responsibility of taking it, revoked the order on the 19th of the same month.

A portion of General Hunter's troops met a severe check at the battle of James Island, where General Benham made an attack, in disobedience of orders from his superior.

General Hunter saw very soon that men of color should not only be made free by military authority, but also enlisted, uniformed, armed and permitted to stand as soldiers of the Union, and so believing he organized negro regiments in his department. For this he and General Phillips were outlawed. As the General-in-Chief of the Confederate armies has recommended the arming of slaves, the Legislature of proud Old Virginia has ordered her Senators to vote for such a law, and the rebel Congress has enacted it. The order of outlawery is here produced as an ancient landmark of the earlier and more knightly days of the "New Nation."

"WAR DEPARTMENT, ADJUTANT AND INSPECTOR-GENERAL'S OFFICE,
RICHMOND, August 21, 1862.

"*General Orders*, *No.* 60.

"*Whereas*, Major-General Hunter, recently in command of the enemy's forces on the coast of South Carolina, and Brigadier-General Phillips, a military commander of the enemy in the State of Louisiana, have organized negro slaves for military service against their masters, citizens of this Confederacy:

"*And, Whereas*, The Government of the United States has refused to answer an inquiry whether said conduct of its officers meets its sanction, and has thus left to this government no other means of repressing said crimes and outrages than by the adoption of such measures of retaliation as shall serve to prevent their repetition:

"*Ordered*, That Major-General Hunter and Brigadier-General Phillips be no longer held and treated as public enemies of the Confederate States, but as outlaws; and that in the event of the capture of either of them, or that of any other commissioned officer employed in drilling, organizing, or instructing slaves, with a view to their armed service in this war, he shall not be regarded as a prisoner of war, but held in close confinement for execution as a felon, at such time and place as the President may order.

"By order, S. COOPER,
"Adjutant and Inspector-General."

Subsequently, General Hunter, in a letter to Dr. Tyng gave his reasons as a soldier for the employment of blacks. In that letter he said:

"But in presence of one great evil, which has so long brooded over our country, the intelligence of a large portion of our people would seemed paralyzed and helpless. Their moral nerves lie torpid under its benumbing shadow. Its breath has been the pestilence of the political atmosphere in which our statesmen have been nurtured, and never, I fear, until its beak is dripping with the best blood of the country, and its talons tangled in her vitals, will the free masses of the loyal States be fully aroused to the necessity of abating the abomination at whatever cost and by whatever agencies.

"This is written, not politically, but according to my profession in the military sense. Looking forward, there looms up a possibility (only too possible) of a peace which shall be nothing but an armistice, with every advantage secured to the Rebellion. Nothing can give us permanent peace but a successful prosecution of the war, with every weapon and energy at our command, to its logical and legitimate conclusion. The fomenting cause of the Rebellion must be abated; the ax must be laid to the root of the upas tree which has rained down such bitter fruit upon our country, before anything like a permanent peace can be justly hoped.

"Already I see signs in many influential quarters, heretofore opposed to my views in favor of arming the blacks, of a change of sentiment. Our recent disasters before Richmond have served to illuminate many minds."

Subsequently to being relieved of the Department of the South, General Hunter commanded in the Shenandoah valley, has been President of an important military commission and has rendered other important services to the country.

THE EIGHTH ILLINOIS CAVALRY.

The following is the original roster of the regiment:

Colonel, John F. Farnsworth; Lieutenant-Colonel, William Gamble; Major, David R. Clendenin; Adjutant, Robert T. Sill; Adjutant 1st Batallion Campbell, W. Waite; Adjutant 2d Battalion, Edmund Gifford; Adjutant 3d Battalion, John Tifield; Quartermaster, Bradley L. Chamberlain; Surgeon, Abner Hard; Assistant Surgeon, Samuel K. Crawford; Chaplain, Lucius C. Matlack.

Co. A—Captain, Patrick G. Jennings; 1st Lieutenant, Bryant Beach; 2d Lieutenant, Nelson L. Blanchard.

Co. B—Captain, Lorenzo H. Whitney; 1st Lieutenant, John G. Smith; 2d Lieutenant, Jacob M. Liglen.

Co. C—Captain, Alpheus Clark; 1st Lieutenant, Daniel D. Lincoln; 2d Lieutenant, John C. Mitchell.

Co. D—Captain, Jacob S. Gerhart; 1st Lieutenant, Henry I. Hotopp; 2d Lieutenant, Carlos H. Verbeck.

Co. E—Captain, Elisha S. Kelly; 1st Lieutenant, Benjamin L. Flagg; 2d Lieutenant, Woodbury M. Taylor.

Co. F—Captain, Reuben Cleveland; 1st Lieutenant, Edward S. Smith; 2d Lieutenant, Alvin P. Granger.

Co. G—Captain, William H. Medill; 1st Lieutenant, George A. Forsyth; 2d Lieutenant, Dennis J. Hynes.

Co. H—Captain, Rufus M. Hooker; 1st Lieutenant, Charles Harrison; 2d Lieutenant, John M. Southworth.

Co. I—Captain, Hiram L. Rapelge; 1st Lieutenant, William H. Sheldon; 2d Lieutenant, John Cool.

Co. K—Captain, Elon J. Farnsworth; 1st Lieutenant, George W. Flagg; 2d Lieutenant, Darius Sullivan.

Co. L—Captain, Daniel Dustin; 1st Lieutenant, Amasa E. Dana; 2d Lieutenant, John M. Waite.

Co. M—Captain, John Austin; 1st Lieutenant, Andrew J. Martin; 2d Lieutenant, John F. Austin.

There is no regiment of which Illinoisans have more frequently spoken with pride than the 8th Cavalry. It comprised much of the *elite* of the Northwest; young men of education and position, and they have borne their battle-flag from the Fox to the Chickahominy without disgrace.

The regiment was organized at St. Charles under the Hon. John F. Farnsworth, on the 18th of September, 1861. In October it proceeded to Washington. December, 15th it left Washington for Alexandria and was assigned to General Sumner's division, and constituted a portion of General Richardson's force which went to the Rappahannock in February, 1862. It was kept scouting on this line until General McClellan's army had been embarked for the Peninsula, when it took transports for Shippings Point, at the mouth of York River, where it was debarked May 1st and 2d and joined in pursuit of the retreating rebel force from Yorktown to Williamsburg, where the men saw the first heavy fighting, of which, though under fire, they were spectators rather than active participants. They were among the first to enter Williamsburg, and to carry into it the "old flag." Here one battalion under command of Major John L. Beveridge was sent on a reconnoissance to Jamestown. After leaving Williamsburg, one squadron was detached as escort to General Keyes, commander of 4th corps, and the rest under their gallant Colonel reported to General Stoneman, and were assigned the perilous honor of leading the advance in McClellan's march on Richmond. On the Chickahominy it held a large picket line and skirmished more with the enemy than any other regiment, and more than once was complimented by Generals McClellan and Stoneman. It participated in all the battles of that remarkable campaign and covered in the retreat to Harrison's Landing. In the "seven days' fights" Captain R. M. Hooker, Co. H, was the first man killed. He fell, when the enemy attacked the pickets on the extreme right, but his brave men fought on. The remainder of the regiment came up to reinforce the pickets, and the 8th alone stood against the rebel infantry, for five hours of bloody battle. At Mechanicsville it was hotly engaged. At Gaines Hill it was placed to keep the infantry stragglers in place, and to rally the broken fragments of regiments, which they did in such manner as to secure official approval. Ex-Governor Wood was visiting the regiment at this time, and was everywhere conspicuous, rallying the desponding and leading them again and again to the conflict. General Porter more than once ordered the old hero from the field, but he could not obey such orders! He would share the destiny of the regiment he loved!

As the army withdrew across the Chickahominy, the 8th was relieved from duty on the picket-line, and found opportunity for a daring exploit which rang through the country. Two or three weeks previously, it made a raid on the enemy's communications, cutting the railroad north of Richmond, capturing a train of cars, destroying supplies, and in every possible way making itself disagreeable to the enemy. Now the foe was attempting to rush in and sever the Federal line of communication. About two miles from Bottom's Bridge were two hospitals unapprised of our retreat, and soon the rebels would be upon them. The 8th would not suffer them to be captured. A squadron fell back to the hospitals, and then coolly marched to meet the advancing columns and engaging them at narrow places along the road they had studied in their raids, fought them as though supported by a whole army, until time was gained for the removal of the inmates and hospital supplies, and then laughing their enemy to scorn, rejoined their comrades!

During the retreat, the 8th was pushed through to Haxall's Landing, in advance of all the troops, and joined in the battle of Malvern Hill, and on the day following, in the retreat from Haxall's Landing to Harrison's Bar, constituted the extreme rear, exposed, of course, to assaults of the enemy. In the incessant skirmishes of the next month, the 8th was constantly engaged. Its sabers were ever drawn, and its tally ho! was learned and dreaded by the bravest of their enemies. When again retreat was ordered, and the grand army of the Potomac marched from Harrison's Bar to Yorktown, the 8th was the extreme rear-guard, again between the flag and the foe.

After coming up the Potomac from the Peninsula, the 8th Illinois, 8th Pennsylvania, and 6th U. S. Cavalry were the advance, marching against Lee at Frederick, Md. Each day they fought, and each day they drove the rebel cavalry before them. The charge of those three regiments was terrible as destiny. Near Poolsville, the 8th captured the colors of the vaunted 12th Virginia Cavalry, a regiment composed of scions of the chivalry.

The flag of the 8th was seen in the thick of the conflicts at Katocin Pass, Middletown, South Mountain, Boonsboro and Antietam. It shared largely in the daily skirmishes which preceded the advance of the army under Burnside, and when the army did move, the cavalry was thrown forward to clear the way. It was no child's play. The 8th fought along that line of march with brave enemies at Purcelsville, Philemont, Union, Upperville, Piedmont, Markham, Barbee's Cross Roads, and Aimsville. At Little Washington, the 8th Illinois and 3d Indiana Cavalry—regiments worthy of being associated, as they were, in many a weary march and desperate battle, in reverse and victory—under command of Col. Farnsworth, without artillery, met, engaged, and drove back Hampton's brigade, with its artillery. It was bravely done. After one or two more skirmishes, Col. Farnsworth's command reached Falmouth with Burnside's advance. They were the only cavalry on the terrible field of Fredericksburg, under fire, but not actually engaged.

Winter brought the 8th little rest, for between skirmishing and picket duty, it was constantly busy. In the spring it joined the cavalry movements, and after raiding toward Richmond, returned in time to witness the closing contest of Hooker's army at Chancellorsville. During this spring, when rapid marches, incessant fighting, and short rations had so reduced most of the cavalry, the fine condition of the horses and the fire of the men of the 8th were commended by officers and admired by spectators. This was owing both to the skill and care of the officers, and the superior *morale* of the men.

Again, at Beverly Ford, the 8th distinguished itself by especial bravery, and was highly complimented upon the field by General Pleasanton. Never was the approval of a commander more richly won. These bold troopers rode fearlessly into the face of death. After this they were placed in General Buford's division, in which they remained until the death of that gallant commander. They commenced the terrific battle of Gettysburg, and it was a proud movement for the boys when General Doubleday thanked them for saving his division from slaughter in the first day's battle. They engaged in the many cavalry skirmishes preceding the crossing of the Potomac by Lee at Falling Waters. At this point Buford's cavalry captured great numbers of the rebel rear-guard of infantry.

Another rapid campaign and the army was again upon the Rapidan, Buford's cavalry leading the way.

The 8th claims the honor of originating veteran enlistments. As early as July, 1863, a majority offered to re-enlist as a regiment. Strange to say, the War Department refused permission until nearly November. It is a marvel how constantly the people and the army have been beforehand with the War Department, and how often brave men have been compelled to beg for the privilege of service. In November a few were sworn in, but the work of making out the veteran rolls delayed the re-enlistment of the regiment until January 1, 1864, when the 8th was again in service.

The veteran furlough having expired, it was ordered to the East and again engaged in scouting in Northern Virginia. When Early's invasion came, the 8th was active in repelling him. With others, it contested the ground foot by foot, fighting heroically and successfully at Middletown and Monocacy Junction. At Urbana the 8th held in check two brigades, opposing a wall of steel to their approach, and so saved the bleeding army of Major-General Lew. Wallace from being destroyed in detail. The service then rendered can hardly be overestimated.

It has been, sorely against its will, retained in the department at Washington, where it has had fatiguing scouting, heavy marching and hard riding, with but small opportunity for distinction. But the record of the 8th *is made*, and a glorious one it is! The cavalry annals have none brighter. Its deeds have the glitter of romance, and yet the hard granite of substantial fact.

A correspondent of the *Chicago Tribune*, writing Feb. 1, 1865, says:

"The 8th Illinois numbers about 1,100 men fit for duty, and is occasionally receiving new recruits. After traveling through the Army of the James and the whole extent of General Grant's lines, noticing all the various camps, I am sure the 8th will compare favorably with any regiment in the service, while the appearance of the camp certainly does credit to the men as well as their officers. Some of the best officers have resigned and gone home to their families. They were almost necessitated to leave, for the simple reason that they could not maintain their families on their pay, which every one knows to be too small for the exigences of the times; but this regiment has about five months' pay due them, and this delinquency is quite an item with an officer who has family incumbrances dependent on his salary for support."

General Jno. F. Farnsworth was the first Colonel who commanded the gallant 8th cavalry. He was a lawyer, residing in St. Charles, and had represented his district (then including Chicago), in Congress. Subsequently Hon. I. N. Arnold was nominated and elected.

Mr. Farnsworth was an intense hater of slavery, and when the slaveholder's rebellion came he had but one thought; viz., to put it down *at once and forever.* Throwing all the energy of his nature into the work, the 8th cavalry was raised and filled with noble fighting material. He led it to the field and participated in its hardships, battles and skirmishes.

He was soon placed in command of a brigade and attracted the attention of his superior officers by his ability and bravery. He was promoted Brigadier-General of volunteers December 5, 1862.

While in command of the 8th, he came home on furlough, and reached Chicago on a day when a vast and enthusiastic war meeting was being held in the court-house square. His presence became known, and incessant cries were made for him. At length he came forward upon the steps of the north front, wearing his dusty blouse, evidently worn with campaigning and travel. It was before the kid-glove policy of fighting had been wholly abandoned, and when one of the worst fears of some commanders seemed to be that of "exasperating our Southern brethren." Especially was there much tenderfootedness in reference to slaves. They were not to be harbored. If they came within our lines they should be restored to the prowling rebel who might claim them. With this the General dealt as matter of fact. It was folly to fight and yet leave slavery to provide Southern food. It was the Southern commissariat and must be broken up. Beside that, Northern soldiers were not to be degraded into Southern slave-catchers. "But," he added, "you cannot keep the negro out of this war. The only question is, who shall use him? He will dig their trenches or ours; he will build their breastworks or ours. Aye," and he drew himself to a loftier hight as he said, in ringing tones, "he will fight in this war; he will cut the throats of us or the rebels, and we must soon decide which." The effect was positively overwhelming.

In the fall of 1862, the Congressional districts having been changed, he was nominated to represent the 2d district, and elected by a large majority. In 1864 he was re-nominated, and elected by the largest majority of any representative in the United States. He resigned his commission March 4, 1863.

He is an uncompromising hater of slavery. It is with him a hate bitter as gall and relentless as death. He lost no chance to deal it a blow from his sinewy arm, and none rejoiced more heartily when Congress declared the day had come when it must die.

Gen. William Gamble, a native of Ireland, was a practical engineer, having been, from fifteen to twenty years of age, engaged in the Queen's surveying office and in the survey of the North of Ireland. Landing at New York when twenty years of age, he enlisted in the 1st U. S. dragoons (regulars). He was soon promoted to Sergeant-Major and so served five years. He was in the Florida war, and was stationed at Forts Leavenworth and Gibson engaged in guarding against the Indians.

He left the army, and removing to Chicago, engaged again in the profession of civil engineering. When war came he resided in Evanston, though his business was in Chicago. He knew his military experience would be of service, and leaving a lucrative business, he enlisted in the service of his adopted country. His services in drilling the 8th were of great value, and did much to make it what it became, a model of discipline and terribleness. He was commissioned Lieutenant-Colonel, Sept. 5th. He was early thrown in command of the regiment and the men knew he was fearless and capable. On the promotion of Col. Farnsworth, he became Colonel. He was through the battles of the Peninsula, and leading a charge at Malvern Hill, August 5, 1862, narrowly escaped with his life, receiving a severe wound in the breast, which for some time disabled him. When the regiment came home to re-enlist, its fame called young men by hundreds to its torn flag. A peril being again upon the capital, the 8th was ordered back to service before its veteran furlough expired, a circumstance which called out a characteristic order from the Colonel.

For two years or more the Colonel was in command of a brigade. In December, 1864, the President designated him Brigadièr-General by brevet, and on the 14th of February, 1865, the nomination was confirmed by the Senate—a tardy act of justice.

Colonel Clendenin, who wears his title yet by brevet, hàs been in actual command of the regiment most of the time for two years and has proved himself a competent commander. While Col. Gamble had charge of a brigade, including some 6,000 men, stretching over a line of more than thirty miles, the care of the regiment devolved upon his junior. It is sufficient for his capacity to say that the regiment, after all it has undergone, numbered, in February 1865, more than 1,100 men fit for duty.

Major Beveridge, after serving the 8th with distinction, was mustered out for the purpose of organizing the 17th cavalry, of which he became Colonel, and has since been promoted Brigadier-General by brevet.

Capt. Elon J. Farnsworth entered the 8th in command of Co. K. He was subsequently detached and rose rapidly until he received the commission of Brigadier-General, June 29, 1863. He fell, mortally wounded, on the field of Gettysburg, and died shortly afterwards. His young life was full of high promise—suddenly going out.

Among the costly gifts of the 8th to the country was Major Wm. H. Medill. He was born in Massillon, Ohio, Nov. 5, 1835. In 1855 he came to Chicago and became one of the proprietors of the *Prairie Farmer*. Subsequently he returned to Ohio and was editor and proprietor of the *Stark County Republican*. He returned to Chicago and obtained a situation in the *Tribune* office. At the breaking out of the rebellion he enlisted in Barker's dragoons, and at Beverly distinguished himself for gallantry, capturing in personal combat a Georgian Lieutenant. When the dragoons were mustered out he obtained permission to raise a company for the 8th cavalry, and declining to be a candidate for Major, was made senior captain, and as such, for several months in the summer and fall of 1861, had command of the regiment, proving his fitness for advanced rank. At Bealton's Station he commanded the leading squadron in a gallant charge upon a body of rebel cavalry, which was broken and fled. He was with "Farnsworth's big Abolition Regiment"—as the 8th was called by both Northern and Southern traitors—in its varied fortunes; led his battalion on a reconnoissance within twelve miles of Richmond. During the pendency of the peninsula battles he wrote home:

"I am disgusted at the way this fine army is employed. One part is ditch digging, and another stands guard over the plantations and property of slaveholders, whose sons are in Lee's army fighting us. Our generals will never put down this slaveholders' rebellion by pursuing a pro-slavery policy. The chief support of the rebellion is derived from the labor of four millions of slaves, who supply the commissary and quartermaster's departments of the enemy, and support the families of the rebel soldiers besides. We must knock away this great pillar of their edifice, else we shall never succeed in putting down the revolt. I am not sanguine of the result of the impending battle; our boys will make a stubborn fight, but McClellan has waited too long. He has neglected his opportunity. Mark my words."

He commanded in the affairs of Damascus, Tenallytown and Boonsboro, which taught J. E. B. Stewart the power of Illinois bravery. Again at Martinsburg he distinguished himself for bravery and skill, and received the commendation of General Pleasanton He was severely ill for a time, but as soon as possible was in the saddle, and participated in the contest at Aldie and Upperville, and had charge of the regiment. It was a brilliant affair when the "Abolition Regiment" defeated, successively, two Virginia regiments and one from North Carolina, and the Major himself captured the Colonel of the 11th Virginia cavalry. A newspaper correspondent thus narrates the incident:

"While the Major was rallying his men, after one of our charges, I saw, at a short distance over the field, a rebel horseman, with drawn sword, chasing our Sergeant Major, who had got mixed up with the rebels. Major Medill, who happened to be near, put spurs to his big bay horse, and in a few bounds was close to the 'reb.,' who raised his sword aloft and shouted 'surrender!' The Major brought his revolver to an aim, and was in the act of pulling the trigger, when the fellow dropped his sword and cried out, 'Don't shoot, I surrender.' He saved his life by just a second, as more than one bullet would have lodged in his body the next instant. The prisoner proved to be the Colonel of the 11th Virginia cavalry, and big enough in a fist fight to have whipped two of our Major; but on the field of battle, size confers but little advantage."

At Gettysburg, Buford's cavalry, in which the 8th was conspicuous had the advance, and kept the foe in check for three hours. Major Beveridge, commanding the right, Major Medill the left of the 8th. The 12th was near the 8th, and Buford's cavalry defied the massed foe. The battle was over and Lee was in full retreat, and the cavalry hung on the rear. July 6th it was discovered by the 8th that the rebels were building a bridge on the Potomac at Williamsport, and though they were in force it was desirable to destroy it. A brigade of regulars were placed on the right and the cavalry on the left of the road. Half the 8th was ordered by Buford to dismount and advance as skirmishers. Major Medill said to Major Beveridge, "A field officer should command the battalion and if you have no objection I will go." Seizing a carbine he galloped after his comrades, reached them, took his place and called, "Come on, boys," and the line surged rapidly forward. Some rebels posted behind a barn and some fences opened fire, but they steadily advanced until the field was more than half crossed, when he ordered a volley and raised his own carbine, when a minnie ball struck him, passing through the breast bone downward, perforating the lung and lodging near the backbone. The wound was seen to be mortal. He was borne to the hospital at Frederick City. Here he lay six days, calmly conversing, making his will and listening eagerly for word of the destruction of Lee's host. When he heard of its escape he was agonized and said he wished he had died without hearing it. His remains were brought to Chicago and interred with all due respect.

So died a brave man, a fearless leader, an officer of promise and a true patriot. General Pleasanton bore testimony to his worth. His brother, Joseph Medill, is editor of the *Chicago Tribune.*

Chaplain Lucius C. Matlack was an eloquent minister, an original anti-slavery agitator, and long an anti-slavery editor. He had been President of the college at Wheaton. Owing to some informality he was mustered out. When the 17th Cavalry was organized he was chosen as one of its majors.

He was succeeded by Rev. Philo Judson, who did good service until failing health compelled him to return. The choice of the regiment was then for a brave fellow-soldier, orderly sergeant W. A. Spencer, who came home and received ordination from a council called by the First Congregational Church of Chicago. Others of the 8th deserve mention, but with the imperfect facts in our possession at present, we cannot do them justice.

THE TWELFTH CAVALRY.

The twin regiment of the 8th has been the 12th. It has passed through many of the same scenes, battles, marches, privations and victories. It seems to be made of the same unconquerable stuff. As originally constituted, the following is the roster:

Colonel, Arno Voss; Lieutenant-Colonel, Hasbrouck Davis; 1st Major, Francis T. Sherman; 2d Major, Thomas W. Grosvenor; 3d Major, John G. Fonda; Adjutant, James Daley; Adjutant 1st Battalion, Jonathan Slade; Adjutant 2d Battalion, Alexander Stewart; Adjutant 3d Battalion, ——— ———; Quartermaster, Lawrence J. J. Nissen; Commissary, Moses Shields; Surgeon, John Higgins; Assistant-Surgeon, John McCarthy; Chaplain, Abraham J. Warner.

Co. A—Captain, Thomas W. Grosvenor; 1st Lieutenant, Philip E. Fisher; 2d Lieutenant, William Luff.

Co. B—Captain, Andrew H. Langholz; 1st Lieutenant, Henry Jansen; 2d Lieutenant, Charles Grimm.

Co. C—Captain, Stephen Bronson; 1st Lieutenant, William J. Steel; 2d Lieutenant, George F. Wood.

Co. D—Captain, Richard N. Hayden; 1st Lieutenant, Charles Roden; 2d Lieutenant, Nathan J. Kidder.

Co. E—Captain, John P. Harvey; 1st Lieutenant, Cephas Strong; 2d Lieutenant, Edward Vasseur.

Co. F—Captain, Ephraim M. Gillmore; 1st Lieutenant, Henry L. Reans; 2d Lieutenant, Dennis Palmer.

Co. G—Captain, Thomas Logan; 1st Lieutenant, John H. Clybourne; 2d Lieutenant, Joseph Logan.

Co. H—Captain, Franklin T. Gilbert; 1st Lieutenant, Charles O'Connell; 2d Lieutenant, Theodore G. Knox.

Co. I—Captain, David C. Brown; 1st Lieutenant, Edwin A. Webber; 2d Lieutenant, George H. Sitts.

Thus organized the 12th joined its fortunes with the armies in the Old Dominion, and had its first serious encounter September 7, 1862, and that with an out-numbering force of Ashby's cavalry. On the 5th, Lieut.-Colonel Davis attacked and drove a detachment of the enemy from Bunker's Hill, between Martinsburg and Winchester. Several prisoners and horses were captured. On the 7th Lieut.-Col. Davis's camp at Fryatt's farm was attacked at daybreak by 800 of the enemy's cavalry and the videttes and pickets driven in. He had with him a small force of Company A, Captain Grosvenor, and a few men of Companies F and G, but with these a stand was made, until Col. Voss sent a company of the 12th to reinforce Lieut.-Col. Davis. This commander ordered his little force to charge, and though the foe was ten to one, the men answered with a shout, and the enemy was forced back to Darkesville on the Winchester pike, where a strong stand was made, the rebels occupying the houses and stone-walls on the flanks, and massing themselves in front of the bold riders of the 12th.

Then occurrred one of the most brilliant saber charges on record. Without firing, the little handful rode, sword in hand, with shouts and ringing blows upon their foe, dashing upon his center, breaking it, throwing it into confusion and actually driving him nearly to Winchester, capturing between forty and fifty prisoners, while the villagers reported the burial of twenty-five or thirty. In this brilliant charge there were actually less than eighty men under Col. Davis! His loss in all was fifteen or twenty wounded, three or four mortally wounded. Among the severely wounded was the brave Captain Grosvenor (later Lieut.-Col.,) who specially distinguished himself for bravery, riding in advance of his men. In the report to Brig.-General White, Captains Grosvenor and Haydon, and Lieut. Logan were commended as worthy of special mention.

September 12, 1862, the regiment marched with General White's command from Martinsburg to Harper's Ferry, Va., where it remained until the night of the 14th, when, the place being surrounded by the enemy, the cavalry had leave to attempt to cut out and reach our lines. The column left Harper's Ferry at 8 P. M., and proceeded at a gallop to Sharpsburg, Md., and thence at a rapid gait to within two miles of Williamsport, Md. At this point it intercepted a rebel supply train and captured 112 wagons loaded with ammunition and provisions, 100 head of beef cattle, and fifty prisoners. The column reached Greencastle, Pa., on the morning of the 15th, after marching 65 miles. The loss of the 12th in killed, wounded and prisoners was fifty men.

The regiment joined the forces on the upper Potomac September 20, 1862, and served there until December 8, 1862, when it marched to Dumfries, Va., as advance and rear guard of General Slocum's column, Army of the Potomac. It served at Dumfries until March, 1863, and on the 28th of December, 1862, defended and held the place against a greatly superior force of cavalry and artillery under the rebel General Stuart.

On the organization of the cavalry corps, Army of the Potomac, the 12th was assigned to the 2d brigade, 3d division. The regiment took an important and conspicuous part in what is known as the "Stonewall raid." Lieut.-Col. H. Davis, with 300 men, marched from Thompson's Cross Roads, where he left the main column, to Gloucester Point, Va., passing in the rear of Lee's army and within two miles of Richmond, although opposed by superior numbers of the enemy. The loss of the 12th in killed, wounded and prisoners was three officers and fifty men.

It was an exciting moment to the brave Illinoisans when they came within sight of the spires of Richmond, the center of rebellion, and they would willingly have essayed the task of galloping down its principal avenues and carrying its usurping chief a present to the President of the U. S., but cooler brains gave other orders.

In May, 1863, the regiment, with the 2d New York Cavalry, under command of Colonel Kilpatrick of the 2d, made a raid into Mathew's County, Virginia, and captured and brought to Yorktown 500 horses, 100 head of beef cattle, 300 sheep and 20,000 bushels of corn and wheat.

The regiment then marched from Gloucester Point to Falmouth, Virginia, moving up the south side of the Rappahannock and crossing at Alabama, and June 18, 1863, formed the 1st brigade 1st division cavalry corps. It shared in the battles of Aldie, June 20th; Upperville, June 22d; Gettysburg, July 1st, 2d and 3d; Boonsboro, July 6th; Burevola, July 7th; Funkstown, July 8th; Williamsport, July 10th; Jone's Cross Roads, July 11th; Falling Waters, July 17th; Chester Gap, Virginia, July 28th; Rappahannock, August 3d; Culpepper, C. H., August 24; Raccoon Ford, August 27th, Madison, C. H., September 12th; Germania Ford, October 10th; Stevensburg, October 13th; Brentsville, October 17th.

At the close of the campaign of 1863 the regiment was sent to Chicago to recruit and reorganize. It immediately filled to the maximum, and on the 9th of February, 1864, left for St. Louis one thousand two hundred and fifty strong. Left St. Louis, March 15th and arrived at New Orleans, April 1, 1864. Left New Orleans, April 20th, for Red River and arrived at Alexandria, La., April 23d. In action at Alexandria, La., April 28th, May 5th, 6th, 7th and 8th; Markville, May 15th; Yellow Bayou, May 17th; Morganzia, May 20, 1864. Arrived at New Orleans, June 1, 1864. Left New Orleans, June 11, 1864, and marched to Napoleonville, La., where it remained on picket and scouting duty until October, 1864, when it marched to Baton Rouge, La.—scouting and picketing here until November 14th, when it formed part of General Lee's column in a raid to Liberty, Miss.; fought at Liberty—a small detachment dismounted with carbines, defeating three times their number. November 27th left Baton Rouge with General Davidson, marched to West Pascagoula, Miss. Arrived at New Orleans by transport, December 20th, at Baton Rouge, December 30th. Left Baton Rouge by transports, January 7, 1865, disembarked at Vicksburg, Miss, and remained a week; re-embarked and went to Memphis, Tenn.; left Memphis by transport, January 26, 1865, and went to Gaines' Landing, Ark.; disembarked and made a raid under Col. E. D. Osband, through Southern Arkansas and Northern Louisiana. Returned to Memphis February 14, 1865. February 28, 1865, being three years from the original organization, 120 officers and 200 men whose time had expired, were mustered out of the service and the organization consolidated into eight companies.

It has never been the custom of the 12th to falter when blows were to be given or taken. It has a brilliant record, and has added to the lustrous glory of Illinois cavalry.

The data for biographical sketches of the officers of this regiment are not in the author's possession.

Col. Voss commanded more than one year, when he resigned, in August, 1863. He was succeeded by Lieut.-Colonel Davis, a son of "Honest John Davis," so long Senator from Massachusetts. He has commanded the 12th in its marches and battles, and has right well won the double designation of the brave soldier and the able officer.

Lieutenant-Colonel Grosvenor was so severely wounded in the sword-arm in the engagement of Darkesville, as to be permanently disabled. He was then Captain of Company A, and was duly promoted Major and Lieutenant-Colonel, but ill health compelled him to resign his commission. He was well worthy the confidence of his men. Surgeon Hard of the first separate brigade sends the author the following touching incident which is well authenticated:

"On the 13th and 14th of September, 1863, the cavalry corps of the army of the Potomac under command of General Pleasanton, drove the rebels in a series of battles, or it might be said almost a continuous engagement from the Rappahannock River to Raccoon Ford on the Rapidan River, a distance of twenty miles. On the 14th of September, while the skirmishers on each side were hotly engaged, two brothers of the 12th Illinois Cavalry, by the name of Kemper, were on the skirmish line, one a 1st sergeant the other a private. The sergeant was shot by a carbine or minnie ball and fell. His brother sprang to his relief, took him in his arms and was carrying him from the field, when he also fell, pierced by a rebel bullet. In a few moments I was called to see them. I found the ball had entered the thorax of the sergeant, and lodged in the lung after having fractured a rib, and that his wound was mortal, of which he was informed. The brother was shot through the lung making his recovery extremely doubtful. They were placed in an ambulance and sent to Culpepper with the other wounded. The train was ordered to move slowly and make frequent stops, in order to give the wounded stimulants and rest. They had traveled several miles when at one of the halts, the sergeant said to his brother: 'I feel that I am dying. The doctor says I cannot recover, but before I go let us sing the Star Spangled Banner.' As if inspired with superhuman power these wounded brothers rallied, raised themselves up, and in a clear and distinct voice sang the piece through, when the sergeant laid back upon the stretcher and expired. I have since learned that the brother lived a few weeks, and then died of his wound in one of the general hospitals in Washington. Such exhibition of *love for the old flag to the last*, it seems to me is worthy of being placed on record."

The following is the roster of the regiment as reorganized:

Colonel, Hasbrouck Davis; Lieutenant-Colonel, Thomas W. Grosvenor; Major, Hamilton B. Dox; Adjutant, William R. Carpenter; 2d Major, Lawrence J. J. Nissen; Commissary, Moses Shield; Surgeon, John Higgins; 1st Assistant Surgeon, John McCarthy; 2d Assistant Surgeon, Charles E. Wentworth.

Co. A—Captain, Wm. M. Luff; 1st Lieutenant, Joseph E. Fisher; 2d Lieutenant, Joseph A. Adlington.

Co. B—Captain, Charles Roden; 1st Lieutenant, Charles F. Vaas; 2d Lieutenant, Henry Losberg.

Co. C—Captain, Wm. J. Steele; 1st Lieutenant, Charles E. Coombs; 2d Lieutenant, Stephen Standish.

Co. D—Captain, Gustavus A. Marsh; 1st Lieutenant, James Daly; 2d Lieutenant, Danford Taylor.

Co. E—Captain, Cephas Strong; 1st Lieutenant, Edward LeVasseur; 2d Lieutenant, Alexander Stewart.

Co. F—Captain, Jackson Drennan; 1st Lieutenant, James Matlock; 2d Lieutenant, Charles Vennard.

Co. G—Captain, John H. Clybourn; 1st Lieutenant, Charles E. Overrocker; 2d Lieutenant, Edson N. Pratt.

Co. H—Captain, Earl H. Chapman; 1st Lieutenant, Isaac Conroe; 2d Lieutenant, Thomas J. Smith.

Co. I—Captain, Frederick W. Mitchell; 1st Lieutenant, William T. Rickard; 2d Lieutenant, Amherst F. Graves.

Co. K—Captain, Henry Jansen; 1st Lieutenant, Edmund Luff; 2d Lieutenant, Charles L. Arnet.

Co. L—Captain, Richard A. Howk; 1st Lieutenant, Carroll Gossett; 2d Lieutenant, James Dickson.

Co. M—Captain, Oliver Grosvenor; 1st Lieutenant, Robert Gray; 2d Lieutenant, Jesse C. Rodgers.

BARKER'S CHICAGO DRAGOONS

Were organized and reported at Camp Yates, and were mustered into State service, and subsequently into the U. S. service. The squadron proceeded to Camp Defiance, Cairo, where it did picket duty six weeks. General McClellan, visiting there, was so much pleased with the dragoons that he adopted them as his escort, and directed them to join him at Clarksburg, Va., which they did. For two months they were actively engaged, first at Philippi, then at Buckhannon, then the severe battle of Rich Mountain, and then the hotly fought and bloody contest of Beverly, where the Union forces gained a substantial victory, routing the foe and chasing him beyond Carrick's Ford, where General Garnett, one of the bravest rebel officers, was killed, and many prisoners captured. During the engagement, at one time the dragoons dismounted and fought as infantry. The way to Richmond, via Staunton, seemed open, but the commanders were *cautious!*

The dragoons remained in service more than a month over their term of enlistment, and returned home and were mustered out. Subsequently most of them re-enlisted, uniting with the 12th cavalry, under Col. Voss. It is doubted whether any more thoroughly drilled squadron of cavalry have been seen on parade, or any cooler and braver under fire.

"THE IRISH BRIGADE."

The war-spirit is not difficult to kindle among the descendants of the Emerald Isle, and yet it is simple truth to say that not so large a proportion of that population has enlisted for the defense of the flag as the early days of the war gave promise. For then, there was a blaze of patriotism. The example of Shields, Meagher, Corcoran and Mulligan kindled the fire to fever heat.

When the call for volunteers was made, James A. Mulligan, an eloquent and popular young lawyer of Chicago, with other leading citizens conceived the idea of an Irish regiment of which certain existing military organizations should be the basis. The "Montgomeries," the "Shields" and "Emmetts," held a public meeting and received the proposition with great favor. The press reported the meeting. Instantly telegrams poured from Lasalle, Ottawa, Grundy and elswhere, tendering companies already formed, to the "Irish Brigade," and within a week, there were twelve hundred Irishmen ready for the service for any length of time.

But it was the era of caution, and slow movements. The War Department only saw rebel armies "as trees walking." The quota of Illinois was full and no more troops would be accepted! The announcement was disappointing and mortifying. The Governor could do nothing. Those interested in the regiment sent Mr. Mulligan at once to Washington to tender it to the President for any service. It was accepted May 17, 1861.

Mulligan returned from Washington, secured "Kane's Brewery" and converted it into a barracks, that was known while occupied by the regiment as "Fontenoy Barracks." The organization also adopted the name of the "Irish Brigade." Its title on the official rolls is "23d Illinois Infantry." The result of the election of officers was as follows:

Colonel, James A. Mulligan; Lieutenant-Colonel, James Quirk; Major, Charles E. Moor; Chaplain, T. J. Butler, D. D.; Surgeon, W. D. Winer; Quartermaster, Thos. I. Ray; Adjutant, Lieutenant James F. Cosgrove.

1st. Detroit Jackson Guards—Captain, P. McDermott; 1st Lieutenant, James F. Cosgrove; 2d Lieutenant, P. J. McDermott.

2d. Montgomery Guards—Captain, Michael Gleeson; 1st Lieutenant, D. W. Quirk; 2d Lieutenant, Ed. Murray.

3d. Chicago Jackson Guards—Captain, Francis McMurray; 2d Lieutenant, Robt. Adams.

4th. Earl Rifles—Captain, S. A. Simison; 1st Lieutenant, T. D. McClure; 2d Lieutenant, James Hudson.

5th. Ogden Rifles—Captain, Frank K. Hulburt; 1st Lieutenant, George D. Kellogg; 2d Lieutenant, H. Pease.

6th. Douglas Guards—Captain, D. P. Moriarty; 1st Lieutenant, L. Collins; 2d Lieutenant, P. O'Kane.

7th. O'Mahony Rifles—Captain, I. C. Phillips; 1st Lieutenant, J. A. Hynes; 2d Lieutenant, Martin Wallace.

8th. Ottowa City Guards—Captain, Charles Coffey; 1st Lieutenant, T. Hickey; 2d Lieutenant, Thomas J. Ray.

9th. Shields Guards (A)—Captain, James J. Fitzgerald; 1st Lieutenant, Wm. Shanley; 2d Lieutenant, P. Ryan.

10th. Shield's Guards (C)—Captain, D. Quirk; 1st Lieutenant, James Lane; 2d Lieutenant, Owen Cunningham.

It was mustered into the United States service by Captain Pitcher, U. S. A., on the 15th day of June, 1861. The 14th of July following, Colonel Mulligan received marching orders to Quincy, Illinois, thence to the Arsenal at St. Louis, and on the 21st day of July his men were fully armed and equipped at that point. On the 22d, seven companies were ordered to Jefferson City, Mo., and arrived there the same day under the command of Colonel Mulligan, to protect the Legislature. The other companies soon followed.

On the 31st of August, 1861, Colonel Mulligan was ordered by Major-General John C. Fremont, to take post at Lexington, a young city on the south bank of the Missouri River. September 1st the 23d left Jefferson City and arrived at Lexington. Colonel Mulligan commenced at once to fortify an elevated hill known as the College Hill. But few hours were allowed him to erect entrenchments. The details of the siege, and the gallant, though unsuccessful defence are given elsewhere, with as much circumstantiality as is possible in the limits of this volume. The officers and men fought well, but were overpowered by numbers and thirst.

The enlisted men were paroled by General Price, and in ten days afterwards the commissioned officers of the whole command were likewise paroled and permitted to return to their homes. Colonel Mulligan alone refused to accept a parole from the rebel chief, and remained a prisoner with General Price during his retreat southward into Arkansas and the famous crossing of the Osage. The enlisted men of the regiment arriving at St. Louis without officers, it was ordered to muster them out of the United States service by Major-General Curtis. Weeks passed on, the members of the regiment were scattered over the country; some returned to their homes, some enlisted in other regiments, and some waited the return of their captured chief, that they might enroll themselves under his banner. Colonel Mulligan was exchanged for Colonel, afterwards Major-General, Bowen. The ovations he received at every point, fully proved the high esteem in which the people held him. But his first care was his old regiment. Upon his release from captivity he immediately proceeded to Washington and asked of the President the revoking of the "muster out" of the "Brigade." The regiment was restored by order of Major-General McClellan, and ordered to fill up the maximum. The head-quarters were established in Camp Douglas, Chicago. Many of the men that enlisted in other regiments returned to their old commander, and recruits came in rapidly. At the same time Colonel Mulligan received permission to recruit a battery of light artillery to be attached to his regiment. It was so recruited, attached to the regiment, and has done good service with the Brigade during a long campaign in Western Virginia. This battery is known in the field as the "Mulligan Battery," or "Mulligan's Cross Band"—officially, as Battery "L," 1st Illinois Light Artillery.

On the 14th day of June, 1862, up to which time Colonel Mulligan commanded at Camp Douglas, he was ordered with his regiment to Annapolis, *en route* by Harper's Ferry. The "Brigade" was detained by the Secretary of War at that place, it then being threatened by the enemy, but remained only a few days at the post. Major-General Wool then commanded the Middle Department within whose limits, at New Creek, Virginia, a large depot of government stores, was situated. The place was threatened by the rebel General Ewell. General Wool ordered Colonel Mulligan to defend it.

The Irish Brigade arrived at New Creek, Va., on the 24th of June, 1862. Colonel Mulligan proceeded at once to establish means of defense. A defensive work which he called Fort Fuller, in honor of the Adjutant-General of Illinois, was constructed, commanding the New Creek Valley. During the last days of September, 1862, Colonel Mulligan moved with the 23d to protect Clarksburg, Va., menaced by the rebel General Jenkins. Parkersburg, Va., on the Ohio River, was threatened at the same time. By rapid movements both towns were saved from the rebel raiders.

In November, the 23d was ordered to attack Imboden who was raiding the country. His camp was reached November 10, 1862, and in a gallant dash his force was scattered to the mountains. The result was forty prisoners and several hundred head of cattle. On the 20th of January, 1863, Colonel Washburn commanding some Ohio troops at Moorefield, Va., was reported attacked by a superior force under General Jones. Colonel Mulligan moved to his support, and after a forced march of forty miles in nineteen hours, arrived at Moorefield with his regiment and the "Mulligan Battery." Jones hearing of reinforcements abandoned his position and fell back on the south fork of the Potomac. Mulligan followed in pursuit at midnight and entered the enemy's camp at daybreak. General Jones had fled. The command fell back to Moorefield, rested one day, and returned to its old camping ground at New Creek. On April 3, 1863, the regiment was assigned to the 5th brigade, 1st Division, 8th Army Corps. The command of the brigade was given to Colonel Mulligan.

While commanding the 5th brigade the conflict at Philippi and Fairmount was lost from want of adequate force to cover that long line, while other points as valuable were saved, the most important being Grafton at the junction of the branches of the Baltimore & Ohio Railroad.

About the 25th of April, one company of the regiment, Company "G," commanded by Captain Wallace, was attacked at Greenland Gap. The gallant Captain took possession of a church near the gap and made a stand. Three thousand cavalry commanded by General Jones, charged some four times unsuccessfully. That gallant little band, held its own Thermopylæ for five long hours, emptying many a traitor's saddle. "Night came on, and what failed by strength of arms was accomplished by treachery. The darkness preventing the movements of the enemy from being discovered, the church was set on fire, and not until the fresh burning brands fell on those brave heads was a thought of surrender received. The roof cracked, the flames hissed, and the demons of treason shouted outside in derision of their victims. Capt. Wallace ordered his men to throw their arms and accoutrements into the burning timbers, and, as he himself, the last man, left the spot, the burning roof crumbled to the ground. The captured command was sent to Richmond, but exchanged in some months after, and rejoined their regiment to the delight of their comrades.

After the battle of Gettysburg had been fought, it was supposed that the rebels would attempt a crossing at a ford near Hancock, Md. General B. F. Kelley commanding the department of West Virginia, was ordered to that point with all the available force at his disposal.

A manuscript before us, says:

"Colonel Mulligan moved with a brigade of infantry, some cavalry and artillery, on the 6th of July, and arrived at Hancock on the evening of the 7th. Troops from other portions of General Kelley's command to the number of about five thousand, arrived on the same day. General Kelley in person was upon the ground. The command of all the forces was given to Colonel Mulligan. In a few days he advanced to Cherry Run, on the Potomac, crossed the swollen river by the aid of a few rafts, and engaged Hampton's North Carolina Legion of Lee's army near Hedgesville. The advance and expected assistance of General Mead was anxiously looked for, but while Lee's army marched west of the Blue Ridge, with no opposing forces but Kelley's under Mulligan, in the valley, General Mead moved the Army of the Potomac east of that range of mountains. Mulligan's force was thus compelled to fall back across the Potomac, thereby preventing him from taking part in what all supposed would be the utter annihilation of the rebel army of Virginia.

"Lee having made good his retreat, General Kelley ordered Colonel Mulligan to recross the Potomac, strike the northwestern turnpike, and march to Burlington, Va., via Romney. Arrived at this point, Colonel Mulligan moved with the old 5th Brigade of which the 23d Illinois formed a part, to Petersburg, Va. This being an advanced and dangerous post Colonel Mulligan fortified it by constructing Fort Mulligan.

"On September 4th, the Irish boys, under the immediate command of Colonel Mulligan, engaged and routed the enemy under Imboden in the gap of Petersburg. September 11th, Captains Fitzgerald and Wallace attacked the rebel forces of the guerrilla McNeal, on the south fork near Moorefield, Va., driving them in confusion to the mountains. October 25, 1862, the 2d division of the department of West Virginia was organized. Colonel Mulligan was assigned to the command. His regiment was assigned to the 2d brigade of the same and was stationed at Petersburg, while the Colonel was ordered to take up his head-quarters at New Creek, West Virginia, November 8th. The same year the regiment moved to the support of General Averill, who engaged and defeated the rebel General Echols at Lewisburg, Greenbrier Co., Va., December 9th. Imboden again fled before the threatening bayonets of the Irish Brigade. In January and February, 1864, he had heavy skirmishing with the advance of the rebel columns. On February 4th Colonel Mulligan moved on Moorfield with 800 cavalry and two pieces of artillery. The rebels were driven out of this city and were pursued some six miles south of the place by Colonel Mulligan. Early's object being clearly to retire into the valley of Virgina, Colonel Mulligan returned to New Creek. The 23d took possession of Greenland Gap, the key of the Northwestern Turnpike."

General Fitzhugh Lee who had seriously threatened the brigade, found it impossible to make headway amid the winter desolations about him, and retired, sending word by a private citizen saying: "Present my compliments to Col. Mulligan, and tell him the severity of the weather will not allow me to call at this time." The Colonel's answer was, "Present my compliments to Gen. Lee and say, 'do not allow the severity of the weather to detain him, for I will be happy to furnish a hot fire on his arrival.'" The invitation was not accepted.

On the 23d of April the "brigade" arrived in Chicago for the purpose of re-enlisting as veterans and marched to Camp Fry. It came with the laurels of Moorefield, Greenland Gap, Gettysburg, Williamsport, Hedgesville, Petersburg Gap, etc., on its banners, and its ranks reduced from 800 to 350 fighting men, told how hardly war had borne upon it. After the expiration of the veteran furlough it returned to the field, and formed part of General Hunter's army in Western Virginia. At 6 P. M., Saturday, the 23d of July, its participation in the battle of Winchester commenced, Mulligan's division of infantry being ordered forward from Stone Mills to Kerntown to support the cavalry. It accomplished the purpose of the advance, and under orders fell back into its original position. Sunday morning, the 24th, the conflict was renewed. Under orders from General Crook, Mulligan's division advanced to occupy a position from which Col. Harris's brigade had been driven by superior force. General Crook supposed the enemy to be but a small force, and formed in line of battle, with Mulligan's division in the center. Advancing at 3½ P. M., into an open country, suddenly the enemy's line of battle, bristling with bayonets and frowning terribly with artillery was displayed, and the Union force found itself face to face with Lieut.-General Early's entire command, numbering 30,000, which stretched a mile beyond our front, and threatening to surround it. This was the force supposed to be in full retreat! Of course the order was given to fall back.

In the hot engagement which became necessary to check the enemy's advance, the 23d did nobly, and it was in this storm of battle that its gallant Colonel fell mortally wounded and was captured by the enemy. Here, too, Lieut. Nugent, Mrs. Mulligan's brother, fell while endeavoring to bring off his commander and brother-in-law.

Since then the "Irish brigade" has been in constant service. They are brave men, and have worthily placed the harp and the shamrock on the azure field of our national flag.

Brigadier-General James A. Mulligan, the popular Colonel of the Irish Brigade, was not born in Ireland as is generally supposed, but in Utica, New York, June 21, 1830. His parents were Irish, and he considered himself in faith and national feeling, a true son of the Emerald Isle. He came to Chicago when he was but six years old, and it was a mere village. He was the first graduate from the University of St. Mary's of the Lake, receiving in June, 1850, the degree of Master of Arts.

After a year spent with Judge Dickey in the study of Law, his love of adventure led him to accompany Stevens, the noted traveler, in his South American expedition. Returning he continued the study of law, editing in the meantime the *Western Tablet*, a Catholic weekly paper. In 1855 he was admitted to the bar, and continued in the practice of his profession until the commencement of the war, with the exception of a few months spent in the Indian Bureau. He had a military taste, and was connected with the Shields' Guards, of which he had command for a time.

He was an ardent democrat, and a warm personal admirer as well as political friend of Senator Douglas. He was a ready and popular speaker whose services were in frequent demand in the city and elsewhere. His adhesion to the country as represented by the administration had much influence.

In the sketch of the regiment and the account of the siege of Lexington,* his activity in organizing the regiment, securing its acceptance, and his service as its commander, have been sketched. He was devoted to his regiment, and when it was thrown out of service, and he was in Washington to secure justice for it, the President tendered him a brigade which he refused, because it would throw the 23d out of service. When he secured its re-acceptance, he desired to share all its fortunes and did so to the last.

In his command at New Creek, great responsibilities were upon him in command of brigade, division, and virtually of a department, and well and nobly he acquitted himself, sealing finally his devotion with his blood. He loved his Irish Brigade intensely and was proud of his men, yet never ungenerously so, as his references to other troops show. His mind was one of rare delicacy and culture. He had a keen critical perception which would have won him eminence in literary criticism.

In the copies of his correspondence before us, we have smiled at the brilliancy of his wit, and been melted to tears by the tenderness of his affections. There is everywhere the unaffected culture of the scholar, and the warm affection of the Irish heart.

From the many, a few extracts are given:

* A letter from Col. Mulligan written March 27th 1862, says: "I did not enter Lexington until the 9th of September last, assuming command on the 10th."

"MARCH 31, 1862.

"TO LIEUT. QUINN MORTON:—I hope to meet them somewhere in Arkansas, beyond Pea Ridge, the land of beautiful water, corn-bread and two meals a day—the land of the ubiquitous Price.

"The brigade is flourishing. I hope to be ordered to St. Louis in two or three weeks. I will move with about 800 men. May we meet—the 23d Missouri and the 23d Illinois, ordered to charge a breastwork together—may the day come, and quickly! Good-by, Colonel; God be with you.

"'Strike till the last armed foe expires,'
"Avenging Lexington and our native land."

He had been invited to deliver an address on the topics of the day, and thus responded from his headquarters at Petersburg, West Virginia, October 8, 1863:

"In reply to your letter of the 6th inst., inviting me to address the citizens of your district on the war and its issues, permit me to say that I am now under an engagement which I am unwilling to disregard—to address the enemy of this district on the same subject.

"The real rostrum of the day is the rifle-pit. And therein we are pleading for the inviolability of the Union with Enfield rifles; we are arguing for the continued honor and nationalty of our government with 6-pounders.

"Argument by mere words has failed and been refused by our adversaries, who are active, resolute men, despising rhetoric, but yielding due respect to the argument of ball and saber.

"By your kind belief that my words would have weight with your citizens, I am honored. I offer them example in place of speech."

He was desirous that the sons of what he considered his nationality should stand by the country. He wrote, and spoke, and urged this. Writing from New Creek, West Virginia, December 21, 1863, he said:

"I see by the *Times* that the war spirit is again filling Chicago with meetings speeches and subscriptions. You must co-operate with this healthy fever, and aid in pressing forward this redeeming work. * * * * *

"Write me particularly of the feeling among the Irishmen at the present time on the subject of enlistment; and if there be a hesitancy among them, from what it arises.

"You must educate the Irish sentiment. You must impress it upon all Irishmen that the future of two countries, the freedom, and the glory, and the happiness of two countries are involved in this struggle. WORK HARD."

Again, still more strongly and eloquently did he push this matter in a letter to a brother officer, written a little later:

"I have noticed with pain Mr. Smith O'Brien's letters regarding this struggle. I am unwilling to believe they represent Irish sentiment at home, and I am confident they are working mischief to Irish interests abroad. Ingratitude does not accord with the Irish character, and it would be well for Mr. O'Brien to remember that the flag he now charges with covering injustice, cruelty and oppression, a few years ago waved over the splendid freights of the Jamestown and the Macedon—offerings of peace and good will from this Union to his and our starving countrymen. It would be well for Mr. O'Brien, before denouncing the flag and the cause of the American Union—before endeavoring to divorce the Irish heart from the hearts of this people—to look calmly about and see where, on all this earth, he will find such another land of shelter, food, protection and appreciation, when again the scourge of God and England lie heavily on Ireland."

It was matter of surprise that so active an officer, and one entrusted with so grave responsibility as the prolonged command of a brigade and then a division, should only wear the ensignia of a Colonel. Hon. Mr. Arnold spoke of it warmly, saying, "that promotion ought to have been given." Yet it was delayed until he who had won it was among the glorious dead, and then only a brevet. How he treated the matter will be seen:

"Promoted! Lord bless you, no. There is not the glimmer of a 'star' in my horizon. I have a big command, a little rank and a contented mind; or, speaking after the manner of godliness [he was writing to a priest], I have a diocese but am no Bishop, wear the *chapeau rouge* but am not a cardinal."

"My Dear Captain:—Your term of service, like my own, is drawing to a close; what have you determined on for the next three years? Not soured, I trust, because a crowd of miserable tricksters, who, though without record in the field, have yet friends in Congress, and have passed you in promotion. Don't mind it. The country will yet think better of the men who have slowly *fought* their way, than of the men who quickly purchased it. The revolution has commenced, and already the political heroes who relied upon their ornamental shoulders for the conduct of campaigns, have found that brains, skill and management are ingredients as necessary for the war as 'stars' and 'eagles.'

"In this hope, bide your time, and 'strike till the last armed foe expires,' and if our country never remembers us, yet our conscience will applaud. So, full of faith in our cause, full of hope for our country, full of animation to cheer our comrades, full of courage to strike the foe, full of charity to forgive him, fallen, let us go forward to VICTORY, UNITY, HAPPINESS."

These utterances were not written for the public, but were the unstudied utterances of confidential friendship. They give the very inside life of this noble young soldier. One extract has in it so much of the spirit of justice, and exhibits his love of honest, fair dealing so strongly that we give it place:

"COLONEL:—The bearer (colored man) informs me that he paid the wagon-master of train arriving from Petersburg, West Virginia, last evening, six dollars to bring him to this post. I know of no order authorizing such exaction, nor permitting wagon-masters to use the government trains for private profit. The money belongs to the government or the negro—I think the negro. I desire you to cause an investigation, do justice and permit no recurrence of these wrongs. The act should have been done as a charity or let alone."

There is another class of letters before us. The romance of war was developed in his life. His young wife accompanied him in his campaigns, and if not on the field was near it with her little ones. His letters and telegrams to his family evince a depth of tenderness and intensity of affection rarely equaled. The relations of home and family are too sacred to be needlessly paraded. Sometimes it was simply a telegraphic "God bless you, darling," and sometimes sending his love to his babes, whom he loved ardently.

When Col. Mulligan returned to Chicago, after his Lexington captivity, he received a grand ovation. When the "brigade" was dropped from the army rolls he sought and secured its restoration, and an order from General McClellan declaring the regiment to have been continuously in the service of the United States. He delivered a series of addresses in principal cities which increased the martial spirit.

After the re-enlistment of his regiment and its return to Virginia, his life was one of ceaseless activity. He desired to see the rebellion crushed, and believed it could only be done by fighting, hence he shunned no opportunity of coming face to face with the foe.

He fell at the battle of Winchester, July 25, 1864. He moved his men into the engagement in splendid style, driving the rebel skirmishers before him, and ascertaining his strength. In the fight on Sunday, he commanded a division. A correspondent of the *New York Tribune* says: "Col. Mulligan was especially conspicuous for his bravery. With his hat off, and sitting erect in his saddle, he cheered his men on, perfectly regardless of the storm of bullets striking around him. Although cautioned repeatedly by the staff officers, that he was recognized by the enemy's sharp-shooters, he still persisted in remaining mounted, and in keeping in the extreme advance of his command.

At length a minnie ball struck him in the thigh and he fell. His staff gathered about him, and his men of the Irish brigade, with swimming eyes, planted their colors near him, and encircling him, determined to carry him from the field. His wife's brother, the brave young Lieutenant Nugent, was killed in the attempt. The Colonel told them not to "lose the colors of the Irish brigade." Finding his life ebbing, and seeing the foe nearing, came his last command, one made immortal, "Lay me down and save the flag." He died the next day.

The news was flashed to Mrs. Mulligan, at Martinsburg, and she started instantly for the field. Lieut.-General Early gave permission to her and her escort, Lieut. Russell, and ordered that "all officers will render Mrs. Mulligan such assistance as may be in their power in reaching Gen. Mulligan and ministering to his comfort, or in obtaining his body and effects." She was taken to the house of Henry M. Brent, in Winchester, where his remains were brought from Kernstown and seen by her. Mrs Mulligan traveled day and night more than a hundred miles. Procuring a coffin, she brought the remains in the ambulance, which had been her conveyance, to Hancock, and then by rail to Cumberland, and thence to Chicago.

The remains lay in state in Bryan Hall, where they were visited by thousands. At the meeting of the Chicago bar, Hon. I. N. Arnold, representative in Congress, said:

"You will remember how, in 1861, the whole country rang with his gallant defense of Lexington. On the 20th of December the following resolution was adopted unanimously by the House of Representatives:

"'*Resolved*, That the thanks of Congress be presented Col. James A. Mulligan and the officers and soldiers under his command who bravely stood by him, against a greatly superior force, in his heroic defense of Lexington.'

"* * * He never complained. Injustice was done him. Honors bravely and fairly earned were withheld, yet uninfluenced by the example of men in high position, he faithfully and patiently performed his duty as a soldier and uttered no word of complaint."

His funeral was one of the most imposing ever seen on the shores of the lake whose voice he so dearly loved. Vast multitudes thronged the streets—the long procession wound its way to the tomb amid the tolling of bells, the slow beat of "funeral drums," and the booming of signal guns. Flags floated at half-mast and each one seemed to repeat the dying hero's last words.

In the cathedral of St. Mary's the requiem of the Solemn High Mass was sung, and the prayer intoned by Dr. Butler, his friend and former chaplain, after which there was an eloquent funeral discourse by Rev. Dr. McMullen. As the procession wound its way the stores were seen draped in mourning. He sleeps the sleep of a brave man!

Brave young Nugent! His grave is unknown. He, too, died bravely, nobly.

THE THIRTY-NINTH INFANTRY.

Another regiment of the best class of men compelled to dance attendance upon the War Department, and literally to beg its way into service, was the "Yates Phalanx," or 39th infantry, organized in Chicago. Its officers incurred heavy expense from the law's delay, the tenacity of the red-tape, and not least, the engrossing idea that the "disturbance would soon be put down,'" and that too many troops would be uneconomical. It failed to secure acceptance under the "six-regiment bill." It retained its primary organization and continued its drill, hoping to have the privilege of fighting under the "ten-regiment bill," but that contained provisions fatal to its hope. Only one company could be accepted from Cook county, and the men, sick and tired, disbanded and went home.

The officers believed more men would be wanted, and retained their skeleton organization and forwarded a messenger to knock at Mr. Cameron's door, which he did unsuccessfully. They sent another, Captain O. L. Mann, who was also unsuccessful for a time, but while he was arguing the case, the battle of Bull Run occurred, and the next day the regiment was accepted. The work of recruiting was resumed, and after some difficulty the regiment was mustered in August, 1861, and officered as follows:

Colonel, Austin Light; Lieutenant-Colonel, Thomas O. Osborn; Major, Orrin L. Mann; Adjutant, Frank B. Marshall; Quartermaster, Joseph A. Cutler; Surgeon, Samuel C. Blake; 1st Assistant Surgeon, Charles M. Clark; 2d Assistant Surgeon, William Woodward; Chaplain, Charles S. Macreading.

Co. A—Captain, Sylvester W. Munn; 1st Lieutenant, Joseph W. Richerson; 2d Lieutenant, Leroy A. Baker.

Co. B—Captain, Isaiah W. Wilmerth; 1st Lieutenant, David F Sellards; 2d Lieutenant, James Haldeman.

Co. C—Captain, John Gray; 1st Lieutenant, Wallace Lord; 2d Lieutenant, Simon S. Brucker.

Co. D—Captain, Samuel S. Linton; 1st Lieutenant, Jonathan F. Linton; 2d Lieutenant, Austin Towner.

Co. E—Captain, James H. Hooker; 1st Lieutenant, Lewis Whipple; 2d Lieutenant, Norman C. Warner.

Co. F—Captain, Amasa Kennicott; 1st Lieutenant, John W. McIntosh; 2d Lieutenant, Patrick Seary.

Co. G—Captain, William B. Slaughter; 1st Lieutenant, Oscar F. Rudd; 2d Lieutenant, Amos Savage.

Co. H—Captain, Casper S. F. Dericks; 1st Lieutenant, Charles J. Wilder; 2d Lieutenant, Charles Flickenger.

Co. I—Captain, Hiram M. Phillips; 1st Lieutenant, Emory L. Waller; 2d Lieutenant, Albert W. Fellows.

Co. K—Captain, Joseph Woodruff; 1st Lieutenant, Oscar S. Belcher; 2d Lieutenant, Donald A. Nicholson.

Colonel Light was the unanimous choice of the officers, and proved himself a successful drill officer. Indeed, the rapid improvement of the regiment under his instruction, was observed by all. His previous service in the regular army had given him a practical knowledge of military routine. On the 11th of October the regiment left Chicago for St. Louis, where it reported at Benton Barracks. Here a disappointment came. The regiment was organized as riflemen, and contained many capital marksmen, whose long expected rifles proved to be old muskets, altered from flint to percussion.

On the 27th the Phalanx left Missouri for Williamsport, Md., via Indianapolis, Pittsburg and Harrisburg. At Williamsport the measles broke out in a malignant form, and the first who died was Lieut. Richardson, from Will county.

Amusing scenes occurred there, as everywhere in drilling raw recruits. The 39th had its share of men of quiet mischief. From Captain Slaughter's MSS. lying upon our table, we take one or two extacts:

"The officer of the day, one morning, instructed the guard respecting the 'courtesies' due the officers. One of them, an inveterate wag, though a good soldier, misconstrued the instructions for his own fun. He waited until the officer approached him, when with a half-roguish, half-innocent look, he dropped a low courtesy.

"'What do you mean?' said shoulder-straps.

"'Why, sir, I was told that when an officer came near me, I must kurchey, and so I kurchied.'

"The officer good-naturedly accepted the explanation, and gave the novice further instruction in salutes."

"A son of Erin found himself doing guard-duty one dark night. The officer of the day, making the Grand Rounds, approached him.

"'Halt! who comes there?'

"'Grand Rounds.'

"'Go to —— wid yer Grand Rounds,' said Pat, and resumed his contemplative walk."

"I had been out of the camp one evening, and was returning, when I was challenged—

"'Halt! who comes there?'

"Not having the countersign, I answered, 'A friend.'

"The indignant answer was, 'Well, if y'er a friend, what you standin there for? Why don't you come along in?'

"Of course this afforded an opportunity to instruct the sentinel in his duty."

Suddenly the regiment was astounded by the abrupt announcement of its Colonel's dismissal from service on some technical ground of former years. He had become greatly beloved and his removal was a sad blow. Lieut.-Colonel Osborn succeeded to the command and became an efficient and most popular officer.

On the 14th of December, the 39th was armed with Springfield rifled muskets, greatly to the delight of the men. On the 17th the regiment moved towards Hancock, via Clear Springs, then into Virginia, where it did guard duty for the Baltimore and Ohio Railroad, and valuable scouting service in the vicinity of Bath.

The last week of January, the 39th had its introduction to the forces of Stonewall Jackson in a sharp skirmish, in which Lieut.-Col. Mann narrowly escaped capture, and nine men were captured. The Union forces were compelled to fall back from Bath before the crushing weight of Jackson's columns. A daring handful of the 39th lay in wait at one point, and poured into the advancing column of the foe marching from Bath on Alpine Station, a deadly fire, causing it to fall back in confusion. Another detachment at Great Cacapon gallantly resisted the advance of picked men, and drove them back. The retreat continued to Hancock, where Gen. Lander was in command. Its surrender was declined, and after a fruitless effort to bombard it the enemy raised the siege. To him it was a fruitless and costly effort. Subsequently, the 39th was stationed at New Creek where sickness raged with terrible fury, the hospital in Cumberland was crowded, and there was fearful suffering.

In February the regiment had the advance in the movement for opening the Baltimore and Ohio R. R. toward Martinsburg. General Lander died. General Banks crossed the Potomac at Harper's Ferry, and General Williams at Williamsport, and the grand advance upon the Shenandoah had begun. The 39th was in the advance of Shields's division, and on the 11th of March passed through Martinsburg, and the next day bivouacked within two miles of Winchester, from which Jackson's forces retired. That wily leader had his own plans, to be developed all too soon.

On the 18th, forward, was again spoken, and the 39th, part of the 2d brigade, advanced toward Strasburg. The rebels still retreated. Strasburg was yielded, and then our troops marched back to Winchester. On the 22d there was active skirmishing, during which General Shields was wounded with a fragment of shell. Shields's division had been left alone in the valley while Banks had moved toward Centerville. Jackson knew this and sought his opportunity, and moved with massed strength, to crush Shields's command. On the 23d the battle raged furiously, and night came down upon our brave men holding the field in spite of a greatly superior force. The 39th did important service, but chafed that it did not come directly into the fight. The morning came, the forces of Jackson had retreated. Our forces pursued them to Strasburg.

The remainder of that campaign is known; the defeat of Kelley at Front Royal, and the retreat of General Banks down the Shenandoah Valley—a retreat admirably conducted, but yet a retreat. From thence to Suffolk, September 1st, where it remained until January 5, 1863, sharing in skirmishes at Black Water, Zurich and Franklin. January 19th arrived at Newbern, N. C., and on the 25th embarked at Moorehead City on transports, sailing with the Foster expedition against Charleston February 1st, it was landed at Hilton Head, and on the 5th at Helena Island. April 1st it again embarked, and on the 5th landed on Folly Island. Here it witnessed the bombardment of Sumter, and participated in the siege and capture of Morris Island. It participated in the siege of Charleston, and was the first regiment to enter Fort Wagner, Lieut.-Col. Mann in command. In this achievement much gallantry was displayed.

Under orders, the 39th returned to Hilton Head, December 7th. Re-enlisting January 1, 1864, as veterans, it returned home to recruit and remained until March 19th, when it started for the front and arrived at Bermuda Hundreds May 6th, and on the 14th had a sharp engagement with the enemy, and Col. Osborne was severely wounded. On the 16th it participated in the battle of Drury's Bluff, losing fifteen killed, seventy-two wounded and fifty-two missing. At the Mier Bottom church, from May 20th to June 19th, the loss in different engagements was 23 killed, 130 wounded and 13 missing. At Deep Bottom and Deep River, Va., August 14–16, the loss was 26 killed, 77 wounded and 8 missing. It was in the advance on Richmond via Deep Bottom, September 29th, October 1st. At Darbytown road, October 13th, it lost 15 killed, 57 wounded and 8 missing. It again met the enemy at Charles City Cross Roads October 27th and 28th. This was its last fighting up to 1865. It has suffered severely from battle casualties, and the ordinary causes of mortality and disability, but has borne its colors proudly, without stain. The 39th has a noble record.

Brev. Brig. Osborn of the 39th, was a native of Ohio, and a graduate of the Ohio University. He studied law with Lew. Wallace (now Major-General), at Crawfordsville, Indiana, and on being admitted to the bar, came to Chicago in the fall of 1857. He was active in raising the Phalanx, and when called to command it, he gave himself so heartily and laboriously to its duties, that his men soon found they had a soldier as leader. His defense of Alpine Station and Great Cacapon against the advance of Jackson, called forth the official approval of General Lander. After the battle of Winchester he marched his regiment over the Massanutten Mountains to protect the bridges of the valley, and then marched it back again to the support of General Banks. During the seven days' battles of the Peninsula, the Shields division was divided into two brigades, one of which was commanded by Col. Osborn. Subsequently the Colonel was stationed at Fortress Monroe. He was with the 39th in personal command, when not in charge of a brigade, in its various wanderings and engagements. On the 14th of May, 1864, he was painfully and severely wounded, so as to endanger, for some time, the loss of an arm, and returned home to his friends in Chicago.

He is an eloquent speaker as well as gallant soldier. A few months ago we heard him speak of the employment of colored soldiers, and of his former prejudices. But he had seen the time when he was thankful for their gleaming bayonets, and from that hour he was "cured of fancy soldiering!" He said this with inexpressible emotion, his arm suspended in a sling, and the large audience made the woods ring with their response.

As soon as his wound would permit he returned to his command, and in March 1865, was appointed Brigadier-General by brevet.

Lieut.-Col. Mann, by his activity and tact in securing the acceptance of the regiment, showed his men that he had the stuff for a leader, and accordingly he was chosen Major. December 1, 1861, he was promoted Lieutenant-Colonel, and was frequently in command of his regiment. He led the charge on Fort Wagner. He was severely wounded at Wier Bottom, May 20th, and compelled to sport a crutch for some months, during which, having returned home, he repeatedly addressed his fellow-citizens on the necessity of bravely fighting the war through to the end. Before his wound had healed he reported for duty, and is, at this time, Provost-Marshal General at Norfolk, Va.

Major S. W. Mann entered as Captain of Company A, and was promoted Major December 1, 1861. He was an efficient officer, but felt it necessary to resign. He was succeeded by S. S. Linton, who was wounded at Drury's Bluff, May 16th; thus within six days were the three commanding officers of the 39th placed *hors de combat.* Its record will show, when published, a large proportion of killed and wounded among its field and staff officers.

THE STURGIS RIFLES.

This was a single company of eighty-three men organized at Chicago, armed, equipped and subsisted for nearly two months by the munificence of Mr. Solomon Sturgis. Its commissioned officers were Captain Steele; 1st Lieutenant, N. V. Sheldon; 2d Lieutenant, ——— Foster.

It was organized in April, 1861, and mustered May 6th. Through the generosity of its patron, the company was armed with Sharpe's rifles. On the 19th of June it started for West Virginia, where it was to serve as body-guard of General McClellan. Every attention had been given to perfection in drill and discipline. It arrived at Parkersburg, and accompanied the General through the West Virginia campaign. It participated in the battle of Rich Mountain, and accompanied the General to Washington, where he went to assume chief command.

It reached Washington, July 26th, and settled into guard duty, not only over the person of its chief, but being entrusted with the care of some ladies of secession proclivities. In this it remained until March 10, 1862, when the quiet of the Potomac was broken by the cry of Forward!

The "Rifles" accompanied the General on the memorable march upon and siege of Yorktown, and thence into the Seven Days' battles of the Chickahominy. Subsequently to the close of that campaign, they returned to Washington.

Many of them were on detached duty. Some as foragers, some as scouts, etc. A few of them were at the battle of Antietam, but the company as a whole, was not present.

They left the army at Falmouth, and on the 27th of November, 1863, were mustered out of the service at Washington. Before leaving Washington, on the Yorktown campaign, nineteen recruits were sent forward. They were a gallant and finely disciplined body of men, and were ready to fight as well as stand guard.

SIXTY-FIFTH ILLINOIS INFANTRY.

The "Scotch Regiment," so called, was organized at Camp Douglas, May 5, 1861. It contained not a few of the descendants of "Old Scotia," for the descendants of the men who had shouted their Slogan, "The Bruce!" "The Douglas!" could not have their sympathies elsewhere than with freedom as against slavery in such a contest. Its organization was as follows:

Colonel, Daniel Cameron; Lieutenant-Colonel, William S. Stewart; Major, John Wood; Adjutant, David C. Bradley; Quartermaster, James C. Rankin; Surgeon, George H. Park; 1st Assistant Surgeon, Ira Brown; 2d Assistant Surgeon, Henry T. Mesler; Chaplain, Charles H. Roe.

Co. A—Captain, John Wood; 1st Lieutenant, James Duguid; 2d Lieutenant, Clandine George.

Co. B—Captain, Robert S. Montgomery; 1st Lieutenant, James W. Ballard; 2d Lieutenant, Henry H. Jones.

Co. C—Captain, John J. Boyd; 1st Lieutenant, Henry Fisher; 2d Lieutenant, Andrew Young.

Co. D—Captain, Van Ness Billings; 1st Lieutenant, Ai D. Ewer; 2d Lieutenant, Benjamin Harding.

Co. E—Captain, George H. Kennedy; 1st Lieutenant, John R. Floyd; 2d Lieutenant, Arthur M. Tanney.

Co. F—Captain, James S. Putnam; 1st Lieutenant, Samuel D. Toby; 2d Lieutenant, Harrison W. Mallory.

Co. G—Captain, Iranoff Willentzki; 1st Lieutenant, Alexander W. Diller; 2d Lieutenant, Louis H. Higgins.

Co. H—Captain, Alexander McDonald; 1st Lieutenant, Lysander Tiffany; 2d Lieutenant, John J. Littler.

Co. I—Captain, William H. Mapes; 1st Lieutenant, William Knowles; 2d Lieutenant, Benjamin B. Adams.

Co. K—Captain, Henry M. Fuller; 1st Lieutenant, William Robertson; 2d Lieutenant, John Blain.

It has been out of the author's power to secure full notes of the history of this gallant regiment. In the sketch of General White the reader will find some record of its early history, of its compulsory surrender at Harper's Ferry, and its subsequent movements in Kentucky and elsewhere. It was with Burnside in East Tennessee at the siege of Knoxville; with Sherman in his "On to Atlanta and Savannah." Was with Thomas in the battles of Columbia, Franklin and Nashville and the chase after Hood's army. It was at the occupancy of Wilmington, and at our last advices was with Major-General Cox's division, 23d army corps. Five companies were recently mustered out by expiration of time, and the field officers were moving earnestly to fill its decimated ranks.

It re-enlisted as a veteran regiment and returned to the field, and has done good service.

Colonel Cameron was born in Berwick-upon-Tweed, but though a borderer by birth, was himself of Highland ancestry, being a descendant of Cameron of Lochiel, whose blood watered the field of Culloden. Coming to this country, Mr. Cameron became actively connected with newspaper life. He was an ardent democrat and warm personal friend of Judge Douglas. During his service he was much of his time in command of a brigade. He has resigned his commission and is now upon his farm.

John A. Bross

COL. JOHN A. BROSS.

ENGRAVED EXPRESSLY FOR 'PATRIOTISM OF ILLINOIS' CLARKE & CO. PUBLISHERS.

CHAPTER XXXIV.

BIOGRAPHICAL.

Major-General John Buford, the Cavalry Marshal—Colonel John A. Bross—Colored Troops—In the Cedars—The 29th U. S. C. T.—Obey Orders—The Mine—Lieut. De Wolf—Lieut. Skinner—Young Durham.

ILLINOIS hath her honored dead among the graves of soldiers of the Republic, in the burial places of our south-eastern armies. Among the first in honor is that of Major-General John Buford. He was a native of Kentucky, but his home was in Illinois. He was a graduate of the military academy at West Point. He was commissioned Brigadier-General of volunteers, July 27, 1862, and was assigned to a cavalry brigade under General Pope. His fitness for this arm of the service soon attracted the attention of his superiors, and he was assigned to the command of the separate cavalry brigade of the entire army of the Potomac.

His genius shone brilliantly, and he was soon recognized as the first cavalry officer of the country. He could deal with masses of horsemen, and with companies and persons. He could restrain the fiery impatience of subordinates, until the right moment, and then launch his troops like resistless thunderbolts upon the foe.

When the cavalry was organized into three divisions, he was assigned the first. He kept near him, as much as possible, the 8th and 12th, with the New York 2d, for he knew their mettle. In the eventful campaigns of 1863, he was almost constantly in the saddle. At Gettysburg, a portion of his command met the brunt of the first onset, and stayed the sweeping, crushing avalanche, and when the retreat came, his men hung upon the flanks and rear of the retreating force of Lee. He proved himself such a cavalry marshal as the service had not yet developed.

In view of important movements pending in that department, he had been ordered, a few days before his death, to the command of the cavalry forces of the army of the Cumberland. Could he have reached it and assumed command, and directed the movements of the Western horsemen, some painful chapters might have been differently written.

But his exposure and overwork broke down his sinewy strength. He was prostrated with typhoid fever, and died in the city of Washington, December 15, 1863, aged forty years. Shortly before his death, he was made Major-General of volunteers, his commission dating from July 4th, or the victory of Gettysburg. His funeral was a magnificent pageant, for he was honored above many.

General Buford was brave. He dared all perils if they were in the way of the necessary victory. At the same time he was careful of the lives of his men, and never sent them into death headlong. They never questioned *his* orders. At his word they would have rode against walls of mason-work or lines of steel.

"He could," said a returned captain who long served under him, "preserve the dignity of the commander, and yet be the soldier's friend. Any one might approach him. He had a smile and cheerful word for the private as well as the officer." No wonder he was an idol with the bold troopers of the Potomac.

He seems to have been among the first to comprehend the true power of a strong cavalry force, and its place in a great army. It is not infantry, is not to do the work of infantry, but to hover upon the flanks and rear of a foe, to cut his communications, cut off his advance, turn the retreat into a route, or at the decisive moment, by a bold charge, decide the fortunes of the day. And in the painful history of waiting and pausing; of politely giving our enemy time to entrench and secure his communications before assailing him, it is refreshing to turn to the chronicles of Buford's cavalry. It is like reading the annals of romance. Now their shout is heard from the hillsides, and now the ringing of their sabers is echoing in the valley. Now they ride defiantly within sight of the spires of Richmond, and discuss the propriety of breakfasting with the "Mrs. President' of the confederacy. Now they confront superior forces and dash them back until the army of the Union is in position, and the Union is saved at Gettysburg.

There were other brave men and gallant officers there—men seamed with scars and wearing well-worn honors, but no injustice is done them when we write that much of the glory of the brave cavalry of the army of the Potomac is due General John Buford of Illinois.

COLONEL JOHN A. BROSS.—It became early evident that colored men could not be kept out of the war, and by degrees the Northern mind was educated to consent to their enlistment. From various causes, the work of raising a regiment in Illinois was difficult. The black laws had thwarted the coming of men of color into the State, and increased prejudice against them. In addition, many of this class had left the State and enlisted elsewhere—nearly two full companies having entered the Massachusetts 59th. Yet it was decided to enlist the 29th U. S. colored troops in Illinois.

To undertake the work of recruiting, and then of drilling such a regiment, Capt. John A. Bross, of Company A, 88th Illinois infantry, was selected. This gentleman was born in Milford, Penn. His father, Deacon Moses Bross, now resides in Morris, Illinois, while his brother William, widely known as one of the editors of the *Chicago Tribune*, is now Lieut.-Governor of the State. He received an academic education and entered the profession of the law. Democratic in politics, he served as assistant U. S. Marshal under Mr. Pierce, and held the office of U. S. Commissioner until his death. He entered heartily into the work of aiding the government in suppressing rebellion, and in the summer of 1862, raised two companies, one of which entered the 75th infantry. The other went into the 88th, and he was chosen its captain.

In his first engagement, that of Perryville, it was seen that he was a soldier, brave and true. He was in the battle of Stone River, where the 88th covered itself with glory, enduring at one time the assault of a whole brigade. After the battle he was introduced to Major-General Negley. As that officer looked at him, a pleased beam of recognition came over his face, and he said: "*Ah! I saw you in the Cedars*," and he gave the Captain's hand a hearty clasp. He was with his command through the long and severe campaign terminated by the hard-fought and bloody battle of Chickamauga.

He assumed the formation and discipline of the 27th U. S. colored troops from conviction of duty. He was in the direct line of promotion in the 88th. He felt God called him to the work he took in hand. His headquarters were established at Quincy. He entered upon the work of recruiting and drilling his men with all his accustomed industry. From the first he decided that his treatment of his troops should be such as became them as *men;* and the result was that he soon established himself fully in their confidence and affections. The undertaking in his hands was at once a success, so far as the proficiency of the troops in their ordiuary duties was concerned. The filling up of the regiment, owing to the causes alluded to, was not rapid. Having raised six companies, he was commissioned as Lieut.-Colonel, April 7, 1864. He was ordered to join the 9th army corps (Burnside's), then moving from Annapolis to the field. He passed through Chicago with his regiment on the 27th of May, 1864. His troops were provided with refreshments at the "Soldiers' Rest," and a number of friends presented the Colonel with a fine horse and equipments, as a token of their high appreciation of his steadfast devotion to the cause of liberty. The presentation address was made by Col. F. A. Eastman, and was briefly replied to by the recipient of the gift. His response being entirely extempore, was not preserved, but a sentence or two is remembered by those who heard it. "When I lead these men into battle, we shall remember Fort Pillow, and shall not ask for quarter. I leave a home and friends as dear as can be found on earth, but if it is the will of Providence that I do not return, I ask no nobler epitaph than that I fell for my country at the head of this black and blue regiment."

The 9th army corps had left Annapolis before the 29th could arrive, and an order was received directing it to proceed to Alexandria. General Casey was in command at Washington, and had issued an order for the regiment to report at his headquarters, near Long Bridge. For some reason the order failed to reach Col. Bross, and and he marched directly past General Casey's office through to Alexandria, and encamped, in ignorance of the General's directions. An order was thereupon sent to him direct, to report immediately at headquarters. He was received with much sternness by General Casey. "Have you seen service before, sir?" "I have, sir." "How came you to disobey *that?*" said General Casey, one of his staff at the same time presenting the order. "Are you accustomed to obey orders?" Said Col. Bross, with emphasis, "General Casey, I obey orders with my life; your order never reached me." The mistake was of course discovered and explanations were soon made. His air of resolute determination favorably impressed the old General, and the Colonel was thereupon placed in command of the colored brigade, then at Camp Casey, near Washington. This position he held until after the battle of Spottsylvania, when, with his brigade, he was ordered forward to White House, where he remained until an opportunity offered to go to the front. At this time the troops were rapidly attaining perfection in drill, and their discipline was every way satisfactory.

His regiment was thoroughly drilled, and on occasions of alarm proved itself ready to stand in its lot amid the thunders of battle.

General Grant was before Petersburg. An order was addressed to Col. Bross to detach one regiment to guard. He selected the 29th and accompanied it, leaving the brigade. He reached the main army and commenced work in the trenches June 19th. In July it was known that an extensive mine was in preparation, and following its explosion, extensive movements were to be made and grand results achieved.

"On Saturday morning, July 30, 1864, at 40 minutes past 4 o'clock, the mine beneath the rebel fort was exploded; and at 5 o'clock and 30 minutes a charge was made and for a while seemed to promise well. The line, for a short distance on each side of the mine, is said to have been brilliantly carried. The second line was gained and held for a time. The colored division, under General Ferrero, including seven colored regiments, was then ordered forward. The fort had been seized, and the order to the black troops was to take the interior line beyond. They had been ordered to take the caps from their muskets and rely on the bayonet. It soon became evident the work claimed to have been done by Ledlie's division was not thoroughly accomplished. The enemy's lines had not been sufficiently cleared, and such had been the delay that the rebels had rallied in full force and were prepared now to dispute, successfully, any further advance of our troops. But they did advance, in face of a fire in front; and in addition, received an enfilading fire upon each flank and also in the rear from portions of the enemy's first line, which had not been taken. They advanced towards Cemetery Hill, which was the key to the entire rebel position. Cemetery Hill commands Petersburg itself, and was, therefore, the objective point of the assault; and without attaining it, the attack, as a whole, must fail. It would seem, therefore, that such a careful disposition of the forces should have been made as would render the attempt a *certain* success. On the contrary, the first assault was so executed that no subsequent bravery could prevent a total failure; and *no* failure of the war, of the same dimensions, has been more disastrous. Not that in a strictly military sense, the loss was so great, though it cost us four thousand of our bravest and best men—the military situation was the same after the attempt as before. In addition to the loss of life the moral effect was intensely calamitous. It spread a gloom over all the land. It was widely felt, as a result, that we were making no progress in the war, and were likely to make none. All the friends of those who died in the undertaking felt that their lives had been sacrificed to the most stupid and criminal blundering. If a soldier falls in a successful battle, his name is imperishably linked with whatever of luster it sheds about it. History, poetry and oratory dwell upon it. But to fall in a failure is to go down in comparative darkness, and history refuses to linger upon the theme."

Lieutenant Chapman says:

"Whenever I recall the scenes of that dreadful day, feelings of sorrow and regret inevitably arise. Before day we were up and ready. Every one felt the danger awaiting him, and there was unusual silence. All seemed occupied with their own thoughts. The Colonel came up to me, and we had a few moments of cheerful conversation. Soon the artillery opened—the musketry was distinctly heard—the conflict had commenced. In perfect silence we moved forward. My last interview with the Colonel was while we were halted in the covered way. Capt. Aiken and Lieut. Gale were also there. Few words were exchanged, our thoughts, as usual at such times, straying homeward. We little knew then that by incapacity and wanton neglect, thousands of lives were to be sacrificed. Again we were moving forward. The outer line of works was passed, and we were hastening up the hill to the fort. Here, friend and foe, living and dying, were heaped together, causing us to halt in the midst of a destructive fire of both musketry and artillery. I well remember how he looked; standing in the midst, his countenance lighted up with steadfast hope and an almost superhuman courage, he cried out, 'Forward, 29th,' and we moved on over the mass. The men were falling thick and fast, and soon my turn came. Lying on the field, I felt the auspicious moment had passed. His form was ever a prominent mark. Turning to Capt. Brockway, he said, 'Bring forward the colors.' Then, seizing them in his own hand, he cried, 'Follow me, my men.' But it was in vain; the enemy were concentrated. It was madness for us to charge where three divisions had already failed. As we were ordered back, the Colonel was seen endeavoring to rescue the colors. Standing upon the parapet, he said, 'The man who saves those colors shall be promoted.' The fatal ball came, and he fell, but the legacy of his bright example and the memory of his noble deeds remain. The intense sorrow and grief of that night I will not attempt to portray."

Capt. McCormick testifies that the 29th first advanced through a narrow strip of timber, and received the rebel fire. Beyond was the first line of earthworks and then an open plain. Across this charged the troops to a mined fort, receiving a terrible cross and enfilading fire, and here the brave Captain Flint was killed. Onward, up to the ditch in front of the rebel lines, and after a brief rest, another advance upon the second rebel line, where was entrenched a force so strong that the unsupported soldiers of the Union could not go farther. The Colonel leaped upon the parapet and planted his colors, but seeing at a glance the strength of the foe, ordered a retreat, but before he could retire a minnie ball struck him on the left side of his brain and crashed through his skull. He exclaimed, "O Lord!" and was dead.

That regiment lost in that charge, one hundred and fifty killed, one hundred wounded, and from seventy to eighty prisoners! It did all that could have been done. Four hundred and fifty men went into the melee—one hundred and twenty-eight came out! Of the officers, the Colonel and Captain Flint were killed; Major Brown was wounded; adjutant Downing was severely wounded and captured; Captain Aikin was mortally wounded; Captains Daggett and Brockway severely, and Captain Porter slightly.

The colored troops did their duty. *Some one blundered*, and they were marched into death. Col. Bross was foremost in the charge and his body was farthest in advance. He sleeps in his soldier grave unmarked, unknown! His pastor delivered an eloquent funeral discourse, from which we make the following extract:

"God will keep his dust, and his memory will grow brighter and brighter in that long catalogue of heroes and martyrs who have given their lives to liberty and to God. It is a little remarkable that he was accustomed to repeat Tennyson's 'Charge of the Light Brigade,' and especially these verses:

"'Forward the Light Brigade!
No man was there dismayed,
Not though the soldiers knew
Some one had blundered—
Theirs not to make reply;
Theirs not to reason why;
Theirs but to *do* and *die;*
Into the valley of death
Rode the six hundred.'

"Mr. Bross was a good husband, a tender father, a kind and generous neighbor. He was also an humble and decided follower of Jesus. His serious attention to the claims of religion was arrested, he used to say, by the fact that his father, with whom he was going to church on a certain occasion, stopped in a lonely place to pray.

"I have reason to know that in the army he was constant in his religious duties, and in circumstances where it required no little degree of moral courage to acknowledge his convictions and do his duty. He had, however, no cant about him. He was simply straightforward and conscientious.

"He was a faithful and much loved member of this Church. Many of us have known him long and well. Quiet, unpretentious, liberal according to his means, genial in spirit, and ready for every good word and work, we could not fail to esteem him, nor regret his loss when he left us for the field of strife. And now we mourn him, as we mourn good men whose lives have been linked with ours and are no more. Nay, as we mourn good men who die for us. Nor are we alone. He has numbered himself with those for whom a nation mourns, and over whose fate the lovers of our country, in all lands, will drop a tear."

He died a Christian soldier. He was a fine singer, and his love of song went with him to the front. The Surgeon of the regiment thus writes:

"HON. WM. BROSS—*Dear Sir:* I would esteem it a great kindness if you would send me a card photograph of my late much lamented and highly esteemed Colonel. * * * We had many happy times together during our—to me, alas! too short—acquaintance. When he visited me at the hospital, we used to make these old Virginia woods ring with auld Scotch songs. 'My Nannie's awa,' was a special favorite of his. He was delighted to hear me recite or read Burns, and many a hearty laugh we had at our 'Immortal Bobby,' and my Scotch pronunciation. Or, we would start some sacred tune: 'Sweet Hour of Prayer,' 'Marching Along,' 'A Light in the Window for Thee, Brother,' etc. The two former he taught me.

"I well remember the night we crossed the James. We had a long hot day's march on foot—his horse was sick. We were resting on an old stump when we received orders directing me to report to the hospital. He said, 'Doctor, I am glad you are going to the hospital; if anything should happen to me or my boys, we shall get the best attention, and if I am wounded, I wish you to attend to my case; I will not have any of these drinking surgeons touch me.' Then turning to an orderly, he said, 'Call the officers.' When they were around him, he said, 'Now, gentlemen, we are expecting to storm those works to-night or to-morrow morning early, and I wish it thoroughly understood that *not a man is to leave his post to assist the wounded—no matter who falls, I, or any body else. Let the wounded lie where they fall, and* PRESS on.' We then lay down on that corn-field—little thought I it was the last night we should spend together.

"This war, and that of the Crimea, have deprived me of many warm friends, but this last is the severest trial of all. Be assured I should prize one of his pictures very highly.

"I am, sir, very respectfully, your obedient servant,

"D. MACKAY, *Surgeon 29th U. S. Colored Troops.*"

The Chicago bar held, on Thursday, August 18th, one of the largest and most affecting meetings ever convened on the occasion of the death of one of its members. As one truly said, they mourned a brother over whom it was necessary to throw no mantle of charity. The following preamble and resolutions were adopted:

"WHEREAS, Our friend and brother, Lieut.-Colonel JOHN A. BROSS, 29th regiment U. S. colored troops, has fallen upon the field of battle—another victim upon the altar of our country—

"*Resolved*, That by his glorious death this Bar has lost one of its most cherished members, his regiment an able and fearless commander, the country a brave soldier, and humanity an earnest advocate and uncompromising friend. While we mourn, we cannot but gather consolation that another of our number (having courageously assumed the chances alike from an open enemy in honorable warfare, and a malignant foe in indiscriminate massacre), ripe in Christian character and manly virtue, and impelled by patriotic devotion, has thus enrolled his name on that long list of heroes enshrined in the hearts of a grateful nation.

"*Resolved*, That though we shall miss Col. Bross in the halls of justice and in the other walks of our common profession, we shall not cease to remember the urbanity of his deportment, the geniality of his companionship, the integrity of his purposes, and the honesty of his heart.

"*Resolved*, That from our earliest acquaintance, our departed brother illustrated the principles of universal philanthropy having their foundation in the gospel he professed; and while his military career gave the highest evidence of his self-sacrificing patriotism and his fidelity to early convictions, leading him to seek a path of danger unequaled in civilized warfare, in his heroic death he has sealed with his blood those great principles of our common humanity, which he believed to be inculcated by his Divine Master.

"*Resolved*, That we do not and will not forget that the dearest and tenderest of ties bound Col. Bross to family, home and earth, and increased the sacrifice thus cheerfully made at the shrine of principle, patriotism and humanity, and that we tender to those he held most dear our cordial sympathy in this bereavement.

"*Resolved*, That a suitable committee be appointed to communicate the above resolutions to the United States Courts and the several courts of record, with the request that they be recorded therein.

"*Resolved*, That copies of the foregoing resolutions, signed by the Chairman and Secretary, be presented to the family and brothers of the deceased, as a testimonial of sympathy and regard."

We would be glad to insert all the addresses which were delivered. He who reads them sees that Col. Bross was no needy adventurer, taking command of colored troops to attain distinction not to be won elsewhere. Said Mr. Herbert:

"Col. Bross entered the army in the 88th Illinois, for which he enlisted a company, leaving this city in August, 1862. The campaigns of Kentucky and Tennessee brought him practically into direct contact with an element in the great contest, which before, he had studied theoretically only at a distance. His conviction of the great fact that "*God had made of one blood all the nations to dwell upon all the face of the earth*," had early been with him a settled principle of faith; and when the Government decided to call forth that great element of power representing four millions of our population, and give them their position as men in this conflict, no one was surprised that Capt. Bross applied for power to enlist a regiment in Illinois. In this he was measurably successful. He needed but the maximum of a regiment to have received a commission as Colonel.

"A man of less principle would have hesitated. He had as much to lose as any other man; as much to bind him to family, friends and home; as much to induce him to temporize and delay; but foremost in this State at the hazard of life—nay, though counting it almost certain death—he engaged in the effort which he believed would demonstrate the truth of the divine statement to the most unbelieving, and would elevate the chattel to the full rank of manhood, and disabuse a public sentiment which he looked upon not only as a reproach upon our State and nation, but upon our common Creator.

"Col. Bross entered on this work with an enthusiasm lighted up by patriotism, philanthropy and religion. With him the great brotherhood of man had its foundation in a common Creator, a common ancestry, and a common destiny, and anything that practically denied that, was to him infidelity.

"I shall ever remember the magnetic grasp of his hand, and the earnest fervor of his mild and determined eye, when he bade me his last farewell. His manner, indeed the whole man impressed me with the feelings from that moment, that John A. Bross would return, if ever, a dead man or a hero. You all know the result. On the 30th of July, before Petersburg, on the parapet of the enemy, planting the flag of the country—the flag he so much loved—he fell, covered with the folds of that flag and with glory, and attested the sincerity of his faith and his philanthropy, by mingling his blood with that of the despised and oppressed race whose welfare and whose elevation he sought with so much earnestness and zeal.

"If the ancients wished to stimulate the Greek, they spoke of his household gods. If they wished to inspire the valor of the Roman, they promised him immortal honors with the heroes of antiquity. If they would urge on the stubborn Jew, they spoke of the altar and the temple—the graves of the prophets and the great Jehovah.

"It was this feeling of religious enthusiasm which moved the sword of the Lord and of Gideon; which nerved the arm of the youthful David to hurl the smooth stone from the brook; that stimulated the infant Hannibal; that beamed in the fervid eye of the maid of Orleans; that sustained the patient courage of Washington. This it was which in our own day gave England her Havelock, and has among ourselves raised up the idols of our army and our navy—our Foote and our Howard—and is now developing a host of minor worthies, each of whom, if not enrolled high in the annals of fame, will be found registered in the hearts of his comrades, and in that great catalogue of Christian martyrs and heroes in the Lamb's book of life.

"This great principle is most happily illustrated in the life and death of Col. Bross. His death, like his life, was the development of a calm and patient pursuit of what he thought a rigorous duty. 'He loved his fellow-men,' and thus attested by the divine law, his love for his country and to his God.

"If, when surrounded by home and by friends—

'The chamber where the good man meets his fate
Is privileged beyond the common walk
Of virtuous life, quite on the verge of Heaven,'

how near to the great white throne above must be that favored spot of earth where, heralded by the thunders of battle and canopied by the smoke and flame of contending armies, with one hand on the flag, the same Christian hero and martyr, with heart full of love for his country, his brother, and his God, yields up his life, and whence his released spirit takes its flight to the bosom of that God who 'is no respecter of persons,' but of whom it is said that 'in every nation he that feareth God and worketh righteousness is accepted with him."

The gallant Major Alex. F. Stevenson who was present, said:

"In battle there was none braver than he. At Stone River and Chickamauga, battles historic for the bravery of our troops against heavy numerical superiority of the enemy, he displayed that coolness and determination which fitted him so much for a higher command.

"But it seems to me Col. Bross had still greater moral courage than we gave him credit for. He has shown it in taking the command of colored troops. To take this step required a man of nerve and fortitude, for he knew that to the officers of colored troops there was no imprisonment like unto others, but certain death awaited them should the chances of war cast them into the hands of the enemy. But with the full knowledge of all this, he went bravely into the contest, because he believed it to be his duty to his country and his God.

> "No doubting, no fearing, the soldier shall know,
> When here stands his country, and yonder the foe;
> One look at the bright sun, one prayer to the sky,
> One glance where our banner floats glorious on high;
> Then on, as the young lion bounds on his prey,
> Let the sword flash on high, fling the scabbard away,
> Roll on as the thunderbolt over the plain,
> We'll come back in glory, or come not again."

We can only give one more quotation, and that is from the address of Hon. I. N. Arnold:

"I remember very vividly my last interview with him. It was the Saturday before he marched from his camp, near Alexandria, to join the forces of Grant, confronting Lee. I drove over with my family from Washington to his quarters. It was a most beautiful sunny afternoon, and I saw him with great pride review his regiment on dress parade. He had received his marching orders, and was full of enthusiasm and very proud of his regiment. He assured me that in capacity for service, endurance, courage, and all the qualities of a soldier, his regiment of negroes would not be outdone by any regiment, white or black, in the service. He took a seat in my carriage and rode with me a short distance towards Washington. I parted with him as the sun sank behind the blue hills of Virginia, and as we shook hands in farewell, I never was more impressed by any man. He was sunburnt and manly—his large, fine manly form full of health and vigor, filled with the martial ardor of the soldier and the hero. He struck his tents that night—led his gallant regiment to Petersburg, and found there the death of a hero and martyr. I can truly say that in all the rich sacrifices of this war there has fallen not one more manly, brave and true: none more patriotic and disinterested: no more worthy *Christian soldier* that JOHN A. BROSS."

If more space is given this officer than to most of his rank whose fall has been chronicled, the author's single apology is, that something of historic mention is due to the commanding officer of the first regiment of colored troops raised in Illinois—to the brave, honorable Christian man and chivalrous officer, who identified his fortune with that of the people of affliction. His death was appropriately acknowledged by various Sunday school and other organizations. His wife and boy cherish his memory as a priceless legacy for he was a good man and died in a good cause.

Lieut. William D'Wolf, who fell in the battle of Williamsburg, Va., May 4, 1862, and died on the 2d of June following, was one of the noble young men the State has given to the Republic. His father, William F. D'Wolf, is a well known citizen of Chicago. William enlisted May, 1861, in Co. B, 1st Regiment Illinois Light Artillery, better known both North and South as "Taylor's Battery." Early in the field, he shared the fortunes and perils of his battery in the hot fights of Frederickton, Belmont and Donelson. In the last he was wounded. He served with his battery nearly a year, when, for gallant and meritorious conduct, he was promoted to a Lieutenancy in the regular army, in the 3d Regiment of Artillery. General McClellan addressed a letter to the Secretary of War requesting his promotion. On the 4th of April, 1862, he joined his regiment. In the battle of Williamsburg he manifested the utmost bravery. A shell exploded under his horse, killing it and wounding the Lieutenant in the thigh. He caught a loose horse and went forward with his battery. He meant to stand by his guns. He was again wounded, this time in the knee of the other leg, but remained with the battery until it was withdrawn. He was conveyed to Fortress Monroe, and thence to Washington City, where, in the home of the patriotic representative from the Chicago district, Hon. I. N. Arnold, he received every possible attention, but sunk under his wounds, and, with his mother beside him, expired on the 2d of June.

Col. Tristam Burges, General Stoneman's aid, reported that he saw the young officer through the whole fight, and that he acted like a veteran. Says Captain Gibson, who commanded the battery:

> "One of my subalterns, a handsome, gallant boy from Chicago, named D'Wolf, was wounded, and, I regret to say, has since died. I was much attached to him, and if your friends know his family, please assure them of my sincere sympathy with them in the bereavement and my high appreciation of his coolness and gallantry in the midst of no ordinary danger. Poor fellow! He joined my battery on the 4th of April, was wounded on the 4th of May, and on the 4th of June was dead."

His remains were brought to Chicago, and an eloquent oration delivered in St. James' Church (Protestant Episcopal) by the Rector, Dr. Clarkson, whence his remains were followed to the grave by a vast concourse.

Lieut. Richard Skinner, of the 10th infantry, regular army, was another costly sacrifice. His great-grandsire, General Timothy Skinner, was a subaltern officer in the war of the Revolution. His grandfather, Judge Richard Skinner, was member of Congress from Vermont during the last war with England, then Chief Justice, then Governor, then declining a re-election, was again placed upon the bench as Supreme Justice, where he remained until within a short time of his death, when he resigned the place.

His father, Hon. Mark Skinner, of Chicago, is an eminent and patriotic citizen, formerly Judge of the Court. He was the first President of the Northwestern Sanitary Commission, giving it his time and labor until compelled, by shattered health, to resign. Much of its efficiency was due to his wise supervision.

His only son, after an academic training, entered Yale College and graduated. He had a fine literary taste and wrote in an accomplished style. With unblemished reputation, native endowments of high order, thorough culture, and a fine physique, he had a brilliant future before him. All was laid upon his country's altar.

He received the appointment of 2d Lieutenant in the 10th U. S. A., and was ordered to report to Major-General Hunter, and became a member of his staff, discharging the duty of commissary of musketeers, and remaining with him during his command in South Carolina.

Subsequently he was ordered to report to Brigadier-General B. S. Roberts, then in command at Davenport, Iowa, whom he accompanied to New Orleans and thence to Pass Caballa and Matagorda Island, where the General was post commandant. He was duly promoted 1st Lieutenant, and was about attaining a captaincy, when he was ordered to join his regiment in front of Petersburg. He went to it gladly, but found it reduced to a hundred men, under the senior Lieutenant, and at that time on picket duty. He arrived on Sunday, June 19, 1864. On Monday he was in the trenches. On Tuesday morning, while conversing with a group of officers, he was struck by a ball, mortally wounded, and died on Wednesday. He had won the confidence and high esteem of the general officers whom he had served. An *only son*—such is one of the many costly offerings made for the government! His honored father said, sadly, "We had only him, and we gave him: he had only his life and he freely gave it!"

Let this chapter close with brief mention of a young man who wore no ensignia of rank—a brave lad, a fine newspaper correspondent, a Christian young man—GABRIEL B. DURHAM, son of Pleasant Durham, of Kankakee City. He enlisted in Barker's Dragoons, and with his company entered the 12th Cavalry. In that obstinate resistance made by Buford's cavalry to the enemy at Gettysburg, he, with others, was dismounted. Placing a rail for rest and barricade, he fired his twenty rounds and started for a fresh supply. While passing to the rear, he was struck by a fragment of shell and mortally wounded. He was placed in the Calvary Hospital and lingered until the 23d July, when he died. He knew he must die, but bravely, nobly said, "I have only done my duty. If I had other lives I would give them to save my country." The Lieutenant-General could utter no grander words. The body was embalmed and brought home and buried from the Methodist Church.

"So sleep the dead who sink to rest
With all their country's wishes blest."

CHAPTER XXXV.

THE ADJUTANT-GENERAL'S OFFICE.

Its Appearance—Its Occupants—Its Contents—Mather—Wyman—Grant—Loomis—Adjutant-General Fuller—Biography—Judge—Adjutant—Governor Yates Testimony—Speaker—Resolution of House—Economy.

IN the dingy capitol at Springfield, is the Adjutant-General's office, where are documents which will be searched in days to come, by the historian, the annalist, the lawyer.

Entering a room about forty feet square, you see double rows of desks, and peering above each is a head variously colored. The clerks are hard at work preserving the facts of our Illinois regiments. In those pigeon holes are documents which in curt official style tell of many a deed of daring, and many a weary march. In the casualty reports are enshrined the names of those who have received wounds or died the soldier's death on the field!

These "Descriptive Rolls" tell you the place and date of birth, place and date of enlistment, hight in feet and inches, color of hair and eyes of each soldier. They state when enlisted, when discharged, and when completed, will tell the story of wounds and death. We doubt if any office is more exact in the arrangement of these details. The best models—American, English and Continental were consulted, and a combined system adopted, covering all the details.

At the commencement of hostilities, Thos. T. Mather, was Adjutant-General. General Wyman was detailed for a time, and then one Ulysses S. Grant, a retired Captain of the regular army. His military information, both in extent and detail astonished all. Did any one ask about a Springfield musket, a Belgian rifle or any other arm, he would quietly rest a moment and state the number of pieces it contained, how they are put together, and the advantages and drawbacks of each. He could enlighten a bewildered quartermaster on the mysteries of rations, how many pounds the soldiers would have to carry if rations of one kind were given, and how much if another, and then what constituents each ration contained, and in what it might be deficient. Quietly stood the retired captain solving the puzzles of men with eagles and stars. His suggestions were invaluable.

A young man, J. S. Loomis, had enlisted. He was judged to have rare qualifications for the duties of the adjutant's office, and he remained in it until near the close of Governor Yates' administration, having received the rank of Colonel. He rendered valuable service in the office, entering upon its duties *con amore*, searching the most minute details, and generalizing admirably.

In his last message, Governor Yates thus alludes to him:

"In March, 1864, I sent Col. John S. Loomis, who had been connected with the State Department from the commencement of the war—first as Assistant Adjutant-General, and recently, as my principal aid-de-camp—to Washington, with instructions to urge final adjustment of all our accounts. His extensive acquaintance with the origin and history of our military organization and contracting and settlement of war claims, enabled him to make full explanation of our vouchers, and prosecute appeals from what was considered erroneous decisions of adjusting officers of the treasury, in disallowing and suspending a part of our claims. He was accompanied by Gen. John Wood, Quartermaster-General of the State, whose services were required to aid settlement of the class of claims originating in his department. From the report of Col. Loomis, and copies of his appeals on suspended and disallowed accounts, herewith transmitted, it will be seen that the claims of the State against the government, filed in the Treasury Department, for war expenses, amounted to three millions eight hundred and twelve thousand five hundred and twenty-five dollars and fifty-four cents (3,812,525.54); of which amount there has been allowed, on various settlements with the Third Auditor, three millions seven hundred and twenty-six thousand seven hundred and ninety-two dollars and eighty-seven cents ($3, 726,792.87); leaving a difference between the claims and allowances, in that department, of eighty-five thousand seven hundred and thirty-two dollars and sixty-seven cents($85,732.67); suspended and disallowed, because, in the opinion of the said Auditor the law did not sufficiently provide for them. Of the amount allowed by the Third Auditor, and passed to the Second Comptroller of the Treasury, it will also be seen, that the Comptroller suspended nearly all of our

State claims upon ground of insufficiency of vouchers, but which decision, upon the appeal of Col. Loomis, the Secretary of the Treasury reversed, and ordered a settlement of the accounts. An appeal was also taken upon the suspension and disallowment of accounts in the Third Auditor's office ($85,732.67), which is set forth in the report.

"I am recently advised, by letter from the Treasury Department, that upon last settlement there was found to be due the State four hundred and sixty-eight thousand two hundred and sixty-five dollars and ninety-eight cents ($468,265.98), and that the amount of suspensions and disallowances has been reduced to twenty-seven thousand three hundred and ninety dollars and seventy-four cents ($27,390.74.)

"Thirty thousand dollars have recently been paid by the government on the balance found due on our accounts; which sum is sufficient to pay off all warrants drawn upon the State Treasury against the war fund.

"In this connection, I desire to call your attention specially to the report of Col. Loomis. It gives a complete history of a necessity for all expenses incurred by the State for the general government, and, in my opinion, clearly establishes the right of the State to the reimbursement of every dollar we have advanced, and which yet remains suspended. Colonel Loomis' labors in the adjustment of our war accounts have been invaluable, and it is recommended that a sufficient appropriation be made for his services and expenses."

But the name of Allen C. Fuller has been more frequently mentioned in State military matters than that of any other man beside Governor Yates. He came to Belvidere in 1846, a young lawyer, without means, without patronage, with nothing upon which to depend, but industry, integrity and capacity. He soon built up a lucrative practice, and by sympathy with and participation in public interests, he became a leading and influential man in Northern Illinois. He was elected Judge of the Circuit Court, the duties of which high office he discharged with much ability. He was upon the bench when the war broke out, and was tendered the position of Adjutant-General. The members of the bar objected to his resignation, and urged him to accept temporarily the appointment. He accordingly entered upon its duties November 11, 1861, and in July following resigned his seat on the bench. That he has faithfully performed its laborious duties, has been attested by the Legislature and Governor.

The House of Representatives at its last session unanimously adopted a report of its committee appointed to inspect the Adjutant-General's office, and from which report we extract the following:

"That we have thoroughly examined the office of the Adjutant-General and find it a model in completeness; one that preserves in all its glory the proud records of our soldiery, and reflects infinite credit upon the great State whose sons they are.

"That in the judgment of this committee, the thanks of every patriot citizen of the State are due to Gen. Fuller for the able and efficient manner in which he has discharged the duties of the office, and for his indefatigable efforts in collecting and preserving this glorious record of a glorious State."

Governor Yates, in his last message of 1863, says: "I refer you to the report of the Adjutant-General, to whose untiring labors, and able and faithful co-operation I acknowledge myself deeply indebted, and in the management of the military affairs of the State." In his last message, after regretting that the Adjutant-General's serious illness in November and December, 1864, had prevented the prepara- of his biennial report, the Governor says: "I have also inspected the Adjutant-General's Office, and deem it proper to say that it is as complete in all its arrangements, and in the perfection of its system and method, as any similar office in the United States. General Fuller has been a most able, faithful and energetic officer, and is entitled to the gratitude of the State."

These official "well dones" are echoed by the officers and boys in blue. They have recognized in the General a true and competent friend. In 1864, the leading Republican journals of the northern part of the State and some from the Central and Southern advocated his nomination as the successor of Governor Yates, but the choice fell upon the brave General Oglesby.

He was elected to represent Boone County in the General Assembly, and on the 1st of January resigned the position of Adjutant-General, and was chosen Speaker of the House of Representatives. Before adjournment, that body by unanimous vote, adopted the following:

"*Resolved*, That we tender our heartfelt thanks to Hon. Allen C. Fuller, our presiding officer, for the kind, courteous, able and impartial manner in which he has presided over us, and as such recognize in his general bearing and demeanor the perfect model of a gentleman."

The Adjutant's office has been most economically managed. Indeed it may be doubted, if in any other department of State service so much labor has been performed for so slight a remuneration. In his report of 1861–2, General Fuller says:

"Under the law of May 2, 1861, the salary of the Adjutant-General is fixed at seven dollars, the first assistant at six, and second assistant at five dollars per day. No express authority was given the Adjutant-General to employ clerks, but the law authorized you to employ such clerks, aids and messengers as the public interests might require, and allow them such reasonable compensation as in your judgment they should be entitled to.

"When I took possession of the office, November 11, 1861, three clerks and a messenger boy were employed, beside the Adjutant-General and his assistants. No injustice is done in saying that such had been the pressure of business upon the office that its affairs were very much behind hand. There were but few rolls on file and few permanent records.

"Notwithstanding the great increase of business, I have endeavored to keep the expenses of the office to the very lowest possible figure, and in this I have had the generous co-operation of my assistants and clerks. The average number of hours which they have actually labored is not less than sixteen out of twenty-four. Under your direction they have been employed, and the average compensation has been a little less than three dollars per day. But it will be seen, by schedule F, that one hundred and sixty-one days have not been charged by both assistants, and their places to that extent have been supplied by these clerks.

"It will also be seen that the number of days' service performed by clerks from April 16, 1861, to January 1, 1863, is 1,779, at a compensation of $5,261. The total amount of salaries and clerk-hire during this period is $14,548. The total amount allowed to the Adjutant-General and his two assistants, by law, for the same period, is $11,250, leaving $2,743 (beside one dollar a day for messenger boy), for clerk-hire, or at the rate of $2.20 per day for two clerks. This is explained by the additional fact that in my salary from November 11, 1861, to January 1, 1863, being 416 days, would amount to $2,912, whereas but $1,288, or pay from the first of July last is charged. The reason for this deduction is that until July last I held the office of Circuit Judge of the 13th Judicial Circuit, and I have not felt at liberty to draw salaries for two offices.

"I trust I have kept the expenses of the department, considering the amount of labor performed, within proper limits. The extent of that labor few can know as well as those who have performed it.

The General has sustained to the boys in blue a sort of paternal relation, and will ever meet from them a cordial welcome. The reader will find copious extracts.

As the writer was dependent upon the reports and archives of the Adjutant-General's office for much of the material woven into the preceding chapters, he has thought proper to introduce the reader into the same office.

General Fuller's successor is Brigadier-General Isham N. Haynie, formerly Colonel of the Forty-eighth, of whom more anon.

TABULAR STATEMENT—Showing the Population, Enrollment, Total Quotas, Credits, Deficits and Excess of each County in the State, July 1, 1864.

NAME OF COUNTIES.	Population in 1860.	FIRST AND SECOND CLASS ENROLLMENT.		QUOTAS.	Credits.	Deficits.	Excess.
		1863.	1864.	Gr. Total.			
Adams	41,144	7,049	8,475	4,853	3,695	1,158	
Alexander	4,652	2,221	2,942	1,178	1,279		101
Bond	9,767	1,465	1,803	1,972	970	102	
Boone	11,670	1,600	1,646	1,168	947	221	
Brown	9,919	1,311	1,558	0,066	1,046		40
Bureau	26,415	4,533	5,233	3,089	2,284	802	
Calhoun	5,143	952	1,175	640	319	321	
Carroll	11,718	2,109	2,172	1,368	962	406	
Cass	11,313	1,610	2,073	1,221	989	232	
Champaign	14,581	2,776	3,061	1,792	2,011		219
Christian	10,475	2,155	2,512	1,372	977	395	
Clark	14,948	1,886	2,029	1,448	1,144	304	
Clay	9,809	1,365	1,444	971	1,311		340
Clinton	10,729	2,056	2,372	1,340	974	366	
Coles	14,174	2,773	3,203	1,793	2,636		843
Cook	143,947	33,471	38,262	20,305	16,177	4,128	
Crawford	11,527	1,561	1,624	1,149	1,003	646	
Cumberland	8,309	903	985	749	864		115
DeKalb	19,079	3,150	3,269	2,120	1,888	232	
DeWitt	10,814	1,604	1,947	1,175	1,453		278
Douglas	7,109	1,481	1,803	952	966		14
DuPage	14,696	1,300	2,188	1,329	1,207	122	
Edgar	16,888	2,671	3,605	1,962	1,812	150	
Edwards	5,379	747	728	536	497	39	
Effingham	7,805	1,302	1,760	937	1,189		152
Fayette	11,146	1,956	2,020	1,282	1,357		75
Ford	1,979	491	607	300	140	160	
Franklin	9,367	1,214	1,363	929	1,199		270
Fulton	33,289	4,169	4,967	3,285	3,012	273	
Gallatin	7,629	1,065	1,191	786	1,325		539
Green	16,067	2,271	2,726	1,694	1,568	126	
Grundy	10,372	1,794	1,984	1,204	1,030	174	
Hamilton	9,849	1,226	1,323	947	1,207		260
Hancock	29,041	4,440	5,280	3,195	2,440	755	
Hardin	3,704	472	561	369	539		170
Henderson	9,499	1,746	1,998	1,153	1,053	100	
Henry	20,658	3,933	4,624	2,583	2,481	102	
Iroquois	12,285	2,204	2,458	1,460	1,485		25
Jackson	9,560	1,586	1,797	1,088	1,361		273
Jasper	8,350	975	998	770	817		47
Jefferson	12,931	1,812	1,845	1,307	933	374	
Jersey	11,942	1,801	2,324	1,355	846	509	
JoDaviess	27,147	2,283	3,709	2,589	1,812	777	
Johnson	9,306	1,219	1,314	919	1,412		498
Kane	30,024	4,530	4,962	3,212	3,561		349
Kankakee	15,393	2,353	2,575	1,659	1,484	175	
Kendall	13,073	1,959	2,921	1,374	1,241	133	
Knox	28,512	4,576	5,212	3,190	3,229		39
Lake	18,248	2,391	2,592	1,805	1,381	424	
LaSalle	48,272	8,333	9,992	5,715	4,590	1,125	
Lawrence	8,976	1,193	1,443	918	1,007		89
Lee	17,643	3,235	3,493	2,107	1,848	259	

TABULAR STATEMENT—CONTINUED.

NAME OF COUNTIES.	Population in 1860.	FIRST AND SECOND CLASS ENROLLMENT.		QUOTAS.	Credits.	Deficits.	Excess.
		1863.	1864.	Gr. Total.			
Livingston ..	11,632	2,307	2,922	1,524	1,310	214	....
Logan	14,247	2,377	2,870	1,655	2,056	....	401
Macon	13,655	2,504	3,245	1,715	1,791	....	76
Macoupin . . .	24,504	4,219	5,093	2,902	2,314	588	....
Madison.....	30,689	6,951	8,598	4,355	2,728	1,627	....
Marion......	12,730	2,051	2,454	1,446	1,782	....	336
Marshall	13,437	2,165	2,866	1,570	1,141	429	....
Mason	10,929	1,529	1,695	1,125	1,506	....	381
Massac......	6,101	965	1,236	698	843	....	145
McDonough..	20,061	3,221	3,458	2,212	2,171	41	....
McHenry....	22,085	3,117	3,194	2,243	1,967	276	....
McLean.....	28,580	5,741	7,229	3,770	3,610	160	....
Menard	9,577	1,403	1,715	1,037	928	109	....
Mercer......	15,037	2,075	2,325	1,540	1,657	....	117
Monroe......	12,815	2,987	3,509	1,826	736	1,090	....
Montgomery .	13,881	2,617	2,976	1,709	1,203	506	....
Morgan	21,937	3,248	3,935	2,381	2,302	79	....
Moultrie.....	6,384	951	970	665	579	86	....
Ogle........	22,863	3,709	3,815	2,509	2,326	183	....
Peoria	36,475	6,238	7,828	4,348	3,791	557	....
Perry	9,508	518	1,554	1,034	1,433	....	399
Piatt	6,124	1,033	1,136	700	1,044	....	344
Pike........	27,182	3,492	3,961	2,687	2,758	....	71
Pope	6,546	1,192	1,249	772	1,207	....	435
Pulaski	3,904	986	1,543	647	552	95	....
Putnam	5,579	916	1,006	626	449	177	....
Randolph ...	16,766	2,743	3,301	1,925	1,735	190	....
Richland....	9,709	1,492	1,483	1,025	1,485	....	460
Rock Island..	20,981	3,007	3,540	2,220	1,953	267	....
Saline	9,161	1,216	1,261	904	1,256	....	352
Sangamon...	31,963	6,226	7,989	4,158	4,451	....	293
Schuyler....	14,670	1,854	2,054	1,430	1,429	1	....
Scott	9,047	1,460	1,739	1,028	1,070	....	42
Shelby	14,590	2,910	3,673	1,917	1,606	311	....
Stark	9,003	1,284	1,602	964	810	154	....
St. Clair.....	37,169	7,159	8,959	4,765	2,778	1,987	....
Stephenson..	25,112	3,998	4,285	2,755	2,476	279	....
Tazewell	21,427	3,598	4,281	2,506	1,787	719	....
Union	11,145	1,501	1,948	1,168	1,819	....	651
Vermillion ..	19,779	3,306	3,669	2,251	2,115	136	....
Wabash.....	7,233	937	910	695	601	94	....
Warren	18,293	3,041	3,627	2,115	1,938	177	....
Washington..	13,725	2,341	2,682	1,594	1,451	143	....
Wayne......	12,222	1,448	1,517	1,140	1,575	....	435
White	12,274	1,611	1,616	1,194	1,963	....	769
Whiteside...	18,729	3,224	3,328	2,129	1,860	269	....
Will........	29,264	5,746	5,338	3,509	2,957	552	....
Williamson..	12,087	1,498	1,620	1,161	1,565	....	404
Winnebago..	24,457	4,072	4,524	2,778	2,409	369	....
Woodford ...	13,281	2,419	2,842	1,616	1,047	569	....
Total	1,704,323	287,941	333,518	197,360	181,178	27,024	10,842

www.ingramcontent.com/pod-product-compliance
Lightning Source LLC
LaVergne TN
LVHW021100110826
845150LV00001B/127

* 9 7 8 1 4 2 5 5 6 6 1 5 9 *